Majestic Quran

Guidance and Good news for the Mindful

Translated by Musharraf Hussein

The Majestic Quran

The Majestic Quran – Guidance and Good news for the Mindful
First edition published April 2020

INVITATION PUBLISHING LTD
512-514 Berridge Road West
Nottingham
NG7 5JU
E-mail: info@invitationpublishing.co.uk
https://majesticquran.co.uk

Distributed by
INVITATION PUBLISHING LTD.
Tel: +44[0] 115 8550961

Cataloguing-in-Publication Data is available
from the British Library

ISBN 979-8746427335

Typeset in Garamond Premier Pro.
Cover design and typesetting by Sajhd Hussain.
Printed in Turkey by: Imak Oset.
Printed on paper from responsible sources.

Contents

Map of Arabia

The revelation of the Quran began in 610 CE when the angel Gabriel appeared to the Prophet Muhammad ﷺ in the cave Hira near Makkah, reciting to him the first verses of chapter Al-ʿAlaq. The Prophet ﷺ continued to receive revelation as and when required until his departure from this world in 632 CE. This map shows the Arabian peninsula and while reading the Quran you will come across the names of certain nations, places and persons.

Helpful tips for studying the Majestic Quran

Our goal is to convey the meaning of the Quran accurately. This translation is easy to read and understand. Here are some useful tips to help you enjoy and benefit from:

1. The Quran is a book of guidance, that impresses the reader, drives home the message deep into the heart and mind. It moulds the attitude and inspires you. Every chapter develops its central theme from the beginning to the end logically, there is a gradual move to completion, sometimes it seems disjointed, but these are digressions, Divine comments. The pattern seems to be: Some chapters open with the mysterious broken letters, others with praise and glorification of the Lord. Followed by arguments for the Lords majesty, reference to His creative power in nature, or description of hell and heaven, rewards, punishment, or reference to human history of disobedience. This form helps in achieving the original goal, which is to impress the reader. So, read the introduction of the chapter.

2. The Quran gives direct instructions, it doesn't speak in abstract terms, often uses the imperative for example: *Anfiqu*, give charity; *Aqeemu-salah*, pray regularly; *Athu-zakah*, pay zakah. When you carry out these Divine orders you will experience a change. Look for God's orders.

3. The Quran routinely keeps things brief, with minimum details, It's concise. Minimalism is the Quranic style. For example, it leaves out names of people and towns, as though it's in a hurry to get to the message, and pronounce the moral and spiritual lessons, pay special notice to this.

4. The Quran is a useful manual not a textbook, it persuades, dissuades, pricks the conscience, flips from present to future and back to the past, reasons using evidence from nature, human experience, and history. Just follow its guidance.

5. The Quran demands the reader's full attention: Applying one's mind, being focused. This leads to reflection and asking pertinent questions; who is the Creator? What does He expect from me? Answer these questions.

6. The Quran persuades through reason. So, when reading, ask yourself: What's the message for me? What does the Majestic Quran want me to believe, accept or do? What does it expect me to learn and understand about God? It's teaching you the bigger picture, so you may understand the deceptive nature of worldly life.

Introduction

Objectives and Methodology

I have undertaken this translation because I owe so much to the Quran; it has given me meaning and purpose in life. I feel indebted, and this translation is a labour of love that I believe will offer fresh insights and understanding for readers living in a global village in an exciting age of science and information technology. The purpose of this translation is to convey the meanings of the Majestic Quran clearly, concisely and in a clear tone of voice, making this 'majestic reading' the most readable and appealing translation of the Quran in English.

I have been a serious student of the Quran for more than fifty years, during this time I have memorised the Quran, and studied the Arabic language, the science of Tafsir and Hadith at Al-Azhar University, Cairo. Prior to this I was a research scientist for more than ten years.

For the past fourteen centuries, Muslim scholars worked hard to understand the Majestic Quran as accurately as possible. My own understanding of the Quran is based on these works of honourable sages, and this translation is underpinned by the accumulated treasury of classical Islamic wisdom. It would not be an exaggeration to say that this translation and the introductions to the chapters is the crystallisation of the traditional understanding of the divine words.

Although I have been guided by the past English translations of the Majestic Quran, I hope I have taken the work of those renowned scholars a bit further. I have learnt a lot from my predecessors and I have tried my best to avoid some of the pitfalls, biases, and inaccuracies they made. However, the most widely read and circulated translations of the Quran were unfortunately published in 'old-fashioned' English: Marmaduke Pickthall, Abdullah Joseph Ali and the Sahih International version, which makes the Quran appear an outdated book that is nothing to do with contemporary society. In this translation, I have attempted to avoid such 'old' terminology as much as possible, while still retaining the original meaning of the Majestic Quran.

I hope this 'majestic reading' will be widely read the world over. The Quran is a living book, its message: Islam is a living message; a message of hope, providing spiritual and material prosperity and a happy life. Muslims are a young community that needs guidance, and is there any guidance better than the guidance of God? That's why this 'majestic reading' must once again be presented with clarity, and this translation attempts to give clarity to the message of the Majestic Quran in plain English; it's to the point, easy to understand and readable in contemporary English.

Plain and Contemporary English

My goal has been to translate the meaning of the divine message, all the time being faithful and accurate in expressing the exact meaning of the Quranic words; by using the root meanings of the words rather than freer interpretation. Mine is an authentic translation, neither liberal nor free, however, I have used interpretation to join ideas together. I believe this is the best way to give readers a true taste of the Quran, so that it can speak for itself. I have used plain English: simple words and avoiding archaic words and turns of phrase. Instead of translating Arabic idioms, I have used English idioms wherever possible. I have aimed for an accurate translation by relying on classical Arabic dictionaries and Quranic commentaries. How successful I have been in providing a meaning that is clear, plain and contemporary is for you, the reader to judge.

The Topical Section Headings

A distinct feature of this translation is the use of section headings for the sake of clarity. These headings correspond to the main themes and subject matter presented in the text. The headings of each section are not just attention-grabbing, but reflect its contents, themes and specific topics that will help the reader to understand the "bursts of revelation" as the Quran was revealed according to the needs of the time. However, this is only an attempt at clarity for the sake of understanding the divine text. They are not there to dictate the interpretation of these verses, although they may possibly give a particular interpretation to some readers. Their main purpose is to join ideas in the section, so helping to contextualise the passages. This allows the Quran to speak for itself. In brief, the headings are a useful device for unlocking the meaning and the purpose of the Quran and to help to make its teachings fully transparent. I believe this is a very convincing way for the reader to get a true taste of the Majestic Quran.

Introduction to the Chapters

The chapters, in the Quran are divided into sections, based on where the subject begins or at the seam between two subjects. These act as 'hinge passages', which are separate units that can be attached to a preceding or following narrative block. These narrative blocks can be very fluid, particularly those that act as buffer zones which allow one passage to merge into the next.

The chapters highlight the period of revelation, the major themes and shed some light on the socio-economic, political, historical and cultural environment of the Arabian Peninsula at the time of revelation, the seventh century.

The Footnotes

I have used footnotes sparingly to add value to the communicative process of translation, where their absence could lead to misunderstandings. I have used them to explain metaphors and the figurative language of the Quran, and to describe circumstances of revelation that will help the reader to understand the background and the context of the events.

Presentation and Layout of the Translation

The Quran is full of dialogue, sometimes between the Messenger peace be upon him (the following honorific ﷺ will be used) the express this, and the Quraysh, with the People of The Book, and sometimes with all of humanity, etc. By using quotation marks I have endeavoured to convey the conversation in the original text. This has also been useful for identifying the start and end of sections.

I have paid special attention to verses concerned with the Majesty of God and to honour the Messenger I have avoided using irreverent words. This also applies to anthropomorphic terms used for God in the Quran, including references to God's face, eyes, hands and expressions of God's response to human folly, like mocking, deception, etc. In places, these have been interpreted and in others I have used English equivalents, as recommended by orthodox commentators.

Capitalisation has been used when reference is made to God; the pronouns, titles, the beautiful names of God, and the major concepts and terms in Islamic studies.

I have used italics rather than brackets for any extra words inserted for the sake of explanation. The reason is that the omission of words and phrases is a common feature of the Quranic style, where things are left unsaid.

For clarity, verse numbers are mentioned at start in this English translation but are usually placed at the end in Arabic.

I am grateful to the Almighty Loving Lord who gave me the opportunity to serve His wonderful book. I pray that God accepts this humble effort. However, it is a fact that no translation of the Quran no matter how accurate it is can express all the meanings of the Divine text, my translation is an attempt to understand the meanings of the Quran, it is not possible to fully translate and grasp the inimitable and powerful words of God. Therefore, it is likely that there will be shortcomings and even mistakes in the translation, so I request my readers to point them out so, they can be corrected in the next edition.

Acknowledgements

I would like to thank all of the people who have helped in this wonderful and sacred project, from those who gave moral support to those who provided finance, may God reward them plenty.

I would like to thank my editorial team, who ensured that the translation is accurate and accessible, they were: Ustadh Yasrab Shah, Maulana Asif Ali, Mufti Muhammad Ismael and my students at the Karimia Institute. I am especially grateful to the following individuals, who provided very useful suggestions and for their audious proof-reading: Atif Hussain, Ghufran Shah, Dr Assam Latif, Majhad Hussain, Nabeela Hussain, Parveen Hussain and Qasim Hussain,

My typesetter and designer, Sajhd Hussain, deserves a special mention for his tireless work. I wish to pay a special thanks to the Dar Al-Iftaa of Cairo, Egypt for approving the translation. Finally, I would like to express my appreciation to my family for their continuous support throughout this journey.

May God bless them all abundantly.

Musharraf Hussain

The Majestic Quran

1. Al-Fatihah
The Opening

The opening chapter of the Majestic Quran summarises the major themes and topics of the Quran: shaping a world view through the belief system; faith in God, His messengers and the Hereafter; the Angels; Predestination and the Day of Resurrection; challenging idolatry and materialism; practising the five pillars; emphasis on obeying the laws: halal and haram; an invitation to embrace spiritual ideals: mindfulness and alertness, reliance on God; the promotion of moral teachings; the condemnation of moral vices; social obligations; the life and beautiful character of the Messenger 鑫; the history of human disobedience; Satan the arch enemy, how he misleads and his snares and traps; human diversity and pluralism; the awe-inspiring nature; vivid descriptions of Heaven and Hell. This is the essence of the Quran.

It is read dozens of time daily in the prayers and is a plea, a prayer that the devout servant makes to the Caring Lord. The rest of the Quran is a response to this, and the blessed Messenger 鑫 praised its virtue: "by Him in whose hand is my life, nothing like this was ever revealed in the Torah, or the Psalms or the Gospel" (Ahmed). A concise prayer that is life transforming, no wonder the Messenger 鑫 described it as: *al-fatihah*, the door to the treasury of wisdom; Umm al-Quran, the Fountain of Quranic wisdom; *al-shifa*, the healing for moral, spiritual and social diseases.

In the name of God, the Kind, the Caring.

THE KEY TO THE QURAN

[1] All praises are for God, the Lord of the worlds.[a] [2] The Kind, the Caring, [3] the Master of Judgement Day. [4] We worship You alone and from You alone we seek help. [5] Guide us on the straight path, [6] the path of those You favoured, not those who are condemned[b] nor the misguided ones.

---

[a] An alternative meaning is "praise be to God".
[b] *"Maghdoob"* literally means "with anger on them", or "those who have failed to win your favour".

2. Al-Baqarah
The Cow

This, the longest chapter in the Quran, was revealed in Madinah after the migration of the Prophet 🕊 in 622 CE (Common Era). It was completed in two years, by now two-thirds of the Quran had been revealed in Makkah, under a tense social and political environment. In Madinah, settling down in a new city with Arabs and Jews, Muslims faced new challenges. There were two main Arab tribes: the Aus and the Khazraj, both with a long history of rivalry and bloodshed, and three main Jewish tribes. The Jewish tribes had moved to Madinah after they were expelled from Jerusalem by the Romans, and were literate, skilled and affluent compared to the Arabs. The Jews also believed that they were "chosen people".

The first action of The Prophet 🕊, to develop trust in his new home city, was to make a treaty with the Jewish and Arab tribes. The treaty stated all the communities were one community and would protect each other, they were guaranteed freedom to practise their religions.

The Main Themes of the Chapter
- The chapter opens by describing the inhabitants of Madinah and dividing them into three groups: the pious believers, the disbelievers and the hypocrites. Imam Razi, in *The Great Commentary,* states:

  > The believer is the one whose heart and conscience are religiously clear and good; the disbeliever is one who stubbornly refuses to believe, the hypocrite is the one who pretends to believe but whose conscience is against it.

- The Five Pillars of Islam: belief in the Oneness of God, the five daily prayers, Zakat, Ramadan, and pilgrimage to Makkah.
- The unity of the Abrahamic faiths: the chapter repeatedly points out that Islam is not a new religion but instead a system which verifies and continues the original teachings of Judaism and Christianity, which also taught belief in one God and of serving humanity. Islam replaces Judaism and Christianity as the final religion of God, and the Quran is The Final Revelation.
- Family matters: the chapter covers various aspects of marital laws and means of resolving family disputes and addressing divorce.
- The social, spiritual and economic principles of a just society.

New Laws Established
In Madinah, Muslims were able to practise Islam with a freedom they had not been allowed in Makkah. There is a lot of emphasis on developing a civil society that is not defined by

blood, but instead by a belief system, by spiritual and moral teachings, and by social and political values. The chapter establishes a clear legal context to support this spiritual and moral social structure and to tackle the sickness of an uncaring society. In addition, political and economic principles are laid out within a legal framework. These include:

- The change of the direction of prayer from Jerusalem to Makkah (verse 142).
- The four forbidden foods (172).
- The obligation to fast during the month of Ramadan (183).
- The morals and rules of Hajj and Umrah (197).
- Family laws: the law of retribution (178); writing down one's will (180); the prohibition of marriage with non-Muslims (222); divorce and marital discord (228–32); the duty of fathers to pay maintenance expenses (233), and the rules and manners of giving charity (261–74).
- Commercial transactions: the prohibition of earning interest (275); business contracts; commercial transactions, and guarantees for loans (282–3).
- The permissibility for Muslims to fight against others in defence (190).

The Story of the Cow

What is the relevance of this story? In a chapter that lays down many laws, it is important to point out that a human society is not just based on laws. A balanced civil society is one which respects moral and social values and spiritual ideals. A legal system is only one part of a flourishing civilisation, and the Story of the Cow highlights the idea that attitudes and values lie at the heart of a just society.

Salvation Lies in Submission to God

An overview of the chapter reveals an important thread woven throughout: "Human salvation lies in complete submission and commitment to the Lord of the Worlds". This is comprised of the following principles:

- Firm faith in God, the One God.
- Belief in His majestic rule and power.
- Belief in God as the Sole Creator of The Universe.
- Belief in His messengers sent to guide humanity, and to make clear the straight path that will help creation to achieve the pleasure of the Creator.

Such belief helps us to live a righteous life: a good life pleasing to the Lord, and conducive to both our own healthy living and the well-being of people. This is not a mechanical performance of ritual exercises. Instead, it is conscious awareness of and attentiveness to The Divine, in such a way that one feels His presence everywhere. A natural outcome of this way of living is a belief in a resurrection and Judgement Day, signifying that this life is an opportunity to gain the pleasure of God, and therefore to secure a place near Him in Paradise.

In the name of God, the Kind, the Caring.

[1] *Alif Lam Meem.*[a]

A DESCRIPTION OF THE FAITHFUL

[2] This is the *Majestic* book, there is no doubt in it, guidance for the pious, [3] who believe in the unseen, perform prayer and spend in charity from what We have provided them. [4] They believe in what is revealed to you and what was revealed before you, and they have firm faith in the Hereafter. [5] Those are the ones who follow their Lord's guidance and those are the successful.

THE LOCKED MINDS OF DISBELIEVERS

[6] Those who disbelieve, it is all the same for them whether you warn or not, they will not believe. [7] God sealed their hearts and hearing; laid a blindfold over their eyes, and they will have a painful punishment.[b]

THEY ARE DECEIVERS AND LIARS

[8] Some people say: "We believe in God and the Hereafter", but they aren't believers. [9] They try to deceive God and the believers, but they are unwittingly deceiving themselves. [10] There's a disease in their hearts, and God has increased their disease, and they shall have a painful punishment because of the lies they told.

THEY MOCK AND MAKE TROUBLE

[11] When they are told *for their own good*: "Don't make trouble in the land", they say: "We are the peacemakers". [12] Beware! They are the troublemakers, but they don't realise it. [13] When they are told: "Believe like other people believed", they say: "Shall we believe like the fools?" It is they who are the fools, but they don't know. [14] And, when they meet the believers, they say: "We believe", but when they are alone with their devilish friends, they say: "We are with you, we were just joking with them". [15] God will punish them for mocking,[c] and He extends their

---

[a]   These are three letters of the Arabic alphabet, and there are twenty-nine chapters that begin with such letters. They are described as "*Muqatta'at*", detached letters or acronyms, whose meaning is known to God and His Messenger ﷺ.

[b]   This is explained as follows; everyone is given the ability to know right and wrong, they have free choice in adopting either one. A person who persists in falsehood and refuses to accept the truth, gradually loses the ability to see it - this is the meaning of "God sealed their hearts..."

[c]   Literally translated as: "God mocks them". However, this is too negative a quality for the Lord, therefore I have translated it to express the holiness of God.

wandering around blindly in their disobedience.

THEY ARE IGNORANT AND MISGUIDED

[16] They have chosen error instead of guidance; their bargain is without profit, and they aren't rightly guided. [17] They are like the one who lights a fire, and when everything is bright, suddenly God takes away their light and leaves them in pitch darkness so they cannot see. [18] Deaf, dumb and blind, they will not return to *the straight path.*

THEY ARE DISORIENTATED AND FEARFUL

[19] Or they are like a raincloud in a sky full of darkness, thunder and lightning. They stick their fingers in their ears for fear of death by thunderbolts. God has the disbelievers surrounded. [20] The lightning nearly blinds them; whenever it lights up they walk *about* in it, and when it falls dark they stand still. If God wanted, He could take their hearing and sight. God controls all things.

THE QURAN'S CHALLENGE TO THE HYPOCRITES

[21] People, worship your Lord Who created you and those before you, so that you may guard yourselves *against evil.* [22] Who spread out the Earth for you and made the sky a roof, and sent down rain by which He produces fruits to provide for you. So, do not knowingly make any rivals equal with God. [23] If you have doubts about what We have revealed to Our servant, then produce a chapter like it and call all your witnesses and supporters besides God; *that is* if you are truthful[a]. [24] If you have not done so – and you will never be able to do so – then fear the Fire whose fuel is people and brimstone, prepared for the disbelievers.

PARADISE IS AN AMAZING REWARD

[25] And to those who believe and carry out good works, give them good news of gardens with running streams beneath them. Each time they are given a fruit to eat from there, they say: "We used to eat this before". They will be given something like it, and they will have chaste spouses and live there forever.

ONLY THE DISOBEDIENT ARE MISGUIDED

[26] God is not embarrassed to give the example of a mosquito or something even smaller. Those who believe know that this is the truth from their Lord, but those

---

[a] The message of The Majestic Quran is brief, inspirational and factual. It's portrayal of the reality. That's why it is free of doubt.

who disbelieve say: "What does God mean by this example?" He allows many to be misguided by it and others to be guided; *yet* only the disobedient are misguided by it, [27] those who break their ties with God after it has been agreed; they break *the ties* that God has ordered to be joined, and they make trouble in the land: these are the losers.[b] [28] How can you deny God when you were dead and He brought you to life, then He will cause you to die and give you life once more, and to Him you shall be returned. [29] It is He who created everything on Earth for you, then He turned to the sky[c] and completed the seven Heavens; He has knowledge of all things.

THE STORY OF ADAM'S CREATION

[30] Remember when Your Lord told the Angels: "I am creating a representative on Earth". They replied: "Are You creating someone who will make trouble there and shed blood? Is it not enough that we glorify You with praises and proclaim Your Holiness?" He said: "I know what you don't know".

PROPHET ADAM'S KNOWLEDGE AND SATAN'S ARROGANCE

[31] He taught Adam the names of all things, then presented them to the Angels and asked: "Tell Me the names of these things, if you are right". [32] They said, "Glory be to You! We only know what You have taught us. You are the Knower and Wise". [33] He said, "Adam, tell them their names". So, when *Adam* told them *all* of the names, *God* said: "Did I not tell you that I know the secrets of the Heavens and the Earth, and that I know what you show and what you hide?" [34] Then We commanded the Angels to prostrate to Adam, they all prostrated except Iblis[d] (Satan); he disobeyed, acted arrogantly and was ungrateful.

ADAM AND EVE ARE TEMPTED

[35] We said: "Adam, live with your wife in Paradise and eat freely from wherever you want, but don't go near this tree, or you will be wrongdoers". [36] But Satan tempted them and had them expelled from where they were. We told them: "Go down as enemies of each other on Earth, you will have a place to live and things

---

[b] A person goes astray because of their attitude and stubbornness not to listen. So, it is a consequence of their choice, God knows the person's choice, so He lets them go astray.

[c] "Turned to the sky" does not imply God physically turning in a direction, but turning His attention to the next phase of His creation.

[d] *Iblis* is the name of the devil, he is the rebel, the one who refuses the command of God to prostrate. He is from the Jinns, an invisible creation of God made from the Fire.

to enjoy for a fixed term".[a] [37] *Then*, Adam received words *of inspiration* from his Lord, so He accepted his repentance; He is Forgiving, Kind. [38] We said: "Go down from here, you all! When the guidance comes from Me, whoever follows it will have nothing to fear, nor to grieve". [39] Those who disbelieved and denied Our verses, these are the people of the Fire, and they will be there forever.

THE JEWS ARE INVITED TO BELIEVE IN THE MESSENGER

[40] Children of Israel, remember My gifts I gave you, and fulfil My contract, and I will fulfil your contract. Fear Me! [41] Believe what I have revealed, it confirms what you *already* have, and don't be the first to deny it or to sell My verses cheaply. Be mindful of Me.[b]

HOW TO BECOME PIOUS

[42] Do not mix the truth with falsehood, nor knowingly hide the truth. [43] Perform prayer, pay Zakat, and bow down with those who bow *in prayer*. [44] You tell people to be righteous but forget yourselves, although you read The Book? Don't you understand? [45] Seek help through patience and prayer; these are burdensome virtues except for the humble, [46] who believe they will meet their Lord. *In the end*, they will return to Him.

GOD'S FAVOURS ON THE ISRAELITES AFTER PHARAOH'S OPPRESSION

[47] Children of Israel, remember the great gifts that I gave you when I favoured you above all other people; [48] and fear the day when no one will be willing to pay even a small ransom for another person, and no intercession will be accepted from the disbelievers nor any compensation allowed, and nor will they be helped. [49] Remember when We saved you from the people of Pharaoh who punished you severely, killing your sons and sparing your women; that was a tremendous test from your Lord. [50] And remember also when We parted the sea for you, rescuing you but drowning the people of Pharaoh before your very eyes.

THE ISRAELITES WORSHIP A CALF

[51] *Remember* when We invited Moses for forty nights, but you began worshipping the *golden* calf, *becoming* wrongdoers. [52] Afterwards We pardoned you so that you might be grateful. [53] Then We gave Moses The Book and told him how to judge

---

[a]   *Shaytan*, the name of the devil when he acts as a tempter, the one who tempted Adam and Eve.

[b]   *Taqwa* is translated as "be mindful": be aware of God's creative power, be conscious of your dependency on Him, and of your shortcomings.

right from wrong so that you may be guided. [54] Remember when Moses said to his people: "My people, you have committed a major sin by worshipping the *golden calf*; so repent to your Maker and *punish the culprits* among yourselves.[c] That is better for you in the sight of your Maker so that He may accept your repentance: indeed, He is Relenting and Kind". [55] *Remember* when you said: "Moses, we won't believe you until we openly see God", and a thunderbolt struck you as you watched. [56] We then resurrected you after death so you might be thankful.

GOD CONTINUED TO BLESS THE ISRAELITES

[57] We sent clouds to give you shade, We sent Manna and quails for you, *saying:*[d] "Eat the pure provision We have provided you". They didn't harm Us, but they harmed themselves. [58] When We said: "Enter this town and eat from wherever you like, and enter the gate with humility saying: 'Forgive us'[e] so We forgive your sins and increase the reward of the righteous". [59] The wrongdoers altered the words to *something* other than what they were taught. So, We sent down a plague from the sky for their wickedness.

THE MIRACLE OF THE TWELVE SPRINGS

[60] When Moses prayed for water for his people. We said: "Strike the rock with your staff", twelve springs gushed out, and each tribe recognised its drinking place. "Eat and drink God's provision, and don't go around making trouble in the land". [61] When you said: "Moses, we are weary of eating the same meal *every day*, so ask your Lord to produce for us, herbs, cucumbers, garlic, lentil and onions". He said: "Why are you swapping something superior for something less? Go back to Egypt, if that's what you want". So, they were disgraced and humiliated, and brought on themselves God's anger because they denied His signs, killed the prophets unjustly, disobeyed and often broke the rules.

---

[c]   Qadi Abdul Jabbar, said that the words "kill yourselves" should not be understood literally, but mean "mortify" or "punish yourselves" (Razi).

[d]   "Manna and quails": Manna is a special type of food, like honey, that was graciously provided by God to the Israelites, along with quails, a type of small game bird.

[e]   Instead of saying *hittah* ("forgive us"), they used a meaningless irreverent word.

ONLY FAITH AND GOOD DEEDS GUARANTEE SUCCESS

[62] The believers,[a] the Jews, Christians and Sabians,[b] whoever believed in God,[c] the Hereafter and did righteous works, shall have reward from their Lord. They shall not fear nor grieve. [63] With the mountain towering over you, We took your contract, *saying:* "Hold firmly to what We have given you and remember what it teaches so you become mindful of God". [64] But you turned away. If it hadn't been for the grace and God's favour, you would be losers. [65] You knew those who broke the law of Sabbath; We said to them: "Be *like* apes, shunned and rejected". [66] So, We made their fate an example for their generation and those who followed them, and a clear lesson for the God-fearing.

THE STORY OF THE COW

[67] *Remember* when Moses said to his people: "God commands you to slaughter a cow". They said: "Are you joking with us?" He replied: "God forbids that I should be so bad-mannered". [68] They said: "Then ask your Lord to explain what sort of cow it is". He answered: "He says she is neither old nor young but in-between, so do as instructed". [69] They said: "Ask your Lord to clarify what colour she is". He said: "God says it is a light-yellow coloured cow, pleasing to the onlookers". [70] They again *repeated*: "Ask your Lord to spell out for us what she looks like, as all cows look similar to us; then, if God wills, we shall be guided". [71] *Moses* said: "He says she is a cow that has not been yoked for ploughing or watering the fields, a healthy cow with no scars". They then said: "Now you have given us the exact description". Eventually they slaughtered it though they disliked doing so.

A MURDERED MAN IS RESURRECTED

[72] *Remember* when you killed a person, and you quarrelled about it; God exposed what you were hiding. [73] So, We told them: "Touch with a piece of the cow's meat *the corpse of the dead* person". That is how God brings the dead to life, and He shows you His signs so you might understand.

HARDENED HEARTS REFUSE TO UNDERSTAND

[74] Afterwards, your hearts became hard like rocks or even harder. There are some

---

[a]   This refers to the followers of the Prophet Muhammad 鷺.

[b]   Sabians were a monotheistic sect of Christianity.

[c]   It has always been a perfectly natural and common practice for Arabic-speaking Jews and Christians to use the name God in their prayers and everyday speech.

rocks from which streams flow, and there are others when split open, water flows from them, and yet other rocks which tumble down out of fear of God, He is not unaware of what you do. ⁷⁵Do you expect them to believe you when a group of them hears the words of God and, after understanding them, deliberately changes them?

Be wary of inventing lies

⁷⁶When *such people* meet those who believe, they tell them: "We believe". However, when they are alone, they say: "Why tell them about what God has granted you so they use it as evidence against you before your Lord. Don't you have any sense?" ⁷⁷Do they not realise, God knows what they hide and what they publicise? ⁷⁸Some of them are illiterate; their knowledge of The Book is *based on* false hopes, and mere guess. ⁷⁹What misery awaits those who rewrite The Book with their own hands and then claim: "This is from God", just to earn a little money! What misery awaits them for what their hands have written, and what misery awaits them for what they have earned!

The false claim of a light punishment

⁸⁰They claim: "The Fire will only burn us for a few days". Ask them: "Have you taken a pledge from God; He never breaks His pledge, or are you making a claim about God, ignorantly?" ⁸¹Rather, the evildoers are occupied in their sins, these are the people of the Fire, there forever. ⁸²But those who believed and did righteous works, these are the people of Paradise, there forever.

The contract of the Israelites with God

⁸³*Remember* when We took the contract from the Israelites: worship God alone, care for parents, relatives, orphans and the needy; speak kindly to people; perform the prayer and give Zakat. Unfortunately, you turned away, objecting to it except a few of you. ⁸⁴We took the contract that you would not shed one another's blood or expel one another from their homes; you accepted and witnessed.

Injustice and oppression are unacceptable

⁸⁵You were killing one another, one group forcing the other out of their homes, or helping one side to commit sin and sow enmity against the other. When you took them prisoners, you demanded a ransom for them, although it was forbidden to evict them in the first place. Do you believe in some parts of The Book and

reject others? The only fitting punishment for those who commit such crimes is disgrace in this life, and on Judgement Day will be dispatched to the severest punishments. God is not unaware of what you do. [86] Such people have chosen this worldly life instead of The Hereafter; their punishment will not be lessened nor will they be helped.

THE ISRAELITES DENIED AND KILLED PROPHETS

[87] We gave Moses The Book and sent messengers *afterwards* to succeed him. We gave miracles to Jesus, son of Mary, and supported him with the Spirit of the Holy One.[a] Is it not *true* that whenever a messenger came to you with a message that you did not like you became arrogant, refusing to believe some *of them* and killing others. [88] They said: "Our hearts are covered". Indeed, God cursed them because of their disbelief. How little they believe!

JEALOUSY BREEDS DOUBLE STANDARDS

[89] When a book from God came to them, the Majestic Quran, confirming what they already have – they used to pray for victory over the disbelievers – when what they recognise *as true* comes to them, they deny it. So, God's curse *falls* on the disbelievers. [90] What a miserable price they have sold themselves for, denying rudely what God has revealed, because God sends down His favour on anyone of His Servants He wills! *That is why* they have brought down on themselves wrath upon wrath; for *such* disbelievers is humiliating punishment. [91] And when they are told: "Believe in what God has sent", they say: "We believe in what was sent to us". However, they deny what came afterwards, even though it is the truth confirming that which they already have. Ask them: "Why then, if you were believers, did you kill the previous prophets of God?"

EXPOSING THOSE WHO LOVE THIS WORLD MORE THAN THE HEREAFTER

[92] Moses came to you with miracles, *but* you started worshipping the calf *soon* afterwards, and became wrongdoers. [93] We took a contract from you, near the Mount Sinai towering over you, *and We said*: "Hold on firmly to what We gave you and listen", *but your forefathers* said: "We hear and we disobey", swallowing *love of* the calf *deep* into their hearts because they were unthankful. Tell them: "How wrong is what your faith tells you to do, if you are believers!" [94] Say: "If

---

[a]   *Ruh ul-Qudus* refers to the Archangel Gabriel.

the Final Abode with God is reserved solely for you and no one else, then *why do you not* wish for death, if you are truthful?" [95] However, they will never wish for it since *they know well* what their hands have stockpiled, and God knows well *who the wrongdoers are.* [96] You will find them and some of the idolators among the most eager of people for *the pleasures of* this worldly life. Every single one of them would love to live a thousand years, even though living so long would not save them from the punishment. God sees what they do.

PRETENDING TO NOT KNOW THE TRUTH

[97] Ask: "Who is the enemy of Gabriel?" He brought the Quran down into your heart by God's authority, confirming what came before it, and as guidance and good news for the believers. [98] Whoever is an enemy of God, His Angels, His Messengers, and Gabriel and Michael, *should know* that God is the enemy of *such* disbelievers. [99] We have sent down to you clear verses, and only the wicked deny them. [100] Every time they enter an agreement, a group of them breaks it; in fact, most of them do not believe. [101] When a messenger from God came to them, confirming what they already had, a group of the People of The Book refused to accept it, pretending that they had never heard of it.

THE BLIND QUEST FOR WORLDLY POWER

[102] They *blindly* followed the devilish people who had fabricated about the kingdom of Solomon. Solomon did not disbelieve; rather, it was the devilish people who became disbelievers by teaching people magic and what had been given to the two *angels*, Harut and Marut, in Babylon. These two angels did not teach anyone until they had warned them: "We are *sent as* a test, so do not disbelieve". From these two *angels*, they learned how to create conflict between husband and wife, but they couldn't harm anyone without God's permission. So, people studied what harmed them rather than what benefitted them, knowing that anyone who gained this *knowledge of magic* will have no share in the Hereafter. How wretched is what they have sold themselves for! If only they knew! [103] Had they believed and feared *God*, the reward would have been far better, if they knew!

THE PROPER MANNER OF ADDRESSING THE MESSENGER 🌺

[104] Believers,[a] do not say: *"Ra'ina,"* but *instead* say: "Look at us,[b] and listen carefully *to him*". As for the disbelievers, a painful punishment awaits. [105] Neither the disbelievers among the People of The Book nor the idolaters desire that anything good should come from your Lord; God chooses for his favour anyone who wants to please Him, He is Gracious.

THE DANGERS OF QUESTIONING GOD'S POWER

[106] If ever We abrogate or postpone any verse, We replace it with something better or similar. Do you not know that God has power over all things? [107] Do you not know that the Kingdom of Heaven and Earth belongs to God; there is no protector and helper for you besides Him. [108] Or do you want to ask your Messenger what Moses was asked *by others* before?[c] *We hope not, because* whoever swaps faith for disbelief has wandered far from the straight path. [109] Many of the People of The Book would dearly love to change you into disbelievers after you have believed; *this is* out of jealousy inside themselves *even* after truth has become clear to them. So, *believers*, pardon and be forgiving until God fulfils His command. God has control over all things.

PARADISE IS FOR ANYONE WHO SUBMITS TO GOD

[110] And perform prayer and give Zakat; whatever good you send ahead for yourselves, you will find it with God. God sees all that you do. [111] They claim that only the Jews, or only the Christians, will enter Paradise; this is their wishful thinking. Say: "If you are telling the truth, prove it". [112] On the contrary, anyone who submits to God and is righteous, their reward shall be with their Lord, and they shall neither fear nor grieve.

RESPECTING FREEDOM OF RELIGION

[113] The Jews say: "The Christians are misguided", and the Christians say: "The Jews are misguided", yet all read the *same* Book the Bible. Similarly, those who know nothing say the same thing as them. God will decide between them on

---

[a]   The vocative phrase "O believers" occurs eighty-eight times in the Quran, and this is the first time it is used.

[b]   The word *"Ra'ina"* has two meanings: "look at us", and "attend to our need". However, by a slight twist of the tongue, it has an insulting meaning (carry on deceiving us). That's why it was banned from being used to address the Messenger 🌺, and the clearer term *"unzurna"* is recommended.

[c]   This refers to verse 55 above, when the Israelites demanded: "Moses, we will not believe you until we openly see God".

Judgement Day regarding their differences. [114] Who can be more wicked than the one who stops people from glorifying God's name in His Mosques,[d] and who tries to destroy them? Yet they should only enter them in the fear *of God*. They shall suffer disgrace in this world and severe punishment in the Hereafter.

The vastness of God's creation is proof of His existence

[115] The East and the West belong to God, so wherever you turn, God's Presence will be there. Indeed, God is Boundlessly Vast, the Knowing. [116] They claim God has adopted a son. Glory be to Him! The Heavens and the Earth belong to Him; everything obeys Him, [117] The Creator of The Heavens and the Earth. When He decides on any matter, He only says: "Be!" And *there* it is. [118] The ignorant say: "If God spoke to us, or sent us a sign, we would believe." People before them said similar things; they think alike. We have made Our signs *abundantly* clear for those who firmly believe.

You cannot please both God and the disbelievers

[119] *Prophet*, We sent you with the truth, as the bearer of good news and a warner; you will not be asked about the people of blazing fire. [120] The Jews and the Christians will never be satisfied with you until you follow their religion. Tell them: "God's guidance is the only guidance". If you Muslims follow their wishes after the knowledge has come to you, then you will have no one to protect you from God and to help you[e]. [121] Those given The Book, recite as it ought to be recited,[f] they are the true believers. Anyone who disbelieves in it, they are the losers.

Do not take God's favours for granted

[122] Children of Israel, remember My gifts to you; I preferred you over all other people. [123] So, fear a day when no one will be able to compensate for anyone else; no ransom will be accepted, and no one's intercession will benefit, and they will not be helped.

Abraham prays for his descendants and for Makkah

[124] Remember when Abraham was put to all kinds of tests by His Lord, he achieved them. His Lord said: "I will make you a leader of humanity", so he asked: "And what about my children?" God said: "My pledge will not benefit the evildo-

---

d   *Zikr ul-llah* here refers to Salah, study, spiritual retreat and all kinds of worship.
e   "If you follow" is an address to the followers of the Prophet ﷺ. The Prophet ﷺ is making the announcement.
f   "Reciting" here means combining reading with understanding and action.

ers amongst them". [125] We made The Ancient House a safe and much frequented place, saying: "Take the place where Abraham stood as a place of prayer". And We told Abraham and Ismael: "Keep My House clean for those who circle it, those who stay there to worship, to bow and to prostrate". [126] Remember when Abraham prayed: "Lord, make this a city of sanctuary, and sustain with fruits those who believe in God and The Last Day". God said: "The disbelievers, We shall let them enjoy themselves a little, then drive them towards the punishment of Fire. What a terrible destination!"

ABRAHAM'S PRAYER FOR A SPECIAL MESSENGER

[127] *Remember* when Abraham and Ismael were raising the foundations of The House, they prayed: "Our Lord, accept *this* from us. You are the Listener, the Knower. [128] Our Lord, keep us committed to You,[a] and make our children a community that submits to You, and teach us our rites, and be relenting towards us: indeed. You accept repentance, the Kind. [129] Our Lord, send them a messenger from their people, who will teach your signs, the Book, the wisdom, and purify them. You are the Almighty, the Wise".

ABRAHAM'S RELIGION IS FOR ALL GENERATIONS

[130] Only a fool can turn away from the religion of Abraham; We chose him in this world, and in the next life he will be among the Righteous. [131] *Remember* when His Lord said to him: "Submit", and he replied: "I submit myself to the Lord of the Universe". [132] He advised his children to *submit*, and *later* Jacob *also* did the same, saying: "My children, God has chosen your religion for you, so till you die remain as true Muslims".

JACOB'S FINAL ADVICE TO HIS CHILDREN

[133] Were you witness when death came to Jacob? *Remember* when he asked his children: "What will you worship after me?" *And* they replied: "We will worship Your God and the God of our forefathers, Abraham, Ismael and Isaac, the One God, and we submit to Him". [134] That community has passed away; they will reap the reward of what they did, and so will you, and you will not be asked about what they did.

---

[a] The Arabic uses "Muslims", referring to people who have chosen to submit and commit to the Will of God and to enjoy a living relationship with God.

Muslims do not pick and choose from the prophets

[135] They say *to you*: "Become Jews...", or: "Become Christians and you will be guided". Tell them: "In fact *our religion is* the religion of Abraham, *who was a true Hanif,*[b] and was not an idolater".[c] [136] Say: "We believe in God and in what is revealed to us, and in what was revealed to Abraham, Ismael, Isaac, Jacob and the Tribes, and in what was given to Moses and Jesus, and in what was given to *all* the prophets from their Lord: we make no distinction between any one of them, we submit to Him".

True faith in God affects the whole of a believer's life

[137] If they *decide to* believe in the same *God* as you believe, then they will be guided, but if they turn away, they will be divided. God will be sufficient for you against them. He is the Listener, the Knower. [138] The dye of God *is the best*, whose dye is better than God's at colouring *our whole being*?[d] We worship Him *alone*. [139] Say: "Do you argue with us about God, when He is Our Lord as well as Yours, when we have our deeds and you have yours, we are absolutely committed to Him?" [140] Or do you claim that Abraham, Ishmael, Isaac, Jacob and the Tribes[e] were "Jews" or "Christians?" Say: "Who knows better, you or God? And who can be more sinful than the one who tries to hide evidence from God? Indeed, God is not unaware of what you do". [141] That community has passed away; they will reap the reward of what they did, and so will you, and you will not be questioned about what they did.

The reason for change in the direction of prayer

[142] Some foolish people will ask: "What has turned them away from the direction they used to pray in?" Say: "The East and The West belong to God. He guides to the straight path anyone who wants to be guided". [143] So We made you a well-bal-

---

[b]   *Hanif* describes a person who believes in One God and rejects all forms of idolatry.

[c]   What is idolatry? None of us would dream of worshipping an idol, but succumbing to things that have no eternal value, pleasures, power and possessions? Isn't this a form of idolatry? Anything we put before God, which dilutes our trust in Him, becomes an idol.

[d]   "Dye of God" refers to the natural state of humans. This natural state is mentioned in *Chapter Ar-Rum: 30* as *"Fitra"*: the original and good nature of humanity that is instinctively receptive to moral virtues and spiritual values.

[e]   Since these prophets, and The Twelve Tribes until the time of Moses, lived before the revelation of the Torah, they could not have been Jews.

anced nation,[a] to be witnesses against humanity, and the Messenger will be your witness. We only established your previous prayer direction *towards Aqsa Mosque* to distinguish[b] those who follow the Messenger from those who turn on their heels. This was indeed a difficult test, except for those whom God has guided; God will never allow your prayer[c] to go to waste. Indeed, God is Most Kind and Gracious to people. [144] We saw you turning your face towards the Heaven, and We shall turn you towards a direction of the prayer that will please you. So, now turn your face towards The Sacred Mosque. Wherever you are, turn your faces towards it. Those who were given The Book know *well* that this is the truth from their Lord, and God is aware of what they do.

Don't try to please others at the expense of God

[145] Even if you were to produce conclusive evidence for the People of The Book, they will not adopt your direction of prayer, nor will you adopt their direction of prayer; *in fact*, they do not even follow each other's direction. If anyone were to follow their desires after the knowledge has come to you then they would be wrongdoers. [146] Those Jews given the Book recognise *The Messenger* just as they recognise their sons, *yet* a group of them deliberately tries to hide the truth. [147] The truth has come from your Lord. Listener, don't be among those who have doubts *about it*.

Each person has a goal and a direction

[148] Everyone has a direction to which they turn, so compete in doing good works. Wherever you happen to be, God will bring you together. God has power over everything. [149] By whichever direction you go out *of Madinah,* turn to face the Sacred Mosque *in prayer*; that is the truth from your Lord, and God is not unaware of what you do. [150] In whichever direction you go always turn to face the Sacred Mosque. All of you, wherever you are, always turn your faces towards it, so that people do not have any evidence *of disunity* against you except, *of course*, the wrongdoers among them. Don't be afraid of them, but fear Me, so I will complete My favours on you, and ensure you are guided.

---

[a] The phrase *"Ummatan wastan"* means "a middle nation" a metaphor for "moderate people", far from extremism.

[b] The primary meaning is "to know", but since God knows everything, it is not an appropriate term to use here so we have used the term "distinguish".

[c] The phrase *"Li-eemanikum"* literally means "your faith". However, commentators translate this as "prayer".

The functions of The Messenger 鬱

[151] For example, We sent to you a *noble* Messenger from amongst you; he recites Our verses for you, purifies you, teaches you the Book and wisdom, and teaches you what you didn't know. [152] So, remember Me, and I shall remember you. Be thankful to Me, and don't be unthankful to Me.

Patience: Coping with life's tests

[153] Believers, find strength through patience and prayer – God is with those who are patient. [154] Don't speak *irreverently* of those who were killed *fighting* in God's way, *that they are* "dead"; rather, they are living, though you don't sense *it*. [155] We will certainly test you: with fear, hunger, loss of wealth, health and harvests. Give good news to the patient [156] and who, when they are struck by misfortune, *softly* say: "We belong to God and are returning to Him". [157] These are the ones who shall be blessed and will be taken care of by their Lord; they are the guided.

A tribute to Hajar's patience

[158] The hills of Safa and Marwa are Symbols of God;[d] whoever comes to *God's* House to perform the Hajj or Umrah, *let him know that* there is no objection in walking between them. Whoever works voluntarily will be rewarded by God, the Knower of all things.

God's teachings are not secrets to be hidden away

[159] Those who hide the clear signs and the guidance We have revealed, after We have clearly explained it in The Book for people, they are the ones whom God curses, as do those who *have the authority to* curse, [160] but if they repent, reform themselves and openly declare faith then I shall accept their repentance; I am the Accepter of repentance and the Kind. [161] Those who disbelieve and die as disbelievers will be cursed by God, the angels and *the rest* of humanity, [162] dwelling therein forever, and their punishment will be neither reduced nor delayed.

The signs of God's creative power

[163] Your God is one God; there is no God beside Him, the Kind, the Caring. [164] In the creation of The Heavens and the Earth, in the cycle of night and day, and in the ships which sail the seas for people's profit; in the rain God sends down from the skies, bringing the dead Earth to life, and causing it to abound with all kinds

---

[d] The Quran pays a special tribute to the patience of Lady Hajar, the wife of Prophet Abraham, as she frantically searched for water between these two hillocks. Making these symbols of God teaches the reward of patience.

of animals; in the movements of the winds, and in the clouds which float between Heaven and Earth: *in all these things,* there are signs for people who understand.

REGRETS ABOUT WASTED LIFE ON JUDGEMENT DAY

[165] Some people take idols[a] beside God, loving them as much as *they* love God, *whereas* those who believe, love God passionately. If only the wrongdoers could see the punishment, they would realise that God possesses all power, and that God's punishment is severe. [166] *On Judgement Day,* the followers *of idols* will be disowned by the idols they served, and they will see the punishment, and their ties *with these idols* torn to shreds. [167] Then the followers will say: "If only we had another chance so we could disown them as they have disowned us *today*". That is how God will show them their deeds, which they will bitterly regret, and they will never get out of the Fire *of Hell.*

HOW SATAN INFLUENCES PEOPLE

[168] People, eat of what is lawful and wholesome on Earth, and do not follow the footsteps of Satan; he is your open enemy. [169] He will direct you to evil, indecency and saying things about God which you don't know. [170] When *the disbelievers* are told, "Follow what God has revealed," they say: "No! We follow what we found our ancestors doing", even though their ancestors lacked both basic understanding and guidance. [171] The disbelievers are like the bleating *sheep being called* loudly *by the shepherd,* they hear nothing but crying and screaming; deaf, dumb and blind, they *simply* don't understand.

MEAT WHICH IS UNLAWFUL TO EAT

[172] Believers, eat the wholesome foods We provide you and thank God, if you truly worship Him. [173] The *few* things He has made unlawful for you are carrion, blood, pork, and animals slaughtered in any name other than God's. However, if anyone is compelled *by circumstance,*[b] not because he desires it or wishes to disobey *God,* then he commits no sin. God is the Forgiving, the Kind.

IT IS WRONG TO USE RELIGION FOR WORLDLY GAINS

[174] Anyone who hides what God has revealed in the Book, or sells it for a small

---

[a] "Idols" refers not only to physical statues that people worship, but any material thing in which one puts trust instead of God. This can include wealth, career, family, technological gadgets and even gangs.

[b] For example, if you hate the thought but are dying of hunger or thirst, are being force-fed by a captor, or told you will be killed if you refuse to do so, then consuming such meat is not a sin.

sum *of money* are filling their stomachs with Hellfire. God will neither speak to them nor purify them on Judgement Day; they shall have a painful punishment. [175] They have chosen *for themselves* error over guidance and punishment over forgiveness. How will they endure Hellfire? [176] That is because God has sent The Book with the truth, *but* those who differ about The Book have digressed with farfetched heresy.

WHAT IS RIGHTEOUSNESS?

[177] Righteousness is not simply turning your face towards The East or The West *in prayer,* rather, righteousness is believing in God, The Last Day, the angels, the *revealed* books and the prophets; spending wealth for the love of God on relatives, orphans, the needy, travellers, beggars and freeing slaves; performing prayer and paying Zakat; fulfilling any contracts one has entered; and being patient in illness, misfortune and in times of hardship. Those *who do these things* are the truthful people, and they are mindful of God.

THE LAW OF TAKING REVENGE FOR JUSTICE

[178] Believers, retribution is prescribed for you in the case of victims of murderers: a free man for a free man, a slave for a slave, and a woman for a woman. *However*, if the *culprit* is pardoned by his *aggrieved* brother, this will be adhered to in accordance with best practice, *the culprit* paying *the next of kin* what is due. This represents a *lightening of the burden* and an act of kindness from your Lord. After this *day* if anyone goes beyond *these limits,* they will suffer a painful punishment. [179] The people of understanding *will appreciate* that in the law of retribution there is *a means for preserving* life, so you›re stopped from being unfair.

INSTRUCTIONS FOR WRITING A WILL

[180] *Also* prescribed for you *is the writing of a will*: when death approaches any of you, who is leaving behind wealth, let him prepare a will in favour of parents and close relatives in accordance with best practice; this is a duty upon those who are mindful *of God*. [181] If any *witness*, after hearing *the terms*, alters them then they – and they alone – has committed a sin. God is the Hearer, the Knower. [182] Anyone who suspects that a testator[c] has made a mistake intentionally or unintentionally, and tries to put things right between the parties, commits no sin in doing so. God

[c] The testator is the person who has made the will.

is the Forgiving, the Kind.

The purpose of fasting in Ramadan

[183] Believers, fasting has been compulsory for you as it was made compulsory for those before you so you become mindful *of God.* [184] *Fast* for a fixed number of days, but if any of you is ill or on a journey then *let him fast* an *equivalent* number of days *later.* The obligatory compensation on those who *do not fast,* is to feed a needy person, *if they* can afford it. However, anyone who voluntarily does good will benefit from that, *but* to fast would be better for you, if you knew.

The Quran was revealed in Ramadan

[185] The Quran was revealed in the month of Ramadan; *the Quran* is a guidance for people, it contains clear teachings and distinguishes *right from wrong*; whoever is present in the month must fast in it, but, if anyone is ill or on a journey, then *let them fast* an *equivalent* number of days *later.* God wants ease for you, not difficulty, and wants to see you complete the *compulsory* number *of fasts. So,* glorify God for guiding you, and be ever-thankful.

God answers our prayers

[186] If My servants ask you about Me, *tell them that* I am near, I answer *the* prayer of the prayerful whenever he prays to Me. So, let them obey Me, and believe in Me so they may be guided.

A rule for married couples in Ramadan

[187] It is permissible for you to sleep with your wives during the nights of the fast – they are *like* a garment for you, as you are for them.[a] God knew that you were deceiving yourselves *by what you were doing in secret*, and He has relented towards you and pardoned you. So now be intimate with them, and desire whatever God has allowed you, and eat and drink until the white streak of dawn is distinct from the blackness of the night, then complete the fast until the nightfall.[b] However, do not be intimate with your wives *on those nights* when you are engaged in a *spiritual* retreat in the Mosque. These are God's boundaries, so do not breach

---

[a]   Literally translated as: "they are your garments and you are their garments". In other words, the sexual intimacy that husbands and wives enjoy helps cover them both in public like clothing, preventing them from acting indecently.

[b]   The white streak of dawn refers to the daybreak when the light is spread horizontally as the sun is 18° below the horizon.

them. This is how God explains His verses for people, so they are mindful.

BRIBERY, FRAUD AND SQUANDERING ONE'S WEALTH ARE ALL IMMORAL

[188] Do not misuse your wealth *by spending it* amongst yourselves for wrong purpose, or by deliberately bribing judges to misuse a part of other people's wealth wrongfully.

EXAMINING SUPERSTITIOUS PRACTICES

[189] They ask you about the crescent moon, say: "It is *to help* people keep track of time, *not least* for the pilgrimage". There is no virtue in entering homes from the back, but virtue lies in piety. Enter homes from front doors, and be mindful of God so you may be successful.

FIGHTING IS ONLY PERMITTED IN SELF-DEFENCE

[190] Fight in God's way those who fight you, but do not attack first. God does not like aggressors.[c] [191] *When in battle,* fight them wherever you find them, and expel them from where they expelled you. *A prolonged campaign of* persecution is far worse than *a decisive battle involving* killing. Do not attack them near the Sacred Mosque until they attack you. If they attack you, fight back; that is the way to deal with the disbelievers. [192] If they cease fighting, God is the Forgiving, the Kind.

JUST RETALIATION TO END PERSECUTION IS ALLOWED

[193] Fight them until there is no more persecution, and people are free to worship God. If they cease fighting, then let there be no hostility except against wrongdoers. [194] A sacred month always remains a sacred month; therefore, any violation of what God has forbidden calls for retaliation. If someone is hostile to you, respond in equal measure, and be mindful of God, and know *for certain* that God is with the pious. [195] Spend generously in God's way, but do not cast yourselves into *the jaws of* destruction by your own hands, and do your best. God loves those who do good[d].

HOW TO COMPENSATE FOR AN INCOMPLETE PILGRIMAGE

[196] Perform Hajj and Umrah for the sake of God. If you are prevented *from per-*

[c] This verse and others which permit fighting are giving permission for self-defence only. This is an agreed opinion of all commentators and jurists. Fighting can only be authorised by legitimately elected governments, not self-proclaimed leaders. This passage was revealed when Muslims were performing the Umrah and were anxious about what to do if they were attacked by the Makkans.

[d] These six verses have four prohibitions; seven restrictions...The prevalent message of the Quran is one of peace and tolerance it allows self-defence (Abdal Haleem).

forming Umrah, then *make* whatever sacrificial offering you can afford. Do not shave your heads until your offering has reached the place of sacrifice *in Mina*. If anyone of you is ill or has a disease of the scalp then he should fast, give in charity or make a sacrifice in compensation. When you are safe, then anyone wishing to combine Hajj and Umrah *must make* whatever sacrificial offering he can afford, *and* anyone who lacks the means to do so should fast for three days during the pilgrimage and seven days after returning home – that is ten days in all. This applies to those whose families do not live near the Sacred Mosque. Be mindful of God, and remember God's punishment is severe.

The rites of Hajj

[197] Hajj takes place in the specified months, and anyone undertaking this duty must not: engage in sexual intimacy *with one's spouse*; commit sin nor quarrel with each other. Whatever good you do, God knows it. Prepare yourselves *for Hajj*, and the best preparation is being mindful *of God*. People of understanding, be mindful of Me. [198] There is no sin in seeking your Lord's bounty *by offering a service whilst performing your Hajj*. When you leave Mount Arafat, remember God at the sacred place *of Muzdalifa*. Remember Him, because He guided you when, in the past, you were misguided. [199] Then set off from where *other* people set off, and seek God's forgiveness. Indeed, God is the Forgiving, the Compassionate.

The pilgrims' prayer

[200] Once you have completed your rites, remember God as you used to remember your ancestors, and even more. There are people who pray: "Our Lord, grant us *wealth* in this world", they will have no share in the Hereafter. [201] But others pray: "Our Lord, grant us good in this world and good in the Hereafter, and protect us from the punishment of the Fire". [202] Such *people* will have a *full* share of what they earned, and God is swift in calculating *good and bad deeds*. [203] Continue remembering God till specified days, but if anyone is in a hurry to leave after two days, *he can,* he will not have sinned, nor will anyone who delays his departure have sinned, so long as he is mindful *of God*. Be mindful of God, and know that you will be gathered before Him.

The troublemaker

[204] There is a *type of* person whose speech will please you, and he even calls on God as a witness to what is in his heart, yet he is the bitterest of opponents. [205] As soon

as he turns away, he makes mischief in the land, destroying crops and cattle[a]. God detests mischief. [206] When he is told: "Fear God!" His pride leads him to sin. Hell will be enough for him. A dreadful place.

THE PEACEMAKER: COMMITTED TO GOD

[207] Yet there is *another type* of person who would give away his life to gain God's pleasure; God is Compassionate to *His* servants. [208] Believers, submit and dedicate fully, and do not follow in the footsteps of Satan; he is your sworn enemy. [209] If you should turn back after clear signs have come to you, then know that God is the Almighty and the Wise. [210] What are they waiting for? God and the angels to come down in the shade of the clouds? By then, *their* fate will have been sealed. *In the end,* all matters will return to God.

SUCCESS IN THIS LIFE IS NO GUARANTEE OF SUCCESS IN THE NEXT

[211] Ask the Israelites how many clear signs We gave them. Anyone who exchanges a gift of God *for something else* after it has been granted to him, *beware*; God is severe in *His* punishment. [212] The worldly life is attractive for the disbelievers; they may mock some believers *now*, but the pious *will rise* above them on Judgement Day. God will provide abundantly to those who He wishes.

GAINING KNOWLEDGE PROMPTS SOME PEOPLE TO ARGUE

[213] Humanity was once a single nation. Then God sent prophets, who brought good news and warnings, and He sent with them the Book containing the truth, providing rulings to help people solve their differences. This was due to the rivalry that arose from differences *of interpretation* after clear signs had come to the People *of The Book*. However, God, by His authority, guided the believers to the truth regarding the point of disagreement. God guides to the straight path anyone who wants to be guided.

EVERY GENERATION OF BELIEVERS HAS BEEN TESTED

[214] Did you think of going to Paradise without experiencing the difficulties of those *who* came before you? They were struck by misfortune and hardships, and were subjected to Earthquakes, even the messenger *of that time* and those who believed him cried out: "When will God's help come?" Beware, the help of God is near. [215] They ask you what they should spend *their wealth* on; tell them: "Spend

---

[a]   *"Al-ḥars wanasl"* is an idiom for human civilisation (Hans Wher), so they raid villages and towns destroying them.

on your parents, relatives, orphans, the needy and the travellers". Whatever good you have done God is the Knower *and is fully aware* of it.

JIHAD IS COMPULSORY

[216] War is ordained though you dislike it. Sometimes, you may dislike something that is good for you, and sometimes you may like something that is bad for you. Only God knows *the whole truth*, not you. [217] They ask you about the sacred months, and *specifically* fighting in them; say: "Fighting in them is a major sin, but blocking the way of God and rejecting Him, *barring* access to the Sacred Mosque and expelling its residents from it – these are even greater *offences* in God's sight. *A prolonged campaign of* persecution is a far greater sin than *a decisive battle involving* killing". The *disbelievers* will go on fighting until they achieve what they want: that you give up your religion. *But beware*. If any of you gives up his religion and dies as a disbeliever, such people's deeds will come to nothing in this world and in the Hereafter. These are people of the Fire, where they will stay forever. [218] The believers, who migrated and struggled in God's way, have *full* hope in God's Kindness. God is the Forgiving, the Kind.

QUESTIONS ON ALCOHOL, GAMBLING, CHARITY AND ORPHANS

[219] They ask you about wine and gambling; say: "Both are major sins, there is a small benefit for people, but the sin in them by far outweighs any benefits". They ask you what they should spend *in charity*, say: "Whatever you can spare". This is how God explains His verses to you so that you may reflect, [220] in this world, and the next. They also ask you about orphans, say: "Keeping *their affairs and accounts* in order is best. If you mix *your investments* with theirs, *remember that* they are your brothers and sisters, and God knows well who is straight and who is dishonest". If God so wished, He could put you in *all kinds* of difficulties. He is the Almighty, the Wise.

GOING TO PARADISE OR HELL MAY BE DETERMINED BY WHO ONE MARRIES

[221] Do not marry disbelieving women[a] until they believe; a female slave who believes is better than an idolatress, even if the idolatress pleases you more. *Similarly*, do not marry *believing women to* any idolater until they believe; a male slave who believes is better than an idolater, even if the idolater is more pleasing. These

---

[a] *"Mushrik"* refers to the idolaters and idol worshippers, and therefore refers to a special kind of disbelief.

idolaters invite you to the Fire, whereas God, by His grace, invites you to Paradise and forgiveness; and He explains His verses for people to remind them.

An answer to a question about menstruation and sexual intimacy

²²² They ask you about menstruation, say: "It is a sore state *that women go through*, so stay away from *sexual intimacy with* women during menstruation, and do not approach them *for that purpose* until they are clean again. However, once they are clean, come to them as God has allowed you. God loves those who repent, and He loves those who maintain cleanliness". ²²³ Your women are like pastures for you, so enter your pastures as you wish, and prepare for yourselves *good deeds*. Be mindful of God, remember you will meet Him, and you, *Muhammad, continue to* give good news to the believers".

Ruling about settling marital disputes

²²⁴ Do not make your oaths in the name of God an excuse to stop you from doing good, being mindful, and reconciling people *who are undergoing some marital dispute*; God is the Hearer, the Knower. ²²⁵ God will not hold your thoughtless oaths against you, but He will take you to task over your heart's *intentions*. God is The Forgiving, The Gentle. ²²⁶ For those who take an oath to *separate from* their wives, the waiting period is four months, but if they go back on their oath, then they will find God Forgiving, Most Kind. ²²⁷ However, if they are determined to divorce, then God is the Hearer and the Knower.

The rights and responsibilities of married couples and of divorcees

²²⁸ Divorced women must wait for three menstrual cycles before they can marry; it is not lawful for them to keep secret what God has created in their womb if they believe in God and the Last Day. Their husbands have the right to take them back during this period, if they wish to be reconciled. Women too have rights and responsibilities in equal measure, according to the custom. However, men have an additional degree of rights and responsibilities over them. God is The Almighty, The Wise.

What to do if marriage guidance and reconciliation fail

²²⁹ A revocable divorce *may be pronounced* twice only; after that *a wife* must either be kept honourably or allowed to leave honourably. It is not lawful for you *husbands* to take back anything that you have given them, except when both par-

ties fear that they may not be able to live within God's boundaries. However, if, *after attempting reconciliation*, you believe that the couple may not be able to live within the bounds set by God, then there will be no blame on either if *the woman* chooses to give back part of her settlement. These are God's boundaries, so do not overstep them. Only the wrongdoers overstep God's boundaries.

THIRD TIME DIVORCE

[230] If *the husband* divorces her *a third time*; she will no longer be lawful for him *to remarry* until she marries another husband. Then, if *the second husband* divorces her, there will be no blame on either of them to return to each other, provided they feel confident that they will keep within God's boundaries. These are God's boundaries which He has explained for people who understand.

DON'T BE UNJUST WHEN GOING THROUGH DIVORCE

[231] When you divorce women, and they reach the end of the waiting period, either keep them honourably or allow them to leave honourably. Don't hold on to them to cause harm or to transgress God's boundaries; whoever does so has wronged himself. Do not play with the commands of God. Remember His favours on you and what He has revealed to you of the Book and wisdom, through which He teaches you. So be mindful of God, and know that He is the Knower. [232] When you divorce women, and they reach the end of the waiting period, do not prevent them remarrying their *former* husbands, if they choose to do so by mutual consent *and* according to the custom. Anyone who sincerely believes in God and the Last Day is instructed to do this. This is a purer and cleaner *way* for you by far. God knows that which you don't know.

A FATHER WILL PAY MAINTENANCE EXPENSES FOR HIS CHILDREN

[233] *Divorced* mothers may breastfeed their children up to full two years; that is if they wish to complete the full term. The father of the child is responsible for *the mother's* food and clothing in accordance with the best practice. *However*, no one is to be burdened over and above their means. Neither should the mother be harmed because of her child, nor the father. The same goes for the *father's* heirs. No one shall be to blame if *the father or the mother* wishes to wean the child, and it is agreed by mutual consent after proper consultation. *Likewise,* if you wish to employ a nanny for your children, you can't be blamed, if you pay as agreed in accordance with the best practice. *Always* be mindful of God, and know that He

sees what you do.

[234] Those who die, leaving behind widows, *their widows* should wait for four months and ten *days* then, once they have reached *the end of* this period, there is no blame on you regarding whatever they choose to do with themselves in accordance with the best practice. God is aware of what you do. [235] There is no blame on you if you propose engagement to *these* women *before the end of the waiting period*, or you keep *your feelings* to yourself. God knows that you intend to propose to them. However, do not make them any promises unless you speak to them in a respectful way, and do not confirm contracting the marriage until the prescribed *waiting* term has ended. Remember that God knows what is in your hearts, so beware. God is the Forgiving, The Gentle.

WHAT TO DO IF DIVORCE OCCURS BEFORE A MARRIAGE IS CONSUMMATED
[236] There is no blame on you if you divorce a woman before either consummating the marriage or paying the marriage gift. Let the rich and the poor each give them generously according to their means; this is a duty on the righteous. [237] If you divorce them before consummation but after fixing the marriage gift, then let them have half of what you had previously settled on, unless *the women* agree to waive their right or the one contracting the marriage tie waives his right, and waiving one's right is nearer to piety. So, do not forget to be gracious to each other, *because* God sees all that you do.

NEVER NEGLECT YOUR PRAYERS UNDER ANY CIRCUMSTANCES
[238] Make sure to perform your *daily* prayers, particularly the middle prayer *Asr*, and stand devoutly before God. [239] If you are fearful *of an enemy*, then pray standing or in the saddle; then, when you are safe and secure once more, then remember God, as He taught you what you didn't know.

FURTHER RULINGS ON MAINTENANCE FOR WIDOWS AND DIVORCEES
[240] Those who die, leaving behind widows, should make a will for their maintenance for one year: they should not be expelled *from the family home*. However, if they *choose to* leave *the family home*, then you can't be blamed with regards to what they have chosen to do in line with custom. God is the Almighty and Wise.

²⁴¹ Divorced women are entitled to maintenance[a] in line with custom; this is a duty on the pious. ²⁴² This is how God explains His verses for you, so that you might understand.

THE STORY OF THE JEWISH KING TALUT

²⁴³ Haven't you seen those who left their homes in their thousands for fear of death, and God said to them: "Die!" And then He brought them back to life?[b] God is very gracious to people, but they are ungrateful. ²⁴⁴ Fight in the cause of God, and remember He is the Hearer, the Knower. ²⁴⁵ Who will offer God a loan, a beautiful loan, He will multiply its reward many times over. God withholds *His favour*, or He gives plenty, and to Him you will return.

THE ISRAELITES DEMAND A KING

²⁴⁶ Have you not considered the Jewish leaders *who came after* Moses. They said to a prophet of theirs: "Appoint a king so that we may fight in God's way". He said to them: "When fighting is ordained for you, will you fight?" They said: "Why would we not fight in the way of God when we and our children have been expelled from our homes?" When fighting was ordained for them, they turned away except for a few of them. God knows the disobedient.

TALUT IS THE KING

²⁴⁷ Their prophet said to them: "God has appointed Talut to be your king". They said: "How can he be our king, when we have more right to kingship than him, he is not wealthy enough?" He replied: "God has selected him for you, given him vast knowledge and physical strength. God gives His kingship to anyone He finds suitable. God is boundlessly Vast, He is The Knower". ²⁴⁸ And their Prophet said to them: "The sign of his kingship is The Ark *of the Contract, which* will be brought to you by the angels,[c] a source of tranquillity from your Lord which contains relics left behind by families of Moses and Aaron. In this there are signs for you, if you believe".

---

[a] Mata'un is the post-divorce financial support a woman receives. According to Tabari it is an obligation on the husband: "Mut'ah is mandatory for all divorced women".

[b] This refers to the story below of a community of the Jews who refused to take part in Jihad as ordered by their king, Talut, known as Saul in the Bible.

[c] The Ark was a wooden chest containing the two stone tablets with the Ten Commandments. The Israelites treasured it as a sacred sign of God's presence among them.

TALUT'S SOLDIERS FAIL THE TEST

[249] When Talut set out with his army, he said: "God will test you near the river. Anyone who drinks from it will no longer be my *soldier*, but whoever does not taste it will be mine, except those who scoop it up in the palm of their hands". So, they all drank from it, except a few of them. When he crossed *the river* along with those who had believed him, they said: "We have no strength today to fight Jalut and his army". But those who believed that they would meet their Lord said: "How many times have small forces defeated large forces with the help of God, and God is with the patient".

THE FAITHFUL ISRAELITES ARE VICTORIOUS

[250] When they advanced to face Jalut and his army, they prayed: "Our Lord, shower patience on us, keep our feet firm *on the ground*, and help us against the disbelievers". [251] So, by the help of God they defeated them, and David killed Jalut, and God gave David kingship and wisdom, and taught him what it pleased Him to teach. If God did not repel one group of people with another there would be lot of conflict on Earth, but God is Most Gracious to His creatures. [252] These are the exact verses of God that We recite to you, and you are one of the Messengers.

GOD HAS PLACED THE PROPHETS IN RANKS

[253] Of these prophets We ranked some above others; God spoke with some, and others He raised *many* degrees. *For example*, We gave Jesus, son of Mary, many miracles, and supported him with the Spirit of the Holy One. If God had so wanted, *the Christians* would not have fought each other after the miracles had come to them, but they disputed. Some of them believed and others disbelieved. If God wanted, they would not have divided into sects, but God does what is just. [254] Believers, spend *in charity* from what We provided you before that day comes when there will be no buying and selling, no friendship and no intercession; the disbelievers are wicked people.

THE THRONE VERSE: A GLORIOUS PORTRAYAL OF GOD

[255] God, there is no god but Him! *He is* The Living, The Everlasting. Neither tiredness nor sleep overwhelm Him. All that is in The Heavens and on Earth belongs to Him. Who dares intercede without His permission? He knows what

they have achieved and what they have failed to do,[a] but they can only grasp what He wishes of His knowledge. His *Majestic* Throne extends over the Heavens and the Earth, and He never tires of protecting them both. He is The Exalted, The Majestic.

FREEDOM OF RELIGION IS A FUNDAMENTAL HUMAN RIGHT

[256] There is no compulsion in religion. Guidance is clearly distinct from error.[b] Whoever rejects false gods[c] and believes *solely* in God has grasped the most trustworthy handhold, which will never break. God is the Hearing, the Knowing.

GOD IS THE FRIEND OF THE BELIEVERS

[257] God is the friend of believers, taking them out of darkness into light. As for the disbelievers, their friends are the false gods, who take them out of light into darkness; these are people of the Fire, where they will stay forever.

EXAMPLES OF GOD'S GUIDANCE: *ABRAHAM DEFEATS THE TYRANT NIMROD*

[258] Have you not considered the one who God made King, when he argued with Abraham about his Lord? Abraham said to him: "It is my Lord Who gives life and death". He replied: "I too give life and death". Abraham replied: "God brings the Sun from the East, so why not bring it from the West, *if you can?*" The disbeliever was speechless, God does not guide the wicked people.

EZRA IS SHOWN GOD'S POWER OVER LIFE AND DEATH

[259] Or take *the example of* the one who passed through a town, its buildings razed to the ground; he *asked himself*: "How can God bring these *ruins* to life once they are dead?" So, God made him die for hundred years and then brought him back to life. *God* asked him: "How long did you remain *dead* in such way?" He replied: "Possibly a day or part of a day". God told him: "In fact you remained dead for a hundred years! Look at your food and drink, they have not gone off; but look at your donkey. We *have done all* this to make you a sign for people, look at the *donkey's* bones, how We put them back together and covered them with flesh".

---

[a] I have used Ibn Abbas interpretation "what they have achieved" as what happened to them in this world, while "what they failed to do" points to what will happen to them in the Hereafter.

[b] The occasion for its revelation is: some Ansar whose children died young would take an oath to devote their children to Judaism if they remained alive, so some of them converted to Judaism. After the Jewish tribe Banu Nadhir was expelled from Madinah, they wanted to convert them to Islam.

[c] All manner of things can be *"Taghut"*, including an unhealthy appetite for money, power and unjust governments etc.

When it had *all* become clear to him, he said: "I now know that God has power over all things".

Abraham witnesses the resurrection of dead birds

²⁶⁰ *Remember* when Abraham said: "My Lord, show me how you bring the *dead* back to life", *God* said: "Do you not believe?" He said: "Yes, of course, but I want my heart to be at peace". He told him: "Take four birds and *tame them first,* then cut them into pieces and put a piece of each of them on different hilltops and call them; they will come hurrying back to you. Know that God is the Almighty, the Wise."

Those who spend in the way of God: Parable of a single grain

²⁶¹ Those people who spend their wealth in God's way are like a grain that sprouts into seven ears, each ear has a hundred seeds, and God will multiply it for them many times more as He pleases.ᵈ God is The Vast, The Knowing.

Parable of the soil-covered rock: do not seek favours in return

²⁶² Those who spend their wealth in the way of God and do not follow it up by reminding the recipients of the favour, or causing them offence, shall have reward from their Lord: they shall neither fear nor grieve. ²⁶³ A kind word and forgiveness are far better than charity that is followed by an insult. God is Self-Sufficient and Most Gentle. ²⁶⁴ Believers, do not invalidate your charity by reminders *of favours done* or by insulting, like the one who spends his wealth to show off in front of people and does not *truly* believe in God and the Last Day; he is like a rock with a layer of soil on the top, when heavy rain comes, it is left clean and bare. They will get nothing from their efforts. God does not guide the disbelievers.

Parable of the orchard that produces fruit regardless of the rain

²⁶⁵ Those who spend their wealth seeking God's pleasure, and for strengthening their faith, are like an orchard on a hilltop; if it rains, it produces double yield, and if there is no rain the dew is enough. God sees all that you do.

Parable of the orchard destroyed by stinginess

²⁶⁶ Would any of you wish to have an orchard of date palms and grape vines beneath which streams flow, producing all kinds of fruits? Then suppose he grows old whilst his children are still small, then *out of the blue* comes a hurricane with

---

ᵈ   God multiplies the reward according to the sincerity and the donors love of God.

lightening and fire that burns *his orchard* to ashes? This is how God makes clear His signs, so that you may reflect.

GIVE THE BEST YOU HAVE IN CHARITY

[267] Believers, give in charity of the good things that you have earned and that We have brought forth for you from the soil. Do not pick out the least attractive things to give in charity, things you wouldn't readily accept yourselves. Know that God is Self-Sufficient, Worthy of all praise. [268] The Satan scares you of poverty, and he urges you to behave indecently, but God promises you a share of His forgiveness and bounty. God is the Vast, the Knowing.

WISDOM IS THE GREATEST GIFT OF ALL

[269] He gives wisdom to whom He pleases, and whoever is given wisdom has received great goodness, but only understanding people are mindful *of this fact.*[a]

WHETHER YOU GIVE OPENLY OR SECRETLY, DO IT TO PLEASE GOD

[270] Whatever you give in charity or vow you make, God knows it. Evildoers will have no helpers. [271] If you give charity openly, that is wonderful, but giving it secretly to the needy is *even* better; *in both cases* it will compensate for your sins. God is fully aware of what you do. [272] It is not for you, *Muhammad*, to guide them, rather God guides anyone who wants to be guided. Whatever good things you give in charity will benefit yourselves; that is, if you give, seeking only God's pleasure. Whatever good things you give in charity will be rewarded, and you will be not short-changed in the least.

HOW TO RECOGNISE THE GENUINELY NEEDY

[273] *Give charity* to the poor who are completely absorbed working in the way of God, unable to travel about the land *to earn their livelihood.* Because of their modest behaviour *some* ignorant *people* consider them wealthy. You can recognise them from their facial expression and the fact that they do not make demands on people. Whatever good things you give in charity, God knows it well. [274] People who give their wealth in charity by night or by day, secretly or openly, shall have their reward from their Lord: they shall neither fear nor grieve.

---

[a] Wisdom is God's gift to those who make the right choices, who make constant effort to better themselves by practicing moral, social and spiritual values.

[275] Those who deal in usury[b] will stand *on the Day of Judgement* like the one who is demented by Satan's touch; that is because they claim: "Trading and usury are alike", whereas God has made trading lawful and forbidden usury. So, whoever takes heed of his Lord's warning and gives up *usurious lending*, he can have *the capital* that he lent back, and his case rests with God. However, whoever goes back *to usury*, then such people will be the companions of the Fire, remaining in it forever. [276] God wipes out *the benefits of* usury, but multiplies *those of* acts of charity. God dislikes every ungrateful sinner. [277] *As for* those who believe, do righteous deeds, perform the prayer and pay Zakat, they shall have reward from their Lord: neither shall they fear, nor grieve.

GOD DECLARES A WAR ON USURERS AND OFFERS A WAY OUT
[278] Believers, be mindful of God and give up any outstanding usury *on debts owed to you*, if you are true believers. [279] If you do not do so, then heed this declaration of war from God and His Messenger. However, if you repent you may keep the capital of your wealth so that you neither wrong others nor are yourselves wronged. [280] If *the debtor* is in difficulty, allow him time to repay when it is easier for him, but to write off the debt out of charity would be better for you, if only you knew. [281] Be fearful of the day you will return to God; then every soul will receive exactly what it has earned, and no one will be wronged.

LOANS AND BUSINESS CONTRACTS: *RECORDING LOAN TERMS TO PREVENT FRAUD*
[282] Believers, when you enter into a loan agreement for a fixed period, then write it down, and let a scribe write it down accurately. A scribe should never refuse to write down *the truth*, as God has taught him. So, let *the scribe* write, and let the debtor be mindful of God his Lord and dictate without any subtraction *the exact terms of what he has borrowed.*

WITNESSES ARE REQUIRED TO PROTECT THOSE LIABLE TO EXPLOITATION
If the debtor has learning difficulties, is feeble or otherwise incapable of dictating by himself, then let his guardian dictate accurately *on his behalf*; and let two men amongst you witness *the agreement*. If two men are not available, then a man and two women of whom you approve can be witnesses so that, if one of *the women*

---

[b]   Usury is the exploitation of the weak by charging interest on money borrowed.

makes a mistake, the other can remind her. Witnesses should never refuse to attend when they are called upon.

ALL COMMERCIAL DEALS SHOULD BE RECORDED, WITH ONE EXCEPTION

Do not consider recording the terms of small amounts and its due date as insignificant compared to large ones; that is fairer in the sight of God. However, an exception exists for on-the-spot transactions which you arrange amongst yourselves, and for which there is no blame on you if you do not record the details, but make sure witnesses are present when you exchange the goods. No pressure should be brought to bear on either a scribe or a witness to any transaction; if you do so, you will be guilty of wrongdoing. So be mindful of God, and follow God's instructions. God knows all things.[a]

THE PLACE OF SECURITIES AND TRUST IN BUSINESS DEALS

[283] If you are on a journey and unable to find a scribe then pledge something as a security. However, if you decide to trust one another, then let the trustee fulfil his trust, and let him be mindful of his Lord. Let none of you hide the truth; whoever does so, his heart is sinful. God is fully aware of what you do.

GOD'S KNOWLEDGE OF ALL THINGS VISIBLE AND INVISIBLE

[284] God owns everything in the Heavens and on Earth. Whether you reveal your innermost thoughts or you hide them, God will hold you to account for them; then He will forgive whomever He pleases and punish whomever He pleases. God has control over all things.

THE ARTICLES OF FAITH

[285] The Messenger accepts as truth what has been revealed to him by his Lord, as do the believers; all of them believe in God, His angels, His books and His messengers. *They say*: "We make no distinction between any of His messengers"[b]. And they say: "We hear and obey. Forgive us, our Lord, to You is the final return".

A PRAYER FOR CONSOLATION, JUSTICE AND KINDNESS

[286] God does not burden anyone beyond their capacity; they will receive the reward they earned, and will suffer the consequences of whatever evil they commit-

---

[a] Why two women witnesses giving witness is not a 'right' it's a duty, real responsibility. The Quran here is not obliging women to take this duty; they can have another woman with them. So, a woman is not being deprived of a right.

[b] All the Messengers are equal in their Prophethood but differ in ranks.

ted. So, pray in this way: "Our Lord, when we forget and make a mistake do not punish us. Our Lord, do not make things hard for us, as you did with those before us. Our Lord, do not burden us with more than we can bear, pardon us, forgive us and be kind to us. You are our Protector, so help us against the disbelievers".

3. Ale 'Imran
The Family of Imran

This chapter was revealed after the battle of Uhud, which took place in Shawwal 624 CE. 'The family of Imran,' refers to Imran, the father of Mary, the mother of Prophet Jesus. Three major themes of the chapter are:

- God's Oneness, *tawhid*, and His unique power and majesty.
- Criticism of certain Jewish and Christian doctrines and practices, especially sectarianism. There follows an invitation to the Jews and Christians to follow the Prophet Muhammad ﷺ who is praised for his brilliant leadership.
- The last part of the chapter deals with the battle of Uhud.

The chapter opens by proclaiming that God's revelation has been continuous from the beginning of time, and that it includes the Torah of the Jewish Scriptures, the scrolls revealed to many other prophets and the Gospel of Jesus. The Quran is a continuation of that chain and therefore the final revelation. So, the People of The Book are invited to embrace this final testament, and to follow it. The Quran warns against erroneous interpretation of metaphorical passages and making interpretations that go against the spirit of the divine message, thus sowing the seeds of conflict, even though, "Only God knows their exact meaning" (7). This kind of 'stretching' the meanings of divine scripture was the root of sectarianism rampant among the Jews and Christians. The Christian doctrine of the divinity of Jesus and the "son ship of God," is an example of this arbitrary interpretation of the message of Jesus. The Quran challenges the Christian doctrine of Jesus being either one with God or the "son" of God. Instead it asserts that "Jesus is like Adam; *God* created him from dust then said to him 'Be!' And he was" (59).

The story of Mary's childhood is beautifully told through the miracles, the Prophet Zachariah, Her guardian, prayed to God for a child of his own and he was blessed with a son: John. This is followed by an account of Mary's virgin conception and the birth of Jesus.

The Battle of Uhud

Since their defeat at the Battle of Badr, the Makkans had been planning to avenge their dead. Within a year, they mustered an army of some 3,000 men to attack Madinah. When the Prophet ﷺ learnt of this, he held a war council. The overwhelming opinion was to leave the city and meet the enemy in the open field. So a thousand Muslims marched to mount Uhud. However, 300 men led by Abdullah ibn Ubayy, the hypocrite, deserted.

The Prophet ﷺ arrayed the bulk of his forces with their backs to Mount Uhud, and posted fifty archers on the nearby hill, to provide cover against outflanking manoeuvres by the enemy cavalry. These archers were ordered not to leave their post under any circumstances. In their subsequent, death-defying assault upon the numerically superior forces of the Makkan idolaters, the Muslims gained a decisive advantage over the former, who turned to flee. At that moment, believing that the battle had been won and fearing lest they lose their share of the spoils, most of the archers abandoned their covering position and joined the skirmish around the encampment of the Quraysh... [They] veered round in a wide arc and attacked the Muslim forces from the rear. Deprived of the cover of the archers and caught between two fires, the Muslims retreated in disorder, with the loss of many lives (Asad).

Amidst all this mayhem, a rumour quickly spread that the Prophet ﷺ had been killed, and this caused some Muslims to flee. Later the Muslims regrouped to defend the Prophet ﷺ. By then, the Quraysh fled in the direction of Makkah. The Muslims were exhausted, so they could not pursue the enemy. The Muslims incurred heavy losses, with seventy men martyred; a devastating blow, due to sloppy discipline. The lesson was learned: "Obey your leader." After a harsh criticism, the Quran reassures the Muslims, "Do not be disheartened or sad, you will come out on top if you are true believers" (139).

––––––––––

In the name of God, the Kind, the Caring.

¹ *Alif Lam Meem.*

THE QURAN IS THE ABSOLUTE STANDARD FOR GOODNESS

² God is the only God, the Living, the Everlasting. ³ Truly He has revealed to you the Book, confirming what *scriptures* already existed, and He revealed the Torah and the Gospel ⁴before that as a guidance for people, and He sent the criterion *for distinguishing right from wrong*. Those who deny God's verses will be severely punished. God is the Almighty, the Avenger. ⁵ Nothing on Earth and in the Heavens is hidden from God. ⁶ He is the one who forms you in *mothers'* wombs as He pleases; there is no God besides Him, the Almighty, the Wise.

SEARCHING FOR HIDDEN MEANINGS OF THE QURAN COULD MISLEAD

⁷ He is the one Who revealed the Book to you: some of its verses are precise in meaning, they are the foundation stone of the Book, whilst others are metaphorical. The people whose minds are sick chase after what is metaphorical, they want to stir up disagreement and to concoct their own interpretations; yet only God knows their exact meaning, and those firmly grounded in knowledge say, "We believe in it, *since* all of it is from Our Lord," only those with understanding pay

heed[a]. [8]"Our Lord, let not our hearts waver *from the truth* after You have guided us, and take care of us. You are the Giver of gifts. [9]Our Lord, You will gather people on for a day in which there is no doubt." God never breaks His promise.

WORLDLY WEALTH AND POWER IS NOT A GUARANTEE OF VICTORY

[10]As for the disbelievers, their wealth and their children will not benefit them in the least against God; they will be fuel of the Fire, [11]just like the people of Pharaoh and those before them who denied Our signs, so God punished them for their sins. God is severe in punishment. [12]Tell the disbelievers: "You will soon be defeated and be herded into Hell." What a miserable place of rest! [13]A sign for you was the meeting at *Badr*; one army fought in the path of God, *and* the others were disbelievers, they saw *the Muslims* as twice as many as themselves. God strengthens with His help anyone He pleases; for those of insight, it had a lesson.

WORLDLY LUXURIES AND THE DELIGHTS OF PARADISE

[14]People's love of worldly pleasures has been made attractive to them: women, children, heaps of gold and silver, well-bred horses, animals and farmland, such are delights of this worldly life, but God has the best place of return. [15]Say: "Shall I tell you of something far better than these? To those who are mindful, their Lord will give them gardens beneath which rivers flow where they will live forever, and pure spouses and the pleasure of God." God watches over His servants [16]who *pray*, "Our Lord, we believe, so forgive us our sins and save us from the punishment of Hellfire," [17]*they are* patient, truthful, obedient, charitable, and seek forgiveness at dawn. [18]God bears witness that there is no god beside Him, as do the angels and those whose knowledge *is used* to uphold fairness; there is no god but Him, the Almighty, the Wise.

RELIGION MEANS SUBMISSION AND COMMITMENT TO THE WILL OF GOD

[19]Islam is the *only* religion acceptable to God. Those given the Book began to disagree amongst themselves out of sheer rebelliousness after knowledge had come to them. Whoever denies God's signs, *let him remember that* God is swift in settling accounts. [20]If they argue with you, then say, "I have submitted myself to God, as have those who follow me", then ask those given the Book and the *Arabs*

---

[a]   Some verses are more direct than others, the less direct ones are metaphorical. They convey multiple meanings or ambiguous meanings. A metaphor compares one aspect of an idea with another to illuminate the idea. So, a metaphor takes you beyond one meaning and opens the mind to many possible meanings.

without any scripture: "Have you submitted *to God*?" If they submit *to God*, they will be guided, but if they turn away, you will have done your job of delivering the message. God watches over His servants.

THE DISOBEDIENT WILL BE PUNISHED

²¹ Those who reject God's verses, unlawfully killed the prophets and killed those who enjoined justice, give them the good news of painful punishment. ²² Their deeds will prove to be worthless in this world and the Hereafter, and they'll have no one to help them. ²³ Haven't you seen those who have been given a share of the Book? When they are referred to the Book of God to judge between themselves, a group turns away, stubbornly resisting. ²⁴ That is because they said, "We will be in Hellfire only for a few days." The lies they used to make about their religion have deceived them. ²⁵ How will it be when We gather them on *the* Day that is certain to come, and everyone is paid in full what they've earned without being wronged *in the least*?

A PRAYER OF SUBMISSION TO GOD'S WILL

²⁶ Say, "God! Master of all power, You give power to anyone You want, and You take it away from anyone You want; You bestow honour and You humiliate anyone You please. All goodness is in Your hands. You have power over all things. ²⁷ You *gradually* merge the night in to the day, and You *gradually* merge the day into the night. You create the living from the dead, and You cause the living to die. You provide without bounds to anyone You want."

EVIDENCE OF GOD'S LOVE: OBEYING THE MESSENGER ﷺ

²⁸ The believers should not make the disbelievers their allies in preference to the believers, and whoever does so will receive no *help* from God unless they have done so to protect themselves out of fear[b]. God cautions you to be mindful of Him, and the final return is to God. ²⁹ Say, "Whether you reveal what is in your minds or you conceal it, God knows it. In fact, He knows whatever is in the Heavens and on the Earth and God has power over all things." ³⁰ Every person that day will find *in front of them* whatever good and whatever evil they had done. They will wish that they had not done their bad deeds. God warns you to be mindful

---

[b]   Ubaidah ibn Samat a prominent disciple of the Prophet ﷺ had a treaty with the Jews of Madinah. At the battle of trenches, he said to the Prophet ﷺ "I have five hundred of the Jews who will fight alongside me against the enemy." These verses were revealed on that occasion (al Sabuni).

of Him, He is kind to His servants. [31] Say: "If you love God then follow me, and God will love you and forgive your sins. God is the Forgiver, the Kind." [32] Say: "Obey God and the Messenger." If they turn away, *remember that* God does not love the disbelievers.

THE STORY OF MARY AND HER SON JESUS

[33] From all the creation, God chose Adam, Noah, the families of Abraham and of Imran, [34] each generation related to the other. God is the Hearer, the Knower. [35] When Imran's wife said, "Lord, I vow to dedicate whatever is in my womb to Your service, so accept *this vow* from me. You are the Hearer, the Knower." [36] Once she had given birth to her, she complained, "Lord, I gave birth to a girl" – God knew well what she had given birth to, the male is not like the female[a] – *then she added*, "I have named her Mary, and I place her and her offspring in Your protection from the accursed Satan."

ZACHARIAH TAKES THE RESPONSIBILITY OF RAISING MARY

[37] Her Lord accepted her and raised her in the best way, and He entrusted her to the care of Zachariah. Whenever Zachariah entered the prayer room, he found fruits around her; so *one day* he asked her, "Where do you get these from Mary?" She replied, "It's from God. Indeed, God provides boundlessly to whomever He pleases."

ZACHARIAH PRAYS FOR A CHILD AND RECEIVES A SIGN

[38] Standing there *in a state of bliss*, Zachariah prayed to his Lord, saying, "My Lord, kindly grant me a righteous child. You are the Hearer of prayers." [39] The angels called out to him as he stood praying in the prayer room, "God gives you good news of John, confirming a Word from God, a chaste and distinguished person, a Prophet from among the righteous." [40] He asked, "Will I have a boy, I have reached old age and my wife is infertile." *The angel* replied, "It will be so. God does what He pleases." [41] *Zachariah* asked, "My Lord, give me a sign." He said, "The sign is that for three days, you will only speak by sign language to people. So, remember your Lord constantly, glorifying Him in the morning and the evening."

---

[a] 'The male is not like the female' is a parenthesis that explained to Mary's mother "the male child she had prayed for could not have been like the female she was granted." This implies that Mary's excellence would go far beyond any hopes, which her mother had ever entertained (Asad).

MARY IS CHOSEN ABOVE ALL THE WOMEN OF HER TIME

[42] *Remember* when the angels said to Mary: "Mary, God has chosen you and purified you from all the women of the world. [43] Mary, worship your Lord, prostrate and bow with those who bow." [44] This is from the reports of the unseen which We revealed to you. You weren't there among them when they cast lots to determine who would be Mary's guardian; nor were you there with them when they argued *about the virgin conception.*

MARY LEARNS OF THE BIRTH AND THE MIRACLES OF JESUS

[45] *Remember* when the angels said: "Mary, God gives you good news of a Word from Him, his name will be the Messiah, Jesus son of Mary, honoured in this world and in the Hereafter, and among those nearest to *God.* [46] He will speak to people from *his* cradle and as a grown-up, and he will be righteous." [47] She asked, "Lord, how can I have a son when no man has touched me?" *The angel* said, "That is how God is; He creates whatever He pleases. If He decides something, He *simply* says, 'Be!' And *there* it is. [48] And *God* will teach him the Book, wisdom, Torah and the Gospel." [49] And, as a messenger to the Israelites, *he will tell them:* "I have come to you with miracles from your Lord. I will create for you a model of a bird from clay, and with God's approval, when I blow on it, it will become a *living* bird. With God's approval, I will heal the blind, the leper, and I will bring the dead back to life, and I will tell you what you ate and what you stockpile in your homes. In that there is a sign for you, if you are believers. [50] I shall confirm what came before me in the Torah, and I will make lawful some things that were *previously* unlawful for you. I have come to you with a sign from your Lord, so fear God and obey me. [51] God is mine and your Lord, so worship Him: this is the straight path."

JESUS CALLS HIS DISCIPLES, AND THEY CONFIRM THEY ARE MUSLIMS

[52] When Jesus sensed rejection from them, he called out, "Who will be my helper for the sake of God?" The disciples replied, "We are God's helpers. We believe in God and bear witness that we submit *to His will.* [53] Our Lord, we believe in what You have revealed and we follow the messenger, so include us among witnesses *to the truth."*

JESUS IS TOLD WHAT LIES IN STORE FOR THOSE WHO DENY HIM

[54] *The hypocrites among the Israelites* plotted, and God prepared a counterplan. God is the Best of the planners. [55] *Remember* when God said: "Jesus, I will receive

you,[a] then raise you up to Me, and I will acquit you of *all the charges invented by* those who deny *the truth*. I will place your followers above those who denied *the truth* until the Day of Judgement; *but for now* you shall return to Me, and I will make judgement about their differences concerning you. [56] The deniers, I will punish them severely in this world and the Hereafter, and they will have no helpers." [57] The believers who do righteous deeds, He will reward them in full, but God dislikes the wrongdoers. [58] That is what We recite to you of *Our* verses from the wise Reminder.

JESUS' NATURE EXPLAINED IN RESPONSE TO CHRISTIAN MISUNDERSTANDINGS

[59] In the sight of God, Jesus is like Adam; He created him from dust then said to him "Be!" And he became. [60] This is the truth from Your Lord, so listener, don't be among the doubters. [61] Whoever argues with you over this once *the* knowledge has come to you, say to them: "Come! Let us call our sons and your sons, our women and your women, ourselves and yourselves; then let us call on God's curse on the liars." [62] This is the true account. There is no god but God, and God is the Almighty, the Wise. [63] If they turn away, *so what*, God knows the troublemakers.

JUDAISM, CHRISTIANITY AND ISLAM: CONVERGENCE AND DIVERGENCE

[64] Say: "People of The Book, let us agree on a common statement *that exists* between us: We worship no one except God; we associate nothing with Him; and we shall not adopt anyone else as lord besides God." Then if they turn away *from this*, say: "Be witnesses that we submit *to God's will*."

ABRAHAM WAS NEITHER A JEW NOR A CHRISTIAN

[65] "People of The Book, why do you argue over Abraham, given that the Torah and the Gospel were not revealed until after him? Why don>t you think? [66] Here you are arguing over something that you know well, but why must you argue over something you don't know?[b] God knows but you don't know. [67] Abraham was neither a Jew nor a Christian, but a person of true faith who submitted *to the Will of God*; he certainly was not from among the idolaters. [68] The closest of people to Abraham are those who followed him *at that time*, and this Prophet and those

[a]   Tabari said "this phrase is back to front, it means Jesus I will raise you up to Me then after your second coming let you die as fixed." This reflects the belief Jesus will return before the world ends, he will establish Islamic guidance before his death.

[b]   This verse helps explain what was mentioned in verse 7, the question of the reason for all the friction and disunity.

who believe *in his Message*. God is the Protector of the believers."

CLEVER ARGUMENTS AND TRICKS ARE NO SUBSTITUTE FOR DIVINE GUIDANCE
[69] Some People of The Book would love to mislead you, not realising that they are only misleading themselves. [70] "People of The Book, why do you deny God's signs when you are eyewitnesses *to their revelation?* [71] People of The Book, why do you dress up the truth with falsehood and knowingly hide the truth?" [72] A group of People of The Book say: "*Go ahead and* believe what has been revealed to the believers early in the day then, at the end of the day, deny it; this way, *the believers* may give up *their faith*." [73] And they say: "Only believe in those who follow your religion." Say: "God's guidance is the only guidance *to rely on that has been given to like.* So why do they dispute with you before your Lord?" Say: "All grace is in God's hand, to give to anyone who wants it. God is Vast, the Knower. [74] He selects for His kindness anyone He pleases." God is Most Gracious, the Almighty.

WARNING AGAINST CHANGING GOD'S WORDS OR THEIR MEANINGS
[75] Among the People of The Book are those who, if you entrust them with a heap of gold, they will return it to you. But there are others who, if you entrust them with a single gold coin, they will not return it to you unless you stand over them *until they give it back*; this is because they claim, "We are under no contract when it comes to non-Jews,"[c] and *in this way* they knowingly tell lies against God. [76] Not so! Whoever fulfils his pledge and is mindful *let him know that* God loves the mindful. [77] Those who sell God's contract and their own vows in return for a small sum of money will have no share in the Hereafter. God will not speak to them nor look at them nor purify them on Judgement Day, *instead* they will have a painful punishment. [78] Some of them twist their tongues *when reciting* from the Book to make you think it is from the Book, even though it forms no part of the Book, and they say: "This is from God," even though it is not from God, and they knowingly tell lies against God.

HOW TO TEST THE VALIDITY OF CONTROVERSIAL DOCTRINES
[79] It is inconceivable for a man who has been given the Book, authority and prophethood by God to then tell people: "Worship me instead of God." Rather he will say, "Be godly, seeing as you used to teach the Book and study it." [80] *Like-*

---

[c]   Literally, the verse says "illiterate", in the sense of having no scripture or revelation from God.

wise he would never command you to adopt the angels and prophets as lords. Would he command you to disbelieve after you have submitted *yourselves to the Will of God*?

The conference of the Prophets

[81] *Remember the time* when God took a pledge from *all* the prophets, saying, "Whatever I give you of *the* Book and wisdom, and later *the final* messenger comes to you confirming what you have, then you must believe in him and lend him your support.[a]" *They were then asked*, "Do you affirm and accept my pledge as it is?" They replied, "We do." So, *God* said, "So be witnesses, and I am a witness with you. [82] So, whoever turns away now, these are the sinners.

Submission to God is the only true religion

[83] Are they seeking something other than God's religion, while all things in the Heavens and on Earth willingly and unwillingly submit to Him, and to Him they will return? [84] Say: "We believe in God and everything revealed to us and to Abraham, Ismael, Isaac, Jacob[b] and *his* children, and in what Moses and Jesus and *other* prophets were given by their Lord. We do not discriminate between any of them, and *we bear witness that* we submit and commit ourselves to Him." [85] Whoever seeks a religion other than Islam,[c] it will never be accepted from him, and in the Hereafter he will be among the losers.

Look out for words and actions that lead to apostasy

[86] Why should God guide people who rejected *faith* after believing? They witnessed that the messenger *sent to them* was genuine and came to them with clear proofs. God will not guide such wrongdoers. [87] The reward for such *people* is the curse of God, the angels and all humanity. [88] They will remain in *Hell* forever; neither will the torment be lightened nor will they be given any respite, [89] except those who later repent and reform themselves. God is the Forgiver, the Kind. [90] Those who disbelieve after believing will increase in *their* disbelief, their repentance will never be accepted; such people are utterly misguided. [91] Those who dis-

---

[a] "The final Messenger" here is our Beloved Prophet Muhammad ﷺ. So, God took a pledge from all the Prophets to believe in him. This pledge was affirmed when all the Prophets prayed behind him in Masjid al Aqsa on the occasion of Ascension (Zia ul Quran).

[b] Israel is a name which was given to Jacob later in life, so it is his sons who were the first of the twelve tribes, or the children, of Israel.

[c] Islam means to surrender oneself, commit to the teachings of God; Religion of Islam.

believe and then die as disbelievers, even if one of them were to offer as a ransom enough gold to cover the Earth, it would not be accepted. For such people, a painful punishment is *in store*, and they will have no helpers.

A LESSON FROM THE ISRAELITES: NOT TO INVENT BELIEFS AND PRACTICES
⁹² You will never achieve goodness until you spend *in charity* from what you dearly love, and whatever you spend, God Knows it. ⁹³ *Initially* all foods were lawful for the Israelites except what Jacob outlawed for himself before the Torah was revealed. Say: "Bring the Torah and read it, if you are telling the truth." ⁹⁴ After this, whoever makes up lies against God, such people are wrongdoers. ⁹⁵ Say: "God has spoken the truth," so together follow the religion of Abraham, a man of firm faith; he was not an idolater.

THE FIRST PLACE OF WORSHIP ON EARTH
⁹⁶ The first house founded for people *to worship in* was that in Bakka,ᵈ as a blessing and *source* of guidance for all people. ⁹⁷ There are clear signs in it, *for example* the place where Abraham stood. Anyone entering it will be given sanctuary. Pilgrimage to the *Ancient* House is compulsory for People who can make the journey, in order to seek God's pleasure. Anyone who denies *this duty should know that* God is Self-Sufficient, *independent* of all the creation.

A WARNING NOT TO DENY OBVIOUS SIGNS OF GOD'S FAVOUR
⁹⁸ Say: "People of The Book, why do you deny God's signs, *knowing that* God is a witness to all that you do?" ⁹⁹ Say: "People of The Book, why do you stop believers from God's path, seeking to make *those signs* appear to be a deviation, even though you are eyewitnesses *to them*. God is not unaware of what you do?" ¹⁰⁰ Believers, if you pay heed to *the teachings of* any sect of the People of The Book, they will urge you to revert to disbelief after having believed. ¹⁰¹ How could you possibly disbelieve when God's verses are being recited to you and His Messenger lives among you? Anyone who holds firmly to *faith in* God will be guided to a straight path.

UNITY AMONG BELIEVERS IS A SIGN OF GOD'S FAVOUR
¹⁰² Believers, fear God as He deserves to be feared, and do not die except in state of submission *to Him*. ¹⁰³ Hold tightly to God's rope altogether, let nothing divide

ᵈ Bakka is the old name of Makkah.

you, and remember God's favour on you when you were enemies and He joined your hearts together *in mutual love* so that, by His favour, you became brothers. You were on the edge of a pit of fire when He saved you from *falling into* it. This is how God makes clear His signs for you, so you may be rightly guided. [104] There should *always* be a group among you that calls *people* to what is best, enjoins the common good and forbids evil; *these people* are the successful.

Sectarianism is condemned

[105] Don't be like those who differed and became divided among themselves after clear signs came to them; severe punishment awaits such people, [106] on a day when some faces will be bright whilst others will be gloomy. As for those whose faces are gloomy, *they will be asked*, "Did you disbelieve after having believed? So taste the punishment for your disbelief!" [107] Those whose faces shine joyfully *will be* in God's care, where they will remain forever. [108] These truly are God's verses that We recite to you, and God does not want to be unjust to His creation. [109] All things in the Heavens and on Earth belong to God, and He determines the outcome of all things.

The special role of the Muslim community

[110] You are the best community to emerge for humanity, *so long as* you enjoin the common good, forbid evil and believe in God.

Disgrace for those who disobey God's commands

Had the People of The Book believed, it would be better for them. Some of them believe, but most of them are evildoers. [111] They will never do you *any* major harm even if they were to fight you, they would soon turn their backs and then no one would help them. [112] They will be disgraced wherever they go, *unless they are loyal to God or loyal to the people.* They have incurred the wrath of God, and they are disgraced. All because they denied God's signs, killed prophets unjustly, were disobedient and overstepped *God's boundaries.*

Do not stereotype people because of religion and race

[113] All of them are not alike; a group among the People of The Book upholds the *teachings of the scripture*, reciting God's verses throughout the night as they prostrate *to Him*. [114] They believe in God and the Last Day, enjoin common good and forbid evil, and always rush to perform good deeds; such people are the righteous.

[115] Whatever good they do, it will never go unrewarded *by God*, God knows the pious.

THE GOOD DEEDS OF DISBELIEVERS WILL BE OF NO VALUE

[116] Neither the wealth nor the children of the disbelievers shall benefit them in the least before God. They are companions of the Fire, remaining therein forever. [117] In this life anything they spend *in charity* is like a biting wind that blows and destroys the crops of the wrongdoers. God did not wrong them but it was themselves.

CHOOSE FRIENDS WISELY

[118] Believers, don't take as your closest friends others apart from fellow believers, they will cause you grief and they'd like to cause you distress. Their hatred is obvious from their mouths, but what they hide in their hearts is even worse. We have clearly explained to you *Our* signs, if you reflect.[a] [119] This is how you are, you love them, but they don't love you *though* you believe in their whole Book. When they meet you, they say: "We believe," but when they are alone they bite their fingertips out of rage. Say, "Die in your rage!" God knows well *people's* innermost feelings. [120] When you have good time, they are saddened, but when you have hard time, they are happy. As long as you are patient and guard yourselves *against them*, their plotting will not harm you. God is aware of what they do.

THE STORY OF THE BATTLE OF UHUD

[121] *Remember* that morning, when you left your home to align the believers in their fighting position. God is the Hearer, the Knower. [122] When your two parties considered giving up *the fight*, though God was their protector; so let the believers put their trust in God. [123] God had helped you in *the battle of* Badr, when you were weak, be mindful of God so that you are thankful *to Him*.

NEWS OF AN ARMY OF ANGELS STRENGTHENS THE BELIEVERS' RESOLVE

[124] *Remember* when you were motivating the believers: "Aren't you glad your Lord helped you with three thousand angels sent down *as reinforcement*?" [125] Of course, God will send five thousand angels swooping down if you are steadfast and mindful, even if the enemy attacks suddenly. [126] God did so to raise your spirits and to reassure you, help comes from God the Almighty, the Wise. [127] *It was done* to cut

[a] The early Muslims of Madinah were cautioned to befriend the People of the Book who could mislead them.

off one of the flanks of the disbelievers' army or to weaken them so much that they fled in disarray. [128] It isn't your concern whether God forgives them or punishes them; they are wrongdoers. [129] All things in the Heavens and on Earth belong to God; He forgives anyone He pleases, and He punishes anyone He pleases. God is the Forgiver, the Kind.

THE TAKING OF COMPOUND INTEREST IS FORBIDDEN

[130] Believers, do not take compound interest,[a] *increasing your wealth unjustly*, and fear God so that you may prosper; [131] protect yourselves from the Fire prepared for the disbelievers, [132] and obey God and the Messenger so you are treated kindly.

BELIEVERS ALWAYS TRY TO PUT THINGS RIGHT

[133] Rush towards your Lord's forgiveness and towards Paradise, which is *as* wide as the Heavens and the Earth, prepared for those who are mindful *of God*: [134] who spend *in charity* in good and bad times, *can control* their anger and pardon people. [135] God loves those who strive to do good. If *by mistake* they act indecently or wrong themselves, at once they remember God and seek forgiveness for their sins – can anyone except God forgive sins? – And never continue doing *the wrong* knowingly. [136] The reward for them is forgiveness from their Lord and gardens beneath which rivers flow, where they'll live forever. What an excellent reward for those who act *righteously*! [137] *Many different* ways of life have existed before you, so travel the Earth and see *for yourselves* what became of those who denied *God's signs*. [138] This is an explanation for humanity, a guidance and warning for those mindful *of God*.

HARD LESSONS LEARNT FROM THE BATTLE OF UHUD

[139] Do not be disheartened or sad; you will come out on top when you are *true* believers. [140] If you were injured, they were injured too. We cause such days to alternate between people, so that God may mark out the true believers among you, and select some as martyrs. *Even if they sometimes win*, God does not love the wrongdoers. [141] *Furthermore*, God *may do this* to put the believers to the test and wipe out the disbelievers. [142] Or did you think you would go to Paradise without

---

[a] Compound interest is a type of usurious practice, where the borrower is forced to pay interest on any accumulated interest as well as on the capital. It is different from simple interest which is interest paid on the capital sum only. It was practised by rich Arabs before the advent of Islam to exploit the poor, who had to borrow money to survive. See *Chapter Al-Baqarah* 275-278 for more on the prohibition of usury.

3. The Family of Imran

God marking out those of you who had struggled *in His path* and those among you who are steadfast? [143] Before coming face to face with it, you were eager to fight,[b] but now you have seen it with your own eyes.

THE SPOILS OF WAR ARE NEVER THE REAL PRIZE

[144] Muhammad is a *noble* messenger, many Messengers came and went before him. If he should die or be martyred, would you turn on your heels *and head back to the old ways*? Whoever turns back will not harm God in the slightest. God rewards the thankful. [145] No one dies without God's knowledge, but dies at the appointed time, as approved by God. Anyone who wants riches of this world, We shall give him some, and whoever wants riches of the Hereafter We shall give him all; and We will reward the thankful.

BELIEVERS ALWAYS STOOD FIRM IN BATTLE

[146] *Muhammad is* like many other prophets alongside whom masses of *devout men* have fought; they were neither disheartened nor weakened, nor did they surrender in face of their sufferings. God loves the patient. [147] They prayed, "Our Lord, forgive our sins and any extravagance of ours, make us steadfast, and help us against the disbelievers." [148] God granted them both the rewards of this world and an excellent reward in the Hereafter. God loves those who strive to do good. [149] Believers, if you obey the disbelievers, they will make you turn on your heels and go back *to your previous ways* as losers. [150] Rather, God is your Protector, and He is the Best of helpers. [151] We will cast terror into the hearts of the disbelievers because *of* all that they associated with God without any revealed authority. Their home is the Fire. What an evil resting place for the wrongdoers!

A BITTER LESSON FOR THE ARCHERS WHO DISOBEYED PROPHET'S ﷺ ORDER

[152] God fulfilled His promise of help, so you defeated them, then you lost courage, argued about the order *you had been given* and disobeyed, even after He had shown you what you desired – *the fact is that* some of you long for the world, whilst others among you long for the Hereafter – and then He saved you from them in order to test you *further*. Now He has pardoned you. God is Gracious to the believers. [153] *Remember* how you fled uphill *in panic* without concern for anyone, yet the Messenger was calling you from behind; so He gave you a lot of

---

[b]   This alludes to the eagerness of some of the Muslims to go to battle.

anguish so that *afterwards you don>t* grieve over your loss and sufferings. God is aware of what you did.

DOUBTS ARE MEANS OF TESTING COURAGE

[154] Then, after the anguish, He gave you a sense of security, drowsiness over-whelmed some of you, whilst others were absorbed in their private thoughts, entertaining false ideas about God, ideas only fit for the Age of Ignorance. They were saying *to themselves*, "Do we have any say in this?" Tell them, *Muhammad*: "All of this rests with God." They conceal in their hearts what they will not reveal to you, saying, "If we had a say in this, we would not have been killed in this spot." Say: "Even if you had stayed at home, those who were fated to be killed would still have come out here to their graves. God did this to test your courage and to prove what is in your hearts." God knows well *people's* innermost feelings.

GOD PARDONED THE ARCHERS WHO DISOBEYED

[155] Those of you who fled on the day the two armies met did so because Satan made some of them err, but God has pardoned them; God is the Forgiver, the Gentle. [156] Believers, do not be like the disbelievers who say of their brothers who *die* on a journey or in battle: "Had they stayed with us they wouldn't have died nor been killed." This is how God sows regret in their hearts. God gives life, and He takes it away, He sees all you do. [157] Whether you are killed for God's cause or you die, God's forgiveness and kindness are far better than what they can gather. [158] If you die or get killed, you will certainly be gathered before God.

YOUR SETBACK WILL LEAD TO YOUR COMEBACK

[159] God made you kind, so you are lenient with them; had you been harsh and hard-hearted they would have deserted you, so pardon, seek forgiveness and con-sult them. Once you have made up your mind, put trust in God. God loves those who put their trust *in Him*. [160] If God helps you, no one can defeat you, but if He humiliates you, then who will be your helper? The believers put their trust in God. [161] A prophet does not cheat *anyone*. Whoever cheats will *be forced to* produce what he gained by cheating on the Day of Judgement; then everyone will be paid their due in full, and they will not be wronged. [162] How can a person who seeks God's pleasure be compared with one who earned His anger, and whose destination is Hell? What a wretched end! [163] For each of them, God has *prepared* different ranks. God sees what they do.

THE MESSENGER ﷺ IS THE GREATEST FAVOUR OF GOD FOR THE BELIEVERS

¹⁶⁴God favoured the believers when He sent them a messenger from among themselves, reciting His verses, purifying them, and teaching them the Book and wisdom, before that they were misguided.

THE DEFEAT AT UHUD DISTINGUISHED THE HYPOCRITES FROM THE BELIEVERS

¹⁶⁵*Strangely*, when a tragedy struck you, after you had inflicted twice as much *damage on your enemies*, you said, "Where did this come from?" Tell them: "It came from yourselves." God has power over all things. ¹⁶⁶What happened to you that day when the two armies met happened with God's permission, and to mark out the believers, ¹⁶⁷and to mark out the hypocrites; when they were told: "Come and fight in God's way, or at least defend yourselves," they answered, "If only we knew how to fight we would have followed you." That day, they were far nearer to disbelief than ever they were to faith, saying with their mouths what wasn't in their hearts. God knows well what they hide. ¹⁶⁸Those who told their brothers to remain behind with them, *and then said*, "If only they had listened to us, they would not have been killed." Say *to them*: "Ward off death from yourselves, if you are telling the truth."

THE MARTYRS OF UHUD; THE DEAD DON'T DIE

¹⁶⁹Don't consider dead those killed in God's way; they're alive *eating and drinking*, in their Lord's presence. ¹⁷⁰Delighting in that portion of grace which God has given them and rejoicing at those who have yet to join them *as martyrs* in succession, *saying* that they should have no fear nor should they grieve. ¹⁷¹They rejoice in God's gifts and favours, God will not lower the value of the believer's reward. ¹⁷²Those *believers* who rallied to the call of God and the Messenger after getting injured will get a great reward, for striving to do good and being mindful *of God*. ¹⁷³When they were told: "The people *of Makkah* have gathered against you, so fear them," their faith increased, and they said: "God's *help* is enough for us. What an Excellent Guardian!" ¹⁷⁴So they returned *home* with God's blessing and favour, without being harmed since they had sought God's pleasure. God is Most Gracious.

CONSOLATION FOLLOWING THE DEFEAT AT BATTLE OF UHUD

¹⁷⁵That was Satan, making *you* fear his cronies. Don't be afraid of them but fear Me, if you are *true* believers. ¹⁷⁶*Muhammad*, do not be distressed by those who

rush headlong into disbelief; they will never harm God in the slightest. God wishes to give them no share in the Hereafter, but their punishment will be severe. [177] They have traded their faith for disbelief,[a] they can never harm God in the slightest; for them is a painful punishment.

THE WEALTH OF THE UNGODLY IS NOT BLESSING BUT A TEST

[178] The disbelievers shouldn't consider Our prolonging their lives as a good thing for them; We prolong their lives so they increase in their sinfulness; for them is a shameful punishment. [179] God will not leave *you* believers as you are now until He has separated the good from the bad; nor will God inform *all of* you about the unseen realm, but God picks out anyone He pleases from His messengers. So, believe in God and His Messenger, and if you believe and are mindful *of God*, then you shall have a great reward.

[180] Don't let those who are stingy with what God has given them of His favours imagine for a moment that it is good for them; rather it is bad for them. On Judgement Day they will be made to wear the wealth they hoarded as collars round their necks. Everything in the Heavens and Earth belongs to God. God is aware of what you do.

THEY HAVE DENIED, MOCKED AND KILLED PROPHETS

[181] God has heard the words of those who said, "God is poor, and we are rich." We shall write down what they said. They killed the Prophets unlawfully, and We shall say to them, "Taste the punishment of the blazing Fire, [182] this is for the misdeeds committed by your hands." God is not unjust to *His* servants, [183] who say, "God has taken our pledge not to believe in a messenger until he comes to you with a burnt offering."[b] Say: "Many messengers came to you before me with clear proofs, and practised what you mention. Why did you kill them, if you are telling the truth?" [184] If they accuse you of lying, many messengers before you were also accused of lying, *even though* they came with miracles, scriptures and the enlightening Book.

TESTS ARE A PART OF LIFE

[185] Everyone will have the taste of death, and on Judgement Day you will be given

---

[a] Literally translated as: "bought disbelief instead of faith".

[b] "A burnt offering" refers to "conforming to the Mosaic Law, which prescribes burnt offerings as an essential part of Divine services." (Asad).

your full reward. Anyone who is saved from the Fire and is admitted to Paradise will be the winner. This worldly life is no more than a deception. [186] You will certainly be tested through your wealth and persons and you will hear many insults from the idolaters and those given the Book before you. If you are patient and mindful *of God*, that is real resolve.

DO NOT HIDE THE MESSAGE

[187] *Remember,* God made a contract with those given the Book: "Proclaim it to the people and do not hide it." So, they threw it behind them[c] and sold it for a small sum of money. How evil was their bargaining! [188] *Prophet,* do not consider those who delight at what they have done and wish to be praised for what they failed to do; don't think they've escaped the punishment; they shall have a painful punishment. [189] Control of the Heavens and the Earth belong to God. God has power over all things.

THE PRAYER OF INTELLIGENT PEOPLE

[190] In the creation of the Heavens and the Earth and the cycle of night and day, there are signs for smart people, [191] who remember God standing, sitting and lying down, and think about the creation of the Heavens and the Earth, *prayerfully saying,* "Our Lord, You haven't created this in vain, Glory be to You! Save us from the punishment of the Fire. [192] Our Lord, anyone You assign to the Fire is humiliated; the evildoers shall have no helpers. [193] Our Lord, we heard a crier calling to faith; 'Believe in your Lord,' so we believed. Our Lord, forgive our sins, delete our evil deeds, and when we die count us among the righteous. [194] Our Lord, give us what You've promised us through Your messengers and do not humiliate us on the Day of Judgement; indeed, You do not break *Your* promise."

THE LORD ANSWERS THEIR PRAYER

[195] Their Lord answered the prayer, *saying,* "I will not allow the deeds of any of you, male or a female, to go to waste; you will both get the same reward. As for those who migrated, those expelled from their homes, those who suffered in My way, those who fought, and those who were killed, I will certainly delete their evil deeds, and I will certainly admit them into gardens beneath which rivers flow. This is their reward from God; and God gives the best reward.

---

c   Literally translated as: "threw it behind their backs".

WHAT IS TRUE SUCCESS?

[196] Don't be deceived by the disbelievers' commercial trade through the land; [197] it's a temporary provision, and their final home will be Hell. What a wretched place! [198] However, those who are mindful of their Lord will have gardens beneath which rivers flow, where they will live forever, a resting place provided by God. Most wonderful is that which God has *prepared* for the righteous. [199] Among the People of The Book are those who believe in God and what has been revealed to you and to them; they are humble towards God, not selling God's verses for a small sum of money; such people shall *find* their reward with their Lord. God is swift in settling accounts. [200] Believers, be patient, encourage each other to be patient, be disciplined,[a] and be mindful of God so that you may prosper.

[a]   To serve God and to defend yourself, like a soldier who stands guard at a border post.

4. An-Nisa'
The Women

This chapter was revealed in Madinah over a period of eighteen months after the Battle of Uhud, in 625 CE. Nearly a third of the chapter discusses family issues, since seventy Muslim men were martyred, leaving behind them orphans, widows and creating a crisis in families. There was a dire need for clear guidance on how to deal with the crisis. The chapter lays out a series of laws concerning: the status of women, marriage, marital discord, inheritance, capital punishment for murder, prohibition of praying under the influence of alcohol, and the rights of orphans. It provides instructions on settling family disputes arising out of what is now called "post-traumatic stress disorder". It lays out clear rulings to ensure justice is done, but still emphasises the need to be caring and loving towards orphans and one's family. In this way, a safe space is created for the nurturing of children.

The chapter sheds light on the tension between Muslims and the Jews, whose persistent mockery of the Muslims is condemned. They are reminded of their iniquities, rebellion, and disobedience against their prophets, and their hostility towards the Prophet Jesus. The Christians are also censured for tampering with Scripture and adopting Trinity as the foundation of Christianity. In the case of the claims of many Jews at that time, the Quran makes it clear that: "They neither killed him nor crucified him but it appeared like that to them." (157)

Regarding jihad, the Muslims "who are willing to swap this worldly life for the Hereafter" are urged to "fight in the way of God" (74). It goes on to explain that jihad is not about fighting and killing people, but standing up for justice against the persecution of those who pray, "Our Lord, take us out of this town with its tyrannical people and, out of Your kindness, give us protectors and helpers" (75).

A portion of the chapter discusses the problem of the hypocrites: people who profess Islam while secretly disbelieving. This was – and remains – the most challenging and troublesome group, sitting on the fence that separates faith from disbelief, and described as "dithering between *this and* that, *they are* neither with these *believers* nor with those *disbelievers*" (143). They were a real menace for the Muslims, an enemy within, always plotting, spreading rumours and sowing doubts.

Their characteristic traits have already been mentioned in *Chapter Al-Baqarah*: troublemakers, sick at heart, and spreaders of corruption. More are added: they obstruct people from believing, and engaged in scheming against the Muslims. By describing their traits, the Quran is cautioning Muslims to beware of them. By enumerating these negative qualities, the chapter stresses the need to adopt values opposite to those of the hypocrites: sincerity, loyalty, kindness and generosity towards fellow citizens and the authorities.

Obedience to the Messenger ❀ is a source of blessing

Good leadership is a powerful glue that holds a society together: "Believers, obey God, the Messenger and those in authority amongst you, if you disagree amongst yourselves over anything, then refer it to God and the Messenger" (59). Those who obey the Messenger are blessed: "Whoever obeys God and the Messenger, such people shall be with those whom God has favoured: the Prophets, the truthful, the martyrs and the righteous. What wonderful companions!" (69).

The advice to counter hypocrisy is: be honest, sincere and genuine to oneself; secondly, care for and serve others, particularly members of one's family; and thirdly, show love and respect for the leadership of the community. These three principles form the basis of a peaceful, harmonious and just society as described in this blessed chapter.

In the name of God, the Kind, the Caring

MAINTAIN FAMILY TIES, AS THEY CONNECT YOU TO GOD

¹ People, be mindful of your Lord, He created you from a single person and created his partner from him, and then from the pair He spread countless men and women *throughout the world*. Be mindful of God in Whose name you make demands from each other, and take care of the relatives. God watches over you.

TAKING CARE OF THE ORPHANS

² Give the orphans *in your care* their belongings, and do not swap *their quality belongings* for worthless ones, nor misuse their wealth *by merging it* with yours; this is a major sin. ³ If you're afraid that you may be unfair to *female* orphans *by marrying them*, you may marry other women as you like: two, three or four. However, if you fear you may be unfair *by marrying two or more*, then *marry just* one or what your right hands possess;ᵃ that is just, so don't deviate *from the right path*. ⁴ Give women their dowers as a marriage gift; however, if they are kind and give you some of it back, then take it and use it as you wish.

ADVICE TO TRUSTEES OF ORPHANS' PROPERTY

⁵ Do not give your wealth, which God has given you for your use, to those with learning disabilities, but provide for them, clothe them, and treat them kindly. ⁶ Assess the orphans to see if they are ready to be married; then, if you find them

---

ᵃ The phrase "what your right hands possess" refers to slaves. The Prophet ❀ received the revelation at a time when slavery was widespread. Although Islam encouraged the freeing of slaves, this was not possible to achieve all at once, therefore rules were revealed on how to treat slaves in the best possible way. *See Chapter An-Nur p688.*

to be mature enough, hand over their wealth to them, and do not squander it hastily before they have grown up. If *their guardian* is wealthy, he should not take *any of the orphans' wealth*, but if he's poor, let him take what is a fair *compensation*. When you hand over their wealth, have it witnessed. God is a sufficient Reckoner.

THE LAW OF INHERITANCE

[7] Men receive a share of what parents and relatives leave behind, and women receive a share in what parents and relatives leave behind, whether *the estate* is small or big, there are fixed shares. [8] If relatives, orphans and the needy are present at the time of distribution, then offer them something from *the estate* and speak kindly to them, [9] and let those who fear leaving their own vulnerable offspring behind show concern *for the orphans*. They should be mindful of God and say what is right. [10] Those who misuse the wealth of orphans are feeding their bellies fire, and will burn in a blazing Fire.

MEN AND WOMEN HAVE DIFFERENT SHARES

[11] God commands you regarding your children: a son's share is equal to the share of two daughters. If there are more than two female heirs, *they will receive* two-thirds of what *the deceased* leaves behind, and if there is only one female she will have one half. Each of *the deceased's* parents shall receive a sixth of what he leaves behind if he had children; *but* if he had no children and his parents are sole heirs then his mother gets one third. If he had siblings, then his mother will get a sixth; *and the above is calculated* after settling any bequest[b] or debt. You do not know which of them are more deserving; your parents or your children. This is an essential *requirement* from God. God is the Knower, the Wise.

THE INHERITANCE OF HUSBANDS, WIVES AND DISTANT RELATIVES

[12] Half of what your wives leave behind is yours, provided they had no children; if they had children, then a quarter of their estate is yours. *This is calculated* after settling any bequest or debt. Wives shall receive a quarter of what you leave behind, if you had no children; but if you had children, then *wives* will get an eighth of what you leave behind. *This is calculated* after settling any bequest you have made or any debt. If a man or a woman's only heir is a distant relative who has a brother or a sister, then each one of them shall receive a sixth; but if they are more *than*

---

[b] *Wasiyya*: Bequest is the written will.

two, then they shall be partners in one third. *This is calculated* after settling any bequest or debt, if *the bequest* is not detrimental.[a] This is a command from God. God is the Knower, the Gentle.

THE REWARD FOR ADHERING TO GOD'S BOUNDARIES

[13] These are the boundaries set by God. Anyone who obeys God and His Messenger will have gardens beneath which rivers flow, living in them forever; that is a great victory. [14] Anyone who disobeys God and His Messenger and oversteps His boundaries will be cast into Fire, remaining in a humiliating punishment forever.

PENALTY FOR ADULTERY

[15] If any of your women commit adultery, and there is testimony of four men against them, then keep them under house arrest until death, or else God provides another way out for them. [16] *Likewise,* if a man and a woman commit adultery among you, punish them both. However, if they repent and reform themselves, then leave them alone. God is the Relenting, Kind.[b]

WHEN IS REPENTANCE ACCEPTABLE?

[17] Those who do wrong ignorantly then repent immediately can expect God to accept their repentance, and God will relent towards them. God is the Knower, Wise. [18] There is no repentance for those who keep on doing evil deeds until death is near, then they say: "Now I repent," nor for those who die as disbelievers. For such We've prepared a painful punishment.

MEN ARE URGED TO BE KIND TO THEIR WIVES

[19] Believers, it is not lawful for you to inherit women against their will,[c] nor to prevent them from marrying so that you may make off with part of what you have given them, that is unless they have committed a clear act of gross indecency. Live with them in a good way. If you *hate* them, it may be that you *hate* something in which God has placed much goodness. [20] If you wish to change one wife for another wife after having given the former heap of gold, do not withhold anything from it. Would you invent a slanderous accusation and an open sin to take it *from*

---

[a]   In Shariah, the maximum that can be bequeathed is a third of the estate.

[b]   Verses 15 and 16 describe the penalty for adultery and fornication, respectively; this was later changed by the ruling mentioned in *Chapter An-Nur*: 1.

[c]   A pre-Islamic Arab custom: a man could inherit a male relative's widow without her consent or the need to renew the marriage.

her? [21] How could you possibly take it after having enjoyed intimacy with each other? They took a solemn pledge from you.

WOMEN RELATIVES FORBIDDEN FOR MARRIAGE

[22] Do not marry women who your fathers married, except *if such a marriage* has already taken place; *from now on* it would count as gross indecency, vile, and leading to evil consequences. [23] It is forbidden for you to marry: your mothers; your daughters; your sisters; your maternal aunts; your paternal aunts; nieces from the brother's or sister's side; your foster mothers who have suckled you, and your foster sisters; your mothers-in-law; the stepdaughters who are in your care from women with whom you have consummated marriage, but if you have not consummated your marriage with them then there's no blame. *Also, forbidden are*: the wives of your sons; and marrying two sisters *at the same time*, except *if such a marriage* has already taken place. God is the Forgiver, the Kind.

THE ENJOYMENT OF SEX IS ONLY LAWFUL IN MARRIAGE

[24] *Also forbidden are* women who are already married, except your slaves.[d] *These prohibited marriages* are God's commandment *to be obeyed*. Whatever falls outside the above-mentioned *prohibitions* is lawful for you to desire, using your wealth to become married men, not fornicators. Whichever of them you wish to enjoy *in lawful marriage* you must give them their bridal gift; there is no blame on you, after fulfilling that obligation, in whatever you may mutually agree to do with *the marriage gift*. God is the Knower, the Wise.

MARRYING A BELIEVING WOMAN IS BEST

[25] If anyone lacks the means to marry chaste believing freewomen then *let him marry* from the believing slave girls you own. God knows best your faith. You are all of the same *origin*; so, marry them with the permission of their owners and give them their marriage gifts according to custom, as with chaste freewomen, not as fornicators or taken as lovers. If, after they are married, they commit an act of gross indecency then their punishment is half that of a chaste freewoman. That *permission* is for those of you who fear *falling into* sin. It is, *of course*, best for you to be patient *and exercise restraint*. God is Forgiving, and Kind.

---

[d] The custom of war in Arabia and elsewhere at the time was that women and children captured on the battlefield were not to be killed or left to die, but taken as hostages or slaves. Their previous marriage became void.

GOD MAKES ALLOWANCES FOR HUMAN WEAKNESSES

[26] God explains and guides you in the traditions of those *believers* who came before you, and to forgive you. God is the Knower, the Wise. [27] God wishes to accept your repentance, whereas people who pursue their lusts want you to deviate far from the course. [28] God wishes to ease your burden, since humans were created weak.

HONESTY IS THE BEST POLICY

[29] Believers, don't use one another's wealth dishonestly, rather only for a business venture through agreement, and do not ruin yourself.[a] God treats you Kindly. [30] Whoever *disobeys God* out of hostility and injustice, shall be thrown in the Fire, that's easy for God. [31] If you avoid major sins that are forbidden, then We shall delete your *minor* sins, and grant you an honourable entry *into Paradise*.

BE CONTENT WITH YOUR SHARE OF THE DECEASED'S ESTATE

[32] Do not wish *to get that* which God has favoured others with. Men *get* a share of what they've earned, and women *get* a share of what they've earned, and ask God for a share of His favour. God knows all things. [33] What parents and relatives leave behind, We have appointed beneficiaries for them, and those whom your right hands have contracted[b] *should be beneficiaries of your wills*, give them their shares. God Witnesses all things.

DEALING WITH MARITAL DISCORD

[34] Men are guardian-carers of women, God granted some more favours then others, because they spend money on their wives. Honourably acting wives are pious and they guard *their chastity* as God expects them to guard it. Those whose ill-conduct[c] you are afraid of, *first gently* warn them, *then* leave them alone in the bed and for a while live separately from them, *if all else fails*, apply *a minimum of*

---

[a] Literally "don't eat one another's wealth" but here it is metaphorical, as we might say, "don't kill yourself," to someone who is throwing all their effort into getting a job done, for example, or saving up money to buy something. Others say it refers to suicide, or it is an order not to kill each other.

[b] In Arabia, contracts like wills became binding not by a signature, but by a solemn oath.

[c] See also verse 128 for advice to women on how to deal with such ill-conduct and high-handedness of husbands.

force on them.^d If, *after taking these steps*, they obey you, then don't behave unjustly in any way against them. God is Most High, the Great.

MEDIATION FOR RESOLVING MARITAL DISPUTES WILL WORK

³⁵ If you fear hostility between husband and wife, then appoint a mediator from his family and one from her family. When both try *sincerely* to reconcile them, God will certainly bring about reconciliation between them. God is the Knower, the Aware.

THE PURPOSE OF RELIGION IS GOD'S WORSHIP AND KINDNESS TO OTHERS

³⁶ Worship God and don't associate anything with Him; be kind to parents, to relatives, to orphans, to the needy, to those neighbours you know well and those you don't, to travellers and to *the slaves* you own. God dislikes the arrogant and the boastful; ³⁷ *and* those who are miserly and advise others to be miserly, hiding His favours that God has blessed them with – for the disbelievers – We have prepared a humiliating punishment. ³⁸ Those who spend their wealth to show off; they don't believe in God and the Last Day. Anyone who has made a close friend of Satan has taken an evil friend!

THE MESSENGER ﷺ WILL BE THE WITNESS ON JUDGEMENT DAY

³⁹ What harm would it do them if they believed in God and the Last Day and spent *in charity* from what God has provided them? God knows them well. ⁴⁰ God wrongs *no one*, not even an atom's weight; and if it is a good deed, He multiplies it and gives an immense reward. ⁴¹ How *will they react* when We bring a witness from every nation and then We bring you, *Muhammad*, as a witness against them all? ⁴² That day the disbelievers and those who disobeyed the Messenger will wish that the Earth would swallow them up; and they won't be able to hide from God anything they had spoken.

RULES ON WHAT INVALIDATES PRAYER

⁴³ Believers, don't come to the prayer whilst you are drunk stay away until you

---

^d   There is an alternative meaning of the word '*Wadrebuhunna*'; apply force on them. When asked to explain this phrase, the Prophet ﷺ took his miswak (a teeth cleaning twig, a traditional alternative to the modern toothbrush) and lightly prodded the Companion sat next to him; a purely symbolic act, like not sharing the bed, which represents the husband's displeasure but does not cause any physical harm. Violence of any kind against women is forbidden.

know what you are saying;[a] nor when you are in the state of major ritual impurity, and when on a journey,[b] until you have bathed yourselves. *However*, if you are ill or on a journey, or if you have relieved yourself or had sexual intercourse with *your spouse*, and you cannot find water, then purify yourselves with some clean sand, wiping your faces and forearms.[c] God is Pardoner, Forgiver.

EXPOSING THE PETTY RUDENESS OF SOME JEWS OF MADINAH

[44] Haven't you seen those given a portion of the Book, *how* they swap it for error, wishing you stray from the path? [45] God is aware of your enemies; and God is sufficient as a Protector and a Helper. [46] Some of the Jews *deliberately* misquote the words *of revelation*, saying, "We hear and disobey," and, "Listen like a deaf man," and, "Look to us,"[d] twisting *the words* with their tongues to insult the religion. If only they had said: "We hear and obey," and, "Listen and look out for us," that would be far better and proper for them. However, God deprives them of his kindness because of their disbelief, and only a few of *them truly* believe.

AN INVITATION TO JEWS AND CHRISTIANS TO ACCEPT THE TRUTH

[47] You who received the Book, believe in what We revealed, it confirms what you already have, before We turn *your* faces back to front, or else We curse you as We cursed the People of the Sabbath. God's command is always fulfilled. [48] God does not forgive those who associate anything with Him, but He forgives anything less than that for whomever He pleases. Whoever associates anything with God has invented a great sin. [49] Haven't you seen those who regard themselves as pure? Rather it is God Who purifies whomever He pleases, and not an ounce of injustice will be done to them.[e] [50] Look how they make up lies about God. That is a blatant sin. [51] Haven't you seen those who were given a portion of the Book and they continue to believe in idols and false gods, saying to the disbelievers that they are more on the right track than the believers? [52] God has cursed them; and anyone God curses, you will find no helper for him. [53] Or do they have a share in

---

[a] In the early days of Islam alcoholic drink was not banned, it was forbidden by the revelation of *Al-Ma'idah: 90*

[b] In the Hanafi school, a person is a traveller when he sets off on a journey of fifty four miles or more, and intends to stay fewer than fifteen days in any one place, in which case he can shorten the prayer.

[c] This is known as *"tayammum"*, a symbolic way of purifying oneself, in lieu of wudu, ablution.

[d] See *Al-Baqarah* 2: 104 for an explanation.

[e] The word *"fateel"* refers to the thin film covering a date stone, a metaphor for an insignificant weight or amount.

God's sovereignty? If so, they would never give people even a tiny bit.[f]

WHY ARE THEY JEALOUS?

[54] Or do they envy *other* people for what God has given them from His grace? We gave Abraham's family the Book, wisdom, and a vast country *to rule over*. [55] Some of them believe in *the Prophet*, and others block the way to him. Hell, with its blazing fire will be enough *for them*. [56] Those who deny Our signs will soon roast in Fire. Whenever their skin falls off, We will replace it with fresh skin so they may taste the torment.[g] God is Almighty, Wise. [57] As for those who believe and do righteous deeds, We will take them to gardens under which rivers flow, living in them forever; there they'll have pure spouses, and We'll let them enter the cool shade.

ADVICE ON OBEYING AUTHORITY

[58] God commands you to return trusts to their rightful owners, and when you judge between people, be just, God reminds you gently! God is the Hearer, the Seeing. [59] Believers, obey God, the Messenger and those among you in authority. If you disagree over something, then refer it to God and the Messenger, that is if you believe in God and the Last Day: that's the best solution.

THE DECEPTIONS OF HYPOCRITES

[60] Haven't you seen those who claim to believe in what is revealed to you and what was revealed before you, yet they turn to false gods for judgements despite having been ordered to reject them. Satan wants to lead them far from the right way. [61] If they are told, "Come *along* to *listen to* what God has revealed to the Messenger, you will see the hypocrites turning to face in the opposite direction from you." [62] But when a disaster strikes them because of what they have done, they turn to you swearing by God: "We only want what is best and *to maintain* harmony." [63] God knows what is in these peoples' hearts, so, forgive them, warn them, and speak eloquently with them so it penetrates their minds.

THE SINNER WHO COMES TO THE MESSENGER ﷺ IS FORGIVEN

[64] We haven't sent a single messenger except that he should be obeyed as commanded by God. If anyone who wronged themselves came to you seeking God's

---

[f] *"Naqeer"* refers to the little groove in date stones, and means the same as *"fateel"* in this context.

[g] The nerves that sense pain are in the skin, without the skin there would be no pain. So, this terrible and painful description shows the nature of that suffering.

forgiveness, Messenger, seek forgiveness for them! They will find God Relenting, Most Kind. ⁶⁵ By your Lord, they aren't believers until they make you the judge in their disputes, accept your decision without reservation, and commit themselves *to your decision.*

THE REWARDS OF OBEYING THE PROPHET ﷺ

⁶⁶ If We had ordered them: "Lay down your lives," or "Leave your homes," for the sake of God only a few of them would have done so.^a Had they done what they were *told,* that would have been better for them and *put them* on a far firmer footing; ⁶⁷ We would have given them a great reward, ⁶⁸ and guided them on the straight path. ⁶⁹ Anyone who obeys God and the Messenger shall be with those God favoured: the Prophets, the truthful, the martyrs and the righteous. What a wonderful fellowship! ⁷⁰ Such is God's grace; and God is sufficient, the Knower.

JIHAD FOR WORLDLY GAINS IS CONDEMNED

⁷¹ Believers, take all precautions and let the battle-hardened march out *in front* or else march out together. ⁷² There are some of you who lag behind and if you suffered a setback, will say, "It was God's favour on me that I wasn't there with them." ⁷³ When God favours you, he will say, "If only I had been with them, I would have gained a great victory," as though there was no love lost between you and him. ⁷⁴ So those who are willing to swap this worldly life for the Hereafter, let them fight in the way of God. Whoever fights in the way of God and is either killed or victorious, We will give him a great reward.

THE PURPOSE OF JIHAD IS TO FIGHT INJUSTICE

⁷⁵ What is the matter with you that you do not fight in the way of God when the weak – men, women and children – are saying, "Our Lord, out of Your graciousness, take us out of this town of cruel people, give us a protector and a helper!" ⁷⁶ The believers fight for the sake of God, whilst the disbelievers fight for the sake of false gods; so, fight the supporters of Satan. Satan's scheming is weak. ⁷⁷ Haven't you seen those who were told: "Hold back your hands *from wrongdoing,* and *instead* perform the prayer and pay zakat"? Since fighting was prescribed for

---

^a This introduces verse 71, encouraging *Jihad* for the defence of faith and freedom.

them, a group of them fears men as they fear God, or even more.[b] They say, "Our Lord, why have You prescribed fighting for us? Couldn't You have delayed it for a while?" Say: "The delights of this world are little, while the Hereafter is far better for the mindful, you will not be treated unjustly in the slightest."

THERE IS NO ESCAPE FROM DEATH WHEN ITS TIME COMES

[78] Death will catch up wherever you may be, even if you are in strong forts.[c] When good things happen to them, they say, "This is from God," and, when bad things happen to them, they say, "This is your fault, *Muhammad*." Say: "All is from God." What is the matter with these people that they hardly understand what they are told? [79] Whatever good things happen to you they're from God, and whatever evil happens to you it's from yourselves. We sent you as a Messenger to people; God is sufficient witness. [80] Whoever obeys the Messenger has obeyed God, but whoever turns away, We didn't send you as a guardian over them.

HYPOCRITES WILL ALWAYS FIND EXCUSES IN THE SHARIAH

[81] They say, "We will obey." However, when they leave your presence, a group of them spend the night plotting against what you said. God writes down how they spend the night, so, ignore them and put your trust in God. God suffices as a Protector. [82] Don't they reflect on the Quran? Had it come from anyone beside God, they would have found many inconsistencies in it.

DON'T BE DISHEARTENED BY THE RUMOURS SPREAD BY THE HYPOCRITES

[83] Whenever a report of war or peace comes to them they broadcast it loudly; whereas, if they had referred it to the Messenger or to those in authority, its significance could be determined by those best suited to interpret it. If it had not been for God's grace and kindness, most of you would have followed Satan. [84] So, *Muhammad*, fight in the way of God – you are only answerable for yourself – and encourage the believers. It may be that God will curb the power of disbelievers. God is stronger in might and more severe in punishment.

---

[b] The pagans used to plunder to enrich their tribe, violence wasn't for defence or a moral cause as in Islam. The Quran repeatedly speaks of war as a means of putting an end to the persecution of the weak by the strong. They were told: "Hold back your hands" from wrongdoing, since they would pick only on weak groups, which tended to run away, leaving their goods behind for the taking.

[c] The Bedouins were used to raids, which they won by a mere show of strength, rather than actual fighting.

Always be courteous

[85] Whoever speaks out for a worthy cause will have a share in its benefits, and whoever speaks out for a wrong cause will share its burden, God is Watchful over everything. [86] When anyone greets you, respond with a better greeting or *at least* return it *in kind*. God keeps account of everything. [87] God is the only God, He will gather you all on Judgement Day, there is no doubt about that. Who is more truthful in speech than God?

The rules of engagement with prowling bands of hypocrites

[88] Why are you divided in two groups concerning the hypocrites? God has driven them back into *disbelief* for what they did. Do you want to guide those who God has allowed to go astray? Anyone who God allows to go astray, you will never find a way out for him. [89] They would love to see *all of* you disbelieve as they have disbelieved, so that you become equal. Don't ally yourselves to any of them until they migrate for the sake of God. If they turn away, seize them and slay them wherever you find them, and take none of them as an ally or a helper, [90] except for those who are related to a people with whom you have a treaty, or who come over to you because their hearts are wary of fighting you or of fighting their own people. Had God wished, He would have given them power over you, so they would have fought you. If they withdraw and do not fight you but make you an offer of peace, then God gives you no excuse *to fight* against them. [91] There are others whom you will find wanting to be on good terms with both you and their own people, but whenever they are put to the test, they return to *fighting*. So, if they don't withdraw or make you an offer of peace, and cease hostility, seize them and slay them wherever you encounter them, We've given you clear authority against such people.

Penalty for accidental death and murder

[92] It is forbidden for a believer to kill another believer, except by mistake. Anyone who kills a believer by mistake must free a believing slave and pay compensation to the *victim's* family, unless they waive it as an act of charity. If *the victim* belonged to an enemy tribe but was himself a believer, then free a believing slave and if he was from a tribe with which you have a treaty, then pay compensation to their family and free a believing slave. Whoever cannot find the means *to pay compensation* let him fast two consecutive months to gain God's forgiveness. God is

the Knower, Wise. [93] The penalty of intentionally killing a believer is Hell, living there for a long time; God's anger and curse will fall on him, and He has prepared for him a terrible punishment.

Do not be judgemental or dismissive

[94] Believers, when you set out on patrol in the path of God, be cautious. When someone gives you a greeting of peace,[a] do not say: "You are not a believer," seeking worldly gains, God has many *other* rewards. That is how you used to behave in the past until God favoured you *with Islam*, so be open and honest. God is aware of what you do.

Believers are rewarded according to their efforts

[95] The believers who stayed behind – apart from those who were physically or financially incapable – are not equal to those who strive with their lives and their wealth in the path of God. God has favoured by degrees those who strive with their wealth and lives above those who stayed behind. God has promised both goodness; *however*, God has favoured those who strive over those who stayed behind with a great reward, [96] high ranks, forgiveness and kindness. God is Forgiving, Most Kind.

Migration for the sake of saving

[97] The *Muslims* whose souls the angels take while they were doing wrong to themselves *since they didn't migrate*,[b] will be asked: "What *state* were you in?" They will say, "We were weak and vulnerable in the land." *Then* the Angels will ask: "Wasn't God's Earth spacious enough for you to migrate?" For such people, their refuge will be Hell. What a wretched destination! [98] Except for the weak among the men, women and children who were unable to come up with a strategy or to find a way out. [99] They may be pardoned by God. Indeed, God is Pardoning, Forgiving. [100] Whoever migrates in the path of God will find a place of refuge *somewhere* in the land and worldly abundance and whoever sets out from home

[a] *Salam*, meaning "peace", a customary greeting of Arab Jews, Christians and Muslims. The verse was revealed after a Muslim had killed someone who had greeted him with *"as-salam 'alaykum"*. Rather than give the stranger the benefit of the doubt, he thought this person was pretending to be a Muslim to save his life. His action was condemned.

[b] A reference to Muslims who stayed behind in Makkah, choosing not to migrate although they had the means, but instead hid their faith and lived an oppressed life. Is this threat of Hell a veiled wake-up call for those who are comfortable with their material life? Muslim by name not by conviction?

to migrate for the sake of God and His Messenger, and dies *on the way*, God will grant him his reward. God is Forgiving, Kind.

Shortening the prayer when travelling

¹⁰¹ When you are travelling in the land, you can shorten the prayer without feeling guilty,ᵃ if you fear being attacked by the disbelievers; the disbelievers are your open enemies.

The prayer in the state of fear

¹⁰² *Messenger*, when you are among them and leading them in prayer, let a group of them stand with you carrying their weapons; then, when they have prostrated, they may *cover* you from behind while another group who hasn't yet prayed come and pray with you, *again* with due precaution and with their weapons. The disbelievers would love to see you neglect your weapons and your possessions so they could descend on you all at once. Nor is there any blame on you if some hardship such as rain or illness makes you put down your weapons, but remain on your guard. Indeed, God has prepared humiliating punishment for the disbelievers. ¹⁰³ When you have completed the prayer, *continue nevertheless to* remember God, be it standing, sitting or lying down. Then, whenever you feel safe again, perform the prayer. The prayer is compulsory for the believers at fixed times. ¹⁰⁴ *So* do not be half-hearted in seeking out the *hostile, disbelieving* people. If you are suffering, then they are suffering just like you, however *there is difference,* while you have hope in God they have no such hope. God is the Knower, Wise.

There is no excuse for treachery

¹⁰⁵ We sent down to you the Book containing the truth so that you may judge between people the way God has shown you. So, don't support the traitors, ¹⁰⁶ but seek God's forgiveness. God is Forgiving, Kind. ¹⁰⁷ And do not argue about those who deceive themselves. God dislikes anyone who is treacherous and sinful. ¹⁰⁸ They try to hide from people, but they can't hide from God; He is with them as they talk late into the night about things that displease Him. God is aware of what they do. ¹⁰⁹ *Believers*, here you are defending them in this worldly life, but who will defend them against God on Judgement Day, or be their lawyer?

ᵃ The shortening of the prayer refers to shortening the 4 *Fardh* of *Dhur, Asr* and *Isha* to two units only. This is a special concession when travelling a minimum of fifty four miles away from home and staying there for less than fifteen days.

The case of a Muslim who lied to avoid punishment

[110] Whoever does an evil deed or wrongs himself but then seeks God's forgiveness, he will find God Forgiving, Kind. [111] Whoever commits a sin will reap its reward. God is All-Knowing, Wise. [112] Whoever does wrong or commits a sin then blames *someone else* for it, he has burdened himself with a slander and an open sin.[b]

To avoid Hell, Muslims must follow the path of God's pleasure

[113] If it wasn't for God's grace and kindness towards you, a group amongst them would have misled you, but as it is they only misled themselves, doing you no harm. God has revealed to you the Book and wisdom, and has taught you what you didn't know. God's favour on you is great. Never plan to harm others

[114] There's very little good in most of their secret meetings, except when they enjoin acts of charity or do common good or reconcile between people. Whoever does these things seeking God's pleasure, We will give them a great reward. [115] Whoever opposes the Messenger after the guidance has been made clear to him and follows a path other than that of the believers, We will let him continue down his chosen path, until We burn him in Hell. What an evil destination!

Satan's way of misleading people

[116] God will not forgive idolatry, but He forgives whatever is less than that to whomever He pleases. Whoever associates anything with God has wandered far, far astray. [117] What they call on apart from Him are nothing but *fabricated* goddesses and *ultimately* what they call on is only a rebellious demon. [118] God has cursed him for saying: "I will take an allotted share of Your servants; [119] and I will lead them astray and give them false hopes and I will order them to slit the ears of cattle and to tinker with God's creation." Whoever takes Satan as a protector beside God will clearly be a loser. [120] He promises them and gives them hopes, but Satan's promises are mere deception. [121] Their home is Hell, and they will find no way out of it.

Submission is the spirit and the heart of Islam

[122] Those who believe and do good works, We will admit them into gardens

---

[b] This refers to an incident of theft by a Muslim who blamed a Jew, so his family asked the Prophet ﷺ to punish the Jew. However, these verses were revealed clarifying the innocence of the Jew.

beneath which rivers flow, living there forever. *This is* God's true promise, and whose word is more truthful than God's? [123] It is neither according to your wishes nor to the wishes of the People of The Book; anyone who does evil will be repaid in kind, but will not find any protector or helper besides God. [124] A believer who does good works whether male or female will enter Paradise and will not be wronged in the least. [125] Can anyone have a better religion than the one who surrenders himself *completely* to God, performs good works and, out of a natural inclination,[a] follows Abraham's way of worshipping? God made Abraham a close friend. [126] Whatever is in the Heavens and on Earth belongs to God. God has full control of all things.

SAFEGUARDING ORPHANS AND CHILDREN IN CARE

[127] They asked you concerning women. Say: "God instructs you concerning them – in addition to what was recited to you in the Book[b] – about female orphans from whom you withhold what is prescribed for them *regarding their inheritance because* you wish to marry them," and likewise helpless children, deal fairly with orphans. God knows whatever good you do.

DEALING WITH MARITAL DISPUTES

[128] If a woman is afraid of her husband's ill-conduct or alienation, both should *try* to reconcile with each other without feeling guilty. Reconciliation is the best *policy*, but humans tend to be selfish.[c] So if you are righteous and mindful *of God, remember that* God is aware of what you do. [129] You will never be able to be *strictly* just *when dealing* with your wives, however hard you try, but do not lean so much towards one that you leave the other as though suspended *between marriage and divorce*. If you can reconcile and be mindful, God is Forgiving, Most Kind. [130] If they separate, God will provide for each of them from His abundance. God is the Vast, Wise.

EVERYTHING BELONGS TO GOD; HE GIVES AS HE LIKES

[131] Whatever is in the Heavens and the Earth belongs to God. We commanded you and the People of The Book before you: "Be mindful of God." Even if

---

[a] *"Hanif"* refers to one who believes in one true God and rejects all false gods, which comes naturally to him or her.

[b] This refers to verses 2–10.

[c] *"Shuh"* implies greed, avarice, self-centredness and egotism.

you deny it, whatever is in the Heavens and the Earth belongs to God. God is Self-Sufficient, Worthy of praise. [132] Whatever is in the Heavens and the Earth belongs to God, and He is sufficient as a Guardian. [133] If He wishes, people, He can get rid of you altogether and replace you with others. God has the power to do that. [134] Whoever desires the reward of this world *only*, then *let him know that* the reward of this world and of the Hereafter are with God. God is the Hearer, the Seeing.

STAND UP FOR JUSTICE AND STRUGGLE AGAINST PREJUDICE

[135] Believers, stand up as God's witnesses for justice even if it's against yourselves, parents or relatives, and *regardless of* whether a person is wealthy or poor, God has more right *to your loyalty* than they. Therefore, do not follow *your* desire instead of being just. If you distort *the truth* or refuse *to give testimony*, God is aware of what you do. [136] Believers, believe *firmly* in God and His Messenger and in the Book that He has sent down to His Messenger and in the Book He sent before. Whoever rejects God, His Angels, His books, His messengers and the Last Day has gone far astray.

THE HYPOCRITES ARE WAITING UNTIL A VICTOR EMERGES

[137] Those who believed then disbelieved, then believed *again*, then disbelieved, then increased *yet further* in disbelief, God will not forgive nor guide them towards *His* way. [138] Give glad tidings of painful punishment to the hypocrites, [139] who have taken disbelievers as their allies instead of the believers. Do they seek strength from them, when strength is God's? [140] God revealed in the Book, when you hear God's verses being rejected or mocked, do not sit with them till they turn to another topic of conversation; otherwise you will be like them. God will gather all the hypocrites and disbelievers in Hell. [141] They are waiting to see what happens to you; if victory from God comes to you they will say: "Were we not with you?" And if the disbelievers gain some success, they will say to them: "Didn't we encourage you and protect you against the believers?" God will decide between you on the Day of Judgement; however, God will never give the disbelievers a way *to a conclusive victory* over the believers.

HYPOCRITES MAKE A SHOW OF PRAYING

[142] The hypocrites try to deceive God, but He leaves them in their deception; *thus* whenever they stand up for the prayer, they do so lazily, making a show for the

people and they remember God little; [143] dithering between *this and* that, *they are* neither with these *believers* nor with those *disbelievers*. Whoever God allows to go astray, you can't ever guide him.

HYPOCRITES WILL BE IN HELL

[144] Believers don't take disbelievers as allies instead of the believers. Do you wish to give God clear proof against yourselves? [145] The hypocrites will be in the bottommost pit of Hell, and you will never find a helper for them; [146] except *that is* for those who repent, reform themselves, hold firmly to *the religion of* God, and become genuine in their worship of God; such people will be with the believers. God will give the believers a great reward.[a] [147] Why should God punish you, if you believe and are grateful? God is Appreciative, the Knower.

THE VICTIM MAY SPEAK PUBLICLY AGAINST THE OFFENDER

[148] God dislikes *anyone* talking openly about a wrongdoing, except the person who has been wronged. God is Hearer, Knower. [149] Whether you do good *work* openly or you conceal it or you pardon a wrong, God is Pardoning, the Powerful.

BELIEVERS DO NOT CHERRY PICK FROM GOD'S COMMANDMENTS

[150] Those who deny God and His messengers, and who wish to separate God and His messengers, claim: "We believe in some *aspects* and reject others"; and they wish to steer a middle course; [151] these people are disbelievers. We have prepared for the disbelievers a humiliating punishment. [152] Those who believe in God and His messengers and make no distinction between any of them, will be rewarded. God is Forgiving, Most Kind.

THE JEWS EXPERIENCE GOD'S WILLINGNESS TO PARDON

[153] The People of The Book ask you for a book to be sent down to them from Heaven. They asked Moses for something even more outrageous than that: "Show us God with the naked eye," so a thunderbolt struck them for their rudeness. Then they adopted the *golden* calf *as an idol*, after clear signs had come to them; nevertheless, We pardoned them for that. We gave Moses clear authority; [154] *whilst taking* their contract with the mountain towering above them, We said, "Prostrate as you enter the gate," and We told them not to violate *the sanctity of* the Sabbath, taking a solemn pledge from them.

---

[a] While a disbeliever must declare his faith to be forgiven, a hypocrite must: repent, reform, practise religion and show sincerity.

JEWS MADE FALSE ALLEGATIONS AGAINST MARY AND JESUS

[155] What about their breaking the contract, their denial of God's signs, their unlawful killing of the prophets, and their saying, "Our minds are locked"?[b] Indeed! God has sealed their hearts and minds because of their disbelief, so that none but a few of them believe [156] and because of their denial, and their spreading a terrible slander against Mary.

GOD RAISED JESUS TO HEAVENS BEFORE THE CRUCIFIXION

[157] They *mockingly* say: "We have killed the Messiah, Jesus son of Mary, the Messenger of God," though they didn't kill him nor crucify him, but it appeared like that to them. Those who differed over *the matter* are *still* in doubt about him. They have no knowledge of it except speculation, and they certainly didn't kill Jesus. [158] In fact, God raised him to Himself. God is Almighty, Wise. [159] There is no one from the People of The Book who will not believe in *the Messiah* before his death,[c] and on the Day of Judgement he will be a witness against them.

THE JEWS WILL BE PUNISHED OR REWARDED, BASED ON THEIR BELIEF

[160] Because of the wrongdoing of the Jews, We prohibited some of the wholesome things that were lawful for them, and they stopped many *people* from following the way of God, [161] and adopted usury despite it being forbidden, and they squandered people's wealth. For the disbelievers among them, We have prepared a painful punishment. [162] But some of them are firmly grounded in knowledge and are believers in what is revealed to you and what was revealed before you; *likewise,* those who perform the prayer, pay Zakat and believe in God and the Last Day will be given a great reward.

THE PROCESS OF REVELATION WAS THE SAME FOR ALL PROPHETS

[163] We revealed to you as We revealed to Noah and the prophets after him; and We revealed to Abraham, Ismael, Isaac, Jacob, the Tribes, Jesus, Job, Jonah, Aaron and Solomon; and We gave David the Psalms. [164] *There were* messengers that We told you about, and *there are other* messengers that We haven't told you about. God spoke directly to Moses. [165] *There have been* messengers bearing good news and warnings so that, after the messengers, people would have no defence against God. God is the Almighty, Wise. [166] God bears witness of what He has sent down

---

[b]   The arrogant Israelites were prepared to use any excuse to evade responsibility for their sinful behaviour.

[c]   This refers to the second coming of Jesus the Messiah, when all will believe in him.

to you – He has sent it down with His knowledge – and the Angels are witnesses *too*. God is a sufficient Witness.

No forgiveness for him who obstructs God's path

[167] Those who deny *the truth* and stop others from the path of God have wandered far, far astray, they deny *the truth* and do wrong, [168] God will not forgive nor guide them along a path, [169] except the path to Hell, remaining there forever and to do so is easy for God.

Christians are warned against offensive beliefs

[170] People, the Messenger has come to you with the truth from Your Lord, so it is better that you believe than to reject *the message*, whatever is in the Heavens and the Earth belongs to God. God is All-Knowing, Wise. [171] People of The Book, do not go to extremes in your religion; always speak the truth about God. The Messiah, Jesus son of Mary, was a *noble* messenger of God, His word, which He blew into Mary, and a spirit from Him. So believe in God and His messengers and talk no more of "three"; it is better that you stop *believing this*. God is the only one God. He is free from such defects, so how can He have a son! Whatever is in the Heavens and the Earth belongs to Him; and God is a sufficient Guardian.

Jesus is not embarrassed to be called the servant of God

[172] The Messiah would never be ashamed of being *called* a servant of God, nor would the angels near *His Throne*. Whoever is ashamed of worshipping Him is arrogant, God will gather them all. [173] Those who believe and do righteous deeds will be repaid in full, and He will grant them an increase from His grace. However, those who are ashamed and arrogant, He will give them a painful punishment and they will find no helper or protector other than God.

The Messenger ﷺ is a clear proof of God's majesty

[174] People, a clear proof has come to you from your Lord and We have sent down to you a shining light. [175] So, those who believe in God and hold firmly to *their belief in* Him, will be kindly treated with His grace, and He will guide them towards Himself along a straight path.

Rule of inheritance for those who die childless

[176] They ask you for a ruling, say: "God instructs about the one who dies without descendants. If a man dies childless, but had a sister, she would inherit half of

what he has left and he would be her only heir, if she were *to die* childless. If *the deceased* had two sisters, they would inherit *between them* two-thirds of what he left. *However,* if the siblings were both male and female, then each male would receive the share of two females." God explains this so that you do not make mistakes. God is the Knower of everything.

5. Al-Ma'idah
The Feast

This chapter was revealed in Madinah in 628 CE, after the Treaty of Hudaibiyah. This marked a new era for Muslims; now they were free to propagate Islam in the Arabian Peninsula, as agreed in the treaty. By now the economic prowess of the Jewish tribes had faded, while the Muslims were confident and upbeat.

This chapter lays out the basis of God's contract with Muslims as the final law revealed. It puts it in the context of the contracts the Jews and Christians had made with God, but who unfortunately broke the law, invented false beliefs, and changed some laws of the Torah and Gospel. Consequently, they lost the privilege of being the favourite people of God. Cautioning Muslims: if you don't abide by the Shariah, then you too will fall out of favour, God has no special preference for any people except those who obey and submit to Him.

The new Muslim state needed laws to function as a well-ordered civil society. In this chapter, eighteen new laws are announced on: contracts; testimony and the importance of honest witnesses; respecting sacred months; slaughtering animals; the lawfulness of seafood; rules of entering into a state of *ihram* for pilgrimage; intermarriage with Jewish and Christian women; apostasy; rules for cleanliness; the penalty for stealing; the penalty for sedition; prohibition of intoxicants and gambling; atonement for breaking an oath; hunting whilst in a state of *ihram*; making a will at the time of death; and the penalty for those who violate divine laws.

These laws are set in the context of various historical events. An example of this is the story of the Israelites' refusal to obey Moses when told to enter the Holy Land. The moral is: disobeying God's messengers merits severe punishment. The second story describes the murder by Cain of his brother Abel, showing that murder is an abominable crime. The relationships of various groups in the Arabian Peninsula are surveyed, and the Christian-Muslim relationship is highlighted in particular:

> You will find the nearest and most affectionate to the believers are those who say, 'We are Christians', because among them are priests and monks who are not arrogant (82).

The chapter's central theme is the fulfilment of contracts. It explains how the Jews and Christians failed to fulfil their contracts, and gives examples of how they violated the divine laws, so they were rejected by God. The Christians are further condemned for violating their contract with God by tampering with the teachings of Prophet Jesus; their adoption of the doctrine of the Trinity in 325 CE, which gave rise to a misunderstanding of the oneness of God. "Those who say: 'The Messiah, the son of Mary, is God' are denying the truth" (17). Furthermore, "Those who said: 'God is the third of three', have committed an act of disbelief" (73). Since the glorious Quran is a final contract of God, both the Jews and the Christians are invited to follow the Messenger 繺.

There is an emphasis on honouring pledges and contracts, which should be taken seriously. However, the contract that humanity has with God is the most serious, belief in His oneness. These laws appear harsh and difficult to apply because they require a high level of self-discipline, and a sense of justice, impartiality and courage. Hence, a stress on their benefits and why they shouldn't be violated. By pointing out weaknesses of the Jews and the Christians, Muslims are in a way being alerted. It is in the best interest of humanity to live by God's laws:

> So beware that they do not tempt you away from what God has revealed to you ... Is it the customary law of the Age of Ignorance that they want? For those who have firm belief, whose rule can possibly be better than God's (49–50).

The key lesson is draw near to God through sincere belief in His oneness, love Him and follow His commandments.

In the name of God, the Kind, the Caring

Honour contracts and keep promises

[1] Believers, fulfil all your contracts and responsibilities. Livestock animals are lawful to eat except what will be mentioned to you in the coming verses, and you are not allowed to hunt while you wear the pilgrim's garb. God commands what He wills. [2] Believers, don't violate God's symbols: the sacred months; the sacrificial animals, and animals with garlands around their necks; and those on their way to the Sacred House, seeking grace and pleasure of their Lord. Once you have removed the pilgrim's garb then you may hunt. Don't let the hatred of people who once blocked your way to the Sacred Mosque lead you to break the rules. Cooperate in matters of goodness and piety, and don't cooperate in matters of sin and hostility. Fear God, He's severe in punishing.

Which kind of meat is forbidden?

[3] You are forbidden to eat: carrion;[a] blood; pork; whatever is slaughtered in a name other than God's; animals killed by strangulation, a blow to the body, fallen from a height, gored; eaten by beasts of prey – unless you are able to slaughter it before it dies – and anything slaughtered on the altars of idols. Nor are you allowed to divide meat by drawing lots using marked arrows; this is clearly sin-

----

[a]   "Carrion" refers to the meat of animals that are found already dead, like road kill.

ful. Today, the disbelievers have lost hope of you abandoning your religion; so don't fear them, fear Me. Today, I have completed your religion for you; I gave My favour in full, and I am pleased that Islam is your religion. So, anyone forced by famine to eat these forbidden meats, without the desire to sin, will find God Forgiving, Kind[a]. [4]They ask you, Messenger, what is lawful for them. Say: "All healthy foods are made lawful for you, including what you have trained birds and beasts of prey to hunt, teaching them as God has taught you; so, eat what they catch for you, as long as you declare God's name over it, be mindful of God. God is swift in settling the account of your deeds. [5]Today, all healthy foods are made lawful for you; the food[b] of People of The Book is lawful for you, and your food is lawful for them.

EXTRAMARITAL AFFAIRS ARE FORBIDDEN, BE PURE AND MARRY

Chaste women from the believers and the People of The Book are lawful to marry after you have given the bridal gift. Live honourably with them, don't engage in sex outside of marriage, or take them as lovers. Anyone who rejects faith, their deeds will be worthless, and in the Hereafter, they will be the losers.

INSTRUCTIONS ON RITUAL CLEANLINESS FOR PRAYER

[6]Believers, when you intend to perform the prayer, wash your face and arms up to the elbow; wipe your head and then wash your feet up to the ankles. If you are in a state of ritual impurity[c] purify yourselves by taking a bath; however, if you are ill, or on a journey, or you have relieved yourselves, or you have touched your wives in a sexual way, and are unable to find water, then take clean Earth and wipe your face and arms with it. God doesn't want to impose hardship on you, but wants to purify and complete His favours on you so you thank Him.[7]Remember God's favour and the contract He solemnly took from you when you said, "We hear and obey." Be mindful of God, He knows well what is in your hearts and minds.

ALWAYS BEHAVE JUSTLY, GIVE UP DISCRIMINATION

[8]Believers, be committed to God as witnesses for justice, and don't let hatred of

---

[a]   Commentators believe this verse was revealed on the 9th Dhul Hijjah during the Messenger's 🕊 farewell pilgrimage in the year 631 CE.

[b]   This refers to the meat of animals slaughtered by the Jews and the Christians, though Muslim scholars disagree, since Christians don't practise biblical laws, but the Jewish Kosher meat is considered *Halal*.

[c]   *"Junub"* is the ritual impurity due to sexual intercourse, a discharge of semen, menstruation, or after childbirth.

a community stop you being just. Be just, that is closest to piety. Be mindful of God. God is aware of what you do. [9] God has promised forgiveness and a great reward to believers who do righteous deeds, [10] and disbelievers who deny Our signs will be the companions of Hell. [11] Believers, remember God's favour when certain people intended to attack you, but He held them back. So, fear God, and let the believers put their trust in Him.

THE ISRAELITES WHO KEPT THE CONTRACT WERE REWARDED

[12] God took a contract from the Israelites when We appointed twelve chieftains for them. Then said, "I am with you so long you perform the prayer, pay the Zakat, believe in My messengers and support them, and give God a beautiful loan, I will erase your sins and admit you to gardens beneath which rivers flow. Anyone who breaks the contract after that will stray from the right path."

THE PROPHET 鑿 IS ADVISED TO OVERLOOK THE FAULTS OF THE JEWS

[13] When the Jews broke their contract, We cursed them, and hardened their hearts. They misquote verses from the Book and neglect parts of what they were taught. Even today you can see treachery in most, except for a few of them. Despite that you should pardon them and overlook their faults. God loves those who benefit others.

BREAKING THE CONTRACT LEADS TO CONFLICT

[14] We took a contract from those who said "We are Christians." When they neglected parts of the teachings, We whipped up enmity and resentment among them, which will continue till Judgement Day. God will inform them of what they invented.[d]

INVITATION TO FOLLOW THE PATHS OF PEACE

[15] People of The Book, Our Messenger has come to clarify a lot of things in the Book that you used to cover up and to pardon your disobedience. A light from God has come to you, and a clear Book, [16] by this God guides anyone who follows the path of peace in search of Divine pleasure. The Quran by His authority takes them out of darkness into the light, and guides them on the straight path.

IT IS IRRATIONAL TO BELIEVE JESUS IS GOD

[17] Those who say: "The Messiah, the son of Mary, is God" are denying the truth.

[d] There are thousands of Christian sects or denominations in the world, and they continue to grow.

Say: "Who has the power to stop God, if He so wished, to finish off the Messiah, son of Mary, his mother and life from the face of the Earth?" God has control of the Heavens, the Earth and whatever exists between them; He creates what He wills. God has the power over everything.

The Jews and Christians cannot deny having been warned

[18] The Jews and Christians say, "We are the children of God and His beloved." Say: "So why does He then punish you for your sins? The reality is you are ordinary human beings from His creation. He forgives anyone He wants, and He punishes anyone He wants." God has control of the Heavens, the Earth and whatever exists between, and finally they will return to Him. [19] People of The Book, Our Messenger came to explain the truth after an interval – when no messengers appeared – so that you can't say: "No herald of good news or warner ever came to us." But now, a herald of good news and a warner has come to you. God has control over everything.

The results of fear

[20] So, when Moses said, "My people, remember God's favour on you, He appointed prophets and kings among you, and gave you what no one else was given in the world. [21] My people, enter the Holy Land God has promised you, and don't turn your backs, or you will become losers." [22] They said, "Moses, fearsome people live there. We won't enter until they leave, once they have left, we'll go in." [23] Two of their God-fearing men said, "March against them and enter through the gate, if you enter through it, you will conquer. Put your trust in God if you are believers." [24] They said, "Moses, we will never enter the land as long as they remain there. Go and fight, you and your Lord, we'll stay here." [25] Moses said, "My Lord, I only have control over myself and my brother, so separate the two of us and these sinful people." [26] God said, "The Holy Land is now forbidden for them. They shall roam the wilderness for forty years, so don't worry about these sinners."

Jealousy led a man to kill his brother

[27] Give them an exact account of the two sons of Adam.[a] When both offered a sacrifice, and it was accepted from one but not from the other, Cain angrily said, "I'm going to kill you." Abel replied, "God only accepts from the pious. [28] If you

---

[a]   A reference to the biblical story of Adam's two sons, Abel and Cain, in the book of Genesis.

raise your hand to kill me, I will not raise my hand to kill you. I fear God, Lord of the universe. [29] I hope you'll be burdened with mine and your sins and become one of the companions of the Fire; that is a fitting reward for wrongdoers." [30] Yet Cain was tempted by his passion to kill his brother Abel, so he killed him and became a loser in this world and the next. [31] God sent a crow, it dug the ground to show him how to bury his brother's corpse. He said, "How pathetic am I! I am no better than this crow, I can't even hide my brother's corpse?" So he was regretful.

EVERY HUMAN LIFE IS MOMENTOUS

[32] Because of that murder, We decreed for the Israelites that whoever kills another person – unless it is in lawful retaliation for taking a life or for creating terror in the country[b] – it is as though he has killed the whole of humanity, and anyone who saves a life, it is as though he has saved the whole of humanity. Our messengers came to them with clear signs, but many of them became extremists in their country.

THE PUNISHMENTS FOR UNREPENTANT TERRORISTS

[33] The fitting punishment for those who start war to destroy the people of God and His Messenger is: the death penalty, or crucifixion, or amputation of their hands and feet on opposite sides, or be exiled from the city. That's how they will be disgraced in this world, and in the Hereafter they will be severely punished, [34] except for those who repent before you arrest them. Know, God is Forgiving, Kind.

DRAW CLOSE TO GOD, WEALTH WILL NOT SAVE YOU

[35] Believers, be mindful of God and search for ways to draw close to Him[c] and strive in His way, so you may be successful. [36] Even if the disbelievers owned everything on Earth twice over and tried to ransom themselves with it from the punishment of Judgement Day, it would not be accepted from them; theirs will be a painful punishment. [37] They will long to come out of the Fire but won't be able to do so; theirs will be a lasting punishment.

[b] *"Fasad"* means a heinous act; violence and conflict that undermines the peace and order of a country.

[c] *"Wasila"* is a means of getting to one's destination, or getting nearer to it (Lisan al-Arab). Faith, good works, charity, good character and worship are all examples of *Wasila*. Similarly having a teacher who guides one to God is a *Wasila*.

Reformed thieves are forgiven

³⁸ The penalty for thieves, male and female, is to cut off their hands to the wrist, a deterrent from God. God is Almighty, Wise. ³⁹ God relents towards him who repents after wrongdoings and reforms himself, He is Forgiving, Kind. ⁴⁰ Don't you know God controls everything in the Heavens and Earth? He punishes anyone He pleases, and He forgives anyone He pleases. God has power over everything.

Beware of hypocrites misquoting the Quran

⁴¹ Messenger, don't be saddened by those rushing headlong into disbelief, they say: "We believe," while there is no belief in their hearts, and likewise some who call themselves Jews. They are listening eagerly to lies and other people who have yet to come to you; they deliberately misquote the verses after the revelation has been laid down, saying, "If you are given this ruling, accept it, but if not, then beware." If God wishes to test anyone, you will have no means to save him from God. God doesn't wish to clean their hearts since they don't want that. They will suffer disgrace in this world, and they will be severely punished in the Hereafter.

A caution: don't follow those who deviated from the Torah

⁴² They listen eagerly to lies and live on deceitfully-earned wealth. If they come, you may either judge them or turn them away. If you decide to turn them away they will not harm you in the least; however, if you judge between them, be just. God loves the just. ⁴³ How is it they ask you to judge when they have the Torah containing God's laws; and after asking you, they still turn away. Those aren't believers. ⁴⁴ He revealed the Torah, which has guidance and light. The prophets who submitted themselves to God's will used to judge the Jews according to it, as did the rabbis and the scholars according to what they had preserved of the Book of God, and they were witnesses. So, don't fear people but fear Me, and don't sell My verses for a small price. Whoever doesn't judge by God's revelation are the disbelievers.

An eye for an eye is just, but to pardon is charity[a]

⁴⁵ In the Torah We commanded: a life for a life; an eye for an eye; a nose for a nose; an ear for an ear; a tooth for a tooth; all injuries like for like. Whoever gives up his

---

[a] The law can be ignored by: not paying attention to it, making up rulings, being excessively harsh or lenient. Setting rates of compensation for certain injuries is not ignoring the law, as is mentioned in the Quran (e.g. *Chapter An-Nisa'*: 92). See Exodus 12:23 for penalties according to Jewish law.

right out of charity, that will serve as an atonement for him on Judgement Day, but whoever does not judge by what God has revealed will be the wrongdoers.

SIN IS THE VIOLATION OF THE LAW OF THE SCRIPTURE

[46] Afterwards, We sent Jesus, son of Mary, to follow in their footsteps. He confirmed what was revealed in the Torah before him, and We gave him the Gospel, in which there is guidance and light, and it confirmed what was in the Torah, as a guidance and clear warning for the mindful. [47] So let the people of the Gospel judge with what God has revealed in it, and whoever doesn't judge by what God has revealed are sinners.

RELIGIOUS DIFFERENCES ARE BY GOD'S WILL

[48] We revealed to you the Quran, full of truth, confirming what was revealed before from the Book, and superseding all earlier revelation. So, judge between them according to what God has revealed, and don't follow their whims that contradict the truth that has come to you. To every community in the past, We gave a specific law and a way of life. Had God wanted, He would have made you one nation, but He chose to test you regarding what He gave you; so compete with each other in doing good works. In the end you will all return to God, and He will clarify your differences.

THE PROPHET ﷺ IS COMMANDED TO JUDGE JUSTLY

[49] Judge between them according to what God has revealed, and do not follow their whims. So beware they don't tempt you away from what God has revealed to you. If they choose to turn away, then you should know that God intends to punish them because of their sins, many are sinners. [50] Do they want the old law of the Age of Ignorance?[b] There is no better rule than God's, for firm believers.

A WARNING AGAINST CHOOSING SIDES OUT OF FEAR

[51] Believers, don't take the Jews and the Christians as protectors;[c] they're only each other's protectors. Anyone who takes them as his protector might as well join them. God doesn't guide people who do wrong. [52] You will see people with

---

[b] The Age of Ignorance refers to the time before the coming of the Messenger ﷺ in 610 CE, when power and wealth ruled in Arabia and customs were based on superstition not the law, and there was a lack of moral, social and spiritual values.

[c] *"Awliya"* is plural of *Wali;* a friend but it can also mean allies, supporters and protectors. The context here suggests it is protectors not friends at the time of war.

sickness in their hearts rushing to join them, saying, "We fear tragedy may strike us." It may be that God will grant us victory or bring about some other positive outcome, causing them to regret what they kept secret in their hearts. [53] The believers will say, "Didn't they swear a solemn oath; by God they were with you?" Their deeds have proved to be worthless, and they are the losers.

VICTORY IS FOR THE LOVERS OF GOD

[54] Believers, if anyone leaves his religion then God will bring forward people He loves and who love Him, who are gentle towards the believers and unflinching against the disbelievers, who strive in the path of God and aren't afraid of the critics' comments. That positive attitude is a favour of God; He gives it to whomever He pleases. God is Vast, All-Knowing. [55] God is your only true protector, along with His Messenger and the believers who perform the prayer, pay Zakat and bow down to God. [56] Anyone who turns to God for protection, His Messenger and the believers, should know God's party will be victorious.

A WARNING TO THOSE WHO POKE FUN AT RELIGIOUS PRACTICES

[57] Believers, do not take as allies those who treat your religion as a joke and a game, whether they are from the people who were given the Book before you or the disbelievers. Be mindful of God, if you are true believers. [58] When you are called to the prayer, they poke fun at it since they don't understand. [59] Say: "People of The Book, what do you have against us, other than we believe in God and in what was revealed to us and to those before us? Most of you are sinners." [60] Say: "Shall I tell you of an even worse kind of reward from God? Anyone incurring the curse and anger of God will become like monkeys, pigs[a] and the worshippers of false gods. They are in a far worse position, and have wandered far from the right path."

BELIEF REQUIRES CONVICTION, NOT MERE WORDS

[61] If they come to you saying, "We believe," they have entered the same state of denial that they were in previously. God knows well what they conceal. [62] You will see many of them rushing towards sinfulness, enmity and consuming unlawful gains. How foul is what they are in the habit of doing! [63] If only the rabbis and scholars would have stopped them from their sinful speech and consuming unlawful gains. How foul is what they do!

---

[a] The phrase "monkeys and pigs", which appears elsewhere in the Quran, is a figure of speech that refers to disobedient people with no sense of morality, becoming like monkeys and pigs in selfish pursuit of their lust.

ARROGANCE LEADS TO DISUNITY AND CONFLICT

⁶⁴The Jews said, "God is tight-fisted."ᵇ May their hands be tied, and may they be cursed for what they have said. God's hands are wide openᶜ, He gives generously as He pleases. What's revealed to you increases their rebelliousness and disbelief. We have cast enmity and hatred between them until Judgement Day. Every time they kindle the fire of war, God extinguishes it; so they move about the country creating terror, and God dislikes those who create terror. ⁶⁵Had the People of The Book believed and become mindful, then We would erase their sins and admit them into the gardens of bliss. ⁶⁶And if only they were to apply the Torah, the Gospel and what has been revealed to them from their Lord, they would be given plenty to eat from the sky above and from beneath their feet. Some of them are moderate in their behaviour, but many behave wickedly.

THE MESSENGER ﷺ PREACHES WITHOUT FEAR OR FAVOUR

⁶⁷Messenger, communicate all that's revealed to you by your Lord, if you don't, you won't have delivered His message. God will protect you from the people who wish to harm you. God does not guide the disbelievers.

GOD WILL REWARD THE FAITHFUL

⁶⁸Say: "People of the Book, you will have no excuse on Judgment Day unless you implement the Torah and the Gospels and what has been revealed to you from Your Lord." What has been revealed to you causes many of them to increase in their rebelliousness and disbelief, so don't feel pity for the disbelievers. ⁶⁹The believers, the Jews, the Sabians and the Christians, and anyone who believes in God and the Last Day and performs honourable deeds, they shouldn't fear, they shouldn't grieve.

A WARNING TO THOSE WHO TURN A BLIND EYE AND A DEAF EAR

⁷⁰We made a contract with the Israelites and sent many messengers to them. However, every time a messenger came to them with a revelation that didn't suit their wishes, they denied some and killed others, ⁷¹and they didn't think it was a test, so they chose to turn a blind eye and a deaf ear. Then God relented towards them, but once again many of them chose to turn a blind eye and a deaf ear. God clearly sees what they are doing.

ᵇ This blasphemous phrase literally means "God's hand is tied", i.e. He isn't generous.
ᶜ "God's hands" is a melonym for the power of God.

CHRISTIANS INVITED TO GIVE UP TRINITY SO THEY MAY ACHIEVE SALVATION

[72] Those who say, "God is the Messiah son of Mary," have committed an act of disbelief. The Messiah said: "Jews, worship God, my Lord and your Lord. Whoever associates anything with God, God will forbid his entry into Paradise, and his home will be the Fire, and there shall be no helpers for the wrongdoers." [73] *Likewise those who say*, "God is one of three," have committed an act of disbelief. There is no god apart from the One God. If they don't stop saying what they say, the disbelievers among them will be severely punished. [74] Why don't they repent before God and seek His forgiveness? God is Forgiving, Most Kind.

JESUS WAS A MESSENGER

[75] The Messiah son of Mary was a messenger, like the many messengers who went before him, and his mother was a truthful woman; both ate like other humans. See how We explain Our signs to them, and look how they ignore the truth? [76] Say: "Why, instead of worshipping God, do you worship what can neither help nor harm you?" God is the Hearer, the Knower. [77] Say: "People of The Book, don't go beyond the bounds of truth in your religion, and don't follow the whims of people who went astray before you, misleading many others, themselves wandering far off the straight path."

NOT CHALLENGING EVIL TURNED SOME JEWS INTO DISBELIEVERS

[78] The disbelievers among the Israelites were cursed by David and Jesus, son of Mary, because they were disobedient and went beyond the limits of the Torah: [79] they didn't condemn wrong in their society. They were wretched! [80] You will see many of them seeking the protection of disbelievers. How wretched is what they've stored for themselves, inviting God's wrath and punishment forever! [81] If they had believed in God, the Prophet and what was revealed to him, and hadn't taken the disbelievers as allies! Alas most of them are shameless sinners.

THE CHRISTIANS ARE MOST FRIENDLY TO MUSLIMS

[82] Of all the people, you will find the most hostile to the believers are some Jews and idolaters,[a] and you will find the nearest and most affectionate to the believers are those who say, "We are Christians" because among them are priests and monks who are not arrogant. [83] When they hear what's revealed to the Messenger, you'll

---

[a] The "*al*" definite article of "*al-Yahood*" is not "*al*" of *Jinssiya*, inclusive of all Jews but can also refer to a specific group mentioned here, the Jews of Madinah.

see their eyes well up with tears as they recognise its truth, saying, "Our Lord, we believe, so count us among the witnesses. [84] Why shouldn't we believe in God and what came to us of the truth, and why shouldn't we long for our Lord to join us with the righteous?" [85] So may God reward them for what they have said, with gardens under which rivers flow, to live there forever: that is the reward of the righteous! [86] Those who disbelieve and deny Our signs are the prisoners of Hell.

Do not make life difficult for yourselves

[87] Believers, don't declare unlawful healthy foods made lawful by God, and don't go beyond the limits set by Him; God dislikes those who go beyond the limits. [88] Eat the lawful and healthy food that He has provided you, and be mindful of God who you believe.

Penalty for breaking an oath

[89] God won't take you to task over oaths you make thoughtlessly, however, He will take you to task over any contracts that you seal with solemn oaths. The atonement for the breaking of oaths is: feed ten needy people the same food as you would typically feed your family; clothe them, or free a slave. Whoever hasn't the means to do this should fast for three days. That is the atonement for breaking oaths that you have sworn, so keep your oaths. This is how God explains His verses so that you might be grateful.

Intoxicants and gambling are unlawful

[90] Believers, wine,[b] gambling by drawing lots, the use of pagan sacrificial altars, or foretelling the future with arrows are filthy works of Satan; reject them so that you may succeed in life. [91] Satan wishes to sow enmity and hatred between you using wine and gambling, and to divert you from the remembrance of God and performance of the prayer. So, won't you stop? [92] Obey God and the Messenger, and beware. If you turn away that will be bad, you know Our Messenger's duty is to deliver the message clearly. [93] The believers who do righteous deeds shouldn't be blamed for what they consumed in the past, so long as they are mindful believers, doing righteous deeds, and thereafter they continue to be mindful and to believe in God, and now they are still mindful and striving for perfection. God

---

[b] Wine is specifically mentioned, but the Sunnah mentions anything that intoxicates is haram to consume – or trade in – including narcotics, drugs and alcoholic drinks. The sad fact that these vices are now rampant in our society demands that we must practise these teachings.

loves the righteous.

PILGRIMS SHOULD NOT HUNT

[94] Believers, God will test you by bringing the animals you hunt within reach of your hands and spears, so God marks out whoever fears Him without ever having seen Him; so whoever after this warning goes beyond the limits set by God will suffer a painful punishment. [95] Believers, don't hunt and kill animals while you are in the sanctified state of pilgrims.[a] The penalty for killing an animal intentionally is: sacrifice a livestock animal near the Kaaba that is judged to be equivalent by two just men; atone by feeding the needy or fast an equivalent number of days to realise the seriousness of his action. God has pardoned what happened in the past, but whoever transgresses from now on, God will punish him. God is the Almighty, the Avenger. [96] Catching fish from the sea and eating it are made lawful for your benefit and for the traveller. However, you are forbidden to hunt on land while you are in the sanctified state of the pilgrim; so be mindful of God, before Whom you will be gathered. [97] God has made the Kaaba a sacred house,[b] built for the benefit of humanity, along with the sacred months, and the sacrificial and garlanded animals. This is so you know God has knowledge of all that is in the Heavens and on Earth. God knows everything.

THE MESSENGER ﷺ DELIVERS THE MESSAGE BUT DOESN'T FORCE IT ON OTHERS

[98] You must realise that God is severe in His punishment, nevertheless Forgiving, Kind. [99] The Messenger's duty is to convey the message, God knows well what you reveal and what you conceal. [100] Say: "The good and bad are not the same, though the abundance of the bad will surprise you. So be mindful of God, you who are understanding, so you may succeed."

DON'T ASK TOO MANY QUESTIONS

[101] Believers, don't ask too many questions, if they were answered they would cause you difficulty, and if you ask while the Quran is being revealed they will be made clear to you. God has kept silence[c] about them. God is Forgiving, Gentle.

---

[a] The sanctified state (*ihram*) of a Muslim pilgrim is two pieces of unsewn white cloth. When a pilgrim enters that state, it becomes unlawful to do certain things like hunting. See also *Chapter Al-Baqarah*: 196–203.

[b] The Kaaba is the cube-shaped building in Makkah, and is mentioned in *Chapter Ale 'Imran*: 96 as the oldest sanctuary on Earth, a holy place.

[c] Literally, "God has passed over them." The story of the cow in *Chapter Al-Baqarah*: 67–71 is an example of what can happen when people ask too many questions.

[102] People before you asked such questions and when they were answered, then they denied it.

RID YOURSELVES OF THE SUPERSTITIONS OF PAST GENERATIONS

[103] God didn't order the veneration of: camels whose ears are split before being turned loose; she-camels which roam free; camels dedicated to idols that can't be slaughtered; and camels which mustn't be mounted;[d] rather it was the disbelievers who invented lies about God, and most of them lack the power of reason. [104] When they are told: "Come closer to what God has revealed and to His Messenger," they say, "What we found our forefathers practising is enough," yet their forefathers knew nothing and had no guidance. [105] Believers, you are responsible for yourselves. Those who are misguided can't harm you if you stay on the right path. You will all return to God, and He will tell you what you did.

THE APPOINTING OF WITNESSES FOR ONE'S LAST WILL

[106] Believers, when death approaches you, get two just persons to be witnesses to your last will and testament. If you are on a journey when the pangs of death strike, take any two witnesses from another tribe. Keep the two witnesses back after the prayer and, should you have any doubts, let them both swear by God: "We will not sell the testimony for any price, even if a close relative is involved, nor will we hide God's testimony, in that case, we would be sinful." [107] If it turns out that the two witnesses are judged guilty of a sin of perjury, then let two other witnesses take their place from amongst those whose right has been taken away, then let them both swear by God: "Our testimony is more truthful then theirs, and we haven't transgressed, in that case, we would be wrongdoers." [108] It's more fitting they produce their testimony in this way or stand in fear that the previous oaths be upheld after they had pronounced their oaths. Be mindful of God and listen carefully. God does not guide the disobedient.

THE MIRACLES OF PROPHET JESUS

[109] On the day when God will gather His messengers and ask, "What response did you get?"[e] They will say, "We have no knowledge. You are the Knower of

---

[d] Names of four types of animals that pagans dedicated to their idols: *bahira*, a she-camel with a cleft ear; *sa'iba*, an animal left to roam; *wasila*, an animal which must not be slaughtered; and *hami*, a camel forbidden for riding. These superstitious practises are condemned.

[e] Meaning, "What response did you get to your preaching?"

the unseen realms." [110] Then God will ask, "Jesus, son of Mary, do you remember My favours on you and your mother: I helped you with the Holy Spirit[a], so you could speak to people when you were in the cradle and preach when you were a young man. I taught you the Book, wisdom, Torah and the Gospel, and gave you miracles: you made clay birds and blew into them so they flew like live birds; you healed the blind and the lepers, and with My permission, you raised the dead from their graves. And remember I protected you from the attacks of Israelites when you preached to them with clear signs, and their disbelievers said, "This is magic!"

The miracle of Jesus; feeding of a large crowd

[111] Once I inspired the disciples "Believe in Me and My Messenger," they said, "We believe, and bear witness we have submitted ourselves to the Will of God." [112] The disciples said: "Jesus, son of Mary, can Your Lord send down from Heaven a table laden with food?" Jesus said: "Fear God, if you are believers." [113] They said, "We want to eat from it for reassurance, to know for certain that you have told us the truth, and we will be the witnesses of this miracle." [114] Jesus, son of Mary, prayed: "God, Our Lord, send down from Heaven a table laden with food, which becomes a festival for the believers of past and future,[b] and a sign from You, and provide for us, for You are the Best Provider."[c] [115] God said, "I will send it down for you. Whoever denies My favour after this miracle, I will punish him with a punishment that no creature has ever been punished with."

Prophet Jesus a witness against disbelievers

[116] On the Day of Judgement, God will say: "Jesus son of Mary, did you tell people, 'Take me and my mother as two gods besides God'?" He will say: "Glory be to you! How could I say something that I had no right to say, had I said it, You would know. You know what's in my innermost being, and I don't know what is in Yours. You are the Knower of the unseen realms. [117] I only told them what You commanded me to say: 'Worship God, my Lord and Your Lord,' I was a witness all the time I lived amidst them. Then, when You took me to Yourself, it was You Who were the Guardian over them. You Witness everything. [118] If You pun-

---

[a] "Ruh al-Quds" refers to the Angel Gabriel.
[b] Literally: 'for the first and last of us.'
[c] This could be the story mentioned in Mark 6:31, dubbed as 'The miracle of feeding the five thousand.'

ish them, they're Your servants, and if You forgive them, You are the Almighty, Wise." [119] God said, "This day the truth of the truthful will benefit them; they will be in gardens under which rivers flow, living there forever. God is well pleased with them, and they are pleased with Him." That is the glorious victory. [120] Control of the Heavens, the Earth, and whatever lies within them belongs to God, and He has power over all things.

6. Al-Anʿam
The Cattle

A late Makkan chapter revealed in its entirety on a single occasion, at a time of severe tension between the Muslims and the idolaters. Ibn Abbas said that some Makkans told the Prophet 鸞: "We shall not believe until you bring us a book which we can touch and accompanied by the angels." (Al-Qurtubi). The chapter presents powerful arguments supporting beliefs in *Oneness, Messengership,* and *Hereafter;* typical subject matter of Makkan chapters, whilst the Madinan chapters deal with law, worship and the organisation of the community. *Al-Anʿam,* "the Cattle", is derived from several references to the idolaters' superstitious practises of dedicating animals to their idols.

The Quran adopts five methods of reasoning to prove the creative power of God; a way of putting forward propositions about the existence of God, and His dominance:

1. Self-evident truths: these maxims are pithy statements of truth: "This worldly life is a sport and an amusement, the home in the Hereafter is far better for the mindful people" (32). Is there a doubt about the fleeting and temporary nature of this life?
2. The Nature: "God cleaves the seed and the fruit-stone; He brings the living from the dead and the dead from the living" (95). How can one fail to see the hand of God in the vast universe?
3. Human history: the stories of the prophets are frequent lines of evidence that the Quran presents to support its teachings (74–110). Prophet Abraham is instructed: "Worship God, there is no God beside Him." Steering stubborn and materialistic people to God by drawing their attention to the helplessness and mechanical nature of their gods.
4. Human conscience: The Quran appeals to human goodness and kindness to awaken the conscience, and frequently condemns human vices of greed, arrogance, and anger.
5. Human interest: people are naturally inclined to knowing what benefits or harms them. The Quran repeatedly demonstrates how idols are incapable of inflicting harm or benefit. So, why would anyone worship idols? Shouldn't they worship their genuine benefactor and creator?

The chapter opened with a powerful verse praising the creative power of God and criticising the idolaters for equating their idols with Him. It reminds the idolaters that its denial will land them into Hell, and that no matter how many miracles they see, they will not be convinced. The only remedy for stubbornness is submission. The Quran is a book of guidance; it reminds the idolaters that on Judgement Day they will regret their idolatry and will want to return to the world to do good.

The blessed Messenger 鸞 is told be humble: know your strengths, weaknesses and purpose in life. So be patient, keep the company of righteous, rely on God and have a deep knowledge of the greatness of God (74–90). The next section, until verse 104, provides powerful evidence for the resurrection.

Possible Reasons for Idolatry

The Quran explains the underlying cause of the idolaters' disbelief: they are close-minded: Stubborn and deaf, refusing to listen to the Prophet 鑾, unwilling to pay attention to human reason. When the Prophet 鑾 pointed out their superstitious and illogical ways, they reacted by mocking him, and employed bully tactics to intimidate him. No miracle could convince them, since their hearts were inclined towards evil. Satan motivates them and makes their works look attractive to them (105–24). On the other hand, the believers are open-minded; "The person God wishes to guide, He opens his mind *to Islam*; and whomever He wishes to go astray, He closes his mind..." (125).

The criticism is to prick the conscience, to encourage them towards awareness of reality and bring them out of their delusion. So, the Quran gives ten new Commandments: don't commit idolatry; care for parents; stop infanticide; avoid sinning openly and secretly; don't murder; look after orphans' wealth; weigh and measure things accurately; be just; fulfil the contract of God; and follow the straight path. The final advice: "He made you representatives on Earth... to test you with what He has given you" (165). The message is that human life is both precious and purposeful, so take it seriously!

The Makkah of seventh century relishes in pride, power and pleasure. Set in opposition to God. In that sense Makkah wasn't too different from London, New York or Dubai of today.

In the name of God, the Kind, the Caring

EVIDENCE FOR THE POWER AND MIGHT OF GOD

[1] Praise be to God, Who created the Heavens and the Earth and made darkness and light; though the disbelievers hold up *others* as equal to their Lord. [2] He created you from clay and fixed your lifespan, a lifespan *firmly* fixed by Him;[a] but you still doubt. [3] He is God in the Heavens and on Earth. He knows your secrets and all that you reveal, and He knows all that you do.

EVERY CIVILISATION THAT DENIED GOD PERISHED

[4] When a sign from their Lord comes they turn their backs on it, [5] denying the truth when it comes to them, *but* news of what they joked about[b] will soon come

---

[a] "Fixed time" in the first instance refers to death, and the second time it refers to the Day of Judgement.

[b] Irrefutable proof of the existence of the Resurrection, Judgement Day, and Hell.

to them. [6] Don't they realise We destroyed many previous generations, We gave them far more power in the land than We gave you, and how We sent abundant rain from the sky, making rivers flow. *Eventually*, We destroyed them for their sins, and raised up other people after them.

MIRACLES FAIL TO CONVINCE THE SCEPTICS

[7] Even if We sent down a book written on paper[a] which they could touch with their hands, the disbelievers would say, "This is nothing but magic." [8] They said, "If only an angel would come down to him," if We were to send an angel, that would *only be to* decide *their fate* and they would have no more time after that. [9] Just as We could have made *the Messenger* an angel, We could equally have made *the angel appear* as a man, thus confusing them with their own attempt to create confusion.[b] [10] Messengers were mocked before you, and the very punishment they once mocked swept away those who poked fun. [11] Say: "Travel about the land and see what happened to the deniers." [12] Say: "Who owns what's in the Heavens and Earth?" Say: "*Is it not* God? He has decreed that He will be kind.[c] Then He will gather you all on Judgement Day; in that, there is no doubt. Those who, *through wrong life choices*, have failed themselves will not believe. [13] Anything that is living – be it during the night or the day – belongs to Him. He is the Hearer, the Knower.

GOD ULTIMATELY DECIDES WHAT HE WILLS, SO SUBMIT

[14] Say: "Should I take a protector beside God, the Creator of the Heavens and the Earth, Who feeds and is not fed?" Say: "I am commanded to be the first who submits and not to be among idolaters." [15] Say: "I fear the punishment of a mighty day if I disobeyed My Lord." [16] Whoever escapes the *punishment* of that day, and is treated kindly; will have a clear victory. [17] If God decides to punish you, no one can remove it except Him, and if He decides to benefit you, He has power over all things. [18] He is the controller of His creatures, the Wise, the Aware.

THE ONENESS OF GOD IS SELF-EVIDENT

[19] Say: "Who could be the biggest witness?" Say: "*It is* God, a witness for you and

---

[a] Literally, "parchment" of leather.

[b] This is because angels are ordinarily only visible at the time of our death.

[c] Literally means, "He decreed kindness *as obligatory* on Himself." My translation expresses the idea that nothing can be imposed on God, other than by Himself. He is independent.

me. This Quran has been revealed to me so I should warn you and anyone *else its message* reaches. Do you believe there are other gods beside God?" Say: "I won't bear witness *to that.*" Say: "There's only One God, and I am not involved in what you associate *with Him.*" [20] Those *previously* given the Book know this is true just as they know their own children. As for those who, *through their choices in life,* have failed, they will not believe. [21] Who is a worst wrongdoer than the one who invents lies about God and denies His signs? Those who have failed themselves will not believe.

THE IDOLATERS' EXCUSES WILL FAIL THEM ON JUDGEMENT DAY

[22] The day We gather them all, We shall say to idolaters, "Where are the partners you claimed? [23] In their confused state they will say, "By God, Our Lord, we never worshipped false gods." [24] Look how they proved themselves liars, and how they deserted those they invented. [25] Some hear you, but We have placed a veil over their hearts so they fail to understand *the Quran,* and there is deafness in their ears.[d] Were they to see all the signs, they still would not believe. When they come to argue with you, the disbelievers say, "These are only the myths of the ancients," [26] they prevent others from *listening to* it and themselves, walk away. They are unwittingly destroying themselves.

ADMISSION OF WASTED LIFE

[27] If you could see them *on Judgement Day* when they stand *staring at* the Fire; they will say, "If only we could be returned and, instead of denying Our Lord's signs, become believers." [28] No way! What they once used to hide will appear before them. Suppose they were returned, they would *simply* go back to doing what they had been forbidden; they are liars. [29] They say, "Only our worldly life exists. We won't be brought back to life." [30] If you could see them as they stand before their Lord. He will ask them, "Isn't this real?" They will say, "By Our Lord, it is." It will be said, "Taste the torment of what you denied." [31] Those who deny meeting God shall be losers when the Final Hour suddenly overtakes them, and they will be carrying a burden on their backs, and say, "Alas for us, we wasted this *life!*" Isn't evil what weighs them down? [32] This worldly life is a sport and an amusement, the home of the Hereafter is far better for mindful people. Don't you understand?

---

[d] This spiritual blindness and deafness is a result of their attitude and stubbornness. They have chosen to shut-off the faculty of believing, the Lord leaves them in their state of delusion.

THE MESSENGER ﷺ IS CONSOLED AND URGED TO BE HUMBLE:

³³ We know, *Muhammad*, you are saddened by what they say. They can't turn you into a liar, but the wrongdoers are disputing God's signs. ³⁴ Messengers before you were also called liars, they were patient in the face of the lies and insults they suffered, until Our help came to them. No one can change God's words, and reports of the messengers have already come to you *confirming this.* ³⁵ If you find it difficult to bear their rejection then, if you can, look for a tunnel in the ground or a ladder to climb to the sky to bring them a miracle. If God wanted, He could have united them all on *the path of* guidance. Followers of the Prophet^a, you mustn't be like the ignorant. ³⁶ Only those who listen will answer. God will resurrect the dead, and they will return to Him. ³⁷ They say, "If a sign were to come down to him from his Lord?" Say: "God has the power to send down a sign," but most of them do not know.

HUMILITY: ANIMALS LIVE IN COMMUNITIES

³⁸ There is no creature on land or a bird flying in the sky that does not belong to a community just like yours. We haven't left anything out of the Book. They will be gathered before their Lord. ³⁹ Those who deny Our signs *might as well be* deaf and dumb, and *groping about* in the dark. Anyone God wills, He lets him go astray, and anyone He wills, He puts on a straight path. ⁴⁰ Say: "Suppose God's punishment, or the Final Hour, was to come now; would you call anyone other than God? ⁴¹ No! You would call Him alone, and if He so willed, He would sweep away whatever made you do so, and you would forget what you associated *with Him.*"

HUMILITY COMES THROUGH SUFFERING

⁴² We sent *messengers* to *many* communities before you, and put those communities through sufferings and hardships so that they might submit *to God.* ⁴³ They should have submitted when the sufferings came but instead their hearts hardened, and Satan made their works appear attractive to them. ⁴⁴ Once they forgot what they should remember, We opened up the floodgates of worldly provisions for them and, just as they were revelling in what they had, We suddenly seized them, and they were left in utter despair. ⁴⁵ The last traces of the evildoers were razed to the ground. Praise God, Lord of *all* the realms. ⁴⁶ Say: "Suppose God

---

^a   This change of address from the Prophet ﷺ to the followers is hinted to in Zia ul Quran.

114

were to take away your hearing and sight, and seal your hearts,[b] which god beside God would make them work for you?" See how We explain the signs, but they turn away. [47]Say: "Suppose God's punishment was to catch you unaware or fully aware *the fact is* only the wrongdoers would be destroyed."

THE HUMILITY OF THE MESSENGER 鐮; NO EXTRAVAGANT CLAIMS FOR HIMSELF

[48]We only sent messengers as bearers of good news and as warners. So, whoever believes and puts his life in order will neither fear nor grieve; [49]whereas those who reject Our signs will taste the punishment for their sins. [50]Say: "I don't say, 'I own the stores of God's riches,' or 'I know the unseen'; nor do I say, 'I am an angel.' I only follow what is revealed to me." Say: "Are the blind and the seeing equal? Why don't you think?"

HUMILITY IN PRACTICE; KEEP THE COMPANY OF DEVOUT PEOPLE

[51]Warn, by means of *the Quran*, those who fear being gathered before their Lord. Beside Him they have no protector or intercessor, so they may be mindful, [52]and don't drive away those who worship their Lord morning and evening, seeking His pleasure. It isn't for you to judge them, nor for them to judge you. Were you to drive them away, you would be a wrongdoer. [53]That is how We test some of them by means of others, so they say, "Are these the ones that God has favoured over us?"[c] Doesn't God know best who is grateful? [54]When believers in Our revelation come to you, say, "Peace be on you." Your Lord has decreed that He will be kind. Whoever unwittingly[d] does evil and then repents and reforms himself, *will find* God Forgiving, Kind. [55]This is how We explain the signs, so that the way of the sinful may be clearly distinguished.

THE PROPHET 鐮 IS EQUIPPED TO RESPOND TO THE DISBELIEVERS

[56]Say: "I am forbidden to worship those you serve beside God." Say: "I will not follow your desires because, if I did so, I would go astray and fail to be guided." [57]Say: "I have clear proof from My Lord, the one you have rejected. What you want to hasten is not in my *control*; the decision is God's, Who tells the truth and is the best Judge *of truth and falsehood*." [58]Say: "If what you seek to hasten were in

---

[b] This means if God made you deaf, blind or mentally disabled no one could heal you except God.

[c] The rich and powerful in society often find it hard to accept that God loves the poor and weak.

[d] Literally, "out of ignorance." Some Companions said that includes any major sin since, if we were in our right minds, we wouldn't do it.

my *control*, then the matter that divides us would have been settled by now." God knows well the wrongdoers.

EVIDENCE OF GOD'S CONTROL; NATURAL OCCURRENCES

[59] He has the keys of the unseen realm, only He knows them. He knows all that is in the land and sea. Not a single leaf falls without His knowledge, no seed *buried* in the darkness of the Earth, nor any fresh or withered plant is left unrecorded in a clear Book.[a] [60] He receives your soul at night[b] and knows what *good or evil* you have done during the day, and He raises you up *every morning* so that your fixed term[c] may reach its conclusion. After that you shall return to Him, and it is then that He will inform you of what you did. [61] He is Dominant[d] over His servants, and He sends forth *angel* guards so that whenever death overtakes one of you Our angels bring back his soul, never failing in their duty. [62] Then they will be returned to God, their True Master. Doesn't the final decision rest with Him? He is the swiftest of reckoners.

EVEN SURVIVING A STORM DOES NOT MAKE THEM HUMBLE

[63] Ask *them*: "Who rescues you from the dark forces of land and sea when you call Him humbly in secret for help, *all the while saying*, 'If He rescues us from this we will, indeed, be thankful'?" [64] Say: "It is God Who rescues you from that and every other danger, but then you go back to associating *false gods*."[e] [65] Say: "*Only* He is able to punish you from above or from beneath your feet, or create conflict and factions; so some may taste the violence of the other." Consider, how We explain the signs so they might understand.

AVOID GATHERINGS WHERE ISLAM IS MALIGNED

[66] Your people, *Muhammad*, deny *all* this, even though it is the truth. Say: "I will not be your guardian *on Judgement Day*. [67] Fulfilment comes to every prophecy, as you will discover *in due course*." [68] Whenever you see anyone mocking Our verses, turn away from them until they change the topic of conversation, and if Satan

---

[a]   This "clear Book" refers to *al-Lawh al-Mahfuz*, God's official record of our deeds, in which everything that has ever happened or will happen is kept.

[b]   Literally, "He causes you to die," or, "He takes you in His custody," or "He puts you to sleep."

[c]   The "fixed time" here means the time of death.

[d]   *Al-Qahir* is a name of God, it refers to His overwhelming power, complete authority, and control.

[e]   This example helps to explain why God refuses the deniers a second chance at life on Earth. Even after staring in the face of death, such people always revert to their old ways.

made you forget, as soon as you remember leave the gathering of the wrongdoers. [69] Those that are *already* mindful *of God* are in no way accountable for the *wrongdoers; their role is to* remind so they might become mindful. [70] Stay away from those who regard their religion as a sport, amusement, and are deceived by *the attractions of* this worldly life.[f] *To prevent* any person being *needlessly* lost to Hell because of the fruits of their actions, mention the fact that they will have no protector or intercessor beside God, nor will any ransom be accepted. They will be in Hell as a result of their actions; they denied so they shall have boiling water and painful punishment.

EXAMPLE OF GETTING LOST IN WORLDLY ATTRACTIONS

[71] Say: "Shall we worship beside God things that can neither benefit nor harm us, and turn back on our heels once God has guided us, like someone who is distracted and tempted by Earthly demons, *even though* he has friends calling him to the truth, saying, 'Come to us'?" Say: "God's guidance is the only guidance; and we have been ordered to submit to the Lord of *all* the realms, [72] and to perform the prayer and to be mindful of Him; before Him you will *all* be gathered." [73] He created the Heavens and the Earth for a purpose. A day *will come* when He says, "Be!" And it will be; His word is the *absolute* truth, all things will *return* to Him on the day when the *last* trumpet sounds. He is the Knower of the seen and unseen realms, the Wise, the Aware.

ABRAHAM EXPOSES THE FOLLY OF IDOLATRY

[74] *Remember* when Abraham said to his father, Azar,[g] "Have you taken idols as gods? I see you and your people are misguided." [75] That's how We showed Abraham the splendour[h] of the Heavens and the Earth, so he became a firm believer. [76] As the night grew dark around him, he saw a star, he thought, "*Could* this be My Lord?" After it set, he said, "I don't like *things* that set." [77] *Similarly*, after seeing the moon rising, he said, "*Could* this be My Lord?" But, after it set, he said, "If My Lord doesn't guide me, I will stray." [78] When he saw the sun rising, he *again* said, "*Could* this be My Lord? This is big." After it set, he said, "My people, I am

---

[f]   This includes people who call themselves Muslims but lack sincerity in their belief and practise of the faith.

[g]   Some commentators translate *Abeehay* as his uncle. They contend that the lineage of the blessed Prophet ﷺ has been free of idolaters from the time of Adam, a pure breed of the Noble Messenger.

[h]   The word *malakut* refers to God's control, authority and power over the operation of the universe.

free from what you associate *with God.* [79] I naturally turn my face to Him Who created the Heavens and the Earth; I won't associate *partners with Him.*"

ABRAHAM USED LOGIC TO DISPROVE THE IDOLATERS' ARGUMENTS

[80] *On hearing this,* his people *began to* argue with him, *so* he said, "Are you arguing with me about God, Who guided me? I am not afraid of those you associate with Him, unless My Lord wants something else. My Lord has knowledge of all things. Will you not listen? [81] Why should I be afraid of things you associate *with Him,* when you are not afraid to associate others with God about which He sent you no authority? Which of *our* two parties, *you or me,* deserves *to enjoy* security, if you have knowledge?" [82] Those who believe without confusing their faith with idolatry[a] who shall enjoy security, and it is they who are guided. [83] Such was the evidence that We gave to Abraham *to use* against his people; We raised him high as We wanted. Your Lord is Wise, Knowing.

ABRAHAM WAS THE FATHER AND THE LEADER OF MANY PROPHETS

[84] We gave him Isaac and Jacob and guided both as We had previously guided Noah – and among Abraham's offspring were: David, Solomon, Job, Joseph, Moses, Aaron – that is how We reward the righteous. [85] Zachariah, John, Jesus, Elijah – each one was upright – [86] Ishmael, Elisha, Jonah and Lot[b] – every one of them, We favoured over all the people – [87] and *some* among their fathers – offspring and brothers – We chose them and guided them along a straight path. [88] Such is God's guidance, by which He guides His servants as He pleases. If *any of* them had associated *partners with God,* then *the reward of* whatever *good* deeds they had done would be worthless. [89] We gave the Book, the law and the prophethood to them. Even if these *people* reject it, We *nevertheless* entrusted it to people who accepted it.[c] [90] God guided them, so imitate *them in* their guidance. Say: "I don't ask you for any reward for this; it's a reminder for all people."

PEOPLE BELIEVED IN SOME PARTS OF SCRIPTURE AND REJECTED OTHERS

[91] When they said, "God has never revealed anything to a human being," they failed to recognise *the true greatness* of God which is His due. Ask: "Who re-

---

[a] *Zulm* is generally wrongdoing, because of the context, it refers to idolatry, as explained in *Chapter Luqman* 31: 13.

[b] The Biblical names of the prophets mentioned in verses 83–86 are, in order: Abraham, Isaac, Jacob, Noah, David, Solomon, Job, Joseph, Moses, Aaron, Zachariah, John, Jesus, Elias, Ishmael, Elisha, Jonah and Lot.

[c] In other words, Muslims who will believe them.

vealed the Book Moses brought as a light to guide people which you keep in scrolls. You openly declare *some of* it and hide a lot *of it*; and you were taught what neither you nor your ancestors knew?" Say: "It is God," then leave them to amuse themselves with their *foolish* chatter. [92] This is a blessed Book that We have sent down, confirming what came before it, so you might warn *the people of* the Mother of Cities[d] and of its surroundings. Those who believe in the Hereafter, they believe in *this Book*,[e] taking care to observe their *daily* prayers.

THE DISBELIEVERS IN DEATH THROES

[93] Who is more wrong than the one who invents lies about God, or says, "It has been revealed to me," when *in fact* nothing has been revealed to him, or says, "I will send down the same as what God has sent down?" Were you to see the wrongdoers in death throes, when the angels stretch out their hands, *saying*, "Let out your souls, today you will be rewarded with the punishment of contempt because of what you falsely said about God, arrogantly rejecting His signs.[94] You will come to Us all alone like the first time We created you. You have left behind the favours We gave you; nor do We see your intercessors with you, those whom you claimed were God's partners. The ties between you *and them* have been severed, and whatever you used to *claim as a partner* has deserted you."

EVIDENCE OF GOD'S INGENIOUS CREATIVITY: SEEDS, BUDS, FLOWERS

[95] God is the one who splits open the seed and the fruit-stone; He brings the living from the dead and the dead from the living. Such is God, so how were you misled *from the truth*? [96] He splits *the darkness with* the dawn, and made the night for resting, and the sun and moon for accurately measuring *time*. Such is the precision with which He reassures, the Almighty, the Knowing. [97] He made the stars for your guidance through the darkness of land and sea. We explained the signs to *a group of* people who know. [98] He created you from a single soul, with a place of settlement *in life* and *another* where you will be buried.[f] We have explained the signs to *a group of* people who understand. [99] He sent down water from the sky, by which We produce blossoms of every kind, and lush greenery. Furthermore,

---

d The "Mother of Cities" is Makkah.

e The pronoun 'it' in the Arabic refers to the glorious Quran.

f The word *mustaqarr* means a fixed term (*Chapter Al-Baqarah* 2: 36). Al-Qurtubi translates it as "depositing" in the grave, where one awaits the Day of Judgement.

We produce *pods* with seeds packed together and from the flowering part of palm trees, low-hanging clusters of dates, and orchards of vines, olives and pomegranates, some look-alike and others different. Look at their fruits as they grow and ripen; there are signs in that for people who believe.

GOD, THE ORIGINATOR OF THE UNIVERSE

[100] *Some people* have taken jinn[a] as partners of God, yet He created them, and falsely ascribed sons and daughters to Him without any knowledge. Glory be to Him! He is Exalted far above what they describe. [101] He's the Originator of the Heavens and the Earth. How could He have a son when He has no mate? He created everything, and He knows everything. [102] Such is God, your Lord; there is no god but Him, the Creator of everything, so worship Him. He governs everything. [103] *Our* eyes cannot perceive Him, but He perceives *what* our eyes see. He is the Subtle, the Aware. [104] *Say, Muhammad*: "Visible proofs have come to you from your Lord; anyone who looks at them, it is for his own benefit, and whoever remains blind *to them*, on *his head* be it. I am not *sent* to watch over you." [105] This is how We explain the signs, but *the disbelievers* say, "You have learnt it[b]." So, We *wish to* make them clear for people who know *the truth*.

MUSLIMS FORBIDDEN TO INSULT THE BELIEFS OF NON-MUSLIMS

[106] *Messenger,* follow what is revealed to you from your Lord – there is no god but Him – and turn away from the idolaters. [107] Had God willed, they would not have associated *anything with Him*. We've not put you *there* to watch over them, nor are you responsible for them. [108] *Believers*, don't insult anything[c] they worship beside God, then they will insult God out of hostility and ignorance. That is how We made every community's actions appear attractive to them, they will return to their Lord, and He will inform them about what they did.

EVEN MIRACLES FAIL TO CONVINCE SCEPTICS

[109] *The idolaters* swear solemn oaths by God that if a miracle came to them they would believe. Say: "Miracles come only from God." What would make you realise that even if a *miracle* came, they still wouldn't believe; [110] and that We would

[a]   The Jinn are an invisible species created from fire. Like humans, they possess intellect and are accountable for their actions, and among them are both believers and disbelievers.

[b]   From the People of The Book, it's not from God.

[c]   The classical commentaries talk specifically of idols, which were relevant to the context of Makkah, but the Quran is general, so it also includes non-religious belief systems: atheism and secularism.

turn their faculties of intellect and sight upside down because they failed to believe in it the first time, leaving them to wander blindly about in their wickedness? [111] Even if We sent down angels, or the dead spoke, or We gathered everything before them, they wouldn't believe unless God so willed. Most of them are ignorant.

HOW DEMONS MISLEAD?

[112] For every prophet We assigned an enemy, demons from humans and jinn, who inspired one another with flowery speech to deceive. If Your Lord wanted, they wouldn't have done this; so, leave them and what they invent. [113] *They do* so that the intellects of disbelievers of the Hereafter might turn towards *their flowery speech,* and be pleased with it, and so that they might get what is coming to them *because of their wicked ways.* [114] *Say:* "Should I seek a judge beside God, when He has sent down the Book to you, clearly explained?" Those given the Book know it has been sent by Your Lord with truth so, listener don't be among the doubters. [115] Truly and justly has your Lord's promise been fulfilled;[d] no power can change His promise. He is the Hearer, the Knower. [116] If you were to obey *the whims of* most of those in the city, they would mislead you from God's way. They do nothing but follow speculation and tell lies. [117] Your Lord knows best those straying from His way, and those guided.

A WARNING FOR THOSE FUSSY ABOUT FOOD

[118] So eat of the *meat* on which God's name has been invoked,[e] if you believe in His signs. [119] Why wouldn't you eat that on which God's name has been invoked, after He has explained in detail what He has forbidden you *to eat* except out of necessity? Many of them are misled because of their desires and lack of knowledge. Your Lord knows best the sinners. [120] Stay away from open and hidden sins; those who commit sins will be punished for what they gained from it. [121] Do not eat that *meat* on which the name of God has not been invoked; to do so is sinful. *Believers,* the *human* demons inspire their followers to dispute with you; and if you were to obey them, you would be *guilty of* associating *partners with God.*

---

[d] *Kalima,* literally "word", here refers to God's promise of judgement in the Hereafter. It could also refer to the Quran.

[e] The verses 118–121 contain a challenge for our times, with so many halal certifiers competing against each other for business. Al-Qurtubi says God revealed them in relation to Muslims who only ate what they slaughtered themselves, refusing any other meat.

Evil works look attractive

[122] *Take for example a* person spiritually dead who We gave a life and a light to walk among people, is he like someone who lives in utter darkness which he never leaves? That is why what disbelievers did appeared attractive to them. [123] In the same way, We have placed sinners in every town who go about plotting *evil*, but *they* are only unwittingly deceiving themselves. [124] When a revelation came to them, they said, "We shall not believe until we are given what God's *earlier* messengers were given." God knows best where to place His Message. Those who break the law will face humiliation in front of God, and severe punishment for their former plotting.

Submission to God is sign of open-mindedness

[125] The person God wishes to guide, He opens his mind[a] to surrender *to God*; and anyone He allows to go astray, He closes his mind, as if he were struggling to climb skywards: by such means God allows evil to come about on those who do not believe. [126] This is the straight path of your Lord, and We have explained the verses in detail for people who are open to reminders. [127] They shall enjoy a house of peace with their Lord, and He shall be their Protector for what they did.

How the sinners can influence others?

[128] On the day when He gathers them all, *He will say*, "Company of jinn, you derived much pleasure from *misleading* humans," and their allies among the humans will say, "Our Lord, we benefitted from each other, but now we have reached the end of the span of life that you appointed for us." He will say, "The Fire is your eternal abode, unless God wishes otherwise." Indeed, *messenger*, your Lord is Wise, Knowing. [129] This is how We give some sinners influence over others because of the deeds they earned. [130] God will ask: "Company of jinn and humans, did messengers not come to you from among your own kind, telling you of My signs and warning you that you would meet *Me* on this day?" They will say, "We testify against ourselves," but the worldly life deceived them, and they testified against themselves that they were disbelievers. [131] Your Lord was never unjust, He would not destroy towns whose inhabitants had no knowledge *of the truth*.

---

[a] *Sadr* means the "chest"; it can be a metaphor for the intellect and emotions, but can also be quite literal when followed by a simile: 'the narrowing of the chest'.

DIFFERENT RANKS IN THE HEREAFTER BASED ON RIGHTEOUS DEEDS

[132] Everyone's rank *in the Hereafter* will be based on what they did *in this life*, and Your Lord is not ignorant of what they do. [133] Your Lord is Self-Sufficient, Most Kind. If He wanted, He could get rid of you altogether and replace you with whomever He pleases, just as He raised you from the offspring of other people. [134] What you have been promised is coming, and you will not be able to stop *it*. [135] Say: "My people, do it your way, and I'll do it my way. Soon you will know who will gain the happy home in the Hereafter." Evildoers don't succeed.

PAGAN CUSTOMS AND SUPERSTITIONS ABOUT LIVESTOCK

[136] They set aside for God a share of the crops and cattle that He has produced, saying, "This is for God," as they claim, "and this is for our partner *gods*." *Whatever* is for their partners doesn't reach God, and whatever is for God reaches their partners. How badly they judge!

THEY COMMIT INFANTICIDE

[137] In this way their partners *in falsehood* have made it appear attractive to many of the idolaters to kill their children.[b] *Their false gods do this* to destroy them and to dress up their religion. Of course, if God had so wished, they wouldn't have done it; so leave them and whatever they have invented.

THE PROHIBITION TO RIDE SOME ANIMALS

[138] They say, "These cattle and crops are set aside. No one may eat them without our authorisation." *Some* cattle are forbidden to ride; and on other cattle they do not invoke God's name *when slaughtering*, falsely attributing these rules to Him. He will deal *appropriately* with whatever *lies* they invented.

SUPERSTITION ABOUT THE STILLBORN

[139] They say, "What is in the wombs of these cattle are exclusively for our men and forbidden for our wives. But, if it is stillborn, then they all share in it." He will reward them *appropriately* for their *false* description *of Him*. He is Wise, Knowing. [140] Those who kill their children foolishly without knowledge, and who forbid

---

[b] These pagan Arab superstitions were to justify infanticide, especially of females, by claiming that it was forbidden to feed this baby girl from the milk of this ewe, for example, but her twin brother can be fed from it. A few verses later, the comparison is made between what the Arabs before Islam used to forbid with what was forbidden for the Jews. In Mark 7: 11, Jesus the Messiah criticised the Jews for refusing to help their parents, claiming that his time was *qurban*: in other words, dedicated to God as a kind of sacrifice.

what God has provided them, falsely attributing it to God, they have *already* lost: they have gone astray; they aren't guided. [141] He grows gardens, both with and without trellises,[a] date palms, plants of different flavours, olives and pomegranates, some alike and others different. Eat of their fruits when they are ripe, give *the needy* their due on harvest day, and do not squander; He dislikes spendthrifts.

Four pairs of animals

[142] Some cattle are for carrying loads and some are for food; so eat what God has provided you and don't follow in Satan's footsteps, *for* he is your open enemy. [143] There are eight *animals in* pairs: two sheep and two goats. Say: "Is it the two males that He has forbidden, or the two females; or is it perhaps what lies within the wombs of the two females? Tell me based on some sound knowledge, which is it if you are telling the truth." [144] *Likewise, there are* two camels and two oxen. Say: "Is it the two males that He has forbidden, or the two females; or is it perhaps what lies within the wombs of the two females? Or were you *even* present when God ordered you to do this? Who is more wrong than the one who ignorantly invents lies about God to mislead people? God does not guide the wrongdoers." [145] Say: "I find nothing in what has been revealed to me that people are forbidden to eat except carrion, blood products, pork, which is impure, or else meat *from animals* slaughtered in the name of anything other than God." However, if anyone is compelled, not because he desires it or wishes to disobey *God*, then your Lord is Forgiving, Kind. [146] We forbade the Jews *from eating* animals with claws; and the fat of oxen and sheep, except whatever *fat* clings to their backs or to the offal, or is stuck to bones. That penalty was imposed because of their rebelliousness. We are Most Truthful. [147] If they accuse you of lying, say: "Your Lord is gracious, and yet His punishment will not be deflected from the sinful people."

The idolaters' practices have no sound basis

[148] The idolaters will say, "If God wanted, neither we nor our ancestors would have associated *anything with God*, nor would we have forbidden *the eating of* anything." In the same way, people before them used to lie outrageously, until they tasted Our punishment. Say: "Have you got any knowledge? If so, produce it for us. You only follow speculation and tell lies." [149] Say: "God has conclusive proof,

---

[a] A trellis is a wooden or metal lattice used to support fruit trees or vines.

If He so wished, He would have guided you all."[b] [150] Say: "Bring your witnesses who will testify that God forbade this." Even if they testify, you do not testify with them. Do not follow the desires of deniers of our signs and those who don't believe in the Hereafter, and hold *others* up as equals to their Lord.

COMMANDMENTS FOR MUSLIMS; THE NEW CONTRACT

[151] Say: "Step forward *and* I will tell you what your Lord has forbidden for you: Associate nothing with Him, treat parents well, don't kill your children due to poverty, We provide for both you and them. Stay well clear of gross indecency, whether openly or in secret. Don't kill anyone, God has made life sacred, unless by some lawful right. This is what He has commanded you, so that you might reflect. [152] Stay well clear of the property of orphans, except if it be to do good *by investing it wisely*, until they come of age. Be honest in *your* weights and measures, *because* We do not task any person beyond its capacity. Whenever you speak, be just even regarding your own relatives. Be true to the contract of God. This is what He has commanded you, so that you might pay attention. [153] This path of Mine is straight, so follow it and do not follow other paths, as they will cause you to deviate from His path. This is what He has commanded you, so that you might be mindful."

GOD'S REVELATION REMOVES DOUBTS

[154] After that, We gave Moses the Book as a comprehensive *manual* for the one who strives for righteousness, explaining everything in detail, and as a guidance and kindness so that people might believe in meeting their Lord. [155] And this *too* is a blessed book that We have sent down, so follow it and be mindful, so that you might be treated kindly *by God*. [156] *This is* just in case you should say, "The Book was only sent to two groups before us, and we were unaware of what they had been taught," [157] or you say, "If only the Book had been revealed to us, then we would have been better guided than them." Now clear evidence has come to you from your Lord, along with guidance and kindness. Who then does greater wrong than the one who denies God's signs and turns away from them? We will

[b] This clarifies the belief about predestination; the relationship between God's knowledge of the future and human free-will. Seemingly, the two are contradictory. That's not so, We believe God's knowledge is infinite and humans have been given a responsibility; the moral choice to be either good or bad. If God wanted He could have made us all righteous, without a free-will. The the Day of Judgement would be meaningless and worldly life no longer a test. From here to the end of the chapter is clarification of this moral choice.

award those who turn away from Our signs the worst of punishments because of what they used to do. [158] Is this what they are waiting for: that angels should come to them, or your Lord, or some signs of your Lord? On the day when some of your Lord's signs come, *there* a person's faith will be of no benefit unless it already believed, or had earned some good because of faith. Say: "Wait *and see*, for we too are waiting."

SECTARIANISM IS CONDEMNED

[159] You have nothing to do with those who divided their religion and made sects; their case rests with God, and He will inform them about what they did. [160] Whoever *on Judgement Day* produces a good deed will have *the reward of* ten like it, and whoever produces an evil deed will be awarded just one like it; and they will not be wronged *in the least*.

FAITH IN GOD CALLS FOR COMPLETE COMMITMENT

[161] Say: "My Lord has guided me on a straight path, an upright religion, tending naturally towards Abraham's way of worship, he wasn't an idolater." [162] Say: "My prayers, my sacrifices, my life, my death; are for God, Lord of *all* the realms; [163] He has no partners. That's what I have been ordered to do, and I am the first to surrender *to Him*." [164] Say: "How can I long for a lord other than God, when He is Lord of everything? No person earns anything except towards its own account, and no one will bear the burden of another; then to your Lord shall you return, and He will inform you about whatever you differed over." [165] He made you representatives on Earth, raising some of you over others in rank in order to test you with what He has given you. Your Lord is swift to punish but always Forgiving, Kind.

7. Al-Aʿraf
The Heights

A late Makkan chapter, revealed possibly a year before the Hijrah and after *Chapter Al-Anʿam*. It deals with the three basic beliefs of Islam, presenting proofs from nature, stories from human history, and evidence from the human condition and experience. Simultaneously, it rejects false beliefs and provides an authoritative critique of idolatry and erroneous behaviour. Concepts, images, stories and powerful metaphors are presented to make the meaning clear, such that it touches the heart and mind.

The Quranic sentence is not the same as sentences in our writings that have clearly defined subject, verb and object sequences. Instead, it is diverse and complex, reflecting the complexity of nature and the world around us. It does not talk in past, present and future sequences either, often flips from past to future, from the present to the past, and vice versa, sometimes with one foot in the present and the other in the future; reflecting the timeless nature of the Almighty Creator.

The stories of the prophets Noah, Saleh, Hud, Lot, Jethro and Moses are a reassurance for the Messenger ﷺ and the Muslims and warning for the Idolaters. In all these cases the prophets were rejected, condemned, and even killed. However, they continued their mission: teaching, preaching and mentoring rebellious people. Finally, the divine punishment destroyed them.

The chapter opens with a powerful description of the Quran as the guidance, and a reminder that should be heeded. Otherwise, the consequences would be devastating. By relating the story of Adam and Satan, the Quran is alluding to the causes of human failure to follow the path of religion. The Satan is the arch enemy, and we are warned to remain alert to his temptations. On the other hand, the weakness of humankind is that it readily falls into temptations that appeal to psychological hungers: lust, food, senses of belonging and honour. This is precisely what Satan did with Adam and Eve. He tempted them and they fell in his trap, but quickly repented.

The chapter flips to the Hereafter, presents a detailed conversation between the people of Heaven and Hell, and introduces a third group of people, "The people of the heights," after whom the chapter takes its name. Most commentators define them as "people whose good and evil deeds are equal." They are in limbo, an undefined state, anxiously awaiting the judgement. Another explanation of Aʿraf is the following:

> The term Al-Aʿraf is the plural of ʿUrf meaning acknowledgement ... and discernment. This interpretation has been adopted by some of the early commentators and cited by Razi ... People thus described were those who in their lifetime could discern between right and wrong but didn't incline to either way; they were indifferent. Their lukewarm

attitude prevented them from doing either much good or much wrong – with the result that as the next sentence shows they deserve neither Paradise nor Hell. A third explanation of people of A'raf is: people who were most pious, the martyrs and the scholars who worked for the glory of God and strengthening Islam and serving humanity. Since A'raf refers to the heights and raised decks, it points to their elevated position from where they can see the delights of Paradise and the horrific punishment of Hell-fire and can comment on it. (Shaikh Muhammad al-Ghazali)

The Divine Laws

The next section of the chapter (59–102) describes the work and lives of six great prophets. The story of Moses is presented at length, giving details of his encounter with Pharaoh, the magicians and the Israelites. God has always guided humanity by sending the prophets, their beautiful character was a model to be followed. Their clean and God-filled lives were attractive role models, their love of humanity – the weak and vulnerable – was heart-warming. Yet as we read these stories we notice human stubbornness, unwillingness to listen, and obey them. The chapter teaches us to dress smartly when worshipping God, see verse 26 but insisting that inner smartness is as important, as it is a way of defending oneself against both indecency and arrogance. By linking clothing with piety, the Quran teaches the relationship of the outer to the inner, the physical to the spiritual, and the connection between words and behaviour.

In verse 172 another important notion mentioned in this chapter is the nature of humankind; it is Divine nature, made by God with the potential of recognising and believing its creator.

However, as mentioned earlier in the chapter, people often fail to resist temptations, and fall into them. This is demonstrated in the story of Bal'am ibn Ba'ura, a follower of Moses who became arrogant and contested his master. The Quran comments: "If We wanted, We could have raised his status because of those signs, but he chose to pursue Earthly matters and follow his whims" (176).

———————

In the name of God, the Kind, the Caring.

[1] *Alif Lam Meem Sad.*

THE QURAN IS A WARNING AND A REMINDER

[2] A book has been sent down to you, *Messenger*, so have no worries about it; through it you warn, it's a reminder for the believers. [3] Follow what's sent down to you by Your Lord, and follow no other masters beside Him. People, you pay too little attention.

IN THE HEREAFTER, ALL DEEDS WILL BE WEIGHED

[4] How many towns did We destroy? Our scourge struck them at night, or during their afternoon nap, [5] and when Our scourge struck, they pleaded, "We were wrongdoers." [6] We'll question both the messengers and their people to whom they were sent. [7] Let Us tell them our side of the story based on *irrefutable* knowledge, for We were not absent. [8] The weighing up *of deeds* on that day is a certainty. Anyone with heavy scales *of good deeds* will be successful, [9] and anyone with light scales will lose out because they used to go against Our scripture. [10] We established you on Earth, and gave you the means to live. People, you give little thanks.

SATAN VOWS TO MISLEAD PEOPLE

[11] *Humanity*, We created you and gave you the present form; then We told the angels, "Prostrate before Adam," they all prostrated, except Satan who didn't prostrate. [12] "What stopped you from prostrating when I commanded you?" *God,* Satan replied, "I am better than him *since* You created me from fire, and him from clay." [13] God said to him, "Get down from here, how dare you be arrogant, so get out, you are despised." [14] *Satan* said, "Give me time until the Day of Resurrection." [15] *God* said, "You shall have your time." [16] *Satan* said, "Since You let me go astray, I shall sit near Your straight path for *a chance to lure* them; [17] then I will pounce on them from the front, behind, and from their right and left, You will find most of them are ungrateful *to You.*" [18] *God* said, "Get out of here, despised and an outcast. Anyone who follows you, I will fill Hell with the lot of you."

HOW SATAN MISLED ADAM AND EVE

[19] "Adam, live with your wife in Paradise and eat from wherever you wish, but don't come near this tree otherwise you will be wrongdoers," *God said.* [20] So Satan whispered to the two of them, in order to reveal their nakedness, of which they had until then been unaware, and said, "Your Lord has only forbidden you from eating *fruit* of this tree to stop you becoming angels or eternal." [21] Then he swore an oath, "I am a sincere adviser for you both." [22] So, by deception, he brought about their fall. On tasting *the fruit of* the tree, they became aware of their nakedness and began to *cover* themselves with the leaves of *the trees of* Paradise. Their Lord called out to them, "Didn't I forbid you from *going near* that tree and warned you Satan is your open enemy?"

ADAM AND EVE PRAY FOR GOD'S FORGIVENESS

²³ Both said, "Our Lord, we've wronged ourselves. If You don't forgive us and treat us kindly we will be the losers." ²⁴ *God* said, "Get down *from here*, each of you the enemy of the other.ᵃ On Earth you shall have a home for a while and a means of livelihood, ²⁵ there you will live and die, and *eventually* be raised from it."

CLOTHING IS FOR MODESTY AND LOOKING BEAUTIFUL

²⁶ Children of Adam, We've inspired you to wear clothing to look beautiful and to cover your nakedness,ᵇ and the clothing of piety is the best. That is one of God's signs *to humans*, so they may pay attention. ²⁷ Children of Adam, don't let Satan tempt you as *he tempted* your parents and had them expelled from Paradise, stripping them of their clothes, exposing their nakedness. He and his type watch you from a place where you can't see them. We made *those* demons the friends of disbelievers. ²⁸ Whenever they perform an act of indecency, they say, "We found our forefathers doing it; God has ordered us to do it." Say: "God does not order acts of indecency. You are saying things about God that you don't know?"ᶜ

SHOW YOUR LOVE OF GOD BY DRESSING SMARTLY FOR WORSHIP

²⁹ *Messenger*, say: "My Lord orders *you* to be just; turn your faces *towards Him* at all *time in* places of worship,ᵈ and call upon Him, reserving your worship for Him alone. As He created you, so you shall return *to Him*." ³⁰ God guided one group, whilst He let the other group go astray *because* they took devils as protectors instead of God, thinking they were rightly guided. ³¹ Children of Adam, dress beautifully when attending the place of worship, and eat and drink, but don't squander; He dislikes the squanderers. ³² Say: "Who has forbidden the adornment which God has produced for His servants, along with the provision of healthy foods?" Say: "It is for those who believed *in God and the Last Day* during this worldly life, reserved for them alone *to wear* on Judgement Day." This is how We explain Our signs for people who know.

ᵃ   Here the story switches from addressing just Adam and Eve to the plural form, meaning that He is now referring to Satan on the one side, and the two humans on the other, being enemies of each other.

ᵇ   *Reesh* refers to a bird's plumage, the beautifully coloured and patterned feathers.

ᶜ   This verse condemns the unlawful sexual acts and also the idolaters' practice of performing the Hajj in the nude.

ᵈ   The Arabic word *masjid* literally means place of prostration, and an "act of worship".

SINS HARM US AND LEAD TO HELL

[33] Say: "My Lord has forbidden acts of indecency, whether openly or in secret; *likewise any* sin; unlawful rebellion; associating with God anything for which He has revealed no authority;[c] and saying things that you have no knowledge about God." [34] Every community has an allotted term, and when their allotted term comes *to an end*, they can neither delay it by a *single* hour, nor can they hasten it. [35] Children of Adam, whenever messengers from among yourselves come to teach you My scripture; whoever is mindful and reforms himself will have nothing to fear nor grieve. [36] *However*, those who deny Our signs and consider *those signs* to be beneath them, such people shall be the companions of the Fire, living there forever.

EACH SUCCESSIVE GENERATION OF DISBELIEVERS WILL BLAME THE OTHER

[37] Who can be more wicked than the one who invents lies about God, or denies His signs? Such people will receive their portion of *enjoyment decreed in* the Book, up until Our *angelic* messengers come to take their souls, saying to them, "Where are those you worshipped beside God?" They will say, "They have deserted us and testified against themselves that they were disbelievers." [38] He will say, "Enter the Fire along with the communities of jinn and humans who've passed away." Whenever a community *enters the Fire*, it will curse its fellow *community*, up until each of them has followed all the others into it, and the last of them will say about the first of them, "Our Lord, here are those who misled us, so double their punishment in the Fire." He will say, "Each *of you* will have double *the punishment*, though you don't know *it*." [39] Then the first *to enter* will say to the last, "You were no better than us, so taste the punishment for what you earned."

THE ARROGANT WILL BE THROWN IN HELL

[40] Those who deny Our signs and consider *them* beneath their dignity, the gates of Heaven will not open for them, nor will they enter Paradise until a camel can pass through the eye of a needle;[f] that is how We punish sinners. [41] They shall have a bed of Hell *fire*, and there will be a covering *of fire* above them; that is how We

---

[c]   It is perfectly acceptable to associate knowledge, for example, or speech with God, since authority for calling these divine attributes exists in the Quran and Sunnah.

[f]   Some commentators translate *jamal* not as camel but as "thick twisted rope" (*Razi*), meaning it will be impossible for an arrogant person to enter Paradise.

punish wrongdoers.

THE RIGHTEOUS RECOGNISE THAT IT WAS GOD WHO GUIDED THEM

[42] The believers who did righteous deeds – We don't task any soul beyond its capacity – will be the inhabitants of Paradise, living there forever. [43] We shall remove malice from their hearts, *and let them enjoy*: rivers flowing beneath them in Paradise, they shall say, "Praise be to God, Who guided us to this, and *we* wouldn't be guided had God not guided us. The messengers of Our Lord came with the truth." They will hear the call: "This is Paradise, you've inherited it because of what you did." [44] The people in Paradise will call out the people of the Fire: "We've found what our Lord promised to be true, have you found what your Lord promised you to be true?" They will say, "Yes!" So, an announcement will be made: "The curse of God is on the wrongdoers [45] who block God's path, wishing to distort it, and who deny the Hereafter."

THE PEOPLE ON THE HEIGHTS

[46] A wall *will appear* between both *groups*, and on the high places there will be men[a] who recognise each *other* from their features, and they will call out to the people of Paradise, "Peace be on you." They won't have entered it, but they will be longing to do so. [47] When their eyes turn toward the companions of Hell, they will say, "Our Lord, don't put us with the evildoers." [48] The companions of the high places will call out to *other* men whom they recognise by their features, and they will say to them, "Your large group and pride hasn't benefitted you. [49] Are these the ones about whom you swore God's kindness would never reach?" *The angels will say*, "Enter Paradise. You shall neither fear nor grieve."

THE PEOPLE OF HELL ASK FOR WATER

[50] The companions of Hell will ask the companions of Paradise: "Give us some water or anything else God has provided you." They will say, "God has forbidden both for the disbelievers, [51] who made their religion a fanfare, a sport and were deceived by worldly life. Today We shall abandon them just as they neglected their meeting *with Us* on this day, they disputed Our signs."

DISBELIEVERS WILL FIND THEMSELVES WITHOUT ANY SUPPORT

[52] We brought them a book, which explained *things* intelligently, a guidance and

---

[a] The phrase A'raf' is "companions of the high places" for more see the introduction to the chapter.

source of kindness for the believers. [53] Are they waiting for its fulfilment? On the day when it is fulfilled, those who had neglected it will say, "Our Lord's messengers came with the truth. Are there any intercessors to plead on our behalf, or *is there a possibility that* we will be returned *to our former life* so we can act differently from how we used to?" They've failed themselves, and things they invented have deserted them.

PRAY HUMBLY TO THE LORD WHO CREATED THE UNIVERSE

[54] God is your Lord, Who created the Heavens and the Earth in six days[b] and then established Himself *as befits Him* on the throne[c]. He causes the night to cover the day, which follows it swiftly. The sun, moon and stars all obey His command. Doesn't *all the* creation and the command *to control it* belong to Him? Blessed be God, Lord of *all* the Universe. [55] Call on your Lord, humbly and in secret. He dislikes transgressors. [56] Do not make conflict in the land after it has been made peaceful but call on Him with fear and longing. God's Kindness is close to the righteous.

A COMPARISON OF RAIN TO RAISING THE DEAD

[57] He sends winds – bearing glad tidings, a sign of His kindness – that carry along heavy clouds driving them towards arid lands, and We send rain, producing fruits of all kind. This is how We will bring the dead *to life*; perhaps you will reflect. [58] Good soil brings forth its crops by its Lord's permission, whereas poor *soil* produces only a little bit. This is how We explain the signs for people who are grateful.

THE PEOPLE OF NOAH IGNORED HIS SINCERE ADVICE

[59] *When* We sent Noah to his people, he said, "My people, worship God; you have no other god but Him. I fear the torment of a dreadful day." [60] The leaders of his community said, "We believe you're mistaken." [61] He said, "My people, I am not mistaken; rather I am a messenger of *the* Lord of the Universe, [62] conveying to you, as a sincere advisor, the messages of My Lord, and I have knowledge from God that you don't have. [63] Are you surprised that a reminder has come from

[b] This period of "six days" is not six lots of twenty-four hours. In the Quran (*Chapter Al-Hajj 22: 47*), a day is equated with a thousand years, this isn't literal either, a thousand represented the largest numerical concept then known to the Arabs, unlike in India at that time where they already had words for 100,000 (*lakh*) and 10,000,000 (*crore*). So this refers to six relatively distinct eras and doesn't conflict with the scientific theory that the universe was created 14 billion years ago, with the Big Bang.

[c] This is interpreted as the completion of the creation of the universe and God has control of it.

your Lord through one of your men, *who* teaches you to be mindful *of God* and wants you to be treated kindly" [64] They called him a liar, but We saved him and his followers aboard the ship, and those who denied Our signs We drowned; they were blind people.

The people of Hud rebelled

[65] And to *the* tribe of Ad, We sent their brother Hud, who said, "My people, worship God; you have no god but Him. Will you not be mindful *of God*?" [66] The disbelieving leaders of his community said, "We think you have gone crazy, and you're a liar." [67] He replied, "My people, there is nothing crazy about me; rather I am a messenger from the Lord of the Universe, [68] conveying to you, as a sincere advisor His messages." [69] Are you surprised that a reminder should come to you to warn you from your Lord through one of your men? *Remember what happened to* the people of Noah, He made you *their* successors and made your body strong. So remember God's gifts, and you will be successful." [70] They said, "Have you come to us *to make us* worship God alone and to abandon what our forefathers worshipped? If so, bring on what you are threatening us with, if you are telling the truth." [71] *Hud* said, "May punishment and wrath befall you from your Lord! Are you arguing with me about simple names that you and your forefathers have made up, and for which God has sent no authority? Wait *for God's decree*, and I shall wait with you." [72] We were kind so We rescued him and his followers, but destroyed the deniers of Our signs; they weren't believers.

Arrogance led the Prophet Salih's people to disobey God

[73] And to *the tribe of* Thamud, We sent their brother Salih who said, "My people, worship God; you have no god but Him. Clear proof has come to you from your Lord; this is the she-camel of God, a sign for you. Let her graze *wherever she wants* in God's Earth, but do not harm her, or else you'll be severely punished. [74] And remember how He made you successors after *what had happened to* Ad, establishing you in the land, where on its plains you *now* build mansions and carved homes in the mountainsides. So, remember God's gifts, and don't spread violence in the land." [75] *Some* arrogant leaders from his community said to the believers from the weak *people*, "Do you know *for certain* that Salih is a messenger from his Lord?" They said, "We believe in the message he's been sent with." [76] But the arrogant leaders said, "We reject what you believe in." [77] So they hamstrung the

she-camel, disobeying their Lord's command, saying, "Salih, bring on what you have threatened us with, if you are a messenger." [78] An Earthquake seized them so violently that they ended up lying face down in their homes. [79] *Salih* turned away from them, saying, "My people, I delivered My Lord's message sincerely to you, but you don't like the one who gives you sincere advice."[a]

THE PEOPLE OF THE PROPHET LOT REJECT HIM AS TOO PURITANICAL

[80] And *remember* Lot, when he said to his people, "Why do you commit indecent acts that have no precedence anywhere in the whole world? [81] You approach men with lust rather than women. You've gone to excess *in satisfying your sexual appetites.*" [82] His people said, "Expel them from your town. They are puritanical." [83] So We saved him and his family, except his wife, who stayed behind, [84] and We pelted them with hailstones. Look at the outcome of the sinners!

PROPHET JETHRO STOPS HIS PEOPLE CHEATING

[85] And to Madyan, We sent their brother Jethro,[b] who said, "My people, worship God; you have no god but Him. Clear proof has come from your Lord, so be honest in *your* weights and measures, and don't deprive people of their rights, and don't create conflict in the land after it has been made peaceful. That's *the* best *advice* for you, if you are believers. [86] Don't sit at the roadside, threatening *people* and preventing believers from *following* the path of God, wishing to distort it. Remember how few you were in number, and how He increased you. Look at the fate of trouble-makers. [87] *A* group of you believes in what I was sent with while the other group doesn't, so let us wait until God decides between us: He is the best judge."

JETHRO AND HIS FOLLOWERS FACE REJECTION AND PERSECUTION

[88] The arrogant leaders of his community said, "We will expel you from our town, Jethro, *you* and *all* those who believe in you, unless you return to our way of worship." He said, "Even if we don't want to? [89] We would be inventing lies about God if we returned to your way of worship after God had saved us. There is no way that we would return unless God, Our Lord, should wish it. Our Lord has the knowledge of everything. We place our trust in Him. Our Lord! Decide justly

---

[a] It may be that dim memories of this story, preserved incorrectly in their folk-tales, form the basis of the pagan Arab superstitions detailed in *Chapter Al-An'am* (6: 136–150).

[b] Jethro is the biblical Jethro, father-in-law of Moses.

between us and our people, for You are the best judge." [90] The disbelieving leaders of his community said, "If you follow Jethro, you will be losers." [91] After that they were seized by an Earthquake so violent that they ended up lying face down in their homes. [92] As though those who treated Jethro as a liar never lived there; the *ultimate* losers were those who called Jethro a liar. [93] So he withdrew from them saying, "My people, I delivered to you the messages of my Lord, and I was sincere towards you. So why should I mourn people who *choose to* disbelieve?"

GOD ALWAYS SENDS A WARNING BEFORE PUNISHING

[94] We haven't sent a single prophet to any community without initially putting its inhabitants through suffering and hardship to humble them. [95] Then We would replace the evil with good until they overtook *their predecessors* and, *without a thought for God*, said, "Hardship and prosperity affected our forefathers too." Suddenly, We would take them unaware. [96] If the people of the communities had believed and been mindful, We would have opened up for them blessings of the Heavens and Earth, but they rejected *Our signs*, so We seized them for what they did. [97] Were the people of the communities confident that Our punishment wouldn't come when they were asleep at night? [98] Or were they confident that Our punishment wouldn't come as they played at mid-morning? [99] Or did they feel secure from God's plan? It is only the losers who are not afraid of God's plan.

THE MORE ONE REJECTS GUIDANCE, THE HARDER IT BECOMES TO BELIEVE

[100] Didn't any guidance come to those who inherited the land from previous inhabitants, if We wished, We could afflict them *too* because of their sins, and We could seal their minds so they would no longer hear? [101] Such communities, We have told you some of what happened to them. Their messengers came to them with clear proofs but, because they had already denied them, they were not *prepared* to believe; that is how God seals the hearts of disbelievers. [102] We found most of them uncommitted to the contract, they were mostly disobedient.

IN THE FACE OF MOSES MIRACLES, PHARAOH PLAYS FOR TIME

[103] After them, We sent Moses with our miracles to Pharaoh and his leaders, but they rejected them. Look what happened to the trouble makers. [104] Moses said, "Pharaoh, I am a messenger from the Lord of the universe. [105] I am duty-bound to speak the truth about God. I have come to you with clear proof from your Lord, so let the Israelites go with me." [106] He replied, "If you have come with a sign, then

show it, if you are telling the truth." [107] So he threw his staff, and straightaway it turned into a snake, everyone saw that; [108] next he pulled his hand out *from his cloak*, and it looked white to the onlookers. [109] The leaders of Pharaoh's people said, "He's an expert magician, [110] he wants to expel you from your land, so what do you command?" [111] They said, "Delay him and his brother and, *in the meantime*, send messengers to the cities [112] to bring every experienced magician *here*."

THE MAGICIANS, CONFRONTED WITH THE TRUTH, ACCEPT IT

[113] The magicians came to the Pharaoh, they asked, "Will we be rewarded if we win?" [114] He said, "Yes! You will join people who are in my inner circle." [115] They said, "Moses, either you go *first*, or let us go first?" [116] He said, "You start." So they went first, with trickery charmed people's eyes to frighten them, and made an impressive magical spectacle. [117] Then We urged Moses, "Throw down your staff," and at once it began to swallow up their fake devices. [118] So the truth came out, and what they had done was shown to be fake. [119] They were defeated there, and humiliated. [120] The magicians threw themselves *to the ground* in prostration, [121] saying: "We believe in the Lord of the universe, [122] the Lord of Moses and Aaron."

THE PHARAOH ORDERS KILLING OF MAGICIANS

[123] Pharaoh said, "How dare you believe before I give you permission! This is some cunning plot that you have *all* devised in this city to expel its people. You will soon know *where true power lies*. [124] I will have your hands and feet cut off on the opposite sides and crucify you all." [125] They said, "We hand ourselves over to our Lord. [126] What reason do you have to take revenge on us except that we believed in signs of our Lord when they came? Our Lord, give us patience, and let us die in submission *to You*."

PHARAOH THREATENS TO PUNISH THE ISRAELITES

[127] The leaders of Pharaoh's community said, "Are you going to leave Moses and his people to wreak havoc in the land, disregarding you and your gods?" He said, "We will slay their sons and let their women live *to show* that we are dominant over them." [128] Moses told his people, "Seek God's help and be patient. The Earth belongs to God, and He gives it to any of His servants to inherit it, and *only* the mindful *of God* shall have *success in* the end. [129] They said, "We suffered before you came and continue to suffer." He said, "It may be that your Lord will destroy

your enemy and make you successors in the land, so that He may see how you will behave."

THE PLAGUES THAT BEFELL THE PEOPLE OF PHARAOH

[130] For years there was a drought, We caused crop failure for Pharaoh's people, *hopeful* they might reflect. [131] In good times they would say, "We deserve this," but in hard times they would take it as an *evil* omen[a] brought on by Moses and those with him. Is it not the case that their omen comes from God? Most of them are ignorant. [132] They said, "Any signs you come up with to captivate us, we will not believe." [133] So We sent down clear signs to them: floods, locusts, lice, frogs and blood, but they were arrogant and sinful people. [134] When caught in a plague, they would say: "Moses, pray to your Lord for us through the contract you have. If you can relieve us of the plague, we will believe you and send the Israelites with you." [135] However, when We relieved them of the plague and gave them a respite, after a while they'd go back on their word. [136] So We took revenge, drowning them in the sea since they denied Our signs and paid no attention to them.

THE ISRAELITES FORGET GOD'S FAVOURS SOON AFTER THE EXODUS!

[137] Those who were once helpless We made them inherit the lands We had blessed from the east to west, and so it was that the gracious word of your Lord to the Israelites came to be fulfilled, because of what they had suffered: and We destroyed what Pharaoh and his people had built. [138] After We had led the Israelites across the sea, they came across people who worshipped idols. *The Israelites* requested, "Moses, let us have a god like their gods." He said, "You are ignorant people. [139] These *people*, whatever *state* they are in is beyond repair,[b] and whatever they have been doing is null and void." [140] He said, "How can I seek a god other than God for you, it is He Who has favoured you over the rest of humanity?" [141] *Remember* when We saved you from Pharaoh's people, who inflicted the worst punishment *imaginable on you:* slaying your sons and leaving your women to live; that was a big test from Your Lord.

MOSES GOES TO MOUNT SINAI TO RECEIVE THE TABLETS

[142] We kept Moses *on mount Sinai* for thirty nights, to which We added ten, so

---

[a] The Arabic word *ta'ir* means "bird". The pagans had lots of superstitious practices: before embarking on a journey they would release a bird into the air, and if it flew towards the right it would signal success.

[b] *Mutabbar* means "broken", like broken pottery or glass that can't be repaired.

he stayed a total of forty nights with his Lord. *When* Moses was *leaving, he* said to his brother, Aaron, "Be deputy over my people, do what is right, and do not follow the path of those who are mischievous." [143] After Moses came to Us according to his appointment, and his Lord spoke to him, he said: "My Lord, let me see You." *God* said, "You will not *be able to* see Me, but look towards the mountain; if it stays in its place, then you will *be able to* see Me." When His Lord appeared in His glory on the mountain, it crumbled, and Moses fell unconscious as though struck by lightning. When *Moses* regained consciousness, he said, "Glory be to You! I seek Your repentance, and I am the first believer." [144] *God* said, "Moses, in *giving you* My messages and My words, I have chosen you above all people, so take what I have given you and be grateful." [145] We wrote everything on the tablets for him as a warning, explaining things in detail: "So hold *the tablets* firmly, and order your people to take hold of the best of *what is in* them.[c] I'll show you the houses of the sinners.

ARROGANCE BLINDS PEOPLE TO THE BLESSINGS OF GOD'S GUIDANCE

[146] Those who behave arrogantly unjustifiably in the land shall be deprived of seeing My signs, even if they saw every single sign, they still wouldn't believe, if they were to see the path of guidance, they wouldn't take it; but if they see the path of error, they follow it. That's because they denied Our signs and paid no attention to them. [147] Those who denied Our signs and meeting in the Hereafter, their deeds will prove worthless. Wouldn't they be rewarded for their deeds?

THE ISRAELITES MAKE A GOLDEN CALF

[148] Meanwhile Moses' people took a calf *as god,* with a mooing sound and a body *moulded* from their jewellery. Wasn't it obvious to them it neither spoke to them nor guided them along any path? *Nevertheless,* they adopted it *as a god* and so became wrongdoers. [149] When the enormity of what they had done struck them[d] they realised they were misled, so they said, "If our Lord isn't kind and forgives us, we will be losers." [150] Moses returned to his people, and *saw what they had done*; he was angry and sad and said, "How foul is what you did after me! Were you so

---

[c]   "The best of *what is in* them," means follow what God commanded and avoid what He forbids or, if two lawful alternatives existed, as with pardoning and retaliation, adopt pardon (Al-Qurtubi).

[d]   *Suqita fi aydihim,* is an idiom meaning, "it fell into their hands," referring to the moment of bewilderment when it is no longer possible to deny the truth, the evidence is in one's hands, "staring one in the face."

keen to hasten your Lord's judgement?" He lay down the tablets and grabbed hold of his brother's head *by the hair*, pulling him towards himself. *Aaron* said, "Son of my mother, they thought I was weak and almost killed me. So do not give *our* enemies any reason to ridicule me, and don't put me *in the same category* with the wrongdoers." [151] *Moses* said, "My Lord, forgive me and my brother, embrace us with Your Kindness, for you are the most Kind. [152] Those who accepted the calf *as a god* will have their Lord's wrath and disgrace in this worldly life. That is how We reward those who invent *lies*. [153] Those who were evil then repented and believed, your Lord will forgive and be Kind."

MOSES RETURNS TO MOUNT SINAI, WHERE HE TALKS ONCE MORE TO GOD
[154] Once Moses' anger had subsided, he picked up the tablets. They contained guidance and *teachings of* kindness for anyone who fears their Lord. [155] *Then* Moses chose seventy men from his people to meet with Us. After a blast had taken them, *Moses* said, "My Lord, if this is what You wanted, You could have killed them and me long before. Will You now kill us *all* because of what the fools among us did? This was Your way of testing to let anyone you wish to go astray and anyone You wish to guide; You are our Protector, so forgive us and be kind to us; You are the best Forgiver. [156] Decree for us in this world what is good and in the Hereafter; we return *in humility* to serve you." *God* said, "I afflict My punishment on whomever I please, while My kindness embraces everything. I shall decree *what is good* for those who are mindful *of Me*, pay Zakat and believe in Our signs."

A PORTRAIT OF GOD'S OBEDIENT SERVANTS
[157] Those who follow the Messenger, the untutored Prophet, they will find him mentioned in the Torah and the Gospel. He who instructs them to do good and forbids evil, declares lawful all that is pure and healthy, and prohibits whatever is unclean, and relieves them of their burden and the shackles that once bound them. So, they believe in him, honour him, support him, and obey the light that was sent with him, they shall be successful.[a]

---

[a] "*Ummi*" is from *Umm* meaning the mother, the Quran calls Makkah 'Umm al-Qura', mother of cities. Since the Prophet ﷺ was born there he is referred to as *Ummi*. A person who is not tutored is also called *Ummi*; here it means that God taught him directly without a human teacher.

THE BELOVED MESSENGER 鬠 IS SENT TO ALL PEOPLE

¹⁵⁸ Say: "People, I am the Messenger to you all from God, sovereignty of the Heavens and the Earth belongs to Him; He is the only God, He gives life and death. So, believe in God and His Messenger, the untutored Prophet, who believes in God and His words, and follow him so that you might be guided."

THE TWELVE TRIBES OF ISRAEL ARE OFFERED A CHANCE TO REPENT

¹⁵⁹ Among Moses' people is a community that guides *others* with the truth and practises justice. ¹⁶⁰ We divided *the Israelites* into twelve tribes, each a community, *and* when his people asked Moses for water We told him: "Strike the rock with your *shepherd's* staff." Twelve springs gushed out, and the people of each *tribe* knew their drinking place. We made the clouds shade them and sent them manna and quails, saying, "Eat of the wholesome things We provided you." *The Israelites* never harmed Us, but they harmed themselves. ¹⁶¹ *For example,* when they were told: "Settle down in this town and eat *of its fruits* from wherever you please, and when you enter the gates, prostrate yourselves and say: '*Forgive us our sins*,' so that We forgive your wrongs, and We will increase the reward of the righteous *ones*." ¹⁶² The wrongdoers among them altered the phrase to something else than what they were told *to say*, so We sent punishment from Heaven because of the wrong they did.

THOSE WHO BROKE THE LAW OF SABBATH WERE PUNISHED

¹⁶³ Ask them, *Messenger*, about the town by the sea; they broke the *law of* Sabbath. On the Sabbath, the fish would appear on the surface *of the sea*, but not on any other days when they were *fishing*. We tested them because they sinned. ¹⁶⁴ Another group from the *Israelites* said, "Why are you preaching to people, who God will destroy or punish?" They said, "It is a plea for clemency from your Lord,^b and in the hope that they might be mindful *of God*." ¹⁶⁵ Once they forgot all they had been reminded of, We punished them severely because of their sinfulness and saved those who warned them against doing evil. ¹⁶⁶ When they disrespectfully continued doing what they were forbidden, We said, "Become like apes, de-

---

^b It is a collective obligation on the community to "enjoin the common good and forbid evil" (*Chapter Al' Imran* 3: 110). In this example, there were three groups: obedient, those who advised the wrongdoers to obey the law; and those who saw no point in advising the wrongdoers (Al-Qurtubi).

spised!"[a]

[167] *Remember* when your Lord declared: "Let there arise against *the wrongdoers, people* who will inflict the terrible torment on them *from now* until Judgement Day." Your Lord is quick to punish, but He is *also* Forgiving, Kind. [168] And so it was that We dispersed *the Israelites* across *the face of* the Earth as *separate* communities – some are righteous and others not at all like them – and We tested them through good and bad times hoping they may return to Us. [169] After them came a successor *nation*, who inherited the Book but practised only the easy parts of the *Book's teachings*, saying, "We'll be forgiven," and if the like of it comes their way *from a source other than the Book*, they *willingly* take that too. Will they not be taken *to task* over the pledge in the Book to say nothing but the truth about God, given that they have studied whatever is in *the Book*? The home of the Hereafter is better for the mindful. Do you not understand? [170] Those who hold fast to the Book and perform the prayer, We do not allow the reward to go to waste for people who strive for improvement *in society*. [171] *Remember,* We shook the mountain *that loomed* over them like a shadow, and they thought it would fall over them; *and We said*, "Hold firmly what We gave you and remember what's in it so that you become mindful."

THE FIRST ASSEMBLY OF HUMAN SOULS; PLEDGE OF LOYALTY

[172] *Remember* when Your Lord took *all* the offspring from the loins of the children of Adam to be witnesses, *saying*, "Am I not Your Lord?" They replied, "Yes, we bear witness." This was so that, on Judgement Day, you would not say, "We were unaware of this *contract*"[b] [173] or say, "It was our forefathers who first associated *partners with God*, and we are *merely* descendants who came afterwards. Will You kill us because of the actions of the falsifiers?" [174] This is how We explain *Our* signs, perhaps they will return *to the right path*.

THE DENIERS OF GOD'S SIGNS ARE LIKE PANTING DOGS

[175] Tell them about the one who We gave knowledge of Scriptures, but he shed

---

[a]   Did they literally turn into apes or is this a metaphor? The most likely meaning is they became objects of ridicule like monkeys often are. However, it is totally wrong to call Jews monkeys.

[b]   The Day of *Alast*, was the first assembly of human souls. While memory of this momentous assembly in the divine presence may have faded from human consciousness, it remains etched in human nature. That's why whenever a person is properly guided, the seed of faith in God sprouts and grows.

them *as a snake sheds its skin*; then Satan made him follow him so that he became disobedient.[c] [176] If We wanted, We could have raised his *status* because of those *signs*, but he chose to pursue Earthly matters and follow his whims. His type is like a dog: if you attack it pants, and if you leave it alone it pants, and the people who deny Our signs are like that. So, repeat these stories to them, perhaps they might reflect. [177] How wretched is that type of person who denies Our Scripture and, in the process, wrongs himself. [178] Anyone God guides is truly guided but anyone He allows to go astray; such people are the losers. [179] *And so it is that* many of the jinn and humans that We've created *are intended* for Hell. They have brains which don't think, eyes that don't see, and ears that don't hear, such people are like cattle, even more dumb, worse than them; they are unaware *of reality*.

THE BEAUTIFUL NAMES OF GOD PROMPT US TO REFLECT

[180] God has the most beautiful names, so call Him by those *names,* and avoid those who take His names in vain, they will be *appropriately* rewarded for what they earned. [181] Among Our created beings there is a community that lives according to the guidance, and practises justice in agreement with the truth. [182] But others who deny Our signs, We will let them edge their way little by little *towards destruction* from where they least expect it. [183] I will give them some respite, but My decision is made. [184] Have they not thought it through? There is no madness in their companion;[d] he is a clear warner. [185] Haven't they seen the realm of the Heavens and the Earth and in all that God has created a single thing *to suggest* that perhaps their end is near? *If not*, then what message will they *ever* believe in after this? [186] Anyone God allows to go astray will have no guide, and *God* will leave them to stumble blindly into wickedness.

PEOPLE'S CONTINUOUS QUESTIONING ABOUT THE FINAL HOUR

[187] They ask you about the Final Hour, "When will it come?" Tell them: "My Lord alone knows it; except for Him, no one can reveal its timing. However, it hangs heavy in the Heavens and Earth and will come to you suddenly." They ask you as though you were thoroughly acquainted with it. Say: "Knowledge of it rests with

---

[c] Al-Qurtubi refers to a traditional Jewish story of a scholar called Bal'am ibn Ba'ura', when he spoke thousands of students wrote down his words until, one day, he chose to write that the world had no maker, and became a disbeliever.

[d] Meaning the Prophet Muhammad 襲.

my Lord alone," but most people are ignorant *of that fact.* [188] Say: "I have no control to bring benefit or harm *even* for myself, except *to the extent* that God wills. If I had full knowledge of the unseen, then I would have amassed a lot of wealth, and no harm to come my way. *As it is,* I am a warner and bearer of good news for people who believe."

Parents' promise gratitude, if blessed with a healthy child

[189] He created you from a single soul, and from that made its spouse to live together. When he slept with her, she became pregnant, *the pregnancy was* a light burden at first, allowing her to go about *her daily life,* but as *the foetus* grew heavier they both prayed to God, their Lord: "If You bless us with a healthy *child,* we will be grateful." [190] When He delivered them a healthy *child,* both set about attributing partners to Him regarding what He gave them. God is exalted above whatever *people* associate *with Him.*

The reality of idolatry is exposed

[191] Do *people* associate *partners with God* that create nothing, but are created; [192] they can't help them, or even help themselves; [193] if you call them towards guidance, they will not follow you? It is all the same for *those partners* whether you pray to them or stay silent. [194] Those you worship beside God are *His* servants just like yourselves, so pray to them and let them respond to you, if you are telling the truth. [195] Do they have legs to walk? Do they have hands to hold? Do they have eyes to see? Do they have ears to hear? Tell *them:* "Pray *to* your idols, plot against me, be quick about it. [196] My protector is God, Who revealed the Book, and He protects the righteous. [197] Those you worship beside Him cannot help you, nor help themselves: [198] if you call them towards guidance, they won't hear. You may think they are seeing you, but they can't see." [199] *Messenger* pardon *them,* enjoin the common good, and avoid the ignorant people.

How the pious avoid being trapped by Satan

[200] When Satan tempts you, seek God's refuge. He is Hearing, Knowing. [201] Whenever Satan tries to run rings around those who are mindful *of God,* they remind each other and at once they see straight *again.* [202] As for their *unmindful* brothers, *the demons* draw them further and further into error, sparing no effort *in doing so.* [203] If you don't bring *a fresh* sign, *such unmindful people* say, "If only you could choose one yourself!" Say: "I follow only what's revealed to me by My

Lord. These are *deep* insights from your Lord and guidance and kindness for the believers."

THE CORRECT WAY TO LISTEN TO THE QURAN

[204] Whenever the Quran is recited, listen carefully to it, and be silent so that you may benefit from it. [205] Humbly remind yourself morning and evening of Your Lord and be in awe of Him, without speaking loud, and don't be one of the neglectful. [206] The *angels* in the Divine Presence do not turn away from His worship arrogantly; *rather* they glorify Him and prostrate before Him.[a]

---

[a] This is one of the verses of prostration.

8. Al-Anfal
The Spoils of War

This chapter was revealed after the Battle of Badr, which took place in Ramadan in the year 624 CE. The new community in Madinah was growing rapidly, both in numbers and economic strength, under the brilliant leadership of the Messenger ﷺ. This growing prowess of the Muslims made the hypocrites and the Jews feel threatened. The Makkans too were uncomfortable, since their trade route to Syria might be blocked. So they repeatedly dispatched small armed bands to attack cattle grazing in pastures outside Madinah, creating "low-intensity conflict". Hence in 624 CE, when the Prophet ﷺ learnt of the Makkan caravan returning from Syria, he openly told his companions of his intention to attack it. This would be retaliation for the repeated raids and the property confiscated from the Muslims who left Makkah. A clear message: give up hostility.

When Abu Sufyan heard of the plan, he sent a fast rider to Makkah with an urgent request for help. On receiving this unpleasant news, the Makkans instantly assembled an army of a thousand fighters to defend their caravan. In the meantime, Abu Sufyan changed his route and veered towards the coastal lowlands, to be further away from Madinah. The Muslim army left Madinah, hoping to catch up with the caravan. They hadn't gone too far when they learnt that Abu Sufyan had safely escaped, and the Makkans were coming with a huge army. After a consultation with the companions, the Prophet ﷺ decided to meet the army at Badr, 150 km southwest of Madinah.

The Outcomes of the Battle of Badr

This chapter effectively draws out the important lessons to be learnt from this first military encounter between Muslims and Makkans. Interestingly, the Quran spiritualises war as a brutal and materialistic activity. It begins by describing the virtues of believers: trust, steadfastness and honesty. Then demonstrates that victory can be achieved against the odds, including the odds of victory against an enemy army many times larger, as well as teaching that believers should be willing to make peace. The question of the spoils of war is raised, and it instructs that spoils should not be the prime purpose of war, as they tended to be during the Jahiliya, or Age of Ignorance. Instead, there must be a higher objective: justice and peace for all.

The Battle of Badr marked a turning point in the life of the Muslims, who had been persecuted till that point. So aptly the chapter calls the event *yawm al-furqan*, "The day of separation", truth is now clearly separate from falsehood. The victory was not just in worldly terms, but also in a spiritual and moral sense. So it marked the beginning of a new era for Muslims, the result delivered a shattering blow to the pride of the Makkans. It boosted the Muslims' morale and credibility in the sight of the Arabs, offering conclusive proof of the words: "Power and might belong to God." This functioned as an indicator of the truthfulness of the message of Islam, and the Muslims began to understand more clearly the socio-political dimension of the religious order that the Messenger ﷺ was proclaiming. As Asad put it:

The spirit of passive sacrifice, so characteristic of their earlier days, received its complement in the idea of sacrifice through action. The doctrine of action as the most fundamental, creative element of life was, perhaps for the first time in the history of man, consciously realized not only by a few select individuals but by a whole community; and the intense activism which was to distinguish Muslim history in the coming decades and centuries was a direct, immediate consequence of the Battle of Badr.

In the name of God, the Kind, the Caring.

Mobilisation for the Battle of Badr

[1] They ask you about the spoils *of war*, say: "The spoils belong to God and the Messenger. So, fear God and make peace among yourselves, and obey God and His Messenger, if you are true believers." [2] The believers' hearts tremble *with fear* at the mention of God, their faith grows stronger whenever His verses are recited, and they put trust in their Lord. [3] They perform the prayer and spend from what We have provided, [4] they're true believers; *reserved* for them are lofty ranks near their Lord, and forgiveness and a generous provision.

The preparations for the Battle of Badr

[5] *It was* your Lord Who led you out of your home *for* a purpose, though a group of the believers disliked it, [6] they argue with you about its purpose that has become apparent, as though they were being led to their deaths as they looked on. [7] *Remember* when God promised that one of the two parties[a] would be yours, while you were longing for the weaker target. God wanted by the power of His words, to establish the truth and to break the back of the disbelievers' *might*, [8] to establish the truth and to overturn falsehood, though the sinful hate it.

The Believers are promised a victory

[9] *Remember* when you prayed to your Lord for help, and He answered: "I will help you with a thousand angels in rows upon rows." [10] God made it glad tidings

---

[a] Either the Makkans' army or their trade caravan.

147

and to boost your morale. Victory is from God alone. God is Almighty, Wise. [11] *Remember* when He caused drowsiness to overtake you, *granting you* of His reassurance, and He sent rain from the sky for you so you could clean yourselves, remove Satan's filth from you, strengthen your hearts, and help you to stand firm. [12] *Remember* when Your Lord revealed to the angels: "I am with you, so make the believers stand their ground, while I strike terror into the disbelievers' hearts. So, beat *your wings* above their necks and beat each of their limbs." [13] Since they opposed God and His Messenger, and anyone who opposes God and His Messenger will have severe punishment, [14] a taste for you *of what is to come* for the disbelievers, the torment of the Fire is waiting.

THE DAYS OF RUNNING AWAY FROM THE BATTLE ARE OVER

[15] Believers, whenever you meet disbelievers in battle advancing towards you, don't turn your backs to them *to flee.* [16] On that day, whoever turns his back except in tactical retreat to attack again, or else to rejoin *another* fighting party, will suffer the fury of God, and Hell will be his home. What an evil destination! [17] You didn't kill them, but God killed them nor did you throw *the pebbles* when you threw, *Messenger*, but it was God Who threw *it*.[a] *This was* as a positive test of the believers from Him. God is the Hearer, the Knower. [18] That was *a sign* for you, that God will weaken the disbelievers' plot. [19] If you are seeking a clear outcome, *disbelievers*, then that was an outcome clearly against you. Were you to put an end *to your harassment*, that would be better for you; *but* if you return *to it*, then so shall We. Your army will not benefit you at all, no matter how large it is. God is with the believers.

A WARNING TO THOSE WHO DON'T LISTEN

[20] Believers, obey God and His Messenger and don't turn away from him while you can hear him calling you; [21] and don't be like those who said, "We have heard," while they were not listening at all. [22] The worst of creatures in the sight of God are the wilfully deaf and dumb who refuse to think. [23] If God saw any good in them, He would have made them hear; but even if He had made them hear, they would still have turned away, rejecting the message. [24] Believers, answer God and

---

[a] At the start of the Battle, the Messenger 鑗 picked up a handful of sand and threw it in the direction of the Makkan army and prayed for their defeat. The lessons for believers is not to be proud of winning, victory comes from God.

His Messenger when they call to that which will give you life; and beware God intervenes between a man and his heart,[b] and that you'll be gathered before Him. [25] Be mindful of a future test that wouldn't just affect the wrongdoers amongst you, and know that God's punishment is severe.

BELIEVERS ARE REMINDED OF FUTURE TRIALS

[26] Remember when you were an oppressed few in the land, afraid of being wiped out; God gave you protection and strengthened you with His help and provided you with wholesome things so you might be thankful. [27] Believers, don't betray God and the Messenger knowingly, nor be disloyal to your trusts; [28] and know that your wealth and children are a test,[c] and that God has a great reward *in store for you.* [29] Believers, if you are mindful of God He will give you the standard to judge *between right and wrong,*[d] and He will cover up your wrongdoings and forgive you. God is Gracious in *His* favour.

DISBELIEVERS CAN'T DECEIVE GOD

[30] *Remember* when the disbelievers plotted to imprison, kill or expel you. They plotted, and God planned something else, and God is the best of planners. [31] When Our verses are recited to them, they say, "We've heard *it all before.* If we wanted, we could have said something similar. These are just legends of old." [32] They said, "God, if this is, indeed, the truth from You then pelt us with hailstones from the sky, or fetch us *some other* painful punishment." [33] But God will not punish them as long as you, *Messenger,* are among them; nor will God punish them if they *repent and* ask forgiveness. [34] However, God will punish them for stopping *people* from the Sacred Mosque even though they are not its *real* keepers. Its *real* keepers are those who are mindful *of God,* but most of the disbelievers don't know. [35] Their worship at the *Sacred* House is merely whistling and clapping. So, taste the punishment for your disbelief.

THE WICKEDNESS OF DISBELIEVERS WILL NOT GO UNPUNISHED

[36] The disbelievers spend their wealth to stop *people* from the path of God, they'll

---

[b]   God comes between a person's desires, attitude and behaviour; this shows God can turn people away from what their desires urge them to do. It is God-consciousness that can stop them from being misled by evil desires. The Messenger 🌟 prayed "O turner of hearts, keep me steadfast on your religion."

[c]   *Fitnah* can mean: a temptation, seduction, trial, test, confusion, dissension, persecution, oppression, sedition, or civil war.

[d]   *Furqan* means, "criterion" the ability to differentiate between truth and falsehood.

continue doing so until it becomes a source of regret, and they are defeated. The disbelievers will be banished to Hell, [37] so that God may sort out the wicked from the good; and He will pile up the wicked, layer on layer, in a heap and bulldoze them into Hell. Those are the losers.

FIGHT TO BRING AN END TO MALTREATMENT

[38] Tell the disbelievers to stop *their wrongdoings* so they may be forgiven *sins* of the past. If they go back *to their evil ways*, the example of the people of old is there *for them*. [39] Fight them so there is no more persecution, and people are free to worship God.[a] But if they stop, then God sees what they do, [40] but if they turn away then, know that God is your Protector. What a wonderful Protector, and what a wonderful Helper!

THE DISTRIBUTION OF THE SPOILS OF WAR

[41] Whatever *spoils of war* you seize, know that a fifth of it belongs to God and to the Messenger and *his* relatives, to orphans, the needy and the traveller. That's if you believe in God and in what We revealed to Our servant on the day of separation of *truth from falsehood*,[b] the day the two armies met. God has power over all things.[c]

THE ARRANGEMENT OF THE ARMIES IN THE BATTLEFIELD

[42] *Remember* when you were *grouped* on the near side of the valley, and Makkans on the far side, and the caravan below you. If you had *tried to reach* a formal agreement to meet *there*, you would certainly have differed over the time and place; but *that occurred* so that God could accomplish what was preordained, so that whoever perished should do so on the basis of clear proof and whoever survived should do so on the same basis. God is the Hearer, the Knower. [43] *Remember* when God showed them to you to be small in number as you dozed. If He had shown them to you as large in number, you would have lost heart and quarrelled over the matter amongst yourselves, but God saved you *from disagreements*. He knows well *people's* innermost thoughts. [44] And when you faced each other, He made them appear to be few in your eyes, and He made you seem even fewer in

---

[a] As in *Chapter al-Baqarah* (2: 193), the words of this verse do not incite Muslims to impose their religion on others, but urges them to fight to bring an end to all persecution, including forced conversions.

[b] The phrase, *yawm al-furqan*, is an apt description for the Battle of Badr; the sincerity of those who called themselves Muslims was put to the test, and truth and falsehood were clearly distinguished.

[c] This verse provides an answer to the question at the very start of the chapter.

number in their eyes, so that He could accomplish what had been preordained. *Eventually* all matters return to God.

Be steadfastness in the battlefield

[45] Believers, whenever you face an army *in battle*, stand firm and remember God a lot so you may triumph. [46] Obey God and His Messenger; don't quarrel among yourselves nor lose heart and become demoralised, but persevere. God is with those who persevere. [47] And don't be like those who set out from their homes pompously, showing off to people and stopping *people* from coming to God's way. God has complete control of what they do. [48] *Remember* when Satan made their action appear attractive to them and said, "No one will be able to defeat you today, with me close beside you." However, when the two armies caught sight of each other, *Satan* turned on his heels, saying, "I have nothing to do with you, I see what you can't see, *and* I fear God. God's punishment is severe."

Angels fought alongside the believers

[49] *Remember* when the hypocrites and those with sickness in their hearts said, "Their religion has deceived these people." Whoever puts his trust in God *shall find* God is Almighty, Wise. [50] If you could see, as the disbelievers' souls were taken from them, the angels striking their faces and backs, *saying*, "Taste the punishment of the Blaze. [51] This is *in return* for what your hands produced. God never wrongs *His* servants." [52] The same happened to Pharaoh's people and those before them: they rejected God's signs, so God punished them for their sins. God is Strong, Severe in *His* punishment. [53] That is because God does not change a favour that He bestowed on a people until they change what is within themselves; and God is Hearing, Knowing. [54] Similar to Pharaoh's people and those before them: they denied their Lord's signs, so We destroyed them for their sins, and We caused Pharaoh's people to be drowned. They were all wrongdoers.

Lessons from the Battle of Badr

[55] The worst of creatures in the sight of God are the deniers, they don't believe; [56] *and* those you made a treaty with, and each time they broke their treaty they weren't mindful *of God*. [57] Whenever you come across them in battle crush them so that those who come after them may learn a lesson. [58] If you fear treachery from someone, then tackle them in the same way. God dislikes traitors.

BE PREPARED FOR WAR, BUT WORK FOR PEACE

[59] Don't let the disbelievers think they have won, they can't undo *God's decree.* [60] *So* prepare whatever force you can against them, and cavalry, to deter God's and your enemies, and others beside them whom you don't know, but God knows them. Whatever you spend in God's way will be reimbursed to you, and you will not be deprived. [61] However, if they incline towards peace you incline towards it, and put your trust in God. He is the Hearer, the Knower. [62] Should they wish to trick you, *Messenger,* then God is sufficient for you, He strengthened you with His support and with the believers. [63] He united their hearts together. Even if you spent all that there is on Earth, you couldn't unite their hearts together, but God united them. He is Almighty, the Wise.

TRUE FAITH CAN GIVE THE BELIEVERS THE STRENGTH OF TEN MEN

[64] Prophet, God is sufficient for you and who follow you *into battle* from among the believers. [65] Prophet, urge the believers to fight *in His way.* It may be that your twenty steadfast men can defeat *a force of* two hundred, and a hundred of you can defeat a thousand of the disbelievers, because they are people who don't understand. [66] *But for* now God has lightened your load, knowing that there is some weakness in you. So it may be that a hundred steadfast men amongst you can defeat two hundred, and that a thousand of you can defeat two thousand with God's help; and *rest assured,* God is with the steadfast.

FIGHTING IN GOD'S WAY SHOULDN'T BE FOR WORLDLY GAINS

[67] It is not fitting for a prophet to take captives until he has won on the *battle* field. Believers, you want what this world offers,[a] but God desires the Hereafter *for you.* God is Almighty, Wise. [68] Had it not been for a decree issued in advance from God, you would have been mightily punished for *the action* that you took. [69] So enjoy of your spoils of war, the lawful and healthy, and be *ever* mindful of God. God is Forgiving, Kind. [70] Prophet, tell the captives you are holding: "If God finds any good in your hearts, He will give you better than what has been taken from you and will forgive you. God is Forgiving, Kind." [71] If they act treacherously towards you, they have done so previously with God, yet He has *given you* control over them. God is the Knower, the Wise.

[a] The purpose of inter-tribal fighting before Islam was mostly to take hostages for ransom rather than to kill the enemy.

THE COMPANIONS OF THE PROPHET ﷺ ARE PRAISED

[72] The believers who emigrated and struggled with their wealth and lives in God's way, and those who offered them refuge and support, they are each other's protectors. Those who believed but didn't emigrate, you are not responsible for them until they emigrate. If they should seek your help on religious grounds, then you must help them except against a people with whom you have a treaty. God sees what you do. [73] The disbelievers protect each other. If you don't do likewise, there will be a lot of persecution and violence in the land. [74] The believers who emigrated and struggled in God's way, and those who offered them refuge and support in Madinah are the true believers; they shall have forgiveness and a generous provision. [75] And those later believers who emigrated and struggled with you in God's way, they are one with you. However, blood relationships give them even greater rights over each other in God's Book. God knows everything.

9. At-Tawbah
Repentance

This chapter was revealed during 630–631 CE following the successful campaign of Tabuk in the month of Rajab. Tabuk is 560 kilometres Northwest of Madinah. The cancellation of treaties with idolaters was announced five months later during Hajj in the same year. This chapter is set against the background of a looming battle, and therefore harsh. This explains why it doesn't begin with the Basmala in the usual way, "In the name of God, the Kind, the Caring". The blessed Messenger ﷺ didn't instruct the writing of Basmala either, and some commentators take this to mean that this is a continuation of the previous Chapter Al-Anfal, the two together constituting a single chapter, since the Basmala is considered as the divider between chapters.

After the Conquest of Makkah in 629 CE, the influence of Islam in the Arabian Peninsula spread rapidly and many Arab tribes embraced Islam. The Messenger ﷺ sent letters to the rulers of neighbouring countries, inviting them to Islam. They began to take notice of this religious and geopolitical change. Until now, foreign powers had shown little interest in the Arabs. The Romans were nervous and planned to attack Madinah, so the planning for the Tabuk campaign started. The Messenger ﷺ, after consultation, decided to meet the enemy on the border. Muslims gave generously, and eventually a 30,000 strong army was mobilised northwards to deter the Romans, who decided to remain in their forts rather than come out. The Messenger ﷺ stayed there for twenty days. He made excursions along the Roman Empire's south-eastern border to win allies and sign treaties with local rulers, including the King of Aila, near Aqaba in Jordan. This increased Muslim influence in that area considerably.

The Themes of the Chapter

The important event with which this chapter begins (1–29) is the immediate cancellation of treaties with those Arab idolaters who had repeatedly breached them, whilst continuing to honour the treaties with the tribes that remained loyal. For the second Hajj after the Conquest of Makkah, the Messenger ﷺ dispatched a delegation under the leadership of Abu Bakr, who made this announcement: "From now on the Kaaba will be in the custody of Muslims; idolaters are no longer its keepers," hinting that the Muslims were now the rulers of the Arabian Peninsula.

The Viciousness of the Hypocrites

God is Kind and Loving, but this chapter clearly shows His anger towards the idolaters and the hypocrites. The wretched character of the hypocrites is vividly described in verses 38–83: they make excuses, have evil motives, and criticise and insult the Messenger ﷺ and the Muslims; they spread rumours, blaspheme and are miserly; they are a lazy bunch, who love only the worldly life; and they constantly lie and break promises. Human beings who have such characteristics cannot be trusted and pose a real threat to the welfare and security of society. They were the enemy within, and their presence in Madinah was so damaging that the Prophet ﷺ was told to take a very harsh position against them; they were no longer to be tolerated. The Prophet ﷺ denounced them as a group, and expelled them from his Mosque. When the hypocrites built a mosque of their own, he was told to demolish it because they wanted to divide Muslims and to build an outpost to fight God and His Messenger (107). When the call came to march to Tabuk, the hypocrites stayed behind in Madinah and didn't take part in the campaign. This partly explains the anger against them. However, as well as the hypocrites who made excuses, there were three sincere Muslims who put off their preparations until it was too late to join the campaign. They were forgiven because of their truthfulness and honest admission, but only after their sincerity had been severely tested over fifty days. The chapter takes its name, At-Tawbah, from God's acceptance of their repentance.

The Vitality of the Faithful

The true believers are honoured as God's property (111); people who "repent, worship, praise God, fast, bow, prostrate, enjoin good, forbid evil, and stay within the boundaries of God" (112). The dedicated companions are congratulated. "God is well pleased with *them, and* they are pleased with Him," (100). Verse 122 urges them to take the learning of religion seriously.

The contrast between the opening passage of the chapter and its end can't go amiss; the beginning shows divine anger towards those who breached treaties, but the ending shows kind and loving nature of the beloved Messenger ﷺ. In some ways explaining the paradox of war and peace, the harshness of the battlefield is a reality of life as long as its purpose is to establish justice and remove human suffering.

———————

[1] God and His Messenger have cancelled any treaty you made with the idolaters. [2] So, you *idolaters* have four months to travel freely in the land; you cannot escape God's grip,[a] God will disgrace the disbelievers. [3] An announcement *of this will be made* by God and His Messenger on the day of the great pilgrimage to all the people: "God and His Messenger are free of *any previous obligation towards* the idolaters. So, if you *idolaters* repent that will be best for you, but if you turn away, then beware you can't escape God's grip." Give the disbelievers glad tidings of a painful punishment. [4] But the idolaters who haven't broken their treaty, nor

[a]   Alternative meaning: "God's purpose cannot be thwarted."

have they supported anyone against you, continue to fulfil your treaty with them for the fixed term. God loves the mindful.

A SECOND CHANCE IS GIVEN TO THOSE WHO REPENT

[5] When the sacred months are over, fight the idolaters wherever you find them, lie in ambush for them, arrest and besiege them.[a] However, if they repent, perform the prayer and pay Zakat, then let them go. God is Most Forgiving and Kind. [6] If an idolater seeks your protection give him protection, he may hear God's Word, then take him to his place of safety; this is because they are people who don't know.

THE DISBELIEVERS HAVE RELATIONSHIP PROBLEMS

[7] How could God and his Messenger have a treaty with the idolaters, except for those whom you *previously* made a treaty with at the Sacred Mosque? So long as they remain true, you must remain true to them. God loves the pious. [8] Were they to have the upper hand over you then they wouldn't show respect for either family relationship or the treaty. They try to please you with their speech, but their hearts reject you, and most of them are criminals. [9] They sell God's words for a small price and stop people from His path. Evil is what they do. [10] When it comes to the believers; they show no respect for family relationship or the treaty. They are transgressors. [11] However, if they repent, perform the prayer and pay Zakat they're your brothers in religion. We explain the verses for people who understand.

TREACHERY WILL NOT GO UNPUNISHED

[12] If they break their oaths once they have made a treaty *with you*, and they criticise your religion, then fight the chiefs of the disbelievers. Their oaths mean nothing to them, so this might stop them. [13] Will you not fight those who have broken

[a] Critics of Islam call this the "Sword Verse", due to an order to kill the idolaters. It is clear from the verses before and after it, that this doesn't refer to all the idolaters, but only to those who had no regard for family ties (8, 10), repeatedly broke the treaties they had with the Messenger ﷺ, and plotted to undermine the stability that followed the Conquest of Makkah. God specifically orders the Muslims to continue to respect their treaties with the idolaters who had not been hostile towards them (4, 7). What is also clear is that anyone who chose to enter Islam should be allowed to go about their lives free of any threat of attack (5). In fact, they should be treated as brothers in faith (11), and anyone who chose to remain idolaters but asked for safe passage must be granted it (6). Some extremist Muslims also use this Sword Verse as a general licence to kill anybody whom they considered to not be a Muslim, young or old, whether a combatant or not. This indiscriminate approach clearly goes against the teachings of the Quran.

their oaths and plotted to expel the Messenger, they were the ones who started the hostilities in the first place? Are you afraid of them? God is far more deserving to be feared if you are *true* believers. [14]Fight them so that God may punish and disgrace them at your hands; God wants to soothe the *aching* breasts of the believers, [15]and remove the fury from their hearts. God forgives whomever He pleases. God is the Knower, Wise. Believers are challenged to prove their faith

[16]Or did you think you would be left *untested*? God has not *yet* marked out those amongst you who are willing to struggle on His path, and those who will keep secrets safe from anyone besides God, His Messenger and the believers. God is well aware of what you do.

WHO IS FIT TO BE THE CARETAKER OF THE MOSQUE?

[17]It isn't right for the idolaters to be caretakers of God's Mosques while they are witnesses of their disbelief. Their deeds are worthless, and they will live in the Fire forever. [18]The Mosques of God are looked after by people who believe in God and the Last Day, perform prayer, pay Zakat and fear none but God; these are the rightly guided. [19]Do you consider providing water to the pilgrims and the maintenance of the Sacred Mosque equal *to piety* of those who believe in God and the Last Day and do Jihad in God's way? In God's sight the two things are not equal;[b] and God does not guide the wrongdoers. [20]Those who believed, migrated and struggled in God's way with their wealth and lives have a special place near God; those are the *real* winners. [21]Your Lord gives them glad tidings of kindness, pleasure and gardens in which they will enjoy everlasting delights, [22]living there forever. Surely, God will give them a mighty reward.

GOD IS DEAREST TO BELIEVERS THAN ANYTHING ELSE

[23]Believers, don't take your fathers and brothers as supporters if they prefer disbelief over faith; anyone who does so is a wrongdoer. [24]Say: "If your fathers, children, brothers, spouses, relatives and the wealth you have gathered, the business whose downturn you fear and the houses that delight you, if *these things* are dearer to you than God, His Messenger and struggling in His path, then you should

[b]   In the battle of Badr, Abbas the Prophet's ﷺ uncle was taken prisoner, someone condemned him for not embracing Islam. He replied "If you're so proud of becoming a Muslim and doing Jihad, we are no less than you, we take care of God's house, and take care of the pilgrims." This verse was revealed to emphasise the superiority of faith and Jihad over isolated good works.

wait until God's Judgement comes to pass. God doesn't guide the disobedient."

The dreadful outcome of the Battle of Hunain

[25] God helped you in many battlefields, including on the day of Hunain[a] when you were proud of your large numbers, but that wasn't any use to you. The Earth, for all its vastness, seemed to close in on you, and you turned back and fled. [26] Then God sent down His stillness[b] on his Messenger and the believers; and He sent down troops that you couldn't see, and He punished the disbelievers; that was the reward of their disbelief. [27] Afterwards, God forgave whom He pleased; God is Most Forgiving and Kind. [28] Believers, the idolaters are *spiritually* unclean; so don›t let them enter the Sacred Mosque after this year.[c] If you are afraid of poverty, soon God will enrich you with His gifts as He wills. God is the Knower, Wise.

The Jews and Christians rejected the original teachings

[29] Fight those among the people who were given the Book; they don't believe in God or the Last Day, don't regard unlawful what God and His Messenger have made unlawful, nor do they accept the rule of justice. Fight them until they agree to pay the tax promptly[d] and submit themselves. [30] The Jews say that Ezra[e] was the son of God, and the Christians say the Messiah was the son of God; these are false claims, they just imitate what the disbelievers said before them, may God destroy them! How misguided they are!

The corrupt practices of their religious leaders

[31] They made lords beside God; their rabbis, monks, and Messiah son of Mary, even though they were commanded to worship only one God, other than Whom

---

[a] Hunain is a valley twenty-two kilometres east of Makkah. A battle took place there in the eighth year of Hijrah, after the conquest of Makkah. The Muslim army numbered 12,000 and the idolaters were only 4,000.

[b] *Sakinah* means tranquillity and calmness, a mental state of placing one's trust in God and being content with God.

[c] Although it seems to indicate the opposite, this verse shows the tolerance of Islam: even after the Conquest of Makkah, idolaters were not told to convert or be put to the sword, but allowed to practise their religion. It was only when many of them chose to abuse that tolerance and to act with treachery that steps had to be taken to banish them from the sacred sites.

[d] *Jizya* is a tax that non-Muslim citizens living in an Islamic state pay in return for the protection of their lives, property, civic rights and religious freedom. It is a compensation paid to the Muslim community for providing these services to the non-Muslim citizens.

[e] *Uzair* refers to biblical Prophet Ezra. It has to be recognised that, unlike the Christian doctrine about Jesus, few if any Jews today hold this belief, which may have been restricted to relatively small and remote Jewish communities like those of Madinah.

there is no God. Glory to Him *Who is far removed* from what they associate with Him. [32] They would love to put out God's light with *the words of* their mouths but God rejects *the thought* that His light should not be perfected, no matter how much the disbelievers hate it. [33] It is He who sent His Messenger with guidance and the true religion to prevail all other religions, no matter how much the idolaters hate it.

THOSE WHO HOARD WEALTH WILL BE PUNISHED

[34] Believers, many rabbis and monks take people's wealth dishonestly and stop people from God's way. So, *those* who hoard gold and silver and don't spend in God's way, give them glad tidings of a painful punishment [35] on the day when it will be heated up in the fire of Hell and their foreheads, sides and backs will be branded with it. *It will be said*, "This is what you use to hoard, so taste the treasures you hoarded."

BENDING GOD'S RULES TO SUIT ONE'S EGO

[36] The number of months *recorded* in God's book since the day He created the Heavens and the Earth is twelve, four of them are sacred; this is the established law of nature, so don't be mistaken regarding them.[f] You may fight the idolaters all out just as they fight you all out, and know God is with those who are mindful of Him. [37] The postponing *of sacred months* is an extreme disbelief, by which the disbelievers cause *others* to be misled, making it lawful one year and unlawful the next. They do it to match the number of months that God has made sacred; but, in doing so, they make permissible what God has forbidden. Their foul deeds seem attractive to them, but God doesn't guide the disbelievers.

THE TABUK CAMPAIGN AND OBEYING THE ORDER TO MARCH

[38] Believers, what is the matter with you? When you are told: "Mobilise[g] yourself in God's way!" Why do you feel weighed down to the ground? Are you happy with this life instead of the Hereafter? The pleasures of this life are nothing compared to the Hereafter. [39] If you don't mobilise, He will punish you severely and replace *you* with other people, and you won't harm Him in any way. God has

---

[f] The four sacred months mentioned in verse 5 provided a time when the Arabs could travel freely without fear of attack. Even the idolaters respected them on the whole, except that they would sometimes cheat by swapping the sacred month of Rajab around if they thought it would give them an advantage in fighting other tribes.

[g] *Infirou* means to mobilise men, the marching off to war and all the preparations for it.

power over all things.

A lesson from the Messenger's ﷺ migration from Makkah

[40] If you won't help him, God has already helped when the disbelievers expelled him *from Makkah*. They were two in the cave when he said to his companion,[a] "Do not worry. God is with us." So, God comforted him and helped him with armies that you didn't see, and He foiled their plan, God's plan is supreme. God is Almighty, Wise.

The hypocrite's response to the order to march on Tabuk

[41] Mobilise whether you are lightly or heavily armed, and struggle with your wealth and your lives in God's way, that's better for you, if you knew. [42] Had there been an instant gain and an easy journey they would have followed you; however, *Tabuk* was too far away and the journey difficult. They will swear by God, "If we were capable we certainly would have come out with you." They have ruined themselves. God knows they are liars.

The attitudes and behaviours of Hypocrites: Making excuses

[43] God pardons you! Why did you allow them *to remain behind* before it became clear who was telling the truth, and you had identified the liars. [44] Those who believe in God and the Last Day won't seek your permission *to stay behind* so as not to strive with their wealth and lives. God knows the righteous people. [45] Only those who don't believe in God and the Last Day will seek your permission to remain behind because their hearts are full of doubts which makes them hesitant. [46] Had they wished to go forth *for Jihad* they would have prepared properly for it. However, because God disliked their going forth, He let them hold back *until* it was said: "Remain with those who are staying behind." [47] Had they gone out with you they would have made trouble for you, scurrying among you to wreak havoc, and some would have listened to them. God knows well the wrongdoers. [48] They tried to stir up conflict among you in the past and turn everything upside down for you until the truth *finally* came out, and God's decree was made clear, even though they detested *being exposed*. [49] Some of them say, "Permit me *to stay* and do not put me to the test." Haven't they already failed the test? Hell will encircle the disbelievers.

---

[a] The companion mentioned here was Abu Bakr, who accompanied him in the cave of Thaur, south of Makkah. He became the first Caliph after the Prophet ﷺ passed away in 632 CE.

HYPOCRITES GLOAT AT THE MISFORTUNE OF OTHERS

[50] When times are good for you, they grieve, but when some tragedy strikes you, they say, "We took proper precautions beforehand," and they go away rejoicing. [51] Say: "We are only affected by what God decreed for us, He is Our Protector, and the believers put their trust in God." [52] Say: "Are you waiting for anything besides two good things to happen to us?[b] We are *also* waiting with you for God to inflict on you some punishment, either by Himself or at our hands. So, carry on waiting, we'll wait as well." [53] Say: "Whether you give willingly or unwillingly, your *charity* will not be accepted, because you are disobedient people." [54] Since they do not believe in God and His Messenger their charity will not be accepted, furthermore, they come lazily to the prayer and give charity grudgingly. [55] Don't be impressed by their wealth and children: God wishes to torment them with these in their worldly life, and allow their souls to perish as disbelievers.

HYPOCRITES ARE ONLY IN IT FOR THEMSELVES

[56] They swear by God: they are with you *all the way*, but they aren't with you; they are cowardly people. [57] Were they to find a place to flee to, a cave or any opening, they would turn to it as they run away *from the truth*. [58] Some of them criticise you over *the redistribution of* charitable donations; if they are given some, they are pleased, but if not, they become angry. [59] They should be content with what God and His Messenger gave them and say: "God is enough for us, and soon God and His Messenger will give us from His bounty. *So*, we place our hopes in God."

THE EIGHT RECIPIENTS OF ZAKAT

[60] Zakat[c] is for the poor, the needy, its administrators, people whose hearts and minds are to be won, freeing the slaves, *helping* people in debt, to *advance* God's cause, and for the *needy* traveller. This is a duty instructed by God, and God is the Knower, Wise.

HYPOCRITES SOW CONFLICT AMONG MUSLIMS

[61] Some people insulted the Messenger saying, "He is all ears."[d] Say: "He has an ear for what is good for you. He believes in God and looks out for the safety of the

---

[b] Either in victory in the battle, or martyrdom and Paradise in the Hereafter.
[c] The commentators are agreed that *Sadaqah* here refers to Zakat, a pillar of Islam.
[d] "He is all ears" means that he believes everything he hears.

believers, and he is kind[a] to those of you who believe. However, those who insult God's Messenger will have painful punishment." [62] They swear by God to please you, yet it is God and his Messenger who they should try to please, if they are *true* believers. [63] Don't they know that anyone who opposes God and His Messenger will live in the Fire, forever? What a terrible disgrace!

THE HYPOCRITES ARE AN ANXIOUS BUNCH

[64] The hypocrites are afraid that a chapter may be revealed about them informing them *and the rest of the Muslims* of what is in their hearts. Say: "Keep mocking. God will produce what you most fear." [65] If you ask them *about some incident*, they will say, "We were just discussing and having fun." Say: "Are you mocking God, His verses and His Messenger? [66] Don't make excuses, you have *clearly* disbelieved after *declaring* belief." Even if We choose to forgive few of you, We will punish the rest because they are sinners.

HYPOCRITES DON'T WALK THE TALK

[67] Hypocrite, men and women, stand by each other; they enjoin evil and forbid good and are tight-fisted. They ignore God, so He will ignore them *in the Hereafter*. The hypocrites are disobedient. [68] God has promised the hypocrites, men and women, and the disbelievers the fire of Hell to be there forever; that's good enough for them. God has cursed them, and they will suffer endless torment.

THE HYPOCRITES TALK BUT DON'T LIVE THE VALUES

[69] *Hypocrites! You are* like those before you, but they were more powerful than you, and had greater wealth and children; they enjoyed their share *of the worldly comforts*, so you too enjoy your share just as they did before you; and go on indulging in idle talk just as they did. Their deeds are worthless in this world and the Hereafter; they were losers. [70] Haven't stories of previous people come down to them, like the people of Noah, Ad, Thamud; of Abraham, of Madyan and the overturned cities? Messengers came with clear signs; God wasn't unfair to them, but they wronged themselves.

THE REWARD FOR BELIEVERS IS PARADISE

[71] Believing men and women, are one another's friends; they enjoin what is good and forbid what is evil; they perform the prayer, pay Zakat, they obey God and

---

[a] Literally "kindness".

His Messenger, so God will take care of them. God is Almighty, Wise. [72] God has prepared for the believing men and women, gardens under which rivers flow, where they shall live forever, and comfortable homes *enclosed by* gardens of everlasting bliss, and the Divine pleasure is the greatest *reward* of all,[b] the supreme achievement.

HYPOCRITES MAKE PROMISES THAT THEY DON'T KEEP

[73] Blessed Prophet, struggle against the disbelievers and hypocrites and be strict with them. Hell is their *lasting* home. What an evil destination! [74] They swear by God they didn't say *what they are accused of*, but they blasphemed and disbelieved after embracing Islam. They worry about what they failed to achieve. They were angry because God and His Messenger enriched them with His bounty. It would be better for them, if they repented. But, if they turn away God will punish them severely in this life and the Hereafter, and no one on Earth would protect or help them. [75] Some of them vowed to God: "If He gives us of His bounty, we will donate generously and be righteous." [76] However, when He blessed them with His bounty, they became miserly and turned away, unwilling to give.[c] [77] Since they broke their promise to God and lied repeatedly, God has put hypocrisy in their hearts until the day they meet Him.

HYPOCRITES MOCK GENEROUS MUSLIMS

[78] Aren't they aware God knows their secrets and private conversations. God is the Knower of the unseen. [79] Those who criticise the believers – who make voluntary donations, and who have nothing *to give* but their *time and* talent – and they poke fun at them, God will make a laughing stock of them; and they shall have a painful punishment. [80] Whether you ask for their forgiveness or not, even if you ask seventy times for their forgiveness,[d] God will never forgive them because they rejected God and His Messenger, and God does not guide the sinners.

---

[b] The Divine pleasure means that God is happy with them, He has approved their worldly achievements and taken them as friends.

[c] This refers to Saliba Ibn Hatib, who came to the Messenger ﷺ and said "pray to God to give me wealth". The Messenger ﷺ cautioned him "O Saliba, a small amount for which you are thankful is better than a lot which you can't appreciate." However Saliba kept insisting that He ﷺ pray for him, and he will give the needy their due. So, the Messenger ﷺ prayed and his wealth grew enormously. Unfortunately, he was miserly and refused to give in charity. (Al Sabuni)

[d] The number seventy here is like "umpteen" in English.

Hypocrites aren't trustworthy

[81] Those who stayed at home were delighted after God's Messenger had left. They hated *the thought of* struggling with their wealth and lives in God's way, saying *to others*, "Don't march in this heat." Say: "The fire of Hell is far hotter." If only they understood. [82] So, let them laugh a little, *soon* they will cry a lot, a reward for what they did. [83] When God brings you back *to Madinah*, a group of them will ask permission to march out with you *next time*. Say *to them*: "You will never march out with me, nor will you fight with me against an enemy. You were happy to stay *at home* the first time, so stay with those who were left behind."

Hypocrisy deprives you of the Messenger's 鬈 prayers

[84] *Blessed Prophet*, never pray for any of their dead nor stand by their grave. They disbelieved in God and His Messenger and died as sinners. [85] Don't be impressed by their wealth or children, God wishes to torment them with these in this world, and their souls will perish while they are still disbelievers. [86] Whenever a chapter is revealed *saying*: "Believe in God and strive along with His Messenger," the wealthy among them seek an exemption from you, saying, "Leave us with those who stay behind." [87] They are pleased to stay with those who remain behind, and their hearts have been sealed so they do not understand. [88] However, the Messenger and believers strive with their wealth and lives. They shall have all the best things, and they're successful. [89] God has prepared for them gardens beneath which rivers flow, here they shall live forever; that is the supreme achievement.

Those who long to defend but lack the means are not to blame

[90] Some Bedouins who stayed behind at home came with excuses, sought exemption, and some lied about God and His Messenger. The disbelievers shall soon be afflicted by a painful punishment. [91] No blame shall rest on the weak, the sick and those who lack the financial means, so long as they remain sincere towards God and His Messenger; the righteous shouldn't be blamed, God is Forgiving, Caring. [92] Nor *does any blame rest* on those who came to you expecting to find mounts,[a] and you said, "I can't find a mount for you," so they turned away, their eyes overflowing with tears of grief since they had no money to equip themselves.

---

[a] A mount here refers to an animal for transportation.

THE WEALTHY ARE TO BLAME FOR NOT CONTRIBUTING

⁹³ Blame is on those who seek an exemption, yet they are wealthy. They are happy to stay with those who remain behind, so God has sealed their hearts, they don't know. ⁹⁴ They will make *all sorts of* excuses when you return to them *in Madinah.* Say: "Don't make excuses. We won't believe you. God has already informed us about you. God and His Messenger will soon see your actions, then you will be turned over to the Knower of all that is seen and unseen, and He will inform you of what you used to do." ⁹⁵ When you return to them they will swear by God to be left alone, so leave them alone; they're wicked people. Their home is Hell, a reward for what they did. ⁹⁶ They will swear an oath to please you, but even if you are pleased with them, God will not be pleased with disobedient people.

MANY BEDOUINS REMAIN UNCOMMITTED, BUT OTHERS ARE SINCERE

⁹⁷ Some Bedouins are the worst in terms of disbelief and hypocrisy and are least likely to understand the limits sent by God to His Messenger. God is Knowing, Wise. ⁹⁸ Some Bedouins regard charity as a fine, and are waiting for your luck to turn. An evil turn of fortune awaits them. God is the Hearer, the Knower. ⁹⁹ There are other Bedouins who believe in God and the Last Day, and regard charity as a means of drawing closer to God and gaining the Messenger's blessings.[b] No doubt it is a means of drawing closer. God will treat them kindly.[c] God is Forgiving, Caring.

PRAISE OF THE COMPANIONS OF THE PROPHET ﷺ

¹⁰⁰ God is pleased with those who were the first Migrants and Helpers, and those who followed them in righteousness, they are pleased with Him. He has prepared for them gardens under which rivers flow where they will live forever; that is the greatest victory.

NO ETHNIC GROUP SHOULD BE STEREOTYPED

¹⁰¹ Among the Bedouins *who live* around you there are some hypocrites, and some people of Madinah are inflexible; you don't know them, but We know them. We will punish them twice and then turn them over to horrendous torment *in the Hereafter.* ¹⁰² *Yet* there are others who have confessed their sins, and have mixed good deeds with the bad, *hoping that* God may forgive them. Surely, God is For-

---

[b] Messengers blessing means His prayers and seeking forgiveness for you.
[c] Literally translated as: "enter you in his kindness."

giving, Kind. [103] Accept charity from their wealth to purify them and to develop them spiritually, and pray for them; your prayers are a comfort for them. God is the Hearer, the Knower.

GOD FORGIVES THOSE WHO STRIVE TO PLEASE HIM

[104] Don't they know God accepts repentance and charitable donations from His servants? He is the Relenting, the Kind. [105] Say: "Keep doing *good deeds*! God and His Messenger sees what you do, *so do* the believers. Then you will be returned to the Knower of all that is seen and unseen, and He will inform you of what you used to do." [106] And there are others who are full of hope for God's decree, as to whether He will punish or pardon them. God is All-Knowing, Wise.

PRAY IN A MASJID FOUNDED ON PIETY

[107] The *hypocrites* who built a Mosque – to incite violence, disbelief and disunity amongst the believers, and as an outpost for those who had previously waged war on God and His Messenger – will swear: "We intended good only." God bears witness, "They are liars." [108] *So* never pray in it. *Without a doubt*, it is more fitting by far that you pray in a Mosque founded on piety from the first day that deserves to be prayed in. In that *Mosque*, there are men who like to be pure, and God loves the pure. [109] Which *of the two* is better: the person who laid his foundations on fear of God and *Divine* pleasure; or the one who lays his foundations on the very edge of a crumbling cliff edge, so it tumbles into the fire of Hell, taking him with it? God doesn't guide the wicked people. [110] The building they have built will always create doubt in their hearts, unless *they feel* their hearts torn apart *with remorse*.[a] God is the Knower, Wise.

WHAT IS THE PRICE OF A BELIEVER?

[111] God has purchased from the believers their lives and their wealth in exchange for Paradise. They fight in God's way, slaying and being slain. This is a valid pledge from Him *recorded* in the Torah, the Gospel and the Quran. And who is more true to his word than God? So rejoice at your bargain. This is a mighty victory for [112] those who repent, worship, praise God, fast, bow, prostrate, enjoin good, forbid evil, and stay within the boundaries set by God:[b] give glad tidings to *such* believers.

---

[a] Literally, "until their hearts are cut to shreds," a metaphor for regret and repentance.
[b] Guardians of God's boundaries.

Why Abraham sought forgiveness for his father

[113] It is not fitting for the Prophet and the believers to seek forgiveness for idolaters, even if they are close relatives, after it has been made clear to them that they are people of the Blazing Fire. [114] Abraham sought forgiveness for his father[c] because of a promise he made to him. However, after it became clear to Abraham he was God's enemy, he immediately dissociated himself from his father. Abraham was soft-hearted and gentle. [115] God would not let people go astray after having guided them, not until He has made it absolutely clear to them what they should be mindful of. God knows all things. [116] Control of the Heavens and Earth belongs to God. He gives life, and He takes it away. You have no protector or helper other than God.

God accepted the repentance of the three believers

[117] God has turned in kindness to the Prophet, the Migrants and the Helpers who stood by him at that time of extreme hardship,[d] after the hearts of a group of them had wavered. Then He forgave them. He was Compassionate and Kind to them. [118] *As for* the three who stayed behind,[e] the Earth seemed to close in on them, despite its vastness, their own souls strangled them, and they realised that the only refuge from God lay in *turning to* Him, it was then God forgave them because they repented. God is acceptor of repentance, the Kind.

None of our good deeds shall ever go to waste

[119] Believers, fear God and stand firmly with the truthful. [120] It was not fitting for the people of Madinah and the surrounding Bedouins to stay behind *instead of marching with* God's Messenger, nor *was it fitting* to prefer their lives over his; that is because whatever thirst, suffering or hunger they endure in God's way, whatever path they tread to the fury of the disbelievers, and whatever advantage they gain over an enemy, it is recorded for them as a good deed. God doesn't waste the reward of the righteous. [121] Whatever amount they spend, large or small, and

[c] According to some commentators, "his father" refers here metaphorically to Abraham's uncle, Azar, and not his biological father. "His father's name was Tharah, and the Prophet ﷺ once said, 'I have been raised among the best in the children of Adam;' it's therefore impossible that any of the ancestors of the Prophet were disbelievers." (Mazhari)

[d] Literally, "hour of distress or difficulty."

[e] The phrase "the three who delayed," refers to companions who admitted their mistake of staying behind: Ka'b ibn Malik, Marrah ibn al-Rabi, Hilal ibn Umayyah.

whatever valley they cross, it's all written down for them, God will reward them for the finest things they did.

The community should invest in religious learning

[122] It isn't right all the believers mobilise for *fighting*; rather a group from each community should stay behind and apply themselves to thorough understanding of the religion to warn their people on their return to them, so that they *too* might be mindful.

Disbelievers would rather mock others than reflect

[123] Believers, fight the disbelievers who are nearest to you.[a] Let them find you tough. Know God is with the pious. [124] Whenever a chapter is revealed, some ask: "Whose faith has been increased by this?" Those who believe, their faith has certainly increased, and they rejoice. [125] But those whose hearts are diseased become more and more sick, and will die disbelievers. [126] Don't they realise once or twice a year they are tested, but they don't repent or pay attention. [127] Whenever a chapter is revealed, they look at each other, saying, "Is anyone watching you?" Then they slip away. God has turned their hearts away *from truth* because they are people who *simply* do not understand.

The Messenger ﷺ who understands and cares for the believers

[128] A *noble* Messenger has come to you from among yourselves. He's grieved by your hardships and cares about your well-being, for the believers he is compassionate and kind. [129] So if they *choose to* turn away, tell them: "God is sufficient for me, there is no god but Him. I have put my trust in Him, the Lord of the mighty throne."

---

[a] Those who fight you, since the Quran only allows war in self-defence

10. Yunus

The Prophet Jonah

This is a late Makkan chapter, revealed possibly in the year 622 CE. This is the first of the six chapters named after a prophet; the others are: Hud, Joseph, Abraham, Muhammad and Noah. The chapter opens by asking why people are surprised that God sent the revelation to a human being. This is followed by verses in which God is introduced as the Creator of the universe: the sun and the moon, that establish daily cycles of night and day on Earth, all for a purpose.

The central theme of the chapter is the truthfulness of the Majestic Quran. The Makkans demanded that the Quran be changed because it criticised their false beliefs and bogus religious practices, the reply was: "Who ... is a greater wrongdoer than the one who makes up lies about God or who denies His verses? Certainly, evildoers will not succeed" (17). When they accused the Messenger ﷺ of making it up, the Prophet ﷺ was told to ask them: "Produce a single chapter like it, then call on whomever you can besides God to act as a witness, if you are telling the truth" (38). The significance of the Quran lies in its life-changing teachings and its solution to human misery caused by lack of morality: "People, your Lord's teachings have come to you; they're a healing balm for the diseases of the heart, and guidance and goodwill for the believers" (57). When the Prophet ﷺ is accused of writing the Quran himself, the answer is they are being deaf, dumb and blind (42–43).

The human habit of turning to God in time of hardship is cited as a proof of "the inbuilt faith in God." At times of need humans, believers or disbelievers, instinctively tend to turn to God, but as soon as the hardship is removed they return to their old ways. The Quran warns against this ungrateful attitude: "People, your disrespect weighs against you" (23). What is the reality of idols? They are "imagined gods," (30) and they are totally helpless and powerless of doing anything: "Say: Can any of your idols begin the creation and then restore it?" (34). If they can't then why don't they turn to God? The stories of prophets Noah, Moses and Jonah are given as examples of past nations that refused to listen to their prophets. Each of them perished, so "listen or else" the Makkans are warned. Even the most arrogant and stubborn disbeliever, like the Pharaoh, eventually submitted when drowning. However, his repentance was not accepted as it was too late (90). The story of the titular character; Jonah is given as an example of people who repented.

The short passage from 61 to 63 vividly describes the qualities of God's friends: people with unshakable faith, righteous deeds, and mindful of their duties towards God. The chapter ends with a persuasive instruction: religion is a serious commitment to God: "I was ordered to be a believer and told, 'Keep your face directed towards the true religion, in tune with your nature, and don't be an idolater'" (104–105).

In the name of God, the Kind, the Caring.

¹ *Alif Lam Ra.*

THE QURAN HOLDS WISDOM

These are the verses of the Book full of wisdom. ² Are people surprised We revealed to one of their men: "Warn the people, and give good news to the believers that they are on sure footing with their Lord"? The disbelievers say, "He's clearly a magician."

GOD HAS CREATED EVERYTHING FOR A PURPOSE

³ God is Your Lord, He created *the* Heavens and the Earth in six days then established Himself *as befits Him* on the throne, overseeing the running *of the entire universe*. No one can intercede without His permission: such is God, your Lord, so worship Him. Won't you pay attention? ⁴ You will return to Him. God's promise is true. He initiates *the process of* creation and *after its death will* restore it, to reward fairly the believers and those who performed righteous deeds. But the disbelievers will have scalding water to drink and a painful punishment because of what they denied. ⁵ He gave the sun *its* radiant glow and the moon *its* light, He determined their phases precisely, so you might calculate the *passing* years and keep time. God created *this* for a purpose; so people of knowledge can understand the signs *of creation*. ⁶ In the rotation of day and night, and in the creation of the Heavens and the Earth, there are signs for people who are mindful.

THE VALUE OF FAITH

⁷ Those who don't expect to meet Us, are pleased with worldly life, feel at ease and have chosen to ignore Our signs, ⁸ their final home shall be the Fire, a consequence of their activities. ⁹ Those who believed and did righteous deeds, their Lord will guide them by strengthening their faith, *and lead them* to the gardens of delight beneath *which* rivers flow. ¹⁰ Here their prayer will be, "Glory to you, God!" And their greeting will be, "Peace," and the closing prayer will be, "Praise be to God, Lord of *all* realms."

GOD DELAYS PASSING JUDGEMENT; HE GIVES PEOPLE TIME

¹¹ If God were hasty in punishing people as they would hasten their reward, their fate would have been sealed, so We leave those who do not expect to meet Us to

wander aimlessly in their disobedience. ¹²Whenever troubles distress a person, he prays to Us sitting, standing or *lying down* on his side; *but* as soon as We remove *the cause of* his hardship, he carries on as though he had never prayed to Us to *ease* his hardship. That is how their activities appear attractive to the extravagant. ¹³We destroyed *many* generations before you when they did wrong, and messengers came with clear signs to them, but *still* they didn't believe. That's how We deal with sinful people. ¹⁴Then afterwards, We made you successors in the land, so We could see how you would behave.

THE PROPHET ☀ CAN'T CHANGE THE QURAN

¹⁵Whenever Our verses are recited, those who don't expect to meet Us say, "Bring us a Quran other than this one, or else alter it." Say: "It is not for me to change it by myself. I follow what is revealed to me; *and* I fear the torment of an overwhelming day, if I disobey My Lord." ¹⁶Say: "If God wanted, I would not have recited it to you, nor would He have informed you of it. I spent my entire life among you before it *was revealed*. Can you not think *it through*?" ¹⁷Who then is a greater wrongdoer than the one who makes up lies about God or who denies His verses? Certainly, evildoers will not succeed. ¹⁸Yet they worship besides God *idols* which can't harm or benefit them, and they say, "These are our intercessors with God." Say: "Are you informing God of what He doesn't know in *the* Heavens and the Earth?" Glory be to Him! He is exalted above *all* they associate *with Him*.

PEOPLE'S DIFFERENCES ARE PART OF GOD'S PLAN

¹⁹At one time *all* people were a single community, then they started to disagree, and if it had not been for an earlier decree of Your Lord, the differences between them would have been settled long ago. ²⁰They say, "If only a sign would come down to him from his Lord," Say: "The unseen belongs to God alone. So, wait *for that sign*, and I shall be waiting with you."

FAITH IS DEEP-ROOTED IN HUMANS

²¹When We let people enjoy Our kindness following a hard time they plot to cover up Our goodness. Say: "God is the swiftest planner." Our messenger *angels* record all you're plotting. ²²He lets you travel by land and sea, and when you are on board a ship, sailing happily along with a favourable wind, *then* suddenly a gale wind blows with waves from every direction and they realise they are trapped; *at that moment* they pray to God, sincerely and faithfully: "If You save us from this,

we will be *forever* grateful." [23] However, no sooner does He rescue them then, unashamedly, they are disrespectful throughout the land. People, your disrespect will only count against you – *How brief is* the enjoyment of this worldly life! – You will return to Us, and We shall inform you what you did.

THE PARABLE OF WITHERED CROPS REPRESENTS EARTHLY LIFE

[24] This worldly life is like the water We send down from the sky, it soaks the soil and the plants, which are eaten by the people and livestock. *They grow* until the land takes on beautiful colours and appears attractive, and its owners think they have control over it, *then* Our command comes, at night or by day, and We leave it looking like stubble *after the harvest*, as though it never existed a day earlier. This is how We explain the signs for people who reflect. [25] God calls *people* to the home of *Heavenly* peace, and He guides the one who pleases Him along a straight path. [26] For those who are righteous, there will be an excellent reward and more beside; neither dust nor disgrace will stain their faces, such people will be the companions of Paradise, living there forever.

THE IDOLS ARE NONENTITIES

[27] The wrongdoers will get a matching reward; disgrace will stain them, and they will have no one to protect them from God's *punishment*. As though their faces are masked bit by bit with the *pitch* darkness of night. Such people will be the companions of the Fire, living there forever. [28] The day We gather them together, We will say to idolaters, "*This* place is for you and your partners." Then We shall separate them, and their partners will say, "You didn't worship us, [29] God is sufficient as a witness between us and you, we were unaware of your worship." [30] There, every soul will *be forced to* confront what it did in the past as they are returned to God, their true Master, all *the idols* they devised will desert them.

THE INEFFECTIVENESS OF IDOLS

[31] Say: "Who provides for you from the Heavens and Earth, and Who has the power of *granting* hearing and sight? And Who brings forth the living from the dead and the dead from the living? And Who oversees the running *of the entire universe*?" "God!" They will say. So, say: "Won't you be mindful *of Him*? [32] Such is God, your true Lord. And, beyond truth, what is there except falsehood? So where else can you turn?" [33] This is how your Lord's statement against the evildoers has been justified, that they don't believe. [34] Say: "Has any of your partners

initiated *the process of* creation and will then restore it *to its original state*?" Tell them: "It is God Who initiates creation and then restores it. Why then are you telling lies?" ³⁵Say: "Does any of your partners guide to the truth?" Say: "Only God guides to the truth. So isn't He deserving to be followed or is it the one who can't act as a guide unless he is guided? So, what's the matter with you, that you make *such* decisions?"

THE SCEPTICS ARE CHALLENGED TO PRODUCE A BOOK LIKE THE QURAN
³⁶Most of them are simply speculating, but speculation is no substitute for the truth. God knows well what they do. ³⁷This Quran could not have been invented independently of God; rather it confirms what came before it and is an explanation of *that* Book in which there is no doubt, which is from the Lord of the universe. ³⁸Or do they say, "He has invented it"? *If so*, say: "Produce a *single* chapter like it, then call on anyone you can besides God *to act as a witness*, if you are telling the truth." ³⁹Rather they deny that which they lack the knowledge to understand, and whose interpretation has yet to reach them. That is exactly how those before them used to *falsely* deny, so wait and see what the outcome will be for the wrongdoers. ⁴⁰Some believe in it, but others don't; Your Lord is aware of the immoral crooks.

HUMAN FREE WILL: EVERYONE IS RESPONSIBLE FOR THEIR ACTIONS
⁴¹If they deny you, say: "For me, my deeds and for you yours! You are innocent of what I do, *just as* I am innocent of what you do." ⁴²Some of them pretend to listen to you. Can you make the deaf hear? Especially those who don't think? ⁴³Some of them look at you but how can you guide the blind, since they can't see? ⁴⁴God doesn't wrong people in any way; rather it is they who wrong themselves. ⁴⁵On the day when He gathers them, and as they recognise each other, it will be as though they had lingered *no more than* a daylight hour. Those who denied they would meet God will *find out they* have lost *everything* and were not *at all* guided. ⁴⁶Whether We show you *in advance* something of what We have threatened them with, or whether We cause you to die *first*, they will return to Us; God is a witness of all they do.

LIFESPAN IS UNCHANGEABLE
⁴⁷Every community had a messenger; and when their messenger came, justice was done *and no one* was wronged. ⁴⁸And they say, "When is this promise *to be ful-*

filled, if you are truthful?" [49] Say: "Even for myself, I have no control over what brings benefit or harm, except *to the extent* that God wills. Every community has a *certain* span of life; and, when their lifespan comes *to an end*, they can neither postpone nor advance *it* by a *single* hour." [50] Say: "Have you considered, if His torment were to come to you, at night or day, what part of it the sinners would want to hasten? [51] Is it then you would believe in it once it has happened, *only to be told*, 'What? Now', when *before* you wanted to hasten it?" [52] The wrongdoers will be told, "Taste the everlasting torment. This is the only fitting reward for what you did."

THE SINNERS' VAIN WISHES ON JUDGEMENT DAY

[53] They question you, "Is it really true?" Say: "Yes, by My Lord, it is true, and you are unable to stop *it*." [54] If every soul that sinned possessed all that is on Earth, it would offer it as a ransom. They will *scarcely* conceal their regret when they see the punishment, and justice will be done *so that* none of them is wronged. [55] Doesn't everything in the Heavens and the Earth belong to God? Isn't God's promise true? Most don't know. [56] He gives life and death, *finally* you will return to Him.

THE QURAN IS A SOOTHING BALM

[57] People, your Lord's teachings have come to you; they're a healing balm for *the diseases* of the heart, guidance and beneficial teachings for the believers. [58] Say: "It's God's grace and kindness, so celebrate, it's better than all *the wealth* they accumulate." [59] Say: "Have you *ever* thought about the provision that God has sent down for you, and which you declare either lawful or unlawful?" Say: "Has God given you permission *to do so*, or are you inventing lies about God?" [60] What do those who invent lies about God think *will happen* on Judgement Day? God is Gracious towards people, yet most of them are ungrateful.

A PICTURE OF THE FRIENDS OF GOD

[61] Whatever matter you are dealing with, *Messenger*, and whatever part of the Quran you are reciting; and whatever you are doing, We are witnessing what you are doing. Not an atom's weight on Earth or in the Heavens is hidden from your Lord; nothing bigger or smaller exists that isn't *recorded* in a clear Book. [62] Beware, God's friends have no fear, nor do they grieve. [63] They believe and are mindful *of God*, [64] for them are glad tidings in this worldly life and in the Hereafter. There is

no change to God's rulings; that's a great victory. ⁶⁵ *So* don't be saddened by what they say. All the power is God's. He is the Hearer, the Knower.

GOD'S CREATION CANNOT BE HIS PARTNER

⁶⁶ Beware, everything in the Heavens and Earth belongs to God! Whatever they follow and who they call on as partners beside God are merely speculations and lies. ⁶⁷ He made the night for you to rest and the day to earn *a livelihood*. In this there are signs for people who listen. ⁶⁸ They said, "God has adopted a son." Glory to Him! He is the Self-Sufficient. Whatever is in the Heavens and on Earth belongs to Him. Do you have any proof for this *claim*? How can you say what you don't know about God? ⁶⁹ Say: "Those who fabricate lies about God never succeed." ⁷⁰ *Let them experience* enjoyment in this world; then they will return to Us, *and* We shall make them taste severe punishment because of their disbelief.

THE STORY OF NOAH

⁷¹ Tell them about Noah, when he said to his people, "My people, if you find my presence and my reminder of God's signs offensive, I put my trust in God. Agree together with your partners a plan *of action*, then do not be hesitant to carry it out, and grant me no respite. ⁷² If you *choose to* turn your backs, then *know that* I have not asked you for any reward; my reward is with God, and I have been told to be with those who submit *to His will*." ⁷³ They rejected him, so We rescued him and his followers in a ship and made them successors *in the land*, and We drowned those who denied Our signs. So, take note of the fate of those who were warned. ⁷⁴ After *Noah*, We sent messengers, *each* to their *own* people. *They* came to them with clear signs, but *they* weren't willing to believe in what they had previously denied. That is how We seal the hearts of offenders.

THE STORY OF MOSES, MAGICIANS AND THE PHARAOH

⁷⁵ After them, We sent Moses and Aaron with Our signs to Pharaoh and his courtiers, but they responded arrogantly, they were wicked people. ⁷⁶ When the truth came to them from Us, they said, "This is clearly magic." ⁷⁷ Moses said, "Is this how you speak about truth when it comes to you? *Do you call* this magic, when *you know that* magicians never achieve anything?" ⁷⁸ They said, "Have you come to turn us away from what we found our forefathers doing, so you two may rule over us? We don't believe you." ⁷⁹ Pharaoh said, "Bring me every expert magician." ⁸⁰ So, when the magicians came, Moses said to them, "Cast your *spells*." ⁸¹ When

they had cast *their spells*, Moses said, "You've performed magic. God will prove it to be fake; God will not allow the actions of those bent on corruption to succeed; [82] *rather* God will uphold the truth of His words, though the sinners hate that."

MOSES MOTIVATES HIS PEOPLE TO BE PRAYERFUL

[83] No one believed in Moses – fearing that Pharaoh and his courtiers will persecute them – except some young people. Pharaoh behaved high-handedly throughout the land, and he was one of those who went beyond the bounds. [84] Moses said, "My people, since you chose to believe in God then put your trust in Him, if you have really submitted *to His will*." [85] They replied, "We have put our trust in God, Our Lord, do not leave us at the mercy of the wicked people [86] and, by Your kindness, rescue us from the disbelieving people." [87] We revealed to Moses and his brother: "Let your people take up residence in Egypt; and, *Israelites*, turn your homes into places of worship, and perform the prayer; and *Moses*, give glad tidings to the believers." Moses' prayer for the destruction of Pharaoh.

[88] Moses said, "Our Lord, You have given Pharaoh and his courtiers splendour and wealth in this worldly life so they are leading *others* astray from Your path. Our Lord, destroy their wealth and harden their hearts so that they do not believe until they see the painful punishment *with their eyes*." [89] *God* said, "Your prayer has been accepted, remain steadfast, both of you, and do not follow the path of those who have no knowledge."

PHARAOH'S BODY IS PRESERVED AS A SIGN

[90] *Eventually,* We led the Israelites across the sea, with Pharaoh and his army following them, full of aggression and hatred, until he drowned,[a] *Pharaoh* said, "I believe there is no god except Him Who the Israelites believe, and I am one who submits *to His will*." [91] "What, now?" *Pharaoh was asked,* "After all your disobedience as one of those bent on corruption? [92] Today We shall preserve your body, as a *warning* sign for whoever comes after you." *Unfortunately,* many people are unaware of Our signs.[b] [93] We settled the Israelites in comfortable houses and provided them wholesome food, and they did not disagree amongst themselves until after knowledge had come to them. Your Lord will judge between them on Judgement

---

[a]   *Idrakahu algharaq,* literally means 'overwhelmed by the sea'.

[b]   Commentators think this Pharaoh was the famous Ramesses II (1303-1213 BC), whilst others say it was his predecessor Tutankhamun (1341-1323 bc), (Asad). His body embalmed now is in the Egyptian Museum.

Day regarding their differences.

DOUBTING WILL NOT DRIVE AWAY THE PUNISHMENT

[94] So, if you are in doubt about what We have revealed, then ask those who read the Book before you, *the Jews.* The truth has come to you from your Lord, so listener don't be one of those who have doubts. [95] and do not be one of those who deny God's signs, *ultimately* becoming the losers. [96] Those against whom your Lord's statement is justified, they will not believe, [97] even if all the signs were to come to them *at once,* until – *like Pharaoh* – they see the painful punishment.

ALL THE PEOPLE OF JONAH BELIEVED

[98] What a pity not a single town believed and benefitted from its faith, except the people of Jonah. When they believed, We removed the *looming* punishment of disgrace from them in this life, and We granted them respite for a while. [99] If Your Lord wanted, everyone on Earth would have believed. Will you force people to believe? [100] No one can believe without God's approval, and He casts doubt in *the minds of* those who do not think.[c] [101] Say: "Look at what's in the Heavens and the Earth." Yet signs and warnings are of no benefit to people who choose not to believe. [102] Do they expect *an outcome* other than what happened to those who passed before them? Say: "So wait *for a sign,* and I shall be with you waiting." [103] We always rescued Our messengers and the believers. That is how it is: the believers rightly expect Us to save them.

DO NOT CHANGE TO PLEASE OTHERS, BUT STICK TO WHAT GOD HAS REVEALED

[104] Say: "People, if you have doubts about my religion, I won't worship those you worship beside God; I shall worship God, Who will *ultimately* take your souls. I was ordered to be a believer, [105] and *told*: 'Keep your face *directed* towards the *true* religion, in tune with your nature, and do not become an idolator. [106] Do not pray to something beside God that can neither benefit nor harm you; if you were to do so, you'll be a wrongdoer.'" [107] If God allows harm to distress you, no one can remove it but Him, if He wishes good for you, then no one can turn aside His grace, which He grants to any one of His servants He pleases. He is the Forgiving, the Kind. [108] Say: "People, the truth from your Lord came. So, whoever accepts the guidance will benefit himself, and whoever goes astray will be harmed by doing

---

[c] The reason God let's them go astray is because they "do not think", were they to use reason they would get God's approval and win His grace.

so; I am not guardian over you." [109] *Messenger*, follow what is revealed to you, and be patient until God makes judgement, He is the best judge.

11. Hud
The Prophet Hud

The central theme of this late Makkan chapter is the history of human disobedience. The Messenger ﷺ and the Muslims are reassured by a narrative based on the experiences of seven prophets.

The story of Prophet Noah is the first of the seven stories, and it outlines his bold preaching. His people were particularly prejudiced against the poor: "It's clear to us that you are a mortal like us, and only the dregs of our society follow you. You have no special quality that we lack." (27). Eventually Noah and his followers are saved from the flood. The story of Prophet Hud follows in the same manner. His people rejected him by saying, "You haven't brought us any proof" (53), re-enacting the same old story of unwilling disbelievers, so finally they are destroyed. The people of Makkah were familiar with the ruins of the People of Thamud, who lived near Sana in Yemen. Their messenger was Salih , who invited them to God. Their moral disease seems to be the caste system, discriminating against people from poor backgrounds. They rejected their prophet and were punished by a blast that killed them all.

The next story is of Prophet Abraham pleading on behalf of his nephew Lot. Lot was sent to the infamous people of Sodom and Gomorrah, plagued by homosexuality. This is followed by the story of Prophet Jethro in Madyan, a prosperous community that refused to listen to him. They were morally corrupt and cheated when doing business. The seventh story in this series is Moses and Pharaoh. Pharaoh, like his predecessors, rejected the teachings of Moses , and was drowned for his injustice and his oppression of the Israelites. The chapter concludes by dividing humanity into two groups: the blessed heirs of Paradise, and the wretched inhabitants of Hellfire. After narrating the stories of the prophets, peacemakers and pious men's struggle against wicked people, the chapter repeats the original instruction: "worship God." The common thread that weaves through these seven stories is the rejection of the prophets, the punishment of the disbelievers, and the final victory of the righteous. The Quran in its matchless way is reassuring the beloved Messenger ﷺ of a victory, but is also instructing him ﷺ to be patient in the meanwhile, to perform the prayer and accept this unfortunate human condition. These stories, of human rebellion were the result of the love of wealth and mindlessness. The antidote: believe in resurrection and reform yourselves; overcome prejudice against the poor, show thankfulness to God.

Abu Bakr once pointed out the grey hair in the Prophet's ﷺ beard, he replied, "Chapter Hud and its sister chapters are the cause of my greying hair" (Tirmidhi). This chapter, like most other Makkan chapters, displays the majestic mode, Jalali, which conveys God's avenging will and unwavering justice. Hinting that like the previous prophets you too will have to abandon your home city, and see its demise. On the other hand, it also includes the Jamali mode: God the Gentle, Compassionate and Generous, but the majestic mode is dominant in this chapter.

In the name of God, the Kind, the Caring.

¹ *Alif Lam Ra'.*

DIVINE GUIDANCE: GENTLE REMINDERS, WARNINGS AND PROMISES

This is a Book whose verses give *clear* instructions, explained by a Wise, Knowledgeable *Lord*: ² "Worship no one besides God, I am a warner to you from Him and a giver of good news. ³ Seek your Lord's forgiveness and turn to Him in repentance, so He grants you good provision for a fixed term and gives His grace to whoever is worthy of it. If you turn away, I fear for you the torment of a terrible day. ⁴ You shall return to God. He has control over all things". ⁵ Isn't it *true* that they try to cover their breasts in order to hide *their innermost thoughts* from Him? Isn't it *true* that when they cover themselves[a] with their clothes He knows what they conceal or reveal? He knows *people's* innermost thoughts.

THE FICKLENESS OF THOSE WITH LITTLE OR NO FAITH

⁶ The sustenance of every animal comes from God, He knows where it lives and where it will die. Everything is *recorded* in a clear Book. ⁷ He created the Heavens and the Earth in six days, His throne is over the water, to test who among you lives morally. *Messenger*, suppose you were to say, "You will be resurrected after death," the disbelievers would say, "This is magic." ⁸ And suppose We were to delay their punishment for a short while, they would say, "What is holding it back?" Isn't it *true* on the day that it does come upon them, it won't be deflected from them, and the very thing they used to mock will engulf them? How quickly people's mood swings from sadness to joy

⁹ If We give people a taste of Our compassion then withdraw it abruptly from them, they become broken-hearted and ungrateful. ¹⁰ And if We gave someone a taste of *Our* favours after hardship they say, "Misfortune has left me," and become thrilled and proud, ¹¹ *all* except the patient and those who perform good works; they'll have forgiveness and a great reward.

ᵃ *Sanun Sudurahum* means to sit with knees folded in front of the chest, to hide ones face, a metaphor for 'hide feelings'.

DISBELIEVERS CHALLENGED TO PRODUCE TEN CHAPTERS

[12] So is it possible that you may *think of* leaving out part of what is revealed to you, since you are troubled because they say: "Why didn't a treasure come down to him, or an angel accompany him." You are a warner. God oversees everything. [13] And they say, "He has invented it"? Say: "Then fetch ten chapters like it *that you have* invented, and call *as helpers* whomever you can besides God, if you are telling the truth. [14] And if *your witnesses* fail to respond to you, *doubters*, then be *certain* what is sent down *comes* with God's knowledge, and there is no god but Him. So will you submit *to God's will*?" [15] Whoever desires the worldly life and its attraction, We shall pay them back in full for their deeds during this life, and they won't be short-changed; [16] but, they will have nothing in the Hereafter except the Fire; their works will be worthless, and whatever they used to do will be null and void.

BELIEVERS AND DISBELIEVERS; CONTRASTING BELIEFS AND PRACTICES

[17] Can they *be compared with* someone who has clear proof from His Lord which he reads, bears witness to it and what came before it, *namely* the Book of Moses, as a guide and *Divine* kindness? These *people* believe in it. Anyone who denies from the groups allied *against you*, the Fire will be his promised destination, be in no doubt about it; it is the truth from your Lord, but most people don't believe.

THE DISBELIEVERS FAILED TO USE THE INNER EYE

[18] Who is more sinful than the one who invents lies about God? Such people will be brought before their Lord, and the witnesses will say, "These are the people who lied about their Lord." Beware, God's curse is on the wrongdoers [19] who block God's path, wishing to make it crooked, and who deny the Hereafter. [20] They couldn't thwart *God's plan* on Earth, and they had no *real* protector besides God. Their punishment will be multiplied. They were unwilling to listen, and they did not *try to* see. [21] Such people have lost themselves, and all that they used to invent has deserted them. [22] Without doubt, they will be the biggest losers in the Hereafter. [23] Those who believed, did noble deeds and were humble before their Lord, they will be the companions of Paradise, and live there forever. [24] The two types are like a deaf, blind person compared to a seeing and hearing person. Can they ever be alike? Won't you pay attention?

STORIES OF SEVEN PROPHETS: NOAH TRIES TO REASON WITH HIS PEOPLE

[25] We sent Noah to his people, *saying*, "I am a clear warner to you. [26] Worship God

alone. I fear for you the torment of an agonizing day." ²⁷ So, the leaders of the disbelievers said, "It's clear to us that you are human like us, and only the lowest of our society follow you, and we don't see you have any special quality that we lack. On the contrary, we think you are liars." ²⁸ *Noah* said, "My people, haven't you considered what if I have the clear proof from My Lord, and that He's blessed me with kindness? If you are blind *to the truth*, could we force it on you against your will? ²⁹ My people, I am not asking you for wealth in return. My reward comes from God alone. I am not driving away the believers. They will meet their Lord, but it's clear to me that you are ignorant people. ³⁰ My people, suppose I drove them away, who would help me against God? Why do you not pay attention? ³¹ I am not telling you I have *access to* God's treasures, or knowledge of the unseen, or I am an angel; and I *will* not tell those you look down on that they will be deprived of God's goodness – God knows best what is in their hearts – *if I said these things*, I would be a wrongdoer."

NOAH'S PEOPLE ASK FOR PUNISHMENT

³² They said, "Noah, you argued with us, and have gone on arguing with us *for a long time*, so now bring us what you promised if you are telling the truth." ³³ He said, "Only God can bring it on you if He wishes, and you won't be able to stop it. ³⁴ Nor will my advice benefit you no matter how much I advise you, if God wants you to go astray.[a] He is your Lord, and to Him you will return." ³⁵ Sometimes they say, "He has invented it"? Say: "If I invented it, then my sins will fall on me, but I am innocent of the sins that you commit."

NOAH IS INSTRUCTED TO BUILD A SHIP

³⁶ It was revealed to Noah: "No one else from your people will believe except those who have already done so, so don't be saddened by what they have done. ³⁷ Build a ship under Our supervision and guidance, and don't ask Me to *sympathize for* evildoers: they are *as good as* drowned." ³⁸ Whenever the leaders of his people passed by him building the ship, they mocked him, and he would say: "If you mock us, we too shall be mocking you in the same way. ³⁹ You will *come to* learn *soon enough* who will be humiliated, and deserves an everlasting punishment."

---

[a]   Literally "He will lead you astray", has been interpreted as "He will punish you for your sins". Here I have expressed this as human choice, God doesn't compel people to believe.

THE FLOOD COMES!

[40] *Finally*, by Our order, the baked Earth started flooding *with water.*[b] We said to *Noah*: "Load the ship with a pair of each *animal*, as well as your family – except those against whom Our sentence has been passed – and whoever believes." Those who believed in him were few. [41] "Board her," he said, "In the name of God, she will sail and weigh anchor *to rest*. My Lord is Forgiving, Kind." [42] As she set sail with them, amid waves as high as mountains, Noah called out to his son, who was standing apart from the rest: "My dear son, come on board with us. Don't stay with the disbelievers." [43] He said, "I will take refuge on a mountain, which will protect me from the *rising* waters." Noah said, "There is no protection from God's order today, except the one who He treats kindly." Then a wave came between them, and *his son* drowned. [44] *A voice* called out: "Earth, swallow your water!" And "Sky, clear away *the clouds* and the water receded!" *God's* order was carried out, and *the ship* came to rest on Mount Judi.[c] A *voice* said: "Away with the wrongdoers!"

NOAH IS TOLD NOT TO MOURN HIS SON'S DEATH

[45] Noah called out to His Lord, "My Lord, my son was a member of my family; Your promise is true, and You are the best judge." [46] *God* said, "Noah, he wasn't *a member* of your family his deeds were evil; so don't ask Me about things which you don't know. I am warning you, in case you become ignorant people." [47] He said, "My Lord, I seek your refuge from asking You about things I don't know. If you don't forgive me and show compassion to me, I will be a loser." [48] *A voice* said, "Noah, disembark with peace and blessings from Us and on the nations *who will be the descendants* of those who are with you. There will be *other* nations We shall grant enjoyment *for a while*, but then afflict them with a painful punishment." [49] This is an account from the unseen that We revealed to you, *Messenger,* neither you nor your people knew it before this. So be patient, the future shall be good for those mindful *of God.*

PROPHET HUD PROMISES PROSPERITY IF THEY REPENT

[50] *We sent* Hud, their brother, to *the people of* Ad, he told them: "My people, wor-

---

[b]   *Tannur* literally means a clay oven or kiln, but here it is the sun-baked river bank or the shore of the lake around which they lived.

[c]   The precise location of Mount Judi is not clear. Some say it's near Lake Van in Eastern Turkey.

ship God. You have no other god but Him. You have invented idols. [51] My people, I am not asking you for any reward, my reward comes from Him Who created me, don't you understand? [52] My people, seek your Lord's forgiveness and turn to Him in repentance, and He will give you plentiful rain and make you stronger. Don't turn away as sinners." The people refused to listen

[53] They said, "Hud, you haven't brought us any proof. We won't give up our gods because of your words. We don't believe you. [54] We think some of our gods have made you mad." He said, "I call God as my witness – and you be witnesses – I am free from those you associate with Him. [55] So plot against me, all of you, and grant me no respite. [56] I have put my trust in God, my Lord and yours. There isn't a single creature whose destiny He doesn't control.[a] My Lord *guides me* along a straight path. [57] If you turn away, *so be it*. I have conveyed what I was sent with to you. My Lord will get other people to succeed you, and you can't harm Him in the least. My Lord oversees everything."

GOD'S CURSE TRACKS THE EVILDOERS

[58] When Our verdict came to pass, We rescued Hud and the believers with him, We were kind and saved them from a severe punishment. [59] Such was *the story* of Ad. They rejected their Lord's signs, disobeyed His messengers, and adopted the way of every stubborn tyrant. [60] They were tracked in this *world* by *God's* curse and *again* on Judgement Day. Didn't Ad reject their Lord? Away with Ad, the people of Hud.

PEOPLE DEFY SALIH'S CALL NOT TO HARM THE SHE-CAMEL

[61] *We sent* their brother Salih *to people of* Thamud, he told *them*: "My people, worship God. You have no other god but Him. It is He Who raised you up in *this* land and helped you to settle in it, so seek His forgiveness and turn to Him in repentance. My Lord is near, and answers the *prayers*." [62] They said, "Salih, before this *preaching* we had pinned our hopes on you, are you forbidding us to worship what our forefathers worshipped? We have grave doubts about what you are calling us to."

[a] Literally means "He has hold of them by their forelocks", which is an idiom for God's control over the destiny of His creation.

THE MIRACLE OF THE SHE-CAMEL

[63] He said, "My people don't you realise I have clear proof from My Lord, He's been kind to me. If I disobeyed Him, Who would help me against Him? *In that case*, you would only add to my loss. [64] My people, this is the she-camel of God, a sign for you. Let her graze *wherever she wants* in God's Earth, and don't harm her, or else you'll be quickly punished." [65] They hamstrung her, so *Salih* said, "For three days, enjoy yourselves in your homes: that's no idle threat." [66] When Our decree came to pass, We rescued Salih and the believers with him from that day's humiliation, an act of Our kindness. Your Lord is the Powerful, the Almighty. [67] A single blast devastated the wrongdoers and, when morning came, there they lay, dead in their homes, [68] as though they never existed. Listen, Thamud rejected their Lord. So away with Thamud!

THE ANGELS VISIT ABRAHAM WITH GOOD AND BAD NEWS

[69] Our A*ngel* messengers came to Abraham with good news, greeting him; "Peace!" He *greeted them* with peace too, and he quickly brought them a roasted calf. [70] However, when he saw their hands were not reaching for it, he felt uneasy about them, which gradually turned to fright. "Fear not," they said, "We've been sent to the people of Lot." [71] His wife, who was standing *nearby*, laughed, so We gave her good news of Isaac and, after Isaac, of Jacob. [72] "How come!" She said, "How will I have a child, when I am an old woman and my husband is an old man? This will be an odd thing." [73] "Are you surprised at God's command?" They said, "May God's compassion and blessings be on you, people of *this* household. He is Praiseworthy, Glorious." [74] Once Abraham's fear lessened, and the good news had sunk in, he began to plead with Us about the people of Lot: [75] Abraham was gentle, soft-hearted and devout. [76] "Abraham," We told him, "put this aside. *The time for* Your Lord's command has come, and the punishment can't be turned back, it will come to them."

THE ANGELS VISIT LOT TO WARN HIM OF HIS PEOPLE'S FATE

[77] When Our *angel* messengers came to Lot, he was sad and anxious about them, saying, "What a dreadful day this is!" [78] His people, who committed evil deeds came hurriedly to him; he said, "My people, my daughters and the tribe's women are far purer for you[b]. So fear God, and don't shame me in front of my guests.

---

[b] Prophet Lot is telling them to behave themselves and satisfy their desires with their wives.

Isn't there a single sensible man among you?" [79] They said, "You know we have no right to your tribes daughters, *just as* you know what we want." [80] "If only I had power against you," he said, "or I had a strong supporting group to protect me." [81] "Lot, we are your Lord's messengers," *the angels* said, "They will not get you, so leave with your family in the dark of the night, and let none of you turn back to look. Only your wife will suffer the fate of the others. Their appointed time is the morning. Won't it be morning soon?" [82] When *at last the time* came for Our command *to be fulfilled*, We turned their town upside down, and We continuously pelted it with stones of baked clay. [83] *The site* has been clearly marked out by Your Lord, and it is by no means far from the wrongdoers *of Makkah*.[a]

JETHRO WARNS HIS PEOPLE AGAINST FRAUDULENT PRACTISES

[84] *We sent* their brother Jethro to Madyan, he told *them*: "My people worship God. You have no god but Him. Don't *cheat by giving* in short measure or weights; you are well off, but I fear for you the punishment of an overwhelming day. [85] My people, be scrupulously honest in your weights and measures, and don't defraud people out of what is theirs or wander around making trouble in the land. [86] The profit margin *permitted* by God should be sufficient earnings for you, if you were believers, and I am not *your guardian*." [87] They said, "Jethro, does your prayer teach you to stop us from worshipping what our forefathers worshipped and doing as we please with our wealth? You are too civil and sensible!"

JETHRO WARNS HIS PEOPLE

[88] He said, "My people, don't you realise that I have clear proof from My Lord, Who has generously provided for me. I don't want to do anything that I forbid you to do; I wish to reform *society* to the best of my ability. My success depends entirely on God, I have put my trust in Him and I turn in repentance to Him. [89] My people, don't let your hostility to me lead you to the same *fate* as the people of Noah, Hud, Salih; and *remember* the people of Lot *didn't live* far away from you.[b] [90] So seek your Lord's forgiveness and then turn to Him in repentance. In-

---

[a]   Lot's town was on the trading route north from Makkah to Syria, and was a terrifying reminder to the passers-by of what happens to those who rebel against God.

[b]   The reference here to the people of Lot is significant. Many commentators interpret the distance as one of time. However, it's possible to see in this verse a sort of moral equivalence is being drawn between the evils of all these peoples: a society that practises wholesale cheating and fraud is every bit as deserving of God's wrath as another that mocks His signs, or one that has given itself over to sexual lewdness.

deed, My Lord is Most Kind, Loving."

EMPTY THREATS FROM JETHRO'S PEOPLE

⁹¹ "Jethro," they said, "We don't understand most of your preaching, and consider you to be the weak one among us, were it not for your clan, we would have stoned you, we have no respect for you." ⁹² "My people," he said, "is my clan dearer to you than God, that you should *ignore Him and* put Him behind you? My Lord is aware of what you do. ⁹³ My people, do as you see fit, and I will do *likewise*. You will come to know *soon* who will suffer a humiliating punishment and who is a liar. *So* watch carefully, and I will watch with you!" ⁹⁴ When Our decree came to pass, We rescued Jethro with dignity and those who believed in him. A single blast devastated the wrongdoers, and when morning came, there they laid in their homes, dead. ⁹⁵ As though they had never existed. Away with Madyan, just as Thamud were done away with!

MOSES IS SENT TO PHARAOH

⁹⁶ We sent Moses with Our signs and clear authority ⁹⁷ to Pharaoh and his courtiers, who *chose* to follow Pharaoh's plan, although Pharaoh's plan was not well thought out. ⁹⁸ On Judgement Day, he will walk ahead of his people and take them to the Fire. What a dreadful pit to be taken to! ⁹⁹ *God's* curse tracked them in this *world* and *again* on Judgement Day. What a dreadful gift to be given!

GOD WRONGS NO ONE, PEOPLE WRONG THEMSELVES

¹⁰⁰ We told you these stories about some of the towns; some are still standing and *others* have been razed to the ground. ¹⁰¹ We didn't wrong them, they wronged themselves. The gods they used to call on beside God didn't benefit them at all when Your Lord's verdict came to pass; they only increased their devastation. ¹⁰² That is how your Lord snatches away towns that are steeped in evil: His punishment is severely painful. ¹⁰³ In this are signs for anyone who fears the punishment of the Hereafter, a day when humanity will be gathered, a day to be witnessed.

PEOPLE WILL BE DIVIDED INTO TWO GROUPS

¹⁰⁴ We will delay it only for a limited time. ¹⁰⁵ *That* day, when it comes, not a soul will speak without His permission, and some of them will be miserably sad whilst others will be happy. ¹⁰⁶ The sad ones will be tossed in the Fire, where *they will* scream and groan, ¹⁰⁷ staying there until the Heavens and Earth remain, unless it

pleases your Lord *to do* otherwise. Your Lord does what He pleases. [108] The happy ones will be in Paradise, staying there if the Heavens and Earth remain, unless it pleases your Lord *to do* otherwise, an infinite gift. [109] So don't be doubtful about what these people worship; they worship what their forefathers worshipped before *them*, and We will give them their share *in full*, without reduction.

MUSLIMS ARE REMINDED TO AVOID SECTARIANISM

[110] We gave Moses the Book, but *his followers* disagreed about it, and if it had not been for an earlier decree issued by Your Lord, *the matter* would have been settled between them; *meanwhile* they remain in grave doubt about it. [111] Every one *of them* will be repaid in full by your Lord *according to* their deeds. He is aware of what they do. [112] So remain firm, just as you have been told, *you* and those who have repented with you, and don't exceed the limits. *God* sees whatever you do.

AVOID WRONGDOING, PRAY REGULARLY AND BE PATIENT

[113] Don't be persuaded by those who do wrong, then you'll be punished with fire; and, as you have no protectors besides God, you won't be helped *in any way*. [114] Perform the prayer at both ends of the day and in some part of the night. Good deeds shall erase evil deeds. That is a *powerful* reminder for the mindful people. [115] Be patient, for God doesn't waste the reward of the righteous. [116] If only there had been *more* righteous people in the previous generations who prevented corruption in the land! We saved few of them whilst the wrongdoers enjoyed the luxuries of life and continued sinning. [117] Your Lord would never destroy a town unjustly whilst its citizens were acting righteously.

RELIGIOUS DIFFERENCES ARE PART OF THE DIVINE PLAN

[118] If your Lord wanted, He could have made people a single nation, but *that's not the case* so they continue to differ; [119] except anyone who is treated kindly by God: that's why He created them. Your Lord's decree: "I shall fill up Hell with jinn and humans," is fulfilled. [120] We tell you the stories of the messengers to make your heart strong, and what has come to you in this *account* is the truth, teachings and a reminder for the believers. [121] Tell those who don't believe: "Do as you see fit, and we will do *likewise*. [122] Wait *and see*, for we too are waiting." [123] God knows the secrets of the Heaven and the Earth, and all that exists will be returned to Him; so worship Him and put your trust in Him. Your Lord isn't unaware of what you do.

12. Yusuf
The Prophet Joseph

This is a late Makkan chapter revealed some time after *Chapter Hud*. It tells the story of Prophet Joseph, and is called "the most beautiful story" (3). It employs a commanding narrative that is lyrical at times, with an outstanding drama woven around moral and spiritual values. Deeply embedded in Quranic guidance, values such as truthfulness, patience, modesty, justice, forgiveness, kindness and courage are presented in a variety of contexts in this story, to show that in the end they will prevail over tyranny and immorality. Joseph was the great grandson of the Prophet Abraham, this would be approximately 1600 bc.

The Bible also tells the story of Joseph, in Genesis 37 and 39. The Biblical story contrasts in tone and tenor with the Quranic narration; it appears as an account of the envy between brothers, the youthful naiveté of Joseph, romance and his triumph over his brothers. It stresses the cleverness of a young bureaucrat against the Egyptians; he takes advantage of the famine and buys the cattle of the Egyptians cheaply for the King. However, the Quranic story is free from such charges against a prophet of God. Through its twenty-seven scenes, Chapter Joseph effectively plots the complexity of human life, and sudden and unexpected changes in fortunes: one moment living at home, the next languishing in a dark, dank well; one moment enjoying life in a palace, the next in prison; one moment a prisoner, the next a Prince. The story of Joseph provides a real-life illustration of a Quranic principle: "Sometimes you may dislike something that is good for you, and sometimes you may like something that is bad for you. Only God knows *the whole truth*, not you" (*Al-Baqarah* 2: 216). The chapter teaches that life on Earth is an extraordinary gift, full of trials and tribulations, and with endless opportunities. The message is patience and perseverance give plentiful fruit; on the other hand, short-term instant gratification can be damaging.

The eloquence and the stylistic features of the chapter consists of series of scenes, one after the other, carrying on with the main narrative which then leads to next. Each scene has a rich dialogue and detail that produce a well-knit passage. Throughout the story, the faith of Prophet Joseph helps him maintain integrity. When he was thrown into a well, God reassured him: "*One day* you will tell them about their conspiracy, at a time when they least expect it" (15). Similarly, when the governor's wife tries to seduce him the Quran demonstrates the delicacy and propriety required for the discussion of sexual matters, and at the same time it reveals the modesty and loyalty of Joseph: "She tried to seduce," yet he said, "God forbid!" (23).

This is a model of self-control, loyalty and restraint. What a difficult test for someone in the prime of his youth! Yet Joseph was no ordinary young man. He feared God, with a religious identity and a sense of personal honour. Young people today can learn a great deal from the modesty of Joseph .

In conclusion, we may have great dreams, but God fulfils them in different ways. The boyhood dream of Joseph was about becoming a king, but God had a far greater plan for him: to be his Prophet, who would teach *Tawhid* and who would save Egypt. So, when life gets tough; and you suffer at the hands of those from whom you least expect it, don't complain! Be patient; remember the patience of Jacob , and Joseph .

In the name of God, the Kind, the Caring.

¹ *Alif Lam Ra.*

THE MOST BEAUTIFUL STORY

These are the verses of a clear Book. ² We revealed it as an Arabic Quran so you may understand. ³ We will tell you the most beautiful story by revealing to you this Quran, *a story of which* you were unaware before.

YOUNG JOSEPH DREAMS

⁴ *Consider* when Joseph said to his father, "My dear father, I saw eleven stars, the sun and the moon, all prostrating before me." ⁵ *Jacob* said, "My dear son, don't tell your brothers your dream, they will hatch a plot against you, Satan is a sworn enemy of humanity. ⁶ This *dream shows* your Lord has chosen you, will teach you interpretations of dreams,ᵃ and fulfil His favour on you and the family of Jacob just as He fulfilled it on your forefathers, Abraham and Isaac. Your Lord is Knowing, Wise.

THE BROTHERS HATCH A NASTY PLOT

⁷ In the story of Joseph and his brothers there are signs for the questioners. ⁸ When *the step-brothers* whined, "Our father loves Joseph and his brother more than us, even though we are a large group; our father is obviously mistaken."ᵇ ⁹ "Kill Joseph," *said one of them*, "or get rid of him in a *far-off* land, so you will have your father's full attention; afterwards you can be good. ¹⁰ Another spoke out, "Don't kill Joseph, if you are determined to do something, throw him into the bottom of a well. Perhaps a *passing* caravan will pick him up." ¹¹ *So* they said, "Our father,

---

ᵃ   'Interpretation of dreams' also implies 'problem-solving'. As we will see Joseph solved the problems of other people.

ᵇ   Joseph and his brother Benjamin were the son's of Jacob's wife Rachel and the other 10 children were his half-brothers.

why don't you trust us with Joseph, though we are sincere *about* him. [12] Tomorrow, send him with us so he may enjoy himself and play, and we'll take good care of him." [13] *Jacob* said, "The *mere* thought of you taking him worries me, and I am afraid that a wolf might *snatch and* eat him whilst you are not paying attention to him." [14] They said, "How could a wolf eat him when we are a large group, then we would be losers."

JOSEPH ACCOMPANIES HIS BROTHERS

[15] So, having taken him, they agreed to leave him at the bottom of a well. We inspired him: "*One day* you will tell them about this conspiracy of theirs, at a time when they least expect it." [16] That late evening they came to their father crying, [17] saying: "Our father, we went off to race one another, leaving Joseph with our belongings, and the wolf *came and* ate him. Though we're telling the truth, you won't believe us." [18] *Then* they brought his shirt, *stained* with false blood. *Jacob* said, "You've made *all* this up. I will bear patiently, patience is a beautiful quality. God is *My only* supporter against what you describe."

JOSEPH SOLD AS A SLAVE

[19] Along came a caravan, sending their water-bearer *on ahead*; as he lowered his bucket, he shouted, "Great news! There's a boy here." *Then* they hid him with their goods, but God was aware what they did. [20] They sold him for a paltry price, a few silver coins, because they weren't interested in him.[c] [21] The Egyptian[d] who bought him said to his wife, "Look after him well. He could be useful to us, or else we could adopt him as a son." That's how We settled Joseph in the land of Egypt, and taught him to interpret dreams; God had complete control of *Joseph 's* situation, but most people are ignorant. [22] When he reached maturity, We gave him wisdom and knowledge; that is how We reward the righteous.

THE CAPTAIN'S WIFE TRIES TO SEDUCE JOSEPH

[23] The lady in whose house he was *living* tried to seduce him, bolting the doors and saying, "Come here!" "God forbid!" He said, "My master has given me a good home, and, *in any case*, wrongdoers never succeed." [24] She lusted for him,

[c] 'Zuhd' is to be indifferent; refuse to have anything to do with someone or something. The people of the caravan weren't at all interested in Joseph, they didn't value him,

[d] In the Bible (Genesis 39: 1), the Egyptian was called Potiphar, the captain of the Pharaoh's guard. Notice the difference Potiphar valued Joseph highly.

and he would have desired her *too* if he hadn't seen *overwhelming* proof from his Lord; that was how We deflected the evil and indecency away from him. He was one of Our devoted servants. [25] They raced to the door, and she tore his shirt from behind; there, at the door, they bumped into her husband. "What should be the punishment for someone who wishes to harm your family," she cried, "except imprisonment or torture?" [26] *Joseph* cried out, "She's the one who tried to seduce me!" A member of her household recommended, "If his shirt is torn from the front then she's telling the truth, and he's lying; [27] but if his shirt is torn from behind then she's lying, and he's telling the truth." [28] When *her husband* saw the shirt was torn from behind, he said, "This *cunning* scheme of yours; is a big trick, [29] Joseph overlook this," *and told his wife*, "Seek forgiveness for your sin, you are wrong."

Rumours of seduction soon spread

[30] Some *prominent* women of the city *began* to say, "The captain's wife was in love with her servant; she has fallen in love. We believe she is wrong." [31] After hearing their gossip, she sent for them, and prepared sofas for them *at a banquet*, giving each of them a knife *before telling Joseph*, "Go out to *present yourself before* them." When they saw him, they were captivated by *his beauty*, and cut their hands and said, "God the Great! This is no mortal. This can only be a splendid great angel." [32] Then she said, "That's the one you blamed me for. I tried to seduce him, but he held back. However, if he doesn't do as I tell him now, he will go to prison and be disgraced."

Joseph prays to God for help

[33] "My Lord," said Joseph, "I prefer prison to what they tell me to do. If You hadn't deflected their *cunning* scheme from me, I would have yielded to them and acted unwisely." [34] His Lord accepted his prayer and deflected their scheme away from him. He is the Listener, the Knower. [35] And so, even after seeing the evidence, of his innocence they thought it is right to imprison him for a short term.

Joseph preaches *Tawhid* in the prison

[36] Two young men entered the prison with him, one asked him, "I had a dream, I was pressing grapes," the other said, "I had a dream, I was carrying bread on my head and birds were eating from it. Tell us their meaning, we see you're a righteous person." [37] He said, "I will tell you their meaning before your *next* meal

arrives, it's one of the things My Lord has taught me. I have kept away from the religion of people who don't believe in God and who deny the Hereafter, [38] I follow *instead* the religion of my forefathers Abraham, Isaac and Jacob. The associating of anything with God is not for us; that is one of God's favours to us and to people *generally*, but most people are ungrateful. [39] My fellow prisoners, tell me, are many gods better or the One, God, the Supreme? [40] Whatever you worship besides Him are only names you and your forefathers coined, God hasn't revealed any authority for them. *Ultimate* authority belongs to God alone; He has commanded you to worship Him alone. That's the true religion, unfortunately, most people are ignorant.

JOSEPH INTERPRETS THE BAKER AND THE BUTLER'S DREAMS

[41] My fellow inmates, one of you will serve wine to his master *once more*; sadly, the other will be crucified, and the birds will peck his head. The matter on which you sought my opinion has *already* been decided." [42] Then *Joseph* asked the one who he knew would be spared, "Mention me to your master." However, Satan made him forget to mention him to his master, and so Joseph lingered in the prison for several years.

JOSEPH EXPLAINS THE KING'S BAFFLING DREAM

[43] The King said, "I had a dream of seven fat cows eating seven lean ones, and of seven green ears *of grain* and *seven* others all dried up. Counsellors, advise me concerning my dream, if you can interpret dreams." [44] They replied, "What baffling dreams! We have no expertise in interpreting dreams." [45] Then the one who had been spared of the two *in prison finally* remembered *Joseph* after a long time, said, "I can tell you how to interpret it, so send me." [46] *Returning to the prison, he said,* "Joseph, you who tells the truth, advise us concerning seven fat cows eating seven lean, and seven green ears *of grain* and *seven* others all dried up, so that I may go back to the people, so they may know." [47] *Joseph* said, "For seven years you will plant *crops* as normal, but you will leave what you harvest in the ears, except for a small amount that you will eat. [48] This will be followed by seven years of hardship, during which you will consume all but a little of what you have stored. [49] After that will come a year of rain aplenty, in which people will press *grapes for wine*."

JOSEPH DEMANDS HIS NAME BE CLEARED

[50] "Bring him to me," said the King, when the King's envoy came to him, *Joseph*

told him, "Go back to your master and let him inquire about the women who cut their hands. My Lord knows all about their *cunning* scheme." [51] So *the King* asked *the women*, "What happened when you tried to seduce Joseph?" They said, "God the Great! We know nothing bad about him." Then the captain's wife said, "Now the truth is out. It was me who tried to seduce him, and he told the truth." [52] *Joseph said, "All* this was so that my master would know I didn't betray him in his absence," and God does not guide the schemers of cunning plots. [53] "I don't claim to be blameless *since* human ego continually incites one to do evil, except when My Lord is kind to me. My Lord is Forgiving, Kind."

JOSEPH IS APPOINTED THE TREASURER OF EGYPT

[54] "Bring him to me," the King said, "I will select him for my personal service." Once he had interviewed him, he said, "From this day *on*, you will hold a position of trust with us." [55] "Put me in charge of the country's stores," *Joseph* said, "*for* I am prudent and knowledgeable." [56] And that is how We gave Joseph power to exercise in the land *of Egypt*, and to live wherever he wished. We treat anyone kindly, and never allow the reward of the righteous to be lost. [57] And the reward of the Hereafter is even better for those who believe and are mindful *of God*.

JOSEPH'S BROTHERS VISIT EGYPT

[58] *Years later,* Joseph's brothers came and entered his office, and he recognised them *at once*, but they didn't recognise him. [59] After he had supplied them with their provisions, he said, "Bring me a *half*-brother of yours from your father's side. Don't you see that I am honest in my measures, and that I am the best host? [60] If you fail to bring him to me then you won't get a single measure from me, nor should you approach me *ever again*." [61] "We will try to persuade his father," they said, "We will certainly do that." [62] And *so Joseph* told his servants, "Put the goods they exchanged with us back in their saddlebags so they recognise them when they return to their family and, hopefully, they will come back."

JOSEPH'S BROTHERS ARE OVERJOYED

[63] When they returned to their father, they said, "Father, we will be stopped from taking *a single* measure next time so send our brother along with us so that we may get more. We will take care of him." [64] He said, "If I entrust you with him, won't it be the same as before, when I entrusted you with his brother? God is the best guardian, and He is the most kind." [65] When they opened their saddlebags, they

found their goods were returned to them, *so* they said, "Our father, what *more* do we want? These goods of ours have been returned to us. We can provide for our family, take care of our brother, and we'll get an extra camel-load. That would be an easy load!"

JACOB RELUCTANTLY SENDS BENJAMIN

66 "I will not send him with you," said *Jacob*, "until you give me *a* solemn pledge by God to bring him back safely to me unless it happens that if you are ambushed." When they had given their pledge to him, he said, "God is the Guardian over what we have pledged *here*."

ADVICE ON HOW TO AVOID THE EVIL EYE

67 He said, "My sons, don't enter together through one gate, but enter from different gates. I can't shield you against anything from God, as *ultimate* authority belongs to Him alone.[a] I have put my trust in Him, so let everyone put his trust in Him. 68 When they entered the way their father had told them, it couldn't shield them against anything from God; but, it satisfied Jacob's wish. He had knowledge that We had taught him, unfortunately most people are ignorant.

HOW JOSEPH GETS TO KEEP HIS BROTHER

69 When they entered Joseph's office again, he took his brother aside, saying, "I'm your brother. Don't be saddened by what they did." 70 After giving their provisions, he placed a drinking cup in his brother's saddlebag, then a herald called out: "*people of the* caravan, you are thieves." 71 "What have you lost?" *The brothers* said, as they turned to face them. 72 "We have lost the King's measuring bowl," they said, "and whoever brings it back will get an *extra* camel-load; I guarantee it." 73 "By God," they said, "you know that we didn't come to make trouble in the land, nor are we thieves." 74 *They* said, "What is the penalty, if you are lying?" 75 "In whoever's saddlebag *the measuring bowl* is found will have to give himself up and *become a slave*," *the brothers* said, "that is how we punish wrongdoers." [b]76 So *Joseph* began by searching their bags before his brother's bag, then he produced *the goblet* from his brothers. That is how We devised a plan for Joseph to succeed.

---

[a] Imam Razi gives two explanations of this order of Jacob: If a band of strong men entered from one gate of the city, it could arouse suspicion and they could be arrested, secondly (the one Imam Razi prefers), to avoid the evil eye. The Messenger 🕌 said "An evil eye can drive a person into a grave and a Camel into a cooking pot".

[b] Joseph gives a gift of a precious drinking cup to his brother. The King's measuring bowl was misplaced by the guards and they suspected it was stolen by the brothers.

It would not have been proper for him to arrest his brother under the king's law, unless God had so willed. We elevate in rank anyone We please; and above every knowledgeable person is the One who knows all.

The brothers plead in vain for Benjamin's freedom

[77] "If he has stolen," the brothers said, "then his full-brother before him also stole." Joseph kept *his feelings* to himself and didn't reveal anything to them. *Instead* he said, "You are *all* in far worse position. God is well aware of what you describe." [78] "Your Lordship," they said, "his father is an old man, so arrest one of us instead. We consider you to be a gracious person." [79] "God forbid! We should arrest anyone other than him in whose possession we found our belongings," he said, "Then we would be *blatant* wrongdoers." [80] When they were hopeless about him *changing his mind*, they went off into a huddle *to talk privately*, and the eldest of them said, "Don't you know that your father took *your* solemn pledge by God because you had previously been negligent with Joseph? I won't leave this land until either my father gives me permission or else God decides for me, He is the best Judge."

The brothers return home bearing sad news

[81] Go back to your father and say, "Our father, your son has stolen." *They told him,* "We are only testifying to what we know, and we could not *be expected to protect* against the unforeseen. [82] Ask the townsfolk where we have been and the caravan with whom we travelled. We're telling the truth." [83] "On the contrary," *Jacob* said, "you have made *all* this up. It's better to be patient! It may be that God brings them all back to me, for it is He Who is Knowing, Wise."

Jacob cries for the loss of his sons

[84] *Jacob* turned away from them, saying, "Oh, how I grieve for Joseph!" His eyes *clouded over*, turning white, such was his sadness; yet he controlled his emotions. [85] "By God," they said, "Will you never stop mentioning Joseph until you become ill or die?" [86] "I am complaining to God of My deep sorrow and sadness," Jacob said, "I have knowledge from God that you don't. [87] My sons, go and search for Joseph and his brother; don't despair of God's kindness, it is only the disbelievers who despair of God's kindness."

The great forgiveness

[88] When they entered *again* into *Joseph's* office, they said, "Your Lordship, severe

hardship has struck us and our family. We have brought but a few goods, so give in full measure and be charitable to us; the reward of the charitable rests with God." [89] He said, "Do you *now* know what you did to Joseph and his brother when you were ignorant?" [90] They said, "Joseph, is that really you?" "I am Joseph," he said, "and this is my brother. God has favoured us. Whoever is mindful *of God* and is patient, God will not waste the reward of the righteous." [91] "By God," they said, "God has preferred you over us, and we are the sinners." [92] Joseph said, "There is no blame on you today. God will forgive you, for He is the most Kind."

THE MIRACLE OF JOSEPH'S SHIRT

[93] *Then Joseph said,* "Take this shirt of mine, and place it over my father's face, and his sight will return; then bring your whole family *here* to me." [94] Once the caravan had set off *from Egypt,* their father said, "I smell Joseph 's breath *in the air,* even though you might think I am senile." [95] *Those around him* said, "By God, you are back to your old love again." [96] But when the bearer of good news came and placed *the shirt* over his face, his eyesight returned, he said, "Did I not tell you that I have knowledge from God that you don't have?" [97] "Our father," *the brothers* said, "seek forgiveness for our sins, we have been sinners." [98] He said, "I will seek my Lord's forgiveness for you," Jacob said, " He is the Forgiver, the Kind."

JOSEPH THANKS GOD FOR THE FULFILMENT OF HIS DREAM

[99] When they entered Joseph's office, he received his parents as honoured guests, saying, "Enter Egypt, God willing, in safety." [100] As he invited his parents to sit on the throne, they fell before him in prostration. *Joseph* said, "My dear father, this is the meaning of my long ago dream, which My Lord has made come true. *God* has been gracious to me, getting me out of the prison and bringing you from the desert after Satan had sown enmity between me and my brothers. My Lord has made it come true as He pleases. He is the Knower, the Wise.

JOSEPH'S PRAYER

[101] My Lord, you have given me power and authority and taught me how to interpret dreams,[a] Creator of the Heavens and Earth, You are my Protector in this world and the Hereafter; let me die submitting *to Your will,* and include me among the righteous."

[a] It also means "taught me to solve problems, to find solutions." Joseph solved the problems of the Butler and the King.

The Prophet ﷺ is reminded

[102] *This is one of the accounts of the unseen that We have revealed to you; and you were not there with them, Messenger, when they conspired to hatch a plot against Joseph.* [103] Most people will never believe, no matter how keen you are *to guide them,* [104] you don't seek reward for it from them. This *Quran* is a reminder for humanity.

Signs of God's Creative power

[105] How many signs in the Heaven and Earth do they pass by and they turn their backs to. [106] Most of them will believe in God whilst also associating partners with Him. [107] Are they insured against being overwhelmed by God's punishment, or being taken all of a sudden and unaware by the Final Hour? [108] Say: "This is the path that I am on: I call others to God. I and those who follow me base our beliefs on clear evidence. Glory be to God! I am no associator of partners with God." [109] Even before you, Messenger, the men who We sent, and to who We revealed Our signs to, were townsfolk. Have the disbelievers not travelled about the land and seen how the end came to those who rejected God's signs before them? The home in the Hereafter is much better for the mindful. Doesn't any one of you understand? [110] When the messengers lost hope in outward signs of success, and the disbelievers believed they were lied to, then Our help came to them.[a] Whoever We wanted was saved, but nothing can turn away Our punishment from the guilty. [111] In the story of Joseph and his brothers, there is a lesson for those who understand. It isn't a made-up account, but confirmation of what happened in the past, it explains all things, a guidance that is useful for those who believe.

---

[a]   Abdullah ibn Abbas used to recite the verse "...even the Messenger *of that time* and those who believed him cried out: 'When will God's help come?' The help of God is near" (2: 214). Meaning they were frustrated with their people and lost hope in them but they were never hopeless of God's kindness.

13. Ar-Raʿd
The Thunder

The central theme of this late Makkan chapter is to grasp the Greatness of God, as stated in scripture and nature. Nature, like the scripture, is an open book, where God's creativity can be seen, felt and experienced. On the other hand, the divine revelation brought by the prophets is a set of general teachings: moral values influencing a person's character and behaviour, and spiritual ideals that fill life with meaning and answer big questions: Who are we? Where do we come from? And where are we going?

Reason, Not Wizardry

The Makkans employed many hostile tactics to oppose the Prophet ﷺ: ran a smear campaign, mocked, ridiculed, and made physical threats. Some Muslims wished that God would send a miracle so that their fellow citizens would see and believe. However, "Even if such a Quran was revealed that could move the mountains or destroy the Earth or make dead speak *they still wouldn't believe*" (31). Miracles are not performed on request, and God doesn't want to persuade people with miraculous wizardry. Instead, the Quran offers logical reasons to believe, as well as evidence from nature, physical phenomena, and human history. These appeals to human intellect and emotions, can stir faith in God and motivate people. In other words, the Quran wants people to decide for themselves: to accept God or reject faith. It's their moral choice. The Quran states that change only comes from within: "God doesn't change the condition *of people* until they change what's in themselves" (11).

The Awesome Creation and the Infinite Knowledge of God

The chapter opens with a list of amazing natural phenomena: the sky without pillars, the rising and setting of the sun and the moon, massive mountains, running rivers, gorgeous groves of palm trees, vast vineyards, and fields of maize and wheat.

The Quran disapproves of the disbelievers' stubbornness and rejection of truth: all of this is the creation of a supreme, powerful Lord. What are their idols in comparison? However, the "intelligent people", believe the Messenger ﷺ. Verses 20–23 highlight eight of their qualities, including how they fulfil their promise with God, and develop good human relationships. The Messenger ﷺ is reassured: continue preaching confidently, already signs of victory are appearing. "Haven't they realised how We are moving forward in the land, shrinking the boundaries *of their territory*" (41). A possible reference to the group from Madinah – who had embraced Islam and were now inviting the Prophet ﷺ to come to their city – a lead up to the Hijrah and the final departure of the Prophet ﷺ from Makkah.

In the name of God, the Kind, the Caring.

[1] *Alif Lam Meem Ra.*

THE AMAZING, DIVERSE CREATION OF GOD

These are the verses of the Book that's come down to you from your Lord; it is the truth, but many people don't believe. [2] It is God Who raised the sky without any pillars that you can see; He established His throne of authority, and made the sun and the moon subject *to His will*, each one orbiting *until it sets* at an appointed time.[a] He manages the running *of the universe*, and explains the signs *of creation* so you are convinced of meeting Him. [3] He laid out the land *with mountains* and running rivers, produced fruits in pairs, and covered the day by *the darkness of* the night. Surely, in this are signs for insightful people. [4] There are neighbouring plots, vineyards, fields and palms, *growing* either in clusters or standing alone; all are fed by the same water, yet some are better to eat than others. Surely, in this are signs for people who understand.

THE DISBELIEVERS REMAIN UNCONVINCED

[5] If you are amazed *at anything*, then what is more amazing than their slogan: "How can we be created anew once we have turned to dust?" They disbelieve their Lord. Such people *shall* have iron collars around their necks, and they'll be the companions of the Fire, remaining there forever. [6] They challenge you to hasten what is bad *for them* instead asking for what is good, even though *many* exemplary punishments have happened before them. Without doubt, your Lord is ever willing to forgive people their evil. But your Lord is *also* severe in *His* punishment. [7] The disbelievers say, "If only a *miraculous* sign were to come down to him from His Lord." You are a warner, and there was a guide for every nation.

CHANGE ONLY COMES FROM WITHIN

[8] God knows what every female carries, *even* the shrinking and the swelling of the wombs. Everything is *calculated* with precision for Him, [9] the Knower of the seen and unseen realms, the Great, the Highest. [10] Whether you call out quietly or loudly, or whether one tries to hide in the darkness of the night or walk in the broad daylight its all the same for Him. [11] A chain of angels in front and behind

---

[a] *Jara* in Arabic means "running" or "coursing" through the sky, however, metaphorically it means "orbiting".

him is assigned by God to watch over him. God never changes the *condition of* a nation until they change what is in themselves, and if God wanted to destroy people, no one could stop Him, and they would have no protector besides Him. [12] He displays the lightning which stirs fear and hope in you as He causes the heavy clouds to build up. [13] *Likewise* the *roaring* thunder glorifies His praise, and the angels *too glorify Him* out of awe of Him, and He sends thunderbolts, striking anyone He wants, as they continue to argue about God, He is Mighty in power.

IT IS POINTLESS TO RESIST WORSHIPPING GOD

[14] A true prayer is for Him *alone*. Those they pray to besides Him never answer, they're like a person who stretches out his hands to *catch* water to put into his mouth, but it doesn't reach it. The disbelievers' prayer is ineffective. [15] All things in the Heavens and the Earth worship God willingly or unwillingly, just as their shadows in the morning and the late afternoon do.[b] [16] Say: "Who is Lord of the Heavens and the Earth?" Say: "It's God." Say: "Have you adopted protectors besides Him that lack the power either to benefit or harm *even* themselves?" Say *to them*: "Are the blind and the sighted equal, or is darkness and light the same?" Or have they assigned partners to God who have created *something* so like His creation, so *this* creation *of theirs* appears indistinguishable to them? Say: "God is the Creator of everything, and He is the One, the Compelling."

ONLY THE VALUABLE THINGS REMAIN

[17] He brings rain from the sky that flood the valleys, as the flash flood flows carrying away the surface froth, and from *the ores* that *blacksmiths* smelt in the fire to make jewellery and tools, a similar froth appears. This is how God illustrates truth and falsehood. The froth is carried away like garbage, but *the* useful *minerals* remain in the Earth for people. This is how God gives examples. [18] An excellent reward *awaits* those who have responded to their Lord, but those who ignored Him, even if they owned everything on Earth twice over, they would try to ransom themselves with it. They'll have an evil reckoning, and remain in Hell, a dreadful resting place!

THE PEOPLE OF UNDERSTANDING OBEY THE LORD

[19] Can the one who knows the truthfulness of what's revealed to you by Your Lord

---

[b]   This is one of the verses of prostration in the Quran.

be compared to the blind? Only the understanding will note the warning. [20] *They* fulfil their contract with God and don't break their pledge, [21] they maintain the ties *of kinship* as instructed by God, fear their Lord, afraid of an evil reckoning, [22] and are steadfast in seeking their Lord's pleasure, performing the prayer, spending in charity openly and secretly from what We have provided them, and warding off evil with good – their reward is a home *in Paradise*. [23] They'll walk into the gardens of Paradise accompanied by their righteous forefathers, spouses and children. The angels will greet and welcome them from every gate, [24] saying, "Peace be on you for your steadfastness." How excellent is the reward of a home *in Paradise*? [25] *However*, those who break their contract with God after making a solemn pledge, and sever the ties *of kinship* God has ordered to be maintained, and spread corruption in the land are cursed, and theirs is a miserable home.

WHAT IS THE SOURCE OF LASTING HAPPINESS?

[26] God allocates sustenance to all as He pleases, measuring *it* with care. They are delighted with worldly life, yet it is only a passing pleasure compared to the Hereafter. [27] The disbelievers say, "Why doesn't a *miraculous* sign come down to him from his Lord." Say: "God allows some to go astray, but He guides to Himself anyone who repents: [28] those who believe, their hearts will find peace in God's remembrance." The fact is, hearts find peace in the remembrance of God! [29] Blessed are those who believe and perform righteous deeds, *for* them is the best place of return.

THIS QURAN IS THE MIRACLE THAT THE DISBELIEVERS SEEK

[30] This is why We've sent you *to be* among a community like many that have passed away, to recite what We have revealed to you, while they continue denying the Kind *Lord*. Say: "He is my Lord; there is no god but Him. I place my trust in Him, and I turn in repentance to Him." [31] If ever there was a Quran to move the mountains, or to tear down the Earth, or to make dead speak, *it would be this one*. Indeed, God has complete control *of the universe*. Haven't the believers realised, if God wanted, He could guide the whole of humanity? The disbelievers will continue to be afflicted by tragedy because of what they've done, or else it will strike near their homes until God's promise is fulfilled. God does not break *His* promise.

The disbelievers' mockery and lies are short-lived

[32] Messengers before you were mocked, the disbelievers were given a brief respite and then I would seize them. How *terrible* was My punishment! [33] Is He Who oversees every person and what it does *comparable to anything*? And they attribute partners to God. Say: "Name them. Do you *pretend to* inform Him of something on *this* Earth that He doesn't know, or is this just play with words?" Their plots appear attractive to the disbelievers, as they block the path *of God*, but those God lets to go stray will have no guide. [34] They'll be punished in this life, but the punishment of the Hereafter will be more severe, and they will have no one to protect them from God. [35] What has been promised to those who are wakeful *of God* is like a garden under which rivers flow, and whose *supply of* food and shade is endless. This is the reward of those who are mindful *of God*, whereas the reward for disbelievers will be the Fire.

People's different reactions to the Quran

[36] Those to whom We gave the Book, the Jews and Christians, are delighted at what is revealed to you, though among *their* groups are those who deny some of it. Say: "I've been ordered to worship God and not associate *anyone* with Him. I call to Him, and I'll return to Him." [37] This is how We revealed the Quran with laws in Arabic. If after *receiving* such knowledge you follow their desires, then you will have no helper or protector against God.

Reassurance for the beloved Messenger ﷺ

[38] We sent messengers before you, and gave them wives and children, they were humans. No messenger produced a miraculous sign without God's approval, and God's decree determines the right time for everything. [39] God either gets rid of things or keeps them as He pleases, and the Original Decree remains with Him.[a] [40] Whether We show you in advance something of what We have threatened them with, or whether We cause you to die first, your duty is to communicate the message, the final reckoning is Ours. [41] Haven't they realised how We are moving forward in the land, shrinking the boundaries of their territory? When God decides, no one can reverse it, and He is swift in reckoning. [42] Those who lived before them

[a]   *Umm al-Kitab* literally means "the Mother of the Decree" or Book, which refers to the *Lawh Mahfuz* (*Al-Buruj* 85: 22), "the Preserved Tablet", containing a complete record of everything that has and will ever happen or exist.

used to plot, but God controls every plot, Who knows what every person will earn. The disbelievers will learn who will have a home in Paradise. [43] The disbelievers say, "You aren't a messenger." Say: "God and those who have knowledge of the Book are a sufficient witness for me and you."

14. Ibrahim
The Prophet Abraham

This chapter was revealed in the late Makkan period, after the Prophet's 鼕 journey to Taif, two years before the Hijrah. He planned to call the Banu Thaqif to Islam, only to be shockingly thrown out of the town and pelted with stones.

The chapter begins and ends with a simple statement of the purpose of revelation: to affirm the Oneness of God, and to bring people out of the darkness of idolatry into the light of *Tawhid*. Why is true belief equated with gratitude, and so deserving of reward (7), while idolatry is associated with ingratitude (*kufr*)? It is because everything upon which we rely for our existence ultimately comes from God. To pretend that it belongs to a carved statue or idol is frankly insulting to human dignity. Those who worship idols, including the modern materialist, are reminded (9–14) of the stories they knew about the disbelievers of Noah, Ad and Thamud. A graphic account of Hell (15–17) should remind them that punishment in this world will not be the end of it.

Followed by two parables: first, the ashes scattered by the wind (18–20) to give ungrateful disbelievers pause to question the lasting value, if any, of the worldly wealth and power of which they're so proud. The second is the parable of two trees (24–27), one firmly rooted and bearing fruit, and the other uprooted and slowly rotting. The chapter ends with an account of the anguished prayer of Abraham (35– 41), seeking forgiveness for himself, his parents, and his family. The impact of these words on the pagan Arabs, who took pride in their forefather, Abraham , could have been considerable.

In the name of God, the Kind, the Caring

¹ *Alif Lam Ra.*

THE PATH OF LIGHT

This is a Book which We revealed so that you may lead humanity out of darkness into light, and on the road *to* the Almighty, *as* you have been authorised by Your Lord, the Praiseworthy, ² God; everything in the Heavens and on Earth belongs to Him. And the misery of a severe punishment *awaits* the disbelievers, ³ who prefer the worldly life to the Hereafter, they block God's path, wishing to obstruct others from it and to twist *its meanings*; such people are misled. ⁴ We never sent a messenger unless *he spoke* the language of his people, so he could explain *the message* to them; God lets anyone He wills to go off track and guides anyone who pleases Him. He is Almighty, the Wise.[a]

GRATITUDE IS GENEROUSLY REWARDED

[5] We sent Moses with Our signs, *telling him*: "Take your people out of the darkness into the light and remind them of the days of God."[b] There are signs in that for every grateful, patient person. [6] Moses said to his people, "Remember how God blessed you when He saved you from Pharaoh's people; they gave you the worst punishment *imaginable*, slaughtering your sons and leaving your women to live; that was surely a most difficult test from your Lord." [7] *Remember* when Your Lord declared, "If you are grateful, I will surely increase *My favours* to you, but if you are ungrateful, then My punishment is severe." [8] Moses said, "Even if you and everyone on Earth were to be ungrateful, God is the Self-Sufficient, the Praiseworthy."

DISBELIEVERS REACT ANGRILY WHEN TOLD ABOUT THEIR FAULTS

[9] Hasn't the story of past generations reached you: the people of Noah, Ad, Thamud, and of those after them whom only God knows? When their messengers came with clear proofs, they put their hands on their mouths *to silence them*[c] and said, "We reject what you have been sent with, and we seriously doubt what you are calling us to." [10] Their messengers replied, "Is there any doubt about *the existence of* God, Creator of the Heavens and the Earth? He invites you, so He can forgive your sins and give you time *to think* till the appointed term." *They* said, "You are a mortal like us, who wants to stop us from *worshipping* what our forefathers worshipped; so bring us a miracle." [11] The messengers said to them, "We may be humans like you, but God favours anyone of His servants He pleases. It's not for us to bring you a miracle except with God's approval, and believers *always* put their trust in God. [12] So why would we not put our trust in God when He has guided us on our paths *to His kindness*. We shall patiently endure your persecution; so let all who trust *in Him* put their trust in God."

---

[a] This is a clear statement about 'free-choice'. The 'moral choice' humans have been given. Those who want to be guided, the Lord supports, encourages and energises them to achieve (Tawfeeq). Anyone who refuses to take the opportunity is left to wonder aimlessly.

[b] "The days of God" means the time when God freed the Israelites from the Pharaoh.

[c] According to Al-Qurtubi, this Arabic idiom refers to a gesture expressing shock or anger, as in *Al 'Imran* 3: 119 ("they bite on their fingertips out of rage").

GOD TELLS THE MESSENGERS NOT TO FEAR THE DISBELIEVERS' THREATS

[13] The disbelievers said to their messengers, "We will expel you from our town unless you revert to our religion." Then their Lord revealed to them: "We will destroy the evildoers, [14] and We will settle you in this town after them. This *reward* is for anyone who's afraid of My punishment and of standing before Me *on Judgement Day*."

SIPPING SCALDING WATER IN HELL

[15] *They* prayed to win *over their people*, and *the scheming of* every stubborn tyrant failed. [16] Hell awaits them, where *only* scalding water will be served, [17] they will sip it but can't swallow it, and death will loom all around them, but they will not die, and beyond that *experience* will be an *even more* severe punishment.

DISBELIEVERS DEEDS ARE WORTHLESS, LIKE THE ASHES SWEPT UP BY THE WIND

[18] An *apt* example of the disbeliever's deeds *is*: ashes scattered by the winds on a stormy day. They will have no control over anything that they owned. That is *the meaning of* going far astray. [19] Have you not considered that in truth God is the One Who created the Heavens and the Earth? If He so willed, He could remove you all and produce a new creation *to replace you*; [20] nor would that be too difficult *a challenge* for God.

SATAN ADMITS HE HAS NO CONTROL OVER PEOPLE

[21] They will all appear before God *on Judgement Day*, and the oppressed will say to their arrogant *leaders*, "We followed you, so will you rescue us from God's punishment?" They will say, "If God had guided us, then we would have guided you. It's all the same to us now whether we are anxious or patient; there's no escape for us." [22] Once the sentence has been passed, Satan will say, "God's promise to you was true, whereas I made you a promise and broke it. I had no control over you, I called you and you accepted my call. So, don't blame me blame yourselves. I can't help you and you can't help me. I have rejected whatever you previously associated with me. For evildoers, is a painful punishment." [23] *Meanwhile* those who believed and performed righteous deeds will enter gardens beneath which rivers flow, living there by their Lord's approval forever, in it their greeting will be: "Peace!"

The parable of the fruit tree

[24] Have you not considered how God likened a good word[a] to a good tree, whose roots are fixed and whose branches *reach* to the sky; [25] every season, it bears fruit by the Lord's favour. God gives people parables so they may reflect. [26] *Similarly*, He likened an evil word to a rotting tree, whose roots have been pulled out lying on the ground. [27] God will firmly ground the believers to stand firm in this worldly life and in the Hereafter by means of well-founded words, whereas *He* allows disbelievers to go astray. God does what He wills.

Disbelievers have short-changed themselves

[28] Haven't you seen those who exchanged God's gift *of belief* for disbelief, and who push their people on towards the house of destruction: [29] Hell is where they'll burn, what a bleak place to stay! [30] They made idols equal to God to mislead *people* from His path. Say *to them*: "Enjoy yourselves *while you can*, for the Fire shall be your journey›s end."

The things that people take for granted

[31] Tell My faithful servants; perform the prayer *regularly,* spend in charity openly and secretly from what We have provided, before *that* day comes when bargaining and friendship will serve no purpose. [32] God created the Heavens and the Earth and sent down rain from the sky, by which He produces fruits to provide for you, and made possible for you to sail by ship across the sea by His command, made rivers for your benefit, [33] made the sun and the moon orbit, for your benefit, He made night and day. [34] He has given you a portion of whatever you have asked Him for. If you were to count God's gifts, you would not be able to count them. Humans are most ungrateful, unjust!

Abraham's prayer for the security of his children

[35] *Remember* when Abraham prayed: "My Lord, make this town safe *and secure*, and keep me and my children away from idol worship. [36] My Lord, *idols* have misled many people. So, whoever follows me is one with me, and the one who disobeys me, well, You are Forgiving, Kind. [37] Our Lord, I have settled my children in a barren valley near Your Sacred House so they may perform the prayer, soften people's hearts towards them and provide them with the fruits *of the Earth* so

---

[a]   "Good word" according to Ibn Abbas is *La ilah illa God* ("There is no god but God"), and by Mujahid either, a believer's faith, or the believer (Al-Qurtubi).

they may be grateful. ³⁸ Our Lord, You know what we conceal and what we reveal. Nothing on Earth or in the sky is hidden from God. ³⁹ Praise be to God Who granted Ishmael and Isaac to me in my old age. My Lord is the Hearer of prayers. ⁴⁰ My Lord, make me and my children steadfast in prayer. Our Lord accept my prayer. ⁴¹ Our Lord, forgive me, my parents and *all* the believers on Judgement Day."

THE DISBELIEVERS' BEWILDERMENT ON JUDGEMENT DAY

⁴² Don't think God is unaware of what the wrongdoers do. He is giving them time *to think* till a day when eyes will stare in horror, ⁴³ rushing to and fro, craning their necks, no one returning their gaze, and their hearts empty. ⁴⁴ *So* warn people of a day when the punishment will come to them, and the evildoers will say, "Our Lord, give us more time so we may answer Your call and follow the messengers." *The reply*, "Didn't you swear an oath that your *power* would never diminish? ⁴⁵ You lived in the homes of those who had wronged themselves, so you clearly knew what We had done with them, and We had made *them* examples for you."

THE EARTH WILL BE MODIFIED FOR JUDGEMENT DAY

⁴⁶ They hatched a plot and God *knew* their plots, their plots could move the mountains, *they couldn't thwart God's plan.* ⁴⁷ So don't think God will break His promise with His messengers. God is Almighty, the Avenger. ⁴⁸ One day the Earth will be exchanged for another Earth, and the Heavens *likewise*, and they will *all* appear before God, the One, the Supreme, ⁴⁹ and on that day you will see the sinners bound together in chains, ⁵⁰ their coats made of tar, and their faces ablaze. ⁵¹ *This is* so that God may repay every soul according to their labour. God is swift in accounting.

THE QURAN'S PURPOSE IS SIMPLE: TO DECLARE GOD'S ONENESS

⁵² This is to convey *a message* to people, to warn them so they realise He is the One God Who *exists*, and people of understanding may pay attention.

15. Al-Hijr
The Rock City

This Makkan chapter was revealed in the final years of the Prophetic mission. The central theme is to expose the Makkans' attitude towards the Prophet 鸞. They are not serious about spiritual matters, and love worldly life: "*Leave them to* eat and enjoy themselves, *preoccupied with self-indulging* long hopes" (3). They were stubborn, and unwilling to listen to reasonable arguments. The Quran's diagnosis of the Makkans was they needed moral and spiritual guidance, since their economic success had made them materialistic individuals, selfish and greedy; the solution was a dose of moral and spiritual values.

The Quran presents the fates of past communities who opposed their prophets, so the Makkans are warned of a similar fate if they continue their rebellion.[a] The story of Abraham is a case in point, he was informed that the people of Lot would be punished. At the same time, it describes the angels bringing him the good news of a son; God's kindness to his servants and His punishment of the disobedient.

Further illustrations of the disastrous fate of the people of the Madyan woodlands and the cave dwellers of Thamud, after whom the chapter gets its name (*Al-Hijr*) are given. The Makkans were familiar with these ancient communities since their ruins were on the trade route to Syria.

The final section offers consolation to the beloved Messenger 鸞 and his harassed followers: you are blessed with the Glorious Quran; this is more valuable than anything the others possess and will help to bring balance to your materialistic lives. The Gracious Lord consoles the Prophet 鸞 with heartening words: "We are sufficient for you against those who mock ... We know what they say distresses you" (95–97). The chapter opened, "*They will regret* ..." but the closing verse instructs: "Continue to worship your Lord until you die."

In the name of God, the Kind, the Caring.

¹ *Alif Lam Ra.*

THE DISBELIEVERS' REGRET ON JUDGEMENT DAY

These are the verses of a Majestic Book, the clear Quran. ² *One day the* disbelievers *will* wish they had submitted *to God's will.* ³ Now they can eat and enjoy themselves *with long* hopes distracting them; soon they will come to know *the truth.* ⁴ We have never destroyed a town until its appointed time; ⁵ no town can go be-

---

[a] This use of references to disobedient communities in the past is a recurrent device in the Quran.

yond its appointed time, nor can they delay it. ⁶They said, "Messenger,^b you are certainly mad. ⁷If you are telling the truth, why don't you bring angels?" ⁸We only send angels with the task *to destroy them,* in which case they would not be spared.

DISBELIEVERS HAVE ALWAYS MOCKED THE TRUTH

⁹We revealed the Reminder, and We are its Protectors. ¹⁰We sent messengers to the ancient communities before you, ¹¹and they mocked every messenger who came to them. ¹²That is how We ease the way of *disbelief* into the hearts of the sinners. ¹³They will not believe in *the truth* despite knowing the example of what happened to previous generations. ¹⁴Even if We opened a gate for them in the sky, through which they could climb up, ¹⁵they would say, "Our eyes are deceived, we've been bewitched."

THE STARRY SKIES AND CROSS-POLLINATING WINDS

¹⁶We positioned constellations of stars in the sky, making it beautiful for the on-lookers,^c ¹⁷and protected it from every doomed demon, ¹⁸except those who try to eavesdrop and are chased away by the fiery flame *of a shooting star.* ¹⁹We have spread out the Earth, set mountains on it, and grew all kinds of plants and animals in a balanced *ecosystem,* ²⁰and We made livelihood on *Earth* for you and others you don't provide for. ²¹There is no *living* thing for which We don't have store-houses, which We release in known quantities. ²²We send winds to cross-pollinate *the flowers,*^d rain from the sky which you drink; you have no control over the water wells. ²³We give life and death, and We are the heirs *of all things.*^e ²⁴We know those who went before you; We know those who will come after you; ²⁵and He's Your Lord, Who will gather all, the Wise, the Knower.

SATAN VOWS TO MISLEAD HUMANITY

²⁶We created the *first* human from dried clay out of dark mud, ²⁷before which We created the jinn from smokeless fire. ²⁸*Remember* when Your Lord said to the angels, "I am creating a human with dried clay out of dark mud. ²⁹Once I have shaped and blown My spirit into him, then prostrate before him." ³⁰So all

---

^b Literally, "You to whom the Reminder has been revealed."

^c Constellations are groups of stars that form recognisable patterns in the night sky.

^d The word *lawaqih* meant "pregnant with rainwater" and the fertilisation of plants by the process of pollination, adding a new layer of meaning and appreciation to the text for modern readers.

^e In other words, everything returns to God in the end, as it says in verse 25.

the angels prostrated, [31] except Iblis,[a] who refused to prostrate. [32] God said, "Iblis, why didn't you prostrate?" [33] He replied, "I'm not prepared to prostrate before a human You created with dried clay out of dark mud." [34] *God* said, "Then leave, you shall be pelted *with stones.* [35] *My* curse will be on you until Judgement Day." [36] *Satan* asked, "My Lord, grant me respite until the day they are resurrected." [37] *God* said, "You are granted respite [38] until the date of appointed time." [39] *Satan* said, "My Lord, since You have left me to go astray, I will make *life* on Earth attractive to them and lead them astray, [40] except some of Your chosen servants."

HELL, COMPARED WITH PARADISE

[41] *God* said, "This is a straight path *that leads* to Me. [42] You shall have no control over My servants, except the misled ones who *chose to* follow you. [43] The promised destiny for all of them is Hell [44] with its seven gates, each gate *receiving* its allotted share." [45] The mindful will be in gardens with fountains. [46] *They will be invited*: "Enter *Paradise* in peace and safety." [47] We shall remove any grudges *they had* in their hearts *towards others,* making them brothers, *relaxing* on sofas face-to-face. [48] They will never feel tired nor be expelled from it. [49] Tell My servants I am the Forgiver, the Kind, [50] but My punishment is painful.

ABRAHAM RECEIVES GOOD AND BAD NEWS

[51] Tell them about Abraham's guests, [52] when they came to him, saying, "Peace!" He answered, "We're afraid of you." [53] *The angels* said, "Don't be afraid. We bring you good news of a scholarly son." [54] He said, "You've brought me good news when old age has caught up with me? What good news have you brought me?" [55] They said, "Don't despair, we bring you good news." [56] He said, "Only the misguided despair of the Lord's kindness." [57] He *then* asked, "Messengers, what's your mission?" [58] They told him, "We've been sent to *destroy* the sinners' community, [59] but we'll save Lot's family [60] except his wife, who'll remain behind."

THE ANGELS TELL LOT TO LEAVE

[61] When the angels came to Lot's home, [62] he said, "You're strangers for me." [63] They said, "We've brought you what they doubt. [64] We've brought the truth, and we are the truthful. [65] Tonight set off with your family, following behind them. Let no one look back, but continue as you are told." [66] We decided this for

---

[a] Iblis is one of the names of Satan.

him; all traces of the *sinners* will be smashed when they wake up at dawn.

The shameless people of Lot destroyed

[67] The people of the town came excitedly *to Lot's home.* [68] Lot told *them,* "These are my guests, so don't shame me. [69] Fear God and don't disgrace me." [70] They said, "Haven't we told you not to interfere *in our affairs*" [71] Lot said, "Here are my daughters of my community[b], if you must do something." [72] *God swears* by your life, *Muhammad,*[c] that they were reeling about in their drunkenness[d] [73] when the Blast overtook them at sunrise; [74] and We turned *their town* upside down and pelted them with stones of baked clay. [75] In this are signs for the intelligent people. [76] It is still *visible* along one of the established *trade* routes. [77] Here are signs for the believers.

Punishment of the people of Madyan and Thamud

[78] The people of the woodland[e] were evil, [79] so We took vengeance on them, and both *towns remain* easily visible off an open highway. [80] The people of the Hijr *region* called the messengers liars. [81] We brought them Our signs, but they turned away from them. [82] They carved houses in the mountains, living safely [83] *until* the Blast overtook them at dawn; [84] and their wealth didn't benefit them in any way.

The Quran is the most valuable gift

[85] We created the Heavens, the Earth and what lies between them for a true purpose. *Messenger,* the Final Hour is coming, pardon them graciously.[f] [86] Your Lord *alone* is the Creator, the Knower. [87] We've given you seven oft-recited verses[g] and the Majestic Quran. [88] Don't look longingly at *worldly pleasures* We gave some of their groups to enjoy, and don't be unhappy about them; *instead* take the believers under your wing, [89] and say: "I'm, a clear warner."

[b] "Here are my daughters" means the women of my community are your wives, so satisfy yourselves with them.

[c] According to Ibn Abbas, The Messenger 靈 is the only human by whose life God has sworn.

[d] This refers to their over-excited state of lust.

[e] This refers to people of Thamud, from whom the Prophet Salih was chosen by God to preach. Thamud lies in North West Arabia, in southern Syria.

[f] Here God is addressing the Prophet 靈 directly, making clear that the purpose of the references to the people of Lot, and to the inhabitants of Madyan and Thamud, is to serve as a warning to the people of Makkah to mend their godless ways.

[g] The Arabic phrase *al-Sab' al-Mathani* could also mean: the first seven chapters of the Quran; *Chapter Al-Fatiha;* or the whole Quran (*Islahi*).

⁹⁰ We have already spoken regarding those who divided the scripture ⁹¹ and those who abused the Quran; ⁹² by your Lord, Messenger, We'll question them ⁹³ about what they did. ⁹⁴ So openly announce what you are commanded, and turn away from the idolaters. ⁹⁵ We are sufficient for you against those who mock, ⁹⁶ who set up another god besides God, they will surely come to know. ⁹⁷ We know what they say distresses you. ⁹⁸ So glorify your Lord with praises, and prostrate, ⁹⁹ and continue to worship your Lord until you die.ᵃ

ᵃ *Al-yaqin* refers to death, literally it means certainty, since it's the only aspect of our lives which is certain.

16. An-Nahl
The Bee

This Makkan chapter was revealed in the last months of 622 CE, before the Prophet's ﷺ migration to Madinah. The tension between Makkans and Muslims had reached its peak, the Muslims were disheartened, while the disbelievers felt confident since Islam was no longer gaining new followers. However, the chapter is optimistic and encourages Muslims to keep faith in the promise of a victory. It tells them: "Be patient, your patience *is a gift* from God. Don't grieve over them nor distress yourself because of their plotting" (127).

The Quran often mentions two kinds of books: the revealed Scripture that presents divine instructions, explanations and a set of beliefs, and an open book: the universe, the sun and stars, the moon, the flight of birds, the seas, pearls and rubies, ships ploughing through mighty waves, the rivers, mountains, cattle, riding animals, rain, plants, fruit and crops. Two nourishing and healing foods are mentioned: milk and honey. It draws our attention to the mystery of their production from the udders of the cow and the stomach of bees. God's wonders and marvels, which He made "for your benefit ..." (14). Despite these clear signs, when the pagans are asked: "What has your Lord revealed?" They say, "Stories of the ancient people" (24). A rejection of the truth expressing their narrow-mindedness. On the other hand, when the believers are asked the same question, they respond, "He has revealed the best" (30).

Chapter An-Nahl is also called *Al-Nia'mah*, meaning, "the gift", since it lists some of God's gifts to humanity. Thankfulness is the only way to appreciate these gifts; this is the very essence of Islam. Its opposite is un-thankfulness, the meaning of *kufr*; the disbeliever fails to acknowledge God's gift.

The following verse accurately captures the essence of Divine Message: "God commands justice, generosity and giving to relatives. He forbids indecency, all *kinds of* evil and cruelty" (90). The Prophet Abraham is mentioned as a model of a thankful person. The Quran tells the Messenger ﷺ: "Invite to the way of your Lord with wisdom and courtesy" (125).

―――――――

In the name of God, the Kind the Caring

CREATION HAS A PURPOSE

[1] God's inevitable judgement is coming, so don't wish for it to come sooner. Glory be to Him; He is far above anything they associate with Him. [2] He sends the

angels with the Revelation[a] to his chosen servants to give warning, *telling them:* "There is no God but I, so fear Me." [3] He created the Heavens and the Earth for a purpose; He is far above what they associate with Him. [4] He created Humans from a drop of semen, so is that why humans are quarrelsome?

Domestic animals are Divine gift

[5] He created the livestock to provide you *wool for* warmth, meat for you to eat, and much more. [6] How beautiful they look when you bring them home in the evening and take them to the pastures in the morning. [7] They carry your loads from one city to another, *without them* you would travel with great difficulty. Your Lord is Compassionate and Kind. [8] He created the horse, the mule and the donkey for you to ride and they make you proud, and He created what you don't yet know. [9] God has signposted the straight path, thus making it distinct from the wrong paths; had He wished He could have guided all.[b]

God's gifts on Earth

[10] He sent water from the sky for you to drink and to grow the grasses on which cattle graze. [11] With rainwater He grows crops: olives, dates, grapes and every kind of fruit. In that are signs for those who reflect deeply. [12] He created the night and the day for your benefit; the sun, the moon and the stars *all* follow His command. In that are signs for those who understand. [13] He produced objects of many colours on the Earth for you; In that are signs for those who accept advice. [14] For your benefit He created the sea; from it you get fresh meat to eat, and extract jewellery that you wear. You see the ships sailing over the waves to seek His gifts, so you may be thankful. [15] He placed the mountains firmly on the Earth, so it doesn't shake beneath you, made the rivers and the tracks so you can find your way, [16] and many other signposts, including the stars for guiding the travellers.

God's gifts are countless

[17] So how can the One who creates be like the one who can't create; why don't you listen? [18] If you were to count the gifts of God; you would not be able to count them; God is the Forgiver, the Kind. [19] God knows what you hide and what you

[a] *Al Ruh* literally means "the spirit" here; it is used for revelation, pointing to the essence of revelation as giving life, reviving individuals and people (cf. *Chapter Ash-Shura*, verse [52]).

[b] God doesn't impose his guidance on people, He lets them choose to become believers or reject it. This is freedom of choice that is the foundation of morality.

expose. ²⁰ The idols they worship besides God didn't create anything; in fact, they are created; ²¹ they are dead, lifeless and unaware of when they will be resurrected. ²² Your God is one God; those who don't believe in the Hereafter have a heart that refuses to accept the truth, because they are arrogant.

THE FATE OF THOSE WHO DENIED GOD'S GIFTS

²³ God knows what they hide and what they reveal. He doesn't like the arrogant. ²⁴ When it is said to them, "What has your Lord revealed?" They say, "Stories of the ancient people." ²⁵ On Judgement Day they will carry the full burden, as well as the burden of those they misled naively. What a wretched burden they bear. ²⁶ Previously people had plotted, so God's punishment came and uprooted them from their foundations, and the roof fell from above them and the punishment came from where they least expected. ²⁷ On Judgement Day they will be disgraced and it will be asked: "Where are my associates that you used to disagree about?" The people given knowledge will say, "The evil and shame of this Day is on the disbelievers." ²⁸ Those whose souls were taken by the angels when they were wronging themselves will fall into submission, saying: "We did no evil." Indeed, God knows well what you did. ²⁹ So go through the gates of Hell to live there forever, a wretched place for the arrogant.

THE FATE OF THOSE WHO VALUED GOD'S GIFTS

³⁰ When the devoutly pious are asked: "What did your Lord send down?" They answer, "He has revealed the best". Those who do good in this world will get the reward; *their* home in the Hereafter will be even better. And how excellent is the home of the pious. ³¹ They will enter gardens of eternity with rivers flowing beneath them; they will have whatever they desire; that is how God rewards the pious. ³² The ones whose souls were taken by the angels while they were in the state of purity; they will be greeted with: "Peace be on you; enter Paradise for what you use to do in the world."

THE MESSENGER 簑 IS EAGER TO GUIDE

³³ Are you waiting for the angels or Your Lord's command to come down? Those before them did the same. God didn't wrong them, but they wronged themselves. ³⁴ The evil they had done caught up with them, and all they used to mock will engulf them as punishment. ³⁵ The idolaters will say, "If God wished we wouldn't have worshipped anyone beside Him; neither our forefathers nor we would have

made anything unlawful without *His permission.*" That's how those gone before them behaved; what else can the messengers do except give clear warning? [36] Indeed to every community We sent messengers who taught: "Worship God and turn away from idols."[a] Some God guided, whilst others remained misguided. Travel around the Earth and see the punishment of the deniers. [37] Though you are keen to guide them, God will not guide the one He's *allowed to* stray, and they will have no Helpers.

THE POWER OF GOD'S WORDS

[38] They swear their strongest oath that God will not raise them from the dead, but it is a true promise, He shall fulfil it – but most people don't realise. [39] *It is* to explain to them *the truth of* what they differed in, and to show the disbelievers they were the liars. [40] Whenever We wish something to happen We say, "Be", and it becomes. [41] Those who migrated for God's sake after facing persecution will soon settle in a pleasant place. But the reward of the Hereafter will be greatest, if they knew. [42] These are patient people who trust their Lord.

ALL PROPHETS WERE MEN

[43] We sent revelations to men before you, ask those who have received the message if you don't know. [44] *They came* with miracles and Scriptures, and We sent down to you the Majestic Message so that you can explain to people what is revealed for them, so they may reflect.

WHY ARE PEOPLE FEARLESS OF GOD'S PUNISHMENT?

[45] Are those who planned to do evil feeling safe from God's *punishment*? He may *order* the Earth to swallow them up or send unexpected punishment, [46] or He may punish them whilst they are busy in their everyday jobs; they can't escape Him. [47] Then again, He may punish them gradually through fear. Indeed, your Lord is the Compassionate, the Kind.

ALL THINGS IN THE UNIVERSE SUBMIT TO GOD

[48] Haven't they seen what God has created? How the shadows turn from right to left and left to right as though they are prostrating before God in complete submission? [49] Everything in the Heavens and the Earth, the animals and the Angels, prostrate before God; they aren't arrogant, [50] *but* frightened of their Lord above,

---

[a] "Taghut" according to the Jalalain means idols they worship.

and they do as they are told. [51] God said, "Don't serve two gods; He is one God so fear me alone." [52] All that is in the Heavens and the Earth belongs to Him, and so obedience[b] to Him is obligatory. So, will you fear anyone other than God?

PEOPLE DON'T APPRECIATE GOD'S GIFTS

[53] All your property is gift from God. In hardship you turn to Him, moaning and groaning. [54] He removes it, but some of you *still* associate others with Your Lord,[55] showing how ungrateful they are for the gifts We gave them, so enjoy for a while, but soon you will know.

HOW THE PAGANS HATE THE GIFT OF A BABY GIRL

[56] They assign a share of sustenance, We gave them to their idols, out of ignorance! By God, you will be questioned about what you concocted . [57] They assign daughters for God, glory to Him, for themselves they want sons! [58] When one of them is given the news of the birth of a girl, his face darkens, full of fuming anger; [59] he hides from the community because of the bad news he received, *feeling* undecided – will he keep her with shame or bury her in the dust? How immorally they judge! [60] Those who don't believe in the Hereafter set a bad example, and God the exalted sets a good example. He is Almighty, Wise.

GOD DOES NOT RUSH TO PUNISH

[61] If God were to punish people *right away* for their wrongs, then there wouldn't be *a single* creature left. But He delays it until the fixed term which can't be delayed nor brought forward. [62] They allocate to God what they dislike themselves. Yet they falsely claim that for themselves is all good, but let there be no doubt the Hellfire awaits them; *they will be* the first to be sent there. [63] By God, We sent messengers to communities before you, but Satan made their deeds look attractive to them, so today he is their Guardian, and for them will be painful punishment. [64] We revealed the Book so you can explain to them what they differed about; it's a guide that is beneficial for believers. [65] God sends rain from the sky to revive the Earth after its death; in that is a sign for those who listen.

MILK AND HONEY: TWO AMAZING GIFTS

[66] You have a lesson in livestock, We gave you a drink from inside their bellies – it is from between the bowels and blood – pure milk, healthy nourishment for its

---

[b] *Al-Din* literally means religion, I have taken its functional meaning.

drinkers. [67] And you make juice from the fruits of dates and grapes, delicious and nourishing; in this is a sign for those who understand. [68] Your Lord gave the bee an instinct to build hives in the mountains, the trees and buildings, inspiring her: [69] "Eat *the nectar* from different fruits and follow the ways of your Lord humbly." *Then* from its belly comes a syrup of different colours in which there is a healing for people, it is a sign for those who think.[a]

THE GIFT OF CHILDREN AND GRANDCHILDREN

[70] God created you and will let you die; some of you will turn back to frail old age, when all they once knew they won't know it anymore. God is the Knower and Powerful. [71] He gave some more provisions than others, those given more are unwilling to share their provisions with their slaves, in case they become their equals. How can they deny the gifts of God? [72] God made for you spouses from your own kind, and from them gave you sons and grandchildren and provided you nourishing sustenance. How can they accept falsehood and deny God's gifts?

WHO ARE THANKFUL AND THE UNTHANKFUL FOR THE GIFTS

[73] They worship helpless idols instead of God that can't provide them *with* any provisions from Heaven or the Earth. [74] So don't make images of God; God knows but you don't know. [75] God gives you an example: a slave who is the helpless property of his master, and on the other hand a man blessed with gifts from which he gives in charity secretly and openly. Are they equal? All praise is for God, but most don't recognise. [76] God gives you another example *of* two men; one of them is dumb, helpless and a burden to his master. Whatever task he sets him, he fails miserably; can he be equal to the man who commands justice and is on the straight path? [77] God *knows* the secret of the Heavens and the Earth. The coming of the Hour of Judgement will be as quick as the glance of an eye[b] or quicker, and God is in command of all things. [78] God brought you out from your mothers' wombs not knowing anything, and then gave you hearing, sight and a mind so you may be thankful.

GOD'S GIFTS OF SHELTER, SHIELDS, AND CLOTHES

[79] Haven't they seen birds flying in the sky? It is God Who keeps them *afloat*; in

---

[a] Scientists estimate that in Britain if there were no bees it would cost farmers £4 billion to pollinate the crops (2017).

[b] I have translated this literally, English idiom, 'twinkling of an eye' would be equally good.

this are signs for true believers. [80] God made for you homes to live in, and from the skins of animals you make tents that are light for you to carry *about* when travelling and camping, and from their wool, fur and hair *you make* furnishings that last for years. [81] God made shade to protect you from what He has created, like the places of shelter in the hillsides, and made for you clothes that protect you from heat, and armour that protects you in battle. God gave you His gifts so that you might submit to Him. [82] But if they turn away, your job is only to deliver the clear message. [83] They know God's blessings but fail to recognise them, most of them are ungrateful.

ON JUDGEMENT DAY THEY WILL ABANDON IDOLS

[84] We will pick a witness from each community that Day; the disbelievers won't be allowed to plead *ignorance* nor to repent. [85] When the wrongdoers see the punishment, *they will realise that* it will not be lightened, nor will they be given respite. [86] When the idolaters see their idols they will say, "Our Lord, these are our idols we worshipped besides you," but they will reply angrily, "Indeed you are liars." [87] That day, they will submit before God and abandon what they had invented as gods. [88] Those people who disbelieved and stopped others from God's path, their punishment will be increased many times over because they were rebellious. [89] On that Day, We will pick a witness from each community against them. We will bring you as a witness against them all. We revealed to you a glorious Book that explains *the truth* about all things; it is guidance, a kindness and good news for the Muslims.

LAW OF FULFILLING A PLEDGE

[90] God commands justice, generosity and giving to relatives. He forbids indecency, all *kinds of* evil and cruelty. He teaches you, perhaps you will accept advice. [91] Fulfil God's pledge, and once you made God a witness of your promise, don't break it after confirming it; God knows what you do. [92] *Sometimes* you make promises to deceive others – don't be like the woman who tears to pieces the cloth she spun – so you might make more profit than others. Surely God will test you by this, and on Judgement Day He will make clear what you were disagreeing about. [93] If God wanted He could have made you *all* one community *of believers*, but he lets go astray anyone who wants to do so, and guides anyone who wants to be guided. You will be questioned about your deeds. [94] Don't take oaths to

deceive others; this will shake you after being steadfast, and you must taste *the* evil consequences of stopping people from God's path, and there will be grievous punishment for you.

The works of men and women are of equal value

[95] Don't sell God's pledge for a small price; what God has for you is good, if you knew. [96] Whatever you have will perish, but what is with God will continue, and We will certainly give the patient people *their* reward for what they did. [97] Whoever – whether male or female – does good deeds, while being a true believer, We shall bless them with a happy life, and give them reward equal to their beautiful deeds.

The Quran is God's greatest gift

[98] When you *start* reading the Majestic Quran, seek God's protection from the rejected Satan. [99] He has no influence over believers who trust in their Lord. [100] But he does have influence on those who befriend him and the idolaters. [101] When We change a verse in place of another – *of course* God knows well what he reveals – they say, "You have made it up." No, most of them don't know. [102] Say: "The Holy One, *angel Gabriel*, has gradually brought it down from your Lord truthfully, to strengthen the morale of the believers; it is guidance and good news for the Muslims." [103] We know they will say, "A certain man teaches it to him." Yet the language of the one who they point to is foreign, whilst this Quran is in plain Arabic. [104] If people don't believe in God's revelation, God will not guide them; for them will be painful punishment.

Faith lies deep in the heart

[105] Those who don't believe in God's verses invented lies; they are liars. [106] The one who disbelieves God after believing him – except the one who is forced and his heart remains secure in faith – their hearts accept disbelief. For them is God's fury and a grievous punishment, [107] because they prefer worldly life over the Hereafter and God doesn't guide the disbelievers. [108] He has sealed their hearts, hearing, and seeing, and they are neglectful. [109] No doubt in the Hereafter they will be the losers. [110] Your Lord is Forgiving and was Kind towards those who migrated after persecution and kept struggling and remained patient. [111] That day everyone will plead for himself, and everyone will be fully rewarded for what they did, and no one will be wronged.

Riches made them forget God's gifts

[112] God gives an example of a city *where people* believed they were safe and comfortable, *as plenty of goods came from all directions*, but they were unthankful for God's gifts. Therefore, God punished them with famine and fear for what they did. [113] A messenger from them came, but they denied him, so punishment came to them whilst they were doing wrong.

Observing the lawful and unlawful

[114] So eat from lawful pure sustenance, and be thankful for God's gifts if you worship Him alone. [115] He has forbidden for you carrion, blood, pork, and anything slaughtered without invoking God's name. However, the one in dire need is exempt from this, if he eats without the intention of disobeying and transgressing; God is Forgiving and Kind. [116] Don't make things up to say, "This is lawful and this is unlawful," thereby inventing a lie about God. Those who invent lies about God will not succeed. [117] *This is unfair; for them is a* painful punishment. [118] What is forbidden for the Jews has been narrated previously to you; We didn't wrong them, but they wronged themselves. [119] Those who ignorantly committed evil then repented and afterwards reformed themselves will *find* Your Lord to be Forgiving and Kind.

Abraham, a role model of thankfulness

[120] Abraham was an exemplary leader, obedient to God, pure in faith and didn't associate anything with God. [121] He was thankful for His gifts, so God selected him and guided him on the straight path. [122] We gave him the best in the world, and in the Hereafter he will be among the righteous. [123] We revealed to you: "Follow Abraham's religion, the pure in faith, who wasn't an idolater." [124] The *rules of* Sabbath were made obligatory only on those who differed about it; your Lord will decide between them on Judgement Day concerning their disagreements.

Invite to God in a courteous manner

[125] Invite to your Lord's way wisely: teaching in a pleasant manner, and debating with courtesy; Your Lord knows the one who strayed from His way and the one guided. [126] If you retaliate, then do so to the same extent, but if you are patient that would be better, being patient is good. [127] Be patient; your patience *is* God's *gift*. Don't grieve over them, nor distress yourself because of their plotting. [128] God is with the mindful and the righteous.

17. Al-Isra'
The Ascension

This late Makkan chapter opens with the miracle of the Ascension: the Prophet's ﷺ night journey from Makkah to Jerusalem, and from there to celestial heights, finishing in the Divine Presence. The journey is an unspoken announcement of the aptness of the message of the Prophet ﷺ for the entire world, and hints to the coming glory of Islam. The Ascension took place on 27 Rajab, seventeen months before the Hijrah in the year of sorrow. The purpose of this two-phased journey was, "To show him Our signs". The hadith literature gives graphic details of this momentous journey. The verse begins with the Divine attribute, "Subhan", 'the one who is flawless without defect or weakness, the Glorified.' The Quran states the One who took His servant on this miraculous journey is the One who is free from every kind of weakness. Whose mere command *'kun'* (be) and *'fa-yakun'* (it becomes), is enough.

The Quran is mentioned eleven times in the chapter, describing its various aspects: a guide to the straightest path; an explanation of divine proofs; why disbelievers cannot understand it so they turn away from it; a test of faith; a recitation at dawn with special effects; a healing and Divine Kindness; an inimitable masterpiece; full of powerful arguments for God's existence; the truth; and revealed in comprehensible bites.

Man's nature is described 'hasty' and why he craves for instant gratification and immediate results. Is that why people love the fleeting world, instead of the everlasting Hereafter? To help humanity overcome this weakness the chapter presents a new, just and peaceful way of living – an outline for a new world order: here people are kind, patient and forgiving. It's summarised in the ten commandments announced in this chapter: worship God; care for parents; give to the needy; give up the Seven Deadly Sins (wastefulness, miserliness, murder, adultery, dishonesty, blind imitation and arrogance).

The Messenger ﷺ of Islam was devout and spiritual, so a special night vigil is recommended for him: "At night, wake up to offer voluntary prayer that is only for you. Soon your Lord will raise you to a glorious station of praise" (79). The Quran warns that Satan will exert maximum effort to misguide, so be on guard. But, the true servants will be protected from his insinuations (64–65).

In the name of God, the Kind, the Caring.

The Ascension of the Messenger ﷺ

¹ Glory to Him Who took His *noble* servant on a night journey[a] from the Sacred Mosque to the farthest Mosque – whose surroundings we made holy – to show him Our signs. He is the Hearer, the Seeing. ² We gave Moses the Book of guidance for the Israelites saying: "Don't take a Guardian besides Me." ³ *You are the* descendants of the people We carried in Noah's ship; he was a thankful servant.

The Israelites will face troubled times twice

⁴ We stated in the Scripture: twice you would create mischief on the land and become arrogant.[b] ⁵ So We sent against them Our servants who were severely brutal, they demolished their homes; hence the first prediction was fulfilled. ⁶ Later on We gave you victory over them and helped you with wealth and children and increased your numbers – ⁷ if you do good it will be for your good, and if you do evil it's against yourselves – when the second promise came, you were again disgraced; they entered the masjid *in Jerusalem* as they entered the first time and destroyed what they could get hold of. ⁸ It is still possible that your Lord may be kind to you. However, if you turn back to evil We will again punish you; We made Hell a prison for the disbelievers.

The Majestic Quran is good news

⁹ This Majestic Quran guides to the straightest *path*[c] it brings good news for the believers who perform excellent deeds; they'll have a great reward. ¹⁰ Those who don't believe in the Hereafter, for them We've prepared a painful punishment. ¹¹ *Sometimes* people pray for evil as keenly as they pray for good; people are hasty.

Man's hasty nature

¹² We made the night and the day two signs; We darkened the night and made the day bright, so you can seek sustenance from your Lord and for calculating the number *of years*. We have explained all things. ¹³ We tied the destiny of every per-

---

[a] This was not all night but for a part of the night.

[b] The two punishments were; 586 bc, the Babylonians under Nebuchadnezzar destroyed the Temple of Solomon and took the Israelites into captivity. The second punishment occurred in 70 CE, at the hands of Roman emperor Titus, who scattered the Jews all over the world.

[c] *Aqwam* means "straightest"; without bends, curves or deviations, it is candid, rather than soft or deceptive.

son around their neck;[a] on Judgement Day, We shall bring out the document and spread it wide open before them; [14] read your own document! You should be able to calculate your *own* account today. [15] Whoever accepts the guidance does for his own good, and whoever strays is in loss; no one will bear the burden of another person. We don't punish people until We have sent a messenger.

THE FATE OF THOSE WHO LOVE THE WORLD

[16] When We plan to destroy a town, first We teach its well-off people *to change*, if they continue to disobey, the judgement comes to pass and We destroy them. [17] How many generations did we destroy after Noah? Your Lord is sufficiently aware and sees the sins of His servants. [18] Whoever wants the fleeting world, We readily give whatever We will to whom We please. We have made Hell for him that will burn him, he will be disgraced and rejected. [19] Whoever wants the Hereafter and works hard for it as a true believer; their works will be fully appreciated. [20] On all – these and those – We give the gifts of Your Lord. Your Lord's gifts are not restricted to one group alone. [21] Notice how We give more to some than others; the Hereafter has far greater status in rank and excellence *than worldly life*. [22] Don't take any other god besides God, as you will end up condemned and rejected.

THE TEN COMMANDMENTS:[B] WORSHIPPING GOD AND CARING FOR PARENTS

[23] Your Lord has commanded that you shouldn't worship anyone except Him, and you must care for parents; if one or both of them become old do not say "Uff[c] to them, nor snap at them; instead, speak to them with respect [24] and be kind; lower your wings with humility for them and pray: "My Lord, be kind to them, as they cared for me in childhood." [25] Your Lord knows well what is in your minds; if you are righteous, He forgives those who repent.

KEEP AWAY FROM THE SEVEN DEADLY SINS: NEITHER BE A WASTER NOR A MISER

[26] Give a relative his due, the poor and the traveller – don't spend your wealth wastefully. [27] Those who waste are the brothers of Satan, and Satan is most un-

---

[a]   This refers to human destiny, fate and the outcome of one's life achievements. Outcome of life is determined by one's beliefs, attitudes and behaviour, since God has ordered man to behave responsibly. This could also allude to the human genome, the code that determines a person's make up and structure.

[b]   The Ten Commandments are: worship God, care for parents, give to the needy, don't waste wealth or be a miser, kill, engage in adultery, dishonesty, blind imitation and arrogance.

[c]   "Uff" is a sound that indicates dislike and annoyance towards parents.

thankful to His Lord. ²⁸ If you must turn them away empty-handed, *due to your poverty*, speak gently with them, since you are full of expectation of kindness from your Lord. ²⁹ Neither be tight-fisted nor wasteful, as you will be blamed and regretful.^d ³⁰ Your Lord gives plentiful sustenance or limited amounts to whom he pleases. He sees and is fully aware of his servants' *needs*.

NEITHER KILL NOR COMMIT ADULTERY

³¹ You shall not kill your children out of fear of poverty. We shall feed them and you; to kill them is a major sin *and a crime*. ³² You must not go near adultery; it is indecency and an evil way of life. ³³ You shall not kill anyone *since* God has made *life* sacred, except for a just cause. However, if someone is wrongly killed, then We give his heirs authority *to take revenge*, but shouldn't exceed in taking life. He shall be supported *by the authorities*.

DO NOT CHEAT ANYONE

³⁴ You shall not go near the wealth of the orphans, except with good intentions, until they are mature. And fulfil pledges; you will be questioned about pledges. ³⁵ When measuring, give in full measure, and weigh with correctly calibrated scales; that is fair, and will produce good outcomes.

DON'T FOLLOW BLINDLY OR WALK ARROGANTLY

³⁶ Do not follow blindly without knowledge, *use your senses:* hearing, seeing and thinking, you will be questioned about *them*. ³⁷ You shouldn't walk about on Earth arrogantly, since you cannot tear it up nor can you reach mountains in tallness. ³⁸ These are evil activities, most disliked by your Lord. ³⁹ These are some of *the pearls of* wisdom revealed by your Lord; do not take gods besides God. Be fearful, you may end up in Hell, condemned and rejected. ⁴⁰ How come Your Lord preferred sons for you, and angelic daughters for Himself? You've said a terrible thing.

IF THERE WERE GODS, THEY WOULD HAVE DEFEATED GOD

⁴¹ We have variously explained *proofs of God* in this Quran for their reminder, but it has only added to their bitterness. ⁴² Say: "If there were other gods beside God as they say, then these gods would have found a way to defeat the owner of the Mighty Throne." ⁴³ Glory to Him, He is far above what they say, Exalted and

---

^d Literally: "do not be tight fisted, nor so open handed."

Great. [44] The Seven Heavens and the Earth and what is in them all glorify Him; there isn't a single thing that doesn't glorify and praise Him, but you don't understand their *way of* celebrating His glory. He is the Gentle and the Forgiving.

AN INVISIBLE SCREEN STOPS THEM FROM SEEING THE TRUTH

[45] *Messenger*, when you recite the Quran We place an invisible screen between you and the disbelievers of the Hereafter.[a] [46] We placed coverings over their minds so they can't understand, and made them hard of hearing. Whenever you mention Your Lord's Oneness in the Quran, they turn their backs hatefully. [47] We know well what they wish to hear when they listen to you and when they meet secretly; these wrongdoers say, "The man you follow is bewitched." [48] Notice how they portray you; they are mistaken and will not be able to find a way.

GOD IS CAPABLE OF GIVING LIFE TO INANIMATE THINGS

[49] They say, "When we have become white washed bones and dust, will we be raised up again, a brand-new creation?" [50] Say *yes*: "*Even* if you turned into stones or iron [51] or any substance you may think unlikely to be given life." They ask, "Who will bring us back?" Say: "The One who created you the first time." They will shake their heads saying, "When will that be?" Say: "It's perhaps near." [52] The day God will call you, and all will answer by praising Him, then you'll realise you only stayed a short while *in the world*.

POLITENESS CAN PREVENT QUARRELS

[53] Tell My servants: "Always be courteous *when speaking*", *or else* Satan will stir disagreement among you; surely Satan is the sworn enemy of humanity. [54] Your Lord knows you best; He will be kind to you or punish you if He wants. *Anyway*, We haven't sent you as a guardian over them. [55] Your Lord knows who is in the Heavens and the Earth. We favoured some prophets over others, and We gave blessed David the book *of Psalms*.

MIRACLES MAY COME AS WARNINGS

[56] Say: "Call those you think are your gods besides Him; they cannot remove harm from you or turn it away." [57] Those who they call are themselves looking for the means to be nearer to Him; they long for His kindness and dread His punishment. Your Lord's punishment is dreadful. [58] Any town We destroy before

[a] This 'screen' is a consequence of a person's persistence not to listen, be stubborn and break the natural bond with the Creator. For further explanation see; 2:7, 2:27, 6:25, and 14:4.

Judgement Day or punish sternly is recorded in the *eternal* document. [59] What stopped Us from sending miracles is people's denial in the past, *for example,* We gave Thamud *the miracle* of the she-camel; it was self-evident but they hamstrung her. So, We now send miracles only as a warning. [60] And remember when We said to you, "Your Lord knows all about the people."[b] The dream We showed you and the cursed tree mentioned in the Quran were for testing people.[c] We warned them, but that made them bolder in their disobedience.

SATAN'S TACTICS TO MISLEAD HUMANITY

[61] Remember, We told the angels, "Prostrate before Adam!" They all prostrated, except Satan. He said, "Why should I prostrate to one You created from clay?" [62] He continued, "Do you see this *human* being who You have honoured over me, if You give me time till Judgement Day then I will have *all* his children under my control, except a few. [63] God said, "Go away! Anyone who follows you will be punished in Hell, a fitting reward." [64] Persuade them with your *enchanting* voice; try winning them over with all the might you can muster[d]; be a shareholder in their wealth and children and make promises to them; Satan's promises are mere deceptions. [65] *But* you will have no power and influence over My servants; Your Lord is their Guardian.

A FALSE SENSE OF SECURITY

[66] Your Lord makes the ships sail across the sea for you to seek His bounty; He is most Kind to you. [67] When you are distressed at sea, those you worship besides God desert you, but He brings you safely to the land yet you turn away. Man, is unthankful. [68] Are you sure that He won't sink you in the ground or send a sandstorm? You won't find any protector. [69] Are you sure when you return to the sea He will not send a violent storm to drown you for your unthankfulness? You will not find any helper in opposition to Us.

THE DIGNITY OF HUMANITY

[70] We honoured the children of Adam and enabled them to travel across land and sea, to seek healthy sustenance and favoured them above all Our creation. [71] The

---

[b]   "Encompasses all people" means surrounds, and knows them well to protect you from their harm.

[c]   The 'dream' here according to commentators refers to the Messenger's ﷺ Ascension mentioned in the opening verse of the Chapter. This miracle became a test of their faith; would they believe that he travelled through space and beyond to be in Divine presence.

[d]   Literally "your soldiers on horseback and on foot".

Day We call the communities along with their leaders, some will be given their book in the right hand, and will *happily* read it; they will not be treated unjustly in the least.[a] [72] The blind in this world will also be blind in the Hereafter, and far away from the path.

TEMPTING THE PROPHET ﷺ UNSUCCESSFULLY

[73] *Messenger*, they tempt you away from Our revelation so you might produce something different, then they would befriend you. [74] Had We not made you steadfast then you might have inclined a little bit towards them. [75] In that case We would have made you taste double punishment in this life and after death; moreover, you will not find a helper against Us. [b][76] They tried hard to scare you, so you would leave the city, they too wouldn't have stayed there for long either. [77] Such was our practice with messengers We sent before you. You will find no change in our practice.

PRAYERS DURING DAY AND NIGHT

[78] Pray regularly from midday[c] until the darkness of the night, and the Morning Prayer, since the recitation of the Quran in the Morning Prayer is witnessed *by the Angels.* [79] At night, wake up to offer a voluntary prayer that is *compulsory* only for you.[d] Soon your Lord will raise you to a glorious station of praise.[e] [80] Say: "My Lord, wherever you take me, let me enter truthfully and let me leave truthfully, and give me power and authority from Yourself."

THE MAJESTIC QURAN: TRUTH, HEALING AND KINDNESS

[81] Say: "The truth has come and falsehood vanished; falsehood is bound to vanish." [82] We revealed the Quran it is a healing and benefits the believers, but for the disbelievers it adds to their loss. [83] Often, when We give gifts to people, they turn away unthankfully, remain indifferent, and despair in hard times. [84] Say: "Everyone behaves according to their character,"[f] Your Lord knows best who follows the

---

[a] *Fatelan* is a cord-like fibre in the groove of a date stone, a metaphor for a tiny amount.

[b] It would be impossible for the Messenger of God ﷺ to disobey. But the verse is making a bigger point; rejection of a fundamental truth is unforgivable. (Asad)

[c] *Daluq ashams* also means sunset. Here it means midday, so from midday to darkness of night includes Zuhr, Asr, Maghrib and Isha prayers.

[d] *Tahajjud*, or night prayer, is a voluntary prayer, but compulsory for the Messenger ﷺ.

[e] *Maqaman Mahmoodan* literally means a glorious station of praise. The Prophet ﷺ explained it to be "the place from where I will intercede for my people."

[f] *Shakilat* means disposition, temperament and character.

best-guided path.

THE MYSTERY OF THE HUMAN SOUL

⁸⁵ They ask you about the soul; say: "The soul is my Lord's command, and you have been given little knowledge about it." ⁸⁶ If We wanted, We could have withdrawn what We have revealed to you. Then you would not find an advocate against Us, ⁸⁷ except for your Lord's kindness; He has indeed been very gracious to you. ⁸⁸ Say: "If all humanity and jinn got together to bring a book like this Quran, they wouldn't be able to bring it, no matter how much they helped each other." ⁸⁹ In this Quran We explained every kind of example for people's *benefit,* but most refuse to acknowledge *the truth.*

DISBELIEVERS' UNREASONABLE DEMANDS

⁹⁰ They said, "We won't believe you until you bring for us a gushing spring from the Earth. ⁹¹ Or until you have a garden of date trees and grapes with a river flowing through it, ⁹² or *you* cause a piece of the sky to fall on us as you claim, or bring God and the angels before us, ⁹³ or have a house decorated with gold, or bring a ladder that goes up to the sky. No, we will not believe your *miracle of* Ascension; *we will believe* if you can bring a book we can read" Say: "Glory to My Lord, I am only a human being, a messenger."

HUMANITY NEEDS HUMAN MESSENGERS

⁹⁴ An argument that stops some people from accepting the guidance is, "How could God have sent a messenger who is a mortal?" ⁹⁵ Say: "If angels walked and lived on Earth then *naturally* We would have sent from the Heavens a messenger who was an angel."⁸ ⁹⁶ Say: "God is sufficient witness for me and you." He is aware and sees His servants. ⁹⁷ The one who God guides is guided, and the one who He lets go astray, you won't find a protector for him beside God. We will gather them on Judgement Day with their faces down, blind, dumb and deaf. Hell, will be their dwelling; when the flames die down We will intensify the blazing flames once again. ⁹⁸ That will be *their* reward, they rejected Our signs and said, "When we become bones and dust will we be resurrected as a brand-new creation?"

GOD'S GENEROSITY AND HUMAN MISERLINESS

⁹⁹ Do they not realise God created the Heavens and the Earth, can't he pro-

---

ᵍ   For their guidance. Since humans live on Earth, We sent human messengers.

duce the likes of them *again*? He has fixed their lifespan. The wrongdoers refuse everything except disbelief. [100] Say: "If you controlled the treasures of My Lord's kindness, you would hold them tightly for fear of spending them. People are tight-fisted, miserly."

MOSES' NINE MIRACLES

[101] We gave Moses nine miracles; ask the Israelites, when he came to them, the Pharaoh said, "Moses, I believe you're under a spell." [102] Moses said, "You know, no one except the Lord of the Heavens and the Earth could have sent these clear signs. Pharaoh! I believe you're doomed." [103] The Pharaoh wanted to wipe them off from the land *of* Egypt, so We drowned him and those with him. [104] Afterwards, We told the Israelites: "Live in the land, and when the promise of the Hereafter comes to pass, We will bring you all together as a mixed crowd."[a]

THE MYSTICAL NATURE OF QURANIC REVELATION

[105] We revealed the Quran with truth, so it came down with truth. We sent you to proclaim good news and to warn. [106] *This is* a reading, revealed in separate sections so that you may slowly read it to the people; We revealed it gradually *over a period*. [107] Say: "*It is up to you* to believe it or not. Those who were given knowledge before this *certainly acknowledge it* when it is read to them; they fall on their faces in prostration." [108] Say: "Glory to Our Lord; Our Lord's promise is fulfilled." [109] They fall on their faces in prostration, weeping as their humility grows.

GOD'S BEAUTIFUL NAMES

[110] Say: "Call God or Rahman by whichever names you call, He has most beautiful names." So, when you pray don't call *Him* too loudly or too quietly; instead seek a middle way. [111] Say: "All Praises are for God. He has no son and no partner in His Kingdom; He needs no such petty protectors – to proclaim His absolute greatness."

---

[a] *Lafeefan* refers to a human crowd that is made up of all kinds of people from different races, groups, cultures and civilisations, and economic backgrounds: a reflection of human diversity. The Quran is making it clear that the Israelites will be part of this mixed crowd; they will have no special privilege on Judgement Day.

18. Al-Kahf
The Cave

This late Makkan chapter was revealed between the eighth and tenth year of the Prophet's 鬱 mission. Its central theme is the contrasting nature of the spiritual and the material world: One permanent, the other temporary, one mysterious the other manifest. Humanity is tempted by the attractions of the material world, but fails to realise the importance of spiritual life. In this chapter, these contrasts are illustrated by five moving stories, each one representing a feature of spiritual and material life. Each story is followed by a terse and helpful commentary, which instils the love, majesty and grandeur of God. The five stories are:

- The story of the sleepers in the cave is about young men of faith, serious believers, unwilling to compromise their faith. They confronted society's evil, and abandoned their families to save their faith from an oppressive ruler. The story illustrates God's power of resurrection, bringing the dead to life.
- The story of the poor and the rich man reveals the nature of a greedy, self-centred and insensitive rich man who is ready to pick a fight.
- The Story of Adam and Satan provides a clue to understanding the cause of spiritual sickness.
- The story of Moses and Khidr, the sage who explains serendipity, "always making discoveries, by accidents and sagacity, of things which they were not in quest of". The paradox of outward actions and inner meanings. What appears to be harmful turns out to be beneficial, and a loss becomes a gain. The lesson is that we should accept God's will, since His plan is mysterious and full of wisdom.
- The story of Zulqarnayn, the mighty ruler who challenges the view that the world must be abandoned for spiritual growth. It shows that's not necessary to gain Paradise. What is needed is God-consciousness.

The Connection Between the Five Stories
The underlying theme in these stories, is the temptations individual's face:
- Faith: the young men feared the Emperor would forcefully convert them. Our faith is always being challenged by society. How well we face this determines its strength. The company of righteous people can help to develop a strong faith that will resist the wrongs of society.
- Wealth: we are tempted by wealth, we love it and when wealth opposes religious duties we often prefer wealth, we are unable to sacrifice it and unable to spend it for others good. The solution; avoid attachment to the world.
- Temptations of Satan: He tempted Adam and Eve. He tempts us all the time. How can

we protect ourselves against these temptations?

- Knowledge, competence and skills, often lead to arrogant behaviour. Resistance against this is found in humility: in recognising one's weaknesses and frailties. The example of the humility of Moses is an excellent model for us.
- Power can corrupt and lead people to commit atrocities and injustices. Protection against corruptive power can be found in being sincere and genuine in one's desire to serve others.

These temptations are the thread binding the stories together. The chapter also features much movement, plodding from place to place: the sleepers of the Cave climb a mountain; the rich man and poor man walk to an orchard; Moses travels by foot and boat, and the adventures of Zulqarnayn wandering from East to West with his army. Hint: goodness is promised in movement and searching for God's gifts.

In the name of God, the Kind, the Caring.

THE MAJESTIC QURAN IS A GUIDANCE

[1] All praises are for God, He who sent down the Book to his servant. It does not bend the truth, [2] but is factual,[a] so He gives warning of severe punishment and good news to the believers who do righteous deeds, they will have Paradise, [3] where they will stay forever. [4] You must warn those who said God has taken a child;[b] [5] neither they nor their forefathers had any knowledge. It is an outrageous insult they spout with their mouths; they are lying. [6] So will you worry yourself to death over their actions, if they don't believe in this message? [7] We've made attractive what is on Earth, to test who is best in deeds. [8] Eventually, We will turn the Earth into a barren land.

THE STORY OF THE SLEEPERS OF THE CAVE

[9] *Messenger*, did you know the People of the Cave and Al-Raqim[c] were our amazing signs? [10] The young men took refuge in the cave and prayed: "Our Lord be kind to us and guide us during our test." [11] While they were inside the cave for many years We blocked their ears, [12] then awakened them, to see which of the two groups was better in assessing the length of their stay.

---

[a] *Qayyiman* literally means "straight", and implies the Quran is factual, as it presents reality.

[b] Literally a son, since the people of Makkah believed in angels as daughters of God. Therefore, I have adopted this context-sensitive meaning.

[c] Al-Raqim refers to either the name of the town, or the valley where the cave was located. Others think it means "the written", referring to the brass tablet with the names inscribed (Zia-ul-Quran).

THE SLEEPERS OF THE CAVE WERE MEN OF STRONG FAITH

[13] We will tell you their story exactly as it happened: they were young men who had faith in their Lord; We increased them in guidance, [14] and improved self-confidence. They stood up boldly *before their people* and proclaimed: "Our Lord is the Lord of the Heavens and the Earth. Never will we worship gods beside Him; that would be an outrageous lie. [15] Our people have taken gods beside Him, without any clear evidence. Can anyone be more wrong than the one who makes up lies about God?" [16] It was said, "You have now separated yourselves from those people and what they worship beside God, so take refuge in the cave and your Lord will be kind to you, He will prepare suitable arrangements for you."

THE MIRACULOUS DEEP SLEEP

[17] *Messenger*, while they laid in the clear opening of the cave, you could see the sun rise then move away from them, and turned to their left as it set. This was from the signs of God. Anyone guided by God is truly guided, and anyone gone astray won't find a guide or a protector. [18] You thought they were awake, but they were asleep. We kept turning them from right to left. At the entrance *of the cave* lay their dog with its forelegs stretched out. Were you to stumble across them, you would be filled with fear, turn your back on them, and flee.

THEIR AWAKENING

[19] *Eventually* We awakened them, and they questioned each other. One of them asked, "How long did we stay here?" They said, "We stayed a day or a part of a day." Others said, "Your Lord knows best how long you stayed, now send someone with the silver coin to town to buy pure food so he may bring it for you. *They told him*, "Be polite and courteous,[d] and don't let anyone know who you are, [20] if they find out who you are, they will torture you, or force you to revert to their religion. Then you will never be successful." [21] In this way We brought them to people's attention, so they may know that God's promise is true, and there is no doubt about the Final Hour. The townspeople disputed about *what to do with* them. Some said, "Erect a building over the cave; their Lord knows best about them." However, those who had an upperhand concerning their matter said, "We'll build a Mosque over the cave."

---

[d] *Walyathalatuf* means to be subtle, hidden, yet exert an influence. The middle letter 'Ta' of this word is exactly the middle letter of the Quran.

How many were they?

[22] Some will say the People of the Cave were three, and their dog was the fourth; others will say they were five and the sixth their dog; these are mere guesses; some will say they were seven and the eighth their dog. Say: "My Lord knows best their number." Only a few have real knowledge of them. So, don't argue or ask anyone else about them, say what's known clearly.

When making a plan say, "God willing"

[23] When you intend to do something don't say, "I will do it tomorrow." [24] *Instead* say, "God willing *I will do it.*" Remember your Lord whenever you forget Him, and say, "I hope my Lord will guide me to the right path closer, and closer."[a]

How long did they stay in the cave?

[25] "People say they stayed in the cave for three hundred years, plus nine." [26] Say: "only God knows exactly how long they stayed. He has the knowledge of the unseen in the Heavens and the Earth. How wonderful is His Seeing and Hearing. They have no helper beside Him, and He does not allow anyone to share His rule." [27] And recite what is revealed to you from your Lord's book; none can change His words, nor can you find beside Him a place of refuge.

Lesson 1: Keep company of good people

[28] Keep yourself with those who worship their Lord morning and evening, longing for His pleasure. Don't turn your eyes away from them to seek the delights of worldly life. Neither follow him whose mind is forgetful of Our remembrance, and follows his whims; his case is beyond limits.[b]

Lesson 2: The contrasting fate of the Sleepers of the cave and the Tyrant disbelievers

[29] Say: "The truth is from Your Lord; so, whoever wants to believe, let him do so, and whoever wishes to deny, let him." We have prepared for the evil doers a fire; its walls will surround them. When they plead for water, they will be relieved with boiling water *hotter than* molten brass that will burn their faces – a dreadful drink, and an unbearable place of rest. [30] *On the other hand*, those who believed

---

[a]   The digression from the story is an explanation of the reason for the revelation of this story. When Makkans asked the Messenger ﷺ about the People of the Cave, he said, "I will tell you tomorrow," but forgot to say, "God Willing."

[b]   The wealthy Makkans told the Messenger ﷺ that they were embarrassed to sit with him, alongside the slaves and poor Muslim. This section was revealed to reject their reservations.

and did righteous deeds, We will not waste the reward of those who did good *work;* ³¹ they will have everlasting gardens with streams running beneath them. Here, they will be wearing golden bracelets, green dresses with silk embroidery, and rich patterns. They will be sitting on couches. What a wonderful reward, an amazing resting place.

Parable of the rich man

³² Tell them the parable of two men; to one We gave two vineyards, hedged by palm trees, with a cornfield lying in the middle. ³³ Both vineyards had a stream running between them, so they produced an abundant crop throughout the year, ³⁴ he had plenty of *agricultural* produce. One day he said to his friend, as they were talking *among themselves,* "I have more wealth and a larger family than you." ³⁵ He walked into his garden with these wrong thoughts and said, "I don't think that these vineyards will ever perish, ³⁶ nor do I think that Judgement Day will come. Even if I was returned to My Lord, I will certainly go to somewhere better than this."

The wisdom of the humble man

³⁷ His friend said to him as they argued, "How can you deny the One who created you from dust and then from a drop of sperm? ³⁸ For me, He is God, my Lord, and I do not associate anyone with my Lord.³⁹ When you entered your vineyard why didn't you say, "There is no power except that of God. Even if you saw that I was less than you in wealth and number of children, ⁴⁰ I am hopeful that my Lord will give me better than your vineyards; He could send a thunderbolt from the sky on them and turn the land barren, ⁴¹ or make its water sink deep into the ground so that you wouldn't be able to reach it."

The vineyards are destroyed

⁴² So his fruits were destroyed. There he was, wringing his hands, regretting what he had spent on it. The trellises had fallen; he sobbed, "I wish I had never associated anyone with my Lord." ⁴³ There was no army that could help him against God, nor could he defend himself. ⁴⁴ This shows, *all* power belongs to God, the Truth. *The belief in Him* produces the best reward and the best outcome.

Lesson 1: The parable of life and death

⁴⁵ Tell them a parable of worldly life; it's like the rain We send down from the

sky, the soil soaks it, plants grow, then turn into dry straw that is scattered by the winds. God has power over all things. [46] Wealth and children are beautiful decorations of this life. However, the fruit of good deeds will remain with your Lord, an excellent reward and hope.

LESSON 2: OPENING OF PERSONAL RECORDS ON JUDGEMENT DAY

[47] The day when We clear away the mountains, you will see the Earth spread out as a *vast* plain, and We shall gather *the dead;* no one will be left out. [48] They will be presented before your Lord in rows, *it will be said,* "You have come to Us as We created you the first time; you thought We wouldn't fulfil Our promise." [49] When the record[a] will be laid out before them, the sinners will be frightened of what they see in it, and they will say, "Woe to us, what kind of record is this that doesn't leave out anything small or big, it records everything." They will find everything they had ever done in front of them. And your Lord is not unjust to anyone.

SATAN MISLEADS

[50] And remember when We said to the Angels, "Prostrate to Adam," they prostrated, though Satan, who was from the Jinns, did not. He disobeyed his Lord's order. So, are you going to take him and his followers as your friends beside Me, yet they are your enemies? What a wretched alternative have the wrongdoers chosen! [51] I didn't make them witnesses at the time of creation of the Heavens and Earth, nor in their own creation. I don't take as helpers those who misguide others. [52] On the Day He will say, "Call upon those who you thought were My partners," they will not answer them. We will place between them an unbridgeable gulf.[b] [53] When the sinners see the Fire they will be convinced they are falling into it, and they will find no other place to turn to.

HUMANITY IS QUARRELSOME

[54] We have *explained* all sorts of lessons for people's benefit in this Quran, *but* humans are quarrelsome *creatures.* [55] What stops people from believing and seeking the forgiveness of their Lord when the guidance has come to them? Are they waiting *for the same fate* as the earlier generations? Or for the punishment to be brought right in front of them? [56] The messengers were sent to give good news and a warning; the disbelievers disputed using false arguments to weaken the

---

[a] Personal record in the Book of Deeds.
[b] *Muabiqan,* according to Ibn Abbas, is a valley in Hell.

truth, and they mocked My verses and warnings.

THE LOCKED MINDS OF DISBELIEVERS

⁵⁷ Who is more unjust than the one who is reminded of his Lord's verses and turns away from them? Forgetting what he is sending ahead of him. We have locked their minds: they cannot understand. We made them hard of hearing, so when you call them to the guidance, they will never be guided. ⁵⁸ Your Lord is Forgiving, Kind. Had He punished them for what they did, then it would have come sooner, but there is a fixed time from which they will find no escape. ⁵⁹ We destroyed these towns because they did wrong; We fixed the time of their destruction.

THE STORY OF MOSES AND KHIDR, THE GREEN MAN

⁶⁰ Remember when Moses said to his young servant, "I will travel on until I reach the place where the two seas meet, no matter how long it takes."ᶜ ⁶¹ When they reached it, they forgot the fish, which quietly made its way into the sea and swam away. ⁶² After travelling for some time, Moses asked his young servant, "Bring our meal, the journey has worn us out!" ⁶³ He replied, "Did you notice, when we rested at the rock I forgot the fish – none but Satan made me forget it – amazingly it made its way into the sea." ⁶⁴ Moses said, "That's *the place* we were looking for." So they turned back, carefully retracing their footsteps. ⁶⁵ They found a servant of Ours there, *Khidr, to whom* We were especially kind – We taught him Our special knowledge.

MOSES ASKS KHIDR FOR PERMISSION TO ACCOMPANY HIM

⁶⁶ Moses asked him, "Can I follow you, so you may teach me something of higher guidance which you have been taught?" ⁶⁷ He replied, "You will not be able to have patience with me; ⁶⁸ how could you have patience about things that you don't fully know?" ⁶⁹ Moses said, "God willing, you will find me patient and I will not disobey your orders." ⁷⁰ The man said, "If you *must* follow me then don't ask questions until I speak about it to you."

THREE BIZARRE EVENTS

⁷¹ So both set off walking along the beach until they got a boat, *but when they got off* Khidr damaged it. Moses said, "Did you damage it to drown those on board? You've done an awful thing." ⁷² Khidr said, "Didn't I say you will never have pa-

---

ᶜ The background to this story is given in Bukhari: Moses was asked a question; who is the most knowledgeable person? Moses replied 'I am'. God rebuked him of Khidr being wiser than him.

tience with me?" [73] Moses replied, "Don't be harsh with me for forgetting; please don't make my task any more difficult." [74] So they travelled on until they met a boy; Khidr killed him, and Moses *angrily* said, "You've killed an innocent person who hasn't done anything wrong; you've done a dreadful thing." [75] He said, "Didn't I tell you, you will never have patience with me?" [76] Moses said, "If I ask anything after this then tell me to leave you. You will have a valid excuse from me." [77] So, they set off till they reached a village, here they asked the villagers for food, but they refused to take them as guests. They found a wall about to fall down, so *Khidr* rebuilt it. Moses complained, "You could have asked for a payment, if you wanted."

Khidr explains the three bizarre events

[78] *He* replied, "We must go our separate ways now! I shall give you an explanation for what you were unable to bear patiently. [79] The boat belonged to poor fishermen, I damaged it because a king was coming after them to forcefully seize all seaworthy boats. [80] The boy, his parents were believers, but we feared he would distress them by being disobedient and unthankful. [81] We hope their Lord will give them a righteous child in exchange, one who will be more caring. [82] The falling wall belonged to two orphan boys in the town; buried beneath it was their treasure, their father was a righteous man. Your Lord wanted them to reach maturity, so they could dig up their treasure; *this was* your Lord's kindness. What I did wasn't done by my will; that's an explanation of those events you couldn't bear patiently."

The story of Zul Qarnayn

[83] They ask you about Zul Qarnayn. Say: "I will tell you part of his story." [84] We established and gave him power on Earth, and gave him the resources to achieve great things.[a] [85] So he set off on an expedition, [86] until he reached the place where the sun sets; he found it setting in a spring of murky water.[b] He found some people there, We said: "Zul Qarnayn, you can reprimand or be kind to them." [87] He said, "Whoever does wrong, we will punish him, but when he returns to his Lord, the punishment will be dreadful. [88] However, whoever believes and does good

---

[a]   *Sabab* here means to achieve something i.e. a resource.

[b]   This is a figurative phrase, illustrating how the sun appears to the observer. It is not a scientific fact that the sun sets in murky water.

deeds will have a beautiful reward, and We will only ask him to do easy tasks."

HIS JOURNEY TO THE EAST

[89] So he *again* set off on another expedition, [90] until he reached the place of sunrise *in the east*. He found people there who lived in the open, without any shelter. [91] So it was; We knew all about him.

DELIVERING PROTECTION FROM GOG AND MAGOG[c]

[92] Then he set off on another expedition, [93] till he reached an area lying between two mountains; here he found people who didn't fully understand him. [94] They said, "Zul Qarnayn, Gog and Magog are making trouble in the land; we shall pay you money if you can build a solid wall between us and them. [95] He replied, "The power given by My Lord is enough, but you give me manpower so I can make a rampart between them and you. [96] Bring me pieces of iron" – when he had filled the gap between the two mountainsides, he said, "Blow the bellows!" And he made it glow like fire; he then said, "Bring me molten brass to pour over it. [97] Now they will not be able to cross over it, nor will they be able to pierce it." [98] He told *them,* "This is my Lord's kindness, so when My Lord's promise comes *the wall* will crumble to dust, and my Lord's promise is true." The terrible scenario of the Final Hour

[99] That Day, the Trumpet will be blown. We'll let them surge like waves against each other, and We shall gather them together. [100] That Day, We shall introduce Hell to the disbelievers – [101] whose eyes were veiled from Our remembrance and they were not able to hear. [102] Do the disbelievers think they can take My servants as protectors beside Me? We have prepared Hell as hospitality for the disbelievers. [103] Say: "Shall We tell you who are the biggest losers with respect to works? [104] Whose efforts were misguided, yet they thought they were doing good work: [105] people who disbelieved *in* the signs and *in their* meeting with their Lord, so their deeds are worthless. Nor would We give them on the Day of Judgement any weight. [106] Hell is their reward, because they mocked My signs and My messengers." [107] Those who believed and did righteous deeds will have *the* hospitality of *the* Gardens of Paradise. [108] They will stay there forever, never wanting a change.

---

[c] These are names of the enemies of God's people, as mentioned in the Bible (Ezkel: 38). Or two nations that plunder other people's lands.

GOD'S COMMANDS, CREATION AND CARE ARE INFINITE

[109] Say: "If the seas became ink for writing down the words of My Lord, the seas would quickly run dry before My Lord's words were finished, even if We added sea upon sea to it." [110] Say: "I am a human being like you. It has been revealed to me: your God is one God. Anyone expecting to meet his Lord, let him do good deeds and not associate anyone with Him from His creation."

19. Maryam
The Mother of Prophet Jesus

This early Makkan chapter was revealed before the first wave of migration to Abyssinia, in the fifth year of the Prophet's 🕌 mission. The chapter is lyrical, most verses ending with a long vowel "aa" – a generous peppering of *Yaa* and *Daa* beautifies a familiar subject. This is complemented with the repetition of the divine name *al-Rahman* ("the Most Kind") sixteen times.

It opens with the solemn prayer of Prophet Zachariah, for a successor. He was old, childless, and worried about who would be his heir. This prayer reflects his deep faith and reliance on God: "My prayer has never gone unanswered by My Lord" (4). God blessed him with John , "The soft-hearted, pure and pious" (13). The story of the miraculous conception and birth of Jesus emphasises the Power, Majesty and Independent nature of the Divine, who is beyond the law of cause and effect. The first words Jesus said: "I am a servant of God; He has given me the Book and made me a prophet, and made me blessed wherever I go" (31). The Quran rejects the Christian belief of Trinity, and states how objectionable and unacceptable this is to God: "What a monstrous thing you have said! Even the skies would crack, the Earth would rip apart and the mountains crumble" (89–91). This outrageous claim shows the extent of God's anger, a powerful condemnation of idolatry.

A highly-charged conversation then follows between a nephew and an uncle: Abraham very gently tries to persuade and win over Azar, his uncle, from idolatry. The courtesy and logic he employs are persuasive enough to prompt even a stone heart to move. However, idolatry makes one deaf, locks the mind and seals the heart. Abraham sets a wonderful example for preachers and obedient sons on how to differ politely. There are four stories mentioned here: Zachariah and John , Mary and Jesus , Abraham and Azar, Moses and Aaron . They reflect a father and son relationship, a mother and son relationship, and two brotherly relationships. The relationships between prophets and their communities also reveal the great importance of human relationships.

Faith forms an important element of relationships. The Quran condemns those generations who were the children of prophets yet: "After them came generations who neglected the prayer and followed their lusts. Soon they will face the consequences of their evil" (59). Salah is a powerful expression of a person's relationship with God, the Lord. Neglecting it demonstrates a lack of commitment to the relationship.

In the name of God, the Kind, the Caring.

[1] *Kaf Ha Ya Ain Sad.*

THE STORY OF ZACHARIAH

[2] This is an account of your Lord's compassion for Zachariah, His servant, [3] when he quietly prayed to His Lord [4] saying, "My Lord, my bones are weak because of old age, my hair has turned grey, but My prayer has never gone unanswered by My Lord. [5] I am afraid of what my relatives might do after me. My wife is childless, give me a gift, a successor, [6] who will be my successor and the successor of Jacob's family. My Lord, make him pleasing *to all.*"

ZACHARIAH IS GIVEN GOOD NEWS OF A SON

[7] Zachariah, We give you good news of a son! He shall be called John, no one has been named like him before. [8] He said, "Lord, will I have a son when my wife is barren and I'm old? [9] *An angel* said, "It will be so; your Lord said, 'That is easy for me, I created you before this when you were nothing.'" [10] Zachariah said, "Lord, make for me a sign." He said, "Your sign is: you won't be able to speak to people for three days and nights." [11] So, he came out of his prayer room and signalled to *the congregation* to glorify God morning and evening. [12] "John, hold the Book firmly," and We gave him wisdom in his childhood, [13] soft-hearted, pure and pious. [14] He was kind to his parents, never a tormentor or disobedient. [15] So God's peace be on him the day he was born, the day he will die and the day he will be resurrected.

THE STORY OF MARY

[16] Mention Mary, when she left her family to go to a place in the East. [17] She separated herself from them *to stay* in an isolated place; We sent the Angel of Revelation to her and he appeared in human form. [18] She said, "I seek the protection of the Kind *Lord* from you if you fear God." [19] He said, "I am a messenger from Your Lord, and I have come to give you a pure son." [20] She replied, "How can I have a son when no man has touched me and I am not loose woman?"[a] [21] He told her, "That is how it will be; your Lord said, 'This is easy for me, and We shall make him a sign of Our Kindness for people, a command, done!'"

---

[a] But a virgin.

MARY GIVES BIRTH TO JESUS

[22] And so it was she conceived him and moved to a far-off place. [23] When the pains of childbirth drove her to the trunk of a date tree, she cried: "I wish I were dead and forgotten long before all this." [24] A voice from below cried out to her: "Do not worry; your Lord has provided flowing water at your feet; [25] shake the trunk of the date Palm and fresh ripe dates will fall. [26] Eat and drink, be happy. When you see someone say, 'I vowed to the Kind *Lord* a fast, so today I shall not speak to anyone.'

JESUS SPEAKS TO DEFEND HIS MOTHER

[27] She came to her family, carrying him. They said, "Mary, you have brought something unheard of; [28] sister of Aaron, your father was not evil, nor was your mother loose woman." [29] She pointed to him. They replied, "How can we speak to an infant in a cradle?" [30] *Jesus* spoke: "I am a servant of God; He has given me the Book, made me a prophet, [31] made me blessed wherever I go, commanded me to pray and to give charity. *I shall do so* as long as I live, [32] and I will take care of my mother. He has not made me overbearing or disobedient. [33] So God's peace be on me the day I was born, the day I die and the day that I am resurrected."

JESUS IS THE SERVANT OF GOD

[34] That was Jesus, son of Mary; that's the truth they have doubt about. [35] God has not taken a son, glory to Him. When he gives an order, He says to it, "Be," and it becomes. [36] Surely God is My Lord and Your Lord, so worship Him; this is the straight path. [37] The sects differed among themselves; anguish awaits the disbelievers when the terrible Day comes. [38] How well they will hear and see the day they come to Us, yet today the evildoers are totally lost. [39] Warn them of a fateful Day when the decree shall be fulfilled; they were neglectful and didn't believe. [40] We shall inherit the Earth and all that's in it, and to Us they will all be returned.

ABRAHAM CHALLENGES IDOL WORSHIP

[41] Mention Abraham in the Book; he was a truthful man and a prophet. [42] When he said to his father,[b] "My father, why do you worship idols that cannot hear nor see nor benefit you in the least? [43] My father, the knowledge that didn't reach you has come to me. Therefore, follow me; I shall guide you on the straight path.

[b] Here, classical commentators take "father" to mean "uncle".

[44] My father, do not worship Satan, he has disobeyed the Kind Lord. [45] My father, I fear that you shall be punished by the most Kind, and become a friend of Satan." [46] His father replied, "Abraham, are you turning away from my gods? If you do not stop this, I will torture you; off you go and leave me alone." [47] He said, "Peace be on you. I shall seek My Lord's forgiveness for you, since He is Most Kind to me. [48] In the meantime, I shall leave you and those you call upon beside God. I shall pray to My Lord and believe that my prayer will not go unanswered." [49] When he detached himself from them and what they worshipped beside God, We gave him Isaac and Jacob, and We made them all prophets. [50] We gave them Our gifts and We gave them fame and honour.

PROPHETS MOSES, ISHMAEL, ENOCH AND NOAH

[51] Mention Moses in the Book; he was a chosen messenger and a prophet. [52] We called out to him from the right-hand side of the mount *Sinai* and brought him closer to speak to him in secret. [53] We treated him kindly and gave him as a *support* Aaron, his brother, a prophet. [54] Mention Ishmael in the Book; he was man of his word, a messenger and a prophet. [55] He used to tell his family to pray and to give Zakat, and his Lord liked him. [56] Mention Enoch in the Book; he was a man of truth, and a prophet. [57] And We raised him to a high rank. [58] God favoured these *wonderful* men; the prophets from the children of Adam, and they came from those We carried with Noah, and they were from the children of Abraham and Jacob. We guided and selected them. When the verses of the Kind Lord were recited to them, they fell in prostration tearfully.

THE IMPORTANCE OF REGULAR PRAYERS

[59] After them came generations who neglected the prayer and followed their lusts. Soon they will face the consequences of their evil. [60] Except those who repent, believe and do righteous deeds – they shall enter Paradise, and they will not be wronged in the slightest. [61] The Kind Lord's Promise to his servants are Gardens of Eternity, the unseen. His Promise will certainly be fulfilled. [62] They will not hear any useless chatter but peace, there will be plentiful provisions for them morning and evening. [63] Such *a marvellous* Paradise We shall bless Our pious servants to inherit.

GABRIEL SPEAKS

[64]"We don't come down except by the command of your Lord.[a] To Him belongs what is in front and behind us, and that which is in between. Your Lord never forgets – [65] Lord of the Heavens and the Earth and what is between them. So, worship Him and be committed to His worship. Is there anyone who is equal to Him?"

DISBELIEVERS KNEELING AROUND HELL

[66] A person queries: "Once I am dead will I be raised up again?" [67] Don't people remember We created them before when they were non-existent? [68] So your Lord will gather them all and the Satan; We will make them kneel around Hell, [69] and from every group We will drag out the bitterest enemy of the Kind Lord. [70] We know who deserves to burn in it. [71] However, every one of you will come near it – a decree of your Lord that will be fulfilled. [72] Then We shall save the pious whilst leaving the wrongdoers on their knees in Hell.

THE BOASTING OF DISBELIEVERS

[73] When Our clear verses are recited to them, the disbelievers say to the believers, "Which of the two groups has better dwellings and who has luxurious clubs?"[b] [74] How many generations did We destroy before them who were more affluent and looked smart? [75] Say: "Whoever is misguided, the Kind Lord gives him time until he sees what has been promised – either the punishment or the Final Hour. Then they will know who was in a bad place and who had the weakest forces." [76] God keeps developing the guided in *their* guidance, and the lasting deeds of goodness are best with your Lord as a reward and the best outcome.

DISBELIEVERS' CONFUSION

[77] Have you seen him, who denies Our signs and boasts: "I will certainly be given wealth and children." [78] Has he got knowledge of the unseen? Or has he taken a pledge from the Kind? [79] No, We shall write down what he speaks and We shall prolong his punishment. [80] We shall divest him[c] of what he spoke when he comes to us alone. [81] They took Gods beside God to gain strength; [82] but it will not be

---

a   This is Angel Gabriel speaking.
b   Affluent disbelievers boasting about their wealth and material prowess.
c   Literally: "inherit from him". This is "a metaphor based on the concept of one person's taking over what once belonged to another" (Asad).

so, their idols will reject their worship and become their enemies. [83] Haven't you realised We sent devils to the disbelievers, who constantly rouse them?

[84] Don't be hasty about them, since We are counting their days. [85] On the Day We shall ceremoniously gather the pious before the Kind Lord, [86] and the sinful will be driven to Hell like thirsty cattle driven to a waterhole, [87] no one will be able to make intercession except the one given permission by the Kind Lord.

WHEN IS GOD MOST ANGRY?

[88] They said, "The Kind Lord has taken a child." [89] What a monstrous thing you have said! [90] The skies would crack, the Earth shudder, and the mountains crumble to dust [91] when they attribute a child to the Kind *Lord*. [92] It is not befitting for the Kind Lord to have children. [93] Everyone in the Heavens and on Earth must come to the Kind Lord as an obedient servant. [94] He has accurately counted[a] them and numbered them exactly. [95] So on the Day of Judgement, each one of them will come to Him alone.

LOVE FOR GOOD PEOPLE

[96] The Kind Lord will put love for those who believe and do righteous deeds *in people's hearts*.[b] [97] We made the Quran easy in your language so you can give good news to the pious, and warn the opponents with it.[c] [98] How many generations have We destroyed before them? Do you find any one of them alive or hear as much as *their* whisper?

---

[a] *Ahsa* is literally "bookkeeping"

[b] In the hadith, the Messenger ﷺ said: "When God loves his servant, He tells Gabriel to love him, so Gabriel loves him, and makes the announcement in Heaven that so and so is God's beloved, therefore you should all love him" (Bukhari).

[c] *Qauman Luddan:* obstinate, stubborn and contentious people. Luddites were people who disliked and rebelled against new forms of technology, a parallel with disbelievers who disliked the new message of the Prophet ﷺ.

20. Ta Ha

Ta Ha

This is an early Makkan chapter, its central theme is how God guides humanity through messengers, exemplified by featuring the life story of Moses . The story begins when Moses is returning from Madyan to Egypt. He is appointed as a messenger and given miracles. The chapter flips back to the time of his birth, recalling how as a baby he was rescued from Pharaoh's murderous plan: "I wrapped you up in My Divine Love so that you may grow up under My Eyes" (39). How loving is God! Moses heads straight for Pharaoh's court. A heated conversation follows and the Pharaoh gets angry, but Moses boldly – yet gently – continues to invite him to God. Despite witnessing the two miracles of Moses , the Pharaoh remains stubbornly unwilling to listen to him. He mistakenly believes Moses is a magician so challenges him to duel his magicians.

A vivid description of the duel offers insights into the working of magic, and why magic failed. These expert magicians realised that Moses was not a magician, so they accepted his victory and his prophethood. The Pharaoh was enraged and had them martyred.

Even after this defeat and witnessing nine miracles, the Pharaoh refused to accept Moses . Finally, Moses led the Israelites out of Egypt. The Pharaoh chased them, but was drowned. Once in the Sinai Peninsula, the Israelites enjoyed freedom and were blessed with the Heavenly gifts of quail and Manna. However, when Moses left them for a short while – he visited Mount Sinai to meet God – the Israelites made an idol to worship. Moses was angry with his brother Aaron for not stopping them. Samiri the Goldsmith, the mastermind of this ordeal, forged a golden calf and Moses cursed him for his blasphemy and evil action.

The conclusion is, Makkans are reminded of the dire consequences of rejecting the Prophet ﷺ.

The chapter opened by telling the beloved Prophet Muhammad ﷺ not to be stressed by sarcasm and scornful attitude of Makkans, at the end he's told: be patient, be calm, and seek help through constant prayer.

In the name of God, the Kind, the Caring.

¹ *Ta Ha.*ᵃ

GOD, THE KNOWER OF ALL SECRETS

² We did not send the Majestic Quran to distress you; ³ but a reminder to anyone who fears God, ⁴ a revelation from the one who created the Earth and the soaring skies. ⁵ The Most Kind established on the throne *as befits Him.* ⁶ The owner of what lies in the Heavens, the Earth and between them, and all that's buried deep in the soil. ⁷ Whether you speak aloud or quietly; He knows all the secrets and all that is hidden. ⁸ God – there is no god but He. His names are the most beautiful.

MOSES GOES TO FETCH FIRE

⁹ Have you heard the story of Moses? ¹⁰ When he saw the fire he said to his wife, "Stay here, I've noticed a fire; perhaps I can bring a live coal for you or find a guide *nearby.*ᵇ ¹¹ When he came near *the bush* a voice called: "Moses, ¹² I am your Lord; take off your sandals you're in the Sacred Valley of Tuwa.ᶜ ¹³ I've chosen you, so listen to the Revelation. ¹⁴ I am God. There is no god but Me, so worship Me. Perform the prayer to remember Me. ¹⁵ The Hour shall come, but I will keep it secret, to ensure paying everyone for what they did. ¹⁶ So don't let the disbelievers who follow their whims stop you from it, otherwise you will be ruined too."

MOSES IS BLESSED WITH MIRACLES

¹⁷ *God asked,* "What's in your right-hand Moses?" ¹⁸ He replied, "This is my walking stick; I lean on it *sometimes,* I gather leaves for my sheep, and I use it for other things." ¹⁹ God said, "Throw it down, Moses!" ²⁰ So he threw it down, and it turned into a snake scurrying about. ²¹ God ordered: "Pick it up and don't be afraid; We will return it to its original state. ²² Now put your hand under your armpit; it will come out white and unharmed – here is another sign, ²³ to show you some of Our great signs. ²⁴ Go to Pharaoh, he's overstepped the limits."ᵈ

ᵃ   Most commentators agree this means, "O man", however, Al-Qurtubi said it is also the name of the blessed Messenger 🕊.

ᵇ   As he was returning from Madyan.

ᶜ   The valley of Tuwa is located near Mount Sinai (Egypt) and it is a sacred valley.

ᵈ   Pharaoh overstepped the limits of being God's servant, claiming to be god.

Moses' prayer for greater understanding

[25] He prayed: "My Lord, expand my chest, [26] make my work easy, [27] and untie my tongue [28] so *people* may understand my speech, [29] and from my family give me a helper, [30] my brother Aaron, [31] to strengthen my back [32] and to help me in my task, [33] so that we may always glorify [34] and remember you. [35] Surely you are Ever-Watching." [36] God answered, "I grant you what you asked for, Moses. [37] We have already done you a favour in the past.

Moses is wrapped up in Divine Love

[38] Remember, We inspired your mother to [39] place you in a basket and let it float in the river. *We told her*: 'The river will take him to the bank from where Mine and your enemy will pick him up.' I wrapped you up in my Divine Love so you may grow up under My watchful eye. [40] Remember, your sister came and told them:[c] 'Shall I tell you who can look after him?' So We returned you to your mother, so that she may be happy and not worry. *Later in your youth* you killed someone, and We saved you *again* from trouble and tested you in various ways; you lived among the People of Madyan *for some time*, then you came here, Moses, as decreed. [41] I have chosen you for Myself.

Moses in Pharaoh's court

[42] Go with your brother and take My miracles; don't lapse in My remembrance. [43] Go to Pharaoh both of you, he has overstepped the limits, [44] speak gently with him, so he might pay attention or fear God." [45] They said, "Our Lord, we dread he will torture us and transgress bounds." [46] God replied, "Don't worry, I am with you, listening to and observing everything. [47] Now go to him and say: 'We are messengers of your Lord, so send the Israelites with us and do not oppress them; we have come to you with miracles from your Lord. Peace on the one who follows the guidance. [48] It has been revealed to us that the punishment will come on those who reject and turn away.'"

Moses and Pharaoh in heated conversation

[49] *Pharaoh* said, "Who is your Lord, Moses?" [50] He answered, "Our Lord is the One Who gave everything that exists, a body and guidance." [51] He asked, "What about the previous generation?" [52] *Moses* said, "My Lord has full knowledge of

---

[c] Pharaoh's wife had just rescued Moses from the river.

them, and *their works* are properly recorded. My Lord never makes a mistake nor forgets." ⁵³ It is He who made the Earth a cradle and made for you means and ways of *livelihood,* and sent down from the sky the rain, so *He* produces with it various pairs of plants, ⁵⁴ *which you* eat and graze your cattle on; such are Our signs for the understanding. ⁵⁵ From the Earth We created you; We shall return you there and *finally* We shall bring you back to life once more. ⁵⁶ We showed him[a] all Our signs, but he denied and refused.

Pharaoh threatens Moses

⁵⁷ He said, "Have you come to drive us out of our country with your magic, Moses? ⁵⁸ We will bring magic to match it, so *let us* set a time for a contest at an agreed place; neither of us shall break the promise." ⁵⁹ Moses said, "Meet me on the day of the festival when people gather at mid-morning." ⁶⁰ Pharaoh withdrew and formalised his plans, and came back. ⁶¹ Moses said to him, "Woe to you, do not make up lies about God, in case He destroys you with punishment; the one who makes up lies will lose." ⁶² So they secretly discussed their plans among themselves. ⁶³ They said, "These two magicians want to drive you out of your country with their magic, and put an end to your cherished lifestyle." ⁶⁴ Therefore, put together your plans and then come organised in rows. Whoever triumphs today will succeed.

Moses' contest with the magicians

⁶⁵ The magicians said, "Moses, either you throw or we'll throw first." ⁶⁶ Moses replied, "You throw first!" So by their magic, their ropes and sticks appeared to him to be moving around. ⁶⁷ Moses was alarmed. ⁶⁸ We told him, "Don't worry, you will have the upper hand. ⁶⁹ Throw down what is in your right hand, it will swallow up what they have made. They performed magicians' tricks, and the magicians are never successful in what they do." ⁷⁰ So the magicians fell in prostration saying, "We believe in the Lord of Aaron and Moses."

Pharaoh opposes freedom of faith

⁷¹ The Pharaoh said, "You have believed him before I gave you permission, so he must be your mentor who taught you magic. I'll cut off your hands and your feet from the opposite sides, and hang you on the trunks of palm trees, so you will

---

[a] Pharaoh.

know whose punishment is more severe and everlasting." [72] They replied, "We will never prefer you, we saw the clear proofs of the One who created us, so decide what you will, and the most you can do is end our worldly life. [b73] We have believed in Our Lord, may He forgive us our mistakes and the magic that you have forced us to practice. God is the Best and the Everlasting." [74] Whoever comes to His Lord sinning, for him is Hell where he will neither die nor live. [75] *On the other hand,* whoever comes to Him believing and doing righteous deeds, they shall have a lofty place. [76] They will live in Gardens of Eternity, with streams flowing beneath them. Such is the reward of those who purify themselves.

Moses leads the Israelites out of Egypt

[77] We revealed to Moses: "Take our servants by night and make a dry way for them across the sea, and don't fear being caught, nor be worried." [78] The Pharaoh and his army followed them, and they were besieged and covered up by the sea. [79] The Pharaoh misled his people, and he didn't guide them. [80] Israelites! We saved you from your enemy and We made a contract with you on the right-hand side of the mountain, and We sent down to you Manna and quails.[c] [81] Eat from the wholesome food We gave you, but don't overstep the limits. Otherwise, I shall be angry with you, and anyone who suffers my anger, falls. [82] *However,* I am Forgiving for anyone who repents, believes, does righteous deeds and remains on the straight path.

Israelites make an idol to worship

[83] "Moses, why have you come hastily ahead of your followers?"[d] [84] He said, "They are coming behind me, I rushed to please you My Lord." [85] God said, "After you left, We tested your people, when Samiri misled them."[e] [86] Moses *quickly* returned to his people; angry and saddened. He said, "My people, didn't your Lord make a contract with you? Or have you forgotten it? Or you wanted to invite your Lord's anger on yourself by breaking the contract with me?" [87] They said, "We didn't deliberately break the promise; we were carrying too much weight from people's jewellery, so we threw it *in the fire* and the Samiri threw likewise." [88] Samiri shaped

[b] *Taqdi* means 'he decided' but also 'he ended something'.
[c] Manna is a special type of food like honey that was graciously provided to them; quail is a small game bird.
[d] When you climbed Mount Sinai.
[e] Samiri, or the Samirian, was from one of the tribes of the Israelites.

for them a statue of a calf that made a mooing sound, so they said, "This is god and the god of Moses, but he deceived them." [89] Why didn't they realise the calf couldn't answer them, and neither harm nor benefit them? [90] Aaron had already told them: "My people, you have been tested with this; your Lord is Kind, so follow me and obey my orders. [91] They replied, "We'll carry on worshipping it until Moses comes back."

MOSES IS ANGRY WITH AARON AND THE ISRAELITES

[92] *Moses* said, "Aaron, when you saw them being misled what stopped you [93] from *leaving them and* following me? Why did you disobey my orders?" [94] Aaron replied, "My mother's son, don't grab my beard or my hair, I was afraid you would say: 'You divided the Israelites and you didn't wait for my decision.'" [95] Moses said, "Samiri, why did you do this?" [96] He said, "I saw what they didn't see, I picked up a handful of dust from the trail of the Messenger[a] and threw it at the statue of the calf; unfortunately that's what seemed pleasing to me." [97] Moses told him, "Go away; your life will be such that you will cry: 'Don't touch me'. There is also a promise *of punishment* for you that will not be broken. Look at your god that you worshipped. We'll burn it! Then scatter it in the sea. [98] Indeed your Lord is God; there is no god but He; His knowledge embraces all things."

THE QURAN IS A REMINDER

[99] In this way We tell you stories of what happened in the past. We gave you a reminder, *the Quran*. [100] Whoever turns away from it will be carrying a heavy burden on Judgement Day. [101] They will remain in that state forever, a dreadful burden to be carrying on that Day.

CATACLYSMIC EVENTS WHEN THE WORLD ENDS

[102] The Day the Trumpet is blown, We shall gather the sinners, blind.[b] [103] They will be whispering among themselves: "You stayed no more than ten days *in the world*" [104] We know best what they are saying when their most intelligent one will say, "You were *there* for no longer than a day." [105] They ask you about the mountains. Tell them: "My Lord will grind them into dust, [106] creating a vast area of flatland [107] where you won't see a valley or hill.

---

[a] Angel Gabriel.
[b] *Zurqan* means blue eyed, dim-sighted and blind.

WHAT WILL HAPPEN ON THE DAY OF JUDGEMENT?

[108] That Day they will follow a caller, who no one will ignore. Their voices will be hushed for the Kind Lord; you will not hear but a whisper. [109] On the Day intercession will not benefit anyone except by the permission of the Kind Lord and whoever He approves. [110] He knows what they achieved and what they failed to achieve, but they don't know that.[c] [111] With long, sad faces they will stand before the Ever-Living, the Everlasting Lord. Whoever carries *an* evil burden will be feeling hopeless. [112] *In contrast,* whoever did righteous deeds and was a believer will have nothing to fear of being wronged or unjustly treated."

PRAYER FOR BOOSTING KNOWLEDGE

[113] This is how We revealed an Arabic Quran, and in it We explained warnings so *people* might fear and pay attention. [114] God is the Highest, the Absolute Controller and the Truth. Do not be hasty with the Majestic Quran before it is completely revealed to you, *Prophet,* and pray: "My Lord, increase my knowledge."

HOW SATAN TRICKED ADAM

[115] Previously We taught Adam, but he forgot; We didn't find him determined *to sin.* [116] When We told the Angels, "Prostrate before Adam," they prostrated, except Satan who refused. [117] So We said, "Adam, this is your and your wife's enemy, so don't let him drive you out of Paradise – in that case you will be in trouble. [118] There is enough provision *in Paradise,* so you won't be hungry or unclothed; [119] here you won't suffer pangs of thirst or the *scorching* heat of the sun." [120] Satan whispered to him and said, "Adam, shall I show you the tree of eternity and power that will never diminish?" [121] So both ate from it, and instantly became aware of their nakedness, so they began covering themselves with the leaves of Paradise. Adam forgot his Lord's command and failed.[d] [122] Then your Lord forgave him, chose him and guided him. [123] God said, "Get down from here, all of you as enemies of one another. If guidance comes to you from Me, whoever follows My guidance will not be misguided nor be miserable."

REMEMBERING GOD AND BEING EVER CONSCIOUS OF HIM

[124] Anyone who turns away from My remembrance will live a difficult life and

[c] This translation is according to Ibn Abbas, literally it means "He knows what is in front and what is behind him".
[d] *Ghawa* also means "go astray" and "fail to achieve one's purpose and ruin the comforts of one's life".

We shall raise him up blind on Judgement Day. [125] He will say, "My Lord, why did you raise me up blind, I was sighted *in the world?*" [126] He will say, "That's because Our signs came to you and you forgot them; likewise, you are forgotten today." [127] This is how We deal with those who wasted the *opportunity*, and didn't believe in their Lord's signs. The punishment of the Hereafter is more severe and everlasting. [128] The fact that We destroyed many generations before them, whose houses they used to walk around, *should be* a source of guidance for them; in this are signs for the understanding. [129] If it wasn't for the previous verdict from your Lord, the inevitable would have happened. But there is a fixed time *for it.*

The importance of prayer throughout the day

[130] So be patient with what they say, and glorify your Lord with praise before sunrise and sunset, and during the night, and at the ends of the day, so you may be happy. [131] Don't look with envy at what We gave them to enjoy from life's worldly luxuries; it's Our way of testing them, and your Lord's sustenance is better and everlasting. [132] Teach your family to pray and perform it yourself as well. We don't ask you for provision, actually, We provide for you, and a good outcome is a result of righteousness.

The Quran is a final reminder, so wait

[133] They said, "Why didn't he bring a book from His Lord? Hasn't a clear sign already come to them in former books of revelation?" [134] Had We destroyed them with a punishment before this they would say, "Our Lord, why did you not send a messenger to us? We would have followed your revelation, so we wouldn't be disgraced and put to shame." [135] Say: "Each one of us is waiting, so you wait as well; soon you will know those who were on the straight path and rightly guided."

21. Al-Anbiya'
The Prophets

This is a late Makkan chapter. The central theme is an explanation of the three basic beliefs of Islam: monotheism, prophethood and the Hereafter, with focus on prophethood. It opens by criticising the Makkans and their drunkenness with worldly life. Divine judgement is presented through the effects of historical disobedience: how past nations who denied prophets were destroyed. The next section is about the creation of the universe, and how all living things were created from water – clear evidence that God can recreate humanity after death.

A frequent theme in the Quran is God's care for his creatures. This is illustrated by constant repetition of His Beautiful Names (the Kind, the Caring, the Loving, the Generous and the Responder). God is Al-Hadi, the Guide, evidence of this is Him sending prophets. The Quran presents an historical record of how God intervened in human history by sending the prophets, and established a clear framework for human salvation. The Quran mentions only twenty-five prophets by name, yet there were more than 124,000 prophets according to one prophetic saying. Five of them are recognised in Islamic theology as commanding a special status: the Prophet Muhammad ﷺ, Jesus , Abraham , Moses and Noah . The prophets Abraham , Joseph , Jonah , Hud , and Noah have full chapters dedicated to their life and mission. Many others, like David and Solomon , are mentioned several times in the Quran. They are a symbol of God's care for humanity, as is their distinct role in guiding people. Seventeen prophets are mentioned briefly, their struggles, sufferings and steadfastness, followed by their pleas to the Lord for help. In each case, the eventual Divine wrath destroyed their detractors. For example, the prayer of Prophet Jonah from inside the whale: "There is no god except You; glory be to You, I was wrong. We saved him and rescued him from distress, and that is how We rescue the believers" (87–88). The conclusion: "This is your community, a single *united* community. I am your Lord, so worship Me. *Unfortunately,* people tore the unity of their religion; all will be returning to Us" (92–93).

The chapter ends with a delightful description of Paradise, and the happiness of believers. Perhaps the crowning verse of the chapter is: "We sent you as Kindness for all the worlds" (107). What a tribute for the blessed Messenger ﷺ! How wonderfully God boosted the morale of beloved Muhammad ﷺ.

––––––––––

In the name of God, the Kind, the Caring.

DISTRACTED MINDS FORGET THE HEREAFTER

[1] The time of reckoning for humanity is drawing closer, yet they turn away

thoughtlessly. ²Whenever a new revelation from your Lord comes to them they listen to it playfully, ³their hearts distracted *by worldly activities*. In private the evildoers say, "Isn't he just a man like you? Are you going to follow the magic *of Muhammad* with your eyes open?" ⁴*The Prophet* said, "My Lord knows every word spoken in the Heavens and the Earth; He is the Listener, the Knower." ⁵They replied, "These are just confused dreams; he's made them up. In fact, he's a poet, so let him bring us a miracle like the prophets of the past brought."

Disbelievers criticise the Prophet ﷺ

⁶The communities We destroyed before them didn't believe either, so will they now believe? ⁷We sent Revelation to communities in the past; if you don't know this ask the people of the Scripture. ⁸We didn't make their bodies to live *on Earth* forever, nor could they survive without food. ⁹ We fulfilled Our promise and saved those who We wanted, and destroyed those who wasted *the opportunity of life*. ¹⁰Indeed We revealed a Book to you that mentions you too!ᵃ Why do you not understand?

The Divine reckoning

¹¹We destroyed many towns of the sinners, and afterwards raised up other people in their place. ¹²When they sensed our punishment coming they fled, ¹³*and We said*: "Do not run away; come back to the places of your enjoyment and homes so you may be questioned." ¹⁴They said, "Suffering has come upon us; we were evildoers." ¹⁵They screamed till We made them like dried up stubble.

Life is not casual, like sport

¹⁶We didn't create the Heavens and the Earth and what is between the two as a sport. ¹⁷If We wanted a pastime then We would have found it within Us, were We to do such a *frivolous* thing. ¹⁸No, We pitched the truth against falsehood, so it wiped it out; falsehood is weak. For you is Hellᵇ for the things you attributed to God. ¹⁹Everything in the Heavens and the Earth belongs to Him; those near Him are not arrogant about worshipping Him, nor do they get tired. ²⁰*They are* always glorifying Him, night and day, never growing weary. ²¹Or have they taken gods from the Earth who can resurrect?

ᵃ *Zikra* also means: fame, honour, and reminder, as well as being a name of the Quran.
ᵇ *Wail* is the name of one of the seven Hells and also means woe, suffering.

THE ORDERLINESS IN THE UNIVERSE IS PROOF OF ONE CREATOR

²²If there were gods other than God, then there would be devastation in *the Heavens and the Earth*. Glory to God, Lord of the Throne, *He isn't the way* they describe Him. ²³He won't be questioned about what He does, but they'll be questioned! ²⁴Or have they taken gods besides Him? Say: "Bring your proof; this is a reminder for those who are with me and a reminder for those before me," but most of them don't know the truth, they have turned away. ²⁵Every messenger before you was inspired to say: "There is no god but Me, so worship Me." ²⁶They said, "The Kind Lord has a child." Glory to Him, they are honourable servants,ᶜ ²⁷who don't speak before He speaks and obey His command. ²⁸God knows what is in front and behind them, and they will not intercede except for him who He is pleased with, since they are in fear of Him. ²⁹If any among them claimed, "I am god beside Him," then We shall punish him in Hell; that's how We treat the evildoers.

THE BEGINNING OF THE UNIVERSE

³⁰Don't the disbelievers know the Heavens and the Earth were joined *at one time?* We split them apart and made every living thing from water; won't they believe? ³¹We made mountains on Earth *for stability*, so it does not shake *beneath* them, and We made wide, open pathways so they can find their way. ³²And We made the sky a roof that gives protection, they *still* turn away from these marvellous signs. ³³He created night and day, sun and moon, each one moving in its orbit. ³⁴In the past We didn't make any human being who lived forever, so if you should die, will they live forever? ³⁵Everyone will taste death; We shall test you all with something good and something bad, and *finally* you will be returned to Us.

MOCKING OTHERS IS THE HABIT OF DISBELIEVERS

³⁶The disbelievers mock when they see you and say, "Is this the one who talks about your gods?" They fail to acknowledge the name of the most Kind Lord.ᵈ ³⁷Man was made hasty *and impatient*; I will show you My signs, so don't ask Me to hasten them. ³⁸They ask, "When will this promise be fulfilled if you are truthful?" ³⁹*If* only the disbelievers knew, a time will come when they won't be able to stop the Fire burning their faces and backs, and they will be helpless. ⁴⁰It will

---

ᶜ The idolaters of Makkah believed that angels were God's daughters.

ᵈ Failure to acknowledge God, they ignore and give the cold shoulder.

come unexpectedly, taking them by surprise, they won't be able to get away, nor get any relief. [41]Messengers were mocked before you, and the jokers were punished by *the punishment* they use to mock.

GOD IS THE ONLY PROTECTOR

[42]Say: "Who can protect you at night and during the day from the Most Kind Lord?" They turn away from their Lord's remembrance. [43]Or do they have gods that can protect them beside Us? They're incapable of helping themselves, or being safe from Us. [44]For a long time, We allowed them and their fathers to enjoy the good things of life. Haven't they noticed how We are gradually reducing the borders of their city? So, are they dominant? [45]Say: "I am warning you with the revelation." Unfortunately, the deaf will not hear the warning call when it's given. [46]If a mere puff of your Lord's punishment strikes them they say, "It's too bad for us; we were wrong." [47]On Judgement Day, We shall set up the scales of justice so that no one is misjudged. Even if there is something as little as the weight of a mustard seed, We shall bring it out; We are good in weighing.

THE MESSAGE OF MOSES AND AARON

[48]We gave Moses and Aaron the standard to distinguish between right and wrong, a light and a message for the mindful people – [49]those who fear their Lord without seeing Him, and they are fearful of the Final Hour. [50]This is a sacred message We have sent down, so will you reject it?

ABRAHAM CONFRONTS HIS PEOPLE

[51]Long before *that* We gave Abraham guidance;[a] We knew him well. [52]Remember when He said to his father and the community: "What are these idols you worship?" [53]They said, "Our forefathers were their worshippers." [54]He said, "You and your forefathers are obviously wrong." [55]They replied, "Have you come with the truth or are you joking?" [56]He said, "Your Lord is the Lord of the Heavens and the Earth Who created them, and I am one of the witnesses to this. [57]By God, I will plan something for your idols after you have turned your backs and *gone away*."

ABRAHAM SMASHES THE IDOLS

[58]He smashed them to pieces except the biggest, which He left *intact* so they

---

[a] *Rushd* means being straight in faith and actions, good conduct, maturity of mind, and reason.

would return to it. [59] They said, "Who has done this to our gods? He must be evil!" [60] Some said, "We heard a young man called Abraham speak *disapprovingly* about them. [61] So they demanded: "Bring him in front of the people, so they will see *him*." [62] They asked, "Abraham, did you do this to our gods? [63] He replied, "It was the big one who did this; ask them if they can speak." [64] So they turned to themselves saying *secretly*,[b] "You are the ones who are wrong." [65] They shook their heads in disbelief and said, "You know they can't speak." [66] Abraham quipped, "So, why do you worship beside God something unable to benefit or harm you? [67] A disgrace for you and what you worship beside God; why don't you understand?" [68] They shouted *angrily*: "Burn him and help your gods if you are going to do something." [69] We ordered: "Fire, be cool and comforting for Abraham." [70] They wished to harm him, so We made them the biggest losers.

Lot, Isaac and Jacob

[71] We rescued Abraham and Lot, and took them to the land We blessed for all humanity. [72] So We gave Abraham, Isaac, and Jacob as a grandson, and We made them righteous [73] and *great* leaders, guiding *others* with Our commandments, and inspired *many* virtues: the performance of the prayer, and the giving of Zakat. They were Our true worshippers. [74] We gave Lot authority and knowledge, and rescued him from a town which practised filthy acts of indecency; they were sinful people. [75] We were kind to *Lot* since he was righteous.

Noah, David and Solomon

[76] Remember the bygone days when Noah called for help. We answered, and rescued him and his followers from a terrible torment. [77] We helped him against people who denied Our revelations. They were evil; so We drowned them. [78] Remember when David and Solomon were making judgement regarding the cornfield where some people's sheep had wandered off to graze. We were Witness of their judgement. [79] We helped Solomon understand *the problem*. Each one We blessed with judgment and knowledge. We made mountains echo and the birds sing our praises together with David; We did all these things. [80] We taught him how to make coats of armour, so that you can protect yourself from others. Will you be thankful for this? [81] Solomon could command the stormy winds *blowing* to the land which We had blessed. We know all things. [82] He also controlled the

---

[b] An idiom for introspection, to do self-appraisal (Suyuti).

jinn that dived deep in the sea for him, and would do other work *for him* too. We were their keepers.

JOB, ISMAEL, ENOCH AND EZEKIEL

[83] And remember Job when He called his Lord: "I am suffering. You are the Kindest of all." [84] We answered and relieved him of the sufferings, gave back his family, even bigger *than before*. For the worshippers, this was a special kindness from Us and a reminder. [85] Ismael, Enoch and Ezekiel – each one was patient and steadfast. [86] We blessed them with prophethood. They were righteous.

THE PRAYERS OF JONAH, ZACHARIAH AND JOHN

[87] Remember Dhan-Nun,[a] when he left *Nineveh* angrily thinking We wouldn't restrain *or question* him. He prayed in the depths of darkness: "There is no god except You. Glory be to You; I was wrong." [88] We saved and rescued him from distress, and that's how We save the believers. [89] And remember Zachariah, when He called to His Lord: "My Lord, do not leave me childless, you are the best of inheritors." [90] We answered him, gave him John and healed his wife. They were always quick to do good works, pray to Us with *profound* longing and fear, they were humble before Us.

ALL THE PROPHETS HAD THE SAME RELIGION

[91] Mention the *lady* who protected her chastity; We breathed in her Our Spirit, and made her and her son a miraculous sign for all people. [92] This is your community, a single *united* community. I am your Lord, so worship Me. [93] *Unfortunately,* people tore the unity of their religion; all will be returning to Us. [94] Whoever does righteous deeds as a believer, the reward of their good efforts will not be denied to them, We record it for them. [95] The communities We destroyed just couldn't turn away from their evil ways.[b]

WHEN WILL GOG AND MAGOG COME?

[96] When Gog and Magog are let loose – rushing down swiftly from every direction - [97] the true promise will draw near, then the disbelievers will watch in horror and say, "Woe to us, we were not aware of this; in fact, we were wrong." [98] *It will be said*: "You and those you worshipped beside God are the fuel of Hell; that is where you will go." [99] If these were really your gods then they wouldn't be here.

---

[a] *Dha-Nun* means "man of fish", and refers to Prophet Jonah .

[b] Another interpretation is, "it is impossible for communities We destroyed to ever rise again."

They will stay there forever, [100] hearing nothing but sobbing.

The delights of Paradise

[101] *The people* We promised Heaven will be *kept* far away from *Hell.* [102] They won't hear the slightest noise of Hell; they will have whatever they want forever. [103] They won't be distressed by the great terror of Judgement Day. The angels will greet them saying, "This is your Day, which you were promised." [104] That Day We will roll up the sky like the writer rolls up the scroll. We will recreate as We created the first time; it's a promise We've undertaken and will fulfil it.

God's Kindness for all the worlds

[105] In the Psalms and the previous Scriptures, We wrote: "My righteous servants will inherit the Earth." [106] In this *Quran* is a message for the worshippers. [107] We sent you, *Messenger,* as a kindness for all the worlds. [108] Say: "It is revealed to me, Your Lord is one, so won't you submit?" [109] If they turn away, say: "I have declared what you've been promised; I am not sure whether it is near or far. [110] He knows what you say openly and what you hide. [111] What do I know? This may be a test for you or *a respite in the form* of enjoyment for a short while." [112] The messenger prayed: "My Lord, make fair judgement. Our Lord the Kind is the One Whose Help is sought against what you say."

22. Al-Hajj
The Pilgrimage

This is a late Makkan chapter (621 CE) that includes some verses revealed in Madinah. The central theme is the spiritual progress of humanity, connecting with God. The opening verses paint a terrifying image of Judgement Day, striking fear in the heart of the reader, to urge belief in resurrection. The Quran doesn't use fear but employs reason to support its claim for resurrection. The seven stages of human life are one such line of rational evidence that reveals divine creative power. Secondly: "You see the dry lifeless Earth, and when We send down rain it stirs and swells, producing colourful pairs of plants" (5). The chapter points out that, "The creation of life is not an unusual accident, brought about by blind chance or by some unintelligible laws of probability."[a] The doubters are warned: disbelief is shrugging off one's responsibility.

The perennial question: "Why are there so many different religions?" Is tackled in the next section: "We prescribed rituals for every community to practise. So let them not argue with you over *such* matters. *Instead* invite them to your Lord" (67). God will pass His judgement on them. The Quran teaches that diversity in religions is part of a Divine plan.

Hajj is the fifth pillar of Islam. It consists of several rites which were familiar to the Makkans since its establishment 4,000 years ago by their forefather Abraham . However, the Quran clarifies the spiritual significance of these rites; circling the Kaaba and slaughtering animals. These rites are not merely mechanical rituals, but purposeful; impacting health, mindset and welfare. "Those who respect God's symbols[b] show true piety of the heart" (32).

Muslims were persecuted in Makkah for thirteen years, and continued to be oppressed even after their migration to Madinah. Here they were attacked several times, and in the second year of Hijra Muslims were given permission to take up arms against their oppressors: "Permission *to fight* is given to those who were attacked *and oppressed*" (39). The consensus among Muslim scholars about war is: it's permissible in defence – offensive invasions are not permitted.

The next part of the chapter reassures the beloved Prophet 鹵 of the success he is to achieve in the near future, and reassures him not to be distressed by the current hardships. Examples of past prophets are given as an assertion of the eternal triumph of truth. The chapter concludes by outlining what needs to be done to achieve salvation, and how to escape the terror of Judgement Day, which is described graphically in the opening of the chapter:

---

[a] Muhammad al-Ghazali, *Thematic Commentary on the Quran.*
[b] *Sha'irallah* symbols of God means all sacred things: the Quran, Kaaba, Mosque, etc.

Believers, bow down and prostrate in worship of your Lord, and do good so you may succeed. Strive for the sake of God *to do what is right*, as much as He deserves. (77–78).

In the name of God, the Kind, the Caring.

[1] People, fear Your Lord. The Earthquake of the Final Hour will be a significant event: [2] you will see every breastfeeding mother forget her suckling baby, every pregnant woman will miscarry, and every person will appear drunk that day, though they won't be drunk, but such will be the severity of God's punishment. [3] There are some people who argue about God without any knowledge, and follow every rebellious demon. [4] It is decreed: Whoever befriends *Satan*, he will misguide him and lead him towards the punishment of the blazing Fire.

THE SEVEN STAGES OF HUMAN LIFE

[5] People, if you are in *any* doubt about the resurrection, We *originally* created you from clay, then from a drop of semen, *this became* a clot of blood, *then* a lump of flesh – some parts recognisable others unrecognisable – then *a foetus. We revealed this* to make *the Resurrection* clear for you. We plant in wombs whatever We choose for a fixed term, then We bring you out as a baby; then you reach maturity, *after which* some of you die *young* while others proceed to feeble old age, to the extent that they know nothing after having known *so much. Likewise,* you see the Earth *appear* lifeless; then, when We send down rain, it stirs and swells, producing beautiful pairs of plants. [c6] *This shows* God is the Truth. He brings the dead back to life, and has power over all things. [7] The Final Hour is coming without a doubt – *when* God will resurrect *all* who are in *their* graves.

ONLY THE THOUGHTLESS CAN REJECT GOD AND HIS CREATION

[8] People argue about God without knowledge or guidance, or any enlightening book, [9] turning aside *disapprovingly* to cause *others* to stray from God's way. *Such a person* will be disgraced in this world, and on Judgement Day We will make him taste the punishment of the blazing inferno. [10] *He will be told*: "That's what your hands produced. God isn't at all unjust to *His* servants."

---

[c] The seven stages of human life are: The semen and the egg; a clot; lump of flesh; foetus; birth of baby; childhood and adulthood; and old age.

[11] People who worship God doubting Him, are satisfied at the best of times, but at the worst of times they go back to their old ways, losing in both, this world and the next; that is a big loss. [12] Instead of God they call on what cannot harm or benefit them. That's straying far away. [13] *In fact*, they call on that which is more likely to harm than benefit them. What wretched allies, and what wretched company! [14] *However*, God will admit into gardens beneath which rivers flow those who believe and do righteous deeds. God does what He wishes. [15] Whoever imagines that God will not help *Muhammad* either in this world or the next, let him hang himself from a rope tied to the ceiling then cut it off and see if his cunning plan has made his anger go away. [16] That is how We have sent *the Quran* down as clear verses; and God guides whomever He wishes.

RELIGIOUS DIFFERENCES SHALL BE SETTLED ON JUDGEMENT DAY

[17] The Muslims, the Jews, the Sabians, the Christians, the Zoroastrians, and the idolaters, We shall decide between them on Judgement Day. God witnesses everything. [18] Don't you see whatever is in the Heavens and on Earth prostrates before God: the sun, the moon, the stars, the mountains, the trees, the animals, and many people; *but* there are many who justly deserve punishment. Anyone God disgraces will have no one to honour him. God does whatever He pleases.[a]

CONTRASTING FATES OF THE PEOPLE OF HELL AND HEAVEN

[19] These are two opposite groups who argue about their Lord, those who disbelieve will have suits cut out of fire, *and* scalding water poured over their heads, [20] causing their insides and their skins to dissolve; [21] and they will be restrained with iron rods. [22] Whenever, out of agony, they try to escape *their torment*, they will be returned into it and *told*: "Taste the punishment of the blazing inferno." [23] However, God will admit those who believe and do righteous deeds into gardens with rivers flowing beneath them; they will be decorated with bracelets of gold and pearls, and their clothes will be of silk – [24] *those who* were guided *in this world* to the very best of speech,[b] and were guided to the path of the Praiseworthy, [25] *but not* those who disbelieve and block *others* from God's way and from

---

[a] This is another of the Verses of Prostration.

[b] "The very best of speech" is the *Shahada*: "There is no god but God" (Ibn Abbas). Others suggest it's the Quran.

the Sacred Mosque, which We established for *all* the people, whether resident or traveller. Anyone who seeks to violate its *sanctity* by wrongdoing, We shall make him taste a painful punishment.

GOD INSTRUCTS ABRAHAM ABOUT THE KAABA AND THE HAJJ

[26] *Remember* when We marked out for Abraham the place of the *Ancient* House,[c] *saying*: "Don't associate anything with Me; keep My House clean for those who circle it, *worship there*, standing, bowing and prostrating. [27] Announce the pilgrimage to people. They will come to you on foot and mounted on all kinds of lean camels, through every deep mountain pass, [28] to take part in *rites* that benefit them and to invoke the name of God on specific days over such livestock as He has provided for them *to sacrifice*. Eat the *cattle*, and feed the needy and poor. [29] Then complete the rites *of cleansing*,[d] fulfil the vows, and circle the Ancient House."

THE RIGHTS OF HAJJ: GOD'S SYMBOLS VISITED

[30] Anyone who respects the sacred rites of God shall fare better in the Lord's sight. Livestock is lawful for you except ones already mentioned.[e] Stay away from the impurity of idols, and words of falsehood. [31] Incline towards God without associating *partners* with Him. The one who associates *partners* with God, is like the one fallen from the sky, and birds snatch at him, or like the wind that carries him off to a faraway place. [32] Anyone who respects God's symbols,[f] displays true piety of the heart. [33] There are benefits for you in those *symbols* for a designated period, *the rites conclude* at the place of sacrifice[g] near the Ancient House.

THOSE WHO SHOW REVERENCE TO GOD'S SYMBOLS

[34] We prescribed a rite *of sacrifice* for every community, so they may invoke the name of God over such livestock as provided for them. Your God is One God, so submit to Him. And, *Messenger*, give glad tidings to humble *servants* [35] whose

---

[c]   The "Ancient House" is the Kaaba.

[d]   Such as shaving one's head and throwing stones at the three pillars.

[e]   "The only things He has made unlawful for you are carcasses, blood, pork, and animals slaughtered in any name other than God's" (*Al-Baqarah* 2: 173 and *Al-An'am* 6: 145).

[f]   The sacred symbols of God in the Hajj are the Kaaba, the Sacred Months, staying at Arafa, walking between the hills of Safa and Marwa, and the sacrifice of livestock.

[g]   Or, as mentioned by Al-Qurtubi, the place where one symbolically emerges from the sanctified state (*ihram*) of a pilgrim with the final circling of the Kaaba.

hearts tremble at the mention of God, respond patiently to any affliction, perform the prayer and spend in charity from what We provided them.

HOW TO SACRIFICE CAMELS, AND WHY

[36] The sacrificial camels you find valuable are included among God's symbols; so invoke God's name on them as they stand ready *for slaughter*; and, once they have fallen *dead* on their side, eat from them and feed the needy, whether they ask or not. That is how We tamed them for you, so you may be thankful. [37] Neither their meat nor their blood reaches God, but it is your piety that reaches God. That's how We made them obedient for you, so praise God for guiding you. Give glad tidings to the righteous.

WAR IN SELF-DEFENCE IS ALLOWED

[38] God will defend the believers, God dislikes ungrateful traitors. [39] Permission *to fight* is given to those who were attacked because they have been wronged; and God has the power to help those[a] [40] who were unfairly driven out of their homes for saying, "Our Lord is God." If God didn't defend some people by means of others, then monasteries, churches, synagogues and mosques where God's name is regularly praised would have been destroyed. God will support whoever supports His *cause*. God is Strong, Almighty. [b][41] *If* We granted some people authority on Earth, they would establish the prayer, collect Zakat, enjoin the common good and forbid evil. The outcome in *all* matters is determined by God.

THE MESSENGER 鑾 IS REASSURED

[42] If *today* they are denying you, then *long* before them the people of Noah, Ad and Thamud denied *their prophets* too; [43] *likewise* the people of Abraham and of Lot, [44] and the inhabitants of Madyan. *Even* Moses was denied. So I gave the disbelievers time to think, then I seized them. How *great* was My rejection *of their actions*! [45] How many towns have We destroyed whilst they were doing wrong, so *today* their buildings are razed to the ground, and wells *are* abandoned; and *how many* lofty palaces? [46] Have they not travelled the Earth, so *you would think* they had either minds with which to reflect or ears with which to hear? *In truth*, it's

---

[a]   This was revealed in Madinah just after the migration. It is the first time that the Quran gives permission for physical fighting. It was further elaborated in verses 190-192 of Al-Baqarah.

[b]   "Military Jihad is prescribed only for self-defence and defence of the oppressed" (M.A.Haleem: Exploring the Quran).

not the *lack of* sight that causes blindness but *lack of* insight, which is *found* in *people's* chests.[c]

Waiting a millennium or a day are the same to God

[47] They ask you to bring forward the punishment, but God will never break His promise. Your Lord's *single* day is like a thousand years by your calculations. [48] I granted respite to many towns whilst they were doing wrong, then I seized them; and to Me is the final return. [49] Say: "People, I'm only a clear warner to you." [50] As for those who believe and do righteous deeds, they will have forgiveness and generous provision; [51] but those who strive against Our signs will be the companions of Hell, in vain.

God thwarts all attempts to lead prophets astray

[52] We haven't sent a *single* messenger or prophet before you who recited *Our revelation*, but Satan suggested *errors* in his recitation. God removes whatever Satan suggests, then God makes clear His verses – God is Knowing, Wise – [53] thereby turning whatever Satan[d] suggests into a test for those in whose hearts is sickness and for the hard of heart. The wrongdoers are far removed *from the truth*. [54] And *God does this* so those given knowledge should know that it is the truth from your Lord and believe in it, their hearts turning to Him in humility. God guides the believers towards a straight path. [55] The disbelievers will continue to be in doubt about *the truth* until the Final Hour comes abruptly, or the punishment of a barren day.[c]

God's promise to victims of persecution

[56] On that Day, God will have the authority to judge between them. Those who believed and did righteous deeds will be in the gardens of delight, [57] but those who disbelieved and rejected Our signs will have a humiliating punishment. [58] Those who migrated for the sake of God, or were killed or died *on the way*, God will provide for them handsomely – and God is the best Provider – [59] admitting

---

[c]   The idea that the mind resides in the brain, not the heart, is relatively modern. However, recent research in neuroscience shows a close link between the heart and the brain. Possibly the mind also resides in the heart.

[d]   According to some commentators, "Satan" here refers not to the Devil himself, but to those humans who try, like Satan, to tempt others away from God's path. One example is when the leaders of Makkah offered the Prophet ﷺ power and wealth, in return for giving up the teaching of Islam.

[c]   Judgement Day is described as "barren" because there will be no further opportunities to add to the fruit of one's actions.

them *to a place* that pleases them. God is Knowing, Gentle.

GOD URGES BELIEVERS TO STAND UP AGAINST OPPRESSION

[60] That *is God's command*, and whoever retaliates in equal measure to any injury received, and is then wronged again, God will support him *to regain his right*. God is Pardoning, Forgiving. [61] God merges night into day and day into night, and God is Hearing, Seeing. [62] That is *also* because God *alone* is Real, and anything else they call on besides Him is false. It is God who is the Exalted, the Great.

THE CREATION IS FOR THE SERVICE OF HUMANITY

[63] Have you not considered how God sends rain from the sky, turning the Earth green? God is Subtle, Aware. [64] Everything in the Heavens and the Earth belongs to Him. God is the Self-Sufficient, the Praiseworthy. [65] Have you not considered how God made everything on Earth to serve you?[a] Ships sail on the sea by His command, and He holds the sky *in place* so that it does not fall on to the Earth; everything happens with His permission. God is Compassionate, Kind to people. [66] It is He who brought you to life, then causes you to die, and will then bring you back to life. How ungrateful are humans!

ENCOURAGEMENT FOR INTERFAITH HARMONY

[67] We prescribed rituals for every community to practise. So let them not argue with you over *such* matters. *Instead* invite them to your Lord, *for* you are guided on a straight path. [68] If they argue with you, say: "God knows best what you are doing. [69] God will decide between you on Judgement Day regarding your differences." [70] Do you not accept[b] that God knows *whatever exists* in the sky and on Earth? *All* is *recorded* in a Book, that's easy for God.

THE PENT-UP VIOLENCE OF THOSE WHO GO ASTRAY

[71] They worship beside God things for which no authority has been revealed, nor do they have knowledge. *Consequently, such* wrongdoers shall have no helper. [72] Whenever you recite Our clear verses to them, you *can* recognise disapproval on the disbelievers' faces, *to the extent that* they are almost violent towards those who recite Our verses to them. Say: "Shall I inform you of something even worse? The Fire which God has promised those who disbelieve. A wretched destination!"

---

[a] The verb means God causing His creation "to submit to the will or power" of human beings, who will then be judged according to how they made use of them, either for good or ill, be it carefully or wastefully.

[b] Literally "know".

A SINGLE FLY IS ALL IT TAKES TO DISPROVE IDOLATRY

[73] People, here is an example, so listen to it *carefully*: the *idols* you worship beside God can't create a fly, even if they all got together to do so. In fact, if a fly were to snatch something from *them*, they would be unable to take it back. How weak are both the devotee and the object of devotion![c] [74] They fail to accord God the power that He deserves. God is Strong, Mighty. [75] God chooses messengers from among the angels and humans; God is Hearing, Seeing. [76] He knows their past, and future deeds, and *eventually* all affairs return to God.

STRIVING AND STRUGGLING FOR THE SAKE OF GOD

[77] Believers, bow down and prostrate in worship of your Lord, and do good so you may succeed. [78] Strive for the sake of God *to do what is right*, as much as He deserves. He chose you and placed no hardship in the religion.[d] *It is* the way of worship of your father Abraham. Long ago he named you "Muslims", as in this *Quran*, so that the Messenger might stand witness against you *if you strayed*, and that you might stand witness against humanity's *vices*. So perform the prayer, give Zakat and hold firmly to *faith in* God your Protector. How excellent a Protector, and how excellent a Helper!

---

[c] The commentators note how the pagan Arabs would put offerings of food out for their gods, only to watch the flies come and spoil it.

[d] There is no hardship in Islam, the Lord knows human weaknesses. What makes Islam easy to believe and practise is, it's free from myths and superstitions, it's rational and appeals to common sense; has no ritualism but simple practises of worship and social habits; allows it's followers to benefit from worldly wealth in moderation but condemns excessive consumerism.

23. Al-Mu'minun
The Believers

This chapter was revealed in the late Makkan period. The central theme is the resurrection, arguing that faith in God and the Hereafter are knotted into the purpose of life: the two are inseparable. This may explain why the believer is ideally contemplative and socially active, rather than an "armchair" faithful. It opens with a description of successful believers: faith, humility, avoiding useless pursuits, generosity, sexual purity, a sense of responsibility, taking care of contracts, and yearning for closeness to the Divine. Seven beautiful traits of the believers that reflect; firm faith, generous spirit, lively conscience: a restless soul ready to produce good works. The Quran gives a glowing tribute to such lucky souls for their truthfulness, boldness and self-sacrifice: the reward is Paradise.

This is followed by proof of God's creative power in the creation of humanity, the universe, and human history, particularly the ancient prophets. It presents a history of disobedience – humanity rejected the prophets, and killed some. The life stories of some prophets inform the blessed Messenger ﷺ that the Makkans are behaving like the ancient people. The Quran also points out the unity of the prophets' message; a universal message. However, God dealt severely with those who rejected it by destroying them. The disbeliever's criticisms of the prophets are rejected as baseless, due to arrogance. They are confused; they hate the truth and doggedly follow their whims.

The disbelievers frequently demanded the Prophet ﷺ to bring about the punishment. However, these demands were rejected; God gave them time to reform, those who persisted in asking for miracles were similarly refused, and are told they should use their God-given faculties of hearing, seeing and feeling. They are warned about the severe punishment of Hell, and how regretful they will be in the Hereafter, then it will be too late.

Three questions are asked: "Who owns the Earth?"; "Who is the Lord of the Seven Heavens?"; And "In whose hands lies the control of all things?" Their natural response is "God", so they're asked why not accept resurrection. The chapter concludes by emphasising the purpose of human life; a time of preparation for the Hereafter.

In the name of God, the Kind, the Caring.

THE SEVEN HABITS OF SUCCESSFUL BELIEVERS; THEY'RE GOAL ORIENTED

¹The believers have succeeded: ²those who are humbly focused in their prayer; ³who turn away from meaningless activities; ⁴who give Zakat; ⁵who guard their modesty and *sexual purity,* ⁶except from their spouses or their slaves, in which case they are free from blame – ⁷but whoever desires *sexual gratification* beyond

that are transgressors – ⁸*who* honour trusts placed in them and their contract; ⁹and regularly perform their prayers. ¹⁰Such people are the *true* heirs, ¹¹they will inherit Paradise, living in it forever.ᵃ

THE SEVEN STAGES OF HUMAN LIFEᴮ

¹²We *first* created humanity from an extract of clay. ¹³Thereafter *born*, We placed him as a drop of semen in the stable environment *of the womb*. ¹⁴The drop of semen turned to a blood-like clot; and, from the blood-like clot, We made the fleshy lump into bones and covered them with flesh; then We produce from it another created being. Blessed is God, the best Creator. ¹⁵After all that, you will die, ¹⁶and on Judgement Day you will be resurrected.

THE SEVEN TYPES OF FOOD

¹⁷We created seven orbits of *the Heavens* above you; and We never neglected *Our* creation. ¹⁸We send rain from the sky in *exact* measure, and We hold it in the Earth; and We are *equally* capable of taking it away. ¹⁹With *water*, We produce gardens of date palms and grape vines. There is plenty of fruit for you to eat. ²⁰*We produced a* tree that grows on *the side of* Mount Sinai, it produces *olive* oil, a seasoning for people to eat. ²¹The livestock offer you a lesson; We give you to drink from what is in their bellies, *not to mention* the many other benefits in them, and you eat their meat, ²²and they carry you *across the land*. And you're transported by the ships.

THE SEVEN HABITS OF THE DISBELIEVERS

²³We sent Noah to his people, he preached: "My people, worship God; you have no other god beside Him. Won't you be mindful *of Him*?" ²⁴The leaders of disbelievers of his community said, "He is only a mortal like yourselves, who wants dominance over you. If God so wished, He would have sent angels. Never have we heard *the like of* this from our forefathers. ²⁵He's just a man who's mad, so bear with him a while *till he recovers*." ²⁶*Noah* said, "My Lord, help me, they've denied me."

NOAH ONBOARD THE SHIP AND HIS PRAYER

²⁷*Eventually* We inspired him: "Build a ship under Our supervision and accord-

---

ᵃ   These seven habits are: faith, humility, avoiding useless pursuits, generosity, sexual purity, having a sense of responsibility, taking care of contracts, and are prayerful.
ᵇ   See Chapter Al Hajj: 5.

ing to Our instructions; then, when Our command comes, and the geysers *begin to* flood, then take aboard two of every kind *of creature* and your family, except those who've already been condemned. And do not speak to me about the evildoers. They are *as good as* drowned. ²⁸ Then, once you and your followers are onboard the ship, say: 'Praise be to God, Who has rescued us from the wrongdoers,' ²⁹ and say: 'My Lord, settle me in a blessed place, for You are the best provider of a home.'" ³⁰ In this are signs. We have always put *people* to the test.

CRITICISMS MADE AGAINST THE MESSENGERS: "THEY ARE ONLY HUMAN"

³¹ We raised another generation after them,^a ³² and sent a messenger from themselves, *who said*: "Worship God; you have no other god beside Him. Will you not be mindful *of Him*?" ³³ The leaders of disbelievers from his community who denied meeting *God* in the Hereafter, and those We lavished *with luxuries* in this worldly life, *said*, "He's only a human like yourselves; he eats what you eat and drinks what you drink. ³⁴ If you were to obey a human like yourselves, you would be losers."

DENIAL OF LIFE AFTER DEATH

³⁵ "Does he promise that, when you die and turn to dust and bones, you will be brought out *of your graves*? ³⁶ What you are promised is utter nonsense! ³⁷ This worldly life of ours is it! We will live, die, and we will not be resurrected. ³⁸ He is only a man who has made up lies about God, *so* we won't believe him." ³⁹ *The messenger* said, "My Lord, help me because they've denied me." ⁴⁰ *God* said, "They will regret, soon." ⁴¹ The Blast took them *by surprise*; and We turned them into dust. So away with the evildoers! ⁴² We raised other generations after them. ⁴³ No community can bring forward or delay its fixed lifespan.

CONTEMPT FOR PROPHETS

⁴⁴ We continued sending Our messengers, one after another. Each time their messenger came to a community, they denied him. So, We made one community succeed another, and We made of them tales *to be told*. So away with people who do not believe! ⁴⁵ After that We sent Moses and his brother, Aaron, with Our signs and a clear proof ⁴⁶ to Pharaoh and his court, but they were arrogant and too proud. ⁴⁷ They said, "Should we believe two men like ourselves, whose people

---

^a From verse 31-80, seven habits of disbelievers are mentioned, they are; critical, deny resurrection, contempt of Prophets, confused, hate the truth, whimsical and stubborn.

are our slaves?" ⁴⁸ So they denied them and were destroyed. ⁴⁹ We gave Moses the Book so they may be guided.

JESUS, SON OF MARY

⁵⁰ We made the son of Mary and his mother a sign; We gave them refuge on a hilltop, a peaceful place with *a natural* spring. ⁵¹ Messengers, eat of what is pure wholesome and do good deeds; I know well what you do. ⁵² This community of yours is a single community, and I am your Lord, so be mindful of Me.

THE DISBELIEVERS ARE CONFUSED, THE BELIEVERS KNOW THEIR GOAL

⁵³ *Their successors* split up into sects, each sect pleased with itself. ⁵⁴ So leave them *wallowing* in their confusion for a while. ⁵⁵ Do they reckon We granted them wealth and children because ⁵⁶ We are in a rush to do whatever is good for them? On the contrary, they have no sense *of what is coming*. ⁵⁷ *However*, those who fear their Lord; ⁵⁸ believe in the signs of their Lord; ⁵⁹ don't associate *partners* with their Lord; ⁶⁰ give charity from what they have been given, while their hearts tremble *at the thought* that they will be returning to their Lord; ⁶¹ they rush to do whatever is good, they are the high fliers.

THE DISBELIEVERS HATE THE TRUTH

⁶² We don't task anyone beyond their capacity, and *We keep* a Book with Us that speaks the truth; *so* they shall not be wronged. ⁶³ However, there's confusion in their minds about this; and *the wrongdoers* have even worse deeds than this, which they continue to do ⁶⁴ until We seize their well-off for punishment; then they will cry out. ⁶⁵ "Don't cry today," *they will be told*, "You will find no help against Us. ⁶⁶ When My verses were recited, you turned on your heels *and walked away*, ⁶⁷ arrogantly talking nonsense late into the night." ⁶⁸ Haven't they reflected on what is said *in the Quran*? Or has something come to them that never came to their forefathers? ⁶⁹ Or is it that they don't recognise their messenger, and so they reject him? ⁷⁰ Or do they say that he's possessed? On the contrary, he has come to them with the truth, but most of them hate it.

THEY FOLLOW THEIR WHIMS

⁷¹ If *God,* the truth[b] was to follow their whims, then the Heavens and the Earth and whatever exists in them would have fallen into ruin. We brought them a re-

---

[b]   According to some commentaries, "the truth" here refers to God.

minder, but they turned away from their reminder. [72] Or did you ask them to pay you something? The payment of your Lord is better by far; and He is the best Provider. [73] *At the same time as* you are calling them to the straight path, [74] those who deny the Hereafter have turned away from the path.

THEY ARE STUBBORN

[75] If We were kind to them and removed *all* hardship from them, they would still wander about disobediently. [76] We punished them *once before*, and they didn't surrender to their Lord, nor showed humility [77] until We opened the gate of punishment on them, and they fell into despair. [78] He gave you hearing, sight and mind. How little did you thank Him! [79] He scattered you all over the Earth, and eventually you will be gathered before Him. [80] He grants life and death, and His is the cycle of night and day. Don't you understand?

HARD-HITTING QUESTIONS FOR DISBELIEVERS

[81] On the contrary, *the Makkans* say the same as *their* ancestors. [82] They said: "When we are dead and turned to dust and bones, will we be resurrected? [83] We and our forefathers were promised this before. These are mere tales of the past." [84] Say, *Muhammad*: "To Whom does the Earth and whoever *lives* on it belong, if you have knowledge?" [85] They will say, "To God!" Say: "Why then don't you pay attention?" [86] Say: "Who is the Lord of the Seven Heavens and the Lord of the Mighty Throne?" [87] *Again* they will say, "God!" Say: "Why aren't you mindful *of Him*?" [88] Say: "In Whose hand lies the control over everything, He protects, but against Him there is no protection, if you have knowledge?" [89] They will say, "God!" Say: "So why are you bewitched?" [90] On the other hand, We brought them the truth, but they deny it.

GOD HAS NEITHER SON NOR PARTNER

[91] God has not taken a son, nor is there any other god with Him. If it had been so, each god would have gone off with what it had created, and some of them would be superior to others. Glory to God, *Who is far removed* from what they ascribe *to Him*! [92] The Knower of all that is seen and unseen, Sublimely exalted above whatever they associate *with Him*!

PRAYER FOR PROTECTION FROM SATAN

[93] Say: "My Lord, if You must show me what they've been promised [94] then, My

Lord, don't include me among the wrongdoers." ⁹⁵ We are quite capable of showing you what We promised them. ⁹⁶ Repel evil with good. We know well what they ascribe *to Us*. ⁹⁷ And say: "My Lord, I seek refuge in You from the murmurings of devils; ⁹⁸ and I seek Your refuge from harm they may cause me." ⁹⁹ Only when death comes to one of them will he say, "My Lord, let me return *to my life on Earth* ¹⁰⁰ so that I may act righteously in whatever I *previously* omitted." Never! What he is saying are *empty* words; and before them lies a vast barrier, *uncrossable* till the day they are resurrected.

THOSE SENT TO HELL WILL PLEAD TO RETURN TO LIFE

¹⁰¹ When the *mighty* Trumpet is blown, that Day there will be no kinship *left* between them, nor will they ask about each other. ¹⁰² Anyone whose scales weigh heavy, will be successful; ¹⁰³ but anyone whose scales are light will be the loser, staying in Hell forever. ¹⁰⁴ The Fire will scorch their faces, leaving them grinning *like skulls*. ¹⁰⁵ "Were My verses not recited to you," *they will be asked*, "and you rejected them." ¹⁰⁶ They will say, "Our Lord, misfortune overwhelmed us, and *so* we went astray. ¹⁰⁷ Our Lord, get us out of here; if we return *to acting sinfully*, we shall *only* be wronging *ourselves*." ¹⁰⁸ *God* will say, "May you be driven *ever deeper* into *the Fire*. Don't speak to Me.

THE PATIENT ARE REWARDED

¹⁰⁹ There was *once* a group of My servants who used to say, 'Our Lord, we believe; forgive us and be kind to us, for You are the most Kind.' ¹¹⁰ However, you took them as a laughing stock, your laughing at them made you forget My remembrance. ¹¹¹ This day I shall reward them for their patience. They are the victors." ¹¹² *God* will ask, "How long did you live on Earth?" ¹¹³ They will say, "We spent a day or so. Ask those who keep count." ¹¹⁴ *God* will say, "You spent but a short while, if only you knew."

CONCLUSION: HUMAN LIFE HAS A PURPOSE

¹¹⁵ Did you reckon We created you without a purpose and you wouldn't be returned to Us? ¹¹⁶ God is the exalted, the True King! There is no god beside Him, Lord of the Honoured Throne. ¹¹⁷ Anyone who worships another god for which he has no proof, His Lord will bring him to account. The disbelievers shall never succeed. ¹¹⁸ And, *Messenger,* say: "My Lord, forgive and be kind, for You are the Most Kind."

24. An-Nur
The Light

This chapter was revealed in Madinah after the campaign of Banu Mustalaq in the fifth year of Hijrah. The central theme is social manners: modesty, and the penalty for adultery and slandering innocent people. The aim is to lay down firm foundations for building relationships between men and women based on modesty and respect. It opens with declaring a severe penalty for adultery, and continues by recommending rules for the mixing of men and women, the Hijab, and personal privacy inside and outside the home. The purpose of these rules is to develop a decent environment, free of sexual exploitation. If sexuality is not properly controlled, it can cause disorder in family life and chaos in wider society. These simple rules are powerful preventative measures that restrict shameful behaviour. Ignoring these rules leads to the spread of all kinds of sexual exploitation, indecency, pornography and prostitution.

The story of the false accusation against Aisha, the Mother of the Believers, highlights the importance of these social regulations. The story concludes by declaring the innocence of the Mother of the Believers, and recommends six effective social rules: we are warned against spreading rumours; penalty for those who spread indecency; develop the value of forgiveness; permission should be sought to enter houses; women covering themselves in public; and assistance for single people to marry.

The parable of 'light' in verse 35 points to God's creative power; making living matter from the darkness of nothing. Evidence of the existence of God. The 'light' is God's guidance the ability to discern right from wrong. The marvellous phenomena in the physical world; rain, rainbows, and earthquakes, fill us with awe that leads to belief in Him. But the disbelievers are deprived of this light (40). This spiritual passage comes in the middle of a legal discussion, and the point is that religious laws are only meaningful if God remains in the centre. The next passage stresses the power of the Almighty, and why we need to observe His rules. Devout believers are promised: "*He will* make the believers and the righteous *His* deputies on Earth as He made those before you *His* deputies" (55).

Four more social manners are pronounced: visiting others; concessions in wearing the Hijab for mature women; eating together; and the company of the Messenger ﷺ.

The Quran's Position on Slavery
Since slavery was deep-rooted in the seventh century, the Quran didn't attempt banning it in one big swoop, it would have been impossible to give it up, instead it adopted a gradual tactic: first ensuring slaves have rights; owners were obliged to feed, clothe and allow them freedom to worship. Secondly, those who freed slaves are praised. It prohibited making Muslims slaves. Thirdly, certain atonements could be achieved by freeing slaves, all of

which encouraged and improved the status of slaves. Moreover, the Quranic subtext of kindness, generosity and justice required its followers to see slavery as incompatible with Quranic justice, since it violated the concept of Human brotherhood and sisterhood: "If any of your slaves asks for an *emancipation* contract, and you see some good in them, draft it for them; and give them of the wealth that God has given you." (33)

In the name of God, the Kind, the Caring.

THE PUNISHMENT FOR FORNICATION

[1] *This is* a chapter that We sent down with laws to be obeyed, and We revealed clear verses so you will pay attention. [2] Flog the fornicators,[a] male and female, each of them one-hundred lashes, and don't let sympathy for them hold you back from *fulfilling* God's orders, if you believe in God and the Last Day; and let a group of believers witness their punishment. [3] A male fornicator only marries a female fornicator or an idolatress; a female fornicator only marries a male fornicator or an idolater; and fornication is forbidden for the believers.[b]

THE PROCEDURE IN ACCUSATIONS OF FORNICATION

[4] *Those* who accuse chaste women *of fornication*,[c] but fail to produce four witnesses, should be flogged eighty lashes; and never accept their witness statement again. They are major sinners,[d] [5] except those who later repent and reform themselves. God is Forgiving, Kind. [6] Anyone who accuses his wife but has no witnesses other than himself, let him swear four times by God: he is telling the truth, [7] and the fifth time he says, God's curse be upon him if he is lying. [8] Punishment will be averted from her if she *also* swears by God four times that he is lying, [9] and the fifth time that God's wrath be upon her if he is telling the truth. [10] *Imagine the*

---

[a]   Zina, like 'fornication', is general and refers to all unlawful penetrative sexual intercourse between men and women, regardless of their marital status. 'Adultery' is specifically fornication by a married person.

[b]   This underlines the heinous crime of fornication, a Muslim convicted of it can't marry a believer of good character.

[c]   The word *muhsanat* literally means "protected" or "fortified", be it by a bond of marriage or their own good name.

[d]   The strict requirement of four independent witnesses of honourable reputation who happen to observe the act of penetration clearly with their eyes. In other words, it is insufficient merely to see two people naked together, or to make assumptions about what may or may not be going on under a sheet. Since it is almost impossible to imagine such a situation, the verse should be interpreted as emphasising the importance of truthfulness, the harmful effect on society of spreading unsubstantiated rumours – even if the rumours are true but do not meet the required level of proof – and the seriousness of making false or unprovable statements before a court of law.

consequences, if it were not for God's grace towards you and His kindness. God is Relenting, Wise.

The slander against Aisha, Mother of the Believers

[11] Those who planned the slander were a handful of you, don't consider it bad for you; in fact, it's good for you.[a] Each person among them will bear the consequence of *his part in* the sin; and the one who played the leading role will receive a mighty punishment. [12] If once they heard it – the believers, male and female – of their own accord should have thought the best *of Aisha* and said, "This is clearly a slander." [13] If they had produced four witnesses, *it would be different*; but they failed to produce the witnesses, in God's sight they are liars.

The story of Aisha, Mother of the Believers; Never spread rumours

[14] Were it not for God's grace towards you and His kind treatment in this world and the Hereafter, then a mighty punishment would have affected you *all* because of the rumour you rushed *to spread*. [15] You gave it *publicity* with your chatter and said things with your mouths you had no knowledge of, thinking it was a trivial, but in the sight of God it was serious. [16] If only, when you heard it, you had said: "It is not *fitting* for us to talk about this. Glory be to Him! This is a terrible slander." [17] God warns you: never repeat such *behaviour* again if you are believers. [18] God is explaining the verses for you. God is Knowing, Wise.

Punishment for people who spread indecency

[19] Those who like to spread indecency among the believers *will suffer* a painful punishment in this worldly life and the Hereafter. God knows what you don't know. [20] *Imagine the consequences*, if it were not for God's grace towards you and His kindness. God is Compassionate, Kind. [21] Believers, don't follow in Satan's footsteps. Whoever follows Satan's footsteps *will find* that he urges indecency and shameful acts. If it weren't for God's grace on you and His kindness, none of you would be pure, God purifies anyone He pleases. God is the Hearer, the Knower.

Muslims urged to forgive one another

[22] Those of you who possess status and means shouldn't vow to stop giving to rel-

---

[a] Since this was a test for the believers, to see who would remain steadfast. Furthermore, for every hardship a person suffers they get a reward. "When a person suffers pain or anxiety, even if it is a prick of a thorn, God forgives their sins" (Bukhari)

atives, the needy and those who emigrated for the sake of God. Let them pardon and overlook *their shortcomings*. Wouldn't you like God to forgive you? God is Forgiving, Kind.[b]

WARNING AGAINST FALSE ACCUSATIONS

[23] Those who falsely accuse careless *but nonetheless* chaste believing women shall be cursed here and the Hereafter, and will be severely punished,[c] [24] on the Day tongues, hands and feet will testify against them for what they did. [25] That Day, God will settle their account for them in full, and they will know God alone is the Truth, the Clarifier. [26] Vile women are *fit* for vile men, and vile men are *fit* for vile women; and *likewise,* moral women are for moral men, and moral men are for moral women. Such people are innocent of what *others* say about them; they will be forgiven and have generous provision.

SEEKING PERMISSION TO ENTER A HOUSE

[27] Believers, don't enter any houses other than your own homes until you have made yourselves known and greeted the occupants; that's best for you, so you may pay heed. [28] If there is no one in, then don't enter until permission is given; and if you are told, "Go back!" Then go back: that is the best *course of action* for you. God knows well what you do. [29] You can enter without permission a non-residential place[d] that provides you amenities, God knows well what you reveal and what you conceal.

MEN AND WOMEN MUST BEHAVE MODESTLY

[30] Tell believing men to lower their gaze and be modest;[e] that is the best for them. God is aware of what they do. [31] And tell believing women to lower their gaze and be modest; they shouldn't expose their beauty *in public*, except what is normally showing; and cover their bosoms with headscarves;[f] they should only display beauty to their husbands, fathers, fathers-in-law, sons, stepsons, brothers, broth-

[b]   This verse was revealed after Aisha's father, Abu Bakr, vowed never to support his cousin, Mistah ibn Uthatha, because he spread the slander against his daughter.

[c]   A shocking crime where a Muslim woman or girl has been seen in the company of non-mahram men is enough for her to become the victim of a horrific attack, or even the so-called "honour killing", at the hands of her closest relatives.

[d]   This refers to a public place like a hotel (Ibn Abbas).

[e]   Literally 'safeguard their private parts.'

[f]   Women's fashion at the time of revelation was to have the ends of their headscarves trailing down their backs, leaving their breasts partially visible through the opening of their dress at the front (Al-Qurtubi).

ers' sons, sisters' sons, female servants, slaves, *any* male attendants who are free of sexual desire, and children who are indifferent to *the sight of* women's private parts; and they shouldn't stamp their feet to draw attention to the beauty which they hide *beneath their clothes*. Believers, turn to God, all of you, so you may be successful *here and the Hereafter*.

ENCOURAGING UNMARRIED PERSONS TO MARRY

[32] Help the unmarried people amongst you to marry, and your righteous male servants and maids. Even if they are poor, God will make them self-sufficient through His grace. God is Vast, All-Knowing. [33] And let those who lack the means to marry keep themselves chaste until God makes them self-sufficient through His grace. If any of your slaves asks for an *emancipation* contract, and you see some good in them, draft it for them; and give them of the wealth that God has given you. For your cravings to make worldly gains do not force your maidservants into promiscuity, if they wish to remain chaste, merely because you desire what this worldly life has to offer. Whoever forces them *into it*, then God will be Forgiving, Kind *to those maidservants* after being coerced *to perform sexual intercourse*. [34] We sent down to you clarifying verses and an example of those who passed away before you, as well as teachings for those who are mindful *of God*.

GOD'S LIGHT SHINES IN THE HEARTS OF BELIEVERS

[35] God is the Light of the Heavens and the Earth. An example of His Light is a niche in which there is a lamp; the lamp *glowing* in a glass; the glass *bright* like a brilliant shining star, fuelled from a blessed olive tree, neither of the East nor of the West; its oil shines even though untouched by any flame; light upon light. God guides whomever He pleases towards His Light. God gives people examples and has full knowledge of all things.[a] [36] *Such lamps are to be found* in houses that God has permitted to be erected, and in which His name is mentioned*; and* where, glorifying Him morning and evening, [37] are men who are not distracted by buying and selling from God's remembrance, performing the prayer, and paying Zakat. They dread a day when hearts and eyes will be wandering, [38] *hoping* God

---

[a] In this example the niche is the human heart; the lamp is the guidance of the Quran; the glass is reason and intellect and the olive oil is the emotions. The example shows that every person has God-given potential and the desire to see and accept the truth. This is a powerful desire in search of the truth, like petrol, a spark can set it aflame. So, whenever the Divine guidance (the light) is presented they accept it.

will reward them according to the best they did and give them more from His grace. God provides without limit for whomever He pleases.

DISBELIEVERS' HEARTS ARE DROWNING IN A SEA OF DARKNESS

[39] However, the disbelievers deeds are like a mirage in a desert: the thirsty *traveller* imagines it to be water until he reaches it, only to find nothing there; but finds God before him, settling *his account* in full. God is swift in calculating *accounts.*[b]
[40] Or *their deeds are* like veils of darkness in the deep sea covered by wave upon wave, over which clouds *loom.* The layers of darkness *lie so densely* over one another that, if one takes one's hand out *of the water,* one can barely see it. Anyone God deprives of light will have no light *at all.*[c]

ALL CREATURES COME FROM WATER

[41] Haven't you considered, everything in the Heavens and the Earth glorifies God? The birds flying in flocks, each one knows how it should pray and glorify Him; and God knows what they do. [42] God controls the Heavens and the Earth, and to Him is the final return. [43] Haven't you considered how God moves the clouds along, joins them together, then piles them up *until* you see rain pouring from them. On mountains, He sends down from the sky hailstones that strike whomever He wills and spare whomever He wills; and the flash of its lightning nearly takes away one's sight. [44] God causes the succession of night and day; in that are lessons for people of insight. [45] *Moreover,* God created every creature from water; some crawl on their bellies, others walk on two feet or on four. God creates whatever He wills. God has power over all things.

THE TWO-FACED ARE NOT BELIEVERS

[46] We revealed verses that clearly explain, and *by them* God guides anyone who

---

[b] There are two types of disbelievers; one who thinks and behaves well, has morals and manners that are pleasing. He believes he would reap full reward for his deeds. What he fails to realise is that in a state of disbelief his deeds are worthless they have no spiritual value. So, like the lonely, thirsty traveller he sees a broadsheet of water in the distance, so he runs towards it. There he finds nothing, it was an illusion. *The second type of disbeliever is mentioned in the next verse.*

[c] The second type of disbeliever is engrossed in the world; drowned in lust, in pursuit of wealth and health. He's sunk in hedonistic pleasures; in darkness. He can't receive the light since he is in pitch darkness. The example describes the four layers of darkness; the pitch dark night, the clouds, the depth of the sea and stormy tides upon tides.

wants to be guided towards a straight path.^a ⁴⁷*People* will say: "We believe in God and in the Messenger, and we obey," but afterwards a group of them turns away: such people are not believers. ⁴⁸When they are summoned to God and his Messenger for judgement, a group of them objects. ⁴⁹Had the decision been in their favour they would have submitted willingly. ⁵⁰Is there sickness in their hearts? Or do they have doubts? Or are they afraid that God and His Messenger will deal with them unjustly? Such people are sinners.

THE DIFFERENT RESPONSES OF BELIEVERS AND HYPOCRITES

⁵¹The believers' response, when they are summoned to God and His Messenger for judgement, is: "We hear and obey." These are the successful. ⁵²Whoever obeys God and His Messenger, and fears God and is mindful of Him, these are the victorious. ⁵³*Hypocrites* swear by God, using their strongest oaths, that if you were to command them, they would march out *to battle.* Say: "Don't swear. Obedience is recognisable!"^b God is aware of your works. ⁵⁴Say: "Obey God, and obey the Messenger. Then, if you *choose to* turn away, he *will answer* only for what he has taken on, and you *will answer* for what you have taken on.^c If you obey him, you will be guided. The responsibility of the Messenger is to convey *the message* clearly."

MUSLIMS PROMISED A VICTORY

⁵⁵God has promised to make the believers and the righteous *His* deputies on Earth, as He made those before you *His* deputies; and He will make their religion strong, which pleases Him; and He will remove their fear and make them feel safe, since they worship Me alone, and don't associate *any partners* with Me. The disbelievers are the evildoers. ⁵⁶*So,* perform the prayer, pay Zakat, and obey the Messenger in order to be treated kindly. ⁵⁷Never think the disbelievers can defeat *God's plan* on Earth. The Fire is their place of refuge. What a wretched home!

SOME INSTRUCTIONS ON MANNERS: *RESPECTING PRIVACY WHEN LIVING TOGETHER*

⁵⁸Believers, your slaves and *children* who haven't yet reached puberty should ask permission *before entering your room* three times *of the day*: before the dawn

---

^a   Alternatively God guides anyone He wills towards a straight path. My translation shows that a person witnesses so many persuasive proofs in nature as mentioned in the preceding verses, will want to be guided. This is empowering and reflects the idea of moral choice.

^b   In other words: "Actions speak louder than words."

^c   Meaning conveying God's message and obeying His Messenger 🌸, respectively.

prayer, at midday when you get undressed, and after the evening prayer – three *times* of your privacy, outside these *times* there is no blame on you or them to wander in and out of each other's *rooms*. That is how God makes *His* verses clear for you. God is Knowing, Wise. [59] When your children reach puberty, they must ask permission like those *mentioned* before. That is how God makes His verses clear for you. God is Knowing, Wise.

CONCESSIONS ON DRESS FOR OLDER WOMEN
[60] Older women who have no desire to marry may remove their *outer* garments as long as they don't display *any* beauty, there's no blame on them. However, even for them it's better to remain modest. God is Hearing, Knowing.

PERMISSION TO EAT TOGETHER
[61] There is no restriction on the blind, the disabled, the sick, or yourselves eating in your own homes, or your fathers' homes, your mothers' homes, your brothers', sisters', paternal or maternal uncles' and aunts' homes, or homes whose keys you hold, or at your friends' *homes*. It isn't blameworthy whether you eat together or separately. Whenever you enter houses, greet each other with a sincere blessing from God. That is how God makes *His* verses clear for you, so you may reflect.

HOW TO BEHAVE IN THE PROPHET'S ﷺ PRESENCE
[62] The believers firmly believe in God and His Messenger, and when they are with him *discussing* any matter of general concern, don't leave without seeking his permission. Those who seek your permission are true believers in God and His Messenger. If they ask your permission to attend to some private matter of theirs, give them permission as you wish, and seek God's forgiveness for them. God is Forgiving, Kind.

DON'T TREAT THE MESSENGER ﷺ LIKE YOU TREAT OTHERS
[63] Do not call out *in a loud voice* to the Messenger as you would call out to each other. God knows those of you who quietly slip away to avoid *being given a task*. Those who disagree with his commandment should beware in case they find themselves tested or are struck by a painful punishment. [64] Doesn't everything in the Heavens and the Earth belong to God? He knows *exactly* where you stand; and, on the Day *all* are returned to Him, He will inform them of what they did. God has full knowledge of all things.

25. Al-Furqan
The Benchmark for Right and Wrong

This Makkan chapter provides powerful arguments for the Oneness of God (*Tawhid*), the communication of His Message (*Risalah*), and life after death (*Akhirah*). These three fundamental beliefs were most at odds with the pagan beliefs. It opens by declaring the power and might of the exalted Lord, the Controller of the universe.

In Makkah, the Messenger ﷺ was constantly criticised. The Makkans accused him of lying, puzzled why the Quran was revealed gradually, rather than all at once, and emphasised that it was merely stories of the ancient people. Similarly, they targeted his person: why would a messenger of God be a mere mortal? The chapter answers them, and warns them of the dire consequences of rejecting faith. The Messenger ﷺ is reassured: "Do you think you can be a guardian for the one who makes a god of his desires?" (43).

The chapter then turns to the natural world, and points out the amazing creative power of God seen in nature: the shadow, the nightfall, the rain, fresh and seawater, blood and marriage relatives, the constellations, the sun and the moon: "a *sign* for anyone who wants to be reminded *of God's power* or wants to be thankful" (62). An excellent example of the Quran's two-pronged approach to answering the disbelievers' criticism: the first is an argumentative approach – an emotional appeal where disbelievers are threatened and warned of their rebellion and mischief. Stories of past communities are told and retold to stress the consequences of their disbelief. The second Quranic approach is a rational, scientific approach drawing attention to God's creative power. These awesome and marvellously created signs are all around us, and directly pointing to their creator; won't you believe?

The final passage catalogues the qualities of the pious: humility, peace loving, worshipful, prayerful, moderate, and penitent. They don't: squander wealth, murder, worship idols, commit adultery, give false testimony, engage in useless activities, nor follow blindly. The chapter concludes with a powerful prayer of the pious servants: "Our Lord, grant us joy in our spouses and children, and make us an example for those who are mindful *of You*" (74). Effectively, recapping the opening statement that God is in control of the universe and His true servant submits and prays for divine intervention.

In the name of God, the Kind, the Caring.

ALL REGIONS OF THE UNIVERSE BELONG TO GOD

¹Blessed is the One Who sent down the benchmark to His *noble* servant: the warner for all communities;ᵃ ²God controls the Heavens and the Earth, has not

---

ᵃ Al Alameen according to Jalalain is "humans, Jinns and excludes Angels".

adopted a child, nor taken a partner in *His* dominion, and has created everything carefully measured out. ³Yet *the disbelievers* have adopted beside Him gods that create nothing but were created, they have no power to harm or to benefit themselves, and don't control death, life or resurrection.

THE DISBELIEVERS' EXCUSES FOR DENYING THE MESSENGER 🏵

⁴The disbelievers said, "This is nothing but an outrageous lie that he has made up with the support of some people." *In truth*, it is they who have come to do wrong and bear false witness. ⁵And they said, "*These are* the tales of the ancients he has written down, that were dictated to him morning and evening." ⁶Say: "He sent it down, Who knows the secrets *concealed* in the Heavens and the Earth. He is Forgiving, Kind." ⁷They said, "What kind of messenger is this who eats food and walks about in the market? If an angel was sent with him as a warner, then *we would believe*; ⁸or *if* some treasure came down to him, or he had an orchard for his livelihood." The wrongdoers say, "You are following a bewitched man." ⁹Look what examples they make of you! They have gone astray, and they cannot find a *straight* path. ¹⁰Blessed is He Who will grant you better than that when He wants; gardens beneath which rivers flow and *luxurious* palaces.

THE CHOICE BETWEEN UNENDING PUNISHMENT AND BLISS

¹¹They have denied *the coming of* the Final Hour, and We have prepared a fiery blaze for anyone who denies the Final Hour. ¹²When it sees them from afar, they will hear it raging and roaring; ¹³and they will be chained together and cast into a narrow pit in it; they will plead to perish. ¹⁴"Do not plead to perish once today," *they'll be told*, "but plead to perish many times over." ¹⁵Say: "Which is better, that or the garden of eternal life that those mindful *of God* have been promised?" That will be their reward and destination, ¹⁶they will have whatever they please forever: a promise which Your Lord will fulfil.

THE IDOLS ARE QUESTIONED ON JUDGEMENT DAY

¹⁷On the Day He gathers them and all they worship beside God, He will ask: "Was it you who led My servants astray, or did they stray by themselves from the path?" ¹⁸*The idols* will say, "Glory be to You! It was not for us to take on protectors besides You. However, You let them and their forefathers enjoy themselves until they neglected the Reminder and were ruined people." ¹⁹"*Your idols* have denied what you said," *He will tell them*, "You can't avert *what's coming* or get

help. So whoever continues doing wrong, then We'll let them taste a dreadful punishment."

THE DISBELIEVERS' EXCUSES ARE ADDRESSED

²⁰ Never before you, *Muhammad*, have We sent any messenger who didn't eat food and walk about in the markets. We made some of you a test for others *to see* how patient you will be. Your Lord is Seeing. ²¹ Those who don't like to meet Us say: "If angels were sent down, or we could see our Lord *we would have believed.*" They are proud of themselves and rude. ²² On the Day they see the angels, it won't be good news for the sinners; *the angels* will say, "*Paradise is* a forbidden place *for you!*" ²³ Whatever deeds they had done, We will turn them into scattered dust. ²⁴ That Day the companions of Paradise will *be living* in a *pleasant* home, a cool resting place.

THE WRONG TYPE OF FRIENDS

²⁵ That Day the sky and the clouds will be torn apart, and at last the angels will be sent down, ²⁶ that Day sovereignty will belong to the Most Kind; it will be a terrible Day for the disbelievers, ²⁷ a Day when the wrongdoer will bite his hands *regretfully*, saying, "If only I had followed the path of the Messenger. ²⁸ Woe to me! If only I hadn't taken so-and-so as a friend; ²⁹ he led me astray from the Reminder[a] after it had come to me." The Satan deceived humanity. ³⁰ The Messenger will say, "My Lord, some of my people regard this Quran as something to be avoided."[b] ³¹ This is how We have made the sinners an enemy for every prophet. Your Lord is sufficient as a Guide and Helper. ³² The disbelievers say, "Why wasn't the Quran sent down all at once to him?" *We revealed it* this way to build your confidence,[c] and arranged it as one book.[d] ³³ Not a single example can they bring you of inconsistency in the book. However, We bring you the truth and the best explanation. ³⁴ Those who will be dispatched face down to Hell will be in the worst place and furthest away from any path.

---

[a] Here "the Reminder" is a synonym for the Quran.

[b] "*Mahjuran*" can be interpreted as; to be shunned, out-of-date, to be discarded. So some nominal-followers regard it irrelevant to their lives.

[c] Literally means "to steady your heart with it."

[d] "*Rattalnahu tartilan*" means to put together parts of a thing consistently. (cf 39:23). The Quran is very consistent, free of contradictions. (4:82).

GENERATIONS WHO DENIED GOD'S SIGNS WERE WIPED OUT

[35] We gave Moses the Book, and We made his brother Aaron adviser. [36] We said, "Go, the two of you, to the people who have denied Our signs," then We destroyed them completely. [37] *Likewise* the people of Noah, after they denied the messengers, We drowned them and made them a sign for people. We have prepared a painful torment for wrongdoers, [38] *such as* Ad, Thamud, the community of the well, and many generations in between. [39] We made examples of each of them; and We destroyed them. [40] They[c] have passed by the city that was struck by the terrible rain. Haven't they seen it? They hope not to be brought back to life.

DISBELIEVERS MADE THEIR WHIMS GODS

[41] When they see you, they mockingly *say*, "Is this the one who God sent as a messenger? [42] If we hadn't been committed *to our idols* he would have lead us away from our gods." They will know, who had gone astray from the path when they see the punishment. [43] Do you think you can be a guardian of someone who makes his desires, god? [44] Do you reckon they listen *to you, or* reflect? They are like cattle. No, *in fact* they are even further astray from the *straight* path.

GOD'S CREATIVE POWER: THE EXAMPLE OF THE SHADOW

[45] Don't you see how Your Lord makes the shadow get longer and longer, if He wanted He could have fixed *its size*. We made the sun a pointer to *His existence*, [46] then We gradually shorten *the shadow*. [47] He made the night a garment to *cover* you, the sleep for your rest, and the daytime for rising up again.

THE RAINWATER GIVES CREATURES LIFE

[48] He sends the winds as a herald before the rain;[f] and We send clean water from the sky [49] to bring barren land back to life, and to provide drink to creatures, a great many cattle and people *alike*. [50] We distribute *the rain* to remind them *of Our power*, but most people turn away ungratefully. [51] If We wanted, We could have sent a warner to every city. [52] So don't give in to the disbelievers, but struggle tirelessly *to convince* them with this *Quran*.[g] [53] And He brings the two seas close together,[h] one sweet and fresh, the other salty and bitter; and He has set a

---

[c] This refers to Makkan traders who passed by the ruins of the people of Lot on their way to Syria.

[f] Literally, His Kindness.

[g] The Prophet ﷺ is told to perform *jihad* with the pagans, not with the sword but the Quran. *Bihi* here, according to Ibn Abbas, is the Quran.

[h] This is the literal meaning, but in Arabic 'sea' can mean any large mass of water, including lakes and rivers.

non-breachable barrier between them. [54] And He created humans from water,[a] and gave them blood relatives and in-laws. Your Lord is Powerful. [55] Yet they worship beside God what can't benefit or harm them. The disbeliever[b] is openly opposed to His Lord. [56] We sent you a bearer of glad tidings and a warner. [57] Say: "I'm not asking you for payment for this *preaching*, all I ask of you is: let those who wish to take the path to their Lord *do so*."

CONSTELLATIONS, THE STARS IN THE SKY

[58] Put your trust in the Ever-Living, Who will never die, glorify Him with His praise. Sufficient is He in being, Aware of His servants' sins, [59] Who created the Heavens and Earth and whatever lies between them in six days, then established according to His Majesty on the Throne. *He is* the Most Kind; the Best informed. [60] If they are told: "Prostrate before the Most Kind," they say, "And what is the Most Kind? Should we prostrate to anything you tell us?" *This reminder* increases their hatred. [61] Blessed is He Who placed constellations in the sky, and made brilliant stars, a shining sun and a bright moon. [62] He made the night and day to follow each other, *a sign* for anyone who wants to be reminded *of God's power* or wants to be thankful.

THE QUALITIES OF THE SERVANTS OF THE MOST KIND

[63] The servants of the Kind walk softly on the Earth, and when ignorant people speak with them, they say *words of* peace. [64] And *they* spend their nights *praying* to their Lord, standing and prostrating. [65] And pray: "Our Lord, turn away the torment of Hell from us; its torment is unending. [66] What a dreadful home and resting place!" [67] And they spend *in charity*, they are neither wasteful nor miserly, but moderate. [68] And *they* call on no other god beside God, and do not kill others that God has made sacred, unless by some lawful right, nor commit adultery – and whoever does that will face penalties; [69] his punishment will be multiplied on the Day of Judgement, forever disgraced and in *torment*, [70] except anyone who repents, believes and does righteous deeds. For them, God will turn their *past* sins into good deeds. God is Forgiving, Most Kind. [71] Whoever repents and does righteous deeds, has indeed returned to God. [72] And *they* don't bear false testimo-

---

[a]   According to Al-Qurtubi, "water" here refers to seminal fluid by which the mother's egg is fertilised.

[b]   According to Ibn Abbas, "the disbeliever" here refers to Abu Jahl, who would make a public show of worshipping idols. However, Ikrima interpreted this as meaning Satan.

ny and, when they pass *people* gossiping, they *pass by* with dignity. [73] And when they are reminded of their Lord's signs, they don't fall for them, deaf and blind *to their true meaning.*

PRAYER FOR THE FAMILY

[74] And they say, "Our Lord, grant us joy in our spouses and children, and make us an example for those who are mindful *of You*." [75] They will be rewarded with the loftiest of apartments *in Paradise* for their patience; they shall be greeted with peace, [76] living forever in a lovely home and leisurely place! [77] Say: "What are you to My Lord without your prayer?" *Since* you have denied *My messenger*, the expected *punishment* will happen.

26. Ash-Shuʿara'
The Poets

This chapter was revealed in the middle of the Makkan period, during the fifth or sixth year of the prophethood of the Messenger ﷺ. The beloved Messenger ﷺ was eagerly teaching and preaching Islam day and night, but only a handful of fortunate souls followed him. Opposition and hostility was growing and deepening. However, the Prophet ﷺ was constantly praying, and hoping the Makkans would accept Islam. Meanwhile, his night vigils, heartfelt prayers for his people, and crying to God for their guidance continued.

The central theme of the chapter is relating the stories of seven prophets and how they were rejected by their people. This is the history of human disobedience: the unchanging character of man's weakness and his proneness to self-deception. This explains why people in all communities readily reject the truth.

Consequently, they lose themselves in worship of power, wealth, and what is commonly described as 'glory', as well as in mindless acceptance of slogans and prevailing fashions of thought' (Asad).

The chapter exposes humanity's weakness as well as its goodness. A dramatic story is mentioned: "Then Moses threw down his staff, and at once it swallowed up their trickery" (45). There were no arguments or debates; since the miracle was compelling, and the magicians could not fail to see Moses was a man of God, a true prophet. However, the Pharaoh was arrogant and refused to believe. This succinct chapter separates each prophetic story with the catchphrase: "In that is a sign; yet most will not believe (8).

The stories make the point: all prophets had the same mission: "Will you not believe? I am an honest messenger for you," (106). The first story is the encounter between Moses and Pharaoh: the debate between a prophet of God and a tyrant king, where Moses convincingly talks about the power and the majesty of God. Similarly, Abraham expresses God's generosity: "But My Lord is Lord of the worlds, Who created and guided me, the One who feeds and gives me to drink, and when I am ill heals me" (78–80). The story of Prophet Noah highlights the discrimination of the wealthy against the poor: "Why should we believe in you since only the poorest people are following you?" (111). Their prophets criticise them for their vanity: "You build monuments on every hilltop to please yourselves, and take castles *as homes* so you might live forever? And, when you seize *others' wealth and land*, you are utterly ruthless in doing so" (128–130). The story of Prophet Lot describes the sexual perversion of his people. He pleads with them to give up their wretched way of life: "*Why*, of all the people of the world do you approach males lustfully, leaving your wives, whom your Lord has created for you? You are people who have crossed the bounds *of decency*" (165–166). The final story is of Prophet Jethro . His people were expert defrauders.

At the end, the chapter rejects the Makkans accusation that the Prophet ﷺ is a poet. The Prophet ﷺ is told; 'they are unreasonable'. There is no comparison between the life-changing message of the Quran and the works of the poets?

In the name of God, the Kind, the Caring.

¹ *Ta Sin Meem.*

Have faith in God's plan

² These are the verses of the Book that clarifies *realities*. ³ Perhaps you are over-worried *your people* won't believe. ⁴ Had We wished, We could have sent down to them from the sky a sign to which their necks will bow humbly; ⁵ and yet no fresh revelation has ever come to them from the Most Kind without them objecting to it. ⁶ They are in denial, but soon news will come to them about their earlier mockery. ⁷ Haven't they considered the Earth, and how We have grown abundantly every kind *of living thing*? ⁸ In that is a sign; yet most will not believe, ⁹ though Your Lord is the Almighty, the Caring.

God sends Moses to Pharaoh's court

¹⁰ *Remember* when your Lord called Moses: "Go to the unjust people, ¹¹ the people of Pharaoh. Will they not be mindful *of Me*?" ¹² *Moses* said, "My Lord, I fear they will deny me, ¹³ and my chest feels tight, and my tongue is unable to speak without stammering; so, send Aaron *with me*; ¹⁴ *furthermore* they have a charge against me, so I fear they will kill me." ¹⁵ *God* said, "Not at all! Go, both of you, with Our signs. We will be with you, listening in." ¹⁶ So the two of them came to Pharaoh and said, "We are bearers of the message of the Lord of the worlds, ¹⁷ so send the Israelites with us." ¹⁸ *Pharaoh* said, "When you were a child didn't we bring you up? And didn't you live with us for many years? ¹⁹ Only you could do what you did, and be ungrateful?" ²⁰ *Moses* said, "I did that by mistake,ᵃ ²¹ and I fled from you because I feared you. Then my Lord granted me wisdom and made me a messenger. ²² What sort of favour do you remind me of? That you have enslaved *my people*, the Israelites?"

ᵃ Moses never intended to kill the Coptic, but it was to save the Israelite.

PHARAOH CHALLENGES MOSES

[23] Pharaoh said, "Who is this 'Lord of the Worlds'?" [24] *Moses* said, "The Lord of the Heavens and the Earth, and of whatever is between them, if you believe." [25] *Pharaoh* said to those around him, "Are you listening? [26] *Moses* said, "Your Lord and the Lord of your forefathers." [27] *Pharaoh* said, "This messenger of yours, who has been sent to you, is clearly mad!" [28] *Moses* said, "The Lord of the East and the West and whatever is in between, if only you would reflect." [29] *Pharaoh* said, "If you take any god beside me, I will imprison you." [30] *Moses* said, "Even if I bring you clear proof?" [31] *He* said, "Then fetch it, if you are telling the truth." [32] So *Moses* threw down his stick, and straightaway it turned into a wriggling snake; [33] then he drew out his hand *from his cloak*, and it appeared to the onlookers *brilliant* white.

PHARAOH IS FRIGHTENED

[34] *Pharaoh* said to the nobles around him, "This *man* is an expert magician, [35] who wants to expel you from your land with his magic. So, what do you suggest?" [36] They said, "Put him and his brother off for a while, and send marshals to the cities [37] to bring you every expert magician *of ours*." [38] So the magicians gathered for a tournament on an appointed day; [39] and people were asked: "Will you be gathering for the *tournament*?" [40] *They replied*, "We'll follow the magicians, if they win." [41] When the magicians arrived, they asked Pharaoh: "Will we be rewarded, if we win?" [42] "Yes," he said, "Then you'll be among my close ones."

THE GRAND TOURNAMENT OF MAGICIANS

[43] Moses said to *the magicians*, "Cast whatever *spells* you have." [44] So they threw down their ropes and sticks, saying, "By Pharaoh's might, we are surely the winners." [45] Then Moses threw down his staff, and at once it swallowed up their trickery. [46] The magicians fell in prostration, [47] saying, "We believe in the Lord of the worlds, [48] the Lord of Moses and Aaron." [49] *Pharaoh* said, "You've believed him before I granted you permission? He must be your tutor, who taught you magic, but you will learn your lesson. I will cut off your hands and your feet from the opposite sides and crucify the lot of you." [50] They said, "it doesn't matter![a] We shall be returning to our Lord. [51] We hope Our Lord will forgive our mistakes, since we were the first believers."

---

[a] Literally "it won't harm us."

MOSES LEADS THE ISRAELITES OUT OF EGYPT

⁵²We revealed to Moses: "Set off with My servants at night, no doubt you will be chased." ⁵³Pharaoh sent *word* to the cities *for his soldiers* to muster, ⁵⁴*saying*, "These *Israelites* are a tiny ragbag bunch ⁵⁵who have enraged us, ⁵⁶*while* we are a united force, well trained and equipped." ⁵⁷So *it was* We brought them out of gardens and springs, ⁵⁸and treasures and comfortable homes. ⁵⁹That is how it was, and *later* We caused the Israelites to inherit it.ᵇ

THE PARTING OF THE SEA

⁶⁰At sunrise, *the Egyptians* set off in pursuit of *the Israelites.* ⁶¹When eventually the two groups spotted each other, Moses' companions said, "We've been caught." ⁶²But *Moses* said, "No way! My Lord is with me, *and* He will guide me." ⁶³We revealed to Moses: "Strike the sea with your staff." The sea parted, each side like a mighty mountain. ⁶⁴We lured *Pharaoh* to approach that place. ⁶⁵We saved Moses and anyone was with him ⁶⁶and drowned the others. ⁶⁷There *was* a lesson in that, but most of them didn't believe. ⁶⁸Your Lord is the Almighty, the Caring.

ABRAHAM QUIZZES HIS PEOPLE

⁶⁹Tell them the story of Abraham, ⁷⁰when he asked his father and community: "What do you worship?" ⁷¹They said, "We worship idols and remain devoted to them." ⁷²He said, "Do they hear you when you pray, ⁷³or benefit or harm you in any way?" ⁷⁴They said, "We found our forefathers doing so." ⁷⁵*Abraham* said, "Have you thought about what you worship, ⁷⁶you and your ancestors? ⁷⁷*These gods* are my enemies, all apart from the Lord of the worlds ⁷⁸Who has created and now guides me, ⁷⁹and Who feeds me and gives me to drink. ⁸⁰And when I am ill He heals me, ⁸¹and will make me die and bring me back to life; ⁸²and I sincerely wish that He will forgive my sins on Judgement Day."

ABRAHAM'S PRAYER

⁸³"My Lord, grant me wisdom and unite me with the righteous, ⁸⁴and grant me a reputation for truthfulness among the later *generations.* ⁸⁵Make me one of the heirs of the Garden of Bliss; ⁸⁶and forgive my fatherᶜ – he's gone astray. ⁸⁷Do not

---

ᵇ   Al-Qurtubi mentions how, after the destruction of the Ancient Egyptians, some Israelites returned to Egypt well before the coming of Islam. Indeed, Jews continued to live there as a thriving community until the mid-twentieth century.

ᶜ   Cf 19:41. This refers to his paternal uncle.

disgrace me on the Day when *humanity* will be resurrected, ⁸⁸ the Day when neither wealth nor children will benefit. ⁸⁹ *Success is* for the one who comes to God with a pure heart."

THE DISBELIEVERS COME FACE-TO-FACE WITH HELL

⁹⁰ Paradise will be brought close to the righteous; ⁹¹ and Hell will be shown to the misguided, ⁹² who will be *asked*: "Where is what you used to worship ⁹³ beside God? Are they helping you or even defending themselves?" ⁹⁴ Then they will be hurled into *Hell*, they and the misguided ⁹⁵ and the soldiers of Satan, all of them together. ⁹⁶ They will say, as they argue among themselves in *Hell*, ⁹⁷ "By God, we were mistaken ⁹⁸ when we made you equal to the Lord of the worlds. ⁹⁹ It was the *brazen* sinners who misguided us. ¹⁰⁰ Now we have no one to plead for us, ¹⁰¹ nor even a close friend. ¹⁰² If we could have a second chance we will be believers." ¹⁰³ There is a sign in that, but most of them will not believe. ¹⁰⁴ Your Lord is the Almighty, the Caring.

NOAH INVITES HIS PEOPLE TO GOD

¹⁰⁵ The people of Noah denied *God's* messengers ¹⁰⁶ when their brother Noah said to them, "Will you not be mindful *of God*? ¹⁰⁷ You have in me a messenger to be trusted, ¹⁰⁸ so be mindful of God and follow me. ¹⁰⁹ I don't ask you for a reward for this. The Lord of the worlds will give me reward. ¹¹⁰ So *again*, be mindful of God and follow me." ¹¹¹ They said, "Shall we believe in you, when only the poorest follow you?" ¹¹² He said, "What knowledge have I of what they did. ¹¹³ Their account rests with My Lord – if only you could sense *that*. ¹¹⁴ I will not drive the believers away. ¹¹⁵ I am a clear warner." ¹¹⁶ They said, "Noah, if you don't stop preaching, you will be tortured."

NOAH'S PRAYER FOR DELIVERANCE

¹¹⁷ *Noah* said, "My Lord, my people have denied me, ¹¹⁸ so judge between me and them, and save me and those who believe me." ¹¹⁹ So We saved him and those with him in the fully-laden ship, ¹²⁰ and We drowned anyone who remained behind. ¹²¹ There is a lesson in that, but many will not believe. ¹²² Your Lord is the Almighty, the Caring.

THE STORY OF PROPHET HUD

¹²³ *The people of* Ad denied the messengers ¹²⁴ when their brother Hud said to

them, "Won't you believe in God? [125] I am a trustworthy messenger to you, [126] so believe in God and follow me; [127] I won't ask you for a fee; the Lord of the worlds will reward me. [128] You build monuments on every hilltop to please yourselves, [129] and take castles *as homes* so you might live forever? [130] And, when you seize *others' wealth and land,* you are utterly ruthless in doing so. [131] So be mindful of God and follow me. [132] Be mindful of Him Who has given you abundantly: what you know, [133] cattle and children, [134] gardens and *freshwater* springs. [135] I fear for you the torment of a dreadful Day." [136] They said, "It is all the same to us, whether you preach or not; [137] these are the customs of the past generations. [138] We will not be punished." [139] They refused to believe him, so We destroyed them. There is a sign in that, but most won't believe. [140] Your Lord is the Almighty, the Caring.

THE PEOPLE OF THAMUD DEMAND A SIGN FROM SALIH

[141] *The people of* Thamud also denied *God's* messengers. [142] When their brother, Salih, said to them, "Will you not be mindful *of God*? [143] You have in me a trustworthy messenger, [144] so be mindful of God and follow me. [145] I don't ask you for a reward for this. The Lord of the worlds will reward me. [146] Will you *really* be left safe and secure with all this, [147] in gardens and springs, [148] and fields and date palms with their ripe fruits, [149] while you skilfully carve houses out of the mountains? [150] So be mindful of God and follow me, [151] don't follow the way of the wasteful [152] who spread corruption in the land rather than acting righteously." [153] They said, "You've been bewitched. [154] You are a mortal like us; so bring a miracle, if you're telling the truth."

SALIH PRODUCES THE SHE-CAMEL AS A MIRACLE

[155] Salih said, "Here is a she-camel. She may drink and you may drink, *each* on fixed days. [156] Don't harm her in case the punishment of a terrible Day befalls you." [157] They hamstrung her, only to wake up *the next day* regretting it, [158] *when* the torment overtook them. There is a lesson in this, though most of them will not believe. [159] Your Lord is the Almighty, the Caring.

LOT CONFRONTS LUSTFUL MEN

[160] The people of Lot denied their messengers. [161] When their brother, Lot, said to them, "Won't you believe? [162] I am a trustworthy messenger, [163] so believe in God and follow me; [164] I won't ask you for a fee, the Lord of the worlds will reward me. [165] *Why,* of all the people of the world do you approach males lustfully, [166] leaving

your wives whom your Lord has created for you? You are people who have crossed the bounds *of decency*." [167] They said, "If you don't stop *preaching* Lot, you will be exiled." [168] He said, "I am disgusted by your actions."

LOT'S PRAYER

[169] "My Lord, save me and my family from what they do." [170] So We saved him and all his family, [171] except an old woman, who stayed behind. [172] Then We destroyed the others, [173] pelting them with a rain of *brimstone*. How dreadful was the rain on those who had been forewarned! [174] There is a sign in that, but most will not believe. [175] Your Lord is the Almighty, the Caring.

THE STORY OF PROPHET JETHRO

[176] The companions of the forest *also* denied *God's* messengers. [177] When their brother, Jethro, said to them, "Will you not fear *God*? [178] I am a trustworthy messenger to you, [179] so be mindful of God and follow me. [180] I won't ask you for a fee for this. The Lord of the worlds will reward me. [181] Be honest in *your* measures, and don't be cheats. [182] Weigh with accurate scales; [183] don't serve people short, and don't spread corruption in the land. [184] Be mindful of Him Who created you and many previous generations." [185] They said, "You are bewitched. [186] You are a mortal like us; and we think you're a liar. [187] Cause a chunk of sky to fall on us, if you are telling the truth." [188] He said, "My Lord knows well what you do." [189] They refused to believe him, so the torment of a Day of *impenetrable* shade[a] overtook them. What a dreadful Day of torment that was! [190] There is a sign in that, but most will not believe. [191] Your Lord is the Almighty, the Caring.

REVELATION OF THE QURAN THROUGH GABRIEL

[192] And this is the Revelation of the Lord of the worlds, [193] which that trustworthy spirit, *the Angel Gabriel*, brought down [194] straight into your heart so you become a warner [195] in a clear Arabic language; [196] and it is *found* in the scriptures of earlier nations. [197] Have they not *received* a sign that the scholars of the Israelites will recognise? [198] If We had revealed it to someone who wasn't an Arab, [199] and he had recited it to them, they still wouldn't have believed it.

---

[a] This "*impenetrable* shade" conjures up images of the darkness that we are told occurred when a meteorite struck our planet and brought an end to the dinosaurs 65 million years ago. Or it may refer to the darkness that follows an Earthquake or a volcanic eruption.

Punishment for those who reject the Quran

[200] That's how We allow *rejection of the Quran* to find its way into the hearts of the sinful. [201] They will never believe in it until they see the painful punishment, [202] which will come upon them all of a sudden, when they are unaware. [203] They will say: "Can we be given some more time?" [204] But are they not currently trying to hasten Our punishment? [205] Suppose We granted them years of enjoyment, [206] then when what they had been promised befell them, [207] would what they had enjoyed benefit them? [208] We never destroyed a city which hadn't *received* warners [209] as a reminder. We are never unjust.

The Quran is uncorrupted by demons and jinns

[210] It is not demons who brought down this *Quran*; [211] nor would it be fitting for them, nor are they capable *of doing so.* [212] They are barred from *even* hearing *it.* [213] Therefore, don't call upon any other god alongside God so you *end up* among the tormented.

Instruction to invite relatives to Islam

[214] Warn your nearest relatives, [215] and take whoever follows you from among the believers under your wing. [216] Then, if they disobey you, say: "I am innocent of what you do," [217] and put your trust in the Almighty, the Caring, [218] Who sees you while you stand *in prayer* [219] and when you change *position to be* amongst those prostrating. [220] He is the Hearer, the Knower.

Some poets are misguided

[221] Shall I tell you who will be visited by demons? [222] They visit every sinful slanderer, [223] who listens readily, and who is a liar. [224] *Likewise* the poets, who are deceived, follow them *too.* [225] Do you not see them wandering about in every valley, [226] *boastfully* saying things they don't do? [227] Except the believing *poets* who are righteous, constantly remember God, and defend themselves against oppression. The oppressors will soon know the fate they will be returned to.

27. An-Naml
The Ant

This chapter was revealed in the middle-Makkan period, either in the fifth or sixth year of the mission of the Prophet ﷺ. It charts part of the history of human spirituality by reference to five prophets: Moses , Solomon , David , Salih , and Lot . The opening verses describe the nature of divine revelation as being guidance and good news. The proof of this proposition: the story of Moses and how he received divine revelation on Mount Sinai.

The story of Solomon – a prophet and king who successfully combined the two roles: worldly wealth and spiritual devotion – sets the scene for understanding divine mysteries. God gave him gifts, including the ability to communicate with various creatures – jinn, birds and even insects like the ant: see verses 17 to 19. The stories of King Solomon and the Queen of Sheba abound with symbolism, and subtly weave together the realities of worldly life and spiritual realities. In some ways, it represents the story of the human soul's spiritual awakening and eventual realisation of moral and spiritual truths. The story of the Hoopoe bird, and the transportation of the mighty throne of the Queen of Sheba thousands of miles in the twinkling of an eye express great truths. There is a certain spiritual truth underlying each one of them:

> The many sided, many layered truths which the Quran invariably brings out, sometimes explicitly, sometimes elliptically, often allegorically, but always with a definite bearing on some of the hidden depths and conflicts within our own human psyche (Asad).

When the Hoopoe told Solomon about the Queen of Sheba, Solomon dispatched a letter inviting her to become a believer and give up her idolatry. The Queen, after consulting her advisers, decided to play it safe, and to pacify Solomon sent him precious gifts and waited for her envoys to bring news about him. Solomon refused to accept her gifts, which convinced her that this was no king in pursuit of worldly gains. She travelled from Yemen to Jerusalem. Solomon, in the meantime, decided to receive her: "Who can bring me her throne before they come to me in submission?" (38). One of his knowledgeable followers was able to bring it in the "blink of an eye." The transportation of the queen's throne from Yemen to his palace in Jerusalem hints at the ephemeral, fleeting nature of material power. The throne is a metonym for power and sovereignty:

> It appears that Solomon intends to confront his guest with an image of her worldly power, and thus to convince her that her throne is as nothing when compared with the awesome almightiness of God (Asad).

In the story of the Hoopoe, the Quran teaches a powerful lesson: the lowliest being can sometimes have knowledge of things that even experts may lack. This is a clear reminder counteracting arrogance and self-deceit. Similarly, the story of the Queen of Sheba entering the hall of Solomon is a symbol of a woman confronting something new. She is full of fear, and does not wish to abandon the realm of what she finds familiar, comforting and secure in favour of venturing into the unknown. Yet the Queen of Sheba takes the leap, and sees that the floor of the hall is not dangerous:

> It is a glass-clear light of truth: and with her perception of the ever[-]existing difference between appearance and reality ... the Queen of Sheba comes to the end of her spiritual journey (Asad).

The chapter quickly moves on to the stories of Prophet Salih and Prophet Lot , who faced serious opposition from their people. Their story contrasts with that of the Queen of Sheba, who eagerly accepted faith and realised the foolishness of idolatry. The severe opposition and the hostility faced by these two prophets is a commentary on the human condition. People are being warned against their thoughtless addiction to materialism and idolatry, and are invited to adopt the attitude of the Queen of Sheba. A subtle hope to the Prophet ﷺ and his small band of followers.

The chapter hints to the appearance of a mysterious creature triggering the beginning of the end of the world (82).

————————

In the name of God, the Kind, the Caring.

¹ *Ta Sin.*

THE GLORIOUS QURAN, A SOURCE OF GUIDANCE AND GOOD NEWS

These are the verses of the Quran, a Clear Book, ²a guide and glad tidings for the believers, ³who perform the prayer, give Zakat and believe firmly in the Hereafter. ⁴As for those who don't believe in the Hereafter, We made their deeds appear attractive to them, so they wander about blindly. ⁵These *people* will have the worst punishment, and they shall be the biggest losers in the Hereafter. ⁶But you have received the Quran from the Wise, All-Knowing.

THE STORY OF MOSES

⁷*Remember* when Moses said to his wife, "I've seen a fire. I will bring you some news from there, or fetch you a burning coal so you can warm yourself." ⁸When he reached there, a voice called out: "Blessed is Whoever is *veiled by* the fire[a] and whoever is close to it. Glory be to God, the Lord of the worlds! ⁹Moses, it is I,

---

[a]   The Arabic literally says, "is in the fire".

God, the Almighty, the Wise, ¹⁰ so throw down your *shepherd's* staff." When he saw it wriggling, he turned and fled, without looking back. "Moses," *the voice said,* "Don't be afraid. Messengers shouldn't be afraid in My presence, ¹¹ even the one who has done wrong but then changes himself to do good; for I am Forgiving, Caring. ¹² Now put your hand inside your cloak *and* it will come out *brilliant* white but unharmed, *yet another of* nine signs *to show* Pharaoh and his people; they are brazen sinners." ¹³ *However,* when Our self-evident signs came to them, they said, "This is magic," ¹⁴ and they rejected them, and yet they were certain of their truth; this was due to their wickedness and pride. So look what happened to those who spread corruption.

SOLOMON'S PRAYER OF THANKSGIVING

¹⁵ We gave David and Solomon knowledge, and both prayed: "Praise be to God, Who favoured us over many of His believing servants." ¹⁶ *Then* Solomon succeeded David, and he said, "People, we have been taught the language of birds, and have been given all kinds of things, a clear *sign of* favour." ¹⁷ Solomon's armies of jinn, men and birds gathered to parade before him; ¹⁸ *and they marched* until they came to the Valley of Ants, *where* one of the ants said: "Ants, get into your anthills so that Solomon and his armies don't crush you unwittingly." ¹⁹ *Solomon* smiled and laughed at her words and said, "Lord, make me grateful to You for the blessings that You have given me and my father; and grant me strength to do righteous deeds to please You; and kindly, include me with Your righteous servants."

THE HOOPOE TELLS HIS AMAZING STORY

²⁰ *One day,* whilst looking for *a missing* bird, *Solomon* said: "Why can't I see the Hoopoe? He's absent? ²¹ Either he brings me a valid reason *for his absence,* or I will punish him severely, maybe even slaughter him!" ²² *The hoopoe* did not stay away for long; *he returned* and said, "I know of something that you don't, and I bring you an accurate report from Sheba. ²³ There I found a woman ruling over them; and, *like you,* she has been given everything and has a mighty throne.

THEIR IDOLATRY PUZZLED THE HOOPOE

²⁴ I found her and her people worshipping the sun instead of God, and Satan had made their deeds attractive to them, and blocked them from the *true* way, so they were not guided. ²⁵ Shouldn't they worship *only* God, Who discloses whatever is hidden in the Heavens and the Earth, and Who knows whatever you *choose*

either to conceal or to reveal? ²⁶There is no god but God, the Lord of the mighty Throne."

SOLOMON SENDS A LETTER TO THE QUEEN OF SHEBA

²⁷*Solomon* said, "We shall see if you are telling the truth or lying. ²⁸Go with this letter of mine and make sure they receive it, then move a little way from them and see what *response* they come back with." ²⁹*The queen* said, "My lords, I have received a gracious letter. ³⁰It is from Solomon and reads: 'In the name of God, the Kind, the Caring. ³¹Do not think yourselves above me, but come to me in submission.'" ³²*So* she asked, "My lords, advise me in this matter. I don't make any decision without your presence and advice." ³³They said, "We possess power and military might, but the *final* decision rests with you; so, tell *us* what to do."

THE QUEEN SENDS GIFTS TO SOLOMON

³⁴She said, "When kings enter a city, they lay waste to it and humiliate its nobility; that is their way. ³⁵So I will send them a gift and wait to see what the envoys come back with." ³⁶When they reached Solomon, he said *to her envoys*, "Do you *think you can* increase my wealth? What God has given me is far better than what He has given you. Only the likes of you rejoice in such gifts. ³⁷Go back to *your people* and tell them We shall come with armies that they can't face, and we shall expel them from *their city*, humiliated and disgraced."

THE QUEEN'S THRONE IS BROUGHT TO SOLOMON

³⁸*Solomon* asked *his courtiers*, "Who can bring me her throne before they come to me in submission?" ³⁹An Efreet from the jinns said, "I can bring it to you before you get up from your place; I am strong *and* trustworthy." ⁴⁰*Another,* who had knowledge *of* the Book, said, "I can bring it to you in the blinking of an eye." When *Solomon* saw it installed before him, he said, "This is by My Lord's favour, to test whether I am grateful or ungrateful. Whoever is grateful is grateful for his own benefit; but whoever is ungrateful *harms only himself*, as my Lord is Self-Sufficient, Generous." ⁴¹He said, "Disguise her throne so that we can see if she is guided or not."

THE QUEEN COMES TO SOLOMON

⁴²After arriving, *the Queen* was asked, "Is your throne like this?" She said, "It

looks just like it." *And Solomon said,*[a] "We were given prior knowledge, and we submitted *to God.* [43] What had *previously* stopped her was what she used to worship beside God, as she came from a disbelieving community." [44] "Enter the *royal* chamber," she was told. When she saw it, she thought it was a pool and so bared her legs *to keep her robes dry. Solomon* said, "The chamber is paved with glass." She said, "My Lord, I have wronged myself, but *now* I submit with Solomon to God, the Lord of the worlds."

THE STORY OF THE PROPHET SALIH

[45] We sent to *the people of* Thamud their brother Salih, *saying*: "Worship God," but they *split into* two groups and began to argue. [46] *Salih* said, "My people, why are you in a rush to do evil rather than good? If you would only seek God's forgiveness, you will be shown kindness." [47] They said, "We feel uneasy about you and those with you." He said, "Your feeling of unease *rests* with God. The fact is that, as a people, you are being tested." [48] There was a gang of nine *men* in the city who would not comply but went around wreaking havoc. [49] They said, "Let us swear by God to attack him and his family by night, then tell his guardian that we were not witnesses to his family's demise and that we are telling the truth." [50] They hatched a plot, and so We countered it; but they remained unaware. [51] Behold the outcome of their plot: We destroyed them all, and their community. [52] These are their houses, razed to the ground because of their wrongdoing. In that, there is a sign for people who know. [53] And We saved those who believed and were mindful *of Us.*

THE STORY OF THE PROPHET LOT

[54] And remember Lot, when he said to his people: "How can you commit *acts of* indecency with your eyes wide open? [55] Do you approach other men with lust rather than women? You people are utterly foolish." [56] The only response they gave: "Expel Lot's household from your city, they are such puritans." [57] So We saved him and his family except for his wife, whom We decreed would stay behind; [58] and We pelted them with a rain *of brimstone.* How dreadful was the rain on those who had been forewarned!

---

[a] Al-Qurtubi offers three alternatives for the speaker of these words: the Queen of Sheba, Solomon , or his followers.

ARGUMENTS ABOUT THE CREATIVE POWER OF GOD
[59] Say: "Praise be to God, and peace be upon His chosen servants! Is God better or whatever they associate *with Him*?" [60] Who is it Who created the Heavens and the Earth and sends down rain for you from the sky with which We have produced delightful gardens. You cannot make its trees grow? Is there *another* god along with God? On the contrary, they are people who have turned away from truth. [61] Who is it Who made the Earth a place *for you* to live, made rivers to flow in it, made mountains, and set a barrier between the two seas? Is there *another* god along with God? No, most of them are ignorant.

GOD RELIEVES HUMAN ANXIETIES
[62] Who answers the distressed when they cry out to Him, removes suffering, and causes you to inherit the land? Is there *another* god beside God? How little do you reflect! [63] Who is it Who guides you through the darkness on land and sea; and Who is it Who sends winds heralding glad tidings of His kindness *in the form of rain*? Is there *another* god beside God? God is far exalted above anything they associate as partners *with Him*!

GOD IS THE ABSOLUTE CREATOR
[64] Who sets in motion *the process of* creation, then returns it *to its former state*; and Who provides for you from the Earth and sky? Is there *another* god beside God? Say: "Fetch your proof, if you are telling the truth." [65] Say: "No one in the Heavens or on Earth has knowledge of the unseen except God; nor do they have any knowledge of when they will be resurrected." [66] Can their knowledge comprehend the Hereafter? On the contrary, they have doubts about it; in fact, they are blind to it.

THE DISBELIEVERS DENY THE RESURRECTION
[67] The disbelievers say, "How can it be that when we and our forefathers have turned to dust we will be brought back *to life*? [68] We and our forefathers were promised this before. This is merely a tale of the ancient people." [69] Say: "Travel on the Earth and see the fate of the sinners." [70] Do not grieve over them, *Messenger*, nor be anxious about what they are plotting. [71] They say, "When will this promise be fulfilled, if you are telling the truth?" [72] Say: "It may be, what you seek to hasten is already close behind you." [73] Your Lord is most gracious towards people, but most are ungrateful.

God's infinite knowledge

⁷⁴ And your Lord knows whatever their hearts conceal, and what they reveal. ⁷⁵ There is nothing hidden in the Earth or sky which is not *found* in a Clear Book. ⁷⁶ This Quran narrates most of the disagreements of the Israelites. ⁷⁷ It is a guidance and kindness for the believers. ⁷⁸ Your Lord will decide wisely between them. He is the Almighty, the Knowing. ⁷⁹ So trust in God, *for* you are clearly in the right. ⁸⁰ You can no more make the deaf hear the call than you can the dead, if they turn their backs on you; ⁸¹ nor are you there to guide the blind away from their error. Only those will hear you who believe in Our signs and submit *to Our will*.

When God's promise against the disbelievers is fulfilled

⁸² When the judgement against them comes to pass, We shall bring forth from the Earth a beast that will tell them *about* the people who didn't believe in Our signs. ⁸³ And on the Day when We gather from every community an army of those who denied Our signs, they will march in ranks. ⁸⁴ And, when they arrive *before Him*, He will say, "Did you deny My signs *despite* not comprehending them? *If not*, what were you doing?" ⁸⁵ And, as the decree is passed against them because of their wrongdoing, they will say nothing.

The Trumpet sounds to mark the start of Judgement Day

⁸⁶ Haven't they seen We made the night for them to rest and the day to give them light? In that, there is a sign for people who believe. ⁸⁷ And on the Day that the Trumpet is blown, all those in the Heavens and the Earth will be terrified except those whom God pleases *to protect*; each of them shall come to Him, humbly. ⁸⁸ And you will see the mountains, which you thought were fixed, floating like clouds. This is the handiwork of God, Who has perfected everything. He is fully aware of what you do. ⁸⁹ Whoever brings good deeds with him, shall receive even better *in return*; and they will be safe from the terror of that Day; ⁹⁰ but anyone who comes with evil deeds will be hurled face-down into the Fire *and asked*: "Have you not been rewarded for what you did?"

The Prophet ﷺ is taught what to say to his community

⁹¹ "I have been ordered to worship the Lord of this city, Who made it sacred, and all things belong to Him; and I have been ordered to be among the committed, ⁹² who recite the Quran." *Thereafter,* whoever is guided it is for his own benefit; and anyone who goes astray tell them: "I am a warner." ⁹³ And say: "Praise be to

God. He will show you His signs and you will recognise them. Your Lord is not unaware of what you do."

28. Al-Qasas
The Story

This chapter was revealed in the late Makkan period, just before the Ascension of the Prophet ﷺ in the tenth year of his mission. It relates several stories from the life of Moses to show that history keeps repeating despite the passage of time. A convincing consolation for the Messenger ﷺ and his followers. It opens by describing the Pharaoh's oppression of the Israelites, and his policy of "divide and rule". This is the amazing story of the survival of baby Moses at a time when Pharaoh's policy to kill all newborns was ruthlessly enforced. The Pharaoh is most likely Ramesses II, roughly from 1300 bc. God not only protected Moses , but made him grow up like a prince in the opulent surroundings of Pharaoh's palace. The story highlights the weakness of a worldly king unable to distinguish between foe and friend, yet claiming to be "Almighty God", revealing the extent to which powerful men and women are deceived. The chapter then relates the incident when Moses killed an Egyptian in defence of an Israelite ... Moses was about to be arrested but managed to escape. He hurriedly left Egypt, and travelled to Madyan in the Arabian desert. The Prophet Jethro gave Moses work, in return for marriage to his daughter, so Moses married a non-Israelite woman.

Moses , who was raised as a prince in a palace, became a poor shepherd in the desert – a sharp contrast in lifestyle. The Divine Plan has its own way of unfolding reality. Moses was being trained for the role of leadership, looking after a flock of sheep. Not much different from caring for an uncouth and undisciplined community.

After ten years, Moses returns to Egypt. On the way he passes Mount Sinai, where he is commissioned as a prophet to invite the Pharaoh to accept guidance. After relating the story of Moses in detail, the Quran reminds the Prophet ﷺ: "You were not *present* on the west side *of the mountain* when We handed down *Our* commandments to Moses" (44).

The Quran rejects the request of the Makkans for a written Quran; and reminds them Moses had the Torah written on tablets, but still people denied it. Those people who believed in it from the Arabs, the Jews and the Christians are praised (53–54).

After describing the fate of the idolaters in the Hereafter, the chapter returns to the story of Moses and speaks of Korah, the wealthiest Israelite in Egypt. It vividly paints his pompous lifestyle, his miserly attitude and pride. Through these stories, the human craving for worldly power and wealth is highlighted. The miserliness of Korah, shows human greed. He ascribed his wealth to his knowledge and expertise in business and prudence in worldly affairs. The leaders of Makkah refused to believe, like Pharaoh, because they feared losing their hegemony and control of the Kaaba. Such reasoning continues today: as many of us fail to live by the Quran due to fear of worldly losses.

In the name of God, the Kind, the Caring.

[1] *Ta Sin Meem.*

PHARAOH ADOPTS THE STRATEGY OF DIVIDE AND RULE

[2] These are verses of the Clear Book, [3] *in which* We recite to you part of the true story of Moses and Pharaoh for those who believe. [4] Pharaoh was unjust to people, and divided them by *their* ethnicity. Oppressing one group of them by killing their sons whilst keeping their women alive, he oppressed others. [5] Our plan was to favour the victims in the land and to make them leaders and heirs; [6] to settle them in the land and, through them, to force Pharaoh, Haman[a] and their armies to face their worst fears.

THE STORY OF MOSES' INFANCY

[7] We inspired the mother of Moses: "Breastfeed him, but when you fear for him then *put him in a basket* and let it float on the river, but don't be afraid or sad. We shall return him to you and make him a messenger. [8] *Members of* Pharaoh's household found him *by chance, little did they know* he would become their enemy and a cause of grief. Pharaoh, Haman and their armies were gravely mistaken. [9] Pharaoh's wife said, "He would be a joy to behold for me and you, so don't kill him he may be useful for us, or we could adopt him. They were unaware of its consequences." [10] By the morning Moses' mother was impatient and she nearly revealed his *identity*, if We hadn't strengthened her resolve to *remain* silent about him. [11] She told his sister: "Follow him." From the river bank she kept an eye on him without letting *the Egyptians* see her. [12] We made him reject *the breast milk of* the wet nurses, so *his sister* said to them, "Shall I show you a household that will look after him for you and take good care of him?" [13] So We returned him to his mother, to be a *comforting* sight for her *sore* eyes, so she wouldn't be anxious and know that God's promise is true. Though most *people* don't know.

MOSES ATTEMPTS TO SORT OUT A RACIAL FIGHT

[14] When he had grown up and reached maturity, We blessed him with wisdom and knowledge; that's how We reward the righteous. [15] One day, he entered the

---

[a] Haman was the high priest of the Egyptian god Amon. Haman ranked second only to the reigning Pharaoh. (Asad)

town while people were resting[a] and found two men fighting, one from his ethnic group and the other from his enemy. The one from his ethnic group cried out to him for help against the one from his enemy's *group*; so Moses punched him, so hard that it finished him off. *Moses* said, "This is the work of Satan. He is clearly an enemy who leads *people* astray."

MOSES' PRAYER FOR FORGIVENESS

[16] *Then* he said, "My Lord, I have done wrong, so forgive me." God forgave him; the Forgiving, the Caring. [17] *Moses* said, "My Lord, because you gave me *favours* I will never stand up for criminals *again*." [18] From then on he became fearful in the town, *constantly* on the lookout. *Next day*, the man who previously sought his help again cried out. Moses said, "You are clearly a deceitful man." [19] *Moses* tried to grab the enemy and *the Israelite* said, "Moses, are you going to kill me like you killed someone yesterday? You want to be an oppressor in the land; you've no wish to do good." [20] A man from the far side of town came running and said, "Moses, members of *Pharaoh's* court are deliberating whether to have you killed, so leave *now*. I am your well-wisher." [21] So he left *the city* in fear and remained wary, he prayed: "My Lord, save me from this nation of wrongdoers."

MOSES HELPS TWO WOMEN AT THE WELL OF MADYAN

[22] Having set out for Madyan, he said to himself: "Maybe, My Lord will guide me on the right path."[b] [23] After he arrived at the water *well* of Madyan, he found a large crowd of people watering *their flocks*. He saw standing apart from them two women, holding *their sheep* back. He asked: "What is the matter with you?" They said, "We can't water *our sheep* until the shepherds move off, our father is an elderly man, *unable to help us*." [24] So *Moses* watered *their sheep*, then he turned *to rest* in the shade, praying: "My Lord, I am in *desperate* need of whatever good You may send down to me."

MOSES ACCEPTS A MARRIAGE PROPOSAL

[25] One of *the two women* came to him, walking shyly, and said, "My father is calling you, to reward you for watering *our flock*." *Moses* went and told him the *whole* story. *He* said, "Do not be afraid. You have been saved from nation of wrongdo-

---

[a] Another meaning could be: "when its residents no longer recognised him."

[b] Madyan is the Biblical Midian, this is the area of the gulf of Aqaba and extended eastward towards the Dead Sea.

ers." ²⁶One of *them* said, "My dear father, *why not* employ him? The best person you can employ is strong and trustworthy." ²⁷ He said, "I wish to marry you to one of the two daughters of mine, on the condition that you work for me for eight years. If you complete ten years, that will be up to you. I won't impose it on you. God willing, you will find me to be upright *in my dealings*." ²⁸ Moses said, "That's *agreed* between you and me. Whichever of the two terms I fulfil, let there be no resentment towards me; and let God be a guarantor of what we *decide*."

MOSES MOVES FROM MADYAN BACK TO EGYPT

²⁹ Once Moses had completed his term in Madyan, he set off with his family *to Egypt*. On the way he noticed a fire *burning* by the side of the mountain, he told his wife, "Wait here for a while. I've noticed a fire. Maybe I'll bring you some news from there or some embers from the fire so that you may warm yourselves." ³⁰ When he reached it, a voice called out from the tree on the right-hand side of the valley in that blessed spot: "Moses, it is I, God, the Lord of the worlds. ³¹ Throw down your *shepherd's* staff." When he saw it wriggling *like a snake*, he turned and fled, without looking back. "Moses, go ahead and pick it up, and don't be afraid. You are safe. ³² Put your hand inside your shirt, and it will come out *brilliant* white and unharmed, and hold it under the armpit *to rid yourself* of fear.^c Here are two proofs from your Lord to show to Pharaoh and his nobles; they are sinners."

MOSES ASKS FOR SUPPORT

³³ Moses said, "My Lord, I killed one of their men, I fear they'll kill me. ³⁴ My brother, Aaron, is more eloquent in speech than I am, so send him with me as a support to confirm *what I say, for* I fear they will reject me." ³⁵ God said, "We shall strengthen your arm with your brother and give you both authority, so that they don't harm you; because of Our signs,^d the two of you and whoever follows you will be victorious."

MOSES MOVES INTO PHARAOH'S COURT

³⁶ When Moses came with Our clear signs to them, they said, "This is nothing but clever tricks of magic; and we never heard this *message* from our forefathers." ³⁷ Moses said, "My Lord knows best who comes from Him with His guidance and who will *enjoy* the Final Abode; *but* the wrongdoers won't succeed." ³⁸ Phar-

^c Shah Waliyallah explained this idiom; "now gather your thoughts, overcome your doubts and anxiety."

^d In the Arabic text, the words "because of Our signs" can go with either the phrase before, or the one after.

aoh said, "*My* nobles, I know of no other god for you than myself. Haman, bake *bricks* of clay and build a tower for me, so that I may ascend to the God of Moses, though I know he's a liar." ³⁹And *so it was that* he and his armies, were falsely arrogant in the country, thinking they would never be returned to Us. ⁴⁰So We seized him and his armies and threw them into the sea. See the fate of the wrongdoers! ⁴¹We made them foremost amongst those who call *others* to the Fire; and on Judgement Day, they will be helpless. ⁴²We tracked them with a curse in this world and, on Judgement Day, they will be the most despised.

MUHAMMAD ﷺ IS A SIGN OF GOD'S KINDNESS FOR THE MAKKANS

⁴³We gave Moses the Book, after We destroyed previous *rebellious* generations, to be examples[a] for *all* people, a guidance and kindness, so they might pay heed. ⁴⁴You were not *present* on the west side *of the mountain* when We handed down *Our* commandments to Moses, you weren't a witness. ⁴⁵However, We raised *successive* generations, who lived long lives. Nor did you live among the people of Madyan, reciting Our verses to them, but We sent *them* messengers nonetheless. ⁴⁶Nor were you on the mountainside when We called *Moses*, but *you have been sent* as a kindness from your Lord to warn those people to whom no warner was sent before you, so they might wake up *to the reality*.

PRIDE PREVENTS THEM PURSUING THE PROPHET ﷺ

⁴⁷When a disaster strikes them due to their *evil* actions they pray: "Our Lord, had You sent us a messenger, we would have followed Your verses and become believers." ⁴⁸However, when Our truth reached them, they said, "Why wasn't he given a book like the one Moses was given?" They also denied what was given to Moses, saying, "Two competing works of magic!"[b] And said, "We reject each *of them*"? ⁴⁹Say: "So produce a book from God for me to follow that is a better guide than either of them, if you are telling the truth." ⁵⁰If they fail to respond to you, then know that they are following their impulses. And who is more misguided than the one who follows his impulses without any guidance from God. God does not guide people who do wrong.

---

[a]   Literally to give them 'insights'.
[b]   The Quran and Torah.

CHRISTIANS AND JEWISH BELIEVERS PRAISED^C

⁵¹ We caused the *message* to reach them so they may pay heed. ⁵² Those given the Book previously believe in it; ⁵³ and when it is recited to them, they say: "We believe in it. It is the truth from our Lord; and *even* before this we had surrendered ourselves *to God's will*." ⁵⁴ Such people will be given double reward because of their patience and *secondly* they stop evil with good, and they spend *in charity* what We provided them; ⁵⁵ and when they hear idle talk they turn away from it, saying: "We have our deeds, and you have yours. Peace be upon you. We don't envy the ignorant." ⁵⁶ *Messenger,* you can't guide who you love. But God guides anyone He chooses. And God knows the guided.

FLOUTING GOD'S CALL DUE TO HOUSEHOLD TASKS

⁵⁷ The *Makkans* say: "If we followed your religion, then we would be unsafe in our city." Haven't We settled them in a safe and sacred place where fruits of every sort are brought, a provision from Us? Yet most don't know. ⁵⁸ How many cities have We destroyed that were disrespectful due to their *lavish* lifestyles? Their homes are there, scarcely lived in since their day, and We took them. ⁵⁹ Your Lord never destroyed cities without first sending a messenger to their affluent people, who recited to them Our verses; nor did We destroy any city unless its population were wrongdoers.

SHORT-LIVED PLEASURES OF THIS LIFE

⁶⁰ What you receive *from God* are the passing pleasures and attractions of this worldly life; but what God has stored for you is far better and long lasting. Don't you understand? ⁶¹ Is the person who We made a beautiful promise *of Paradise* the same as the person who enjoys the pleasures of worldly life? On Judgement Day he will be summoned *to account for his deeds*?

FALSE GODS ARE UNABLE TO HELP

⁶² On that Day God will call them: "Where are the partners you associated with Me?" ⁶³ Those questioned will say, "Our Lord, here are the ones we led astray. We led them astray since we were misguided. We declare ourselves innocent before You. They were not worshipping us." ⁶⁴ *Then* they will be told: "Call on your partners *for help*," and when they call them they will not answer. When they see

^C This refers to the group of Jews like Abdullah ibn Salam and some Christians who became Muslims.

the punishment *they'll wish they had*, if only they had been guided. [65] On the Day that He calls them, saying: "How did you respond to the messengers?" [66] They will be so confused by the events of the Day that they won't be able to consult one another.

THERE IS HOPE FOR THOSE WHO REPENT

[67] Those who repented, believed and performed good deeds will be among the successful. [68] Your Lord creates whatever He wills and *then* makes His selection; the choice is not theirs. Glory be to God! Far exalted is God above whatever they associate *with Him* as partners. [69] And your Lord knows what their hearts conceal and reveal. [70] He is God. There is no god but Him. All praise in this world and the next is His. The *Final* Judgement rests with Him, and to Him you will return.

CAN ANYONE OTHER THAN GOD RECREATE NIGHT AND DAY?

[71] Say: "Have you considered if God plunged you into unending night until Judgement Day; which god beside God could bring you light? Do you not hear?" [72] Say: "Have you considered if God were to make your daylight unending until Judgement Day; which god is there beside God to bring you night in which to rest? Do you not see?" [73] Through His kindness, He has made for you both night and day so you may rest in one and seek his bounty *in the other*, and be thankful. [74] On the Day that He calls them, saying: "Where are the partners that you ascribed to Me?" [75] On that Day, We shall take from each community a witness and say, "Fetch *Me* your proof," so they know the truth belongs to God, and that whatever they invented has deserted them.

THE SMUGNESS OF KORAH, THE RICH ISRAELITE

[76] Korah was from Moses' people, but unkind to them[a]. We gave him so much treasure that the keys alone would have weighed down a dozen or so strong men. His people told him, "Do not be proud *of your wealth*. God dislikes those who brag. [77] Instead use some of what God has given you to secure *your place in* the Final home, at the same time not losing your share of this world. Treat *others* as well as God has treated you; and do not wreak havoc in the land. God dislikes those who wreak havoc." [78] *Korah* said, "I've been given it because of *my expertise and* knowledge." Didn't he realise that God destroyed *people of* previous generations

---

[a] Korah is the Biblical Korah.

who were far stronger and wealthier than him? The guilty won't be asked about their sins.

A LESSON FOR THOSE WHO ENVIED KORAH

[79] *So one day* he went out among his people, *dressed* in his finery; and those who yearn for this worldly life said, "Oh, if only we had been given the same as Korah. He's most fortunate!" [80] But those who had been given knowledge said, "Woe to you! God's reward for believers and the righteous is better; the patient will achieve that." [81] So *it was* We made the Earth swallow him and his mansion; there was no *rescue* party to help him beside God, nor was he able to protect himself. [82] Those who only the other day had longed to be in his place said, "Alas! It seems God gives in abundance to whichever of His servants He pleases, and in strict measure. If God hadn't been gracious to us, He might have destroyed us *too*. Alas! It's apparent the ungrateful fail."

[83] Such is the Final Abode; We grant it to those who desire neither grandeur nor wreak havoc in the land. And the *best* outcome is for those mindful *of God*. [84] Anyone who does good deeds will be generously rewarded with something wonderful; and anyone who does evil deeds will be rewarded for what they did.

THE GIFT OF THE QURAN AND THE PROMISE OF RETURNING HOME ONE DAY

[85] The Legislator of *the laws of* the Quran will return you *to Makkah*. Say: "My Lord knows who is guided and who is misguided." [86] You weren't expecting to be given the Book, it was due to your Lord's kindness. So, don't be a helper of the disbelievers; [87] and let no one distract you from *acting on* God's verses after they are revealed to you. Call *people* to your Lord, and don't be an associator of partners *with God*. [88] Don't call others god beside God. There is no god but Him. Everything will perish except His being.[b] He will make the *Final* Judgement, and to Him you will be returned.

---

[b] Literally: Except His face.

29. Al-'Ankabut
The Spider

Most commentators class this as the last Makkan chapter. This is apparent from its confrontational character tempered by rational and historical evidence warning the people of Makkah against their folly. The intense persecution made it dangerous to be a follower of the beloved Messenger 🙼. The chapter opens with a reminder to the believers: life is full of tests and success comes by passing them. The reward for their Jihad, hard work and tireless effort is nothing less than victory; mentioned in the closing verse of the chapter: "Those who strive *hard* for Our sake, We shall guide them along on Our ways. God is with those who do good" (69).

What lies between these two ends are details and processes for achieving success. The central theme is the constant confrontation between belief and disbelief – symbolised by the antagonism between Abraham and Nimrod; the tussle between Moses and Pharaoh, and the struggle between Noah and his people. So, the Prophet 🙼 is bolstered to face hostility from the likes of Abu Jahl and Abu Lahab.

The metaphor of the spider's web is used to convey the weak and fragile nature of worldly power, in contrast to the enduring nature of God's religion. The Quran says: "An example of those who adopt gods beside God is like a spider that spins a web – and a spider's web is the weakest of homes" (41). A sharp criticism of idolatry, love of the world, and denial of the truth, but what is at stake is so precious that the Quran employs such devices to awaken the dead conscience of idolaters, and people drunk with the material world.

Two instructions stand out: perform the prayer regularly, and be polite to People of The Book:

> "Recite the Book revealed to you, *messenger*, and perform the prayer. Without doubt, prayer protects from indecency and evil; and to remember God is greater *still*; and God knows well what you do. *Believers*, debate courteously with People of The Book" (45–46).

•

In the name of God, the Kind, the Caring.

[1] *Alif Lam Meem.*

CHOOSING TO BELIEVE DOES NOT MEAN AN INSTANT END TO SUFFERINGS
[2] Do people think they will be left alone because they say, "We believe," then will not be tested? [3] We tested those before them. God knows the truthful and the liars. [4] Or do evildoers think they can beat Us? How wrong they judge! [5] Anyone

expecting to meet God *should know:* God's appointed time is *fast* approaching; and He is the Hearer, the Knower. [6] Whoever strives hard he strives for his benefit. God is Self-Sufficient, *independent* of all creation. [7] The believers who do good works will have their sins erased and We shall reward them *in* the best way for what they did.

Caring for parents is a socio-spiritual duty

[8] We urged humanity to treat their parents well, but if they strive to get you to associate with Me anything you have no knowledge of, then do not obey them. You will return to Me, when I shall inform you of what you did. [9] The believers who do good works, We shall join them with the righteous.

Hypocrites lack resolve

[10] Some people say, "We believe in God," but when they are persecuted for the sake of God, they consider people's persecution like God's punishment. But if help arrives from Your Lord, they say, "We were with you *all along.*" Surely God knows best what is in people's minds. [11] God knows the believers and the hypocrites.

Disbelievers make promises they cannot fulfil

[12] The disbelievers say to the believers: "Follow in our footsteps, and we will bear *the burden of* your sins," though they won't carry *the believers'* sins. They are liars. [13] *However,* they will carry their own burdens and other burdens beside; and on Judgement Day they will be questioned about whatever *falsehoods* they made up.

Two examples of those who rejected God

[14] We sent Noah to his people; he lived amid them for one thousand years less fifty. Then the flood destroyed them, they were still *unrepentant* wrongdoers; [15] We saved him and the companions of the Ark, which We made a sign for all people. [16] And Abraham *too*, when he said to his people: "Worship God and be mindful of Him. That is better for you, if only you knew. [17] Whatever you worship beside God are nothing but idols, you create a lie.[a] Those you worship beside God have no power to provide for you; so seek provision from God, worship and thank Him; *eventually* you will return to Him." [18] *Makkans,* if you reject *the message, you will be like* so many other nations before you. The Messenger's task is to convey

---

[a] The idol is a physical structure, a visible shape that the disbeliever gives to a false idea, hence "you create a lie".

the message clearly.

[19] Have they not considered how God sets creation in motion and then *periodically* restores it? That is easy for God. [20] Say: "Wander about the land and see how He *previously* set creation in motion. Then God will bring into being the life of the Hereafter." God has power over everything. [21] He punishes whomever He wills, and He shows kindness to whomever He wills; and *eventually* you will revert back to Him. [22] You can't defeat *God*, either on Earth or in the sky; you have no protector or a helper beside God. [23] People who deny God's signs and meeting Him despair of *receiving* My kindness, and they will have a painful punishment.

MAKKANS ARE INVITED TO REFLECT ON ABRAHAM'S WORDS

[24] The only response *Abraham's* people gave was: "Kill him," or "Burn him." But God rescued him from the fire. There are signs in that for the believers. [25] *Abraham* said, "The reason you adopted idols beside God is the love of this life, something that you have in common. On Judgement Day, you will disown and curse each other when *you see that* your home will be the Fire, and you will have no help."

LOT IS REJECTED BY HIS PEOPLE

[26] Lot believed in *Abraham* when he told him: "I am migrating to my Lord. He is the Almighty, the Wise." [27] We granted *Abraham* Isaac and Jacob, planting prophethood in his offspring and *knowledge of* the Book; and We rewarded him in this life, and in the Hereafter he will be amid the righteous. [28] And Lot, when he said to his people, "You approach gross indecency in a way no one in the whole world has done before you. [29] How can you approach men, kidnap *them*, and perform repulsive acts in the clubs where you meet?" His people's response was: "Fetch us God's punishment, if you are truthful." [30] *Lot* prayed: "My Lord, support me against people who are spoilers."[a]

ANGELS COME AS TERMINATORS

[31] Our messengers came to Abraham with the good news *of a child*, then they told him, "We came to destroy the people of this city, its residents are wrongdoers." [32] He quipped, "But Lot is *living* there." They said, "We know who is *living* there.

---

[a] 'Mufsideen' here refers to people who damage human society by indulgence in evil.

We will save him and his household, except for his wife, who will remain behind."
³³ When Our messengers came to Lot, he felt distressed since he couldn't protect them, but *the angels* said, "Don't be afraid or sad. We are *here* to save you and your household, except for your wife, who will remain behind. ³⁴ We are to bring down a plague from the sky against the residents of this city because of their habitual sinfulness." ³⁵ We have left *enough remains* of it behind to be a clear sign for people who understand.

A REMINDER TO REFLECT ON THE RUINS OF EARLY COMMUNITIES
³⁶ To Madyan, We sent their brother Jethro, who said: "My people, worship God and long for the Last Day, and don't roam the land, wreaking havoc." ³⁷ Yet they rejected him, so an Earthquake took them *all of a sudden* and by the next morning they lay dead in their homes. ³⁸ Similarly, Ad and Thamud, *what happened to them* is quite clear from *the ruins of* their homes. Satan made their deeds appear attractive to them, preventing them from the path *of God*, though they could see *right from wrong.*

FOUR EARTHLY PUNISHMENTS INFLICTED ON THE ARROGANT
³⁹ Moses came with clear proofs to Korah, Pharaoh and Haman, but they were arrogant in the land, they weren't the first. ⁴⁰ So We punished each one of them for their crime. We sent sand storms; the Blast; swallowed them *in the bowels of* the Earth; and others We drowned. God did not wrong any of them; rather, they wronged themselves.

THE LIES OF IDOLATERS ARE AS EASILY DESTROYED AS A SPIDER'S WEB
⁴¹ An example of those who adopt gods beside God is like a spider that spins a web – and a spider's web is the weakest of homes – if only they knew.[b] ⁴² God knows what they call on beside Him is nothing. He is the Almighty, the Wise. ⁴³ We give people such examples, and the knowledgeable understand them. ⁴⁴ God has created the Heavens and the Earth, *and* in that there is a sign for the believers.

PRAYER PERFORMED PROPERLY IS A SHIELD AGAINST SINFULNESS
⁴⁵ Recite the Book revealed to you, *messenger*, and perform the prayer. Without doubt, prayer protects from indecency and evil; and to remember God is greater *still*; and God knows well what you do.

[b] "A symbol of false beliefs and values, which in the long run are bound to be blown away by the winds of truth." (Asad)

Advice on interfaith dialogue

⁴⁶ *Believers*, debate courteously with People of The Book – except the oppressors among them – and tell them: "We believe in what's revealed to us and what's revealed to you, Our God and your God is One, and we submit to Him." ⁴⁷ That is how We have revealed the Book to you; and those to whom We *previously* gave *a share of* the Book believe in it, just as some of them believe in it; only the disbelievers reject Our signs. ⁴⁸ You did not recite *any* book before, nor did you ever copy it out with your right hand; had you done so then the fault finders would have a reason to doubt. ⁴⁹ On the contrary, *it contains* clear verses in the breasts of knowledgeable people. Only wrongdoers reject Our signs.

Why demand miracles when one has the Quran?

⁵⁰ They say: "If only miracles were sent down to him from his Lord." Say: "Miracles come from God, and I am a clear warner." ⁵¹ Isn't it enough that We revealed the Book to you so it may be recited to them? There's kindness and a reminder in that for people who believe. ⁵² Say: "God is sufficient witness between me and you. He knows whatever is in the Heavens and the Earth. As for those who believe in falsehood and reject God, they are the losers."

Hell has room enough for all who deserve it

⁵³ They ask you to hasten the punishment, but the punishment would have already come, if the appointed time hadn't been fixed. And it will strike them suddenly, when they least expect it. ⁵⁴ They ask you to hasten the punishment; but Hell is *big enough* to contain the disbelievers ⁵⁵ on the Day when the punishment envelops them from above and below their feet, and *God* says: "Taste the fruit of your deeds."

Believers allowed to migrate

⁵⁶ My believing servants, My Earth is vast, so worship Me *wherever you are*. ⁵⁷ Every soul tastes death, then to Us you will be returned; ⁵⁸ and *the* believers who perform good deeds shall settle in lofty homes of Paradise under which rivers flow, living there forever. What a wonderful reward for the hard workers, ⁵⁹ who were patient and trusted their Lord.

The contradictions of those who believe in God but reject His message

⁶⁰ Animals don't carry their provisions around; God provides for them and you.

He is the Hearer, the Knower. [61] If you were to ask them: "Who created the Heavens and the Earth, and harnessed the sun and the moon?" Without doubt, they will say, "God!" So why do they spread lies? [62] God distributes *His* provision to anyone He wills among His servants, and He measures it out for him. God has knowledge of everything. [63] And if you were to ask them: "Who sends water from the sky, and gives with it life to the Earth after its death?" They'll say, "God!" Say, "Praise be to God!" And most of them still don't understand.

THE IDOLATERS SWING BETWEEN SINCERITY AND DISBELIEF

[64] This worldly life is *little* but fun and games; the home of the Hereafter is *true* life[a], if they knew. [65] When they are on board a ship, they call God sincerely in devotion. Then, when He brings them safely back to the land, they associate partners *with Him*, [66] unthankful for what We gave them. Let them enjoy, soon they will realise.

GOD REWARDS THE HARD WORKERS

[67] Haven't they considered *how* We made *Makkah* a safe place, while all around them people *live in fear of* being kidnapped. Will they *continue* believing in falsehood and deny God's gifts? [68] Who is a greater sinner than someone who makes up lies about God or *flatly* rejects the truth when it comes to him? Isn't Hell a *fitting* home for the disbelievers? [69] Those who strive *hard* for Our sake, We shall guide them along on Our ways. God is with those who do good.

---

[a]   Had they used reason they would have realised the transient and fleeting nature of life.

30. Ar-Rum
The Romans

This chapter was revealed in the fifth or sixth year of the mission of the Prophet 🌸, at a time when tensions were intense. The chapter opens with a remarkable prediction: "The Romans were defeated in a nearby country, but within a few years of their defeat they will be victorious.' (2–4) In 615 CE, the Persians defeated them. Their defeat made the Quraysh happy; they took this as an omen that the Muslims would be similarly defeated. The idea that the Romans would recover from this terrible defeat was not credible to them. However, the Quran predicted otherwise:

> At the time this prediction is said to have been delivered no prophecy could be more distant from its accomplishment, since the first twelve years of Heraclius announced the approaching dissolution of the Empire (E. Gibbon, *The Decline and Fall of the Roman Empire*, Vol. 4, p. 514).

The Quranic prediction was fulfilled on the same day as Battle of Badr (624 CE). The central theme of the chapter is the creative power of God that reinforces the belief in the resurrection. It explains the underlying problem with the disbelievers' materialistic mindset: "People know the outer nature of worldly life, but are unaware of the Hereafter" (7).

Fitrah, the natural human character, is how God created us: "So set your face towards the religion *of God* sincerely, in accordance with human nature, which God shaped." (30). Islamic teachings nurture this pure heart. Others have translated this as "natural disposition, sound human nature", which means "man's inborn, intuitive ability to discern between right and wrong, true and false, and sense God's existence and oneness" (Asad). A positive vision of Humanity, a far cry from Hobbs (d.1679) image of beastly, brutal and selfish humanity.

We can't fail to see all around us wonderful and awesome signs that point to God's creative power. Seven signs are brought to our attention: the creation of humanity from elements, the love between husband and wife, differences in language and people's colour, the functions of night and day, the lightning and the winds. These natural phenomena point to their Creator, and the Quran urges readers to progress onto the next stage – that of recognising God as the Creator, worthy of worship.

There is another prediction: "If pollution has appeared on land and sea it's because of what people have done with their hands, it is to make them taste something of the fruits of what they have done" (41). The reference can be to the climate crisis. There is another remarkable prediction:

Verse 55 predicts: Islam will continue until the end of the time; there will always be true believers to the Last Day. This is good news: despite setbacks, the Ummah will thrive.

In the name of God, the Kind, the Caring.

[1] *Alif Lam Meem.*

THE POWER STRUGGLE BETWEEN ROME AND PERSIA

[2] The Romans were defeated [3] in a nearby land; but after their defeat, they will be victorious [4] within a few years. Whether *it occurs* sooner or later, the decision is God's; that day the believers will rejoice [5] at the victory *from* God. He grants victory to anyone He wants; the Almighty, the Caring. [6] God's promise; God never breaks His promise, but most people don't know.

THE DEEPER MEANING OF LIFE

[7] *People* know the outer nature of worldly life, but are unaware of the Hereafter. [8] Haven't they thought about themselves? Everything God created – in the Heavens and the Earth and what lies between them – is for a purpose and a fixed timespan. Despite this, many people are in denial about meeting their Lord. [9] Haven't they travelled around and seen what happened to those before them? They were more powerful than them; they farmed the land and populated it even more than it is now, and their messengers came to them with clear proofs. God did not wrong them, but they wronged themselves; [10] and the outcome of evil was bound to be evil. They rejected God's signs and mocked them.

PEOPLE WILL BE SEPARATED ON THE LAST DAY

[11] God starts the creation, then He will restore it *to its original state*, then you will be returned to Him. [12] The Day the Final Hour comes, the sinners will despair. [13] Their idols will not intercede for them, but reject them. [14] When the Final Hour comes, that Day *all humanity* will be divided: [15] the believers who did good deeds will be celebrating in Paradise; [16] but the disbelievers who rejected Our signs and Our meeting in the Hereafter will be in everlasting torment. [17] So *say:* "Glory be to God!" When you settle down for the evening and when you rise in the morning, [18] and: "Praise be to Him in the Heavens and the Earth!" At night and noon.

THE GROWTH OF PLANTS ON DRY LAND AFTER RAIN; A SIGN OF RESURRECTION

[19] He brings the living from the dead, and He brings the dead from the living, that's how He revives the Earth after it *appears* dead. That's how you will be brought to life. [20] And among His signs is He created you from dust, and scattered

you *around the world.*

THE LOVE THAT EXISTS BETWEEN HUSBAND AND WIFE IS GOD>S SIGN

[21] Among His signs is He created spouses for you from your own kind, so you can live together peacefully;[a] and He commands you to love and care for each other[b], in that are signs for thinkers. [22] Among His signs is the creation of the Heavens and the Earth, and the differences in your languages and skin colour, there are signs for those who know.

DAY AND NIGHT, AND LIGHTNING AND RAIN AS SIGNS

[23] Among His signs is you sleep at night and *during* the day you seek His bounty. There are signs for people who hear. [24] Among His signs is that He shows you the lightning, *filling you* with fear and hope, and He sends water from the sky, reviving the Earth after it *seemed to have* died. In that there are signs for those who understand.

THE UNIVERSE IS GOD'S GREATEST SIGN

[25] Among His signs is the sky and the Earth that exist by His command. Then, when He makes the call, you shall come out of the Earth. [26] Everything in the Heavens and the Earth belong to Him; they are all obedient to Him. [27] He starts the creation, then restores it *to its original state*; and that's easy for Him. And His greatest example is the Heavens and the Earth. He is the Almighty, the Wise.

GOD IS NOT LIKE ANY OF HIS CREATURES

[28] *God gives* you an example from yourselves. Do you take any of your slaves as your partners, in what We have provided you, so you are equal in *shares*, do you worry about them as you worry for yourselves? That's how We explain *Our* signs to people who think. [29] But those who do wrong ignorantly follow their whims. Who can guide the one whom God has allowed to go astray, and who has no helpers?

TO BE HUMBLE IS IN HARMONY WITH HUMAN NATURE

[30] So stand firmly for the religion *of God* sincerely. That is the human nature, which God made. There is no change in *the laws of* God's creation. That is the

---

[a] '*Letaskunoo*' is derived from '*Sakana*', which means 'to live in a home'. So I have taken the literal meaning rather than the implied meaning of 'with tranquillity'.

[b] An alternative meaning is "He planted love and kindness between you."

upright religion, most people don't know.[c] [31] *Believers, turn* in repentance to Him, be mindful of Him, perform the prayer, and don't be an idolater. [32] Don't be like those who divided their religion and became sects, each sect happy with the *beliefs* they follow.

THE REACTION IN GOOD AND BAD TIMES REVEALS CHARACTER

[33] In bad times people call on their Lord, longing for Him; He treats them kindly, but a group of them continues to associate *partners* with their Lord, [34] being ungrateful for what We gave them. So enjoy yourselves, soon you shall know *the truth*. [35] Or have We sent them any authority that talks about what they associated with Him? [36] When We treat people kindly they're happy; but when they fall into bad times due to what they have done, they despair. [37] Haven't they considered that God distributes *His* provision to whomever He wills, and that He measures it out? For the believers, there are signs in that.

ZAKAT BRINGS LASTING BENEFITS

[38] Give relatives, the needy and the travellers their due. That's a good thing to do for those who seek God's pleasure, and they will have *lasting* success. [39] The wealth you lend people with interest for an increase[d] will not increase in God's sight; but what you give in Zakat, seeking God's pleasure *will increase*, such people will be rewarded many times over. [40] God created you, provided you, then will cause you to die, and then resurrect you. Which of these, if any, can your *false* idols do? Glory be to Him! He is exalted far above what they associate *with Him* as partners.

POLLUTION OF EARTH: THE ENVIRONMENTAL CRISIS

[41] Pollution has appeared on land and sea it's what people have done with their hands, it is to make them taste something of the fruits of their work, so they may turn back *from their wicked ways*.[e] [42] Say: "Travel about the land and observe what became of those before *you*." Most of them associated *partners with God*. [43] Stand firmly for the upright religion before a Day comes from God that can't be postponed; that Day, *humanity* will split in two: [44] the disbelievers will answer for

---

[c] Human nature refers to our ability to distinguish good from bad, we are ever-capable of doing good. The third century Chinese sage Mencius (Mang Tzu) said "all men have a mind, which cannot bear to see the sufferings of others."

[d] In this verse, God links two words that are clearly related in Arabic: 'usury', and 'increase'.

[e] *Fasad* is 'to become bad', to be spoiled, corrupt, weaken and undermine. Isn't the environmental pollution we see so wide-spread *Fasad*?

their disbelief; and the righteous will have a comfortable place arranged for them. [45] So He may reward with His bounty those who believed and did good deeds. *God* dislikes the disbelievers.

THE CYCLE OF WIND AND RAIN: GOD'S BOUNTIES

[46] Among His signs is the winds bearing glad tidings, to give you a taste of His kindness, and ships that sail by His command, enabling you to seek His bounty and show gratitude. [47] We sent messengers before you, *each* to their people, with clear proofs; and We punished the sinners and helped the believers. [48] God sends the winds, which scatter clouds across the sky as He pleases; then He causes *the sky* to break so that you see rain come down; and if He makes it fall on whomever of His servants He pleases, they become happy. [49] Before it was sent down, they were in despair. [50] So observe the effects of God's kindness; the revival of the Earth after its death. *God* resurrects the dead. He has power over all things. [51] Had We sent wind that turned *their crops* yellow, they still wouldn't believe. [52] You can't make the dead hear the call any more than you can the deaf, if they turn their backs to leave; [53] nor can you guide the blind to turn away from their error. The believers are the only ones who will listen to you and accept Our signs, they submit *to Our will.*

HUMAN LIFE: BIRTH, YOUTH, OLD AGE, DEATH, THE GRAVE AND RESURRECTION

[54] God created you weak; after weakness He made you strong, and after being strong He made you weak *again* in old age. He creates whatever He pleases and He is the Knower, the Powerful. [55] The Day the *Final* Hour comes, the sinners will swear they lingered no more than a short while *in their graves*; that is how they were deceived. [56] And those given knowledge and faith will say, "According to God's Book, you have lingered until the Day of Resurrection; and this is the Day of Resurrection, but you were unaware." [57] That Day, the wrongdoers' excuses will not benefit them, nor will they *have a chance to* beg for favours.

THE QURAN CONTAINS SUFFICIENT EXAMPLES, EVEN FOR DOUBTERS

[58] We gave people all kinds of examples in this Quran. Were you to produce a miracle for them, the disbelievers would still say, "You are fake." [59] That is how God seals the hearts of those who don't know. [60] So be patient, God's promise is true; and don't let the deniers frighten you.

31. Luqman
Luqman the Wise

This chapter was revealed in the middle Makkan period. It bears the name of the legendary sage, the wise Luqman from Southern Egypt. By narrating his polite and educational teachings, the Quran is promoting diversity of cultures, races and languages. The central theme of the chapter is: be thankful to God for His gifts.

The chapter starts with a vivid description of the "devout Muslim": he benefits from the teachings of the Quran; stays away from useless activities that distract from the worship of God.

Sometimes the blessed Messenger 🕊 would teach the Quran sitting around the Kaaba. A Makkan storyteller, Nadhar ibn Harith, would also gather people around himself to distract people from the Messenger 🕊. He would tell Persian stories, and to entertain his audience he hired dancers. Verse 7 was revealed to condemn him.

God's visible and hidden gifts that people enjoy are mentioned, and the question is asked: "What have the idols created?" Luqman the wise teaches his son the correct beliefs about God: how to worship Him, how to behave justly with others, especially parents, and how to be humble. The final passage describes the natural world and several signs of God's creative power and contrasts it with human feebleness.

In the name of God, the Kind, the Caring.

[1] *Alif Lam Meem.*

THE GLORIOUS QURAN OFFERS GUIDANCE TO BELIEVERS

[2] These are the verses of the Book full of wisdom, [3] a guidance, beneficial for the righteous; [4] who perform the prayer, pay Zakat and believe firmly in the Hereafter. [5] They *follow* their Lord's guidance and are the successful.

THE FALSE STORYTELLER

[6] Some people pay for false stories *to be told* to divert *people* from God's way,[a] treating it as a joke; they will have a humiliating punishment. [7] When Our verses are recited to him, he arrogantly turns away as though he had not heard it, as though his ears were blocked; so cheer him up with news of a painful punishment. [8] The believers who do righteous deeds will have gardens of delight, [9] living in them

----

[a]   This refers to a Makkan, Nadhar ibn Harith, who was paid to narrate Persian stories in competition with the Quran.

forever. God's promise is true; and He is the Almighty, the Wise.

WHAT HAVE THE FALSE GODS EVER CREATED?

¹⁰ *God* created the skies without any pillar that you can see; and has fixed mountains *like pegs* in the Earth, so you don't feel it's tremors; and spread all animals across it. And We sent rain from the sky, growing plants of every kind all over it. ¹¹ This is God's creation. Now show me what others beside Him have created. Nothing! The wrongdoers are clearly misguided.

LUQMAN TEACHES HIS SON TO REJECT THE FALSE GODS

¹² We gave Luqman wisdom: "Be thankful to God." Whoever is thankful benefits himself; and whoever is unthankful *harms himself.* God is Self-Sufficient, Praiseworthy. ¹³ *Remember* when Luqman said to his son, as he advised him, "My dear son, don't associate *anything* with God. Associating is a major sin."

WE SHOULD RESPECT OUR PARENTS

¹⁴ We commanded *every* human to care for his parents; his mother carried him in pain *during pregnancy*, and breastfed him for *nearly* two years. So be thankful to Me and your parents, *your* destination is to Me. ¹⁵ However, if they force you to associate something with Me of which you have no proof, then don't obey them. Despite this care for them in this life. Follow the path of those who turn to Me, eventually you will return to Me, and I shall inform you of what you did.

LUQMAN TEACHES HIS SON: BELIEFS AND VALUES

¹⁶ "My dear son, *everything* – even as small as a mustard seed *hidden* inside a rock, or in the Heavens or under ground – God will bring out *on Judgement Day*. God is the *infinitely* Subtle, the All-Aware. ¹⁷ "My dear son, perform the prayer regularly, enjoin good, forbid evil, and be patient in times of *hardship*; these are *the marks* of determination. ¹⁸ "Don't look down on people or swagger about. God dislikes every rude boaster. ¹⁹ Walk humbly and keep your voice down. The most disliked sound is the *braying* of the donkey."

APPRECIATING GOD'S GIFTS

²⁰ Haven't you considered how God made everything in the Heavens and the Earth serve your needs, and bestowed His gifts on you, visible and hidden? *Yet* there are people who argue about God without any knowledge, guidance or book to enlighten *them*. ²¹ When they are told: "Follow what God has revealed," they

say, "No! We follow what we found our forefathers doing." What? Even if it is Satan who is calling them to the torment of the *fiery* Blaze? [22] Whoever turns his face in submission and righteousness towards God has grasped an unshakable handhold. *Thereafter,* the outcome of events rests with God. [23] The disbelievers' disbelief shouldn't grieve you. They will return to Us, and We'll tell them what they did. God knows well their innermost thoughts. [24] We let them enjoy themselves a little, then force them in to a severe punishment.

God's words and works are limitless

[25] If you ask them: "Who created the Heavens and the Earth?" They will say, "God." Say: "Praise be to God!" Most don't have any knowledge. [26] Whatever is in the Heavens and the Earth belongs to God. He is the Self-Sufficient, the Praiseworthy. [27] If all the trees on Earth were pens, and the sea and seven more seas beside were ink, the words of God would not end. God is Almighty, Wise. [28] *For Him*, creating and resurrecting *all of* you is just like *creating and resurrecting* a single soul. God is Hearing, Seeing.

Observing God's signs without believing

[29] Haven't you considered how God causes night to merge into day, and day to merge into night; and how He has made the sun and the moon for your benefit, each coursing *through the sky* until *their* appointed time *to set*; and how God is fully aware of what you do? [30] Since God is the Truth, while whatever *disbelievers* call beside Him is false. God is the Exalted, the Great. [31] Haven't you considered how ships sail across the sea by the grace of God to show you *some* of His signs? In that there are signs for every patient *and* thankful person. [32] Whenever a wave covers them like shadows they call God, sincere in their devotion; but when He brings them safely to land, some of them hesitate *to believe*.[a] Anyone who disputes Our signs, is disloyal, unthankful.

Concluding thoughts

[33] People, be mindful of your Lord and fear a Day when a parent will not benefit his child, nor a child benefit his parent. God's promise is true; so make sure this worldly life doesn't deceive you, and make sure *Satan*, the arch-deceiver, doesn't deceive you *either*. [34] God *alone* has knowledge of the Final Hour; He sends rain

---

[a] Muqtasid according to Suyuti is "someone who wavers between faith and disbelief."

and He knows what is in wombs. Nobody knows what he will earn tomorrow, and nobody knows where on Earth he will die; *but* God is the Knower, Aware.

32. As-Sajdah
The Prostration

This chapter was revealed in the middle Makkan period, when debates raged about three key beliefs of Islam: oneness of God, *Tawhid*; prophethood, *Risalah*; and the Hereafter, *Akhirah*. The three beliefs are interconnected and arguments for one support the other. The chapter opens with a confident assertion that refutes the disbeliever's objection that Muhammad ﷺ fabricated his message: "The revelation of the Book is, without a doubt, from the Lord of the worlds" (2). It is a universal message that is not confined to the Arabian Peninsula, but will eventually reach every corner of the globe. The central theme is: God the Supreme Ruler, the Absolute Governor and Commander has full control.

The Quran warns the disbelievers about the punishment to be meted out to them, not only in the Hereafter but in this life. When they see Hellfire they will believe, but it will be too late then. Similarly, the unimaginable delights awaiting the believers are highlighted to motivate people: "No one knows what blissful delights have been set aside for them as a reward for what they did" (17).

Finally, the Prophet ﷺ is told that he and Moses are alike: both are receivers of Divine Revelation. The chapter returns to the repeated theme of the confrontation between truth and falsehood, and compares the glorious Quran with life-giving rain; the latter gives life to dry, parched land. Similarly, the Quran gives life to dead hearts, and the dry minds.

In the name of God, the Kind, the Caring.

¹ *Alif Lam Meem.*

THE QURAN IS REVELATION, NOT FICTION
² The revelation of the Book free from any doubt, is from the Lord of the worlds. ³ They say: "*Muhammad* has made it up"? On the contrary, it is the truth from your Lord, *revealed* to you to warn a people to whom no warner has come before you, so they may be guided. ⁴ God created the Heavens and the Earth and what's between them in six days, and then established Himself *as befits Him* upon the Throne. You have no helper or intercessor beside Him. Will you not pay attention?

GOD GOVERNS THE UNIVERSE
⁵ He oversees the running *of everything* from the sky to the Earth, which will then go up to Him on a Day whose extent shall be *like* a thousand years by your

counting. [6] Such is the Knower of the seen and the unseen *realms*, the Almighty, the Caring, [7] He created everything perfectly; He began the creation of the *first* human from clay, [8] and then made his offspring from a drop of semen.[a] [9] Then He gave *Adam* his form, and blew into him of His spirit; and gave you hearing, sight and awareness. Little do you thank!

THE EVILDOERS WILL BE CONVINCED WHEN THEY SEE HELL

[10] *The disbelievers* say: "How is it *possible* when we have decomposed in the Earth, we shall be created anew?" They are in denial of meeting their Lord. [11] Say: "The angel of death assigned to you will take your soul, and you will be returned to your Lord." [12] If only you could see the evildoers bowing their heads before their Lord *and saying*: "Our Lord, we've seen and heard *the truth*, let us go back *to the world* and we shall do good deeds; we are convinced *now*." [13] If We had so wished, We could have given every person guidance; but My declaration will be fulfilled: "I will fill Hell with jinn and humans, [14] so taste *the punishment,* because you ignored the coming of this Day. We shall now ignore you. Taste this everlasting torment for what you did."

THE DELIGHTS OF PARADISE ARE BEYOND IMAGINATION

[15] When some people are reminded of Our signs they believe and fall in prostration, glorify and praise their Lord, and aren't arrogant. [16] They drag themselves out of bed to worship their Lord, with fear and hope, and they spend *in charity* from what We provided them. [17] No one knows what blissful delights have been set aside for them as a reward for what they did. [18] So, can a believer be compared to a sinner? They aren't equal. [19] Those who believed and were righteous shall be in the gardens of *Mawa,*[b] hospitality for what they did.

DISBELIEVERS WILL BE PUNISHED IN THIS WORLD AND THE NEXT

[20] The major sinners will have a home, the Fire; *and* every time they try to escape it, they will be thrown back, and told: "Taste the torment of the Fire you denied." [21] We'll make them taste the lesser torment *in this life*, and the greater torment *in the Hereafter*, so they may return *to the straight path*. [22] Who can do *himself* greater wrong than the one who is reminded of his Lord's verses and turns his back on them. We shall punish the evildoers.

---

[a] Literally 'humble water', that interestingly contains the entire human genome.
[b] *Mawa* is the name of one of the Heavens; it means a place of refuge and perpetual rest.

MUHAMMAD'S 靐 EXPERIENCE OF REVELATION IS SIMILAR TO MOSES'

²³ We gave Moses the Book; don't doubt receiving it; and We made it a guide for the Israelites. ²⁴ Some of them We made leaders, guiding others patiently with Our Command; and they were convinced of Our signs. ²⁵ Your Lord will judge between them on Judgement Day concerning what they differed about. ²⁶ How many generations before them We destroyed in whose *former* homes they walk, isn't there a lesson for them? In that are signs. So *why* don't they listen? ²⁷ Haven't they considered how We move the clouds towards dry land, thereby producing crops from which they and their livestock eat? Have they no insight?

THE DISBELIEVERS' ANXIETY ABOUT JUDGEMENT DAY

²⁸ They say, "When will this judgement come to pass, if you are telling the truth?" ²⁹ Say: "On Decision Day, their *new-found* faith will not benefit the disbelievers, nor will they be given time *to repent*." ³⁰ So take no notice of them; wait, as they are waiting.

33. Al-Ahzab
The Confederates

This chapter was revealed in the year 626 CE. After the indecisive Battle of Uhud, the Makkans wanted to defeat the Muslims, so in collaboration with the expelled Jews of Banu Nadhir, living in Khyber, they planned to attack Madinah. They gathered an army of 10,000 strong, consisting of many tribes, the confederates.

Background of The Battle of the Trench

When the Prophet ﷺ heard about the Makkan plan, he called a meeting of the disciples to discuss the impending danger. Various ideas were presented and the proposal of Salman the Persian was preferred: to dig a trench between the long stretches of fortress-like houses on the outskirts of the city, whilst in the Northwest there were high rocks that were difficult to cross. So, a trench five metres wide, five metres deep, and seven kilometres long must be dug in three weeks.

When the army of the confederates reached the outskirts of Madinah and saw the trench they were baffled. So they camped outside the city near Uhud, and lay siege on Madinah. The only way to enter the city was if the Jews of Banu Nadhir were to attack from inside. So, the Quraysh and the Jews of Banu Qurayda put together a strategy to win over Banu Nadhir and eventually a pact was agreed; Banu Nadhir would help. The plan went horribly wrong, and the confederates received no help from them. The siege was difficult to maintain, the winter nights were long and bitterly cold, and the horsemen tried several times to cross the trench, but failed miserably. A violent sandstorm blew the tents; the camels and horses of the Makkan forces ran wildly. The besiegers, dispirited and frightened, fled, after three weeks this Divine Intervention saved the Muslims.

This was a testing time for the Muslims. It required wise and brave leadership and committed followers. A large part of the chapter deals with the personal life and wonderful character of the Prophet ﷺ, and his relationships with disciples and family. He is addressed on six occasions with the refrain: "O Prophet!" The Prophet ﷺ is presented as 'a beautiful example for you'.

True followers practise self-control, a key to success in life, so special advice is offered to the Disciples, who faced all kinds of tests: criticism from the hypocrites; the siege; lack of food and water; and the continuous threat of attack. They had to control anger, frustration and fear. The challenge was to resist Satan's whispers, and refrain from losing self-control.

Some outstanding qualities of the believers are: unwavering faith in the mission of the Prophet ﷺ; grateful to God; truthful. Whose purpose in life is the proper use of "free will" and "moral responsibility". How we fulfil this responsibility will determine our eventual fate; Hell, or Heaven.

In the name of God, the Kind, the Caring.

BE MINDFUL OF GOD

[1] Prophet, be mindful of God, and don't listen to the disbelievers and the hypocrites. God is the Knower, the Wise. [2] Follow what is revealed to you from your Lord. God is fully aware of what you do [3] Put your trust in God, He is a sufficient Guardian.

THE FALSE RELATIONSHIPS OF PAGAN TIMES ARE ABOLISHED

[4] God has not set two hearts in any human chest; He doesn't turn your wives that were given divorce into your mothers;[a] nor does He turn your adopted sons into sons. These are *empty* words from your mouths; God speaks the truth, and He guides along the *straight* path. [5] Call *the adopted children* by the names of their *biological* fathers; that is fairer in God's sight. And if you don't know *who* their fathers *are*, then they are your brothers in faith and your clients *deserving protection*. You won't be blamed for any mistakes you make, but only for deliberately planned activities. God is Forgiving, Caring.

THE PROPHET'S ☀ SPECIAL RELATIONSHIP WITH BELIEVERS

[6] The Prophet cares for the believers far more than they care for themselves, and his wives are their *spiritual* mothers. Although blood relatives are still closer to each other than are the believers and the emigrants – in God's Book – you should still act with common decency towards your dependants. All this is written in the Book. [7] *Remember* when We took a contract from the prophets, and you, Noah, Abraham, Moses and Jesus, son of Mary; We took a solemn contract from *all of* them: [8] He would test the claim of truthfulness of the truthful; He has prepared a painful punishment for the disbelievers.

THE GATHERED TRIBES POSED SERIOUS THREAT

[9] Believers, remember God's favour when the armies gathered *against* you, We sent a wind-*stoked sandstorm* against them that you couldn't see. *Meanwhile*, God saw whatever you did. [10] They came *against* you from above and below, *your eyes*

---

[a]   In Arabia, if a husband told his wife: "You are like my mother's back to me," that was a suspended divorce, it deprived her of sexual intimacy and the freedom to remarry. A cruel practice, also condemned in *Chapter Al-Mujadilah* 58: [2].

rolled, your hearts leapt to *your* throats, and you had wild thoughts about God;[a] [11] the believers were tested and severely shaken.

THE HYPOCRITES LACKED LOYALTY AND COURAGE

[12] The hypocrites and those with sickness in their hearts said, "God and His Messenger promised us nothing but deception." [13] A group of them said, "People of Yathrib, you will not be safe anywhere, so retreat," while another group sought the Prophet's permission *to go back*, saying, "Our homes are exposed," yet they were not exposed; they wanted to flee. [14] If *the enemy* had attacked *the city* from *all* sides, and they had been offered an incentive *to switch sides*, they would have done so without hesitation, [15] despite previously having sworn by God that they would not turn tail *and flee*. They will be questioned about *the* oaths sworn in God's name. [16] Say: "Fleeing will not benefit you, if you run away from death or fighting you will have limited enjoyment *in life*." [17] Say: "Who can hold back God from you, if He willed harm or kindness?" They will not find any supporter or helper beside God.

THE HYPOCRITES WERE DISLOYAL

[18] God knows those who obstruct and those who said to their brothers: "Why don't you come over to our side?" They hardly entered the battlefield. [19] *They are* envious of you; and when fear strikes, you see them looking to you *for reassurance*, their eyes flitting back and forth like someone dazed by *dread of* dying. Then, when the fear ebbs, they abuse you with sharp words. They resent you, expecting to gain something good. Such people haven't believed, so God will render their deeds worthless *on Judgement Day*, that's easy for God. [20] They reckon the confederates haven't gone yet; and if the confederates should return, they would then love to be mingling with the Bedouins, seeking news about you. Even if they were on your side, they would barely fight.

THE MUSLIMS WERE LOYAL AND CONFIDENT

[21] You have an excellent role model in the Messenger of God, particularly for anyone who longs for God and the Last Day and remembers Him abundantly. [22] When the believers saw the confederates, they said, "This is what God and His Messenger promised us. God and His Messenger spoke the truth," and *this expe-*

---

[a] "The eyes rolled, the hearts leapt and you had wild thoughts..." this is an idiom that expresses the serious life-threatening situation the disciples faced, it shook their faith.

rience increased their faith and submission. ²³ Amid the believers are men who fulfilled their promise to God, some fulfilled their vow *by dying as martyrs*, while others are waiting; they didn't change. ²⁴ So God will reward the truthful for their truthfulness and punish the hypocrites *for disloyalty* as He pleases, or forgive them, God is Forgiving, Caring. ²⁵ God turned back the disbelievers, who were furious for not achieving any material gain; and God was sufficient *in His support* for the believers throughout the battle. God is Strong, Almighty.

JEWS WHO ACTED DISLOYALLY WERE EXPELLED

²⁶ The People of The Book who backed *the confederates* came out of their forts, but He cast terror into their hearts, *enabling* you to kill some and take others captive, ²⁷ and made you the heirs of their homes, wealth and land, the land that you had never set foot on. God has power over everything.

THE PROPHET'S 襚 WIVES LIVE A SIMPLE LIFE

²⁸ Prophet, tell your wives: "If you desire worldly life and its luxuries, then come forward, I'll ensure that you get them, and release you *from marriage* in a dignified manner. ²⁹ But if you desire God and His Messenger, and the home of the Hereafter, then God has prepared a great reward for your righteousness." ³⁰ Wives of the Prophet, if any one of you commits a flagrant act of indecency, she will suffer double the *usual* punishment. That's easy to do for God; ³¹ but whoever is dedicated to God and His Messenger and does good works shall have double the reward; and We have prepared a generous provision for her.

ADVICE ON HOW TO PREVENT GOSSIP

³² Wives of the Prophet, you are not like other women, you are more mindful. Don't speak softly, in case someone with sickness in his heart should build up his hopes; be polite *but assertive*; ³³ stay home; don't dress to show off, like the custom of the Age of Ignorance; perform the prayer, give Zakat, and obey God and His Messenger. God wants to remove *all* blemish from you as you are the *Prophet's* household, and to purify you. ³⁴ And think about the wonderful verses of God recited and the Prophetic wisdom that's practiced in your homes. God is Subtle, Aware.

A DESCRIPTION OF THE WOMEN AND MEN OF GOD

³⁵ The Men and the women who submit *to the Will of God* are: believers, devout,

truthful, patient, humble, charitable, keep fast, are chaste and *pure* and remember God frequently. God has prepared forgiveness and a mighty reward for them.

THE STORY OF ZAYNAB AND ZAYD

[36] A believing man and a woman have no choice in a matter that is decided by God and His Messenger; and anyone who disobeys God and His Messenger is wrong[a]. [37] *Remember* when you said to the one God had favoured, and you also favoured: "Remain *married* to your wife, and be mindful of God." You kept to yourself what God had made clear *to you*, because you feared people*'s reaction*, though God is to be feared more. When Zayd formally dissolved his marriage to her, We married her to you so that believers might feel no shame regarding *marrying* the *ex*-wives of their adopted sons, if they had formally dissolved their marriages to them, so that God's command is fulfilled. [38] The Prophet should feel no embarrassment regarding what God has made obligatory on him. *This is* the practice *of* God regarding those *prophets* who lived previously – and God's command is fulfilled – [39] delivering the messages of God, fearing Him *alone*, and fearing no one else but God; and God is sufficient Reckoner.

MUHAMMAD ﷺ IS THE LAST AND THE FINAL PROPHET

[40] Muhammad is not a father of anyone of your men, he is the Messenger of God and the seal of the Prophets, *the final Prophet*. God has knowledge of all things. [41] Believers, remember God frequently, [42] and glorify Him in the morning and evening. [43] He blesses you, His angels pray to bring you out of darkness into the light; and He cares for the believers. [44] Their greeting on the Day they meet Him will be: "Peace!" And He has prepared for them a generous reward.

THE PROPHET'S ﷺ CLEAR MISSION

[45] Prophet, We sent you as a witness, a herald of good news, and a warner, [46] calling *people* to God by His permission, and a shinning lamp. [47] *So* bring the believers good news of the bounty they will receive from God [48] and don't follow the disbelievers and hypocrites; ignore their harassment and put your trust in God. God is sufficient Guardian.

---

[a] When the Messenger ﷺ asked Zaynab, who was his cousin to marry Zayd ibn Harith she refused because she thought he was not her equal, however upon hearing this verse she agreed to marry him. The Messenger ﷺ had brought up Zayd like a son.

DIVORCE BEFORE CONSUMMATION

[49] Believers, if you marry believing women, then before the consummation of your marriage you *decide to* divorce them, there is no waiting period for them.[b] Provide for them and release them *from their marriage* in a dignified manner.

CLARIFICATION ON MARRIAGE TO PREVENT MALICIOUS GOSSIP

[50] Prophet, We made lawful for you: your wives who you gave a bridal gift; a *maid* you own from what God allotted you; the daughters of your paternal and maternal uncles and aunts, who emigrated with you; and any believing woman who offers herself to you, *and* you also want to wed; *this last ruling is* solely in relation to you, as distinct from the *other* believers – We know what We made obligatory on *other believers* regarding their wives and what their slave maids – so that there is no embarrassment for you. God is Forgiving, Caring. [51] You may postpone *the turn of* whomever of *your wives* you wish and receive back *into your intimacy* whomever you wish, *including* those you had withdrawn from, there should be no blame on you. That will reassure them, not sadden them; and please them with whatever *intimacy* you *give* them. God knows what is in your hearts. God is Knowing, Gentle. [52] From now on, no *other* women will be lawful for you, nor can you exchange them for other wives, even if you like their beauty, except a slave maid. God is the Observer of all things.

HOW TO BEHAVE IN THE PROPHET'S 🌸 HOUSE

[53] Believers, don't enter the Prophet's apartments to eat without permission, and don't *come early and* wait around for it *to be cooked*. However, if you are invited, then come, and once you have eaten, leave without staying on to chat. Such *behaviour* offended the Prophet, he's embarrassed to tell you; but God is not embarrassed of *telling* the truth. And if you ask *his wives* for something, do so from behind a curtain; that is purer for your hearts and theirs. It isn't right for you either to cause offence to the Messenger of God or marry his wives after him, ever; such *behaviour* would be outrageous in God's sight. [54] Whether you reveal or conceal something, God has knowledge of everything. [55] There is no blame on *the Prophet's wives* being visited by their fathers, or their sons, or their brothers, or the sons of their brothers and sisters, or their *servant* women, or their servants. Be

---

[b]   The waiting period before a divorcee or a widow can marry is three months, to ensure that a child born after the divorce will know its father. This doesn't apply to an unconsummated marriage.

mindful of God, God sees everything.

Send blessings on the Messenger ﷺ

[56] God and His angels *continually* bless the Messenger; *so* believers, you too bless and greet him with peace. [57] Anyone who insults God and His Messenger, God curses them in this world and the next, and has prepared for them a humiliating punishment. [58] Similarly, those who insult believing men and women for no reason will carry the burden of *their* slandering and sinfulness.

Women to dress modestly

[59] Prophet, tell your wives, daughters, and the believers' wives to draw their overcoats close around;[a] that will ensure they are recognised and will not be harmed. God is Forgiving, Caring. [60] If the hypocrites and the troublemakers with sickness in their hearts don't stop *harassing women* in the city,[b] then We will instruct you *to act against* them, after which they won't remain your neighbours for long. [61] They are cursed, *and in the past*, wherever they were found, they were seized and slain. [62] *This was* the practice *laid down* by God regarding those who lived previously; and you will never find any change in the law of God.

The regret of the disbelievers on Judgement Day

[63] *When* people ask you about *the time* of the Final Hour, say: "God Knows that." And who knows the Final Hour could be near? [64] God cursed the disbelievers and prepared a *fiery* Blaze for them [65] in which they will live forever, they won't find a protector or a helper. [66] On the Day that their faces will be distorted in the Fire, they will say, "If Only we had obeyed God and the Messenger." [67] And they will say, "Our Lord, we obeyed our leaders and the elders, and they led us astray. [68] Our Lord, give them double the punishment and put a great curse on them."

Concluding instructions for the believers

[69] Believers, don't be like those who insulted Moses, yet God declared him innocent of what they alleged; *Moses* was honourable in God's sight. [70] Believers, be mindful of God and speak straight to the point, [71] so God may improve your deeds and forgive your sins. Anyone who obeys God and His Messenger has won

---

[a]   The *jilbab* is a loose outer garment, the overcoat draped around the body. See *Chapter An-Nur* 24: 31.

[b]   This verse is best understood in the context of *Chapter An-Nur* 24: 33, which refers to the practice of forcing slave women into prostitution, leading some young men to harass even free women as they left their homes to answer the call of nature in the open fields at night.

a mighty victory.

HUMANITY IS ENTRUSTED WITH FREE WILL

[72] We presented the Trust to the Heavens, the Earth and the mountains,[c] but they declined to carry it *since* they were fearful; but humans *decided* to carry it – humans were wrong and ignorant *of the demands* – [73] God would punish them *for this failure, especially* the hypocrites and the idolaters, both men and women; but God will relent towards the believers, both men and women, *for their failures.* God is, Forgiving, Caring.

---

[c] This Trust is comprehensive: including faith, prayers, moral character, caring for the environment, etc. Compare with the first assembly of prophets, *Chapter Ale ʿImran* 3: 81, and the first assembly of human souls, *Chapter Al-Aʿraf* 7: 172 .

34. Saba'
The Kingdom of Sheba

This chapter was revealed in the middle-Makkan period, and its central theme is the evidence for resurrection. The scenes of Judgement Day are presented in vivid terms, as if they are unfolding before the reader. God's Glory and Power is emphasised as displayed on Judgement Day, when humanity will be held accountable for its actions.

David and Solomon , received many extraordinary gifts from God, which they appreciated. Consequently, God rewarded them even more. In contrast, the people of Saba' were blessed with a dam and fertile land, and the towns built in the area prospered economically. However, they were ungrateful.

> The kingdom of Saba was situated in South Western Arabia, Yemen, and at the time of its greatest prosperity (the first millennium BC) comprised Yemen and a large part of Ethiopia. Its capital was Marib. The Sabaeans had built over the centuries an extraordinary system of dams and dykes, and became famous in history, with its astonishing remnants extant to this day (Asad).

This invited Divine retribution, the dam burst and the unstoppable flood destroyed everything in its wake. This devastated the agricultural land, and left them impoverished. Since the Makkans were familiar with this story, the Quran doesn't describe it in too much detail.

An outline of the conversation between disbelievers on Judgement Day shows the horrific landscape. At the end, the Messenger ﷺ is proclaimed as a prophet for all humanity: "We sent you to all the people as a messenger of good news and a warner, but most people do not know this." (28). Clearly an announcement of the universality of Islam.

In the name of God, the Kind, the Caring.

PRAISE FOR GOD'S KNOWLEDGE AND JUSTICE

¹ Praise be to God, everything in the Heavens and the Earth belongs to Him; and the praise will be His in the Hereafter, the Wise, the Aware. ² He knows what goes inside the Earth and what comes out of it, and what comes down from the sky and what goes up. He is the Caring, the Forgiving. ³ The disbelievers say, "the Hour won't come for us." Say: "Not so! By my Lord the Knower of the unseen, it will strike you. Not an atom's weight in the Heavens and the Earth is hidden from Him; nor *does* anything smaller or bigger than that *exist* that is not written

down in a Clear Book. [4] God will reward the believers who did righteous deeds, they will be forgiven and blessed with generous provision. [5] Those who tried desperately to undermine Our *Quran*[a] will be severely punished.

THE DISBELIEVERS MOCK THE RESURRECTION

[6] Those given the knowledge *of earlier revelations* consider as the truth what is revealed to you by your Lord, and accept that it leads to the path of the Almighty, the Praiseworthy. [7] The disbelievers say, "Shall we show you a man who says, when you *die and you* are decomposed, you will be created anew? [8] He has either invented a lie about God, or is possessed." Not at all, those who don't believe in the Hereafter will *end up* in torment, they're wandering far *from the truth*. [9] Haven't they considered all that is around them in the Heaven and Earth. If We so wanted, We could make the Earth swallow them, or drop a chunk of the sky on them. In that are signs for the servant *of God* who repents.

DAVID AND SOLOMON'S SPECIAL POWERS

[10] We gave David Our favours: "Mountains and birds! Echo *My praises* with him"; and We made the iron soft to his *touch*. [11] *We told him*: "Make coats of armour, and be precise with the links *of chainmail*, and do good. I see what you are doing." [12] To Solomon, *We gave control of* the wind, its outward and its return journey each covered the distance *of* a month; and We made a stream of molten brass to flow for him. By the authority of His Lord some jinn worked under his control, and if any one of them deviated from Our command, We punished them with the *fiery* Blaze. [13] They worked for *Solomon*, building whatever he wanted: lofty chambers, statues, basins as big as water tanks, and *huge* fixed cauldrons. *We said*: "Work, children of David, be thankful. Not many of My servants are thankful." [14] When We decreed *Solomon's* death, the only way *they knew* he was dead was when the woodworm ate his staff and he tumbled *to the ground*. The jinn then realised that if they had knowledge of the unseen, they would never have continued with their demeaning, punishing *tasks*.[b]

---

[a] "Our signs" refers to the Quran (Suyuti).

[b] This hints to Solomon's death whilst sitting on his mighty throne, leaning on his staff. His death went unnoticed until his staff eaten by termites gave way and fell to the ground. An allusion to the fleeting and feeble nature of human life.

THE UNTHANKFUL PEOPLE OF SABA'

¹⁵ *The dam* had gardens on both sides, the right and the left, and between them were their houses. A sign for the people of Sheba. "Eat of the provision of your Lord," *they were told*, "and be thankful to Him. *You have* a fertile country and a Forgiving Lord." ¹⁶ They turned away from Our *call*, so We sent the floodwater of the *broken* dam against them, and We turned their gardens into gardens that *now* produced bitter fruit, Tamarisks, and the sparse *thorny* Lote tree. ¹⁷ That's how We repaid their ingratitude. Would We reward anyone *in this way* except the ungrateful?

SABA' AFTER THE FLOOD

¹⁸ We allowed the growth of towns that were easily visible all the way from *Yemen* to *Greater Syria,* they were blessed *with fruit trees and water*, making travelling between them easy; *and We said*: "Travel this *land* in safety by night or by day." ¹⁹ Despite this they said, "Our Lord has made our journeys even longer." They were unthankful. We made them a legend, destroying them. In that are signs for the patient and thankful. ²⁰ Satan's assessment of them proved right, they followed him; except for a group of believers ²¹ over who he had no power. We will distinguish believers in the Hereafter from those who were doubtful. Your Lord is the Protector of everything.

THE MESSENGER ﷺ TESTS THE DISBELIEVERS

²² Say *Messenger*: "Call those you claim to be gods beside God. They don't control an atom's weight in the Heavens or on Earth; they have no share in them, nor do they have any helper." ²³ No intercession *by angels or others* will benefit in His presence, except for the one granted permission. Only when *the terror of Judgement Day* is released from their hearts will *the angels on high* ask: "What did your Lord say?" *Those below* will say, "The truth! And He is the Exalted, the Great." ²⁴ Ask, *Messenger*: "Who provides you *sustenance* from the Heavens and the Earth?" Say: "God. *It is* either you or us: since only one can be guided, the other must be misguided." ²⁵ Say: "You will not be questioned about what *you think* we are guilty of, nor shall we be questioned about what you did." ²⁶ Say: "Our Lord will gather us all, then He will judge us justly. He is the Supreme Judge, the Knower." ²⁷ Say: "Show me those you associate as partners with God. Never! God is Almighty, the Wise."

THE MESSENGER ﷺ IS SENT TO ALL OF HUMANITY

²⁸ We sent you to all the people *of the world* as a messenger of good news, and a warner; but most people don't know *this*. ²⁹ And they say, "When will this promise *be fulfilled*, if you are telling the truth?" ³⁰ Tell them: "You have a fixed day, which you can't delay nor bring forward even by a single hour."

THE DISBELIEVERS WILL BICKER AMONGST THEMSELVES

³¹ The disbelievers say, "We won't believe in this Quran, or in *the scriptures* that came before it." If only you could see the wrongdoers standing before their Lord, each criticising the other, some of the oppressed will say to the arrogant, "If it hadn't been for you, we would have been believers." ³² The arrogant will reply, "Was it really us who blocked your *path* to guidance after it came to you? Not at all, you were sinners." ³³ The oppressed will say to the arrogant, "Not so! *This is* a trick of *calling day night and* night day. *Remember* when you used to order us to disbelieve in God and set up rivals with Him?" They will conceal their remorse when they see the punishment, and We shall put iron collars around the necks of the disbelievers. Shouldn't We reward them for what they did?

THE WEALTHY RELIED ON THEIR POSSESSIONS

³⁴ Never did We send a warner to a city without the well-to-do saying, "We reject what you are sent with." ³⁵ And also added, "Because we have plenty of wealth and offspring we won't be tormented." ³⁶ Say *to them*: "My Lord is the one Who either increases or withholds the provision as He pleases," but most people don't know. ³⁷ It is neither your wealth nor your offspring that will bring you closer to Us, but belief and the righteousness; the reward of such people will be doubled due to their deeds, and they will be safe in lofty apartments. ³⁸ Those who tried desperately to undermine Our signs shall be tormented forever. ³⁹ Say: "My Lord increases or withholds the provision of any one of His servants as He pleases. Whatever you spend *in charity*, He shall repay it. He is the Best Provider."

THE ANGELS DENY ENCOURAGING DISBELIEVERS

⁴⁰ On the Day He gathers them together, He will ask the angels: "Are these the ones who worshipped you?" ⁴¹ *The angels* will say, "Glory be to you! Only you are our patron, not them. Rather, they worshipped the jinn, and most of them had faith in them." ⁴² On this Day none of you will have the power to benefit or to harm the other, and We shall say to the wrongdoers: "Taste the torment of the

Fire, you denied." [43] Whenever Our clear verses are recited they say, "This man wants to stop you from worshipping what your forefathers worshipped." And they say, "This *Quran* is fabricated lies." When the truth came to them the disbelievers said, "This is clearly magic."

THE ONLY PROPHET SENT TO THE ARABS

[44] Before you We never gave them books to study, or sent them a warner. [45] Those before them also denied *the truth*, though they haven't got more than a tenth of what We gave them, still they rejected My messengers. So, *imagine* how terrible My condemnation will be. [46] Say: "I will give you one piece *of advice*: stand for God, whether *you are* alone or in pairs, *and* then think deeply. Your companion is not possessed; rather, he is warning you about the severe punishment about to come." [47] Say: "Whatever reward I may have asked from you, keep it; God will reward me. He is the Witness of everything."

FINDING FAITH AFTER ONE HAS DIED WILL BE USELESS

[48] Say: "My Lord, the Knower of all mysteries, launched the truth." [49] Say: "The truth has come, falsehood has vanished and will not return." [50] Say: "If I went off course, then I am only leading myself astray; *however*, if I am guided, then it is due to what my Lord has revealed. He is a Hearer, near *at hand*." [51] If only you could see *the disbelievers* in a state of terror. There will be no escape when they are snatched from nearby. [52] They will say, "We believe!" How can they *possibly* receive *faith* now, [53] when previously they had denied it? They are stabbing in the dark from far away[a], [54] and a barrier is put up between them and their desires, as happened with their type before; *because* they were deeply suspicious.

---

[a] Literally: They were throwing arrows in the dark from a long distance.

35. Fatir
The Originator of the Universe

This is an early Makkan chapter, revealed possibly in the third or fourth year of the Prophet's mission 鑿. The central theme is God's numerous gifts: the wonders of His creation in nature is a display of his Kindness: "People, remember the gifts God gave you. Is there any other creator beside God who provides for you from the Earth and the sky?" (3). Imam Ghazali observes:

> Human beings are in urgent need of understanding this universal law of creation, since many of them are under the illusion that what nature provides bears no relation to God Almighty whatsoever. Some have dared to eliminate God from life, giving the wildest explanations of the nature and purpose of existence.[b]

But intelligent and thoughtful people can't fail to see the created world as the handiwork of God. For them, God is everywhere: "Among his servants, only the knowledgeable fear God. God is the Almighty, the Forgiver" (28).

The Makkan people were stubborn in their denial of the Prophet 鑿, so he is reassured: "If they think you are a liar, *so what*? Those before them treated their messengers as liars when they came to them with clear signs, with writings and the enlightening Book" (25). He is told to be patient and resilient, since God gives respite and time for people to think. The stubborn disbelievers are given a warning; whilst He is the Kindest, He is an Avenger who takes exact retribution. "Were God to punish people for the wrong they did; He wouldn't have left a single creature on the surface of *the Earth*" (45).

In terms of faith and good deeds, the chapter divides the believers into three grades: "Some wronged themselves, others were good and some by the grace of God were foremost in good works" (32). The implication is that the Ummah of Muhammad 鑿 will include a group who makes mistakes and pays no attention to their duties, here called "*zalim*", the wrongdoers. The second group are "*muqtasid*", the good: the moderates who fulfil religious obligations and avoid the forbidden, but are sluggish with regards to voluntary activities. The third group are "*al-sabiq*", who are committed to "seeking the pleasure of God, avoid worldly luxuries, the trappings of the world, and never forget God" (Ibn Kathir).

---

[b]   Al-Ghazali, *A Thematic Commentary on the Quran.*

In the name of God, the Kind, the Caring.

GOD'S GLORY, MAJESTY AND POWER

[1] Praise be to God, the Originator of the Heavens and the Earth, Creator of the messenger angels with two, three and four *pairs* of wings. He adds to the creation whatever He pleases. God has power over everything. [2] How He treats people kindly *is up to Him*, no one can withhold it; and what He withholds, no one can take it after His *decision*. He is the Almighty, the Wise. [3] People, remember the gifts God gave you. Is there any other creator beside God who provides for you from the Earth and the sky? There is no god but Him. How then can you turn away *from the truth*?

MAKKANS ACCUSE THE MESSENGER ﷺ OF LYING

[4] If they deny you, *so what*? Messengers before you were denied *too. In the end* all matters will be returned to God. [5] People, God's promise is true, so don't let this worldly life deceive you, and don't let *Satan*, the arch-deceiver, draw you away from God. [6] Satan is your enemy, so treat him as such. He invites his followers to become companions of the *fiery* Blaze. [7] Those who disbelieved will *suffer* severe punishment, but those who believe and do righteous deeds will be forgiven and granted great reward. [8] Evil deeds look attractive to some people, so they like them. God allows some people to go astray, and He guides others as He pleases; so don't be overcome by *pity and* regret over them. God knows what they do.

NEW CREATION IS LIKE THE RESURRECTION

[9] God sends winds that move the clouds, which We drive towards dead regions, and We revive dead land *with rain*. The Resurrection will be like that. [10] Anyone seeking power *should know*, all power belongs to God, an eloquently pure speech rises up to Him, and He elevates all good deeds[a]. However, those who plot evil, theirs will be a severe punishment. Their plot will fail. [11] God created you from dust, then from a drop *of semen*, then He made you into pairs, *male and female*. No female becomes pregnant or gives birth without His knowledge, no one grows old, or has their life cut short but is written in a *celestial* Book. *All* that is easy for God.

---

[a] This Arabic idiom in plain English means "God hears good words and rewards good works."

SALTY SEA WATER, THE CYCLE OF NIGHT AND DAY PROVE RESURRECTION

¹² *Take* two bodies of water, *they* are not the same: one fresh, sweet and pleasant to drink, the other is salty and bitter; *from these waters*, you eat the tender flesh *of fish*, and extract pearls to wear. *Similarly,* you see ships ploughing through *the sea* to seek *a share* of His bounty, and maybe you will appreciate *God.* ¹³ He merges night into day and day into night and has caused both the sun and the moon to travel *through the sky* for a fixed period. That's God, your Lord, all power belongs to Him; those you call beside Him don't possess even the tiniest amount.ᵇ ¹⁴ If you call them they don't hear your call, and even if they were to hear they can't answer you; and on Judgement Day, *your idols* will reject your association of *partners with God.* So, *messenger*, no one can enlighten you *with truth* like the All-Aware.

THERE IS NO SHIFTING OF BLAME ON JUDGEMENT DAY

¹⁵ People, you need God, and God is Self-Sufficient, Praiseworthy. ¹⁶ If He wanted He could get rid of you and bring about a new creation; ¹⁷ that wouldn't be too difficult for God. ¹⁸ No one will bear another's burden. If a *person* with a heavy load were to cry out *for help*, no one – not even a close relative – would accept it. Those you can warn are fearful of their Lord without seeing Him, and they perform the prayer regularly. Anyone who purifies himself, does for his own good; and to God is the final return.

A REMINDER THAT GOD GUIDES, AND THE MESSENGER 襚 WARNS

¹⁹ The blind and the sighted are not the same, ²⁰ nor darkness and light, ²¹ nor *cool* shade and *sweltering* heat. ²² The living and the dead are not the same *either*. God lets him hear, who wants to hear; *messenger*, the one who is in the grave, you cannot make him hear.ᶜ ²³ You are a warner. ²⁴ We sent you as a messenger of good news and a warner. No community was without *its* warner. ²⁵ If they think you are a liar, *so what*? Those before them treated their messengers as liars when they came to them with clear signs, with writings and the light giving Book. ²⁶ After that, I seized the disbelievers. So, *imagine* My terrible displeasure!

THE PEOPLE OF TRUE KNOWLEDGE FEAR GOD

²⁷ Haven't you considered, how God sends rain from the sky, that produces fruits of different colours; *look at* the mountains with streaks of white and red *rock*

ᵇ   Literally the thin filament covering the date pit.
ᶜ   Since the disbelievers refused to listen to the Messenger 襚 they are referred to as dead, their fate is sealed.

of various shades, some pitch black? ²⁸ In the same way, colour differences exist among people and wild and domesticated animals. Among His servants only the knowledgeable fear God. God is Almighty, Forgiving. ²⁹ Those who recite God's Book, perform the prayer and spend publicly and privately from what We provided them, they long for a business that will never be in loss, ³⁰ so He will fully reward them for their *deeds*, and bless them extra from His bounty. He is Forgiving, Appreciative *of their efforts*.

THREE GRADES OF BELIEVERS

³¹ What We revealed to you from the Book is the truth, it confirms what came before it. God is Aware *and* sees His servants' *actions*. ³² We chose some servants to inherit the Book: some wronged themselves *by ignoring its teachings*, *others* have good intentions, and yet others are ahead in doing good deeds by God's permission; that's the great favour. ³³ *These believers* will enter Gardens of Eden, where they will be decorated with bracelets of gold and pearls, and silky clothes. ³⁴ They will say, "Praise be to God, Who has relieved us of distress. Our Lord is Forgiving, Appreciative, ³⁵ Who by His grace has settled us in the everlasting home, here there's no hard work or weariness."

THE TERRIBLE FATE OF DISBELIEVERS

³⁶ The disbelievers will be in the Fire of Hell, they won't die and the punishment will not be reduced for them. That is how We reward every ungrateful *person*. ³⁷ There they will cry loud, "Our Lord, let us out to do good works, not like what we used to do." *God will say*, "Did We not give you long enough to live? Whoever wished to reflect had enough time to do so. And the warner came to you. So, taste *the Fire of Hell*. There is no helper for the wrongdoers."

THE DISBELIEVERS' CLAIMS ARE BASELESS

³⁸ God Knows *the* unseen in the Heavens and the Earth, He knows *people's* innermost thoughts. ³⁹ He made you successors *of people* on Earth. Anyone who disbelieves must bear the consequences of his disbelief; the disbelief of disbelievers increases the dislike of their Lord; the disbelief of disbelievers only increases loss. ⁴⁰ Say: "Have you *really* thought about the *false* partners you call beside God? Show me what they have created on Earth. Do they have a share of the Heavens, or have We given them a book on whose guidance they rely?" On the contrary, the wrongdoers promise nothing but false hopes to each other.

WHAT GOES AROUND COMES AROUND

[41] God keeps the Heavens and Earth from disappearing, were they to disappear, could anyone else preserve them? He is Gentle, Forgiving. [42] They swore solemn oaths by God that if a warner came to them, they would be the most rightly guided people. When a warner came to them, it increased their hatred *of the truth*, [43] behaving arrogantly in the land and plotting evil – and evil plots only ever rebound on those who devise them. So, what else can they expect but what happened in practice to the people of the past? And you will never see change in God's *good* practice, nor will you see a modification in God's *good* practice. [44] Haven't they travelled the Earth and seen how those before them met their end, though they were far greater than them in strength? Nothing in the Heavens or the Earth can weaken God. He is Knowing, Powerful. [45] Were God to take people to task for what wrong they did, then He wouldn't leave a single creature on the face of *the Earth*, but He grants a delay for a fixed period *for reflection*; when their time comes, *that's it*, God observes His servants.

36. Ya Seen
Ya Seen

This is an early Makkan chapter, revealed at a time of severe tension between the Muslims and the idolaters. The Prophet ﷺ called it, "The heart of the Quran." Its central theme is convincing arguments for the doctrines of *Tawhid*, *Risalah* and *Akhirah*. Reading Chapter Ya Seen in times of hardship calms the nerves and reassures one, restores health in sickness and at the time of death eases the pain of death.

It opens by reassuring the Messenger ﷺ of the importance of his role in guiding humanity, and laments the history of human disobedience. The story of three messengers, who were rejected by the people of the town, is told to warn the Makkans; the chief reason identified for their disbelief is arrogance, which they expressed as stubborn behaviour. The brave supporter in the story, who stands up for the messengers, symbolises the small band of Muslims in Makkah, thereby reassuring them of Divine Help. The Makkans are warned of dire consequences of the denial of truth: "Haven't they considered how many generations We destroyed before them?" (31).

The second section of the chapter describes God's amazing creative power, and invites the reader to reflect on creation: a marvel of incredible complexity and beauty. Attention is drawn to the lifeless Earth and how it comes to life after it rains, producing lush vegetation. The lesson is God will bring the dead to life.

A description of Judgement Day follows: The Trumpet is blown, justice done; evidence of one's good and bad deeds won't only come from records kept by the angels, but human limbs will speak. The accuracy and veracity of this evidence will be unquestionable. A vivid account of the delights of Paradise shows how its residents will see God in His Glory and Majesty.

The chapter opened with two claims: The Messenger ﷺ is divinely appointed to guide humanity, and the reality of resurrection. To prove this, it presented historical, rational, and moral evidence. The conceptual boundaries of the readers' mind are prompted to ponder the paradoxical: sparks of fire that come from rubbing together fresh twigs. Seven proofs are presented for God's amazing creative power: The wonder of dry earth becoming lush green after rainfall (33-35); the cycle of day and night (37); the orbits of Sun and Moon (38-40); the ships sailing on seas (41); the livestock (71-73); the mystery of human creation (76); fire from green twigs (80).

Indeed: "When He wants to do something all He says is 'Be,' and it is! Glory to Him Who controls everything and you shall be returned to Him" (82–83).

In the name of God, the Kind, the Caring.

¹ *Ya' Seen.*

THE BELOVED MESSENGER ﷺ IS HONOURED

² By the Quran, full of wisdom. ³ You are a Messenger, ⁴ on the straight path. ⁵ *This is* a Revelation from the Almighty, the Caring, ⁶ to warn a community whose ancestors were not warned, so they're unaware.

WHY IS IT HARD FOR THEM TO BELIEVE?

⁷ The sentence against most of them is justified, because they don't believe. ⁸ *As though* We've placed iron collars around their necks, right up to their chins, so their heads can't move; ⁹ and We've placed a wall in front and behind them and hooded them so that they can't see. ¹⁰ It makes no difference whether you warn them or not, they won't believe. ¹¹ You can only warn someone who follows the Reminder[a] and fears the Most Kind, *the* Unseen. So, make him happy with the news of forgiveness and a generous reward. ¹² We will resurrect the dead and record all they achieved and the *legacies* they left behind; and We recorded everything in a Clear Book.[b]

THE STORY OF THE THREE MESSENGERS

¹³ As an example, tell them about the people of the town, where the messengers came. ¹⁴ We sent two *at first*, they rejected them; so We strengthened *them* with a third; and they said, "We are messengers sent to you." ¹⁵ *They* said, "You're mortals like us. The Most Kind hasn't sent anything, you are lying." ¹⁶ *They* said, "Our Lord knows we are messengers *sent* to you, ¹⁷ and our duty is to communicate *the Message* clearly." ¹⁸ *They* said, "you are an evil omen for us. If you don't stop, we'll torture you, and punish you severely." ¹⁹ *The messengers* replied, "The evil omen is with you. Are you annoyed because you've been reminded? You've gone beyond the limits."

A BRAVE MAN STANDS UP FOR THE MESSENGERS

²⁰ A man came running from the far side of the town, and said, "My people, follow the messengers. ²¹ Follow those who don't ask you for any payment, and they are

---

[a] In other words, the Quran.
[b] The word "imam" here has the meaning of a guidebook, and refers to the Divine Tablet.

guided. [22] Why shouldn't I worship the One Who created me and to Whom you will be returned? [23] Should I take beside Him gods whose intercession[a] would not benefit me in the slightest if the Most Kind willed to harm me? Nor would they be able to save me. [24] Obviously I would be misguided. [25] I *chose to* believe in Your Lord, so *please* listen to me."

THE BRAVE MAN IS MARTYRED AND TAKEN TO PARADISE

[26] "Enter the Garden *of Paradise*," he was told. "If only my people knew," he said, [27] "the extent to which My Lord has forgiven me and placed me among the honourable." [28] Thereafter, We didn't send an army against his people from the sky, We don't do that. [29] Just one Blast, *that's all*, and there they were, *lying* dead. [30] What a shame, whenever a messenger came to a community, they mocked him. [31] Haven't they seen how many generations We destroyed before them, none will come back to them. [32] Yet they will all be presented before Us.

THE WONDER OF THE LIFELESS EARTH; EVIDENCE OF RESURRECTION

[33] A proof *of the Resurrection* for them is the dead Earth. How We give it life and make it produce cereals, which they eat, [34] and here and there We have grown palm groves and vineyards and caused *fresh water* springs to flow, [35] so they might eat its fruit even though they had no hand in making it.[b] Won't they be grateful? [36] Glory be to Him who created every variety *of living things in pairs* from the Earth: *humans* themselves, and others which they *still* don't know.[c]

THE ORBITS OF THE SUN AND THE MOON, THE SAILING OF SHIPS; FURTHER EVIDENCES

[37] Another sign for them is the night, from which We *gradually* peel the daylight away, and there they are in pitch darkness; [38] the sun travels in its orbit that is precisely determined by the Almighty, the Knower.[d] [39] Similarly the moon, We determined its phases from *full moon* to *crescent* that is *slim* as a dry date-stalk. [40] The sun can't overtake the moon, nor the night outpace the day; all are floating in their fixed orbits. [41] Another sign for them is *the story of* their forefathers who

---

[a]   "Intercession" means to put in a good word for someone, or to plead on someone's behalf.

[b]   An alternative meaning preferred is "and what their hands have produced."

[c]   Scientists estimate there are more than twelve million living species on Earth, only two million have so far been identified; the rest remain to be discovered.

[d]   Alternatively *'Dhaalika takdirul Aziz'* means: That's laid down by the Will of the Almighty.

We carried in the heavily-laden ship,^c ⁴² and We created for them similar *modes of transport* which they ride. ⁴³ If We wanted We could drown them, and they will have no help, nor will they be saved, ⁴⁴ unless – *that is* – We show kindness and give brief respite.

Disbelief: an arrogant attitude and selfish behaviour

⁴⁵ When they are told: "Be careful about your past and future *deeds* to deserve kind treatment." ⁴⁶ They turn away from every sign of their Lord that comes to them. ⁴⁷ When they are told: "Spend what God has provided you," the disbelievers say to the believers, "Why should we feed someone who God could have fed, if He wanted? You are clearly misguided." ⁴⁸ And they say, "When will this promise *be fulfilled*, if you are telling the truth?" ⁴⁹ What they are waiting for is a Blast that will seize them while they argue among themselves. ⁵⁰ Then they won't be able to make a will or return to their families.

The Trumpet is blown: Judgement begins

⁵¹ The Trumpet will be blown, and they will emerge from their graves, rushing to their Lord, ⁵² saying: "Woe to us! Who woke us up from our graves?" *They will be told* "This is what the Most Kind promised, and the messengers kept reminding you about." ⁵³ It will be a single Blast, and quickly they will be made to stand before Us. ⁵⁴ On this day, no one will be wronged in the least; and you will only be repaid for what you did.

Separation of the righteous from the wicked

⁵⁵ Today the companions of Paradise will be enjoying themselves; ⁵⁶ sitting beside their spouses on comfortable sofas relaxing in the shade, ⁵⁷ *surrounded* with fruit they like ⁵⁸ *and the greeting*: "Peace!" Spoken by the Caring Lord.^f ⁵⁹ The evildoers" *will be told*: "Step aside today. ⁶⁰ Didn't I command you, children of Adam, not to obey Satan, he is your open enemy, ⁶¹ and worship Me? This is the straight path, ⁶² but *Satan* led masses of you astray. Didn't you think? ⁶³ This is Hell about which you were warned, ⁶⁴ burn in it today, because of your disbelief."

God's patience with humanity

⁶⁵ Today We shall seal their mouths; their hands will speak, and their feet will bear

^c A reference to the Ark of Noah .

^f This greeting of "Salam!" Will come directly from God, and will be the height of all the pleasures of Paradise.

witness to what they did. [66] If We wanted, We could have taken away their eyesight so how could they see it, as they struggled along the path? [67] If We wanted, We could have paralysed them, so they wouldn't move to and fro[a]. [68] Anyone We allow to age, We reduce them in size bit by bit.[b] Will you not reflect? [69] We didn't teach *the Messenger* poetry, it isn't appropriate for him. This *Quran* is a reminder and a clear recitation. [70] So *he* can warn anyone who is alive, and to confirm the sentence against the disbelievers.

EVIDENCE FOR RESURRECTION FROM DOMESTICATED ANIMALS

[71] Haven't they considered how We created their livestock, made by Our hands; [72] and how We tamed *animals* to give in to them, so they ride some and eat some of them? [73] And they derive other benefits from them, *like milk to* drink. Won't they be grateful? [74] Yet they take *other* gods beside God, *hoping* to be helped *by them*. [75] But *they* are incapable of helping them, even if they were standing to attention for them, like an army. [76] So don't let what they say sadden you. We know what they do secretly and openly.

EVIDENCE FROM HUMAN BIRTH

[77] Haven't humans considered how We created them from a drop of fluid, so they openly argue *against Us*? [78] They make up comparisons about Us whilst forgetting their own creation, saying, "Who will give life to *these* bones when they have turned into dust?" [79] Say: "The one Who produced them originally will bring them back to life – and He has full knowledge of every creature – [80] *and* Who, for your *benefit*, placed *the energy of* fire in green trees, from which you get fuel?"

GOD'S PERFECT POWER IS LIMITLESS

[81] Isn't the Creator of the Heavens and the Earth capable of recreating the like of these *quarrelsome humans*? Of course, He is the Creator, the Knower. [82] When He wills something, His command is: "Be!" And it is![c] [83] Glory to Him Who controls everything, to Him you shall be returned.

---

[a]   "We could have blinded their eyes" is a metaphor for "We could have created them morally blind" and thus devoid of all sense of moral responsibility (Asad). This would be tantamount to human life being purposeless and empty of spiritual value.

[b]   An elderly person in their sixties can lose two centimetres in height.

[c]   "It is" means it comes into being.

37. As-Saffat
Arranged in Rows

This chapter was revealed in the middle-Makkan period. Its central theme is proving the truthfulness of the Islamic doctrines: *Tawhid, Risalah,* and *Akhirah.* It opens with three attention-grabbing oaths that describe the mysterious and the perennial Heavenly battles between the angels and Satan, but comes back to Earthly battles of Prophets and their disobedient communities.[d] It tells the stories of six messengers, describing their heroic and courageous efforts to guide their communities. In the dream of Abraham and his willingness to sacrifice, it points to the inner battle: love of children versus love of God.

Two scenes from Judgement Day are described: leaders and their followers are at loggerheads, blaming each other for their dreadful fate; a pious person finds his friend in Hell, and reminds him how he tried to misguide him, but failed in doing so. Zaqqum, the food of the people of Hell is described as:

> A tree that grows in the middle of Hell. Its fruit is like the heads of Satan. They will eat from it to fill their bellies, then drink boiling water; their home is Hell (64–68).

The Zaqqum tree resembles the desert cactus, with a poisonous sap and a foul smell, that causes blistering and even death. The chapter returns to the role of the angels and how they are organised in Paradise, and ends by stressing the significance of the beliefs of *Tawhid* and *Risalah.*

In the name of God, the Kind, the Caring.

Heavenly battles between the angels and Satan

[1] By *the angels* – arranged in rows, [2] who stop people from evil [3] and by those who recite the word [4] that your Lord is One, [5] Lord of the Heavens and the Earth and what is between them, the Lord of the Easts. [6] We have decorated the lower sky with the stars [7] and protected it from every disobedient devil. [8] They cannot eavesdrop on the higher assembly *of angels,* they will be attacked from all sides [9] and driven out. Theirs is everlasting punishment. [10] The snatcher of information is chased by a fiery comet.

---

[d] Razi gives three other subjects of these oaths; the scholars; the soldiers conducting Jihad; and the Majestic Quran. About the Quran he says: "The verses of the Quran are arranged in an orderly way, they cover different topics; arguments for Tawhid, Divine predestination, Wisdom, Prophethood, the Resurrection, Human responsibilities, Moral virtues. These verses are arranged coherently resembling well-arranged rows of people."

[11] Ask: "Are they more difficult to create than the rest of the creation?" We created them from a sticky clay. [12] Are you surprised they mock, [13] if they are reminded they take no notice; [14] when they see a sign they poke fun at it, [15] saying, "This is magic; [16] when we are dead and become dust and bones will we [17] be raised to life with our forefathers?" [18] Say: "Yes, *and* you will be despised!"

THE DISBELIEVERS BLAME EACH OTHER ON JUDGEMENT DAY

[19] It will be a single blast as they look on *terrified*. [20] With regret they will say, "This is Judgement Day." [21] Indeed, the Day of Decision that you denied. [22] *The angels will be ordered*: "Gather the wicked people, *including* their spouses and whatever they worshipped [23] beside God, and lead them on the path to the Blazing Fire. [24] Stop them for questioning, [25] why are you not helping each other *today?*" [26] No, today is the Day that they submit fully. [27] They will confront each other, quarrelling. [28] "You overpowered us," [29] they will reply, "No! You didn't *want* to be believers; [30] we had no power over you, you were rebellious *anyway*. [31] Our Lord's judgement against us is fair. We'll taste the *punishment*. [32] We misguided you since we were misguided." [33] That Day they will share the punishment; [34] that's Our way of dealing with sinners. [35] The arrogant people, when they were asked to say: "There is no God but God," [36] said, "Should we give up our gods for the sake of a mad poet?" [37] No, he came with the truth and confirmed the *previous* prophets. [38] Now taste the painful punishment. [39] You'll be repaid fully for what you did.

THE DELIGHTS OF PARADISE

[40] The sincere servants of God [41] will have *plenty of* provisions; fruits they were familiar with. [42] They shall be honoured [43] in Gardens of Delight, [44] sitting on comfortable sofas facing each other; [45] they shall be served *drinks* in cups filled from a flowing fountain, [46] white and delicious for the drinkers; [47] *this wine* won't cause headache or confusion; [48] sitting with their spouses of modest gaze and lovely eyes; [49] like *precious* eggs, well-preserved.

THE CONVERSATION OF A PIOUS PERSON WITH A DISBELIEVER

[50] They will turn to one another asking questions; [51] one of them will ask, "I had a friend [52] who would ask me, 'Do you really believe: [53] when we are dead and turned to dust and bones we shall be brought back for judgement?' [54] He will say, 'Would you like to see him?' [55] So when he looked down, he saw him in the mid-

dle of the blazing Fire. ⁵⁶ He said, 'By God, you nearly ruined me; ⁵⁷ hadn't it been for the gift of my Lord, I would have been in Hell too. ⁵⁸ Aren't we to die except for our first death? ⁵⁹ Shall we never suffer?'" ⁶⁰ This is a real victory. ⁶¹ Everyone should work for this.

THE TREE OF ZAQQUM

⁶² Is this better hospitality or the tree of Zaqqum? ⁶³ We made this to chastise the wicked. ⁶⁴ It is a tree that grows in the middle of Hell. ⁶⁵ Its fruit is like the heads of Satan. ⁶⁶ They will eat from it to fill their bellies, ⁶⁷ then drink boiling water, ⁶⁸ their home is Hell. ⁶⁹ They found their forefathers misguided, ⁷⁰ and *thoughtlessly* followed in their footsteps; ⁷¹ previously, most of them were misguided. ⁷² We sent *many* warners to them. ⁷³ Look, what's the fate of those who were warned; ⁷⁴ only the sincere servants of God *were saved*.

A TRIBUTE TO PROPHET NOAH

⁷⁵ Remember when Noah prayed to Us, so We responded graciously ⁷⁶ and saved him and his followers from a terrible suffering. ⁷⁷ We made his offspring continue *in the world,* ⁷⁸ and we kept his praise in the future generations. ⁷⁹ Peace be upon Noah of all people. ⁸⁰ This is how We reward the righteous. ⁸¹ He was our faithful servant. ⁸² The others We drowned.

ABRAHAM CHALLENGED HIS PEOPLE

⁸³ Abraham was from the same group; ⁸⁴ he turned to his Lord with a heart free of evil. ⁸⁵ He asked his father and people, "What do you worship, ⁸⁶ do you take false gods beside God? ⁸⁷ What do you think about the Lord of the worlds?" ⁸⁸ He looked at the stars ⁸⁹ and said, "I'm sick."ᵃ ⁹⁰ So people turned away and left him alone.

ABRAHAM SMASHED THE IDOLS

⁹¹ So he quietly went to *the temple full* of idols and spoke with the idols: "Don't you eat? ⁹² Why don't you speak?" ⁹³ He turned on them striking them with full force.ᵇ ⁹⁴ *His people* came to him hurriedly. ⁹⁵ He said to them, "Why do you worship something you shape with your hands? ⁹⁶ God created you and all you do." ⁹⁷ They decided: "Let's make a pile of wood and throw him into a blazing fire." ⁹⁸ They plotted against him but We ruined their plot.

ᵃ "I'm sick" of your idol worship, shows Abraham's annoyance that he felt ill of seeing their evil way.
ᵇ *Bi Yameen* literally means "with the right hand", a metaphor for "with force".

ABRAHAM'S SCARY DREAM

[99] He said, "I'm going to my Lord, He will guide me; [100] Lord, give me *a* pious *son*." [101] So We gave good news of a son with strong character.[a] [102] When he was old enough to work with him, *one day* he told him: "My son, I saw in a dream I'm sacrificing you; tell me what you think?" He replied, "Father, do as you were told; you'll find me patient, God willing." [103] When both submitted and Abraham laid him face down, [104] We called out: "Abraham [105] you have fulfilled the dream. This is how We reward the righteous." [106] It was a clear test *of faith*. [107] We saved *Ismael* in exchange for a slaughtered *ram*, [108] and left his tribute among future generations. [109] Peace be on Abraham. [110] That's how We reward the righteous, [111] he was Our faithful servant. [112] We *later* gave him good news of Isaac, a righteous Prophet. [113] We blessed him and Isaac; some of their children were righteous, others wrongdoers.

MOSES AND AARON WERE THE WINNERS

[114] We favoured Moses and Aaron *too*; [115] We rescued them and their people from a dreadful suffering, [116] and helped them to become the winners. [117] We gave them the Book that explained things clearly, [118] We guided them on the straight path, [119] and left their praise among the future generations. [120] Peace be on Moses and Aaron. [121] That's how We reward the righteous, [122] Our faithful servants.

TRIBUTE TO PROPHET ELIJAH

[123] Elijah was also from the messengers. [124] He said to his people: "Won't you believe? [125] How can you worship Baal and turn your back on the best Creator? [126] Isn't God Your Lord and Lord of your forefathers?" [127] But they denied and will be brought *before Us*, [128] except for the devout servants of God. [129] We left his praise among the later generations. [130] Peace be on Elijah. [131] That's how We reward the righteous, [132] Our faithful servants.

THE PROPHET LOT ACKNOWLEDGED

[133] *Similarly,* Lot was Our messenger. [134] We saved him and all his followers, [135] except the old lady who remained behind. [136] Then We destroyed all others. [137] *Quraysh!* You pass through their ruins in broad daylight, [138] and *sometimes* at night, don't you understand?

---

[a] Haleem means gentle, a moral virtue that represents a strong character.

THE PROPHET JONAH WAS FORGIVEN

¹³⁹Jonah was also from the messengers. ¹⁴⁰When he fled on board the heavily-loaded ship, ¹⁴¹they cast lots, he was the loser, thrown overboard. ¹⁴²A whale swallowed him, as he blamed himself. ¹⁴³Had he not been among those who glorify God, ¹⁴⁴he would have stayed in its belly till the Day of Resurrection. ¹⁴⁵Eventually, We flung him out, sick, on to an empty shore. ¹⁴⁶We caused a gourd tree to grow over to shade him, ¹⁴⁷and sent him back to one hundred thousand or more people. ¹⁴⁸They believed, so We allowed them to enjoy their lives fully.

A DIFFICULT QUESTION FOR THE DISBELIEVERS

¹⁴⁹So ask the disbelievers: "You assign daughters for your Lord and sons for yourself? ¹⁵⁰Were you witness when We created the angels?" ¹⁵¹Beware! This is another of their *concocted* lies, they say, ¹⁵²"God has begotten;" they are liars. ¹⁵³Did He choose daughters over sons? ¹⁵⁴What has come over you that you judge *in this way*? ¹⁵⁵Do you not pay attention? ¹⁵⁶Or do you have evidence? ¹⁵⁷Bring your book if you are truthful. ¹⁵⁸They declare a relationship between Him and the jinn, and the jinn know they will be brought *before him*. ¹⁵⁹Glory be to God, He is far above what they imagine. ¹⁶⁰The true servants of God don't do such things. ¹⁶¹Neither you nor what you worship ¹⁶²can tempt anyone away from God ¹⁶³except him who will burn in the Blazing Fire.

THE ANGELS ARRANGED IN ROWS

¹⁶⁴The angels will say, "each one of us has a role; ¹⁶⁵we are organised in ranks ¹⁶⁶and we glorify God. ¹⁶⁷The disbelievers used to say, ¹⁶⁸"If we had the Scripture like the past people, ¹⁶⁹we would have been like the devout servants of God." ¹⁷⁰So they disbelieved *the Quran*; soon they will know.

THE MESSENGERS ARE VERY SPECIAL

¹⁷¹Our promise to the messengers, Our servants, was fulfilled; ¹⁷²they were helped ¹⁷³and our armies were the winners. ¹⁷⁴So leave them for a while. ¹⁷⁵Watch them, they will see *the reality* soon. ¹⁷⁶Do they want our punishment to come sooner? ¹⁷⁷When it comes into their courtyards it will be a terrible morning for those warned. ¹⁷⁸Leave them for a while ¹⁷⁹and watch, soon they will see *the reality*. ¹⁸⁰Glory be to Your Lord, Lord of Might and Power far above their claims. ¹⁸¹And peace be on the Messengers ¹⁸²and all praises are for God, Lord of the worlds.

38. Sad
The Letter Sad

This early-Makkan chapter was revealed in the fourth or fifth year of the mission of the Prophet ﷺ. It opens by describing the role of the Quran as a reminder, creating awareness and consciousness of a greater reality, its central theme. This is developed by relating the stories of previous communities and the tireless efforts of prophets, starting with an account of the excellent qualities of David and his son Solomon . They were rulers, but also devout and pious servants of God. The heartbreaking story of the sufferings of Prophet Job concludes the chapter.

According to Tabari, Satan surmised that Job would not remain faithful if he encountered difficulties. God allowed Satan to test him. So disaster struck Job: his house subsided, his livestock were killed, his family were killed in an accident and he became ill with a contagious disease so people abandoned him. Satan attempted to shake Job's faith through his wife: she put forward an idea that for him to recover, he must sacrifice a baby goat for Satan. Job refused to do so; he swore an oath to give her one hundred lashes for the blasphemy, once he recovered. In that despair and anguish he prayed: "Satan has brought hardship and pain" (41). Job is presented as model of patience and endurance, and is honoured as "An excellent servant!" He didn't despair, he cried to God for relief and placed his trust in Him. This is what makes this story a lesson, *zikra*, for those with understanding (43).

This passage can be read in the wider context of the chapter. In the beginning, it mentions the arrogance and the hostility of the people of Makkah to the Prophet ﷺ, resulting in the warning: "How many past generations have We destroyed before them! They cried out; there was no time for escape" (3). The chapter presents other objections of the disbelievers to the message of Muhammad ﷺ. The stories of previous communities who rejected prophets alternate with passages about the Makkans, facilitating comparison between them. The chapter ends as it began: "This is a reminder for all people, and after a while you will come to know its truth" (87–88).

———————

In the name of God, the Kind, the Caring.

¹ *Sad.*ᵃ

DIVINE REVELATION IS A REMINDER
By the Quran full of reminders, ²the disbelievers are haughty and hostile. ³How

ᵃ The deep voiced Arabic letter '*Sad*' stands for '*As Siddiq*', the truthful friend referring to the Prophet ﷺ or human conscience that like a truthful friend tells everything, whether you like it or not. The Prophet ﷺ said "ask your heart". The voice of conscience.

many generations We destroyed before them? They all cried out *for help*, but there was no time to escape. [4] They are surprised that a warner came from them, they say, "This is a fraudulent magician. [5] He's turned *all* the gods into one god? How strange!" [6] Their leaders hastily set out *to tell people*, "Walk away and stick to your gods. That's what you must do, [7] we've not heard of this in *any* religion of recent times. This is a fabrication. [8] Did *this* reminder have to be sent down to him of all people?" So, they doubt My reminder? Then *wait* till they taste My punishment. [9] Do they hold *the keys to* the coffers of your Lord's Compassion, the Almighty, the Giver? [10] Or do they have control over the Heavens, the Earth and whatever lies in between? *So let them climb the ropes*[b].

TODAY'S ENEMIES OF THE TRUTH WILL LOSE, LIKE THOSE BEFORE THEM

[11] The armies of the confederates that *oppose you* will be defeated. [12] Before them, the people of Noah, Ad and Pharaoh of the columns,[c] they *all* denied *their prophets*, [13] as did Thamud, the people of Lot and the forest dwellers. Those were the confederates *of their day*; [14] they denied the messengers and so My punishment was justified. [15] And the *Makkans* can expect a single Blast that will not be postponed.

BE LIKE DAVID IN HIS FORTITUDE AND WISDOM

[16] *Your opponents* said: "Our Lord, give us our share in advance *of either Heaven or Hell* before the Day of Reckoning." [17] Put up with what they say, and remember Our servant, the *strong*-handed David: he was devout. [18] We made the mountains *echo* with him, glorifying Us in the evening and in the morning, [19] and the birds in flocks, each of them obedient to *David*. [20] And *so* We strengthened his rule, and We gave him wisdom and *the ability to reach* decisive judgements.

IN RESOLVING DISPUTE, DAVID REALISED HIS MISTAKE

[21] Has the report of the *parties to a* dispute reached you? They climbed over the wall of *his* private chamber [22] and came to David, he was frightened to *see* them; they said, "Don't be afraid. We have a dispute; one *party* has wronged the other. So, judge between us without deviating and guide us towards a fair solution." [23] *One of them said*, "This brother of mine has ninety-nine sheep, whereas I have

---

[b] 'Let them climb the ropes', is an idiom meaning "allow them to continue on their course and suffer its consequences."

[c] Reference to Pharaoh's temples with massive columns.

one. He demands: 'Let me look after it,' and he's putting pressure on me." ²⁴ *David* said, "He is wrong to ask for your sheep. Business partners often take advantage, one of the other – except the believers who are righteous, but they are few!" *When* David realised We had tested him, he begged forgiveness of His Lord, fell in prostration and repented.ᵃ ²⁵ So We forgave him. *David* will *enjoy* closeness to Us in the most beautiful of homecomings.

LESSONS TO LEARN FROM DAVID'S STORY

²⁶ "David, We appointed you Our vice-regent on Earth, so judge fairly between people and don't act on a whim that may lead you astray from the path of God. Those who wander away from the path of God will have severe punishment for neglecting the Day of Reckoning."

GOD'S WORKS ARE PURPOSEFUL

²⁷ We didn't create the Heavens and the Earth and what lies between them purposeless, though the disbelievers may think so. Woe to those who disbelieve, *they will suffer* in the Fire! ²⁸ Should We put those who believe and do righteous deeds on par with those who wreak havoc in the land, or those who are mindful *of God* on par with outright sinners? ²⁹ This is a Book that We sent down to you, a blessed *Book*, so *people* might think about its message, and the intelligent might pay attention.

AFTER A LESSON IN MORTALITY, SOLOMON IS BLESSED WITH GIFTS

³⁰ We granted David *a son*, Solomon. What an excellent servant! Truly devout. ³¹ *One evening,* when the pure-bred horses were paraded before *Solomon,* ³² he said, "my love of fine things increased my Lord's remembrance. He watched them till they disappeared out of sight. ³³ Bring *the horses* back to me." He patted their legs and necks. ³⁴ We tested Solomon with an illness, so he became thin as a skeleton sat on his throne, then turned devoutly to Us.ᵇ ³⁵ He said, "My Lord, forgive me, and grant me a kingdom the like of which no one after me will ever see. *Only* You are the Giver." ³⁶ So We made the winds compliant to him, blowing gently at

---

ᵃ   A verse of prostration. Regarding David's realisation that God was testing him, commentaries mention the dispute over the ewes. David understood the similarity between that case and when he demanded that a man break up his engagement so he could marry his fiancée.

ᵇ   Razi said "Solomon became seriously ill, he lost so much weight he looked like a skeleton. The huge throne he used to sit on with splendour and authority no longer had that majesty, now he looked like a skeleton placed on a large chair".

his command wherever he wanted them *to go*; [37] and demons *from the jinn*, their builders, divers; [38] and others bound in chains. [39] *God said*: "This is Our gift *for you to* give it to *others* or withhold it as you like." [40] *Solomon* will *enjoy* closeness to Us in the most beautiful of homecomings.

JOB'S LEGENDARY PATIENCE IS PRAISED

[41] Mention Our servant, Job, he cried out to his Lord: "Satan has wreaked sorrow and torment on me." [42] *God said*: "Stamp your foot *on the ground*. This is a cool place to wash and drink." [43] We treated him kindly and cured him, so We gave him his family *back* and an equal number of others with them, as a reminder for those gifted with understanding. [44] *God told him*: "Take a handful of grass and strike *your wife* with it so you don't break your oath."[c] We found him to be patient. What a wonderful servant! So devout.

GOD COMMENDS MORALLY COMPETENT PEOPLE

[45] And mention Our servants Abraham, Isaac and Jacob; they were strong men with insight. [46] We chose them for the special task of reminding *others* of the Abode *of the Hereafter*. [47] In Our Sight, they are the best of the chosen ones. [48] And mention Ishmael, Elisha and Ezekiel; they were the chosen ones. [49] This is a *brief* reminder; and for those mindful *of God*, there will be a beautiful homecoming, [50] the Gardens of Eden with open gates waiting for them; [51] *and* reclining there *on sofas*, asking for fruits of all kind and for drinks, [52] and beside them *spouses* modest in their glances and of equal age. [53] This is what you are promised for the Day of Reckoning. [54] This provision of Ours will not end.

AN EXAMPLE OF HOW THE PEOPLE OF HELL WILL QUARREL

[55] This is *for the righteous,* the tyrants will have a most terrifying of homecomings, [56] Hell, where they will burn. What a dreadful resting place! [57] Let them taste, scalding water and pus, [58] coupled with other similar *torments*. [59] This *here* is another crowd rushing headlong with you *into Hell*. No welcome for them. They will burn in the Fire. [60] *The newcomers* will say, "No! It is you, there is no welcome for you, you got us in to this. What a dreadful place to stay!" [61] *Then* they will say, "Our Lord, whoever got us in to this, double his punishment in the Fire." [62] And they will say, "What is *happening* to us? Why don't we see *those* men whom we

---

c   When Job's wife blasphemed, he swore to give her 100 lashes. He was spared from doing this and told to use a handful of grass, so she wouldn't be physically harmed.

considered evil? ⁶³ We took them as a laughing stock? Or did we overlook them?" ⁶⁴ That is how the people of the Fire will quarrel among themselves.

THE MESSENGER'S 🕌 JOB IS TO WARN

⁶⁵ Say, *Messenger*: "I am a warner; and there is no God but God, the One, the Supreme, ⁶⁶ the Lord of the Heavens and the Earth, and whatever lies in between, the Almighty, the Forgiving." ⁶⁷ Say: "It's news of great importance ⁶⁸ which you reject. ⁶⁹ I have never had knowledge of the assembly on high when a dispute arose among them. ⁷⁰ The revelation to me is that I am a warner." Satan refused to bow, he was arrogant

⁷¹ *Remember* when your Lord said to the angels, "I am creating a human being from clay. ⁷² So once I have formed him and blown My spirit into him, prostrate before him." ⁷³ So the angels prostrated all together ⁷⁴ except Iblis; he was arrogant and ungrateful. ⁷⁵ *God* said, "Iblis, what stopped you from prostrating to the one I created with My Hands? Were you arrogant then, or were you already from the haughty?" ⁷⁶ *Iblis* said, "I am better than him. You created me from fire, and You created him from clay." ⁷⁷ *God* said, "Get out of here! You are an outlaw. ⁷⁸ My curse will be on you till Judgement Day."

GOD PERMITS SATAN TO DO HIS WORST TO LEAD HUMANITY ASTRAY

⁷⁹ *Iblis* said, "My Lord, give me time till the day they're resurrected." ⁸⁰ *God* said, "You have it ⁸¹ until the Day of the Appointed Hour." ⁸² *Iblis* said, "*I swear* by Your Might, I will try to mislead them, ⁸³ except the devout servants of Yours." ⁸⁴ God said, "That's right; and I too speak the truth: ⁸⁵ I will fill Hell with you, *Iblis*, and those who follow you." ⁸⁶ Say *messenger*: "I don't ask you for any reward for this, nor am I claiming what I'm not. ⁸⁷ This is a reminder for all people; ⁸⁸ and in due course you will know its *truth*."

39. Az-Zumar
The Crowds

This chapter was revealed in the middle Makkan period. It reinforces belief in the Oneness of God and the dreadful consequences of denying Him. Professor Sells eloquently captures the mood of that early time:

> What gives the early Makkan chapter's their depth, psychological subtlety, texture and tone is the way the future is collapsed into the present; the way the day of reckoning is transferred from the fear and hope of a moment in the future to a sense of reckoning in the present moment. The centrality of the day of reckoning to the early revelations is based on a prophetic impulse to remind humanity of the moment of truth.[a]

The graphic scenes of the Hereafter are presented in a variety of ways to emphasise the enormity and the terror of Judgement Day. Whilst the severity of Divine Punishment is stressed repeatedly in the chapter, verse 53 helps to dispel the pessimism of the sinners: "Say, 'My servants who have wronged themselves, do not be hopeless of God's kindness; indeed God forgives all sins. He is the Forgiver, the Kind'" (53).

The chapter opens with a commanding reference to God's Majesty, and questions how such a wonderful and generous Lord could be ignored and denied. God's marvellous gifts are poured on us day and night: the air we breathe, the delightful foods we enjoy and the spouses that give us friendship and comfort. "If you are unthankful, then God has no need of you; He is not pleased with the ungratefulness of his servants. But if you are thankful, He will be pleased with you" (7). The chapter identifies thankful servants and congratulates them: "Good news for those who avoid serving evil forces and turn genuinely to God..." (17–18).

Such fortunate ones are blessed by God in an incredible way:

> So the one whose mind God opens with *the light* of Islam will have light from His Lord. But those whose minds[b] are closed to the remembrance of God will be ruined; they are wholly misguided (22).

The ability to see, feel and speak the Truth is a great gift. The next passage again compares the person of faith to the idol worshipper (the latter could well include the modern materialist): "Can a servant devoted to many masters who are at odds with each other be the same as the one who is devoted solely to one master?" (29).

The unthankful person is the one who is selfish, follows whims and lowly desires; "The

[a]   M.A. Sells, *Approaching the Qur'an: The Early Revelations.*
[b]   *Lil-Qasiyati Quloobhuhum* literally means their hardened hearts. The heart is a metaphor for the mind since it is the organ of both understanding and emotions.

evil of what they did will distress them. The sinners will suffer the distress as a result of their deeds and they will not escape" (51). The final section of the chapter describes the crushing manner in which crowds of the wicked people will be hurled into Hell. The angels will ask them, "Didn't messengers from among you come to recite your Lord's verses and warn you of this Day's meeting?" (71). How they will regret that day. This is the purpose of presenting the Hereafter in the present: to jolt us, and fill us with awe. The end of the chapter presents a dignified entry of believers into Paradise, and the masses of angels praising the Lord.

In the name of God, the Kind and Caring.

GOD IS THE MIGHTY CREATOR

¹ This Book is revealed by God, the Almighty, the Wise. ² We revealed to you the Book of the Truth, so worship God sincerely with commitment. ³ Take heed! Sincere commitment should be for God alone. People who take protectors beside Him, *claiming that* we just worship them to achieve nearness to God, God will judge their disagreement. God will not guide the lying thankless person. ⁴ Had God wanted to take a son, He would have chosen from His creation as He pleased, glory be to Him. He is God, the One, the Dominant. ⁵ He created the Heavens and the Earth for a purpose; He merges the night into the day and the day into the night; and made the sun and the moon for a specific task,ᵃ each floating in its orbit of a fixed time. Indeed, He is the Almighty, the Forgiving.

THE THANKFUL AND UNTHANKFUL

⁶ He created you from a single being, then made from it its spouse, and gave you eight pairs of livestock.ᵇ He creates you in the wombs of your mothers, developing stage by stage inside three layers of darkness. That is God your Lord, the Absolute Controller; He is the only God so how can you turn away from Him? ⁷ If you are unthankful, then God has no need of you; He's not pleased with the unthankfulness of His servants. If you are thankful, He will be pleased with you. No one will carry the burden of another person, then to your Lord you will be returned and He shall tell you what you did. He knows *your* innermost thoughts.

ᵃ *Sakhkhara* means, "to force something to do a special task"; in this case, the moon and the sun both provide light and a means of measuring time.

ᵇ This refers to the four pairs of livestock: camels, cows, sheep and goats.

[8] When a person suffers a hardship he calls His Lord devoutly, then when He eases the suffering he forgets that a short while before he had prayed to Him, and he sets up rivals with God which misguide him from His path. Say: "Enjoy your ungratefulness for a while; you are people of the Fire." [9] Can such a person be compared to the obedient, prostrating and standing during the night, fearful of the Hereafter and hopeful of his Lord's *kindness*? Say: "Can those who know be equal to those who don't know? Only the understanding people pay attention."

THE REWARD FOR THE THANKFUL

[10] Say: "My believing servants, be mindful of Your Lord." Those who are righteous in this life will have goodness. God's Earth is vast; He shall fully reward the patient without limits. [11] Say: "I have been commanded to worship God, sincerely committed to His religion, [12] and I was ordered to be the first to submit." [13] Say: "If I disobey my Lord, I fear the punishment of a Great Day." [14] Say: "I worship God sincerely committing myself to Him, [15] so worship whoever you please beside Him." Say: "The losers are those who lose themselves and their families on Judgement Day. That is a big loss!" [16] Smoke of fire above and smoke beneath them; with that God frightens His servants, so My *sincere* servants, be fearful of Me. [17] Good news for those who avoid serving the idols and turn genuinely to God, so give My servants good news: [18] *Those* who listen attentively to what is said and follow the best of it, God has guided these, the one's with understanding. [19] The one who God has passed sentence against, how can you rescue him? He's already in the Fire. [20] But those who fear their Lord, they will have lofty apartments luxuriously furnished and streams flowing beneath them; *this is* God's promise. God doesn't break His promise.

THE MIND OF THE THANKFUL OPENS TO ISLAM

[21] Don't you see that God sends rain from the sky. He lets it seep into the ground, where it forms springs. Then with it He produces plants of different colours, then they become dry, so you see them turn yellow, and then He turns it back into soil. In this are lessons for the understanding people. [22] So the one whose mind God opens with *the light* of Islam will have light from His Lord. But those whose minds are closed[c] to the remembrance of God will be ruined; they are wholly

---

[c] *Lil-Qasiyati Quloobhuhum*, means their hardened hearts. The heart is a metaphor for the mind, since it is the organ of both understanding and emotion.

misguided.

They tremble when reading the Quran

[23] God has sent down a beautiful set of teachings *in* a Book that is consistent, proclaiming promises and warnings[a]. The skin shivers of those who fear their Lord. Then, their skin and hearts relax with the remembrance of God; that is God's guidance. He guides with it who He pleases. Whoever God allows to go astray, will have no guide. [24] So the one who must shield his face from the terrible punishment of Judgement Day, the evil, will be told: "Taste what you have earned." [25] Others before them also disbelieved, and they were unaware of where the punishment came from. [26] So God made them taste humiliation in this worldly life, and the punishment of the Hereafter is even greater. If only they knew.

The believers only have one Master

[27] In this *Majestic* Quran, We give examples for people of all kinds so they pay attention, [28] to an Arabic Quran, free from any defect so they may be mindful *of God*. [29] God gives this example: can a servant devoted to many masters who are at odds with each other be the same as the one who is devoted to only one master? All the praises belong to God! Unfortunately, the majority don't know.

The believer in the Quran will be satisfied

[30] You shall die, so shall they die; [31] then on Judgement Day you will argue with one another, near Your Lord. [32] Who can be more wretched than the one who lied about God and denied the truth when it came to him? Isn't Hell the final home of the disbelievers? [33] The one who came with the truth and the one who accepted him, such are the mindful people. [34] They shall have whatever they want *from* their Lord. That is the reward of the righteous. [35] God will remove their wrongs and give them an excellent reward for what they did. [36] Isn't God enough for His servant? Yet they threaten you with *idols* they worship beside God; anyone God allows to go astray will have no guide. [37] And anyone God guides no one can misguide him, isn't God the Almighty, the Avenger?

The helplessness of idols

[38] If you ask them: "Who created the Heavens and the Earth?" They will say, "God". Say: "What do you think about those you worship beside God; can they

---

[a]   "Masani" according to Suyuti is the promises and warnings.

relieve my distress if God wished to harm me, or if He wished to be kind to me could they stop Him being Kind?" Say: "God is enough for me, those who trust put their trust in Him." [39] Say: "My people, do what you want to do and so will I; soon you will know [40] who will be humiliated by sufferings in the world and finally thrown in an everlasting punishment."

THE MYSTERY OF SLEEP

[41] We sent down the Book for people, *it has* the truth. Whoever follows *its* guidance will benefit himself, and whoever goes astray will fail himself. You aren't their caretaker. [42] God takes away the souls of people dying and the souls of *the living* during their sleep. He keeps hold of those whose time of death has come, but sends back others, so *they will die* at their fixed time. In this are lessons for thinkers.

THE IDOLS ARE INCAPABLE OF HELPING YOU

[43] Have they chosen intermediaries beside God? Say: "Though they haven't got power nor understanding?" [44] Say: "God has complete authority for intercession." He controls the Heavens and the Earth, then to Him you shall be returned. [45] When God's Oneness is declared, the disbelievers of the Hereafter hate[b] it intensely, yet when their gods beside God are mentioned they are thrilled. [46] Say: "God, Creator of the Heavens and the Earth, Knower of the unseen and the seen worlds, You shall decide between Your servants about their differences."

A DESCRIPTION OF AN UNTHANKFUL PERSON

[47] If everything on Earth plus twice as much belonged to the wicked, they would happily offer it as a ransom against the terrible punishment of Judgement Day. God will show them what they couldn't have imagined. [48] Their evil deeds will be disclosed, and their mocking will track them *as punishment*. [49] When people are distressed they call on Us, but when We give them Our gifts, they claim: "We've been given this because of our knowledge." No, it is a test but most do not know this. [50] Those before them said the same. Their works will not save them *that Day*. [51] The evil of what they did will distress them; the sinners will suffer the distress because of their deeds, and they will not escape. [52] Don't they know God provides plentifully to *some* and sparingly to *others* as He pleases. In that are lessons for the

---

[b] *Ishma'azzat Quloobuhum* literally means "to hate and despair."

faithful.

INVITATION TO CONFESS SINS PRIVATELY

[53] Say: "My servants who wronged themselves, don't be hopeless of God's Kindness; God forgives all the sins, He is the Forgiver, the Kind." [54] Turn devoutly to your Lord, and submit to Him before the punishment overtakes you – then you shall not be helped. [55] And follow the best teachings sent down to you by your Lord before the unexpected punishment overtakes you when you are unaware [56] and a soul will cry out: "Woe to me since I disobeyed God and mocked *His revelations*." [57] Or he will say, "Had God guided me I would be among the pious," [58] or when he sees the punishment he will say, "If I could live again I would be among the righteous." [59] No, My signs came to you but you denied them; you were arrogant and among the disbelievers. [60] You will see on Judgement Day those who denied God, their faces darkened – isn't Hell the final home for the arrogant? [61] And God will save the pious in a safe place where they won't be harmed, nor will they worry.

HUMAN FAILURE TO UNDERSTAND THE GREATNESS OF GOD

[62] God is the Creator and Guardian of all things. [63] He has the keys to the Heavens and the Earth. Those who disbelieve in God's revelations will be the losers. [64] Say: "Ignorant ones! Are you telling me to worship others beside God?" [65] It was revealed to you and those before you: if you commit idolatry all your deeds will come to nothing and you will be the losers. [66] No, worship God and be among the thankful ones. [67] They don't understand God's true greatness; on Judgement Day, the entire Earth will be in His grip and the Heavens will be rolled up by His command[a]. Glory be to Him, He is exalted above what they associate with Him.

THE END OF THE WORLD

[68] When the Trumpet is blown, whoever is in the Heavens and the Earth will fall unconscious, except him whom God wills. Then when it is blown again they will stand up looking *dazed*. [69] The Earth will shine with the light of its Lord, the Book of Deeds will lay open, the prophets and other witnesses will be brought forward, judgement will be made, and they will not be wronged. [70] Every soul will be fully rewarded for what it did; *God* knows best what they did.

---

[a] "Biyameenhey" literally means by his right hand, however Suyuti interprets it as "by His power and command".

DRIVEN TO HELL IN CROWDS

[71] Those who denied their Lord will be driven into Hell in crowds. When they reach it, the gates will be opened and the gatekeepers will ask them, "Didn't messengers from among you come to recite your Lord's verses and warn you of this Day's meeting?" They will say, "Yes," but the sentence of punishment will come to pass against the disbelievers. [72] It will be said, "Enter through the gates of Hell; remain in it forever." What a miserable home for the arrogant!

DRIVEN TO PARADISE IN CROWDS

[73] Those who were mindful of their Lord will be led into Paradise in crowds. When they reach there, its gates will be opened, and the gatekeepers will greet them: "Peace be on you, you were good so enter it and stay here forever." [74] They will say, "All the praises are for God Who kept His promise for us, and gave us this place, we shall live in the Garden wherever we want." What a wonderful reward for those who worked hard. [75] You will see the angels around the Divine Throne glorifying and praising their Lord. A just judgement will be passed between them and it will be said: "All the praises are for God, the Lord of the worlds."

40. Mu'min
The Believer

This Makkan chapter was revealed around the sixth year, at a time of intense persecution of the Muslims. The name Mu'min comes from verse 28, "A believing man from Pharaoh's family who kept his faith secret...". Its other name is chapter Ghafir, it is mentioned in verse 3, "the forgiver of sins...". The chapter opens with a claim: "This is a revelation from God the Almighty, the Knower" (2). The disbelievers rejected this, so arguments from human history, experience and the natural world around them are presented. The underlying cause of their rejection is false pride in their knowledge and wealth, which leads to delusion and conceit. They mistakenly think material things will save them, and that they have no need of the Almighty: "So when Our Messengers came to them with clear signs, they smugly continued to boast about their knowledge and *eventually* were engulfed by the punishment they mocked" (83).

The central theme of the chapter is false pride; humans think they're the centre of the world, they're deceived in thinking they're independent and self-sufficient. Their wealth, talents and networks make them smug and self-satisfied.

The chapter opens by acknowledging the dignity of the faithful through prayer of the angels:

> Our Lord, everything is under the cover of Your Kindness and Knowledge, therefore forgive those who repent and follow Your way, and protect them from the punishment of Hell (7).

Scenes from Judgement Day: Divine Justice in full swing, people's limbs testifying against them, disbelievers being hurled into Hellfire, conversations with angels and graphic depictions of Hellish torment – all combine to strike fear into hearts.

A prominent verse is: "Your Lord said, 'Call on me, and I shall answer you'" (60). God is Mujeeb, the Answerer, a Responder, a lovely way of encouraging us to seek His goodwill, care and friendliness. There is diversity in the stories, scenes and subjects of the chapter, but the common thread running through them all is: God is the Almighty, able to resurrect the dead.

In the name of God, the Kind the Caring.

¹ *Ha Meem.*

THE FORGIVING AND GENEROUS LORD
² This is a Revelation from God the Almighty, the Knower, ³ the Forgiver of sins,

Acceptor of repentance, Severe in punishment and the Bestower of favours.[a] There is no god but Him. To Him is the return. [4]Only the disbelievers argue about God's revelations, so don't be surprised by their toing and froing in the land *for trade.*[5]The people of Noah before them and other parties after them also denied; each community tried to defeat their messenger and disputed desperately to crush the Truth with falsehood. I punished them, so look what became of them! [6]Your Lord's sentence against the disbelievers was carried out: "They are people of the Fire."

THE ANGELS' PRAYER FOR THE BELIEVERS

[7]The angels who maintain the Divine Throne and those around it glorify and praise their Lord. They are faithful, and seek forgiveness for the believers; they pray: "Our Lord, all good happens because of Your Kindness and with Your Knowledge, so forgive those who repent, follow Your way and protect them from the punishment of Hell. [8]Our Lord, admit them into Everlasting Gardens, which You have promised them and anyone who reforms himself, including their forefathers, spouses and children. You are Almighty, the Wise. [9]Protect them from the consequences of evil; whoever You have protected from punishment that Day, You will be kind to them, and that's the supreme victory."

THE DISBELIEVERS WILL CONFESS THEIR SINS

[10]The disbelievers will be told: "When you were invited to faith you disbelieved, God's dislike of you was far greater than your dislike of yourselves this day. [11]They will say, "Our Lord, twice you put us to death and twice you gave life[b]; we now confess our sins, so is there a way out?" [12]That is because when you were called to God you disbelieved but accepted idolatry, so *today* the decision is God's, the Exalted, the Great. [13]He will show you His Signs, and sends provision down from the sky for you. But only the devout pay attention. [14]So serve God, sincerely serving His religion, though the disbelievers dislike it.

THE TERRIFYING EVENTS OF JUDGEMENT DAY

[15]High above all ranks is the Lord of the *mighty* Throne. The Revelation is sent by His Command to His servants with whom He is pleased to warn *people* of the Day

---

[a] *Zul Fadl* shows kindness, gives gifts freely.

[b] You were non-existent; you were dead, then God gave you life; you then died for a second time and you will be resurrected on Judgement Day a second time.

of Meeting. [16] The Day when they will come out and nothing of theirs will be hidden from God. "Whose is the *absolute power and* control today?" "God, the One, the Dominant." [17] Today every soul will be rewarded for what it did; there will be no injustice today. God is quick in reckoning. [18] Warn them of a fast-approaching Day, when hearts will come up to the throats chokingly. The evildoers will have no friend or an intercessor who will be listened to. [19] God knows the cheaters[a] and what the minds conceal. [20] God will judge justly, but those they served beside God will make no judgment at all; indeed God is the Hearing, the Seeing.

GOD IS THE ONLY PROTECTOR

[21] Haven't they travelled about in the land to see the fate of those before them? They were far stronger than them, and they left behind many remains on the land. So God punished them for their sins; no one can protect them from God. [22] That *happened* because messengers came to them with clear signs, and they disbelieved, so God punished them; He is Strong, severe in punishment.

THE PHARAOH IS TERRIFIED OF MOSES

[23] We sent Moses with Our signs and a mandate [24] to Pharaoh, Haman and Korah. They called him, "a magician, a liar!" [25] He came to them with Our Truth, and they replied, "Kill the children of the believers with him and spare their women." However, the disbelievers' plot was bound to fail. [26] The Pharaoh said, "Leave me to kill Moses, and let him call upon His Lord; I fear he will change your religion or spread disorder[b] in the land." [27] Moses replied, "I seek protection from my Lord and your Lord from every haughty person who disbelieves the Day of Reckoning."

A SECRET BELIEVER DEFENDS MOSES

[28] A believing man from Pharaoh's family, who had kept his faith secret, said: "Are you going to kill a man because he says God is my Lord, and has come with clear signs from your Lord? If he is a liar then let it fall on his head, and if he is truthful then some of what he threatens you with will fall on you." God does not guide the one who is a lying rebel.[c] [29] *He continued*: "My people! Today you rule this land and have power, but who would help if God's punishment came on us?"

---

[a] *Khainat ul Ayun* literally means fraudulence of the eye: betrayal, sly, sneaky and secret.

[b] Cause an uprising against us.

[c] Literally, one who wastes God's gifts of guidance and witnessing His miracles.

The Pharaoh replied, "I have told you what I believe, and I am guiding you to the right path." [30] The believer answered, "I am fearful about your fate, it will be same as those people who opposed *the messengers*, [31] the fate of Noah's people, Ad, Thamud and those after them. God does not want injustice for human beings. [32] My people, I fear for you the Day of Lament.[d] [33] the Day you will turn back and flee with no one to defend you against God's *wrath*. Whoever God lets go stray, will have no guide."

He reminds them of Joseph

[34] "Previously Joseph came to you with clear signs, but you doubted what he brought until his death, then you said, "Now God will not send a messenger after him." That is how God leaves in error the doubting rebel; [35] they dispute God's revelations without His endorsement. That's loathsome to God and the believers. So God closes the mind[e] of every proud tyrant. [36] The Pharaoh said, "Haman, build a tower for me, so I might find pathways reaching [37] to the skies to look for the God of Moses; I think he is a liar." That is how Pharaoh's evil deeds appeared attractive to him, and he was prevented from reaching the path – and Pharaoh's plot led him to ruin.

The believer continues to preach

[38] The believer said: "My people, follow me and I shall guide you to the right path. [39] My people, the life of this world is a brief *period of* enjoyment whilst the Hereafter is the lasting home. [40] Whoever does evil will be punished proportionally, and whoever does righteousness, whether male or female, and is a believer will enter Paradise, there they will have unlimited provision. [41] My people, how come I am calling you to salvation and you are calling me to the Fire? [42] You invite me to disbelieve in God and associate with Him what I have no knowledge of. I *will continue to* invite you to the Almighty, the Forgiver. [43] Undoubtedly what you call me to worship is unfit for worship here and in the Hereafter. We will all be returning to God, and the rebels will be the companions of the Fire. [44] Then you will soon remember what I am saying to you; I rest my case with God. God sees His servants." [45] God protected him from being harmed, but Pharaoh's people

---

[d] *Yaum at-Tanaad* refers to Judgement Day, literally to, "cry out to one another for help". The next verse explains it further.

[e] Literally, "seals the heart".

were overwhelmed by terrible sufferings.

THE PUNISHMENT OF THE GRAVE

[46] The Fire of Hell will be there[a] all the time[b] for them until Judgement Day, and *the angels are told*: "Enter Pharaoh's people into the severest punishment." [47] In the Fire they will quarrel with each other, and those who were oppressed will say to the arrogant leaders, "We were your followers, now save us from burning in the fire." [48] The arrogant will say, "We are all in it together; indeed God has decided among His servants." [49] Those in the Fire will say to the gatekeepers of Hell, "Ask your Lord to reduce our punishment *at least* for a day." [50] They will say, "Didn't your messengers come to you with clear signs?" They will answer, "Yes." They will reply, "So call them! The prayers of the disbelievers are ineffective." [51] We support Our Messengers and those who believe both in this life and on the Day when witnesses will stand up *to testify* – [52] the Day when no excuses will benefit the wrongdoers – and they will be cursed and *given* a dreadful home.

THE ARROGANT DISPUTE TRUTH AND DO NOT REFLECT

[53] We gave Moses the guidance and made the Israelites heirs of the Book, [54] a guidance and a reminder for the understanding. [55] So be patient, since God's promise is true, seek forgiveness for the sins of your people, glorify and praise your Lord evening and morning. [56] Those who dispute the revelations of God without any authority given to them have only *a desire for* greatness in their hearts that they will never achieve. So seek God's protection, He is Hearing, Seeing. [57] The creation of the Heavens and the Earth is far greater than the creation of humans, but most people don't know. [58] The blind and the seeing are not the same; the righteous believers are not same as the wicked. How little you reflect.

THE LORD ANSWERS YOU

[59] There is no doubt that the Final Hour will come, but most people don't believe. [60] Your Lord said: "Call on me and I will answer you." Those who are arrogant about worshipping Me will soon enter Hell disgraced. [61] God made the night for you to rest in and the day for you to see *His bounties*; God is graciously generous to people, but most people are unthankful. [62] That is God your Lord, Creator of

---

[a] Literally, "The fire will be presented to them", refers to the punishment of the grave. It will be a "pit of fire or a garden of Paradise" (Hadith).

[b] Literally, "evening and morning" in their graves.

everything; there is no god but Him! So how then can you turn away from *Him*? ⁶³ But that is how those who dispute God's Scriptures turn away.

SOME FAVOURS OF GOD

⁶⁴ God made the Earth for you to live on, and the sky a roof. He fashioned you in the best forms and gave you enjoyable provision. That is God your Lord! Blessed is God, the Lord of the worlds. ⁶⁵ He is the Living; there is no god but Him, so worship Him sincerely, wholly committed. All praises are for God, the Lord of the worlds. ⁶⁶ Say: "I am forbidden to worship those you pray to beside God, since clear signs have come to me from My Lord, and I have been commanded to submit to the Lord of the worlds."

HE SAYS: "BE," AND IT COMES INTO EXISTENCE

⁶⁷ He created you from dust, then from semen, then from a clot of blood and then He brought you out as a baby. Then you reached maturity, eventually becoming old – though some of you will die earlier – so you reach a fixed time so you might understand. ⁶⁸ He gives life and death, and when He decides an affair He says to it: "Be," and it comes *into existence.*

THE DISGRACE AND TORMENT OF DISBELIEVERS

⁶⁹ Haven't you seen those who dispute God's revelations – how they turn away? ⁷⁰ They don't believe the Book that We sent with Our Messengers – they will know *the consequences.* ⁷¹ With iron collars around their necks and chains *on their feet* they will be dragged ⁷² into boiling water, then burned in the Fire. ⁷³ They will be asked: "Where are those you associated with ⁷⁴ beside God?" They will say, "They have deserted us, those we worshipped in the past were nothing." That is how God lets the disbelievers go astray. ⁷⁵ This is all because you were happy with falsehood in the Earth and lived merrily. ⁷⁶ Enter through the gates of Hell to stay there forever, a terrible place for the arrogant. ⁷⁷ So be patient; God's promise is true. Whether We let you see some of the punishment promised to them or We cause you to die *first* it does not matter; finally, they will be returned to Us.

SOME MORE FAVOURS OF GOD

⁷⁸ We sent messengers before you; some We told you about and others We haven't *yet* told you about. A messenger only brings miracles by God's permission. When God's command comes on Judgement Day justice will be done; there the follow-

ers of falsehood will be losers. [79]God made livestock for you to ride on and to eat from, [80]there are other benefits too for you in them. You can get to any destination you wish riding on them, and ships also carry you. [81]He shows you His signs, so which of God's signs will you deny?

DISBELIEVERS' BELIEF WILL NOT BENEFIT THEM

[82]Haven't they travelled about the land and seen the outcome of the deniers of past times? They were greater in numbers, mightier than them and *moreover* left behind bigger remains on the land, yet all they accomplished will not benefit. [83]So when Our messengers came to them with clear signs, they smugly continued with what little they knew, and were *finally* engulfed by the punishment they mocked. [84]So when they saw Our punishment they declared, "We believe in God; the One and we reject any partner we associated with Him." [85]Their belief won't benefit them now, since they have seen Our punishment. This was the Way of God among His servants in the past, the disbelievers will be *utter* losers there.

41. Ha Meem Sajdah
Ha Meem Prostration

This chapter was revealed in the middle Makkan period, a few days after Hamza, the uncle of the Messenger ﷺ, accepted Islam. Persecution against the Messenger ﷺ and his small band of followers was at its worst. The acceptance of Islam by this prominent young Qurayshi substantially strengthened the Muslims. After this momentous conversion, the Quraysh held a meeting about the growing threat from Islam. Utbah ibn Rabiah, a wealthy leader, took the responsibility of 'striking a deal' with the Messenger ﷺ, so he went and said to him:

> My nephew ... you have brought to your people something of grave concern whereby you have created a rift between the community ... here is a proposal, see if you can accept it; if it is wealth that you seek then we will put together a fortune for you ... if it is honour you seek we will make you our overlord ... and if it is that you cannot rid yourself of the spirit that appears to you we will find the best physician until you are cured (Lings).

The Prophet ﷺ replied: "Father of Walid, now listen to me," and began reciting this chapter. Utbah listened attentively; he was captivated by the words of the Quran. Utbah put his finger on his mouth and requested the Prophet ﷺ to stop reciting when the Prophet ﷺ came to the line: "If they turn away say, 'I warned you of a thunderbolt like the thunderbolt of Ad and Thamud'" (13). Utbah returned to the group and told them: "I've heard some words the like of which I have never heard before. It is not poetry, by God, neither is it a sorcery nor a soothsaying ... come not between this man and what he is about, but let him be."

The central theme of the chapter is the fundamental doctrines of Islam: *Tawhid (oneness of God)*, *Risalah (prophethood)* and *Akhirah (hereafter)*. The chapter opens with an introduction to the Quran: "*This is* a revelation from the Kind, the Caring; a book whose verses are clearly explained, an Arabic Quran for a people who have knowledge; it gives good news and warnings" (2–4). It then explains why the disbelievers are unable to listen and benefit from the Quran: they have locked minds and are intolerant. To open their mind, they are told to look at the wonderful signs of God's Majesty in nature. The power, wisdom, kindness, providence, organisation and management evident in the vast universe is a testimony that this is no drama or play of an imagined god, but the handiwork of the Almighty and the Knower.

The Quraysh are warned if they do not stop their mockery and rudeness they will face dire consequences like previous nations. The chapter refutes recurrent objections against *Tawhid*, the Oneness of God, such as questions about how dead bones can be raised to life, and how a man can be God's messenger.

The early Makkan Chapters are conversational and speak directly to the listeners, each listener is asked to think, reflect and interrogate himself, for example it poses questions like, "Say: "Consider *this*," or "Haven't you seen" or "Haven't you heard". This is a powerful teaching style where facts and figures aren't being taught but critical thinking is being encouraged and awareness of the Reality is being raised.

The Quraysh once asked, "What is the need for a new revelation when the Quran already accepts the Psalms and the Gospels as divine revelations?" The Quran answered: "We gave Moses the Book, but disagreement arose about it too" (45). The Messenger ﷺ is reassured, he has a lofty, pure, beneficial, life-changing message, and if the ignorant fail to listen, then his response should be gentle.

———————

In the name of God, the Kind, the Caring.

The Prophet ﷺ can't be accused of being power-hungry

[1] *Ha Meem.* [2] *This is* a Revelation from the Kind, the Caring; [3] a Book whose verses are clearly explained, an Arabic Quran for people who know. [4] It gives good news and warnings, though most of them will turn away and won't listen. [5] They say, "Our hearts are hardy to what you invite us to; we are hard of hearing and there is a barrier between us and you, therefore do as you like, and we shall do what we like." [6] Say: "I am a human like you; except that I receive revelation: your Lord is One God, so take the straight path to Him and seek forgiveness. Woe to the idolaters. [7] Those who don't give charity and deny the Hereafter. [8] But the believers who are righteous will have a never-ending reward."

The stages of the creation of the Heavens and the Earth

[9] Say: "Do you deny the one Who created the Earth in two days? You have set up rivals to the Lord of the worlds." [10] He made the mountains, blessed it, and in four days determined its provisions for seekers.[a] [11] Then He focused on the sky and it was smoke[b] so He said to it and the Earth: "Come *into existence* whether willingly or unwillingly." They replied, "We shall come willingly." [12] In two days He formed them into seven skies, and to each sky He assigned its functions. We decorated the nearest sky with stars and made it safe. That's the plan[c] of the Almighty, the

---

[a] Literally, "in front and behind them", but implies "all things everywhere".

[b] Provisions from mountains include: gold and precious metals, minerals, marble, coal, and much more.

[c] *Taqdeer* is precise calculation, accurate measurement and strategic planning.

All-Knowing.

DIVINE PUNISHMENT: OUTCOME OF DISBELIEF AND ARROGANCE

¹³ If they turn away say: "I warned you of a thunderbolt like the thunderbolt of Ad and Thamud." ¹⁴ When their messengers came to them from all sides *saying,*ᵈ "Worship God alone," they replied, "Had Our Lord so wanted He would have sent angels; we refuse to accept what you have been sent with." ¹⁵ The *people of* Ad behaved arrogantly and unjustly on the land, and boasted, "Who is stronger than us?" Didn't they realise God created them, He is stronger than them? But they still rejected Our messages. ¹⁶ So, over a few ill-fated days We sent a violent roaring wind to give them a taste of the shocking punishment in this life and an even more shameful one in the Hereafter, and they won't be helped. ¹⁷ Similarly, We gave *the people of* Thamud guidance, but they preferred blindness instead of guidance, so they were struck by a thunderbolt of a shocking punishment for what they did. ¹⁸ But, We saved the obedient believers.

EARS, EYES AND SKIN WILL GIVE EVIDENCE

¹⁹ The Day all enemies of God are gathered in Hell, they will be divided into groups, and ²⁰ when they reach it, their ears, eyes and skins will testify against them for their misdeeds. ²¹ They will ask their skins, "Why did you testify against us?" They will reply, "God is the One Who taught everything to speak and has taught us to speak too, and He created you the first time and to Him you will be returned." ²² You didn't try to hide your evil deeds from your ears, your eyes and your skin. But you thought that God didn't know what you did. ²³ That's what you imagined about your Lord and it ruined you, so you became losers. ²⁴ Even if they are patient now, the Fire will be their home. No matter how much forgiveness they seek, they won't be pardoned.

SATAN MISLEADS BY MAKING THINGS SEEM GRATIFYING

²⁵ We appointed companions for them that make things seem attractive for them everywhere.ᵉ Sentence was passed against them, the jinns and people before them: "They will be the losers". ²⁶ The disbelievers shouted, "Don't listen to this Quran; *you can* drown it out with noisy laughter so you would prevail." ²⁷ We shall give

ᵈ It literally means, "from the front and the behind", an idiom employed for persuading with powerful arguments from all sides.

ᵉ Literally, "in front and behind them", but implies "all things everywhere".

the disbelievers a taste of severe punishment and repay them for the worst deed they did. ²⁸ A payback for the enemies of God: Hell, where they will be forever, a reward for rejecting Our messages! ²⁹ The disbelievers will say, "Our Lord, show the jinn and humans who misguided us, so we may crush them under our feet to make them lowest of the low."

THE ANGELS MOTIVATE THE STEADFAST

³⁰ People who say, "God is Our Lord," and are steadfast are visited *and motivated* by the angels: "Don't fear nor be sad, be happy with the news of promised Paradise. ³¹ We are your friends in this life and the Hereafter, and you will have whatever your souls want in Paradise: every wish fulfilled. ³² A warm hospitality from the Forgiver, the Caring Lord."

THE PREACHERS ARE POLITE, APPROACHABLE

³³ Whose speech can be better than the one who calls to God and acts righteously and openly says: "I am a Muslim." ³⁴ Good and evil aren't the same; counter evil with goodness, and if there was *any* enmity between you and the other, he will become a dearest friend. ³⁵ Only the patient are like this; they are fortunate. ³⁶ If Satan tempts you, seek God's protection. He is the Listener, the Knower.

RAIN GIVES DRY LAND LIFE; GOD GIVES THE DEAD LIFE

³⁷ The night and the day, the sun and the moon are among His signs. Don't worship the sun or the moon; worship God their Creator, if you *truly* worship Him. ³⁸ If they are arrogant about worshipping God, so what, there are many in His service who glorify Him day and night, they never get tired. ³⁹ You will see among His signs a dry, barren land[a]; when We send rain it swells and plants grow there – the One Who gives life to it will bring the dead to life. He has power over all things. ⁴⁰ Those who reject Our verses aren't hidden from Us. So how can the one thrown in the Fire be better than the one who comes safely through on Judgement Day? Do what you like; He sees what you do.

THE QURAN: THE PROTECTED, A GUIDANCE AND A HEALING

⁴¹ Those who deny the Quran when it comes to them *do not realise* that it is a honourable book[b] ⁴² that cannot be influenced by falsehood from any angle,[c] a

---

[a]   *Khashiatan* literally means calm and serene, a metaphor applied to barren land.

[b]   *Kitabun aziz* can also mean indomitable and unassailable, sound and irrefutable.

[c]   *Mimbain yadihe wa min khalfihi* means "from front and behind", an idiom for "from all angles".

revelation from the Wise, the Praiseworthy. [43] Messenger, what is said to you was said to the messengers before you; Your Lord is the Forgiver and the Lord of a painful torment. [44] Had We written the Quran in a foreign language they would have complained: "If only its verses were made clear." What, in a foreign language yet he is an Arab: "It is a guidance and a healing for those who believe, but those who don't believe are hard of hearing and blind to it, as *though* they are being called from far away." [45] We gave Moses the Book, but disagreement arose about it too. If Your Lord's sentence had not been passed against them, their disagreements would have been settled. They are doubtful and distrustful.

NOTHING IS HIDDEN FROM GOD

[46] Whoever does good does so for himself, and whoever does evil harms himself. Your Lord is not unjust to His servants. [47] God alone has the knowledge of the Final Hour: no fruit comes out of its cover, neither a female conceives nor gives birth except with His knowledge. On that Day He will ask them: "Where are my partners?" They will say, "We declare *before* You we aren't their witness." [48] Those they worshipped before will have vanished, and they will know there is no escape.

HOW QUICKLY PEOPLE'S MOOD CHANGES

[49] Man never tires of praying for good, but at times of difficulty he becomes hopeless and sad. [50] When We are kind to him[d] after a misfortune he claims, "This is all my doing, and I don't think that the Final Hour will come, and even if I'm returned to my Lord I'm sure to receive Paradise from Him."[e] We will tell them what they did and torment them with a severe punishment.[f] [51] When We are gracious to a person he turns away and stays aloof, but at times of difficulty he prays and prays.

WHAT DOES THE QURAN EXPECT OF US?

[52] Say: "Consider *this:* if this *Quran* is really from God and you deny it, who would be the biggest loser other than the one who opposed it openly?" [53] Soon We shall show them Our signs in the horizons and in themselves so the Truth becomes clear to them. Isn't Your Lord enough, a witness over all things? [54] Beware! They are in doubt about meeting Their Lord. Beware! Everything is in His grasp.

---

d   Literally, "When We make him taste".

e   *Husna* is Paradise, according to most commentators.

f   Literally it is "make them taste".

42. Ash-Shura
The Consultation

This chapter was revealed in the middle Makkan period, at a time when the Muslims were being severely persecuted. The Makkans didn't just object to the belief in the Oneness of God, but denied that a human being could be a prophet. This awesome objection is refuted: "The Heavens are about to cleave" (5), so absurd and insulting was their conviction. The central theme is the truthfulness of prophethood. In describing the unique, distinctive and the otherness of God the Quran states: "There is nothing like Him" (11).

A list of tips for encountering the other is given: invite people to the way of God; be patient; don't follow others' whims; believe firmly; be just; be tolerant; be responsible; don't argue; and finally, "God will gather us together and all will return to Him" (15).

"You will see *the wrongdoers* in a state of terror because of what they did and its consequences will unfold before them. But the righteous believers will be in the gardens of Paradise" (22). The message is one of making the right choice: do you want the harvest of this life, or the Hereafter? The mission of the Prophet ﷺ is to help us make the right choice: "Say, 'I don't ask you for any reward for this work, except, "love one's relatives"'" (23). The next few verses explain the wisdom behind differences in human abilities and talents. Without this difference between the rich and poor and varying abilities, there would be no rank and file, no discipline and no organisation; people would be unwilling to cooperate with each other. Consequently, human civilisation wouldn't flourish. The next section (36–39) gives nine tips for social harmony; "the works one ought to do" (41): avoid major sins, indecency and anger; forgive; obey the Almighty; pray; mutual consultation; give charity; be courageous in standing up for the rights of others. A powerful appeal is made to humanity: "Come back[a] to your Lord before the Day when there will be no turning back from God. You will find no place to escape that Day, nor will you be able to deny your sins"[b] (47).

At the end the subject of prophethood, God's channel of communication, is covered briefly, dispelling the Makkans' cynicism and doubts. Since not all human beings can speak to God directly, He sends His prophets, with whom He communicates by revelation, from behind a screen, or by sending an angel with revelation (51).

---

[a]   Literally an instruction to answer, but the implication is "come back". That's how I translated it.
[b]   *Nakeer* means helper, supporter, and changer: someone who could change the punishment.

In the name of God, the Kind the Caring.

The Quran is God's Revelation

[1] *Ha Meem,* [2] *Ain Seen Qaaf.* [3] This is what God the Almighty, the Wise revealed to you, and those before you. [4] Everything in the Heavens and the Earth belongs to Him; the Exalted, the Great. [5] The Heavens above nearly collapsed, the angels glorify and praise their Lord and seek forgiveness for those on Earth. God is the Forgiving, the Caring. [6] Those who have taken lords[c] beside God know that He watches over them; you aren't their keeper.

The Quran cautions

[7] We revealed an Arabic Quran, so you may warn the people of Makkah[d] and its surroundings of the Day of Gathering, in which is no doubt; a group *will be* in the Garden and *another* group in the blazing Fire. [8] Had God wanted He would have made them one community, but He allows into His Care whom He pleases. The disobedient have no friend, no helper. [9] Have they taken lords or protectors beside Him? God is the only Lord, He gives life to the dead and controls all things. [10] Whatever you disagree about, the final decision will be God's, that's God, My Lord; I trust Him, and I turn to Him *sincerely.*

There is nothing like God

[11] Creator of the Heavens and the Earth. He made the pair of you, the human species, so you may multiply *on Earth,* and a pair of each livestock. Nothing is like Him and He is the Hearing and the Seeing. [12] The keys to the Heavens and the Earth belong to Him. He increases or decreases the provision as He pleases. He knows all things.

The unity of the Divine Message over the ages

[13] He made the *same* religion for you as for Noah; We revealed the same to Abraham, Moses and Jesus, to accept this religion and not be divided. What you call them to, the idolaters dislike. God selects and guides to Himself anyone He wants.[e] [14] The conflict among people, despite having knowledge, was caused by

c   *Awliya* is the plural of *wali*: near, friend and patron. Here, it means *Mutawalli li umur al alam,* "Lord of worldly affairs".

d   Literally *Umm ul Qura* refers to "mother of towns", a name for the city of Makkah.

e   Two ways in which God blesses people: He selects some; the prophets, truthful, and martyrs; secondly anyone who earnestly turns to God.

jealousy. Had your Lord's sentence, *that* they will be given respite for a fixed term, not been passed, then the Judgment would have come *sooner.* Those who were made heirs of the Book, *Jews and Christians,* are in doubt and are making others doubt too.

MANNERS FOR INTERFAITH DIALOGUE

[15] Therefore, continue inviting *people to the truth;* remain steadfast as you have been commanded; do not follow their whims, *but* say: "I believe in what God has revealed from the Book; I have been commanded to be fair to you; God is our Lord and your Lord; our works are for us and yours for you; there is no argument between us and you; God will gather us all and we'll return to Him."

DEBATING ABOUT GOD IS DISLIKED

[16] Those who debate God's *being and attributes* after He has been accepted, their arguments are meaningless in the sight of their Lord, upon them is wrath, and they shall have a severe punishment. [17] God sent down the Book with truth and scales of justice, and the Final Hour is near. [18] The disbelievers want to hasten its onset, and the believers are fearful of it, since they know it's the truth. But those in doubt have gone far astray.

THE BIG QUESTION: HARVEST OF THIS LIFE OR THE HEREAFTER?

[19] God is most Caring to His servants, provides sustenance as He pleases, He is the Strong, the Almighty. [20] Those who want the harvest of the Hereafter, We shall increase its harvest for them, and those who want the harvest of this life, We shall give its harvest to them, but they won't have a share in the Hereafter.

PEOPLE REAP WHAT THEY SOW

[21] Did their idols start a religion without God's permission? Had the judgement not been passed, their fate would have long been sealed, and for the wrongdoers is a painful punishment. [22] You will see them in a state of terror because of what they did, as they face its consequences. But the believers who were righteous will be in the Gardens of Paradise, where their wishes will be fulfilled; they'll have whatever they wish from their Lord. What a great bounty! [23] God gives this good news to His believing, righteous servants. Say: "I don't ask you for any reward, except, 'love one's relatives'. And whoever does a good deed We shall increase its positive impact for him. God is Forgiving, Rewarding. People deny and disobey

but God is ready to forgive

²⁴ How dare they say, "He has invented a lie about God." In that case God would have sealed your heart and blotted out the falsehood, and established the truth with His Words. He knows what's in people's minds. ²⁵ He accepts the repentance of His servants, forgives evil deeds, knows what you are doing, ²⁶ answers the righteous believers, and increases His bounty for them. But for the disbelievers there is a severe punishment.

WHY SOME PEOPLE HAVE MORE WEALTH THAN OTHERS

²⁷ Were God to give all the people same amount of sustenance in the city, they would be indifferent to each other, but God gives it in right measure as He pleases; He is Aware and watching His servants. ²⁸ He sends the rain when they lose hope, and spreads His kindness all around. He is the Helper, the Praiseworthy.

HUMANS CAN'T DISRUPT GOD'S PLANS

²⁹ Among His signs are the creation of the Heavens and the Earth, and the living things He has spread out. He will gather them together when He likes. ³⁰ The misfortune you face is due to your own fault.ᵃ However, God forgives much. ³¹ You can't disrupt *God's plan*ᵇ on Earth; you have no protector and helper beside Him. ³² Among His signs are the ships sailing on *open* seas, *appearing* like mountains. ³³ He could stop the wind blowing if He wished, so they would stand still on the surface *of the sea*. In that are signs for every patient and thankful person. ³⁴ Or else He could wreck *their ship*, because of what they have done, but God forgives a lot. ³⁵ Those who argue aboutᶜ Our message, *let them know* there's no escape for them.

THE WORKS ONE OUGHT TO DO; NINE SOCIAL AND SPIRITUAL ACTIONS

³⁶ What you are given is passing enjoyment of the worldly life, and what God has is lasting and excellent; it will be given to the believers who: trust their Lord; ³⁷ avoid major sins of indecency; forgive readily when angered; ³⁸ respond by obeying their Lord; perform the prayer; consult each other to settle their affairs; spend what We have provided them; ³⁹ when oppressed they defend themselves. ⁴⁰ A revenge against a wrong could turn into an equal evil, therefore be careful and forgive and put things right through reconciliation; such a person will have

---

ᵃ   Literally, "a result of what your hands have done".

ᵇ   *Mu'jizeen* literally, to debilitate and to weaken something; escape and frustrate.

ᶜ   An alternative meaning is "who question".

his reward from God directly. God does not like the wrongdoers. [41] Anyone who defends himself against injustice mustn't be blamed; [42] the blame is on those who commit injustice and oppress people in the city. For them will be a painful punishment. [43] Whoever is patient and forgives, *now* these are things one ought to do.[a]

DISBELIEVERS WILL BE DISGRACED IN DUNGEONS

[44] Whoever God allows to go astray will have no helper after that, and you will see the wrongdoers when they see the punishment; they will say, "Is there any way of going back?" [45] And you will see them offered to Hell, overwhelmed and disgraced, looking around ashamedly,[b] whilst the believers will say, "Today, on Judgement Day, the losers ruined themselves and their families." Beware, the wrongdoers will have eternal punishment. [46] They will have no protectors beside God to help them, and whoever God allows to go astray will not find his way.

A CALL TO COME BACK

[47] Come back[c] to your Lord before the Day when there will be no turning back from God. You will find nowhere to escape that Day, nor be able to deny your sins.[d] [48] If they turn away from you *Prophet*! Know, We didn't send you as their keeper; your responsibility is to deliver the Message. When We give people a taste of Our kindness they are joyful, but when times are difficult because of their fault they are ungrateful. [49] The Heavens and the Earth belong to God; He creates what He pleases, He gives daughters or sons as He pleases to whom He pleases, [50] to some He gives boys and girls and others He leaves childless as He pleases. He is the Knower, the Powerful.

THE QURAN GIVES DETAILS OF FAITH

[51] God doesn't speak to any human being *directly*, except by revelation from behind a screen, or an angel brings the revelation by His permission. He is the Exalted, the Wise. [52] So, We revealed to you the essence of Our command when you didn't know *the details of* faith or the Scripture. We made it a light and We guide with it whom We please from among Our servants. And you are guiding them to

---

[a] *Azmi-l-'umuur* literally means determination and resolution; to show resolve.

[b] Or with a furtive glance.

[c] Literally this is an instruction to answer or respond, but the implication is "come back"; that is how it has been translated here.

[d] *Nakeer* also means helper and supporter, or someone who might change the punishment.

a straight path, [53] the path of God – His is what is in the Heavens and the Earth[c] – in the end, all things will return to God.

---

[c]   *'A laa* is a participle meaning: is it not? Are they not? It implies "the fact" is and "but".

43. Az-Zukhruf
The Golden Ornaments

This chapter was revealed in the middle Makkan period, at the height of the tension. The darkest days of the Prophet's ﷺ struggle. It opens by demonstrating the unconditionally loving and forgiving nature of God: "Shall We turn away from you and deprive you of this Reminder because you are people who've gone beyond limits?" (5) No matter how heartless and unwilling people are to God's Message and His messenger, He continues to provide guidance.

The contradictory beliefs of the disbelievers are exposed: on one hand they believed in God as the Creator, but on the other they worshipped idols. "If you ask them who created the Heavens and the Earth they will certainly say they were created by the Almighty, the Knower" (9). Another one of their contradictory beliefs was the idea that the angels were God's daughters. They felt shamed if they had daughters, but they happily assigned angels as God's daughters.

They criticised the Prophet Muhammad ﷺ because he was poor and therefore unfit to lead. The Quran rejects their criticism; "if it were not for the prospect of everyone becoming a disbeliever, He would have given the disbelievers so much wealth that the roofs, the staircases and the furnishing of their homes would be made of gold and silver" (33–35).

The chapter also teaches the wisdom behind differences in individuals' capabilities and skills: "Do they distribute your Lord's kindness? We distribute among them their livelihoods in this worldly life, and We raise some among others in ranks so that some may take others in employment" (32). Without this there would be no rank and file to help civilisations to flourish. To illustrate how wealth and power can corrupt people, the Quran gives the example of the Pharaoh: "The Pharaoh declared to his people, 'My people, is not the country of Egypt and all these rivers flowing beneath my feet mine?'" (51). The Pharaoh despised Moses simply because the latter did not have "golden bracelets". The Quran teaches, this is a mean and miserly attitude.

Their persistent objection to the Glorious Quran is rejected: "This Quran is a great honour for you and your people; you will be questioned about it" (44). The Makkans were rude about the Prophet Jesus : "Whenever the example of the son of Mary is given, your people kick up a fuss about it, and say, "Are our gods better or is he?'" (57–58). The Quran praises him and announces his return as the sign of the Final Hour.

The purpose of revelation is to caution people about the consequences of their actions in this life, and to motivate them to accept the truth. To achieve this it presents vivid descriptions of life in Paradise and life in Hell: "*They will be told,* 'Enter the Garden, you and your spouses *together* happily.' *Food and drink* in golden trays and cups shall be passed around. Everything that one desires and the eyes delight in will be there; here you will live forever. This is the Garden you are made heirs of, *a reward* for what you did. *Here* you will have plenty of fruit to eat from" (70–73). This is vividly contrasted with the misery of Hell (74–78).

The chapter opened with the loving and the forgiving nature of God, and ends by advising: "*Prophet,* forgive them and say, 'Peace'; they will come to know" (89).

In the name of God, the Kind, the Caring

[1] *Ha Meem.*

GOD WILL NOT STOP GUIDING HUMANITY

[2] By the Book whose teachings are clear, [3] We sent an Arabic Quran so you may understand. [4] Preserved in the Divine Tablet, securely with Us; it is majestic and full of wisdom. [5] Should We turn away and deprive you[a] of this reminder because you are people who have gone beyond limits? [6] We sent many prophets to the past generations; [7] when a prophet came to them they mocked him, [8] so We destroyed them. They were stronger than them, and now they are part of history.

THE PRAYER FOR TRAVELLING

[9] If you ask them who created the Heavens and the Earth they will say they were created by the Almighty, the Knower, [10] Who made the Earth flat[b] and in it made many paths so that you may find your way around. [11] He sent rain from the sky in *carefully* measured amounts; with it We bring dead land to life, similarly you will be brought out *alive from graves.* [12] He created all kinds of things, made ships and livestock for you to ride on, [13] sitting comfortably on their backs remembering the bounties of your Lord, and when you are mounted comfortably on them you *should* pray: "Glory to Him Who made this for our benefit; we weren't capable of controlling it, [14] and we are returning to our Lord."

DISAPPROVAL OF THE DISCRIMINATION AGAINST DAUGHTERS

[15] Do *the idolaters* think some of His servants are *His* offspring? Humans are openly unthankful. [16] So God chose daughters for Himself from His creation and preferred sons for you? [17] When one of them is given the good news of what he

---

[a] *Dharabtu anho safhan,* an Arabic idiom used when someone turns away from something, ignoring it (Al-Qurtubi).

[b] *Mahdan* literally means flat and small. However, commentators say this is not contradicting the fact that the Earth is a sphere, because it is so big and vast that the roundness is not felt as far as the eye can see.

ascribes to the Most Kind, his face turns dark and he is furious: [18] "What!" One who is brought up in fine jewellery and incapable of presenting a case clearly.[a] [19] They describe the angels who are servants of the Most Kind as females. Were they present at their creation? Their false claims are recorded and they will be questioned.

THE IDOLATERS DENY FREE WILL

[20] They say, "If the Most Kind wanted, we wouldn't have worshipped the idols." They don't understand what they are *saying* and guessing. [21] Or have We given them a book before this which they follow? [22] No; they say, "We found our forefathers on this path and we are guided by their footsteps." [23] Similarly, when We sent a Warner before you to a town, the affluent people[b] said, "We found our forefathers on this path and we are followers in their footsteps." [24] The Prophet said, "If I bring you a better guide than what you received from your forefathers, even then?" They said, "We are deniers of your message." [25] Consequently, We punished them; look what was the fate of the deniers.

THE IDOLATERS WOULD LIKE A CELEBRITY TO BE A PROPHET

[26] Remember when Abraham told his father and his people, "I reject what you worship [27] and I worship the One Who created me, and He guides me." [28] And he implemented *this* word[c] among his children so they may return *to it.* [29] I let them and their forefathers enjoy life, until the truth *eventually* came to them and a noble messenger who explained clearly. [30] When the truth came to them they said, "This is magic and so we deny it." [31] And said, "Why was this Quran not sent down on a famous personality from one of the two towns?"[d] [32] Are they distributing your Lord's Kindness? We Ourselves distribute among them their livelihoods in this worldly life, and We raise some among others in ranks so some may take others in employment. Your Lord's Kindness is more excellent than the treasures they gather.

HOUSES OF SILVER AND GOLD

[33] And if it weren't for the prospect that people would become one *disbelieving*

---

[a] These are the attitudes of the Arab idolaters about women, and not the Divine Teaching.

[b] *Mutraf* means "one who enjoys a life of plenty" and "indulges in pleasures".

[c] *Kalimatan* here means "declaration of the unity of God".

[d] This refers to the two towns of Makkah and Taif.

community, We would have made for the deniers of the Most Kind, houses with silver roofs and stairways to climb; [34] the gates of their houses and the couches on which they rest would be made of silver, [35] and they would be *surrounded* by golden ornaments. These are mere enjoyments of worldly life. *The delights* of your Lord in the Hereafter are for the pious.

WHOSE COMPANION IS SATAN?

[36] Anyone who turns a blind eye to the Most Kind's reminder, will have a Satan appointed as their close companion. [37] They will stop them from following the straight path but they will believe they are guided. [38] Until he comes to Us and says, "Woe! I wish we were poles apart[c]" what an evil companion. [39] *This criticism* today will not benefit you at all since you have sinned and now you will share the punishment together. [40] Can you make the deaf hear or guide the blind? Or the misguided. [41] Even if We took you away We would certainly punish them, [42] or We shall show you the punishment We have promised them, and We can do so. [43] So, hold firmly what's revealed to you, since you are on the straight path. [44] This Quran is a great honour for you and your people; you will be questioned about it. [45] And ask Our messengers We sent before you: did We ever allow gods beside God to be worshipped?

MOSES WAS SIMILARLY INSULTED BY THE PHARAOH

[46] We sent Moses with Our signs to Pharaoh and his nobles. *Moses* said, "I am a messenger from the Lord of the worlds". [47] When he came to them with Our miracles they laughed at him. [48] Every miracle We showed them was greater than the previous one, and each time We punished them *for rejecting it,* hoping they might return. [49] And they kept saying, "Magician! Pray for us to your Lord through the contract you have with Him; we will certainly accept guidance." [50] However, as soon as We removed the punishment from them, they broke the promise.

THE PHARAOH BOASTED LIKE THE MAKKANS

[51] The Pharaoh announced to his people: "My people, isn't the kingdom of Egypt and the rivers flowing under my feet mine? Can't you see? [52] Am I not better than this wretched person who can barely express himself? [53] Why hasn't he been given golden bracelets? Why are there no angels sent down with him?" [54] So he fooled

c   "There was between me and you the distance of the two Easts".

his people[a] and they followed him. They were a sinful people. [55]Then when they roused Our anger, We punished them by drowning them all, [56]We made them a thing of the past and an example for those coming after them.

The Prophet Jesus is a sign of the Final Hour

[57]Whenever the example of the son of Mary is given, your people kick up a fuss about it[b] [58]and say, "Are our gods better or him?" They say this just to annoy you; they really are a quarrelsome lot. [59]He was Our blessed servant who We made a model for the Israelites. [60]Had We wanted, We could have made angels on Earth to succeed you. [61]He is indeed a sign of the Final Hour, so don't doubt it and follow me; this is the straight path, [62]let not the Satan stop you, since he is your open enemy. [63]When Jesus came with clear signs he said, "I have come with wisdom to you and to clarify for you those things in which you differ, so be mindful of God and obey me; [64]indeed God is Mine and Your Lord, worship Him. This is the straight path." [65]Then groups began bickering amongst themselves. So woe to the wrongdoers when they will suffer the punishment of a painful Day. [66]Are they waiting for the sudden coming of the Final Hour when they are unaware? [67]Even best friends on that Day will be each other's enemies – but not the pious.

The delights of Paradise

[68]My servants, today don't fear nor worry. [69]Those who believed in our Scriptures and were true Muslims, [70]*they will be told*: "Enter the Garden; you and your spouses *together* happily." [71]*Food and drink* in golden trays and cups shall be passed around. Everything that one desires and the eyes delight in will be there; here you will live forever. [72]This is the Garden you are made heirs of, *a reward* for your works. [73]*Here* you will have plenty of fruit to eat from.

The wicked will stay in Hell forever

[74]The wicked will be punished in Hell forever. [75]It will not be lightened for them, so they will lose all hope. [76]We didn't wrong them, they wronged themselves. [77]"Angel," they will call out, "If only your Lord would finish us off." He will reply, "You are here to stay forever!" [78]We brought the truth to you, but most of you disliked the truth. [79]Yes, if they have made a final decision, let them know We have

---

[a] *Fastakhaff qaumahu* can also mean: "he incited his people". It could also mean, "make a fool of someone."

[b] The Makkans would argue our worship of Angels is like the Christian worshipping Jesus as 'the son of God', so why do you object? Since you call them the People of the Book. Their line of reasoning is rejected.

also made a final decision. [80] Or do they think We don't hear their secret chats and private discussions? No, Our messengers *standing* by their sides are recording them. [81] Say: "If the most Kind had a son, I would be *his* first worshipper. [82] Glory be to the Lord of the Heavens and the Earth, the Lord of the Throne, from what they ascribe to Him." [83] Leave them in idle talk and amusement until they meet their Day, which they have been promised.

Only the truthful are allowed to intercede

[84] He is the only God in the sky, and He is the only God on Earth, the Wise, the Knower. [85] Blessed is He to Whom the Heavens and the Earth belongs and all that is between them, and He knows the coming of the Final Hour and to Him you will be returned. [86] Those they worship beside Him have no right of intercession; only those who bear witness to the truth will have the right to intercession, and they know that. [87] If you ask them: "Who created them?" They will certainly say, "God," so why are they deceived? [88] And I swear by what He says, "My Lord, these are a people who don't believe." [89] *Prophet* forgive them and say: "Peace," they will come to know *the reality*.

44. Ad-Dukhan
The Smoke

According to some commentators, this Makkan chapter was revealed after a famine struck Makkah; the dust blew, and Makkah was covered with a cloud of dust. The Makkans came to the Prophet 鐮 and asked him to pray for relief from the famine, they promised to believe if they were relieved. He 鐮 prayed and it rained, but the Makkans didn't keep their word, like the people of Pharaoh they broke their promise. The Quran tells the story as a deterrent. Some commentators believe the smoke cloud refers to a catastrophe that will occur near the Final Hour, possibly a nuclear explosion.

The chapter paints a frightening picture of the people of Hell; fed from the tree known as Zaqqum, when its fruit enters the stomach, it boils. What a contrast to the delights that await the pious people of Paradise. The purpose of the Quran is to awaken God-consciousness in people: "So wait, they *the disbelievers* are also waiting" (59).

In the name of God, the Kind, the Caring.

¹ *Ha Meem.*

THE QURAN WAS REVEALED ON A BLESSED NIGHT

² By the clear readable book, ³ We revealed it on a blessed night and have been warning *humanity*. ⁴ In it every matter is decided wisely; ⁵ all the commands come from Ourselves, We send *Message and messengers,* ⁶ a favour from Your Lord – the Hearer, the Knower, ⁷ the Lord of the Heavens and the Earth and what is between them – if only you are firm believers.

MAKKANS' ARE TESTED BY A FAMINE

⁸ There is no god but Him, He gives life and death, Your Lord and the Lord of your forefathers. ⁹ *Unfortunately*, they are in doubt, dilly-dallying.ᵃ ¹⁰ So wait for a Day when the sky brings clouds of smoke ¹¹ that will cover up people *and they will cry*: "This is painful punishment! ¹² Our Lord, relieve us, and we will believe." ¹³ They will not learn a lesson even when a Messenger has come to them, ¹⁴ they turn away from him and say, "He's been taught by someone and is possessed!" ¹⁵ Shortly We shall remove the punishment, but they will turn back *to their disbelief.* ¹⁶ The Day We seize them brutally, We shall take full revenge.

ᵃ *Fee shakkin yal'abun* literally means "toying with doubt".

The Makkans are reminded of Pharaoh's fate

[17] Long ago We tested Pharaoh's people, when a noble messenger came saying to them, [18] "Hand over to me the servants of God; I am a trustworthy messenger sent to you. [19] Don't regard yourself greater than God; I've come with distinct authority to you. [20] I've sought protection from my Lord and your Lord from your abuse;[b] [21] if you don't believe me then leave me alone." [22] Moses called out to His Lord, "These are wicked people." [23] So *We ordered him*: "Take my servants by night, *though* you will be chased, [24] *after crossing* the sea leave it parted,[c] they will be a drowned army." [25] They, *the Pharaoh's lot,* left behind many gardens, springs, [26] cornfields and spacious homes and [27] clubs where they had fun. [28] We raised other people to inherit them, [29] neither the Heavens nor the Earth wept over them, they weren't given respite.

God favoured the Israelites

[30] We delivered the Israelites from the shameful punishment [31] of the Pharaoh; he was arrogant and had gone beyond limits. [32] We knowingly favoured them above other people *of their time.* [33] We showed them many miracles; in them was a clear test.

Life has a purpose

[34] These *Makkans* say: [35] "There is only one death for us; we won't be resurrected. [36] Why don't you bring to life our forefathers if you are truthful." [37] Are they better, or the people of Tubba[d] and the people before them? We destroyed them since they were wicked. [38] We didn't create the Heavens and the Earth and what is between them as an amusement *park.* [39] We created them for a purpose, but most don't know. [40] The Day of Decision is the fixed time for all of them, [41] a Day when no friend will benefit a friend in the slightest, nor will they be helped, [42] except anyone God wants to be kind to. He is the Mighty, the Caring.

The sinners' punishment in Hell

[43] The tree of Zaqqum [44] will be the sinners' food, [45] like molten copper that boils in the stomach, [46] bubbling like boiling water. [47] It will be said: "Seize him and drag him to the middle of Hell! [48] Then pour the punishment of boiling water

---

b   *Tarjumun* literally means to stone, abuse and expel.
c   *Rahwan* according to Al-Qurtubi means cleft or parted.
d   *Tubba* is the historic title of the Kings of Yemen of southern Arabia.

over his head. [49] Taste it! You were the honourable influential one![a] [50] This is what you doubted!"

THE PIOUS WILL ENJOY PARADISE

[51] The pious will *live* in a safe place; [52] of gardens and water fountains, [53] wearing embroidered silken dress enjoying each other's company. [54] That's how it will be, We shall wed them with pure spouses with gorgeous eyes. [55] Safe and satisfied, they will enjoy every kind of fruit. [56] They will taste death only once and will be protected from the punishment of Hell, [57] a bounty from your Lord! That is the supreme victory. [58] We made the Quran easy to understand in your language, so they may pay attention. [59] So wait, they're waiting *too*.

[a] This is irony and an example of covert contempt for them.

45. Al-Jathiyah
Kneeling

The central theme of this Makkan chapter is to acknowledge *Tawhid*, the Unity of God, and depose idols. This seminal teaching of the Quran sums up the mission of Islam. A passage about nature opens the chapter: marvellous signs in the creation clearly point to a Creator, from the plant kingdom to animals, the celestial bodies and the rain cycle. Attention is drawn to Divine creativity, and the idolaters are invited to reflect on the helplessness of their idols: "This Quran is full of insights for humanity, a guidance and beneficial for faithful people" (20).

The leaders of Quraysh vehemently opposed the Messenger ﷺ because he was too radical, and posed a serious threat to their status, wealth and belief systems. They opposed him to preserve their hegemony and customs: they sought to defend their gods, protect the status quo and the wealth they earned from pilgrims who visited the shrines. They weren't prepared to accept the Sovereignty and the Oneness of the God of Muhammad ﷺ. Too much was at stake; loss of status and power.

The disbelievers are warned of the consequences of their rebellion: "When you will see all the communities kneeling down. Today, each community will be summoned to its Book of Deeds" (28). They "mocked God's verses and were deceived by worldly life" (35) to their own detriment. The chapter ends as it began, by emphasising the greatness of God.

In the name of God, the Kind, the Caring.

¹ *Ha Meem.*

Signs of God's greatness in nature

² This *Majestic* Book is revealed by God, the Almighty, the Wise. ³ There are *plenty* of signs for the believers in the Heavens and the Earth; ⁴ and in your creation and the way creatures have been dispersed *around the globe, there* are signs for people of firm faith. ⁵ In the alternation of the night and the day, and *the rain* which He sends from the sky and the blowing winds, *a* delivery that brings the dead Earth to life. These are signs for intelligent people, ⁶ *clear* signs *of* God's *creative power;* We described them exactly as they are. So what kind of message will they believe in once God has explained His Signs?

Signs of God's greatness in the Scripture

⁷ Woe to every liar and sinner ⁸ who hears the verses of God recited in front of

him, but remains stubbornly arrogant as though he hasn't heard them. So give him the good news of a painful punishment. ⁹When he hears something about Our Scripture he mocks it. They deserve a humiliating punishment. ¹⁰Hell is waiting for them – nothing they did nor those who they took as friends beside God will benefit them – they will have a painful punishment. ¹¹A painful punishment for those who deny *this Quran*, a guidance, the Scripture of their Lord.

GOD CREATED NATURE FOR HUMAN BENEFIT

¹²God laid open the sea for you, so ships sail in it by His command, making it possible for you to seek His bounty and be thankful. ¹³*As a favour,* He has subjected everything for your benefit in the Heavens and the Earth; there are signs for reflective people. ¹⁴Say to the believers: "Pardon those who have no hope of God's days," God will reward people for what they earned. ¹⁵Whoever does good deeds will benefit himself and whoever does evil will harm himself. Then, you will be returned to Your Lord.

THE ISRAELITES ALSO DISAGREED

¹⁶We gave the Book, the law, prophethood, and plenty of wealth to the Israelites, and *furthermore* favoured them over other folks. ¹⁷We gave them clear proofs for the law, and though they had knowledge they still disagreed among themselves, they were jealous of each other. On Judgement Day, Your Lord will make the judgement about their disagreement.

THE QURAN GIVES ENLIGHTENMENT TO THE FAITHFUL

¹⁸*Prophet,* We established a Shariah for you,[a] so follow it and don't follow the whims of those who don't know. ¹⁹They won't benefit you in the slightest against the Will of God. The wrongdoers are each other's helpers while God is the helper of the pious. ²⁰This Quran is full of insights for humanity,[b] and a guidance and other benefits for faithful people. ²¹Or do evildoers think We will make them like the righteous believers, so they are like them in their living and dying? They've made a bad judgement.

---

[a] *Shariah* literally means "the path to a watering hole", and technically refers to the system of Islamic law, moral values, social manners, and spiritual principles.

[b] *Basaa'ir* literally means insights, understanding underlying truths and meanings; seeing beyond the visible and being able to understand the character and the context.

THEIR DESIRES ARE THEIR GODS

[22] God created the Heavens and the Earth for a purpose: to reward each person for what they did and they won't be wronged. [23] Have you seen him who made desire his god despite knowing otherwise? God let him go astray, sealed his hearing and heart and covered his eyes. Who will guide him now beside God? Don't you pay attention? [24] They say, "There is no life except our worldly life, we die, we live and *eventually*, time will kill us." They have no understanding of the reality, and they are merely guessing.

THE BOOK OF DEEDS WILL BE PRESENTED

[25] When our clear verses are recited before them they're unable to *find* proofs against them, but they still say, "Bring back to life our forefathers if you are truthful." [26] Tell them: "God gave you life, then will let you die and then gather you on Judgement Day, there is no doubt in that. But most people don't know." [27] The control of the Heavens and the Earth belongs to God. When the Final Hour comes the followers of falsehood will be the losers that Day. [28] You will see all communities kneeling. Today, each community will be summoned to its Book of Deeds, and told: "You shall be rewarded for what you did, [29] this is Our record, it speaks the truth, everything you did We wrote down." [30] So those who believed and did righteous deeds, their Lord will be kind to them; that will be the clear victory. [31] Those who disbelieved will be asked: "Were My verses not recited to you? No, you were arrogant and a wicked lot."

THE LIFE OF THE WORLD DECEIVED THEM

[32] When it was said: "God's promise is true and there is no doubt *in the coming of* the Final Hour," you replied, "We don't know what the Final Hour is; we assumed it's an idea, and we weren't convinced at all". [33] The evil consequences of their deeds will become clear to them as they are tracked by what they mocked. [34] They will be told: "Today We'll abandon you since you forgot the meeting of this Day of yours; this is your destination – Hell. You have no helpers. [35] That is because you mocked God's verses and were deceived by worldly life." So today they won't be taken out of it, nor given an opportunity to explain themselves.[c]
[36] All the praises are for God; the Lord of the Heavens, the Lord of the Earth and

---

[c]   *Yusta'thabun* literally means "to demand repentance from a sinner". Here it means, on Judgement Day, when the reality dawns on them and they see Hell, they will want to repent, but that won't happen.

Lord of the worlds. [37] All greatness in the Heavens and the Earth is His and He is the Almighty, the Wise.

46. Al-Ahqaf
The Sand Dunes

This chapter was revealed before the migration of the Prophet ﷺ to Madinah, the tone and tenor of the chapter makes this clear. The Prophet ﷺ is advised: "be patient like the strong-willed messengers" (35). The boycott faced by the Muslims in the valley of Abu-Talib for three years had been lifted. Here they had languished in abject poverty and starvation, which left them with physical and psychological scars.

A group of jinn visited the Prophet ﷺ on his return from the torturous journey to Taif. If so, then this chapter would have been revealed in the tenth or eleventh year of his mission in Makkah. The opening describes the helplessness of the idols, and contrasts it with the creative power of God. Then it explains how God's channel of communication was always open with humanity through His messengers, therefore the coming of Prophet Muhammad ﷺ was nothing new or odd. In fact, his coming was foreseen by Moses :

An Israelite witness has already testified to the coming of one like him, and has believed, why are you being arrogant? God does not guide the wrongdoers (10).

This refers to Deuteronomy 18, verses 15–18. The Quran comments on the suspicious mind of the disbelievers: "The disbelievers say to the believers, 'If this *religion* was any good then you wouldn't have believed in it before us'" (11).

Verses 15–19 encourage the development of parent-child relationships, by describing how the mother bears the child and then suckles and rears it until the child becomes strong and mature. Just as we should be grateful to our parents and appreciative of what they have blessed us with, we should be thankful to God, our Lord and Creator. The chapter goes on to warn the Makkans of the demise of the People of the Sand Dunes, who were rebellious, and then towards the closing of the chapter relates the story of a band of jinn who visited the Prophet ﷺ as an encouragement to believe in him: the loyalty and submission of the jinn is a mark of being Muslims among the invisible creatures of God.

In the name of God, the Kind, the Caring.

¹ *Ha Meem.*

THE HELPLESSNESS OF IDOLS

² This glorious Book is sent down by God, the Almighty, the Wise. ³ We created Heavens and the Earth and what lies between them with a purpose only, for a fixed term. The disbelievers turn away from the warning given to them. ⁴ Say:

"Have you seriously considered those you worship beside God? Show me what they have created on Earth, or were they partners in *the creation* of Heavens? Bring me a book from the past or any remnants of knowledge[a] if you are truthful." ⁵Who is more misguided than the one who worships things that don't answer him beside God, till Judgement Day they will be unaware of their worship. ⁶When they're gathered they will be their enemies, and will reject their worship.

THE COMING OF PROPHET MUHAMMAD ﷺ IS NOT A NEW THING

⁷When Our verses are recited before the disbelievers, they speak about the truth *saying*, "This is plain magic!" ⁸Or they say, "he has made this up." Say: "If I made it up you can't save me from God; He knows very well what you say about it. He is a sufficient witness between me and you. He is Forgiving and Most Caring." ⁹Say: " I am not the first of the messengers nor *do I claim* that I know what will happen to me and you, I only follow what is revealed to me and I am a clear warner." ¹⁰Say: "Have you considered: if this was from God and you denied it, *what would be the consequences?* A witness from the Israelites testified to the coming of one like himself and has believed, yet you are being arrogant.[b] God does not guide the wrongdoers.

CONTRASTING ATTITUDES OF BELIEVERS AND DISBELIEVERS

¹¹The disbelievers say to the believers, "If this *religion* was good, then you couldn't have believed it before we did." Since they didn't get any guidance from the Quran, they say, "This is an old lie," ¹²although before this Moses' Book came as a guide and a useful manual; and this Book too confirms it in the Arabic language to warn the wicked people, and to give good news to the righteous. ¹³The people who say, "Our Lord is God," remain steadfast without fear, without worry – ¹⁴these are people of Paradise, where they will live forever, a reward for what they did.

IMPORTANCE OF CARING FOR PARENTS

¹⁵We advised humanity to care for parents; in pregnancy, his mother carried him

---

ᵃ *Asaratam min ilm* is an idiom for "knowledge that has been handed down by scholars and the sages" (Ibn Hayyan Undlasi).

ᵇ This refers to Moses forecasting the coming of Prophet Muhammad ﷺ in Deuteronomy 18 : 18 : "I will raise up for them a prophet like you from among their own people; I will put My words in the mouth of the Prophet, he shall speak to them everything that I command. Anyone who does not heed the words that the prophet shall speak in My name I Myself will hold accountable."

with difficulty, and with greater difficulty she gave him birth. The pregnancy and the weaning took thirty months; when he reached his full maturity and *the* fortieth year, he prayed: "My Lord, inspire me to thank You for the gifts that You have blessed me and my parents with, and give me the ability to be righteous, to please You; make my children righteous, too. I turn towards You, and I am a Muslim." ¹⁶ These are the people whose good deeds We shall accept and forgive their sins, and they shall be people of Paradise. This is a true promise, God made with the faithful.

A DISOBEDIENT SON DENIES RESURRECTION

¹⁷ *There's the one who angrily* said to his parents, "How come! You threaten me with being brought out *of the grave,* yet generations have passed away before me." Both parents beg God for help and say to *the son,* "Woe to you! Believe in God's true promise." He replies by saying, "These are stories of the ancient." ¹⁸ These are the ones who justly deserve the fate of the bygone nations of jinn and humans. They were losers. ¹⁹ People will have rank according to their works, and will get full reward for their works, and they won't be deprived *of their rights.* ²⁰ The Day when the disbelievers will be brought in front of the Fire *it will be said*: "You wasted the precious gifts of worldly life and indulged in pleasures, so today you will be rewarded with a humiliating punishment for your arrogance without any right on Earth, and for your disobedience.

THE PEOPLE OF THE SAND DUNES REJECTED THE MESSAGE

²¹ And remember *Prophet* Hud of the tribe of Ad. When he warned his people living near the sand dunes[c] – and many messengers had come to them before and after him – telling them, "Do not worship anyone except God. I fear for you the punishment of a mighty Day," ²² they said, "Have you come to turn us away from our gods? If that is so, then bring upon us what you threaten us with, if you are truthful." ²³ Prophet Hud said, "God alone knows *it's time*; however, I will keep delivering what message is given to me, but you are stubbornly ignorant people." ²⁴ When they saw the punishment coming, *it was* a cloud moving towards their valleys; they said, "This cloud will bring us rain." *Hud said,* "Yes, it's what you eagerly wanted, a sandstorm carrying painful torment. ²⁵ It will destroy everything

---

[c] *Ahqaf,* from which the chapter takes its name, refers to the sand dunes in the southern part of the Arabian Peninsula, where the empty quarter is north of Yemen. The modern cities of Tarim and Hadramaut are in this area.

in its path by the Lord's command." Next morning, there was nothing to see except their ruined homes. That is how We repay the sinners.

THE MAKKANS ARE WARNED

²⁶ We made them stronger than you, and gave them ears, eyes and hearts, yet they didn't benefit the slightest from their ears, their eyes and their hearts, since they denied God's verses. What they used to mock overwhelmed them as punishment. ²⁷ We destroyed many towns that once flourished around you, and made clear to them the Scripture, so they may return. ²⁸ So why weren't they helped by the idols they took for nearness to gods beside God? In fact they deserted them, and this was the lie they invented.

JINN CONVERTED TO ISLAM

²⁹ Remember when We sent a group of jinn[a], they came and listened to the Quran, and said, "Listen silently." When the recitation had finished, they returned to their people to warn them. ³⁰ They told them, "Our people! We have heard a Book revealed after Moses, confirming previous Scriptures, and it guides to the truth and to the straight path. ³¹ They *continued*, "Accept the invitation of the one who calls you to God, and believe him and God will forgive your sins and save you from a painful punishment." ³² Whoever does not answer the one who summons to God, cannot escape the plan of God on Earth, and will have no helpers. They are clearly misguided.

DISBELIEVERS WILL ACCEPT THE TRUTH

³³ Don't they see that God created Heavens and the Earth, and its creation didn't tire Him out, and He is capable of giving life to the dead. Yes, He has control over all things. ³⁴ The Day when the disbelievers will be brought in front of the Fire, it will be said: "Isn't this the truth?" They will say, "By our Lord, this is truth." God will say, "Taste the punishment for your disbelief."

THE PROPHET ☷ IS ADVISED TO BE PATIENT

³⁵ Be patient, like the strong-willed messengers[b] were patient, and don't wish to hasten *the punishment* for them. The day they see the punishment they were

---

[a] Abdullah ibn Masud said "the Prophet was reading the Quran at Batan-Nakhla when a group of Jinn came; they listened quietly" (Jalalain). Batan-Nakhla is a place south of Makka near Taif.

[b] *Ulul azm* literally means "people of determination and resolve", referring to the resilience and the patience of the prophets in response to fierce persecution.

warned about, they will think they only lived an hour of the day. *This is* a true message. Only the disobedient will be destroyed!

47. Muhammad
The Beloved Messenger Muhammad ﷺ

Muslims were persecuted and oppressed in Makkah for thirteen years, and even after the migration to Madinah they were attacked. So, in the second year of Hijra Muslims were given formal permission to take up arms against oppressors: "Permission to fight is given to those who were attacked and oppressed" (*Chapter al-Hajj*: 39). Muslim scholars' unanimous opinion about war is: it is only permissible in defence. Offensive invasions are not permitted except in special circumstances. *Chapter Muhammad* was revealed in Madinah, before the Battle of Badr. It reflects the new era of hostility, at the threshold of war, and its other name is "fighting".

The chapter opens by describing the perennial conflict between truth and falsehood and urges believers to be steadfast, since the life of a believer is, in one way or another a constant battle. The chapter makes clear that Islam does not surrender to oppressors, and urges its followers to stand up against oppression and support the victims. War becomes necessary to defend people's rights and freedoms, and to defeat evil. "When you encounter the disbelievers *in battle* beat their necks ... God will never let the works of those killed in his way go to waste" (4). This is followed by images of the luxuries of Paradise: "rivers of water with never-changing taste and smell; rivers of milk whose taste never changes; rivers of wine that give pleasure to their drinkers; and rivers of pure honey; for them are all kinds of fruits" (15).

The chapter alludes to the signs of the final hour, many Ahadith give lists of these signs; the Prophet ﷺ said: "people will distribute booty among themselves, things in trust will be misused, the Zakah will be regarded as a tax, knowledge will be learnt for worldly purposes, a husband obedient to wife but disobedient to his mother; a person will be closer to his friend than father; mosques will be noisy places; wicked persons will be leaders; people will be respected to escape their harm; singers will be popular; alcohol common; people will curse ancestors; storms and Earthquakes common" (Tirmidhi).

The hypocrites were a group who were confused, unsure and disliked the new community of believers. Their malicious plots, attitudes and disgraceful behaviour is exposed. They were cynical about the Prophet ﷺ and terrified of fighting for the truth. The Prophet ﷺ is warned about them and they are identified for him, so he was made aware of them, but he did not name or shame, until after the Battle of Tabuk in the eighth year of Hijra.

Just as the chapter opened by highlighting the human tendency to war, it closes by encouraging the faithful to be ever-vigilant, willing and prepared to defend themselves against tyranny. This is a costly business, so they are urged to spend in the path of God to defend their rights. Miserliness, selfishness and self-centredness is sternly condemned.

In the name of God, the Kind, the Caring.

BELIEVING IN THE TRUTH

[1] The works of the disbelievers - who obstruct people *from accepting* God's religion - are wasted, [2] but the believers who are righteous and convinced of the truth revealed to Muhammad from His Lord, will be forgiven their sins, and God will improve their current situation. [3] This is because the disbelievers follow falsehood and the believers follow their Lord's truth. This is how God presents examples for people.

PERMISSION TO FIGHT THE AGGRESSORS

[4] When you encounter the disbelievers *in battle* beat their necks until they are thoroughly weakened, then tie them up with ropes as captives. Afterwards, you can release them gracefully or take a ransom from them, but they must have surrendered their weapons. That is an order[a]. Had God wanted, He could have taken revenge Himself from them, but he wishes to test some of you with others. God will never let the deeds of those killed go to waste. [5] He will guide and improve their situation. [6] And He shall admit them into the Paradise He guided them to.

BELIEVERS URGED TO HELP GOD'S RELIGION

[7] Believers, if you help God's *religion* then he will help you and make you firm and strong-minded. [8] On the other hand, the disbelievers will be ruined and their works will go to waste; [9] this is because they dislike what God reveals and wasted their works. [10] Haven't they travelled about in the land so they may see the fate of those people before them? God destroyed them and the same fate awaits *these* disbelievers. [11] This is because God is the protector of believers, but the disbelievers have no protector. [12] God will admit the righteous believers into Paradise, with running streams. The disbelievers today are enjoying themselves and eating like cattle, although the Fire is their final home. [13] There were many towns more powerful than the town that expelled you, yet We destroyed their residents and they had no helper.

THE FOUR RIVERS OF PARADISE

[14] Is the one who accepted the Lord's clear arguments like the one whose evil

---

[a] Literally: This is it!

deeds seem attractive and he follows his desires? [15]The Paradise promised to the God-conscious will have: rivers of water whose taste and smell never changes; rivers of milk whose taste never changes; rivers of wine that give pleasure to their drinkers; and rivers of pure honey; for them are all kinds of fruits as well as forgiveness from their Lord. Can these be like those who will be in the Fire forever, given boiling water to drink that cuts through their bowels?

THE HYPOCRITES PRETEND TO LISTEN

[16]Some of them listen carefully to you until they leave you, and say to those who were given knowledge,[a] "What was he saying just now?" These are people whose hearts God sealed and they followed their desires. [17]Those who followed the straight path, God increased their guidance and blessed them with piety. [18]So are they waiting for the Final Hour to overwhelm them suddenly? Its signs have already appeared, so what use will it be to pay attention then?[b] [19]Know, there is no God but God, and pray that God protects your people from sins,[c] and seek forgiveness for the sins of all believing men and women. God knows your places of work and rest.

THE HYPOCRITES ARE TERRIFIED OF FIGHTING

[20]And the believers say, "Why hasn't a chapter been revealed *about fighting*?" When a decisive chapter is revealed that mentions fighting, you will see people with a disease in their hearts looking at you like the one who is in death throes. It would be far better for them [21]to obey and to say a good thing when the commandment came to pass. If only they were sincere about God, that would be far better for them. [22]So if you turn away now perhaps you would create corruption on the land and sever your blood ties. [23]God cursed these people, made them deaf, and blinded their eyes. [24]Haven't they reflected on the Quran? Or are there locks on their minds?

THE HYPOCRITES HAVE FALSE HOPES

[25]Those who turn their backs after the truth was made clear to them have been fooled[d] by Satan, and given false long hopes. [26]That is because they say to those

---

[a] "Those given knowledge" refers to the true believers, the practising Muslims.

[b] See introduction to chapter.

[c] Al-Qurtubi says this means, "ask God to protect you from sins". I have translated accordingly, since the Prophet ﷺ we believe is always free from sins.

[d] *Sawwal* also means to deceive, dupe and trick.

who hate what God has revealed, "We will follow you in some things only." God knows their secrets. ²⁷ What will it be like when the angels take their souls at the time of death, and they will be striking them on their faces and backs. ²⁸ That *punishment* will be because they followed what angers God, and they disliked *seeking divine* pleasure, so their works are now worthless.

THE HYPOCRITES ARE FULL OF HATRED

²⁹ Or do those with disease in their heart think God will never expose their hatred? ³⁰ If We wanted we can show them to you, and you will *easily* recognise them from their faces and from the tone of their speech. God knows your works. ³¹ We shall test you in order to see who among you strives hard and is patient and test *the sincerity* of your claims. ³² The disbelievers who stop others from God's way and oppose the Messenger after the truth is made clear to them are incapable of harming God in the slightest. And their works will be worthless.

BELIEVERS WILL BE INFLUENTIAL AND PREVAIL

³³ Believers! Obey God and obey the Messenger and don't ruin your works. ³⁴ Surely, the disbelievers who stop others from God's way will not be forgiven if they die as disbelievers. ³⁵ *Believers*! Never lose heart nor beg for peace; you shall be dominant and God will be with you, and He will not deprive you of *the reward* for your works.

MISERLINESS CONDEMNED

³⁶ Indeed, the life of this world is an amusement and pleasant pastime. However, if you believe and are mindful, you will be have rewards, and He will not ask you to give all of your wealth. ³⁷ Were He to demand from you to spend all of your wealth, you would be miserly and your dislike to spend would then be exposed. ³⁸ You are called upon to spend some of it in God's way, but some of you are miserly, and whoever is miserly deprives himself *of goodness*. God is Self-Sufficient, whereas you are in need of Him. And if you turn away, He will bring others in your place, and they will not be the likes of you.

48. Al-Fath

The Victory

This chapter was revealed in the sixth year of Hijra, just after the Treaty of Hudaibiyah. The Prophet 鬱 had a dream, he was performing Umrah, and the next day he informed the disciples of this. The central theme of the chapter is this dream of the Prophet 鬱. There was lot of excitement, and preparations began for the sacred journey. The Prophet 鬱 also invited some new Muslims and Bedouins from around Madinah to join, though only a few joined him. Nearly 1,400 devotees participated, with their sacrificial animals that had clear marks on their flanks and garlands around their necks. Men wore two-piece unstitched uniforms and carried only a sheathed sword. They left Madinah in Dhul-Qada. When the Makkans heard of this they were bewildered, and suspicious of the Muslims. They faced the dilemma of whether to violate the time-honoured Arabian custom of allowing anyone to enter Makkah for the pilgrimage, or to stop them entering the city. When the Muslims reached Hudaibiyah, 13 km outside the city, they were stopped by the Makkan army led by Khalid ibn Waleed. This was an unprecedented move in their history.

The Quraysh sent their envoy, Urwah, to negotiate with the Muslims. This is what he reported back:

> O people, I have been sent as envoy to kings, the Caesar, Chosreo of Persia, and Negus, but I have not seen a king whose men so honour him as the disciples of Muhammad honour him. If he gives a command they almost outstrip his words in fulfilling it; when he washes himself they compete for the water that falls off his hands; when he speaks their voices are hushed in his presence... He has offered you a goodly concession; therefore, accept from him. [M. Lings]

Usman ibn Affan was sent as an envoy to seek the Quraysh's permission to perform the Umrah. He told them they were unarmed and not willing to fight. However, they refused to listen and held him captive. During this tense period of negotiation, a rumour spread that he was martyred. When the Prophet 鬱 heard this, he announced the Muslims would not leave until they had avenged the blood of Usman. Sitting under a green acacia tree full of fresh spring foliage, the Prophet 鬱 took a pledge of loyalty from everyone present. They pledged to die for the blood of Usman. A few days later the rumour proved to be false, and Usman safely returned to the Muslim camp.

Soon the Quraysh realised their mistake, and sent their envoy to conclude the negotiation with a peace treaty. The salient features of this were:
- The two parties will not engage in any kind of warfare for the next ten years
- The Muslims must return this year, and will be allowed to come back next year for three days to perform the Umrah.

The Muslims were furious with these conditions. However, the Prophet ﷺ signed the treaty. He ordered the disciples to rise and sacrifice their animals, and to shave their heads. After this, many set off to return to Madinah. This chapter was revealed during this journey, and announcing the expedition was a great victory. Mohammed Asad summed up the benefits of this victory:

> The truce of Hudaibiyah proved to be beneficial for to the future of Islam; for the first time in six years peaceful contacts were established ... Thus the way was open to the penetration of Islamic ideas into the citadel of Arabian paganism ... As soon as the perennial warfare came to an end and people of both sides could meet freely, new converts rallied around the Prophet, first in tens, then in hundreds, then in thousands – so much so that when the pagan Koresh broke the truce two years after its conclusion, the Prophet could occupy Makkah almost without resistance. Thus the truce of Hudaibiyah ushered in the moral and political victory of Islam over all Arabia (*The Message of the Quran*).

In the name of God, the Kind, the Caring.

THE PEACE TREATY WAS A VICTORY

[1] Indeed, We opened up a *path to* a clear victory for you [2] in order that God may forgive the past and the future sins of your people,[a] and perfect His favours on you, and guide you to the straight path; [3] and God will help you in a mighty way. He gave the believers' hearts an inner peace so their faith grew ever stronger. [4] The forces of the Heavens and the Earth belong to God, the Knower, the Wise. [5] Believing men and women's sins will be deleted, and admitted to Paradise, beneath which rivers flow, to live there forever. This is a great achievement from God.

FATE OF THOSE WHO THINK ILL OF GOD

[6] The hypocrites: men and women, and idolatrous men and women, who think wrong thoughts about God will be overwhelmed by God's wrath and curse, and evil from all sides; and He has prepared Hell for them; a miserable place of no return. [7] The forces of Heaven and the Earth are God's, the Almighty, Wise.

BELIEVERS SUPPORT AND HONOUR THE MESSENGER ﷺ

[8] We sent you as a witness, a giver of good news and a warner, [9] so you *people* will

---

[a]   Since the Messenger ﷺ is sinless and protected from all sins, the only appropriate translation is to assume there is an ellipsis: your people. For further discussion see the introduction to the chapter.

believe in God and His Messenger, and support him and honour him. And glorify God morning and evening. [10]Those who took your pledge of loyalty, really took God's pledge of loyalty, since God's Hand of power is over their hands. Anyone who breaks his pledge will face dreadful consequences. And whoever fulfils his pledge, He will richly reward him.

THE HYPOCRITES STAYED BEHIND

[11]The Bedouins who stayed behind *in Madinah* will come and say to you, "We were busy with our jobs and families, ask God to forgive us." But they say things with their mouths that aren't from their hearts. Say: "Who can intervene for you if God wanted to harm you or to benefit you?" Indeed, God is fully aware of what you do. [12]You thought the Messenger and the believers will never return to their families, and you were delighted with this thought, and you kept thinking these evil thoughts. You are wicked losers.[a] [13]The ones who did not believe in God and his Messenger – We have prepared for such disbelievers a blazing Fire. [14]God has the control of the Heavens and the Earth, and forgives and punishes who He pleases. And God is Forgiving, Caring.

THE HYPOCRITES ARE CHALLENGED

[15]Those who stayed behind will say, "When you go somewhere *next time* which promises rich booty, do let us follow you." They want to change God's words. Say: "You will never follow us; that is what God has told beforehand." They will say, "You are jealous of us." They understand very little. [16]Tell those Bedouins who stayed behind: "Soon you will be called upon to face people of great prowess in war; *you may* fight or they may surrender. If you obey, then God will give you a wonderful reward, but if you turn away as you turned away before, He will punish you with painful punishment. [17]It is not a sin for the blind, the lame and the sick to stay behind. Anyone who obeys God and His Messenger will be admitted into Paradise, beneath which rivers flow, and anyone who turns away will be punished with painful punishment.

THE PLEDGE OF LOYALTY UNDER THE TREE

[18]God was pleased with the believers when they took a pledge of loyalty with you under the tree, and He knew what was in their hearts, so He gave them inner

---

[a] *Qaumum boura* literally means ruined person who has not a speck of goodness in him or her.

peace, and as a reward will give them a victory soon,[b] [19] and in the near future they'll have many rich booties. God is Almighty, Wise. [20] God promised you many rich booties, which you will have in the future. He quickly gave you *this victory* and protected you from the harm of others,[c] so this becomes a sign of help for the believers and they can be guided on the straight path. [21] Many other victories await you are not yet capable of, but God has control over them; God has power over all things.

God doesn't want people to fight

[22] Had the disbelievers fought you, they would have turned their backs *and fled*, then they would have found no protector and helper. [23] This was God's practice in the past; *truth will succeed* and you will never find God's practice changing. [24] He stopped them attacking you, and you from attacking them, in the valley of Makkah after giving you capability to conquer them. God sees all you do. [25] The disbelievers stopped you from entering the Sacred Mosque, and your sacrificial animals from reaching their place of sacrifice. If it were not for the believing men and women *in Makkah* – *about* whom you were unaware – you may have trampled them, thereby unwittingly incurring guilt.[d] So God may admit in to His kindness who He pleases. Had *the believers* separated themselves from *the Makkans* then We would have severely punished the disbelievers.

The Makkans' stubborn disdain

[26] While stubborn disdain filled the disbelievers' hearts, their superiority complex, God gave inner peace to His Messenger and the believers, and made them firm in the word of God-consciousness,[e] which they rightly deserved and were worthy of it. God knows all things.

The Prophet's ﷺ dream was true

[27] God fulfilled His Messenger's true dream; by the Will of God, you will enter the Sacred Mosque in peace with your heads shaven or hair trimmed, fearing no one. You don't know what he knows; soon beside this you will have a near vic-

---

[b]   This predicts the victory of Khybar that occurred immediately after this. (Ibn Abbas)

[c]   Literally this means, "he held back people's hands from you", simply put this means "protected you".

[d]   Otherwise God would have allowed you to fight them.

[e]   *Kalimat tutaqwa* means "there is no God but God and Muhammad is the messenger of God" according to Imam Ali.

tory.[a] ²⁸ He sent His Messenger with guidance and a true religion to override all religions. And God is a sufficient witness.

THE DISCIPLES ARE PRAISED

²⁹ Muhammad is the Messenger of God, and those with him are tough with the disbelievers and caring among themselves; you will see them bowing and prostrating, seeking the grace of God and His pleasure. They bear marks on their faces, an effect of their prostration. These qualities of theirs are mentioned in the Torah and the Gospels; they are like a seed from which a shoot sprouts. He strengthens it so it rises stout and stands straight on its stem. The sower loves it, but the disbelievers become enraged. God promised the believers and the righteous among them forgiveness, and a great reward.

---

[a] This may refer to either victory in Tabuk, which took place a few months after this or the victory of Makkah.

49. Al-Hujurat
The Living Quarters

This Madinan chapter was revealed in the ninth year of Hijra, following two events: a delegation of new Muslims from the Bedouin tribe of Bani Tamim visited the Prophet 攤, they called out to him from outside his living room. The chapter disapproved of their behaviour, and laid out simple rules for respecting the leader. The second event concerned the misinformation given to the Prophet 攤 by one of the Zakat collectors about the tribe of Bani Mustalaq (verses 6–8). He wrongly informed the Messenger 攤 that the tribe was unwilling to pay the Zakat. However, upon investigation, this turned out to be untrue. This kind of behaviour was condemned.

This chapter is also called the "chapter of morals and manners," since it offers moral guidance for living in the community: how to develop trust and overcome suspicions. In verse 13, the unity of humanity is stressed, uprooting any kind of discrimination based on colour, creed and caste. It points out our common origin: Adam and Eve. It teaches that honour and nobility is achieved through being God-conscious, mindful of Him, and having a strong character. This is the foundation that creates equality and fairness in a society. It is these values that lead to peace and trust among people.

The last passage of the chapter returns to the ill-mannered Bedouins, and seeks to clarify the difference between true faith and mere ritual formalities of religion, urging them to acknowledge God's favour. Faith is a special favour of God.

––––––––––

In the name of God, the Kind, the Caring.

MANNERS OF MEETING AND GREETING THE MESSENGER 攤

[1] Believers, do not put yourselves ahead of God and His Messenger; be fearful of God. Indeed, God is the Hearer, the Knower. [2] Believers, don't raise your voices above the voice of the Prophet, nor talk loudly with him as you might talk loudly with each other, your deeds will be ruined without you knowing. [3] Those who lower their voices in the presence of the Messenger of God are the ones whose hearts God has selected[b] for piety. Forgiveness and a great reward awaits them. [4] Most of those who called out to you from outside your home[c] don't understand. [5] It would have been far better for them had they waited patiently till you came

––––––

[b] *Imtahana Allahu* literally means "God has tested", in other words proved that they are fit and deserving to be selected. I have accordingly translated it.

[c] The living quarters, means the Prophet's 攤 home.

out. God is Forgiving, Caring.

WHEN YOU HEAR NEWS, CHECK THE FACTS

[6] Believers, if a discredited person[a] brings you news, then check *it* in case you cause harm to others ignorantly, and then later regret what you did. [7] Remember, the Messenger of God is among you. If he frequently followed your wishes then you would suffer *badly*; however, God has made faith beloved and highly attractive for your hearts, and made disbelief, sin and disobedience dislikeable to you. These are the rightly guided, [8] *given* grace as a gift from God, the Knower, Wise.

STANDING UP FOR JUSTICE AND CREATING PEACE

[9] If two groups of believers fight, then *you must* make peace between them. If one of them is unjust to the other, then fight the unjust until he accepts God's judgement. If he accepts it then make peace between them fairly, and be just. Indeed, God loves the just. [10] The believers are brothers,[b] so make peace between your two brothers; be mindful of God so you might be cared for.

BEHAVIOURS THAT LEAD TO CONFLICT

[11] Believers! Let no man make fun of another,[c] he might be better than him; no woman should make fun of other women, they may be better than them; nor speak ill, nor use offensive nicknames for one another. How bad it is to be called "a trouble maker," after accepting faith. Those who don't turn away from such behaviour are wicked.

SUSPICIONS UNDERMINE RELATIONSHIPS

[12] Believers, do not be suspicious, since some suspicions[d] are sins. Neither spy on one another nor backbite about each other. Would anyone of you like to eat the meat of his dead brother? Never! You would hate it. So be fearful of God. God is indeed Forgiving, Caring.

OUR COMMON HUMANITY

[13] People, We created you from a male and female; *then* made you into different races and tribes so you may know each other. The most honourable in the sight of

---

[a]   *Fasiq* means a transgressor who commits major sins, is uncouth, and a mischievous law breaker.

[b]   Also sisters to each other.

[c]   *Quamun* here means a group of men.

[d]   *Zann* means to suspect and to assume about others: to be inclined to accuse others, and doubt their innocence.

God is the most mindful of God, the Knower, the Aware.

THE TRUE NATURE OF FAITH

[14] The Bedouins say, "We believe," tell them: "You haven't believed yet, you should say, 'We have surrendered.'" Faith hasn't fully entered their hearts. Had they obeyed God and His Messenger, none of their deeds would be lost. Indeed, God is Forgiving, the Caring. [15] The true believers are those who believed in God and His Messenger, and have no doubts. They strive with their wealth and their lives in God's way. They are the truthful. [16] Are you teaching God your religion? God knows what is in the Heavens and the Earth; God knows all things. [17] They think they have done you a favour by embracing Islam; say: "By embracing Islam you haven't done me any favour; *in fact* God has done you a favour. He has guided you to the faith, if you are true in faith." [18] God knows the secrets of Heaven and the Earth, and God sees all you do.

50. Qaf

The Arabic Letter Qaf

This chapter was revealed in the middle Makkan period, and this is apparent in its subject matter: arguments for Resurrection and Divine Judgement. The sceptics are surprised by the idea of new life after death. The Quran responds to them by providing visible evidence from nature, the creation of the Heavens and the Earth, and the mountains and date groves from which they eat. This is followed by another line of visible evidence from human history with which Makkans were familiar: the ruins of previous rebellious nations. The chapter eloquently asks: "Has the first creation tired Us out? Not at all, but they are doubtful about *the possibility* of a new creation" (15).

The next section makes reference to the ego and lower self of human consciousness: "We created man, and We know exactly what his desires are urging him *to do*;[a] in fact, We are nearer to him than his jugular vein" (16). The chapter warns: everything humans say and do is accurately recorded, and on Judgement Day this will lead either to Paradise or Hell. Here, the chapter vividly paints contrasting scenes from Paradise and Hell. In the end is a reminder of God's creative power. Humanity is advised to celebrate the glory and praise of God. The Prophet ﷺ is reminded: continue to remind people, and you can't force religion into people's hearts.

———————

In the name of God, the Kind, the Caring.

¹ *Qaf.*

THE RESURRECTION WILL BE A SHOCK FOR DISBELIEVERS

By the Majestic Quran. ² How is it that they are surprised that a warner has come from among them? The disbelievers say, "This is a strange thing! ³ When we are dead and turned into dust will we be returned; a far-fetched *idea*." ⁴ Indeed, We know what the Earth consumes of their bodies.[b] We have a Book in which everything is carefully recorded. ⁵ In fact, they denied the truth when it came to them because they are confused.

GOD'S CREATIVE POWER IN NATURE

⁶ Haven't they looked at the sky above them, how We made it beautiful and flawless, ⁷ and the Earth how We spread it out and firmly set mountains on it, and

---

[a] The literal meaning is "what his soul whispers to him".

[b] Literally this means "we know what the Earth diminishes of them".

produced all kinds of beneficial plants there? [8] They offer an insightful lesson and a reminder for every human being who willingly turns to God. [9] And how We sent down blessed water from the sky, and with it We grow gardens and crops that are harvested, [10] and tall palm trees loaded with clusters of dates – [11] a sustenance for people, and that is how We bring a dead place back to life with rain. The coming out *of graves* will be like that too!

God never gets tired

[12] Previously the truth was denied by the people of Noah, the Rass, Thamud, [13] Ad, Pharaoh and the brothers of Lot, [14] the people of Iekah and Tubba. All of them denied the messengers, and so what they were threatened with actually happened to them. [15] Has the first creation tired Us out? Not at all, but they are doubtful about *the possibility* of a new creation.

Guardian angels record

[16] We created humans, and know exactly what their desires urge them *to do*; in fact, We are nearer to them than their jugular vein. [17] When the two recording angels, one sitting on their right and the other on their left, record. [18] Not a word they speak goes *unrecorded* by a vigilant observer. [19] Death throes will bring the truth with it: "This is what you tried to escape." [20] The Trumpet will be blown; that is the Day you were warned about. [21] Everyone will be escorted by an angel and a witness. [22] *They will be told*: "You paid no attention to this Day, and We removed your veil, so today your sight is razor-sharp." [23] Their lifelong companion will say, "I prepared, this *file of yours*."

Who will be thrown into Hell?

[24] "Throw him into Hell,[c] every rebellious disbeliever, [25] everyone who obstructed others from good, every aggressor, every doubter [26] who had set up other gods with God. So throw him into the terrible punishment." [27] His devil companion will say, "Our Lord, I didn't lead him to evil; he had already gone far astray." [28] God will say to them, "Do not squabble in My presence; I sent you a warning. [29] My Word does not change, and I am not unjust to any creature." [30] Remember the Day I shall ask Hell, "Are you full?" It will reply, "Are there more?"

---

[c]   This address is to the angels.

Who will enter Paradise?

31 Paradise will be brought near the righteous; it won't be far away from them. 32 This is what you were promised; it is for the one who turned to God, and was ever mindful of Him. 33 The one who feared the Kind without ever seeing Him and came with a devout heart, 34 *he shall be told*: "Enter Paradise peacefully, for this is the Everlasting Day." 35 They will have anything they want there, and We will have much more for them.

To witness God's power requires senses and feelings

36 We destroyed people in the past who were far stronger than them; they used to travel everywhere – did they escape? 37 In this is a reminder for anyone who has a heart, or listens attentively. 38 We created the Heavens and the Earth and what lies between them in six days only, and We were not tired. 39 So bear patiently what they say. Glorify and praise your Lord before the sunrise and sunset, 40 and during the night, and glorify him after the *set* prayers *too*.

The Day people come out of graves

41 Listen carefully about the Day when the caller from nearby will call out, 42 when people hear a Blast. That shall be the Day of the coming out *of graves*. 43 We give life and death, and the Final Return will be to Us. 44 The Day when the Earth will split open, letting them rush out, that gathering will be easy for Us. 45 We know well what they say, and you can't force them *to believe*. So keep reminding through the Quran anyone who fears My Warning.

51. Ad-Dhariyat
Gale-force Winds

A series of oaths referring to the wind opens this chapter. Wind is a fundamental element of life on Earth. Its function is the maintenance of the water cycle. The sun heats the oceans, and water evaporates into the air as vapour. With rising height, the air temperature falls and water vapour condenses into tiny droplets. These droplets over a large area join to form clouds. The winds blow them towards the land, where they fall as rain. The implied question is: since wind is life-giving and is created by God, why can't the disbelievers accept God's power to bring back the dead to life?

The chapter reveals two more facts: "And in the sky is your promised sustenance" (22); and secondly, "We built the universe with *our creative* power, and We are ever expanding it (47). The sun provides all the energy for photosynthesis for plants to grow, which becomes human food. Astronomers believe the universe is expanding, so how could the Prophet Muhammad 襚, who lived in seventh-century Arabia, know this extraordinary fact? Isn't this evidence that the Quran is God's Word?

The Makkans are reminded about their forefather Abraham , blessed with a child in his old age, so He can give life to an infertile couple. Another instance of the Quran challenging conceptual boundaries, which made belief in the Resurrection difficult for them. Then a reminder of the fate of those who denied; a warning to them that their fate could be the same if they persist in their denial. At the end, the Messenger 襚 is encouraged: "Reminder benefits the believers" (55), so carry on reminding humanity of the purpose of their creation: "I created jinn and human beings only to worship Me" (56).

In the name of God, the Kind, the Caring.

THE LIFE GIVING WIND

[1] By the gale-force winds that scatter dust; [2] by the winds that carry heavily-laden clouds; [3] by the winds that sail ships with ease; [4] by the winds that distribute rain as commanded; [5] no doubt, what you have been promised is true; [6] the *Day of Judgement* will certainly come. [7] By the sky with its paths.[a]

FATE OF THE DENIERS OF THE QURAN

[8] You have different views about *this Quran*. [9] Those who turn away from *the Quran* are deceived. [10] The liars are ruined, [11] who are numb and unaware *of real-*

---

[a] *Hubuk* also means ripples, waves and trails (Zia-ul-Quran).

ity. [12] They ask, "When will the Judgement Day come?" [13] That Day they shall be punished with Fire. [14] "Taste your punishment; this is what you were so impatient for."

FATE OF THE BELIEVERS OF THE QURAN

[15] The mindful will be in Gardens with flowing fountains; [16] they will take what their Lord gives them. In the *world,* they were gracious; [17] they slept little at night, [18] and at dawn sought God's forgiveness. [19] They set aside a share in their wealth for beggars, and the needy. [20] And for those who believe firmly there are signs in the Earth [21] and in themselves. Don't you see? [22] And in the sky is your promised sustenance. [23] By the Lord of the Heavens and the Earth, this is as true as what you speak.

ABRAHAM IS VISITED BY ANGELS

[24] Did you hear the story of Abraham's honourable guests? [25] They came and said, "Peace;" he replied, "Peace." *He thought,* "these are strangers." [26] He quietly slipped away to his family and brought a *roasted* fat calf [27] which he placed before them, and said, "Won't you eat?" [28] He felt afraid of them, and they replied, "Don't be afraid." They gave him good news of a knowledgeable son. [29] His wife stepped forward and struck her face *at this news,* she was amazed and said, "*Who me?* A barren old woman!" [30] They said, "That's how your Lord has decreed. Indeed, He is Wise, the Knower."

THE ANGELS DISCLOSE THEIR ASSIGNMENT

[31] Abraham asked, "What's the purpose of your coming, messengers?" [32] They replied, "We've been sent to the wicked people,[a] [33] to pelt them with clay stones [34] marked by your Lord for those who've gone beyond limits." [35] We rescued the believers from there; [36] We only found a single household of believers. [37] And We left behind a sign for those who fear the painful punishment.

EXAMPLES OF OTHER PEOPLE WHO WERE DESTROYED

[38] Also in the story of Moses *is a sign,* when We sent him with a clear authority to Pharaoh. [39] He turned away because of his military might[b] and said, "Moses is a magician or a madman." [40] So We seized him and his army and threw them into the sea; he was guilty. [41] And in the story of Ad *is a lesson* too, when we sent dev-

---

[a] This refers to the people of Lot , who lived in the towns of Sodom and Gomorrah.

[b] *Rukn* means army, bureaucrats and citizens.

astating wind upon them. [42] In its wake it left behind everything crushed and torn up. [43] And in the story of Thamud when it was said to them: "Enjoy yourselves for a while." [44] They disobeyed the Lord's command, so were seized by a blast as they watched. [45] Neither could they bear the punishment nor defend themselves against Us. [46] The people of Noah before *them faced a similar fate.* They too were sinners.

THE EXPANDING UNIVERSE

[47] We built the universe[c] with *our creative* power and We are ever expanding it.[d] [48] And the Earth We spread out and levelled it smoothly. [49] We created everything in pairs so that you may reflect. [50] So come to God quickly. I am a clear Warner to you. [51] Don't set up gods beside God, I am a clear Warner to you. [52] This is exactly what previous people did when a messenger was sent, they called him "a magician or a mad man." [53] Did they tell one another to do this? No. They were transgressors.

PURPOSE OF HUMAN CREATION

[54] So ignore them, you are not to blame; [55] continue reminding, a reminder benefits the believers. [56] I created jinn and human beings only to worship Me. [57] I don't want any sustenance from them nor for them to feed Me. [58] God is surely the Sustainer, the Superpower and strong. [59] The wrongdoers will have the punishment like their ancestors, so they shouldn't ask Me to hasten it. [60] It will be too bad for the disbelievers that Day, which they've been promised.

---

[c] *Al sama* literally means the sky, the Heavens, including all stars and galaxies, i.e. the cosmos or the universe.
[d] Astronomers now believe that the universe is expanding. It is very interesting to note the Quran described God as the expander of the universe.

52. At-Tur
The Mountain

This is a late Makkan chapter that emphatically provides evidence from both nature and human history for the truthfulness of Islamic beliefs: the Oneness of God, the messengership of Muhammad 變, and Resurrection. It opens with five powerful oaths as witnesses of the message of the Prophet 變, and threatens the disbelievers of Makkah, warning them of the consequences of their persistent denials: "Your Lord's punishment will certainly come to pass" (7), followed by a description of the luxuries of Paradise. Verse 21 lends some credence to a common proverb: you reap what you sow. "Each person is answerable for his deeds". However, a concession is made for righteous people: their faithful children will join them in Paradise, despite not being as righteous as their parents.

This is followed by a passage that poses ten challenging questions. These range from challenging the mistaken notion about the Prophet 變 being a poet and soothsayer, to the question of who holds the treasures of God. The Quran masterly asks tag questions: Questions at the end of a statement in a way that invites agreement. By asking several questions in a row, where the reader gets used to answering in agreement, so this makes it easy for them to agree to the next suggestion or order.

The chapter concludes: the Makkans are a stubborn bunch of people, intolerant and close-minded. The Prophet 變 is urged to continue his mission despite their rejection and hostility: "Therefore wait patiently for your Lord's judgement; you are *always* in Our Eyes, and glorify and praise your Lord whenever you stand *for the prayer*" (48).

In the name of God, the Kind, the Caring.

THE CERTAINTY OF SUFFERING AND PUNISHMENT OF HELL

[1] By the mountain, [2] and by a Book written down [3] on open pages, [4] and by the visited house,[a] [5] and by the soaring roof, [6] and by the over-full, ferocious sea – [7] your Lord's punishment will come to pass; [8] no power can stop it! [9] Even the sky will shudder and judder that Day, [10] and the mountains will float. [11] Ruined that Day will be the deniers, [12] who were absorbed in useless projects. [13] That Day they will be thrust into the fire of Hell. [14] "This is the Fire you use to deny. [15] Is this magic? Or do you not see? [16] Burn in it! Whether you are patient or not it is the same; you are being rewarded for what you did."

---

[a] The visited house is *Al Bait al Ma'mur,* refers to the Kaaba of the angels in the Heavens, visited by 70,000 angels morning and evenings (Bukhari).

THE RIGHTEOUS WILL ENJOY THE LUXURIES OF PARADISE

[17] The righteous will be in Gardens full of luxuries, [18] enjoying what the Lord gave them, and protected them from the punishment of Hell. [19] *They shall be told*: "Eat, drink and be merry, a reward for what you did." [20] *They will* rest on *comfortable* sofas *gracefully* arranged in rows, and We shall marry them with spouses with beautiful eyes.[b]

CHILDREN OF RIGHTEOUS PARENTS JOIN THEM IN PARADISE

[21] The believers whose children followed them in faith will be united with them in Paradise without their parents' good deeds being diminished in value. Each person is answerable[c] for his deeds. [22] We shall feed them with all the kinds of fruits and meat they desire. [23] A cup of *wine* passed around will not cause drunken uproar or a sin. [24] Serving them will be young people as *beautiful* as hidden pearls. [25] Turning to each other, they will ask, [26] "were we not fearful about the fate of our families? [27] God has favoured us and spared us the punishment of the Intense Fire. [28] We used to pray to Him; the Good, the Caring."

TEN CHALLENGING QUESTIONS FOR THE DISBELIEVERS

[29] So, remind them, by the grace of your Lord; you aren't a soothsayer nor a madman. [30] They call you, "A poet, and we are waiting to see what time will do to him."[d] [31] Tell them: "Wait if you wish, and I shall wait with you." [32] Or do their minds tell them to say this? Or are they simply a *bunch of* unruly people? [33] Or they say, "He has made it up." Never will they believe. [34] So let them bring a book like it if they are truthful. [35] Were they created without a creator? Or are they themselves creators? [36] Or did they create the Heavens and the Earth? No, they will never be convinced. [37] Or is it that they possess the treasures of your Lord, or have control over them? [38] Or do they have a ladder that allows them to eavesdrop on *the secrets of the Heavens*? Let their eavesdropper bring clear proof. [39] Or is it that He has daughters and you have sons? [40] Or do you ask them for a wage *for this guidance* that would make them heavily indebted? [41] Or do they have the knowledge *of the unseen* they write down? [42] Or do they want to deceive you? The

---

[b] *Hurin ein* literally means "an eye that has a black iris and large white eyeball" (Qamus). According to Hassan al-Basri, it simply refers to "righteous women" (Tabari).

[c] *Raheen*: pawned, mortgaged, given as security. Implying that the person is responsible for his deeds.

[d] *Raib el manun* is an Arabic idiom which means, "evil happenings of time" (Zia-ul-Quran).

disbelievers only deceive themselves. ⁴³Or do they have a god besides God? Glory be to God; He is far above what they associate with Him.

THE DISBELIEVERS HAVE NO ANSWERS, AND THEY ARE STUBBORN

⁴⁴Even if they saw a part of the sky fall, they would say, "It's merely heaps of cloud." ⁴⁵So leave them till they encounter the Day they'll die.^a ⁴⁶A Day when their plots will not benefit them at all, neither will they be helped. ⁴⁷For the evildoers there is another punishment *in this world* before that one, but most of them don't know.

GOD WATCHES HIS BELOVED MESSENGER

⁴⁸Therefore, wait patiently for your Lord's judgement; you are *always* in Our sight, so glorify and praise your Lord whenever you stand *for the prayer*, ⁴⁹*and also* at night glorify Him till the stars fade away.

---

^a *Sa'aqa* has two meanings: to become unconscious or to die. This translation uses the latter.

53. An-Najm
The Star

This chapter was revealed in the late Makkan period. When the Messenger ﷺ recited this chapter to the Quraysh near the Kaaba, they were mesmerised by its tempo and fell in prostration. The chapter opens by rejecting the Quraysh's allegation that the Messenger ﷺ was misguided.

According to the commentators verses 1-18 are descriptions of the Messenger's ﷺ vertical phase of the ascension. The Messenger ﷺ goes beyond the celestial realm into the Divine presence, he ﷺ is honoured, he ﷺ sees the Divine Majesty.

Detailed narratives of the ascension are found in Hadith books. The Messenger ﷺ said, "One night I was asleep, in the Haram near the Kaaba, I was woken by Gabriel, he informed me of the Divine plan and took me to the well of Zam Zam, and opened my chest and filled it with wisdom and faith. Afterwards a beautiful Buraq was presented: an animal larger than a mule but smaller than a horse. I mounted it. Soon the Messenger ﷺ was at the Masjid al-Aqsa in Jerusalem. Here prophets were eagerly waiting for him. He led them in congregational prayer. This marked the end of the horizontal part of the journey. From here, accompanied by Gabriel, the Messenger ﷺ travelled on the Buraq ascending the heavens. In the first heaven, He met Adam; in the second Jesus and John; in the third Joseph; the fourth Enoch; in the fifth Aaron; and in the sixth Moses; and in the seventh Abraham. The journey continued beyond the heavens until He reached the *Bait al-Mamur* - The Kaaba of the Angels, from where He ﷺ ascended to the Lote tree (*Sidratul Muntaha*) of the uttermost boundary. Chapter An-Najm describes this mysterious part of the journey: "Then he drew near, very near, like two bows lengths or even closer (An-Najm: 8).

The Prophet ﷺ witnessed the delights of Paradise and the Punishments of Hell during his celestial journey, he ﷺ saw the grandeur and the Majesty of his Lord.

It ends with a warning: "The Judgement Day is near and draws ever nearer ... Are you surprised about this? Laughing at it rather than crying?" (58–60).

———————

In the name of God, the Kind, the Caring.

THE PROPHET'S ﷺ ASCENSION: THE CELESTIAL JOURNEY
¹By the *shining* star when it came down, ²your master[b] is neither misguided nor deluded. ³He doesn't speak from his desire. ⁴This is a Revelation sent down ⁵and taught to him by the most powerful, ⁶the most wise. When he appeared *to him,*

---

[b]   *Sahib* means companion, master and owner, since this refers to the beloved Messenger ﷺ I translated it as master.

⁷He was on the uppermost horizon. ⁸Then they drew near, very near. ⁹The distance between two bows held together.ᵃ ¹⁰So He revealed to His servant what He revealed. ¹¹His heart didn't deny what he saw. ¹²So why are you disputing what he saw? ¹³And on another occasion he saw him coming down ¹⁴near the far side of the Lote Tree, ¹⁵nearby was the Paradise of *Mawa*.ᵇ ¹⁶The Lote Tree was covered with *indescribable* splendour;ᶜ ¹⁷his eyes didn't wander nor turn to the side ¹⁸as he witnessed the greatest signs of His Lord.

THE IDOLS ARE THE PRODUCTS OF MATERIALIST MINDS

¹⁹*Disbelievers!* Have you thought about Al-Lat, Al-Uzza ²⁰and Al-Manat, the third of them? ²¹*You chose* sons for yourselves and daughters for God, why? ²²How unfair is this division! ²³These are merely names you and your forefathers gave them; God hasn't given them any authority. They are following suspicions and their whims. The Lord's guidance has come to them. ²⁴Does a person always get his wish? ²⁵Both the Hereafter and this world belong to God.

INTERCESSION IS BY GOD'S PERMISSION ONLY

²⁶There are many angels in Heaven, their intercession cannot benefit anyone, except after God allows it for anyone He wants. ²⁷The disbelievers of the Hereafter give the angels female names. ²⁸They have no knowledge but follow speculation, and speculation is no substitute for the truth. ²⁹So pay no attention to the one who has turned away from Our remembrance and pursues only the life of this world. ³⁰This is the sum total of their knowledge. Indeed, your Lord knows who strayed from His path and who is guided.

WHY A PERSON SURRENDERS TO DESIRES?

³¹Everything in the Heavens and the Earth belongs to God. He shall punish the evil, and richly reward the righteous: ³²who avoid major sins and shameful deeds, but *may* stumble *into minor sins*. Your Lord is infinite in forgiveness. He knows you from the time He created you from the Earth, and when you were a foetus

---

ᵃ Literally "the distance between two bows held together". When two Arab chiefs agreed a treaty they would hold their bows together and then release a single arrow from it. An expression that the two chiefs were united. This expression is used now to convey this sense of closeness.

ᵇ *Mawa* is the name of one of the seven Paradises it means "a restful place".

ᶜ A description of "the inconceivable Majesty and splendour attaching to this symbol of Paradise, which no description can picture and no definition can embrace" (Asad).

in your mothers' wombs, so don't admire yourselves too much.[d] He knows well who is mindful.

EACH PERSON WILL HAVE WHAT HE WORKED TOWARDS

[33] Have you seen him who turned away? [34] He gives little *anyway* then becomes more stingy. [35] Does he know the Unseen? Is he seeing it? [36] Does he know what's in the Scriptures of Moses, [37] and Abraham? He fulfilled *his responsibility of preaching.* [38] No one bears the burden of another, [39] and each person will have what he strived for. [40] Soon *the outcome* of his work will be shown, [41] and will be fully rewarded. [42] The Final Destination is to your Lord.

THE ONE WHO MAKES YOU LAUGH

[43] He makes you laugh and cry, [44] He gives death and life, [45] He created the male and the female, [46] from a drop of spurted semen. [47] He is responsible for the second creation, [48] who gives wealth and poverty.[e] [49] The Lord of the star Sirius![f] [50] He destroyed the first Ad [51] and Thamud, and didn't leave a single one of them, [52] and the people of Noah before *that since* they were evildoers and rebellious. [53] He destroyed the Mu'tafikkah[g] [54] and covered them *with rubble* so they're hidden from sight. [55] So which favours of your Lord will you doubt?

PAY ATTENTION TO THE MESSENGER 繠

[56] This warner is like the previous warners. [57] The *Judgement Day* is near, and draws ever nearer, [58] there is no one beside God who can disclose *its time.* [59] Are you surprised about this? [60] Would you laugh and not cry? [61] You are careless and ignorant.[h] [62] Prostrate before God and worship Him.

---

[d] *Falatazaku anfusakum* means don't claim to be pure, it's an idiom for "don't flatter yourself, don't justify yourself".

[e] *Aqna* has several meanings, I have followed the meaning given in Zia-ul-Quran.

[f] Sirius is the 'dog star' that appears in springtime and was worshipped by the pagan Arabs.

[g] This refers to the city of the Prophet Lot, Sodom and Gomorrah.

[h] *Samidun* means "a person who is neglectful and carelessly walks with his head high" (Raghib); someone not bothered about anything.

54. Al-Qamar
The Moon

One night on the plains of Mina outside Makkah, the Prophet ﷺ was with a group of Quraysh, and they demanded a miracle: "split the moon in two parts, and we'll believe". Abdullah ibn Masood reports that the Prophet ﷺ raised his hands and pointed at the moon with his index finger, and lo and behold, it split into two parts. The Makkans were stunned, and the Prophet ﷺ called out to each one of them by their names: you have now seen the miracle with your eyes, so be a witness. Unfortunately, instead of believing they retorted, "This is a powerful magic" (2).

The miracle of splitting of the moon took place in the seventh year of the mission of the Prophet ﷺ. The Makkans are warned about the dire consequences of their stubbornness, disbelief and foolishness. The stories of four ancient people are presented to drive the point home; those who oppose God's prophets always lose. Each story ends with the refrain, "How terrible were My punishment and warnings? We made the Quran easy to learn, so will anyone pay attention?"

———————

In the name of God, the Kind, the Caring

MAKKANS DENY THE MIRACLE

[1] The Final Hour[a] is drawing near and the moon has split into two. [2] And after seeing the miracle they turned away saying, "This is a powerful magic." [3] They denied and followed their whims. For every action produces a specific outcome. [4] The reports *of ancient people* have come to them containing lessons [5] with far-reaching wisdom, but those warnings didn't benefit them. [6] *Messenger,* turn away from them, one Day a caller will call them to something terrible; [7] with eyes lowered they will exit their graves like swarms of locusts, [8] rushing in terror towards the caller, and the disbelievers will say, "This is a difficult Day."

THE PEOPLE OF NOAH REJECTED HIM: SO THEY DROWNED

[9] Previously, the people of Noah denied Our servant, and called him a mad man and severely scolded him. [10] He cried out to His Lord: "I am weak and beaten, so help me!" [11] So We opened the sky's floodgates with torrential rain, [12] and caused the Earth's springs to surge, and the two waters met as pre-designed. [13] We carried

---

[a]   *Al-sa'a* literally means "the hour", and refers to the coming to end of worldly life.

him on a *boat* made of wooden planks *held together with* nails, [14]floating under our watchful gaze. A *magnificent* reward for the one denied. [15]We left that as a sign; will anyone pay attention? [16]How terrible were My punishments and warnings? [17]We made the Quran easy to learn and understand,[b] so will anyone pay attention?

The people of Ad face are punished with a storm

[18]The people of Ad also denied, so how terrible were My punishment and warnings? [19]We sent a howling storm wind on a Day of bitter misfortune, [20]which blew people away like uprooted palm trunks. [21]How terrible were My punishment and warnings. [22]We have made the Quran easy to learn and understand, so will anyone pay attention?

The Prophet Salih was denied: People blasted

[23]The people of Thamud also denied Our warnings. [24]They said, "We must be misguided and mad people if we follow one man from among us. [25]How could he be given a Revelation? He is a big-headed liar." [26]Tomorrow they shall know who is a big-headed liar. [27]We shall send a she-camel to test them, so patiently watch over them. [28]And tell them, the water shall be divided equally among them, and each will come to it when it's their turn. [29]So they called for their leader who cut the hamstrings of the she-camel. [30]How terrible were My punishment and warnings? [31]We sent a single Blast to destroy them, and they were like the scattered sticks of a broken fence. [32]Indeed We made the Quran easy to learn and understand, so will anyone pay attention?

The people of Lot are punished with a sand storm

[33]The people of Lot denied the warnings. [34]We sent a sandstorm of stones; the only exception was the family of Lot, We saved them at dawn, [35]a favour from Us. This is how We reward the thankful. [36]He warned them clearly about Our punishment, but they doubted the warnings. [37]They also demanded from him his guests, so We blinded them and told them, "Taste My punishment and the warnings." [38]So early one morning, a lasting punishment seized them. [39]*It was said*: "Taste My punishment and warnings." [40]We made the Quran easy to learn and understand; so will anyone pay attention?

[b]   *Li zikr* also means remembrance, a reminder, a lesson; to memorise.

The Quraysh are warned: Listen to the Messenger ﷺ

[41] Warners came to the people of Pharaoh, [42] but they denied all Our signs, so We grabbed them with force and power. [43] Are your disbelievers, *the Quraysh*, stronger than them, or have they been promised protection in Divine Scriptures? [44] Or do they say: "We are a united people bound to be victorious." [45] Soon they will be defeated, and they will turn their backs and flee. [46] The Judgement Day is their appointed time, and it will be a terrifying and most difficult *Day*. [47] The sinners are indeed misguided and foolish. [48] The Day when they are dragged on their faces and thrown into Hell, *it will be said*: "Taste the burning of Hellfire."

God's creative and precise power over all

[49] We created everything in a precisely-measured way. [50] Our order is carried out instantly, like the blink of an eye. [51] We destroyed the likes of you, so is there anyone who will pay attention? [52] Everything they did is in the Records – [53] whether big or small – all was written down. [54] The righteous will be in Paradise with *flowing* streams, [55] a delightful place in the presence of the All-Powerful King.

55. Ar-Rahman
The Most Kind

This Makkan chapter begins with the most beautiful name of God: Ar-Rahman, the Kind. The beautiful names of God are word-portraits of the loving and caring Lord. Each portrays an aspect of majesty. Ar-Rahman as a word-portrait shows countless gifts, bounties and favours of God and asks a simple question: "So which favours of your Lord will you deny?" This refrain is repeated thirty-one times after mentioning two favours, so effectively sixty-two favours of God are listed in this chapter. People are challenged about how they deny the Majestic, Creative, Almighty and Powerful Lord. Sells hints to the mystery of the refrain, which "resounds through the chapter each time as a reminder of the creative re-duplication of compassion, tying that core message into the morphology and the acoustics of language itself" (*Approaching the Quran*).

This refrain is in a form of a question, but at a deeper level it's a command. This is the Quranic style, which avoids giving direct instruction but makes the reader think; can you imagine that? Or have you seen that? Do you know? The question also invites agreement, since who can deny the obvious gifts of the Lord.

The first section of the chapter draws attention to universal spiritual principles that underpin the existence of the universe, and maintain, control and regulate it. Just as the orbits of the moon and the sun are determined by God, so are the colours of flowers and the flavours of fruits. The farthest stars and planets in space are firmly under His control: "The sun and the moon move in exactly measured orbits, and plants and trees bow before Him" (5–6). Everywhere in the universe, there is symmetry and balance. In human society, balance can take the form of just dealings with each other, family relations, business dealings, and transactions where everything must be weighed and measured accurately.

The second section presents a frightening and terrifying picture of Judgement Day, and the punishment meted to disbelievers and those who deny the favours of God. The tenor of this passage is harsh and terrifying, reflecting Divine Anger. The image is a contrasting one to the luxuries, cool shade, delightful foods and flowing streams of Paradise. This is followed by another section that describes a further two gardens for ordinary believers. So, ranks will exist among the people of Paradise, as they will among the people of Hell.

In the Name of God, the Kind, the Caring.

HIS FAVOURS COME FROM THE HEAVENS

[1] The Most Kind [2] taught *the beloved Messenger* the *Majestic* Quran. [3] He created human beings [4] *and* taught them the *art of* communication. [5] The sun and the

moon *orbit* in set paths, ⁶plants and trees bow before Him. ⁷He raised the sky and finely balanced everything, ⁸so don't disturb the fine balance. ⁹Give due weight and *measure,* don't short change *one another.*

His favours are everywhere on Earth

¹⁰He created the Earth for living creatures, ¹¹fruits and date trees with sheathed bunches, ¹²husked grains and fragrant flowers. ¹³So which favours of your Lord will you deny? ¹⁴He created human beings from oven-baked clay, ¹⁵and created jinn from smokeless flame. ¹⁶So which favours of your Lord will you deny? ¹⁷He is the Lord of two risings and settings.ᵃ ¹⁸So which favours of your Lord will you deny?

His favours also lie in the sea

¹⁹He combined the seawater and the freshwater, ²⁰there's an invisible barrier between them which stops them mixing. ²¹So which favours of your Lord will you deny? ²²Pearls large and small come from there. ²³So which favours of your Lord will you deny? ²⁴The ships sail on the seas looming high like mountains. ²⁵So which favours of your Lord will you deny?

How God is involved in human life

²⁶All things on Earth will perish; ²⁷all that will remain is your Lord,ᵇ the Majestic and the Giver of honour. ²⁸So which favours of your Lord will you deny? ²⁹All those in the Heavens and the Earth depend on Him; every day He appears in *wondrous* waysᶜ. ³⁰So which favours of your Lord will you deny? ³¹We'll give you attention, humans and jinnᵈ. ³²So which favours of your Lord will you deny?

Space travel is possible

³³Humans and jinn! If you have the capability of passing beyond the regions of Heaven and the Earth then do so; but, you won't be able to pass without authority.ᵉ ³⁴So which favours of your Lord will you deny? ³⁵Flames of fire will lash at

---

ᵃ "Two risings and settings" refers to the rising of the Sun and the Moon.

ᵇ *Wajhu rabika* literally means "your Lord's face", obviously a metonym for God; the face refers to "the self", the whole being of a person.

ᶜ He is engaged in the running of the affairs of the world e.g. creating new life, causing death, honouring or humiliating, giving and responding to the seekers (Jalalain).

ᵈ So you can carry out your work.

ᵉ *Sultanin* is also translated as "my power"; perhaps referring to the power of a space rocket?

you, cover you with smoke, and leave you defenceless.[f] [36] So which favours of your Lord will you deny?

THE FRIGHTENING SCENE OF JUDGEMENT DAY

[37] When the sky splits up it will be *bright* red, like red leather. [38] So which favours of your Lord will you deny? [39] That Day neither human nor jinn will be asked about their sins. [40] So which favours of your Lord will you deny? [41] The sinners will be recognised by the marks *on their faces,* and they shall be grabbed by their forelocks and feet. [42] So which favours of your Lord will you deny? [43] This is Hell that the sinners denied. [44] Here they will wander *aimlessly* between Hell and *cauldrons of* boiling water. [45] So which favours of your Lord will you deny?

THE TWO SPLENDID GARDENS FOR THE MOST PIOUS

[46] The person who feared standing before his Lord will have two gardens. [47] So which favours of your Lord will you deny? [48] Both with thick foliage. [49] So which favours of your Lord will you deny? [50] Both with two flowing fountains. [51] So which favours of your Lord will you deny? [52] Both with fruits of two kinds. [53] So which favours of your Lord will you deny? [54] Sitting relaxed on sofas lined with brocade, with their low-hanging fruit gardens. [55] So which favours of your Lord will you deny? [56] In them will be ladies with lowered gazes who no man or jinn would have touched. [57] So which favours of your Lord will you deny? [58] Like *glamorous* rubies and pearls. [59] So which favours of your Lord will you deny? [60] What's the reward for kindness except kindness? [61] So which favours of your Lord will you deny?

THE TWO OTHER GARDENS FOR ORDINARY BELIEVERS

[62] Beside these there are two other gardens. [63] So which favours of your Lord will you deny? [64] Both with deep green *foliage.* [65] So which favours of your Lord will you deny? [66] Both have two gushing fountains. [67] So which favours of your Lord will you deny? [68] Both gardens will have plenty of fruit dates and pomegranates. [69] So which favours of your Lord will you deny? [70] In them will be ladies with *charming* character and beauty.[g] [71] So which favours of your Lord will you deny? [72] With beautiful eyes living in *tall* tents. [73] So which favours of your Lord will you deny? [74] Never touched before by a human or a jinn. [75] So which favours of your

[f] This seems like the description of a space rocket hurtling through the stratosphere into space.
[g] *Khayrat,* interpreted as strong character; and *Hisan,* as pretty face (Zia-ul-Quran).

Lord will you deny? [76] Sitting relaxed on green cushions and fine carpets. [77] So which favours of your Lord will you deny? [78] Blessed is the name of your Lord, Most Majestic and Giver of Honours.

56. Al-Waqi'ah
The Inevitable Event

This Makkan chapter is paired with the previous chapter, which described two kinds of Paradise; here more details are provided. The Quraysh are challenged and warned of the dire consequences of their denial. After describing the cataclysmic events of the Final Hour and the coming to pass of Judgement Day, it describes the three groups into which humanity will be divided. The rest of the chapter deals with each one of them: the group blessed with the highest level of Paradise, people who struggled and strived with all their might to achieve the nearness of God; the group of the right hand, living in a delightful Paradise, but a rank below the first – their Paradise will be lesser compared to that of the foremost; and the third group, the people of the left hand, living in Hell.

Followed by questions about the beginning and ending of life, they expose the folly of those who deny Resurrection, and urge the reader to examine closely some powerful phenomena. Who makes the semen? Who grows the seed when it is in the depths of the soil? Who sends the rain down? Who made the fire? The chapter teaches that human resurrection is similar to the birth of a baby created from a spermatozoon, nutritious cereals growing from a dead seed, flames of fire coming from wood, and rain from clouds enabling so much to live. Behind them all is the power of God. He creates and destroys what He wills. The frequent reference to Resurrection in the Quran is to remind people of the purpose of their lives, and to protect them from the deception of the fleeting world. The Quran wants to save humanity from falling into its trap. The rampant selfishness and individualism common in our society today can only be corrected by accepting resurrection. The belief that your actions bear consequences. One day you will have to face your evil deeds. This gives life meaning and purpose. The lack of this belief has made modern society nihilistic; aimless and purposeless, that›s causing so much misery and pain.

The chapter ends with the frightening scene of a person in death throes; can anyone prevent his death? After reminding humanity of their helplessness in such situations, "This is the certain truth, Messenger! Glorify the name of your Mighty Lord" (95–96).

In the Name of God, the Kind, the Caring.

THE THREE GROUPS OF PEOPLE ON JUDGEMENT DAY

¹ When the Inevitable Event[a] happens, ² no one will be a denier. ³ Some will be humiliated, others honoured. ⁴ When the Earth trembles violently, ⁵ the mountains

---

[a] *Al-Waqi'ah*, the inevitable event, refers to Judgement Day

will crumble [6] and become scattered dust. [7] That Day you will be sorted out into three lots: [8] *first* will be people of the right hand; how wonderful will be those of the right hand! [9] *Second* will be people of the left hand; how wretched will be those of the left hand! [10] And *third* will be in the first rank, the foremost; [11] closest to God. [12] They will enjoy the delights of Paradise. [13] Many from the earlier generations, [14] but a few from the later generations.[a]

The foremost in a luxurious Paradise

[15] Resting on couches decked with jewels, [16] they will *enjoy each other's company* face to face. [17] Served by young people of timeless youth [18] carrying glasses and jugs full of the purest wine, [19] which doesn't give headache nor drunkenness, [20] they will choose *to eat* fruit of all kinds [21] and relish *roasted* bird's meat. [22] Their spouses will be beautiful, [23] like hidden pearls. [24] A reward for what they used to do. [25] They will hear neither idle talk, nor sinful conversation, [26] only the greetings of peace!

The people of the right hand in a delightful Paradise

[27] And the people of the right hand, how wonderful are the *people* of the right hand, [28] living among thornless cedar trees, [29] bunches of bananas, [30] widely-spread cool shade, [31] water fountains, [32] lots of fruit [33] never ending, never out of reach. [34] They will have the most beautiful partners [35] We *especially* created for them, [36] made them virgins, [37] passionately loving and young – [38] especially for the people of the right-hand. [39] Many from the earlier generations, [40] and many from later generations.

The people of the left hand in a blazing Hellfire

[41] The people of the left hand, how wretched will be those of the left hand. [42] *They will be* living in *surroundings of* scorching winds and boiling water [43] in the shadow of dark smoke, [44] neither cool nor comforting. [45] In the past life they lived in luxury, [46] and kept committing *the* grave sin *of idolatry*.[b] [47] And said, "What, when we are dead and turned to dust and bones, will we be resurrected? [48] And our forefathers too?" [49] Tell them: "Those of the past and the later generations [50] will be gathered together at a fixed time on a known Day. [51] Then, you the misled and

---

[a] The fact that "the foremost people" of Paradise will mostly be from the earlier generations of the faithful and only a few from the later generations hints to the progressive decline in human moral and spiritual intelligence.

[b] *Hinsil azeem* refers to idolatry; this is the biggest sin of all major sins.

the deniers, [52] you will be forced to eat *fruit* from *the* Zaqqum tree,[c] [53] filling your bellies with it, [54] forced to drink boiling water, [55] you'll drink it like thirsty camels." [56] This is their hospitality, on Judgement Day!

THE BEGINNINGS; SEMEN, SEED, WATER AND FIRE

[57] We created you, why don't you accept this? [58] Haven't you considered the semen you emit? [59] Did you create it yourselves, or are We its Creator? [60] We decreed, death will surround you, and nothing can stop Us [61] from changing you and recreating you anew, something you don't know. [62] Since you know well your first creation *in the mother's womb*, why don't you pay attention? [63] Haven't you considered what you sow? [64] Do you make it grow, or are We its growers? [65] If We wanted, We could have turned it into a stubble *after harvest*, and you would be left to wonder: [66] "Why are we debtors! [67] No, in fact we have been robbed." [68] Haven't you considered the water that you drink? [69] Do you send the rain from clouds or are We the senders? [70] If We wanted we could make it bitter, so why don't you thank *God*? [71] Have you considered the fire you light? [72] Did you make the wood or are We its makers? [73] We made fire a reminder of Hell and a beneficial thing for the traveller. [74] So glorify the Name of your Mighty Lord.

THE SPECIAL STATUS OF THE MAJESTIC QURAN

[75] I swear by the positions of the stars, [76] if only you knew, this is indeed a mighty oath. [77] Indeed this is a Majestic Quran, [78] *stored* in a hidden Book; [79] only the clean ones can touch it.[d] [80] A Revelation from the Lord of the worlds. [81] So how can you disrespect Scripture like this? [82] And *from its blessings* all you could receive is denying it? [83]

THE FINAL DESTINATION

Why, then, when *a dying person's* last breath comes to the throat, you can't return it? [84] You watch *helplessly*? [85] Though We are closer to him than you, though you can't see. [86] Why do you think that you are not dependent on Us? [87] If you are truthful, why can't you cause that ebbing life to return?

THE FINAL DESTINATION

[88] So *the dying person if they were* from the closest to God, [89] they shall be comfortable in fragrant and blissful Paradise. [90] And if they are from the people of

---

[c]   *Zaqqum* refers to one of the trees of Hell, resembling a thorny cactus.
[d]   An order to be in pure state i.e. to wash oneself before touching the Quran.

the right hand, [91] they shall be greeted with: "Peace be with you from people of the right hand." [92] But if they happen to be one of the deniers, misguided, [93] their welcome will be boiling water, [94] a blazing fire of Hell! [95] This is the convincing truth, [96] *Messenger*; glorify the Name of Your Mighty Lord.

57. Al-Hadid
The Iron

This Madinan chapter was revealed in the year 629 CE, before the victory of Makkah. The previous chapter divided humanity into three groups: the companions of the right hand, companions of the left hand, and the foremost. The central theme of this chapter is encouragement to become the foremost, achieving higher status and nearness of God through spending in God's path. The chapter outlines the importance and the rewards of charity. Wealth has been granted as a trust; it is natural that we should spend it in God's way. It demonstrates a person's faith in God, and acknowledgment of His kindness. Charity is a mark of faith, it is likened to giving loan to God. In the Hereafter, charity will be the light that will lead the believers into Paradise. Charity givers are given the honorific titles of the "truthful" and the "martyrs".

Next the issue of the hypocrites, those in two minds, an uncharitable bunch neither with Muslims nor with non-Muslims; neither here nor there.

Believers are challenged: "Hasn't the time come for the believers, that their hearts humbly submit to God's remembrance and the revealed truth?" (16) The sense of urgency imparted by this verse encourages the giving of charity without delay. A major hindrance to giving in charity is love of the world, so the next section describes the fleeting and short-lived nature of worldly life, and cautions: don't be tempted by the world. The image used to describe the fleeting nature of life is that of a plant; it grows, dries, and withers away becoming dry stubble. Similarly, human life has its blossoming period, a vibrant youth, old age, a time of decline and finally death.

The theme of spiritual development is continued by revealing another divine principle: predestination. Whatever happens in the world, or to people, is all written down by God. Its purpose is to help people to persevere, endure difficulties and show patience at times of difficulty. The chapter ends with how God will reward the generous.

The question of predestination

The knowledge that whatever happened, had to happen - nothing could stop it from happening since God willed it - That's His plan for us. This ought to enable us to face the reality of good and evil. This is predestination; *Taqdeer*, the relationship between God's knowledge of human actions and human free-will. On the face they seem to be contradictory but that's not so.

God is the Knower, who has given humans free-will. But with this free-will He gave them the huge responsibility of being His representative (*Khalifa*). He gave them a moral choice: to be good or bad. God could have made all good or all bad, but He chose to give us free-will so we become masters of our destiny, so we can choose to do good. This now gives human life a meaning and a purpose, it is a probationary period, preparation to meet the Kind Lord. In addition to this moral discretion, He gave us the revelation to enable us to live "a good life". Furthermore, He has blessed us with the ability to use natural resources. The best example of this is the Iron; the strength of the iron enables engineers to make vehicles, build one hundred storey buildings, weapons and tools of all kinds.

How did the Iron come down?

Interestingly, the Quran mentioned the scriptures were sent down, '*Anzalna*' and so was the Iron. Traditional commentators translated this as "We made the Iron", however, astrophysicists believe that all the elements including Iron 'came down' from the stars, they are 'stardust'. The Quran's choice of '*Anzalna*' we sent down Iron is not accidental. It shows it's from the Lord who created the stars and the universe. Here the Quran is inviting us to use the spiritual (scripture) and the material (iron) to succeed. One without the other would be disorder.

In the name of God, the Kind, the Caring.

A MAJESTIC DESCRIPTION OF GOD

[1] All things in the Heavens and the Earth glorify God; the Almighty, the Wise. [2] The Heavens and the Earth are in His control; He gives life, death and has absolute control over all things. [3] He is the First and the Last, the Evident and the Unseen and the Knower of all things. [4] He created Heavens and the Earth in six days, then established Himself on His Throne *as befits Him*. He knows what goes inside the Earth and what comes out from it, and what comes down from the sky, and what goes up. He is with you wherever you are, and sees whatever you do. [5] He has the control of the Heavens and the Earth and all things will return to God. [6] He extends the night into the day, and the day into the night, *so varying the length of day and night*. He is the Knower of the secrets of the mind.

ENCOURAGEMENT TO GIVE CHARITY

[7] Believe in God and His Messenger, and spend from what He has handed over to you. The believers who spend in God's way will have a great reward. [8] What is the matter with you that you don't believe in God, when the Messenger calls you so that you may believe in your Lord? He has already taken a pledge from you, if you are believers. [9] He reveals clear teachings to His servant, to take you out of darkness into light, and treats you kindly. [10] Why don't you spend in God's way? All *things* in the Heavens and the Earth belong to God. None of you can be equal

to him who spent and fought before the victory *of Makkah*. Their status is far higher than those who spent and fought afterwards. However, God promised to be generous to all. He is fully aware of what you do.

CHARITY WILL BE LIGHT IN THE HEREAFTER

[11] Who will give God a beautiful loan so that He may multiply it for him, and reward him generously? [12] On that Day you will see believing men and women with their lights shining ahead of them, and on their right-hand side. *Believers! Here is good* news for you today: *a home in* Paradise with streams running beneath it, where you will live forever. This is the supreme victory. [13] That Day, hypocrite men and women will ask the believers, "Wait a moment, let us benefit from your light." They will be told, "Go back and get the light." Then a wall with a gate will be put up between the believers and them. Inside *the wall* is *divine* benevolence and comfort, outside is pain and suffering.

THE WEAKNESSES OF UNCHARITABLE HYPOCRITES

[14] The hypocrites will then call *to the believers*: "Weren't we with you?" "*Yes*, but you succumbed to your temptations, you were hesitant to believe, full of doubts, and you were deceived by false hopes until the Divine Command came. The deceiver deceived you! [15] Today, no ransom will be accepted from you or from the disbelievers. Your home will be the Hellfire; that will be your residence, and a wretched destination."

LACK OF CHARITY AND HARDNESS OF THE HEART

[16] Hasn't the time come for the believers, that their hearts submit humbly to God's remembrance and the revealed truth? Don't be like the ancients, who were given the Scripture, and with passing of time their hearts hardened; they were mostly lawbreakers. [17] Know, God gave life to Earth when it was lifeless, that's how We explain for you the signs, so you may understand.

CHARITABLE PEOPLE ARE TRUTHFUL AND MARTYRS

[18] Men and women who gave charity as a beautiful loan to God will have it multiplied for them, and will be generously rewarded by God. [19] The believers in God and His messenger are the truthful and the martyrs in the Sight of God.[a] They will have a *special* reward and a light. The deniers of Our Scripture are the people

---

[a] *Shuhada* means witnesses. Here I've used the technical meaning, "martyrs", those killed in the path of God.

of Hell.

THE SHORT-LIVED NATURE OF WORLDLY LIFE

[20] *You should* know, the worldly life is a sport and an amusement, an attraction, showing off among yourselves and wanting more wealth and children. The rain is an illustration of it; the farmer delights in the *rapid* growth of his crops, then they dry and he sees them turning yellow, then turn into *dry* stubble. In the Hereafter there will be severe punishment *for the disbelievers, but for the believers* forgiveness and His Divine pleasure. The life of this world is a provision that deceives. [21] Therefore, compete with each other for Your Lord's forgiveness and Paradise, its breadth is like the breadth of the Heavens and the Earth, prepared for the believers of God and His messengers. That's God's grace; He gives it to who He pleases. And God is the Most Gracious.

BELIEF IN PREDESTINATION PREVENTS HOPELESSNESS

[22] Any disaster on Earth or to yourselves is written down before it happens; this is easy for God. [23] Its purpose: to *ensure* you don't become hopeless because of your loss, nor boast about your gain. God doesn't like the show-offs, [24] or those who are miserly and tell others to be miserly. If anyone turns away, *remember* God is Self-Sufficient, deserving of all Praise. [25] We sent our messengers with clear proofs, the Book, and Scales of Justice so people may establish justice. We sent down iron; a strong *metal* with many benefits for people, to see who uses this to help God and His messengers, without seeing *Him*. Indeed, God is the Strong, Almighty.

THE CHRISTIANS INNOVATED SELF-DENIAL

[26] We sent Noah and Abraham, and blessed their children with prophethood and the Book; some of them were guided, but most were lawbreakers. [27] We sent more messengers in their footsteps, including Jesus son of Mary, to whom We gave the Gospel. We filled his follower's hearts with compassion, and they invented self-denial,[a] which We hadn't prescribed for them. They *invented* this to seek God's pleasure, but failed to fulfil its requirements. Those who believed, We rewarded them, but many were lawbreakers.

---

[a] Rahbaniyat, asceticism, monkhood, retreat from worldly activities. An innovation by the fathers of early Christianity, the Quran doesn't disapprove of it, an evidence for permissibility of good innovations in Muslim culture and society.

DOUBLE REWARD FOR THE CHARITABLE

[28] Believers, be mindful of God and believe in His Messenger, so you are given a double share of His Kindness. He will offer you a light to walk in, and forgiveness. God is the Forgiving, the Caring. [29] Let the People of The Book know, they don't control God's grace, that's in God's hand; He gives it to anyone He wants. God's grace is vast.

58. Al-Mujadilah
The Woman at Odds

This Madinan chapter is entitled Al-Mujadilah as well as Al-Mujadilah. Aisha reported that Khawla bint Sa'laba came to the Messenger 🕊, and pleaded with him about the injustice her husband had done to her. He divorced her by the Arabian custom of *Zihar*, when the husband tells his wife: "You are to me like the back of my mother." This declaration could not be revoked, so the woman would be left in limbo, in an indeterminate state – neither married, nor divorced. So Khawla appealed to the Messenger 🕊: he told her that until God revealed a new law about *Zihar*, it remained normative. She was disappointed and continued to argue with him, she said, "When Aws married me, I was young and wealthy, and my parents were alive. Now that I am old, my parents dead, and my wealth finished – now he divorced me. Is there any room for us to live together?" The Prophet 🕊 said, "Until I receive revelation, this is the normative." She kept complaining, until finally this chapter was revealed to provide a way out for her from this difficult situation. This story reminds us that God is deeply engaged with His people. It shows that God's speech can be elicited by anyone who earnestly pleads to Him.

The chapter offers instruction on the manners of having private conversations. The secret conversations of the hypocrites and Jews alarmed the Muslims, unaware of what they were plotting. So they complained to the Messenger 🕊, and these verses were revealed as a warning. Another social manner highlighted is how to make room for others in gatherings. The chapter ends by describing the dedication and loyalty of true believers.

In the Name of God, the Kind, the Caring.

THE WOMAN WHO PLEADED

[1] God heard the woman who pleaded with you about her husband and complained to God, and God heard your conversation. God is the Hearer, the Seeing. [2] Those of you who divorce their wives by Zihar[a] *should know* that they are not their mothers. Their mothers are those who gave birth to them; they are saying something horrible and false. Indeed, God is Pardoner and Forgiver. [3] Those who divorce their wives by Zihar, and then *decide* to take back what they have said, must free a slave before they sleep together. This is what you have been ordered to do. God is fully aware of what you do. [4] Anyone who can't do this must fast

---

[a]   This refers to the pagan Arab custom of rejecting a wife. See, the Introduction.

for two consecutive months, before sleeping together. If he is unable to do that, then he should feed sixty needy people. This will be a proof of your faith[b] in God and His Messenger. These are the boundaries of God. And for the disbelievers is painful punishment.

THE DISBELIEVERS WILL BE HUMILIATED

⁵ Those people who opposed God and his Messenger have been disgraced, like those disgraced before them. We sent clear signs, and for the disbelievers is humiliating punishment. ⁶ The Day God raises them up they will be told what they did. God has taken account of all *they did,* but they forgot it. And God is Witness of all things.

RULES ABOUT SECRET TALKS

⁷ Don't you realise God knows what is in the Heavens and the Earth? There is no private conversation between three people but He is their fourth, if five He is their sixth; whether they are few or more, He is with them wherever they are. Then, on Judgement Day, He will tell them what they did. Indeed, God knows all things. ⁸ Haven't you seen those who were forbidden to hold private conversations, yet they return *again and again* to do what they were forbidden? When they talk privately, they conspire to do that which is sinful, hostile and disobedient to the Prophet. When they come to you, they greet you with what God doesn't greet you with, and they tell themselves: "Why doesn't God punish us for what we said?" Hell will be sufficient for them; they will burn in it. What a wretched place of rest. ⁹ Believers, when you talk in private, do not plot to sin, *create* hostility towards, or disobedience of the Messenger, but talk about goodness and being mindful of God. Be aware of God; you shall be gathered before Him. ¹⁰ Any other kind of private conversations are the works of Satan, *which* makes the believers unhappy; he can't harm them except by the Will of God. So the believers should put their trust in God.

HUMILITY AND KINDNESS

¹¹ Believers, when you are asked to make room in congregations then do so, God will make it spacious for you. If you are told to get up *from your place* then do so; God will raise the ranks of the believers among you, *particularly* those who have

---

ᵇ   According to Al-Qurtubi, "to believe" here means to confirm.

knowledge. God is aware of what you do.

PAYING CHARITY AS A CONSULTATION FEE TO THE MESSENGER 鑅

[12] Believers, before you consult the Messenger privately, offer charity for the consultation. That's a good practice and purification for you. If you can't offer anything, then you *will still find* God Most Forgiving, Most Kind[a]. [13] Are you afraid of offering charity before your private consultation? If you haven't done so, God has forgiven you; so perform the prayer, and pay the Zakat and obey God and his Messenger. God is fully aware of what you do.

THE HYPOCRITES USE OATHS AS SHIELDS

[14] Have you seen those who befriend a group with whom God is angry? They are neither from you nor from them, and knowingly take false oaths. [15] God has prepared a severe punishment for them. What they are doing is evil. [16] They take their oaths as shields, so they can stop people from the path of God; for them is a humiliating punishment. [17] Neither their wealth nor their children will benefit them in the slightest against God. These are people of the Fire; they shall live there forever. [18] The Day God raises them up, they will swear before Him as they swear before you now, thinking it will help them. Be aware, they are liars. [19] Satan has control over them, and has made them forget the remembrance of God. They are the party of Satan. Be aware, these are party of the Satan, they are the losers. [20] Those who opposed God and his Messenger are the most despised.

TRUE BELIEVERS ARE DEDICATED TO GOD AND HIS MESSENGER 鑅

[21] God has declared: "I and My messengers will always be the winners." God is Strong and Almighty. [22] You won't find those who believe in God and the Last Day dedicated to those who oppose God and His Messenger, even if they are their parents, or children, or brothers or relatives. These are the ones whose hearts God has strengthened with faith, and helped them with a spirit from Himself. He will take them into gardens with rivers flowing beneath them, where they will live forever. God is pleased with them, and they are pleased with Him. These are the party of God. Be aware, the party of God will win.

---

[a] When people began to demand private audience with the Messenger 鑅 too frequently, this order was given. However, it was quickly abrogated within a short time (Al Sabuni).

59. Al-Hashr
The Gathering of the Forces

This Madinan chapter was revealed after the Battle of Uhud, in the fourth year after Hijra. The central theme is the expulsion of the tribe of Banu al-Nadir from their fortresses, in the south of the city. Historians believe the Jewish tribes settled in Madinah after the sacking of Jerusalem in 587 BC by Ebenezer. The two Arab tribes of Aws and Khazraj are thought to have moved to Madinah centuries later, following a flood in Yemen.

When the Messenger ﷺ arrived in Madinah, he created a bond of brotherhood between the Arab tribes, through their faith in Islam. The Treaty of Madinah was also made with the three Jewish tribes of Banu al-Nadir, Qaynuqa and Quraza:

> The aim was to create a single community of believers but allowing for the differences between the two religions. Muslims and Jews were to have equal status ... In case of war against them they must all fight as one people ... There was no express stipulation that the Jews should formally recognise Muhammad ﷺ as the Messenger of God, though he was referred to as such throughout the document.[b]

The Jews welcomed this new arrangement, which guaranteed them peace. However, some elders found this treaty frustrating, and took every opportunity to create discord among the two communities. They were joined in their intrigues and conspiracies by Abdullah ibn Ubayy, the leader of the hypocrites in Madinah.

A Muslim woman selling her goods at the market was insulted by a Jewish goldsmith. A young Muslim stood up for her and in the scuffle that ensued he killed the offender. Rather than referring the case to the Messenger ﷺ, the Jews took the matter into their own hands and killed him. The Messenger ﷺ asked them for the payment of blood money. Instead of honouring the treaty, Banu al-Nadir conspired to kill the Messenger ﷺ. The Angel Gabriel informed him of their plot, so he immediately left their castle. This was a clear violation of the treaty, so the Messenger ﷺ gave them ten days to leave. Most of the tribe began preparing to leave, however Ibn Ubayy came to them promising them help if they were attacked. So, they refused to leave their fortresses. This was a declaration of war. The Muslims marched and laid siege, then the Messenger ﷺ ordered the cutting of palm trees, a signal that they will be attacked, so they agreed to leave. The Prophet ﷺ allowed them to carry as much as they could on their camels. What they left behind was taken as spoils of war. The Messenger ﷺ gave the palm groves, land, homes and other possessions to the emigrants. The Helpers' were happy with this distribution.

The chapter then returns to Banu al-Nadir, who were betrayed by the hypocrites, who had promised to help them. They are compared to Satan, who will also relinquish respon-

[b] M. Lings, *Muhammad: His Life Based on the Earliest Sources.*

sibility for those he misled.

This chapter contains twenty-two beautiful Names of God. Eighteen of them are mentioned at its close.

In the name of God, the Kind, the Caring.

THE BANU AL-NADIR ARE EXPELLED FROM MADINAH

[1] All things in the Heavens and Earth glorify God, He is the Almighty, the Wise. [2] He is the One Who drove out the disbelievers of the People of The Book from their homes, by the forces gathered, for the first time. You thought they would never leave, since they believed their fortresses would protect them from God. But God came upon them from where they didn't expect, and put fear into their hearts, and they destroyed their homes with their hands and by the hands of the believers. So, learn a lesson from this, people of insight! [3] Had God not decreed exile for them, He would have severely punished them *in some other way* in the world. In the Hereafter, they will have the punishment of the Fire. [4] That is because they opposed God and His Messenger, and whoever opposes God *should know* that God's punishment is severe. [5] The palm trees you cut down or left standing on their roots was done by the permission of God, to humiliate guilty people.

THE MESSENGER'S ✸ AUTHORITY TO MAKE LAWS

[6] Whatever God returned *of the booty* to His Messenger from them *wasn't due to* your swift horses or camels, but God gave authority to His Messengers to overwhelm anyone He wills. God has control over all things. [7] So whatever God returned to His Messenger from the *booty* of the townspeople really belongs to God; the Messenger, *his* relatives; the orphans; the needy; and the travellers. This is *to ensure* wealth does not circulate among your wealthy *only*. Whatever the Messenger gives you take it, and whatever he forbids you avoid it; be mindful of God, His punishment is severe.[a]

THE SELF-SACRIFICE OF THE HELPERS OF MADINAH IS PRAISED

[8] *This booty* is for the poor *Makkan* emigrants, who were expelled from their homes, and their wealth *confiscated;* they are seeking the bounty and pleasure of

---

[a] This gives the beloved Messenger ✸ the mandate to make laws and whatever he ✸ says has Divine authority. Thus, his Sunnah, his way, is being endorsed.

God, and are helping God and His Messenger. These are honest people. ⁹The settled people of Madinah have firm faith, love the emigrants who came to them, and they don't envy what was given to the emigrants. *In fact,* they give them preference over themselves, yet they are poor themselves: anyone who is saved from the greed of his selfish *desires,* is successful.

THE PRAYER OF FORGIVENESS FOR PAST GENERATIONS

¹⁰People who come afterwards will pray for them: "Our Lord, forgive us and our brothers in faith who passed away, and don't leave any hatred in our hearts of the believers. Our Lord, you are the Compassionate, the Kind."

THE HYPOCRITES' FALSE PROMISES

¹¹Haven't you seen the hypocrites saying to their disbelieving brothers among the People of The Book, "If you are expelled, we will also leave with you, and we shall not obey anyone else. If you are attacked, we will help you." God is a witness, they are liars. ¹²If they are expelled, neither will they leave with them, nor help them if they are attacked. If they came to help them, they would soon turn their backs and flee, they wouldn't be helped. ¹³They really fear you more than they fear God; that's because they are a people who don't understand. ¹⁴Even if they were all together, they would not fight you except in fortified settlements or behind *strong* walls. The enmity among them is severe. You would think they are united, but their hearts are divided; they are an unreasonable people.

HYPOCRITES COMPARED WITH SATAN

¹⁵Their example is like the people who were recently punished;ᵇ they tasted the consequences of their *bad* behaviour, and for them is a painful punishment *in the Hereafter.* ¹⁶Another comparison *of the hypocrites* is Satan; he says to man, "Don't believe," and when he disbelieves, Satan says to him, "I disown you, I fear God, the Lord of the worlds." ¹⁷The punishment for both is the Fire where they will live forever, the reward for the wrongdoers.

THE BELIEVERS PREPARE FOR PARADISE

¹⁸Believers, be mindful of God, and let everyone consider *carefully* what they carry forward for tomorrow. Fear God! He is fully aware of what you do. ¹⁹Don't be like those who forgot God so He made them forget themselves. Those are the

ᵇ This could refer to the Jewish tribe of Banu Qaynuqa, who were banished after the battle of Badr for their betrayal of the treaty.

sinners. [20] The companions of the Fire and the companions of Paradise are not alike; the companions of Paradise will be the winners. [21] Had We revealed this Quran on a mountain, you would have seen it humble itself and turn to dust out of fear of God. We give these examples so people may reflect.

EIGHTEEN BEAUTIFUL NAMES OF GOD

[22] He is God: there is no God but Him. He is the Knower of the hidden and the open, the Kind, the Caring. [23] He is God, there is no God but Him, the Sovereign, the Holy, the Peace Giver, Security Giver, the Guardian, the Almighty, the Compeller, the Greatest. God is far above the partners they ascribe to Him. [24] He is God: the Creator, the Originator and the Fashioner. He has beautiful Names, all things in the Heavens and the Earth glorify Him, the Almighty, the Wise.

60. Al-Mumtahinah
The Woman Investigated

This chapter was revealed in the eighth year after Hijra, well after the Treaty of Hudai-biyah. The practice of the Prophet ﷺ was to keep his expeditions and campaigns secret, to prevent information leaking to enemies. The Prophet ﷺ planned action against the Quraysh leaders. However, a companion by the name of Hatib ibn Balata sent a letter via a woman who was travelling to Makkah to disclose the plan to the Quraysh. Hatib ibn Balata's family was under the control of the Makkans, and he engaged in this information leak in an attempt to secure their safety. When the Prophet ﷺ learnt about this he sent some disciples to find her and confiscate the letter. They found her and seized the letter which Hatib had given her. The Prophet ﷺ summoned Hatib and asked for an explanation. He admitted his mistake, but declared his strong and true faith in Islam. His excuse was to win favour from the Quraysh so that his family was not harmed. Since Hatib had fought in the Battle of Badr, the Prophet ﷺ forgave him. We learn a few important lessons from this incident: do not base judgements on guesswork; the forgiving nature of God; the need to be loyal to one's community.

The central theme of the chapter is the relationship between the Muslims and non-Muslims. The Quran teaches diplomacy: If attacked defend yourself, but strive for peace and friendship with them, "God will make friendship between you and your current enemies one day" (7). The beautiful example is given of Prophet Abraham who lived in a multi-faith society. However, faith will make us different and we must accept this difference so we can live in peace and harmony.

In the name of God, the Kind, the Caring.

THE OBLIGATION TO BE LOYAL AND FAITHFUL

[1] Believers, don't take as allies those who are Mine and your enemies. How can you fondly send reports about Muslims to them? Yet they disbelieved the truth that came to you; they expelled the Messenger and you because you believed in God, your Lord. If you truly emigrated in My path seeking My pleasure, then how can you correspond secretly with them? I know well what you have concealed and what you have revealed. Whoever did so has lost the straight path. [2] If they could suppress you, they would be your bitter enemies who would stretch out their hands and tongues to destroy you, and they wish you would disbelieve. [3] Neither your relatives nor your children will benefit you on Judgement Day. There, God

will separate you out. God sees what you do.

ABRAHAM AND HIS FOLLOWERS ARE ROLE MODELS

[4] There is a beautiful role model for you in Abraham and those with him; when they said to their people, "We disown you and those you worship beside God; we reject you; there will be hostility and hatred between us until you believe in God alone." Except for what Abraham said to his father: "I will seek forgiveness for you, although I can't protect you from God in the slightest. Our Lord, we rely on You, and we turn devoutly to You, and the final return is to You. [5] Our Lord, do not make us a prey[a] for the disbelievers; forgive us our Lord. Our Lord, You are the Almighty, the Wise." [6] What a beautiful role model they are for you *and in fact* for anyone who hopes to meet God on the Last Day. Anyone turning away *should know* God is Self-Sufficient, Praiseworthy.

FRIENDSHIP WITH NON-MUSLIMS ISN'T FORBIDDEN

[7] God will make friendship between you and your current enemies *one day*; God is Powerful, Forgiving, Caring. [8] God does not forbid you from being good and just to those who have not fought against you due to religion, nor expelled you from your houses. God loves the just people. [9] However, God does forbid you from befriending those who fought against you due to religion, expelled you from your houses and helped to drive you out *of Makkah.* Those who befriend them are wrong.

KINDNESS TO MIGRANT WOMEN

[10] Believers, when believing migrant women come to you, investigate them. God knows well their faith. If you find them to be believers, then don't return them to the disbelievers. Neither are they lawful for them, nor *believing women* lawful for them. Give the disbelievers what they have spent *on them.*[b] There *would be* nothing wrong if you were to marry them after giving their bridal gift. You should not hold on to marriage ties with disbelieving women; ask for what you have spent on them, just as *the Makkan disbelievers* will ask for what they have spent on them.[c] That is God's judgement. God makes *fair* judgements between you, and God is the Knower, the Wise. [11] If any of your wives went *back* to the disbelievers *in Mak-*

---

[a]   *Fitna* literally means a test; here it is used metaphorically, hence my translation, "prey", a victim.

[b]   The bridal gift.

[c]   When a woman seeks divorce, the man can demand back the bridal gift he gave at the time of marriage.

kah, and afterwards you gained victory over them, pay those whose wives fled the equivalent of the bridal gift they had given them. Fear God, the One you believe.

Women's oath of allegiance

[12] Prophet! When believing women come to you to take an oath of allegiance, accept their oath: they will not associate any partner with God, nor steal, nor commit adultery, nor murder their children, nor lie about who has fathered their children, nor disobey you in common good. And seek God's forgiveness for them. God is the Forgiving, the Caring. [13] Believers, don't befriend a people with whom God was angry; they are hopeless of *success* in the Hereafter, just like the disbelievers are hopeless about the dead people in the graves.

61. As-Saff

The Rows

This short Madinan chapter motivates the believers to be brave: to practice what they say, and not be like the hypocrites who say one thing and do another. It encourages them to stand up for justice when called to do so, and not to shy away from the momentous responsibility of defending the truth. The hypocrites who had deserted the Muslims in the battle of Uhud are reprimanded.

The central theme of the chapter is to encourage Muslims to keep their word; a unity between professed faith and practical life. The believers are warned of the vicious intentions of the Makkan disbelievers to extinguish God's light. However, God promises that Islam's light will prevail and spread. There is nothing that the disbelievers can do to stop this religion of truth being triumphant. A Divine promise and good news of victory to encourage them to continue with the struggle in God's path. Naturally, the Prophet was disheartened by the hypocrites' actions, but the Quran comforted him by giving examples of two great Prophets: Moses and Jesus, who were similarly let down.

By giving the example of Moses and Jesus , the chapter challenges Jews and Christians to examine their heritage and conscience: their prophets had already predicted the coming of Muhammad 🕮 as the final Messenger. In the Gospel of John 14: 15, Jesus speaks to the Disciples and tells them, "If you love me keep my commands, and I will ask the Father to give you another advocate to help you and be with you forever." Who was this advocate? We believe it is our beloved Prophet Muhammad 🕮.

The next section gives a method of achieving salvation: faith and Jihad, firm belief in God and His Messenger 🕮, and practical and persistent efforts to obey them. Those who do so are honoured with the title, "the helpers of God."

In the name of God, the Kind, the Caring.

Do as you say

¹All things in the Heavens and the Earth glorify God, He is the Almighty, the Wise. ²Believers, why do you say things that you don't do? ³It's disliked by God that you say things that you don't do. ⁴God loves the ones who fight in His way in rows upon rows, *standing* like a solid building.

Denouncing hypocrites who offended Messengers

⁵Remember when Moses said to his people, "My people, why do you insult me? Yet you know I am the messenger of God *sent* to you." When they deviated from

the path, God lets them go astray[a]. God doesn't guide the sinful people. [6]Also remember when Jesus, son of Mary, said, "Israelites, I am God's messenger *sent* to you confirming the Torah that you already have, and I give you good news of a messenger who will come after me; his name will be Ahmad." Jesus showed them clear signs, but they said, "This is wizardry."

THE TRUTH OF GOD'S RELIGION WILL PREVAIL

[7]Who can be more wicked than the one who invents lies against God, whilst he is invited to embrace Islam? God doesn't guide the wrongdoers. [8]They want to extinguish God's light with their propaganda, but God will spread His light everywhere,[b] no matter how much the disbelievers dislike it. [9]He is the One Who sent His Messenger with guidance and the religion of truth, so it will prevail over other religions, no matter how much the idolaters dislike it.

SUCCESS LIES IN FAITH AND ACTION

[10]Believers, shall I show you a course of action[c] that will save you from a painful punishment? [11]*It is:* you believe in God and His Messenger, and strive in His path with your wealth and lives. This is good for you. [12]God will forgive your sins and take you into gardens beneath which rivers flow, and into wonderful mansions in the gardens of Eden. That is the greatest achievement. [13]*You will also get* something else that you dearly love: help from God and a speedy victory. Give good news to the believers.

BELIEVERS ARE URGED TO BECOME HELPERS OF GOD

[14]Believers, become helpers of God, like Jesus son of Mary invited his disciples: "Who will be my helper for God's sake?" The disciples replied, "We are God's helpers." So, one group of the Israelites believed and another denied. We helped the believers against their enemies, so they prevailed over them.

---

[a] Literally this means, "God led their hearts astray."
[b] Literally this means, "will complete or perfect."
[c] *Tijara* literally means "business, commerce, bargain and transaction".

62. Al-Jumuʿah
The Day of Congregation

This is a Madinan chapter, revealed after the Treaty of Hudaibiyah in the sixth year after Hijra. It opens with the glorification of God and four important roles of the Prophet ﷺ: teaching; recitation of the verses of the Quran; purification and development of the character of his followers; and explaining the Book with wisdom. The Arabs are referred to as "*Ummiyeen*," unlettered people, as opposed to the literate Jews and Christians who were People of Scripture. The Quran is critical of the Jewish Rabbis who regarded themselves above others because they were literate, People of The Book, and the children of prophets. The question is, what is the point of being literate if you don't read and follow the instructions of the Torah. This is not merely a criticism of the Rabbis of Madinah, but a clear message to Muslims: if you don't read and follow the message of the Quran, you are like "a donkey carrying books."

The central theme of the chapter is the importance of the Friday prayer, a way of glorifying God. It was revealed to reprimand those people who had rushed out during the Friday sermon when they saw a caravan carrying grain arrive in Madinah. The chapter urges Muslims to attend the Friday prayer promptly. "*Fasʾaw*" means running; the use of it here imparts a sense of urgency and importance to the call for prayer, stressing the significance of the weekly learning time, the sermon. The Friday prayer is not only devotion, but an important socio-political gathering where the leader of the community addresses the congregation. The tone of this passage makes clear that a true believer will always give precedence to worship of God over worldly things. The Prophet ﷺ said:

> "When one of you takes a bath on Friday, brushes their teeth, wears beautiful clothes, puts on perfume and then attends the Masjid and prays there until the Imam begins the sermon, all these things will be an atonement for his sins from the previous to this Friday". (Abu David)

In the name of God, the Kind, the Caring.

THE MESSENGER'S ﷺ RESPONSIBILITY TO UNITE HUMANITY
[1] All things in the Heavens and the Earth glorify God, the Sovereign, the Holy, the Almighty, the Wise. [2] He sent a Messenger to the unlettered people. He recites His verses to them, purifies them, teaches them the Book and the wisdom. Before that they were misguided. [3] *He has been sent* to them and others[a] who hav-

---

[a] "Others" refers to all non-Arabs (Ibn Kathir); the Messenger ﷺ came to unite all humanity.

en't yet joined them, and He is the Almighty, the Wise. [4]That is God's grace;[b] He gives it to whom He pleases, and God possesses immense grace.

ACT ON THE TEACHINGS OF GOD'S BOOKS

[5]*Look at* the example of the people who were burdened with the Torah but didn't practise its *teachings; they* are like a donkey carrying books. Shameful is the example of the people who deny God's revelations. God doesn't guide the wrongdoers. [6]Say: "Israelites, if you claim sincerely that you alone out of all the people are the friends of God, then you should wish to die." [7]But they will never wish death, because what their hands have sent before, and God knows the wrongdoers. [8]Say: "The death you are running away from will soon catch up with you, and you will be returned to the One Who knows the seen and the unseen. Then He will inform you of what you did."

THE FRIDAY PRAYER IS A COMPULSORY WEEKLY ASSEMBLY

[9]Believers, when the call for the prayer is made on Friday, come hurriedly to God's remembrance and stop all work.[c] That certainly is good for you. [10]When the prayer is finished, then disperse in the city, seeking God's grace, and frequently remember God so you may be successful. [11]When they saw a *commercial* bargain or entertainment, they rushed towards it and left you standing. Tell them: "What God has is far better than the entertainment and the bargain." God is the Best Provider.

---

[b]   *Fadhl* in Arabic means grace, undeserved, unearned and unmerited reward.

[c]   This verse makes Friday prayer compulsory for all believers. However, there are some exemptions to this: women, travellers and the sick. The *Dhikr-God* here is interpreted as the Friday sermon, not the usual remembrance.

63. Al-Munafiqun
The Hypocrites

This chapter was revealed in Madinah after the campaign of Banu Mustalaq in the sixth year of Hijra. It is a commentary on an incident that took place after this campaign. The Muslims were camped in an oasis near a well. A fight between two men broke out. One of them called out: 'Ansar! Come to my help!' The other called out: 'Emigrants! Come to my help!' Both sides responded, swords were drawn out and a battle about to follow. The Prophet ﷺ rushed to the site and cautioned them: "Why have you started shouting the slogans of the Age of Ignorance? After embracing Islam, this is criminal behaviour." The Prophet ﷺ calmed the belligerents, and everyone dispersed. However, the hypocrites were annoyed by this. They were jealous of Muslim unity and began to scheme. Abdullah ibn Ubayy, the leader of the hypocrites stated: "When we get back to Madinah, the strong will expel the weak," meaning his forces were the strong, and would expel "the weak" Muslims. Some Muslims heard this insulting threat, the Helpers in particular were furious. They went to Abdullah ibn Ubayy and asked him to retract his words and apologise to the Messenger ﷺ. Instead, he responded angrily: "You told me to believe in him, so I believed in him. You said pay Zakat and I donated money. What do you want me to do now – prostrate before him?" When he approached Madinah, his son stood tall with his sword drawn out in front of his father, and stopped him from entering. He swore an oath: "I will not let you enter Madinah until the Messenger ﷺ allows you." Upon hearing this, the Prophet ﷺ said, "Let him enter Madinah."

The Muslims are warned about the appalling behaviour of the hypocrites, their insults, betrayals and plots to create conflict among Muslims. Hypocrisy is vehemently condemned in the Quran on numerous occasions, because it smacks of an unprincipled attitude, indecisiveness and disloyalty. The final section of the chapter provides a powerful antidote to hypocrisy: give charity, and seek closeness to the Divine before time passes away.

In the name of God, the Kind, the Caring.

THE CONTRADICTORY BELIEFS AND BEHAVIOUR OF THE HYPOCRITES

¹When the hypocrites come to you they say, "We bear witness you are truly the Messenger of God." *Of course*, God knows you are His Messenger, and God bears witness that the hypocrites are the liars. ²They take their oaths as a shield, then they stop others from *coming to the* path of God. What they are doing is evil. ³*First* they believed, then they denied, therefore their hearts are sealed so they

no longer understand. [4] When you see them their outward appearances please you, when they speak, you listen to them, but *in reality,* they are like propped-up wooden posts.[a] They think any outcry is against them. They are the enemy, so be careful of them. May God destroy them; they are utterly lost!

THE HYPOCRITES ARE ARROGANT AND MISCHIEVOUS

[5] When it is said to them, "Come so the Messenger of God so he may ask forgiveness for you," they shake their heads and you see them turn away arrogantly. [6] Whether you seek forgiveness for them or not it is the same; God will not forgive them. Indeed, God does not guide disobedient people. [7] They say, "don't spend on those who are with the Messenger of God until they leave *him.*" The treasures of the Heavens and the Earth belong to God, but the hypocrites don't understand. [8] They claim: "When we return to Madinah, the strong will expel the weak." All strength belongs to God, His Messenger and the believers, but the hypocrites don't understand *this.*

THE ANTIDOTE TO HYPOCRISY: GIVE CHARITY

[9] Believers, don't let your wealth and children turn you away from the remembrance of God; those who do so are the losers. [10] Spend from the provisions We gave you before death comes, and you say, "My Lord, if you delay my death for a little while I will *go and* spend in charity and become righteous." [11] God won't delay death for anyone once its time has come. God is aware of what you do.

---

[a]   The simile of 'propped-up wooden posts' shows hypocrites as a useless bunch. Wooden posts are useful if they are beams or joists in a roof or if they are made into doors and furniture.

64. At-Taghabun
The Day of Winning or Losing

The central theme of this Madinan chapter are Islamic beliefs, especially the life Hereafter. The majesty and grandeur of God's power opens the chapter. It points out the benefits of faith: believers will be successful, whilst disbelievers will be ruined, as is apparent in the fates of past generations. The believers are directed to carry out duties that will lead them to success: being charitable, obedient and ever mindful of God. It also warns how wealth, spouses and children can be a temptation that can lead to breaking Divine laws: "Whoever can save themselves from greed, then those are the successful ones" (16).

Yaum At-Thaghabun means 'the day of winning or losing'; the believers will be winners as they enter paradise; but the disbelievers will be losers, thrown in hell. However, everyone will have a sense of being cheated, some believers will feel loss, because they could have worked harder for the Hereafter. The disbelievers will be utterly devastated as they realise the world had cheated them. The noun *ghibn* means, "To take something without paying its price." In other words, to cheat[a]. So, the world and its trappings cheat those who pour themselves into it but get nothing in return in the Hereafter.

In the name of God, the Kind, the Caring.

HUMAN CREATION HAS A PURPOSE

[1] All things in the Heavens and the Earth glorify God. He rules over all things and all praise is for Him. He has control over all things. [2] He is the One Who created you; but some of you chose to be disbelievers, and others choose to be believers, and God sees what you do. [3] He created the Heavens and the Earth for a true purpose and shaped you, then He perfected your forms, and to Him is the final return. [4] He knows what is in the Heavens and the Earth, and He knows what you conceal and what you reveal. God knows what lies in *people's* minds.

THE LIFE OF THE HEREAFTER IS HUMANITY'S FINAL DESTINATION

[5] Hasn't the news of the disbelievers of the past reached you? They tasted the consequences of their deeds, and for them is a painful punishment. [6] That was because when their messengers with miracles used to come to them, they *disapprovingly* said, "How can *mere* humans guide us?" So, they denied and turned away. God has no need of them. God is Independent and Praiseworthy. [7] The disbelievers

---

[a] M. A. Sabuni, Sawatut Tafsir, Dar-ul'Ilm al Arabi.

claimed they will not be resurrected; say *to them*: "Of course My Lord will resurrect you, and then you will be told what you did." That is easy for God. [8] So believe in God and His Messenger, and the light that We have sent down. God is aware of what you do.

SOME WILL GAIN, OTHERS WILL FACE LOSS ON JUDGEMENT DAY

[9] He will assemble you on the Day of Gathering, that's the Day of gain and loss. Whoever believed in God and did righteous deeds, He will erase his sins and take him into gardens with rivers flowing beneath them, to live there forever – the great success. [10] But the ones who disbelieved and rejected our revelations, will be people of the Fire, to live therein forever. What an evil place!

HOW TO AVOID LOSS

[11] No misfortune befalls anyone except by the permission of God. Whoever believes in God, God will guide his heart, and God knows all things. [12] *Therefore* obey God, and obey the Messenger; were you to turn away *you would lose,* since Our Messenger's responsibility is only to deliver the message clearly. [13] There is no god but Him, so let the believers put trust in God alone.

HOW TO ACHIEVE SUCCESS

[14] Believers, some of your spouses and your children could be enemies, so beware of them! However, if you forgive, tolerate and pardon *their conduct* then *you will find* God too is Forgiving, Caring. [15] Your wealth and children are a test; with God is a great reward. [16] So be mindful of God as much as you can, and listen, obey, and give in charity; that is good for you. Whoever can save themselves from greed, then those are the successful ones. [17] If you lend God a beautiful loan, He will multiply it for you, and forgive you. God is Most Appreciative, Gentle, [18] Knower of the unseen world and the seen, the Almighty, the Wise.

65. At-Talaq
The Divorce

This Madinan chapter deals with the subject of divorce: proper method, prescribed waiting term, maintenance expense, the custody and breastfeeding of the child. It was revealed after *Chapter Al-Baqarah*'s passage on family law (222–242). The blessed Messenger 襐 described divorce as, "the most abhorrent of permissible things" (Abu David). Ali, the fourth caliph, said, "The Divine Throne trembles when someone gives divorce." Islam allows divorce only when life as husband and wife becomes unbearable and could lead to damaging welfare and the quality of life. The Islamic divorce as described here specifies that divorce should be given at the end of the menstruation period. Once the husband has given the notice of divorce to his wife, in the presence of two just witnesses, she must stay in her home and must not leave. This is not the end of the marriage. What happened during the heat of the moment in a state of anger may dissipate; reconciliation may occur. The prescribed waiting time of three menstruation periods is effectively a cooling-off period. This is the revocable divorce, and husband and wife can resume their marital life without a new wedding contract (*Nikah*) within the waiting term.

The divorce according to Shariah is a simple, straightforward, short and equitable procedure compared to the complicated , expensive and torturous procedure in other legal systems. It's good to notice how the recent changes in British Law are catching up with the Shariah.

Further rules for pregnant women are outlined: prohibiting divorce during pregnancy, the prescribed waiting term is the end of her pregnancy and the birth of the child. Every opportunity is being provided to help keep the family together, and several warnings are given: "Those are God's boundaries; whoever exceeds the boundaries of God has wronged himself" (1). People going through divorce are reminded, "Be mindful of God." He shall provide them a means out of this dreadful situation, and He will provide for them sustenance. The final section of the chapter warns against disobeying God's commands. It cites the example of previous communities who disobeyed and were severely punished.

In the name of God, the Kind, the Caring.

SAFETY MEASURES WHEN DIVORCING

[1] Prophet, when someone *intends to* divorce a woman, let *him* divorce her at a time when their waiting term[a] can begin, and accurately count the waiting term.

---

[a] *'Idda* is the legal waiting term. It is three menstruation periods, or the end of pregnancy, or three months and ten days for a widow.

Fear God, your Lord. Do not drive them out of their houses, nor should they leave *by themselves* except if they had committed a shameless indecency. Those are God's boundaries; whoever exceeds the boundaries of God has wronged himself. You don't know what new circumstances God may bring about after that. [2]So when they have completed their waiting term, you may keep them honourably, or let them go honourably. *On this occasion* appoint two just witnesses amongst you, and establish witnesses for the sake of God. A guidance *for* believers in God and the Final Day. Whoever is mindful of God, He shall make a way out for him, [3]and provide him sustenance from where he wouldn't expect. Whoever puts trust in God is enough for him. God will complete His task. God has made a precise amount *of sustenance* for all things.

RULES ABOUT DIVORCE DURING PREGNANCY

[4]Your older women in menopause should complete the *waiting* term of three months if you are in doubt. The same applies to those who aren't menstruating. The prescribed term for pregnant women is the end of their pregnancy. Whoever fears God, He will make his circumstances easy. [5]That is the command of God, which He has sent down to you. Whoever is mindful of God, He will forgive his evil deeds, and increase for him *his* reward. [6]House them *during the waiting period* where you live, according to your *financial* means, and do not harass them in order to make their lives miserable. If they are pregnant, then spend *generously* on them until they have delivered the newborn. If they breastfeed *the child* for you, then give them a payment *for that*. Deal in a good way with each other. If you find yourselves in difficulty, then let another woman breastfeed the child for him.[b] [7]Let the wealthy man spend according to his wealth, and let the one whose income is limited spend from what God has given him. God doesn't burden anyone except with what He has given him. God will soon make ease after hardship.

SEVERE PUNISHMENT FOR THOSE WHO DISOBEY GOD'S RULES

[8]How many cities have rebelled against its Lord and His messengers' command? We sternly brought them to account, and severely punished them. [9]So they tasted the evil effects of their disobedience, and their works finally came to nothing.

---

[b] The time of childbirth marks the end of the prescribed waiting term for a divorced pregnant woman. She is now free to marry and therefore will be like a stranger to her former husband. It is the duty of the father to make the arrangements for the newborn; that is why she can negotiate in maintenance fees.

[10] God has prepared a severe punishment for them. So be mindful of God, understanding people who believe! God has sent down a reminder to you, [11] a Messenger who recites God's clear verses to you, to take those who believe and do good deeds out of the layers of darkness into the light. Whoever believes in God and does righteous deeds, He will admit him into gardens beneath which rivers flow; they will live therein forever. God has perfected for them *their* provisions. [12] God is the One Who created the seven Heavens and the Earth in a similar *number* to them. *His* commandments come down between them, so that you may come to know that God has control over all things, and that God's knowledge encompasses all things.

66. At-Tahrim
The Prohibition

This Madinan chapter was revealed in the eighth year of Hijra. There are differing reports surrounding the circumstances of its revelation. The most likely is the following story: One day, Zainab, the wife of the Prophet 🌸, offered him some honey. She knew he was very fond of it, and thoroughly enjoyed it. As a consequence, he spent extra time with her. Later that night, he 🌸 met Aisha, who felt upset and complained that his breath smelled of *Maghafir*, a wild tree on which bees feed. The Prophet 🌸 was disappointed, and promised to refrain from eating honey, and that they should keep this a secret. However, Aisha disclosed it to Hafsah.

Whatever the circumstances here, the Quran teaches five general principles: not to make unlawful that which God has made lawful; how to amend and atone for vows; not to betray trusts and give away secrets; the whole family should work together to save themselves from the Hellfire; and seeking repentance for sins committed intentionally or unintentionally.

The solution given for the human condition of sinning is "*Taubatan Nasuhan*" (8) – sincere and genuine repentance. This means regretting the sin, feeling ashamed of it, resolving not to repeat it, and then asking for God's forgiveness.

The wives of the Prophet 🌸 are gently reprimanded here for this marital tiff, a petty quarrel. They are asked to be more caring and considerate towards each other. There is possibly a warning implied in the mention of the wives of two other prophets, Noah and Lot : if they are to be disobedient and unmindful of God and the Messenger 🌸, they will be the losers like those two women. Finally, it gives them the example of two wonderful women; Asiya, the wife of the Pharaoh, and Mary the Virgin , the mother of Jesus .

In the name of God, the Kind, the Caring.

The importance of keeping secrets

¹ Prophet, why do you – desiring to please your wives – avoid[a] things that God has made lawful for you? God is Forgiving, Caring. ² God has ordered for you that you make up for your *unfulfilled* oaths. God is your Master; He is the Knower, the Wise. ³ Remember when the Prophet shared a secret with one of his wives, and when she disclosed it *to another* God informed him about it; he confirmed part of

---

[a] *Al-Tahreem* literally means "to prohibit and make unlawful". However, here it refers to the Prophet 🌸 avoiding eating honey, rather than regarding it as unlawful.

it and kept the other secret. So when he informed her about this she said, "Who has told you this?" He replied, "The Knower, the Aware told me." ⁴Both of you *wives* should repent before God; your hearts have *already* inclined towards *seeking forgiveness.* Were you to assist one another against him, *remember* that God is his Protector, so is Gabriel; the righteous believers and *all* the angels after that are *his* helpers. ⁵Were he to divorce you, his Lord would give him better wives in your place, those who are submitting, believers, obedient, repentant, devout, fasting, and *some* previously married and *others* virgins.

The responsibility of saving one's family from Hellfire

⁶Believers, protect yourselves and your families from a fire whose fuel is humanity and *their* stone *idols*; *it will be* controlled by fierce, stern angels who don't disobey God in what He commands them to do, and they do what they are told to do. ⁷Disbelievers, don't make excuses today; you will only be repaid for what you used to do. ⁸Believers, turn to God in sincere repentance. Your Lord may forgive your sins, and admit you into gardens with rivers flowing beneath them, the Day that God will neither humiliate the Prophet nor those who believed. Their light will be beaming in front of them and on their right, and they will pray: "Our Lord, perfect our light for us and forgive us, You control all things."

The two disobedient wives

⁹Prophet, strive against the disbelievers and the hypocrites, and deal with them firmly. Hell is their resting place; what a terrible home! ¹⁰God gives an example to the disbelievers of the wife of *the Prophet* Noah and the wife of *the Prophet* Lot; both *women* were married to two of our devout and righteous servants, but they betrayed them. *So* their husbands couldn't save them from God at all. It will be said, "Both of you enter into the Fire along, with the other entrants."

The example of two pious women

¹¹God gives an example to the believers of Pharaoh's wife, when she said, "My Lord, build for me a house near you in Paradise, and save me from Pharaoh and his works, and save me from the evildoers." ¹²And *the second* example is of Mary, the daughter of Imran, who protected her chastity, and We blew in her Our spirit, and she accepted the truth of Her Lord's Words and the Scriptures, and she was an obedient woman.

67. Al-Mulk
The Control

The central theme of this chapter is the purpose of life: an opportunity to earn God's pleasure, falling in love with Him, and doing good works. The chapter points to a common failure to understand this simple fact, for which desperate regret will be felt on Judgement Day by the negligent: "If only we had listened or understood *the message,* we would not be among the companions of the Blazing Hell" (10). The chapter effectively draws our attention to Divine Power as displayed in the splendour of nature, affirming the existence of the spiritual reality beyond the material world. A stern warning is given against failing to see beyond the material world: "Which forces beside the Most Kind can possibly help you? The disbelievers are only deceived" (20). The chapter opened with the purpose of human life, and ends by pointing out that human life is dependent upon water. To emphasise God's control over all, it poses a question: "Have you considered: if your *drinking* water level went low, who could bring back running water for you?" (30)

_____

In the name of God, the Kind, the Caring.

THE PURPOSE OF HUMAN LIFE

[1] The Blessed One has authority, *complete* control, and power over all things. [2] He created death and life to test you – who among you is best in good works. He is the Almighty, the Forgiver; [3] He created the Seven Heavens, layer upon layer. You will not see the slightest defect in the creation of the Most Kind. Look *at it* again; do you see anything wrong? [4] Then look once more; your sight will come back weary and fatigued. [5] We decorated the lowest sky with stars,[a] and made them projectiles hurled at the devils. We have prepared the punishment of Blazing Hell for them.

THE DISBELIEVERS' REGRET FOR NOT HEEDING THE MESSAGE

[6] The disbelievers of the Lord will have the punishment of Hell, a miserable home! [7] When they are thrown into it, they will hear roaring as *Hell* boils bubbling noisily, [8] about to explode with rage. Every group thrown into it will be asked by its guards: "Didn't any warner come to you?" [9] They will say, "Yes, a warner came to us, but we denied and told them, 'God hasn't revealed anything, you are grossly

_____

[a] Literally "lamps", but denotes stars. It can also refer to the shooting stars, which act like missiles against the devils.

misguided." [10] They will *regretfully* reply, "If only we had listened or understood *the Message,* we wouldn't be among the companions of Blazing Hell." [11] So they will confess their sins; away with the companions of Blazing Hell. [12] The people who feared their Lord without seeing Him will be forgiven, and have a great reward.

[13] Whether you hide your words or make them public, He is the Knower of what is in *your* innermost thoughts. [14] Does He not know who He created? He is the Subtle, the Aware. [15] He made the Earth accessible for you, so you could travel through its vast expanses, and eat from His provision, and before Him you will be gathered, alive. [16] Do you feel safe from the One in the Heaven that He wouldn't command the Earth to swallow you up when it shakes violently? [17] Or do you feel safe from the One in the Heaven that He wouldn't send a sandstorm *to destroy* you? Then you will soon know *the seriousness of* My Warning! [18] Those before them also denied, so how terrible My Condemnation!

ARROGANCE LEADS TO DENIAL OF DIVINE GIFTS

[19] Have they not seen the birds flying over their heads arranged in rows, flapping their wings in harmony? It is the Most Kind Who holds them there; indeed He sees all things. [20] Which forces beside the Most Kind can possibly help you? The disbelievers are only deceived. [21] Who can give you provision if He withholds His provision? *Unfortunately,* they persist in *their* arrogance and hostility. [22] Who is more guided: the one who walks grovelling, *looking down* and falls flat on his face, or the one who walks upright on a straight path? [23] Say: "He created you and made hearing, sight and intellect for you; how little you thank!" [24] Say: "He dispersed you throughout the Earth, and you will be gathered before him."

DISBELIEVERS WILL BE GRIEF-STRICKEN

[25] They ask, "When will this promise be *fulfilled,* if you are telling the truth?" [26] Say: "Only God knows it's *timing,* and I am a clear warner." [27] When they see *Hell* come close, the disbelievers' faces will be grief-stricken, and it will be said, "This is what you used to ask for." [28] Say: "Consider this – whether God destroys me and those with me or He treats us kindly, *the question is*: so who will save the disbelievers from a painful punishment?"

BELIEVERS ACCEPT GOD CONTROLS EVERYTHING

[29] Say: "He is the Most Kind; We believe in Him and we put trust in Him, and soon you will know who is misguided." [30] Say: "Have you considered: if your *underground* water level went low, who could bring back running water for you?"

68. Al-Qalam
The Pen

The central theme of this early Makkan chapter is a warning to the people of Makkah: if you refuse to believe in the Messenger ﷺ, then be prepared to face severe consequences like previous disobedient nations did. To affirm that the Messenger ﷺ is trustworthy, and that his Message should be accepted by the Makkans, the chapter opens by acknowledging the beautiful character of Prophet Muhammad ﷺ. He possesses truthfulness, kindness, generosity, patience, forgiveness, humility, justice, modesty and thankfulness. This is contrasted with the vices of al-Walid ibn al-Mughira, a ruthless opponent of the Messenger ﷺ.

The story of the owners of the orchard highlights how much miserliness is disliked by God. The gross injustice of the owners of the orchard is contrasted with the arguably smaller error of Prophet Jonah , who left the city of Nineveh without Divine permission, and was reprimanded severely. The suggestion is that God will not tolerate even minor misdemeanours from His chosen, let alone those who openly oppose God and the Messenger ﷺ.

The final verse gives us an idea of the dislike with which the Makkans listened to the Majestic Quran. The beloved Prophet ﷺ is consoled: their evil eye will not impact him. According to a saying of the Prophet ﷺ: "If there is anything that can overcome destiny, it is the evil eye" (Tirmidhi).

––––––––––

In the name of God, the Kind, the Caring.

¹*Noon.*

THE MESSENGER'S ﷺ STRONG CHARACTER IS A PROOF OF HIS TRUTHFULNESS

By the pen and everything they write. ²By the grace of your Lord, *Prophet*, you aren't possessed. ³Indeed, you shall have an everlasting reward, ⁴and you have a strong character.

THE EVIL CHARACTER OF THE OPPONENTS OF THE MESSENGER ﷺ

⁵Soon you will see, and so will they, ⁶who is really demented. ⁷Your Lord knows best who strayed from His path, and He knows best who are the guided. ⁸So don't compromise with the deniers; ⁹they would love to see you compromise with them so that they may compromise. ¹⁰Don't yield to every[a] despicable swearer of oaths – ¹¹a fault-finder, dashing around backbiting, ¹²obstructing the common

[a]   This refers primarily to al-Walid ibn al-Mughira, a leader of the Quraysh and a staunch opponent of the Prophet ﷺ.

good, an aggressor, a sinner, [13] an oppressor, and moreover of doubtful birth. [14] He has plenty of wealth and children. [15] When Our verses are recited to him he says, "These are ancient stories." [16] We shall soon put a mark on his nose.[b]

THE STORY OF THE MISERLY LANDLORDS OF THE ORCHARD

[17] We test them as We tested the owners of the orchard, when they promised they would pick the fruits early in the morning [18] and they made no exceptions.[c] [19] While they slept, a disaster from your Lord struck *the orchard*, [20] so by the morning it was a desolate place. [21] They woke up in the morning and called out to each other, [22] "Hurry to your harvest, if you are going to pick its fruits." [23] So off they went, whispering to each other, [24] "Absolutely no needy person will enter it today and bother you." [25] They went early, purposefully and determined. [26] However, when they reached there they saw it *utterly desolate*, they said, "We are lost, [27] rather we are prevented *from picking the fruit!*" [28] The middle one said, "Didn't I tell you to glorify God?" [29] They replied, "Glory be to Our Lord, we were wicked!" [30] So they turned to one other and began blaming each other. [31] They cried, "Woe to us! We were shamelessly disobedient, [32] perhaps Our Lord will give us something better in exchange for the orchard; we turn genuinely in hope to Our Lord." [33] Such was the punishment, *but* the punishment of the Hereafter is even greater. If only they knew.

THE PUNISHMENT OF HELL WILL BE SEVERE

[34] The righteous will have attractive Gardens near their Lord. [35] So are We to treat those who have submitted themselves like the sinners? [36] What is the matter with you; what makes you judge in this way? [37] Or do you have a book from where you have learnt [38] that you will get whatever you choose? [39] Or do you have solemn oaths with Us that are binding till Judgement Day – you will have whatever you decide? [40] Ask them: "Who will guarantee this? [41] Or do they have partners *beside God?*" So let them bring their partners if they are truthful. [42] The Day things will be extremely difficult, they will be invited to prostrate, but they won't be able to do so, [43] their eyes lowered and *faces* covered with humiliation. They were invited to prostrate when they were safe and sound. [44] So leave those to Me who deny this

---

[b]   To disgrace him.

[c]   Either they failed to say "if God wills," or they promised not to leave any fruits hanging on the trees for the poor.

Revelation. So gradually We shall lead them to their ruin, and they will not know it, [45] and We shall give them more time. My plan will work.

THEY WANT TO HARM THE MESSENGER 🌸 WITH THEIR EVIL EYES

[46] Or do you ask them for a wage, which will burden them heavily with debt? [47] Or do they have knowledge of the unseen that they write down? [48] So wait patiently for your Lord's judgement and do not be like the companion in the *belly of the whale*[a] who prayed whilst in distress. [49] Hadn't a blessing from His Lord reached him, he would have been abandoned on the barren shore, condemned forever. [50] So His Lord *accepted his plea and* selected him, and He made him among the righteous. [51] They wish to strike you down with their *evil* eyes; when the disbelievers hear the Reminder they say, "He is mad!" [52] This is a clear Reminder for all people.

---

[a]   This refers to the Prophet Jonah .

69. Al-Haqqah
The Reality

The core teaching of the Majestic Quran is: Hereafter is the reality, and worldly life is a mere shadow of it. The physical world is the apparent, and the underlying reality is the Hereafter. Some have translated the title of this chapter as the inevitable hour, referring to the Final Hour. The Quran, in its inimitable style, presents it as "here and now". The central theme of the chapter is the question: what is the reality of human life? The chapter is a direct challenge to human materialist tendencies, and invites the reader to consider the horrors and reckoning of Judgment Day. By offering examples of previous disobedient communities, the Quran warns the neglectful and belligerent Makkans that it would be wise to accept the reality.

In the name of God, the Kind, the Caring.

THE HEREAFTER IS THE ULTIMATE REALITY

¹ The ultimate reality – ² what is the ultimate reality? ³ What could explain to you what is the ultimate reality? ⁴ *The people of* Thamud and Ad both denied that the striking blow *would ever happen.* ⁵ *The people of* Thamud, they were destroyed by the thunderous storm. ⁶ And as for *the people of* Ad, they were destroyed by a violent and furious cold wind, ⁷ which He forced against them for seven nights and eight days in succession. So you would have seen the people therein dead, lying prostrate as if they were like the hollow trunks of palm trees. ⁸ Do you see their remains *today*? ⁹ Then the Pharaoh and those before him brought habitual sin from the overturned cities,ᵇ committed great sin. ¹⁰ So they disobeyed the Messenger of their Lord, and He seized them with a punishment. ¹¹ When the floodwater rose high, We carried you in the sailing ship ¹² to make it a lasting reminder for you, and so attentive ears may understand it.

THE EVENTS OF THE FINAL HOUR

¹³ So when the Trumpet is blown, it will be a single blast, ¹⁴ the Earth and the mountains will be raised high and crushed to powdered dust; ¹⁵ on that Day, the Inevitable Event will happen; ¹⁶ the sky will be split apart, looking flimsy. ¹⁷ On that Day, *a group of* eight angels *standing* along its edges will carry your Lord's

---

ᵇ 'Overturned cities' could refer to Sodom and Gomorrah where the prophet Lot preached.

Throne above them. ¹⁸On that Day, you will be brought *for Judgement,* and nothing of your deeds will remain hidden.

THE DELIGHTFUL LIFE OF THE PEOPLE OF PARADISE

¹⁹The one given the Book *of Deeds* in his right hand, will say, "Here, take it and read my Book! ²⁰I believed that I would be held accountable." ²¹So he will have a happy life, ²²in a lofty garden, ²³with its low-hanging bunches of fruits, easily *plucked.* ²⁴*He will be told*: "Eat, drink and be merry for what you did in the days gone by."

A PORTRAIT OF WASTED LIFE

²⁵*However*, the one given the Book *of Deeds* in his left hand, will say, "I am ruined! I wish that I had not been given my Book, ²⁶and I never knew I would be held accountable; ²⁷how I wish death would have ended this. ²⁸My wealth hasn't benefited me ²⁹and my influence has disappeared." ³⁰Seize him, handcuff him, ³¹then let him burn in Hell ³²and drag him with a seventy-metre long chain! ³³He didn't believe in God, the Almighty, ³⁴nor would he encourage others to feed the needy. ³⁵Today, he has no close friend here, ³⁶neither any food except from filthy bodily discharges, ³⁷that only the sinners will eat.

THE GLORIOUS QURAN IS GOD'S REVELATION

³⁸No, I swear by what you can see ³⁹and what you can't see. ⁴⁰*The Majestic Quran* is the speech of a noble Messenger; ⁴¹not the speech of a poet, little do you believe! ⁴²Neither is it the speech of a soothsayer, little do you reflect! ⁴³A Revelation from the Lord of the worlds. ⁴⁴Had *the Prophet* made up a lie against Us, ⁴⁵We would have seized him by the right hand, ⁴⁶and then cut the major artery *in his heart,* ⁴⁷so none of you would have been able to stop *Us* from him. ⁴⁸Indeed *the Quran* is a reminder for the pious. ⁴⁹We know some of you will deny *it,* ⁵⁰and it will be *a source of* severe regret for the disbelievers. ⁵¹*The Quran* is the absolute truth, ⁵²so glorify the name of your Lord, the Almighty.

70. Al-Maʿarij
The Stairways to Heaven

This chapter was revealed in the middle Makkan period, and its central theme is criticism of the Makkan sceptics who wanted punishment to come sooner. According to Ibn Kathir, the Messenger ﷺ once warned a Makkan storyteller, Nadhr ibn Harith, of the punishment of Hell. He mockingly demanded, "Why don't you bring a sandstorm that will destroy us?" The chapter was revealed in response to his tactless demand.

The chapter opens with a critical reprimand of the questioner who makes such a foolish request. It reminds him of God's Power, Majesty and the stairways leading to the Heavens that can take people to their spiritual heights. The section vividly captures the terrifying moments of the end of time: the sky turning red, mountains hanging like fluffed tufts of wool, and the Day when everyone will be anxious. The next section praises the person who accepts Judgement Day; he is described as a dutiful worshipper who has a good moral character. He cares for others, spends generously, and controls his sexual appetite. The final section questions why disbelievers are unable to believe in the Creator, and gives a stern warning.

In the name of God, the Kind, the Caring

THE END OF TIME

[1] *A sceptical* questioner demanded a punishment to fall [2] upon the disbelievers; nothing can ward it off *once it comes* [3] from God, the Lord of the spiritual stairways to the Heavens, [4] by which the angels and the *Noble* Spirit ascend to Him on a Day with a time-span of fifty thousand years. [5] So *Messenger*! Be patient in a beautiful manner! [6] Indeed, they consider it a long way off, [7] *yet* We know it is near. [8] The Day when the sky will be like molten brass, [9] and the *hanging* mountains will be like masses of *fluffed* wool.

THE DAY OF SORROW, DREAD AND REGRET

[10] *It will be a Day* when no close friend will bother to ask *anything of* his close friend, [11] yet they will be within sight of one another. The wicked person will wish to give away everything to save himself from punishment that Day, even his children, [12] his spouse, his brother, [13] his blood relatives who sheltered him, [14] and everyone on Earth, to save his own skin. [15] That will not *happen*! There will be a raging flame [16] that peels away the skin. [17] *Hell* shall call out to all who turned their

481

backs and turned away, ¹⁸ the one who gathered *wealth* and hoarded it.

A GLOWING DESCRIPTION OF WORSHIPPERS

¹⁹ Humans were created anxious; ²⁰ when misfortune befalls them, they are impatient, ²¹ and when good fortune befalls them, they are selfish; ²² except the worshippers, ²³ who perform their prayer constantly, ²⁴ in whose wealth is a due share ²⁵ for the beggar and the deprived, ²⁶ who believe in Judgement Day, ²⁷ who are fearful of their Lord's punishment, ²⁸ their Lord's punishment from which no one is safe. ²⁹ Who guard their sexual purity, ³⁰ except from their spouses, or their slave maids; for that they can't be blamed. ³¹ But those whose lustful desires go beyond that, they are the transgressors. ³² Who fulfil their trusts and promises, ³³ who give honest testimonies, ³⁴ who are focused and regular in their prayers. ³⁵ They will be honoured in *delightful* gardens.

WHY ARE THE DISBELIEVERS SURPRISED?

³⁶ What is the matter with the disbelievers? They all stare at you *Prophet*, ³⁷ from the right and the left. ³⁸ Does each one of them expect to be admitted into a Garden of Delight? ³⁹ *That will* never happen; We created them from something they know. ⁴⁰ So I swear by the Lord of the Eastern and the Western horizons, indeed We are fully capable ⁴¹ of replacing them with people better than them, and no one can stop Us. ⁴² So leave them *pandering* to their idle talk and playing *games*, until they face *Judgement Day*, which they are promised. ⁴³ The Day they will quickly come out of the graves, as if racing towards goal posts, ⁴⁴ their eyes cast down and *faces* covered with humiliation. That is the Day, which they were promised.

71. Nuh

Noah

This Makkan chapter sketches the life and works of one of the great prophets of God, Noah . The archaeologists of the Bible believe he lived approximately 10,000 years ago, on the Southern shores of the Black Sea. Its central theme is his struggle against unbelievers. The story comes as a reassurance for the Prophet Muhammad ﷺ and the early Muslims: they would be saved and their enemies destroyed, as happened with the people of Noah in the past.

For nine and a half centuries, Noah preached bravely in a variety of ways, with determination. He presented convincing evidence from their lives, the natural world around them, and from history, but his words fell on deaf ears. They were stubborn, materialistic idolaters who could not see beyond the physical realm. The chapter presents a heart-rending prayer, his moving sermon, and finally his prayer of desperation in the final section.

In the name of God, the Kind, the Caring.

NOAH WARNED HIS PEOPLE

[1] Indeed, We sent Noah to his people *with a message*: "Warn your people before a painful punishment comes to them." [2] He told them, "My people! I am a clear warner to you, [3] so worship God, be mindful of Him and obey me, [4] then He will forgive your sins and spare you until your appointed time. When God's deadline comes, it cannot be delayed, I *wish* you understood."

NOAH'S HEART-RENDING PRAYER

[5] He prayed: "My Lord, I called my people day and night, [6] my calling has only increased them in fleeing further and further away. [7] Each time I invited them to Your forgiveness, they put their fingers into their ears, covered themselves up with their garments, persisted *in their disbelief* and were thoroughly arrogant. [8] I invited them openly, [9] then in public, and in private with the utmost discretion.

NOAH'S COMMANDING SERMON TO HIS PEOPLE

[10] I told them, 'Seek your Lord's forgiveness; He is Most Forgiving. [11] He will send plenty of rain for you from the sky, [12] and bless you with wealth, children, provide for you gardens, and provide for you rivers. [13] What's the matter with you that you don't fear the Majesty of God? [14] Yet He created you in stages. [15] Haven't

you considered how God created the Seven Heavens one above the other? [16] He placed the moon as a light, and the sun as a lamp. [17] God produced you from the Earth *like* plants, [18] then He will return you to it, and will bring you out *from it.* [19] And God spread out the Earth for you, [20] so you may travel over its broad paths and valleys.'"

NOAH'S PRAYER OF DESPERATION

[21] *Eventually* Noah prayed: "My Lord, they disobeyed me and followed those whose wealth and children increased them in loss. [22] They devised a scheme of great magnitude: [23] *they* tell them, 'Don't abandon your gods and don't abandon Wadd, Suwa', Yaghuth, Ya'uq or Nasr.'[a] [24] They have misled many; *My Lord,* do not increase the wicked except from going further and further astray *from the Truth.*" [25] Due to their sins, they were drowned and then thrown into Hell; they couldn't find any helper for them against God. [26] Noah prayed: "My Lord, don't leave any disbelievers on Earth; [27] if you left them, they will misguide Your servants, and breed *more* wicked disbelievers. My Lord, forgive me and my parents and whoever enters my house as a believer, believing men and women. Don't increase the wicked except in utter destruction."

---

[a]   These were five idols they used to worship.

72. Al-Jinn
Jinn

According to Ibn 'Abbas, a group of jinn visited the Prophet ﷺ after he returned from his journey to Taif, in which case, the chapter was revealed in the tenth or eleventh year of his mission in Makkah. The central theme is challenging the stubbornness and disbelief of the Quraysh. By telling the story of a group of jinn who believed in the Messenger ﷺ, the Quraysh are made to feel jealous of them. The chapter presented a direct report from the mouth of a jinn accepting faith in the Messenger ﷺ and the Revelation, whilst the materialistic disbelievers think the Quran is merely poetry, or the words of a soothsayer or madman. It also reassured the Messenger ﷺ of the truthfulness of his message, building his confidence and self-esteem, so that he isn't upset.

The jinn are an invisible and intelligent creation of God, made from smokeless fire, a high-energy form. Like humans, they can be either believers or disbelievers. The chapter outlines some of their characteristics, and some similarities and differences to human beings. It reveals their amazement and surprise at the inability of Makkans to believe in the Majestic Quran. Finally, it shows the humility of the Messenger ﷺ who proclaims: "I have no control over harming or benefiting you" (21). God is protective of His messengers by providing them with guardians, who look after them all the time.

––––––––––

In the name of God, the Kind, the Caring.

A GROUP OF FAITHFUL JINN

¹ Say *Prophet*: "It was revealed to me that a group of jinn listened *to the Quran* and said *to their people*, 'We heard an amazing recitation, ²which guides to the right path and we believed it, and will not associate anyone with Our Lord.' ³'Our Lord's majesty is exalted and He hasn't taken a wife nor a child, ⁴as some fools claimed such an outrageous lie against God. ⁵We never thought human beings and jinn would utter *such* lies against God.'

WHAT DO JINNS BELIEVE AND DO? HOW POWERFUL ARE THEY?

⁶'Men used to seek protection from male jinn, but all they have done is increased them in evil practices, ⁷and they believed as you believed that God will not resurrect anyone. ⁸When we snooped at the secrets of the sky, we found it was full of powerful guards and comets.ᵇ ⁹We sat in there waiting to eavesdrop, but now

ᵇ   *Shihab* means a shooting star, flaming fires and a luminous meteor.

whoever listens in will have comets lying in wait for him. [10] So we don't know whether it is evil that is intended for those on Earth, or if their Lord wishes to guide them. [11] Some of us righteous and others not so, we follow many different paths, [12] and we know we won't frustrate God on the Earth, nor manage to run away from Him.'

The jinn are surprised at the Makkans' attitude toward the Prophet

[13] 'When we heard the guidance, we instantly believed it, and whoever believes in His Lord need not fear loss nor oppression. [14] Some of us have submitted, and others are unjust. So the one who submits *to Him*, has received true guidance. [15] The unjust shall be fuel for Hell.'" [16] Had they remained steadfast on the straight path, We would have given them plenty of water to drink, [17] so that We could test them regarding it. Whoever turns away from his Lord's remembrance, He will thrust him into ever-increasing difficulties. [18] The places of worship are for God, so don't worship anyone beside God. [19] When the servant of God stood up to worship Him, they packed around him in crowds.

The Messenger ﷺ humbles himself before God

[20] Say: "I worship my Lord, and I don't associate anyone with Him." [21] Say: "I have no control over hurting or benefiting you." [22] Say: "No one will save me from God, nor will I find a refuge beside Him; [23] my mission is only to deliver His Messages. Whoever disobeys God and His Messenger will be in the fire of Hell forever." [24] Eventually, when they see what they are promised, they will instantly know who is the weakest helper and the smallest in number. [25] Say: "I don't know whether *the scourge* you are promised is near, or if My Lord has postponed it.

God protects His Messengers from all harm

[26] He is the Knower of the unseen and doesn't reveal His secrets to anyone, [27] except the messengers of His choosing. To protect *the messengers,* He sends guardians who walk in front and behind them, [28] to ensure they *can freely* deliver the messages of their Lord. God knows what they have, and He keeps an exact count of all things."

73. Al-Muzammil
The Enwrapped

This is an early Makkan chapter, possibly the second after *Chapter Al-'Alaq*. The first part of the chapter highlights the worries of the Prophet 鬱 about his mission, and his devoutness. The final long verse was revealed in Madinah. This final verse came as a concession to the Prophet 鬱 and the companions with regards to the length of their night vigils. The chapter opens by describing the devotion of the Messenger 鬱, his longing for God, and his recitation of the Quran. He is urged to read the Quran slowly, and articulate each letter clearly in a rhythmic and beautiful tone. The Prophet 鬱 used to say, "Beautify the Quran with your voices" (Al-Hakim). The chapter illustrates that the blessed Messenger 鬱 is a beautiful example of the ultimate worshipper of God, who stands all night in worship, whilst others sleep.

The final lengthy verse gives instructions with regards to night vigils. The Quran is relaxing previous, more demanding instructions, since the situation of the Muslims in Madinah demanded they engage in carrying out other tasks during the day, including those concerned with their livelihoods, preaching and spreading Islam, and protecting their land.

––––––––––––

In the name of God, the Kind, the Caring.

THE MESSENGER'S 鬱 NIGHT WORSHIP IS EXEMPLARY

¹The Enwrapped! ²Pray standing during the night for a little while; ³half the night or even less; ⁴or a bit more, and read the Quran with clear pronunciation.ᵃ ⁵Soon, We will send you a weighty Revelation. ⁶*Prayer* during the night makes a strong impact on the mind and makes the speech effective, ⁷since all day long you remain busy; ⁸remember the Name of your Lord and wholly devote yourself to Him. ⁹The Lord of the East and the West, there is no God but Him, so take Him as *your* Protector.

THE MAKKANS ARE WARNED OF A PUNISHMENT

¹⁰And bear patiently what they say, and avoid them in a goodly manner. ¹¹Leave Me to deal with the deniers who selfishly enjoy comfort, and bear with them for a little while. ¹²Indeed, We have prepared chains, a blazing Fire, ¹³food that chokes and a painful punishment. ¹⁴The Day when the Earth and the mountains will shake violently, then turn into heaps of sand.

ᵃ Ali defined *Tarteel* as pronouncing clearly each letter of the words of the glorious Quran.

[15] Indeed, We sent to you a *noble* Messenger, *who is* a witness for you, like We sent a messenger to Pharaoh. [16] *But* Pharaoh disobeyed the messenger, so We punished him severely. [17] So how will you protect yourself *from the suffering* of a Day which will turn children's hair grey, how can you deny it? [18] The sky will be torn into pieces, and His promise fulfilled. [19] This is a reminder, so anyone who wants to take a path to his Lord, let him do so.

THE NIGHT WORSHIP; THE MESSENGER ﷺ PERMITTED TO RELAX HIS WORSHIP

[20] Your Lord knows, you stay awake worshipping Him with a group of *disciples*, sometimes for nearly two-thirds of the night and *other times* half of it or a third of it. *It is* God Who determines the length of the night and the day. He knows you won't be able to keep this *practice* up for too long, so He is kind to you: from now on, recite the Quran as much as you are able to with ease. He knows there are some who are ill, others travelling on business trips,[a] and others fighting in God's path. So recite from the Quran what is easy for you. *Furthermore,* establish the prayer regularly, pay the Zakat and give God a beautiful loan. *Remember,* whatever good you stock up is for yourselves; *in the Hereafter* you will find it with God. You will be greatly rewarded. Seek God's forgiveness; God is Forgiving, Caring.

·

[a] *Fadhu-l-God*, or "God's grace", is a metaphor for business.

74. Al-Muddathir
The Cloaked One

After the first revelation of *chapter Al-'Alaq* the Angel Gabriel stopped coming to the Prophet 襐. This break in revelation may have lasted for a year, and this chapter was the first to be revealed after the break. In this case it's a significant revelation. The Prophet 襐 is reminded of his important position and crucial role in transforming humanity. The opening verses clearly instruct him to be energetic and forthright in preaching the Message, without fear of anyone.

However, it also contains scores of new constructions, expressions, linguistic patterns, metaphors, statements that allow multiple interpretations, and elegantly concise turns of phrase, not to mention the new intellectual and cultural dimensions that intersect with *this* linguistic and rhetorical development.[b]

The Messenger 襐 is being prepared for the hostility he will face, and Walid ibn al-Mughira, his opponent, is severely criticised, and his gloomy future in Hellfire vividly described. The proverb, "You reap what you sow" is mentioned in this context. The Quran also presents this principle: "Every person is endangered by the evil he has done, except the companions of the right hand" (38). In other words, every person is held hostage by the wrong they do; evil leads to evil results, vice creates vice, and wrong actions lead to wrong outcomes. An empowering verse; people can touch their own destiny. At the end the Messenger 襐 is reassured and cautioned that the jealousy of some will prompt their opposition to him.

———————

In the name of God, the Kind, the Caring.

THE MESSENGER 襐 IS INSTRUCTED TO PREACH OPENLY

[1] *Messenger*, the cloaked one, [2] stand up and warn *people*, [3] and magnify *the praise* of Your Lord. [4] Keep your clothes clean, [5] and steer clear of evil. [6] Don't expect any gains in return for the favours you do, [7] and be patient for the sake of Your Lord. [8] When the Trumpet is blown, [9] it will be a difficult Day, [10] not at all easy for the disbelievers.

A STUBBORN OPPONENT IS CONDEMNED FOR DISBELIEVING

[11] Let me deal with the one I created a lone child;[c] [12] I gave him lots of wealth, [13] many sons around him, [14] and I made his *material* progress smooth. [15] He is

---

[b] B. Saeh, *The Miraculous Language of the Qur'an: Evidence of Divine Origin.*
[c] This is al-Walid ibn al-Mughira, a staunch opponent of the Messenger 襐.

full of hopes that I shall increase *it*. [16] No! He is a determined opponent of Our Revelations. [17] I shall soon lay upon him increasing punishment. [18] He thought and plotted. [19] He is ruined for what he plotted. [20] Again, he is ruined for what he plotted. [21] Then he looked, [22] then he frowned and scowled, [23] then he turned his back and was arrogant, [24] declaring: "This is magic of the ancients; [25] the speech of a mere mortal!"

THE MISGUIDED IS PUNISHED

[26] I shall burn him in Hellfire. [27] What will explain to you the Hellfire? [28] It neither spares nor leaves anyone, [29] constantly scorching the skin; [30] there are nineteen *guards* over it. [31] We appointed the angels over the inmates of Hell, and made their number only as a test for the disbelievers and to assure the ones who were given the Book, and to increase the faith of the believers. So, the believers and those given the Book will have no doubt about your truthfulness. But the disbelievers and the ones in whose hearts there is a sickness will say, "What does God mean by this example *of the nineteen angels*?" That is how God allows some to be misguided and others to be guided. No one knows the forces of your Lord except Him. It is a *Majestic* reminder for humanity.

WHY PEOPLE WILL END UP IN HELL

[32] Yes, by the moon, [33] by the night as it fades away, [34] by the morning as it shines! [35] It's a great thing; [36] a warner for humanity, [37] for those wanting to progress *spiritually* and those who wish to stay behind. [38] Every person is held hostage[a] by the evil he does, [39] except the companions of the right hand [40] *living* in gardens; they will ask each other [41] about the sinners: [42] "What *deeds* brought you into Hellfire?" [43] They will answer, "We neither worshipped, [44] nor fed the needy, [45] busy doing evil and friends of those who were frivolous. [46] We denied Judgement Day [47] until the inevitable, certain, *death* came to us." [48] The intercession of the intercessors, *the idols,* won't benefit them.

WILD FRIGHTENED DONKEYS

[49] So what's the matter with them, they turn away from the Reminder? [50] Like frightened donkeys [51] fleeing from a lioness. [52] Rather, each man among them wants a revelation to be rolled out and handed over to him. [53] No! They don't

---

[a]   *Rahina* literally means "to be held in pledge" or "hostage". I have translated it accordingly.

fear the Hereafter. [54] No! This is a Reminder, [55] so let him who wishes to listen to it do so. [56] They will listen if God wills. He alone should be feared, the Lord of forgiveness.

75. Al-Qiyamah
The Day of Judgement

This is an early Makkan chapter with the central theme of the Day of Judgement. It describes some of the scenes from that Day: disintegrated human bones will be brought to life, a lunar eclipse will occur, people will be astonished and confused. It will dawn upon them that they are standing in front of the Mighty Lord Who will do justice. They will see their whole life unfold before them like a film, and they will make excuses for their wretched behaviour.

Abu Jahl, the Makkan leader, bitterly opposed the Prophet ﷺ. He would bring decaying bones to the Prophet ﷺ and ask, "Can this be brought back to life?" The chapter answers that query, and further explains Abu Jahl's problem: "You love the fleeting world *dearly*" (20). His other problems include his disbelief, lack of worship, and arrogance (31–33). He is warned about his death throes, when he will be dying and no one will be able to cure him. Finally, the Quran asks, "Isn't He capable of bringing life to the dead?" (40).

In the name of God, the Kind, the Caring.

THE HORRORS OF JUDGEMENT DAY

[1] I swear by the Day of Judgement, [2] and I swear by the self-critical soul! [3] Do people think We won't put together their *disintegrated* bones? [4] Of course, We are capable of restoring even their fingertips. [5] Yet they openly commit evil in front of Him, [6] and *mockingly* ask: "When will Judgement Day come?" [7] *When it comes* eyes will be dazzled, [8] the moon eclipsed, [9] the sun and the moon *will appear to* be joined together, [10] and man will ask that Day: "Where can we flee to?" [11] No, there is no safe place. [12] That Day, *you will* be brought before your Lord: [13] people will learn what they achieved and what they failed to do. [14] They will have evidence against themselves, [15] but still offer excuses.

THE PRESERVATION OF THE QURAN IS THE CONCERN OF GOD

[16] *Messenger*, don't read *the Quran* too fast to *memorise* it. [17] We are responsible for its compilation and recital. [18] So when We recite it, then follow its recitation. [19] It is also Our responsibility to explain it clearly *to you*.

LOVE OF THE WORLD MAKES PEOPLE FORGET THE HEREAFTER

[20] You love the fleeting world, [21] and dislike the Hereafter. [22] That Day, some faces

will be shining, ²³*happily* watching their Lord. ²⁴That Day, other faces will be gloomy and grave, ²⁵sensing the occurrence of a back-breaking sufferings. ²⁶No, when the soul reaches the breastbone, ²⁷it will be said, "Where's the charmer *doctor who can heal*?" ²⁸He will know it's time to leave, ²⁹the legs will be straightened and brought together;^a ³⁰then that Day he will be driven toward Your Lord.

GOD WILL RESURRECT

³¹He didn't believe or pray,^b ³²instead he denied and turned his back, ³³walked arrogantly amid his people. ³⁴Yet, *the Hereafter* is drawing closer and closer to you, ³⁵and even more and more closer to you. ³⁶Do people think they aren't *answerable to God*? ³⁷Weren't they a drop of emitted semen? ³⁸Then a germ cell that *God* created and perfected? ³⁹Then He made from it the pair: the male and the female. ⁴⁰Isn't He *the One Who did* that? So, isn't He capable of bringing back to life the dead?

---

^a When a person is dead, the legs are straightened before rigor mortis sets in.
^b This refers to a bitter opponent of the Prophet ﷺ, Abu Jahl, and describes his arrogance and disbelief.

76. Ad-Dahr
The Time

According to some commentators this is a Madinan chapter. Its central theme is: humanity is blessed with the ability to intelligently distinguish between right and wrong, and therefore will be held accountable; a terse reminder of the purpose and meaning of human life. These introductory comments are followed by a lively description of the good people: they fulfil their vows, fear Judgement Day, are generous and selfless, and take care of the needy and the poor. For these wonderful works, they will have the delights of Paradise. The chapter makes it clear that this is a reward for their patience and hard work. Finally, the Messenger ﷺ is reminded to continue his work patiently and diligently.

———————

In the name of God, the Kind, the Caring.

THE PURPOSE OF HUMAN CREATION

¹ Hasn't there been a phase *in human history* when humans were nothing worthy of mention? ² We created human – from a drop of mixed fluid – to test. We gave them hearing and sight; ³ We showed the straight path, *to see* whether they would be thankful, or an unthankful denier. ⁴ For the disbelievers We've prepared chains, iron collars and a Blazing Fire. ⁵ The righteous will drink wine mixed with fragrant herbs,ᵃ ⁶ a drink from a freely-flowing spring, *made for* the servants of God.

WHO ARE THE RIGHTEOUS?

⁷ They fulfil *their* vows, fear a Day whose horror is widespread, ⁸ they feed the needy, the orphan and the prisoner for the love *of God,* ⁹ *saying,* "We feed you for His sake; we don't want some payment or thanks from you. ¹⁰ We fear a Day of calamity and destruction, coming from Our Lord." ¹¹ God will protect them from the distress of that Day, their faces will shine with joy.

A GLOWING DESCRIPTION OF THE DELIGHTS OF PARADISE

¹² He rewarded them with *breathtaking* Gardens and silk *clothing* for the patience they showed; ¹³ *they will* rest on *comfortable* sofas and they won't have extreme heat or bitter cold; ¹⁴ low-hanging *branches* will give them shade and clusters of fruits will be close at hand. ¹⁵ They will be served in crystal-like silver cups, ¹⁶ se-

---

ᵃ *Kafur* literally means camphor and fragrance.

lecting the size of the cups to drink from. [17] They will have a drink mixed with ginger, [18] from the spring of Salsabil[b]. [19] Eternal youth will serve them, and when you see them you will think they are pearls; [20] when you look around these delightful scenes, you will see an immense *blissful* kingdom. [21] Their *fine clothes* will be made of green silk and brocade; they will be adorned with silver bracelets, and their Lord will give them pure drinks. [22] *It will be said*: "This is the reward for you, and today your *tireless* efforts are gratefully acknowledged."

THE MESSENGER 🕌 IS URGED TO BE PATIENT

[23] We gradually revealed the Majestic Quran to you, [24] so wait patiently for the judgement of Your Lord, and don't obey any of them: the sinner or the ungrateful person. [25] Remember the Name of your Lord in the morning and evening, [26] and prostrate to Him, and glorify him throughout the night. [27] These *people* love the *short-lived* world, and dislike a Weighty Day ahead of them. [28] We created them, and strengthened their ligaments and joints; if We wanted, We could have totally replaced the likes of them. [29] This is a Reminder for anyone who wants to take the road to his Lord. [30] You can't have it unless God wills to show you that way,[c] and God is Knowing, Wise. [31] He cares for anyone He wants, and for the wrongdoers He has prepared a painful punishment.

---

[b] *Salsabil* is the fountain in paradise (Suyuti).

[c] This means you have it because God wanted to guide you. He has given you reason and revelation to see the truth. This means that humans have the choice to willingly accept the guidance or reject it.

77. Al-Mursalat
The Winds

Five oaths open the chapter: the first four refer to the incredible power of the wind, its movement of the air, that it is an amazing natural phenomenon: from the calm and pleasant morning breeze, to the gale-force winds that create storms on land to sea, and the gusty winds that move the clouds to become hurricanes and cyclones. The fifth refers to the angels responsible for the Divine Revelation. The phrase, "That will be a Day of big loss for the deniers!" Is repeated ten times. Such refrains warn stubborn people and open their eyes, so they can overcome their ignorance and egotism. Threats are employed, warning the disbelievers of the consequences of their disbelief. This is a powerful rhetorical device for conveying the message. The first time it occurs is after warning the disbelievers of "the Day of Distinction".

The chapter points out the humble beginnings of a human being: from a sperm and an egg a human baby is produced. The One Who can perform this can also resurrect the dead: "Didn't We make the Earth a place for holding back the living and the dead?" (25–26)

In the name of God, the Kind, the Caring.

The immense power of the wind is testimony to God's creative powers
[1] By the winds that blow non-stop,[a] [2] the strong gusty winds, [3] the scattering winds, [4] the shearing winds that forcefully separate, [5] and I swear by the angels who deliver a reminder, [6] sometimes a prayer and sometimes a warning, [7] what you've been promised will happen.

The Day of Decision; the winners and the losers are separated
[8] When the stars' light is faded, [9] when the sky is split, [10] when the mountains are crumbled to dust, [11] when the appointed term for the messengers *finally* comes – [12] for which Day has this been set for? [13] The Day of Decision. [14] What will explain to you what the Day of Decision is? [15] A Day of great loss for the deniers!

Lessons from history and nature
[16] Didn't We destroy the previous generations? [17] We shall do the same to this one; [18] Our way of dealing with the sinners. [19] A Day of great loss for the deniers! [20] Didn't We create you out of an embarrassing fluid? [21] That We lodged in the

---

[a] Literally "that which is sent forth".

womb [22] for a fixed period, [23] precisely determined by Us; we are excellent at determining its length. [24] A Day of great loss for the deniers! [25] Didn't We make the Earth a place for holding back [26] the living and the dead? [27] *Didn't We* make lofty fixed mountains and give you sweet water to drink? [28] A Day of great loss for the deniers!

THE LOSERS DRIVEN TO BURNING FLAMES

[29] "Go to the place, you used to deny! [30] Go in to the shade of the smoke that rises in three columns!" [31] *This will provide* neither cool shade nor safety from the heat of the flames. [32] It throws out columns of sparks like tall towers, [33] like *pieces of* copper. [34] A Day of great loss for the deniers! [35] Today, they won't speak, [36] nor be allowed to make excuses for themselves. [37] A Day of great loss for the deniers. [38] This is the Day of Decision, We'll gather you and all the previous generations. [39] If you've devised a plot against Me then try it! [40] A Day of great loss for the deniers!

THE WINNERS IN THE COOL SHADE OF PARADISE

[41] The righteous will enjoy themselves in *cool* shade and *gushing* springs, [42] and their favourite fruits. [43] *They will be told*: "Eat, drink and be merry for what you did." [44] That's how We reward the righteous people. [45] A Day of great loss for the deniers! [46] *Tell the disbelievers*: "Eat and enjoy yourselves for a while; you are sinners". [47] A Day of great loss for the deniers! [48] When they were told, "Bow for prayer," they didn't bow. [49] A Day of great loss for the deniers! [50] So which revelation after this will they believe?

78. An-Naba'
The News

This early Makkan chapter is critical of the Arab pagans who believed in the Almighty God, God, yet worshipped many idols. They did not believe in life after death, so they questioned the Prophet ﷺ again and again about the life Hereafter, and bitterly disagreed with him. Unfortunately, they didn't see the importance of this belief in ensuring a peaceful, just and purposeful life on Earth. What they could not comprehend was how the dead can be brought back to life. The Quran continually reminds them about God's creative power. The chapter opens with a rich description of the natural world: vast landmasses and oceans, lofty mountains, pairs of living things, the mysteries of sleep and nightfall, and so on. After mentioning these eleven pieces of evidence of God's creativity, people are warned about the Day of Judgement: the Day of Distinction; the Day when justice will be done and people will be rewarded according to how they lived. Then follows a description of the horrors and pain of Hell. The final section beautifully captures the delights and pleasures of Paradise.

In the name of God, the Kind, the Caring.

THE INCREDIBLE DIVINE CREATIVE POWER

¹ What are they questioning one another about? ² Is it the awesome news ³ that they are disputing? ⁴ No, soon they will know, ⁵ indeed very soon they will know. ⁶ Didn't We make the Earth a vast expanse, ⁷ the mountains *like* mighty stakes? ⁸ *Didn't We* create you in pairs, ⁹ made your sleep for resting, ¹⁰ made the night a covering, ¹¹ and made the day for earning a livelihood? ¹² *Didn't* We build seven durable *skies* over your head, ¹³ *the sun* a brightly burning lamp, ¹⁴ and sent down abundant rain pouring from storm clouds? ¹⁵ So We produced cereals, plants, ¹⁶ and gardens of dense greenery.

A SHOCKING DESCRIPTION OF THE PUNISHMENT OF HELL

¹⁷ The *time for the* Day of Distinction is fixed; ¹⁸ the Trumpet will be blown that day and you will come in crowds; ¹⁹ when the sky is opened becoming a gateway, ²⁰ and the mountains will move as if they were a mirage. ²¹ Hell lies in waiting, ²² to receive the disobedient, *their* home; ²³ they will live there for ages and ages. ²⁴ There will be nothing cool to taste, nor anything to drink ²⁵ except boiling water and a dark foul fluid; ²⁶ a fitting reward! ²⁷ Since they never expected any kind of

accounting, [28] and denied our Scriptures. [29] Yet We took account of everything in a Book, [30] so it will be said to them: "Taste *the punishment*. We won't add anything except punishment for you!"

THE RIGHTEOUS IN THE GARDENS

[31] The mindful will have a splendid success: [32] gardens, vineyards, [33] beautiful young companions of similar ages [34] and an overflowing cup. [35] They won't hear idle talk or lies, [36] a *fitting* reward and a gift from Your Lord, [37] Lord of the Heavens and the Earth and what is between the two. The Most Kind will not allow them to speak [38] on the Day when the Spirit *Gabriel* and the *other* angels will stand in rows, they won't speak either without the Most Kind's permission, and they will speak the truth. [39] That's the *Day of* Truth! So, anyone who wishes, let him take the road leading to His Lord. [40] We certainly warned you of a punishment so near, the Day when every person will see what their own hands have produced, and the disbeliever will say, "Oh, I wish I were dust!"

79. An-Naziʿat
The Snatchers

This is an early Makkan chapter; its central theme is the Resurrection. The story of Pharaoh highlights why some people don't believe: because of pride, selfishness and love of the world (15). The chapter opens with five oaths – five descriptive active participles that are enigmatic and unclear, making them difficult to translate. However, commentators have variously interpreted them as referring to warhorses, different winds, various stars, the souls of the righteous, and the angels. The evidence invoked here leads to the conclusion, "You will certainly be resurrected."

In the name of God, the Kind, the Caring.

RESURRECTION IS A GRAND PLAN WITH FAR-REACHING OUTCOMES
[1] By the angels who snatch *human* souls, [2] the angels who take away human souls nimbly, [3] the angels floating naturally, [4] the angels speeding ahead, [5] the Angels managing Heavenly affairs. *You will certainly be resurrected,*[a] [6] on the Day the Trumpet is sounded for the first time, [7] then followed by the second blast. [8] Hearts will beat fast that Day, [9] their eyes downcast. [10] *Today* they ask, "Will we be returned to *our* previous state, [11] when we are rotten bones?" [12] Commenting on it *they say,* "That would be a useless exercise!"[b] [13] It will only take a single *Trumpet* blast, [14] and they will be back on open ground.

TAKE LESSONS FROM THE STORY OF THE PHARAOH
[15] Has the story of Moses reached you? [16] When His Lord called out to him in the blessed valley of Tuwa: [17] "Go to the Pharaoh, he is arrogant, [18] and say *to him,* 'Would you like to purify yourself *spiritually*? [19] I shall guide you to your Lord so that you may be mindful.'" [20] So he showed him the greatest miracle, [21] but he denied and disobeyed; [22] then turned his back and rushed [23] to gather together *the magicians,* and announced: [24] "I am your highest lord". [25] So, God punished him by making an example of him in this world and the Hereafter. [26] There are lessons for the one who fears *His Lord.*

---

[a] This is the implied conclusion, in italics, of the five oaths or the evidences presented in verses [1] to [5].
[b] Literally "a purposeless return".

²⁷ Are you more difficult to create, or the sky, which He raised up? ²⁸ He raised and perfected its canopy, ²⁹ and darkened its night and brought about bright morning light, ³⁰ and the Earth after that, which He spread out. ³¹ He produced its spring water and its green pastures. ³² He fixed the mountains in their place; ³³ *all this is* a provision for you and your animals. ³⁴ So when the mighty catastrophe comes, ³⁵ that Day humans will remember what they accomplished, ³⁶ when they will see the Blazing Flames clearly – ³⁷ *then the* one who was disobedient, ³⁸ and preferred the worldly life, ³⁹ the Blazing Fire will be *his* home. ⁴⁰ But the one who feared standing before His Lord and stopped himself from following his lusts, ⁴¹ he will be at home, in Paradise. ⁴² They ask you *Prophet* about the Hour: "What is its fixed time?" ⁴³ What can you tell them about that? ⁴⁴ Only your Lord knows its fixed time. ⁴⁵ You are a warner for the one who fears it. ⁴⁶ The Day they see it, they'll realise, *the worldly life* was only an evening, or a morning.

80. ʿAbasa
Frowning

One day, the Messenger ﷺ was preaching to the leaders of Makkah, hopeful they would accept his message. He was extremely concerned to bringing them into the fold of Islam, and saving them from the Hellfire. However, Abdullah ibn Umm-al Maktum, a blind Muslim, came unexpectedly and wanted the attention of the Prophet ﷺ, saying: "Messenger! Teach me what God has taught you." The Messenger ﷺ did not like this interruption and frowned at him, turning away from him and towards the Makkans leaders. The chapter commented on this incident, and thereafter the Messenger ﷺ used to say to him, "You are the man for whom my Lord censured me." It is obvious that Abdullah was in error when he interrupted the Messenger ﷺ, who was conveying the Message. So why does the Quran censure him? A closer look at the passage reveals that the Quran wants to remove the Makkan leaders' misunderstanding; they thought Islam needed them. However, the Quran tells them they are wrong, Islam doesn't need them. On the other hand, it appreciates sincere people like the blind man. Whenever the Prophet ﷺ left Madinah, he would appoint Ibn Maktum as the governor. The Quran teaches respect and equality for the blind and disabled.

The next section highlights how God has blessed humanity with life, food, and a rich land, but unfortunately people fail to thank Him for His generosity.

In the name of God, the Kind, the Caring.

WHO IS MOST DESERVING OF THE PROPHET'S ATTENTION?

¹He frowned and turned away ²because the blind man came to him. ³For all you know, he might have developed *spiritually*, ⁴or listened, and the Reminder benefitted him. ⁵*But* as for the one who *thinks he* is self-sufficient, ⁶you paid special attention. ⁷You aren't responsible if he fails to purify himself *spiritually*. ⁸*But* as for the one who came rushing to you, ⁹whilst fearful *of his Lord*, ¹⁰you ignored him. ¹¹Indeed *the Quran* is a Reminder, ¹²for the one who wants to be reminded; ¹³*it is kept* in scrolls, which are honoured, ¹⁴raised and purified, ¹⁵*written* by the hands of angels ¹⁶who are noble and righteous.

HOW CAN PEOPLE BE SO UNGRATEFUL?

¹⁷Humans have ruined themselves by being unthankful. ¹⁸What sort of thing did He create them from? ¹⁹A drop of semen, He created them then assigned their

destiny,[a] [20] then by making their way smooth *in life* enabled them. [21] Then He lets them die and be buried. [22] Then when He wants, He shall resurrect them. [23] Unfortunately, they didn't do what God commanded them. [24] So let humans look at the food they eat *closely*; [25] We let the rain pour down, [26] then We split open the ground [27] to produce cereals, [28] grapes, vegetation, [29] olives, date palms, [30] densely-populated orchards, [31] fruits and fodder [32] what a sustenance for you and your animals.

A WARNING FOR THE UNTHANKFUL

[33] When the Deafening Blast comes, [34] that Day a person will flee from his brother, [35] mother, father, [36] spouse and children. [37] That Day, everyone will be concerned just about themselves. [38] Some faces that Day will be shining, [39] laughing and rejoicing. [40] *But other* faces that Day will be covered with dust, [41] darkness restricting them. [42] The darkened *faces of* the disobedient disbelievers.

---

[a]   Razi interprets *Qaddara* as: his provision, span of life, accomplishments in worldly life.

81. At-Takwir
The Shrouding

The central theme of this early Makkan chapter is the truthfulness of the Majestic Quran and the validity of its teachings. It opens with twelve oaths, each signifying one of the cataclysmic events prior to the Day of Resurrection. In the second section, another set of oaths about time of celestial bodies is presented. I translated *Wal-Kunnas* (Verse 16) as, "By the dying stars", this is a star whose light is diminishing – astrophysicists call this a dying star.

The Quran is keen to stress the truthfulness of the Messenger 鷺 and the source of his message, so it describes the power, authority and reliability of the Angel Gabriel, responsible for bringing the Divine Message. Finally, it challenges its audience with this verse: "So where are you going?" (26).

In the name of God, the Kind, the Caring.

THE OCCURRENCE OF OVERWHELMING EVENTS BEFORE JUDGEMENT DAY

[1] When the sun is covered, [2] when the stars are dimmed, [3] when the mountains are moved, [4] when pregnant camels are left untended, [5] when wild beasts are gathered, [6] when the seas boil, [7] when the souls are paired, [8] when the baby girl buried alive is asked [9] for which crime she was murdered, [10] when the scrolls *of deeds* are unrolled, [11] and when *a layer of* the sky is peeled, [12] when Hell is set ablaze, [13] when Paradise is brought near – [14] *then* everyone will know what they achieved *or failed to achieve in life.*

THE ANGEL GABRIEL BRINGS THE REVELATION

[15] So, I swear by the shining stars,[a] [16] by the dying stars, [17] by the fall of the night, [18] by the morning breeze.[b] [19] Certainly, *the Quran* is the recitation of a noble Angel, [20] who possesses *immense* power, and has a firmly-established rank with the Possessor of the Divine Throne, [21] who is obeyed *by other angels* and is trustworthy. [22] Your companion isn't mad; [23] he saw him clearly on the horizon. [24] He doesn't hide *the news of* the Unseen. [25] It isn't the word of a rejected devil. [26] So where are you going? [27] It's a reminder for all people, [28] *especially* for the one who

---

[a]   *Khunas* literally means stars that shine brightly at night but are invisible in the daytime. They can also refer to five planets: Saturn, Jupiter, Mars, Venus and Mercury.
[b]   Literally this means, "breath", however metaphorically it refers to morning breeze.

longs to be *guided* on the straight path. [29] But how can you long for it unless God, the Lord of the worlds, so wills, to show you that way.

82. Al-Infitar
The Cleaving

This is an early Makkan chapter. Its central theme is self-deception that turns a person away from God. After taking the oaths of the events leading to Judgement Day, a question is gently asked: "people, what deceived *and misled* you from your generous Lord?" (6) The qualities of the Lord of all creation are recalled to prick the conscience. Humanity is warned: you are monitored by the Angels who record your every move. On Judgement Day, all will give an account.

In the name of God, the Kind, the Caring.

WHY ARE YOU DECEIVED?

[1] When the sky is cleaved, [2] when the stars are scattered, [3] when the oceans surge and merge, [4] when the graves are turned inside out – [5] *that Day*, every person will know what it did and what it failed to do. [6] People, what deceived you from your generous Lord? [7] He created you, assigned you a provision, and perfected you [8] with *a beautifully*-shaped physical appearance as He pleased. [9] Yet, you still deny the Judgement. [10] The guardians standing over you are [11] the noble scribes, [12] who know what you do.

THE TERRIBLE FATE OF SELF-DECEPTION

[13] The righteous will enjoy the delights *of Paradise*, [14] whilst the wicked will be *damned* in Hell. [15] They will enter in it on Judgement Day, [16] and they won't ever be able to leave. [17] What can explain to you the reality of the Day of Judgement? [18] Again, what can explain to you the reality of Judgement Day? [19] The Day when no one will be able to do anything for another person; only God's command will prevail that Day.

83. Al-Mutaffifin
The Cheats

This is a late Makkan chapter, condemning cheating traders and shopkeepers who were dishonest in their dealings with others. This picture of a dishonest person isn't limited to commercial transactions, but is also relevant to people who are dishonest in other aspects of life, both in seventh-century Arabia and today.

The chapter, interestingly, doesn't mention the rope makers, tanners and perfume sellers working in Hijaz. Why does it single out the merchants, bankers and bookkeepers? Possibly because they have more opportunities to cheat, exploit the weak and perpetrate injustices. Recall the financial crisis of 2008, which affected economies around the world. Who was responsible for the that? Such injustices are committed by those who deny Judgment Day, and feel they can swindle and cheat without consequence. "Don't they believe they will be resurrected on a Grand Day?" (4–5) The chapter speaks of the effects of such conduct on hearts and minds: "their hearts are coated *with rust*, because of what they did" (14). The Messenger ﷺ said, "When a person commits a sin, a black spot appears on the heart. If he repents it will be removed, but if he continues doing evil, more spots appear until the entire heart is covered" (Ibn Majah). This encrusted, rust-coated, stained heart will lead to dishonesty and evil actions. The consequences in the Hereafter will be dire: those guilty of such crimes will burn in Hell. These are contrasted with people of faith and honest behaviour, who will enjoy the delights of Paradise.

In the name of God, the Kind, the Caring.

OBSERVATION ON THE BEHAVIOUR OF THE CHEATS

[1] Woe to the cheats; [2] the ones who demand full measure from people, [3] but when they measure and weigh for others, they give less. [4] Don't those *double dealers* believe they will be resurrected [5] on a Grand Day? [6] The Day when people will stand before the Lord of the worlds.

HOW EVIL DEEDS HARDEN THE HEART

[7] The written record of the wicked is in Sijjeen – [8] and what can explain Sijjeen to you? [9] *It's* a written document. [10] It will be too bad for the deniers that Day, [11] who deny Judgment Day. [12] Only the wicked transgressor denies it. [13] When Our Scriptures are read to him, he says, "*These are* fables of the ancients!" [14] Moreover, their hearts are coated *with rust* because of what they did. [15] Never! On that Day,

they will be shut out from *seeing* their Lord, [16] then they will enter Hell. [17] It will be said *to them*: "This is what you used to deny."

FAITHFUL PEOPLE IN THE SERENE SURROUNDINGS OF PARADISE

[18] The written record of the righteous is *kept* in 'Illiyeen. [19] What can explain 'Illiyeen to you? [20] *It's* a written record, [21] which is witnessed by those brought close *to God*. [22] The righteous will be enjoying *the delights of* Paradise, [23] sitting *relaxed* on sofas watching *the tranquil scenery*; [24] you will see brightness on their faces in Paradise. [25] They will be served sealed wine, pure [26] musk its after-taste – let the competitors compete for that – [27] mixed with *the water of* Tasneem, [28] a spring from which those brought close *to God* will drink.

A WARNING TO THE DISBELIEVERS WHO MOCK OTHERS

[29] The wicked used to laugh at the believers [30] when they passed by them, they would wink at each other teasingly. [31] Back with their families they made fun of them [32] and when they saw them, they would say, "These are misguided!" [33] They weren't sent as their guardians. [34] But today, the believers are laughing at the disbelievers, [35] sitting on the sofas watching *them in misery*: [36] "Have the disbelievers *not* been repaid for what they used to do?"

84. Al-Inshiqaq
The Splitting Open

This is a late Makkan chapter, of which the central theme is the connection between actions and consequences. It opens by stressing the instinctive obedience of the inanimate; the Sky and the Earth. An indirect disapproval of the Makkans, who refused to obey their Lord despite having intelligence.

Working hard for one's livelihood is a universal human value. However, to limit life to this is a folly; the workaholic is being challenged in this chapter. He is advised not to forget the Hereafter and the meeting with the Lord Who is the true Sustainer and Provider. However, those who work hard for their Hereafter are guaranteed progress: "You will develop stage by stage." (19)

In the name of God, the Kind, the Caring.

WHAT ARE YOU STRIVING FOR?

[1] When the sky splits open, [2] duly obeying its Lord; [3] when the Earth is flattened [4] and throws out its contents and becomes empty, [5] duly obeying its Lord. [6] People, you strive and struggle[a] *gradually moving* towards your Lord; finally you'll meet Him! [7] So anyone given the written record in his right hand [8] will have an easy reckoning, [9] and will return happily to his family. [10] But anyone who is given the written record from behind his back [11] will cry out for death, [12] and will go in the Blazing Fire. [13] He used to be happy amid his family. [14] He was convinced he wouldn't return *to His Lord.* [15] Yes, His Lord was watching him.

PROGRESS IN LIFE IS GUARANTEED TO HARD WORKERS

[16] So, I swear by the red horizon *at sunset*, [17] and by the night and all that it covers up, [18] and by the full moon: [19] you will develop stage by stage. [20] What's the matter with them that they don't believe, [21] and when the Quran is recited to them they don't prostrate. [22] The disbelievers deny. [23] God knows best what they hide *in their minds*, [24] so give them good news of a painful punishment, [25] except for those who believe and do righteous deeds; for them, there is a never-ending reward.

---

[a]   Strive and struggle may refer to the worries, anxieties, happiness and the drudgery of daily life.

85. Al-Buruj
The Constellations

This Makkan chapter marks the beginning of the second phase of the mission of the Prophet 🕊, around the third year; the start of tensions. Its central theme is the support of the faithful. The story of the "diggers of the trench" (4) is recounted in the Hadith collection of Muslim, where the Jewish King of Yemen burnt the Christians of Najran in a trench. This story would have given reassurance to the believers, and a clear warning to the Quraysh, the persecutors.

The chapter opens with a series of oaths, "By the sky full of constellations." A constellation is a recognisable group of stars which appear to be located close together in the sky, and form a picture of imaginary lines that connect them. Constellations are usually named after an animal, a character from mythology, or a common object. Muslim astronomers discovered several constellations and named them in Arabic, such as Ursa Major, and Ursa Minor.

In the name of God, the Kind, the Caring.

BELIEVERS FACE PERSECUTION

¹ By the sky full of constellations, ² by the promised Day, ³ by a witness and what is witnessed. ⁴ Cursed are the diggers of the trench, ⁵ *who lit* the well-fuelled fire; ⁶ when they sat around it, ⁷ watching what they were doing to the believers. ⁸ They punished them because they believed in God, the Almighty, the Praiseworthy, ⁹ the One Who controls *all things in the* Heavens and the Earth, and God is the witness of everything. ¹⁰ The persecutors of the believing men and women didn't repent, so they will be punished in Hell, in the Burning Flames.

THE PERSECUTORS CANNOT ESCAPE THE PUNISHMENT

¹¹ The believers who were righteous will have gardens *of Paradise,* beneath which rivers flow. That will be the great achievement. ¹² Your Lord's punishment will be severely harsh. ¹³ He started the creation and will reproduce it once more, ¹⁴ He is the Forgiving, the most Loving, ¹⁵ Possessor of the Majestic Throne, ¹⁶ the Most Able to carry out what He pleases. ¹⁷ Has the story of the armies reached you? ¹⁸ *About* the Pharaoh and Thamud? ¹⁹ Yet the disbelievers are *still* in denial,

[20] while God surrounds them from all sides. [21] But this is a Majestic reading, [22] in the Protected Tablet.

86. At-Tariq
The Night Visitor

A Makkan chapter a with central theme about the truthfulness of Judgement Day. After taking the oath of the shining stars, people are reminded, "There is a keeper over you" (4). Those who denied the Judgement Day are invited to reflect about their humble beginnings. Where do you come from? The evidence from the shooting stars, the spurted semen and the blooming plants and flowers are perfect illustrations of God's ability to bring the living from the dead; a proof of resurrection. The next important question for the thoughtful is, "Where are we going?" A simple statement contains the answer: "Indeed God is fully able to return him *to life*" (8). Finally, the Makkans, who were busy insulting the beloved Messenger ﷺ are warned, "I too have a plan" (16). In the final verse, the Prophet ﷺ is gently instructed to relax.

In the name of God, the Kind, the Caring.

WHERE DO YOU COME FROM?

[1] By the sky and the night visitor[a] – [2] what can explain the night visitor to you? [3] A piercing comet. [4] There is a keeper over every person. [5] Let humans look at what they were created from; [6] they were created from spurted semen [7] that comes from *bodily organs* in the torso.[b]

WHERE ARE YOU GOING?

[8] God is fully able to return them *to life*, [9] on the Day when secrets will be exposed; [10] they won't have any power and no helper. [11] By the sky and its repeated *rain cycle*, [12] and the Earth splitting open with *new growth*. [13] Indeed, this *Majestic Quran* is a decisive speech; [14] no joking matter. [15] They are continually plotting, [16] and I have a plan too. [17] *Messenger*, put up with the disbelievers; let them off for a short while.

---

[a] *Al-tariq* is the comet or shooting star, a meteor that burns up on entering the Earth's atmosphere forming a bright streak in the night sky. They were considered as supernatural omens by the Makkans.

[b] Literally, "the backbone [or] the loins and the breastbones."

87. Al-A'la
The Highest

An early Makkan chapter, its central theme is the role of the Majestic Quran and the Messenger as reminders. By referring to the early Scriptures of Moses and Abraham , the Quran makes it clear that this is a continuation of the same mission of past prophets. What blinds humanity to this reality? The answer is love of worldly life. These verses express contempt for the love of the material world, since it distracts people from their Lord.

In the name of God, the Kind, the Caring.

PRAISE AND GLORIFY YOUR LORD

[1]Glorify the Name of your Lord, the Most High. [2]Who created and made *you* complete; [3]Who fixed destiny[c] and gave guidance, [4]Who produced green pasture, [5]then turned it into dry dusty debris.

THE JOURNEY OF SPIRITUAL GROWTH

[6]We will teach you *the Quran* so you will not forget *it*, [7]except what God may wish. He knows the open and the hidden. [8]We shall make your *journey* easy, [9]so give reminder; the reminder is beneficial. [10]The one in awe *of his Lord* will listen, [11]but the wicked will ignore, [12]he will enter the Great Fire, [13]not dying and not living. [14]Successful indeed is the one who purifies himself, [15]and remembers the Name of his Lord, and performs the prayer *regularly*. [16]You prefer the worldly life, [17]yet the Hereafter is far better and everlasting. [18]This fact is also *mentioned* in the previous Scriptures, [19]*and in* the Scriptures of Abraham and Moses.

---

[c]   Qaddara refers to the sustenance, life span, choices and lifestyle of the individual (Razi).

88. Al-Ghashiyah
The Awe-inspiring Event

This chapter was revealed in the middle Makkan period. The three fundamental doctrines of Islam are emphasised. The Day of Judgement is introduced in an unusual manner: "Has the news of the Overwhelming Event reached you?" This is followed by a harrowing account of what will happen to the disbeliever who toiled, struggled and worked hard in his life but ignored God, and never thought about the Hereafter. This is contrasted with the fate of a believer who worked to please his Lord. Humanity is invited to enjoy the delights of Paradise, its elegant surroundings, its comforts and luxuries. The price is strong faith. To conclude, the chapter comforts the Prophet 鑫 by telling him not to worry, since he cannot compel people to believe. His mission is to remind: "To Us is their final return, then it will be up to Us to call them to account" (25–26).

In the name of God, the Kind, the Caring.

THE MISERABLE FATE OF DISBELIEVING HARD WORKERS

¹ Has news of the Awe-inspiring Event reached you? ² *Some* faces that Day will be humbled, ³ *looking* tired and exhausted. ⁴ They will walk into an intensely-hot Fire, ⁵ and drink from a boiling water spring. ⁶ They will have no food except bitter thorns, ⁷ which won't nourish or satisfy *their* hunger.

THE DELIGHTS OF PARADISE

⁸ *Some* faces that Day will be beautiful and bright, ⁹ well-pleased with their efforts, ¹⁰ *living* in an elegant Garden, ¹¹ where they won't hear any idle chat, ¹² *watered by* a flowing spring, ¹³ *furnished with* raised and comfortable sofas, ¹⁴ wine glasses *gracefully* arranged, ¹⁵ *silken* cushions set in rows, ¹⁶ and *luxurious* soft carpets laid all around.

INVITATION TO OBSERVE THE WORLD AROUND US

¹⁷ Don't they see the camels, how they were created? ¹⁸ And the sky, how it was raised? ¹⁹ And the mountains, how they were fixed? ²⁰ And at the Earth, how it was spread out? ²¹ So remind, *Prophet*, your job is to remind. ²² You aren't their controller. ²³ The one who turned away and disbelieved, ²⁴ God will give him terrible punishment. ²⁵ They will finally return to Us, ²⁶ and We will call them to account.

89. Al-Fajr
The Dawn

The chapter begins by taking four oaths to draw our attention: the dawn, the time when the first light appears, the ten sacred nights of the twelfth lunar month of Dhu'l-Hijja, the month of pilgrimage, and the mystery of odd and even numbers. The odd may hint to God, who is the One, the Unique and cannot be compared with anything. In contrast, the even reminds how creation is not singular or one, only God is One. The chapter reassures the Messenger ﷺ after mentioning these awesome phenomena: what you face in Makkah is what earlier prophets faced, so be patient. Reference is made to the ancient cities of Iram in the Arabian desert, Petra in modern-day Jordan, and the splendid temples of ancient Egypt with their tall columns. The city of Iram, deep in the Arabian desert, was discovered in the early 1990s by a group of archaeologists. Their ruins demonstrate that these were master masons who had fantastic advanced technology to build enormous buildings. However, their arrogance and denial of God brought them to ruin.

The chapter points out how humans are ungrateful to their Lord. At the slight loss of wealth or pain, they grumble and become impatient. They are sternly warned, and told to renounce their bad habits. However, those who are mindful of God are promised a joyous welcome and a life of utter bliss.

In the name of God, the Kind, the Caring.

REMINDERS FROM PAST CIVILISATIONS

¹By the dawn, ²by the ten *holy* nights, ³by the even and the odd *numbers*, ⁴and by the night as it slips away! ⁵Isn't there a *convincing* oath for an intelligent person? ⁶Haven't you considered how your Lord dealt with *the people of* Ad; ⁷*of* Iram with *its* lofty pillars, ⁸the likes of which haven't existed in *other* lands; ⁹and *the people of* Thamud who carved *homes out of* rocks in the valley; ¹⁰and the Pharaoh, *his temples* with massive columns? ¹¹Those who transgressed in the lands, ¹²who brought about havoc throughout them – ¹³Your Lord let loose a scourge of suffering against them. ¹⁴Your Lord is ever watchful.

INGRATITUDE AND DISBELIEF ARE LINKED

¹⁵The *mortal* man, when His Lord tests him with honour and blessings says, "My Lord has honoured me." ¹⁶However, when He tests him by lessening his provision he says, "My Lord has shamed me." ¹⁷On the contrary, it is you *Makkans* who

don't honour orphans, [18] and don't urge others to feed the needy, [19] while you consume the whole of the *orphans'* inheritance [20] with your insatiable love of wealth.

The harshest of harsh punishments

[21] So, how will you fare when the Earth is ground to dust, [22] and Your Lord's command comes, and the angels *stand* in rows upon rows. [23] That Day Hell will be brought close, people will then remember. But how will remembering *benefit* them now? [24] They will say, "If only We had something to show for our lives!" [25] Then on that Day, He will punish as no one will ever punish, [26] and He will chain them as no one will ever chain.

A joyous welcome from the Lord

[27] God will say: O happy soul! [28] Return to Your Lord cheerfully and loved; [29] now join *the company of* My servants [30] and come into My Paradise.

90. Al-Balad
The City

The mountain is a permanent feature of our landscape, an effective metaphor for the smallness of humans. The Majestic Quran uses the mountains to provide a dramatic setting: "Had We revealed this Quran on a mountain, you would have seen it humble itself and turn to dust out of fear of God." (*Chapter Al-Hashr* 59: 21). The Prophet ﷺ lived in a city surrounded by black rugged mountains, so here is an oath of a city of mountains. The metaphor of the steep mountainous track describes the difficulties of life: a constant Jihad, "Every human We created *experiences* hardship." This might refer both to people in general, or to Usaid ibn Kalda, a famous wrestler. When he stood on a leather hide and men tried to pull it away from under his feet, it would tear into pieces, but he would not budge an inch.

Here Divine Dislike is expressed for people who are deceived by their strength and influence. Usaid thought no one had power over him, not even the angel of death. The Quran warns against such delusions, life is symbolised by a steep path. Following the story of Usaid, this would imply this foolish man made no effort to obey the Lord, the steep path; he hadn't gone beyond physical existence and failed to understand the higher purpose of life.

In the name of God, the Kind, the Caring.

PEOPLE EXPERIENCE HARDSHIPS

[1] I swear by this city, [2] where you, live freely? [3] And by a father, and all his offspring! [4] Every human We created *experiences* hardship. [5] Does he *really* think no one has control over him? [6] He boasts, "I have spent a huge amount of wealth!" [7] Does he *really* think no one has seen him? [8] Haven't We given him two eyes, [9] a tongue and two lips? [10] We showed him the two steep paths *of good and evil*?

THE WAY TO SUCCESS IS HARD

[11] He hasn't yet set foot on the steep mountain track. [12] What can explain to you the mountain track? [13] *It is* to free a slave, [14] to feed on a day of severe hunger [15] an orphan relative, [16] or a penniless and distressed person. [17] Only they are believers, who instruct each other to be patient and kind. [18] They *will get their Book of Deeds* in the right hand. [19] But those who denied Our signs, *will get it* in the left hand, [20] the Fire closing in around them.

91. Ash-Shams
The Sun

This early Makkan chapter opens with eleven oaths. The first four relate to the sun and the last six to the sky, the Earth and the human soul. The purpose of these oaths is to support the claim, "Then He inspired it to follow *either* its vice or virtue" (8). The central theme is developing human potential, either to be conscious of God or remain unaware of Him. "He inspired" means that the human conscience has been endowed with the ability to distinguish between right and wrong, between good and evil. The one who develops the moral values, spiritual beliefs and social norms presented in the Quran will flourish, and the one who disregards them will inevitably fail.

This is further proved by reference to the tribe of Thamud. The Makkans often went past their ruins in the old city of Petra on the southern border of Jordan. They called it a "Red Rose City". The chapter points out that just as an individual may deny and ignore the Divine Commandments, similarly whole communities can deny the truth. They refused to listen to their prophet and that led to their ultimate destruction. They killed a she-camel; an outrage in Bedouin culture. This chapter has a beautiful rhyme – "ha" at the end of each verse, making it lyrical and poetic.

In the name of God, the Kind, the Caring.

POWERFUL OATHS

[1] By the sun and by the morning brightness, [2] by the moon that follows it, [3] by the day that it brightens up, [4] by the night that covers it. [5] By the sky and by Him who designed it, [6] by the Earth and by Him who levelled it out. [7] By the human and by Him who perfected him; [8] so inspired him to follow *either* its vice or virtue.

SUCCESS AND FAILURE IS IN HUMAN HANDS

[9] Whoever purified himself succeeded, [10] and whoever was immoral failed himself. [11] The *people of* Thamud cruelly treated *their Messenger*. [12] When the most wicked among them was dispatched *against him*. [13] God's Messenger told him, "Let God's she-camel have her share of the water." [14] But they denied him, and hamstrung her, so due to this crime their Lord destroyed them. [15] He didn't fear its consequences.

92. Al-Layl
The Night

This is an early Makkan chapter with the central theme of diversity in human endeavours, enterprises and efforts. However, the primary choice confronting people is between good or evil, and practising moral values. The chapter identifies righteous people as those who have three outstanding qualities: generosity, mindfulness of God, and appreciation for the good – the three inner dimensions of human life: the moral, spiritual and social, respectively. As a reward for goodness, "We shall soon make his work easy" (8). This is the Quranic hero, the champion and Beloved ﷺ of God. In contrast, the miserly, the forgetful, and the denier of good. For such a wretch, "We shall make his work hard" (10).

These two contrasting statements, "We shall make his work easy" and "We shall make his work hard," clearly show that God has given free will to humanity. However, He aids and supports those who wish to do good, and hinders those who do wrong. Once a habit is developed that brings pleasure or material gains, many become comfortable with it and adopt it as a way of life. The same applies to being mindful of God. The more a person worships, the easier his path to God becomes.

In the name of God, the Kind, the Caring.

DIVERSITY AND DIFFERENCES IN CREATION

¹By the night as it conceals; ²by the day as it reveals; ³by the male and the female He created! ⁴Indeed your works are different *from each other's*: ⁵so the one who gives, is mindful *of God* ⁶and believes in common good, ⁷We shall make his work easy. ⁸But for the miserly, who thinks he is self-sufficient ⁹and denies common good, ¹⁰We shall make his work difficult. ¹¹His wealth will not benefit him when he falls *into Hell.*

HUMANS ARE SPOILT FOR CHOICE

¹²Our role is to provide guidance; ¹³the Hereafter and the world are Ours. ¹⁴I have warned you about a raging Fire; ¹⁵where the wicked will go, ¹⁶who denied and turned away. ¹⁷*But* the one who was mindful will be kept away from it, ¹⁸he gave his wealth *in charity* to purify himself. ¹⁹Not as a payment for favours received, ²⁰but because he longed for the pleasure of His Lord, the Highest, ²¹and he will be pleased *with the outcome.*

93. Ad-Duha
The Morning Brightness

This is an early Makkan chapter. According to Suyuti, there was a short period when the revelation stopped and the Messenger ﷺ did not preach, prompting the Makkans to say mockingly, "Your Satan has deserted you." The Messenger ﷺ was upset, and the chapter was revealed to reassure him. To cope with this stressful personal experience, he is given a four-point strategy to overcome stress and sorrow: get rid of negative thoughts, be determined that you will succeed, recall your past successes and set yourself clear targets. The basic message it contains is an amazing force field of energy, which can heal our anxieties. Furthermore, it gives a snapshot of the orphan life of the Messenger ﷺ, his dire poverty, deep spiritual experience, and marriage with a wonderful lady, Khadija the Great.

In the name of God, the Kind, the Caring.

OATHS HIGHLIGHTING GOD'S LOVING CARE OF THE PROPHET

¹ By the *brightness of* mid-morning, ² by the night's darkness. ³ Your Lord hasn't deserted you, nor is He displeased with you. ⁴ Your future will be better than the past. ⁵ And your Lord will give you so much that you will be well-pleased.

PAST FAVOURS GUIDE THE WAY

⁶ Didn't He find you an orphan and shelter you? ⁷ *Didn't He* find you absorbed in Divine love, and guide you? ⁸ And *didn't* He find you needy and made you prosperous? ⁹ So, don't be harsh with the orphan, ¹⁰ nor chase away the beggar, ¹¹ and speak positively about the gifts of your Lord.

94. Al-Inshirah
The Expansion

This Makkan chapter builds on the previous chapter's consolation of the Messenger 繼 in a tone that displays friendship and love. The opening, or expansion, of the chest of the Prophet 繼 occurred twice: once in his childhood, and again at the start of the Night Journey, his Ascension. The Angel Gabriel carried out a remarkable procedure in which the heart of the Prophet 繼 was taken out, purified, filled with wisdom, and put back in his noble chest. This miracle prepared it to be the container of Divine Revelation. The chapter expresses the incredibly elevated position of the Messenger 繼, but despite this honour he is told to strive enthusiastically in God's worship.

In the name of God, the Kind, the Caring.

GAIN AFTER STRAIN

¹Didn't We expand your chest, ²and lift your burden, ³which was breaking your back. ⁴We raised high your honour. ⁵Indeed, *every* hardship is followed by ease, ⁶indeed, *every* hardship is followed by ease.[a] ⁷Once you finish your daily chores, ⁸seek your Lord passionately in worship.

---

[a] *Inna ma'-al-'usr yusran* could also mean, "Gain after strain", and "The storm before the calm".

95. At-Tin
The Fig

This Makkan chapter opens with four oaths: two of the valuable trees and two sacred places. These splendid symbols are used as a testimony to the truthfulness of its theme: the 'inherent goodness' of human nature, and how this is ruined. This vivid description of the splendour of God's creation and the nobility of humanity is an elegant piece of rhetoric. The reference to human nature being as the "most beautiful" (4) is an important Quranic teaching, which offers hope in a world ravaged by wars and human greed. It refers to the upright and beautiful human figure, possessing beneficial intelligence, moral goodness and yearnings for the Divine. In other words, humans have the potential to be good, kind and generous, but can easily be ruined by disregarding faith in the Hereafter. This "most beautiful" nature can be easily damaged. The concept of *Din* (creed) or Judgement Day acts as a deterrent.

———————

In the name of God, the Kind, the Caring

How wonderful is the human physique?

¹By the fig, by the olive, ²by Mount Sinai ³and this safe city. ⁴We created humans in the most beautiful form, ⁵then reduced them to the lowest of the lows, *due to disobedience*, ⁶except those who believed and performed honourable deeds; they shall have a never-ending reward. ⁷So after *knowing this* what makes you deny Judgement Day? ⁸Isn't God the most Just Judge?

96. Al-'Alaq
The Clot of Blood

The Messenger ﷺ used to take spiritual retreat in the cave of Hira, seven kilometres south-west of the Kaaba. Here, in the stillness and solitude of the Mountain of Light, far away from the hustle and bustle of a busy city, he had ample opportunity to meditate on his Lord and reflect on the waywardness of his fellow citizens. He loathed their idolatry, corrupt business practices, uncaring behaviour towards the poor and needy. It was during one such moment that the Holy Spirit, Gabriel , brought him the first revelation, comprising the first five verses of this chapter, commanding him to recite in God's name. The second part of the chapter comes as a clear warning to all disbelievers, but in particular to one of his staunchest opponents, Abu Jahl, since he frequently mistreated the Messenger ﷺ verbally and physically.

In the name of God, the Kind, the Caring

THE FIRST REVELATION

¹Recite in the name of your Lord Who created, ²created humans from clustered germ-cells.ª ³Recite! "Your Lord is the most Generous", ⁴Who taught with the Pen, ⁵He taught humans what they didn't know.

ABU JAHL IS WARNED OF DREADFUL CONSEQUENCES

⁶But humans go beyond *boundaries of God*, ⁷considering themselves to be self-sufficient. ⁸*Yet* the *final* return is to your Lord. ⁹Have you seen the one who stops ¹⁰a servant *of Ours* from praying? ¹¹Don't you realise he is rightly guided, ¹²and issues commands based on fear *of God*? ¹³Have you considered, when he denies *the truth* and turns away, ¹⁴doesn't he know God sees *everything*? ¹⁵No! If he doesn't end *this behaviour*, We shall drag him by the forelock, ¹⁶*that* lying and sinful forelock.ᵇ ¹⁷So let him call out to his supporters; ¹⁸We shall summon the angel guards *at the gates* of Hell *to take care of him*. ¹⁹No! Don't follow him, *Prophet*, but prostrate *before Us* and draw *ever* closer.ᶜ

ª The word in Arabic literally means "congealed blood", and it is used figuratively as a label for the early embryonic stage in the womb.

ᵇ The "forelock" is the hair of the forehead that some vain people, when they choose to grow it long, are constantly tossing or pushing back, typically with extravagant and self-conscious gestures, in order to distract others and draw attention to themselves.

ᶜ This is the last of the Verses of Prostration in the Quran.

97. Al-Qadr
The Night of Destiny

This early Makkan chapter praises the splendour of the night on which the Majestic Quran was revealed, a night in the blessed month of Ramadan. On this night of power, glory and splendour, the Quran was transferred from the Protected Tablet in the upper Heaven to the lower Heaven, from which it was gradually and in piecemeal fashion revealed to the Messenger ﷺ over a period of twenty-three years. This explains why this night is very special. Three things come down during the night: angels, human destiny and peace.

_____

In the name of God, the Kind, the Caring.

THE NIGHT OF POWER

¹We sent down *the Quran* on the Night of Destiny, ²and what can explain the Night of Destiny to you? ³The Night of Destiny is better than one thousand months;ᵃ ⁴the angels and the Spirit, *Gabriel,* come down by the order of their Lord, bringing with them *each person's* destiny. ⁵Peace *descends everywhere* until the break of the dawn.

ᵃ This means that worship during this night is more valuable than the worship of over a thousand months, a lifetime of worship.

98. Al-Bayyinah
The Clear Proof

This is a late Makkan chapter, and the central theme is how to deal with the scepticism, resistance and disbelief of the Makkan idolaters, as well as the Christians and the Jews. The Messenger ﷺ initially thought that the People of The Book would readily accept Islam. However, they resisted his call, except for a few. In many ways, this chapter was a consolation to the Prophet ﷺ and his followers: they need not be disappointed at such reactions from the People of The Book. The Jews did the same to the Prophet Jesus, when they refused to acknowledge his prophethood and handed him over to the Romans, accusing him of treason.

In the name of God, the Kind, the Caring

People are given an opportunity before being condemned

[1] The disbelievers among the People of the Book and the idolaters were not condemned until the clear proof had come to them[b] – [2] the Messenger of God recited pages of pure teachings *from the Quran,* [3] containing clear commandments. [4] Those given the Book became divided after the clear proof had come to them. [5] They were commanded: worship God sincerely, turn away from false gods, establish the prayer, and pay the Zakat. That is the religion of truth. [6] The disbelievers from the People of The Book and the idolaters will be in the Hell-Fire forever. These are the worst of the creatures.

Believers are richly rewarded

[7] The believers who did righteous works are the best of the creatures. [8] Their reward is with the Lord: Gardens of Eden beneath which rivers flow; *they will live* there forever. God is pleased with them, and they're pleased with Him. That's for the one who fears His Lord.

---

[b]   Then they knowingly reject it.

99. Al-Zilzal
The Earthquake

This is an early Madinan chapter, its central theme is accountability on the Day of Resurrection. The chapter opens with the advent of the Day of Resurrection, marked by a devastating Earthquake that will flatten the Earth; mountains will turn into rubble, and the seas will surge and merge as described elsewhere. However, the focus in this chapter is the Earth, and what it will reveal of its history. The mindless human will spend his life without a thought for the Hereafter, indulging in evil. The chapter reminds him that on Judgement Day, he must stand before his Lord and give an account. The chapter carries you into the future, inspiring and exciting you.

In the name of God, the Kind, the Caring.

THE DIVINE JUSTICE
¹ When the Earth is shaken violently, ² it *will* throw up its burden; ³ people will ask, "What's the matter with her?" ⁴ That Day, it will tell all its news, ⁵ inspired by her Lord. ⁶ That Day, people will come separately in groups to be shown their deeds. ⁷ So, anyone who did an atom's weight of good will see it. ⁸ And anyone who did an atom's weight of evil will see it *too*.

100. Al-'Adiyat
The War Horses

This is a late Makkan chapter that concisely describes the human condition of ungratefulness. The Arabic is *Kufr*, a key theme in the Quran, as it often warns people of the dreadful consequences of human ingratitude. A *Kafir* is an unthankful person, who fails to acknowledge the gifts of the Generous Lord. The *Kafir*, the disbeliever, is condemned for this ingratitude. Hell is the only place that will cleanse humanity of the filth of this sin. The chapter strongly condemns unthankfulness, and reminds people of the Day when everything will be revealed, and no secrets will remain.

––––––––––––

In the name of God, the Kind, the Caring.

THE UNGRATEFULNESS OF HUMANS

[1] By the snorting war horses, [2] *their hooves* striking sparks, [3] charging in dawn raids [4] scattering dust *clouds* [5] then dashing into the centre *of the enemy.* [6] Human beings are most unthankful to His Lord. [7] He is a witness to this, [8] and passionately loves wealth. [9] Doesn't he know everything in the graves will be thrown out, [10] and the *secrets* of hearts will be revealed? [11] That Day their Lord will be aware of them.

101. Al-Qari'ah
The Sudden Calamity

This is a Makkan chapter that starts with a question about Judgement Day in order to open our eyes to the reality of it. It describes the momentous events of that Day and then points out the root of a successful life: good deeds, a guarantee for success. Those who lack good deeds will have "a blazing fire" (11).

———————

In the name of God, the Kind, the Caring.

GOOD DEEDS ARE THE BASIS OF SUCCESS

¹The Sudden Calamity! ²What is the Sudden Calamity? ³What can explain the reality of the Sudden Calamity to you? ⁴The Day when people will *look lost,* like scattered moths, ⁵and the mountains *will sway* like fluffy wool. ⁶So the one who has heavy scale of deeds ⁷will have a happy life. ⁸But the one who has light scale of deeds ⁹his home will be a bottomless Pitª. ¹⁰What can explain what it *looks like* to you? ¹¹A Blazing Fire!

———

ª *Hawiya* is one of the names of Hell, and means a bottomless pit.

102. At-Takathur
The Competition for More and More

This is a Makkan chapter that concisely highlights human greed and obsession with material things. It is trying to shock that person who is deeply immersed in the love of the world. Therefore, particularly relevant for our affluent societies. It lays bare the fact that this diversion and distraction from the reality of the Hereafter cannot save us from dying and going into our graves. The solution is simple: believe in the Resurrection and Divine Justice. Such moving revelation can awaken readers to the dangers of worldliness and forgetfulness of the Hereafter.

In the name of God, the Kind, the Caring.

HUMAN GREED

[1] The competition for more and more *wealth* preoccupied you,[b] [2] until you went down into your graves. [3] Surely, you will know; [4] Eventually you will understand. [5] If only you had knowledge of certainty. [6] You will certainly see Hell; [7] you will see it with the eye of certainty; [8] that Day, you will be questioned about all the gifts.

[b] From the worship of God, being kind to others and mindful of reality.

103. Al-'Asr
The Age

The short and pithy message of this Makkan chapter is moving description of those who are mindful. Imam Shafie (d.1417 CE) expressed this eloquently: "If people thought deeply just about this one chapter, it would be enough for them." This is because it simply states the obvious: as time passes, man is at loss, except those blessed ones who do four things: believe, act righteously and encourage each other to be truthful and patient.

––––––––––

In the name of God, the Kind, the Caring.

HUMANS ARE AT A LOSS UNLESS THEY ARE RIGHTEOUS

[1] By the age,[a] [2] humans are at a loss, [3] except the believers who are righteous, and encourage each other to be truthful and patient.

––––––––––

[a] *'Asr* also means evening time, and the twilight hours of the day. It may also refer to the age of the beloved Messenger, how incredibly blessed it was.

104. Al-Humazah
The Faultfinder

This is a Makkan chapter that condemns people who have a negative attitude towards others, and are obsessed with wealth. The belief that money can give them health, longevity, happiness and freedom from difficulties is a delusion. Many wealth-obsessed people are so out of touch with reality that they forget their mortality. The only fitting place for such people is what the chapter calls "the Crusher" (*al-Hutama*), Hell, described as a vault of fire. That will be an agonising realisation of a wasted life.

――――――――

In the name of God, the Kind, the Caring

BEWARE OF THE IDOLISATION OF WEALTH

[1]Wretched is every backbiting fault-finder, [2]who gathers wealth and counts it over and over, [3]thinking his wealth will make him live forever. [4]No, he will be thrown into the Crusher! [5]And what can explain to you what the Crusher is? [6]God's blazing Fire, [7]which rises over *their* hearts. [8]Indeed, it is closed over them from all sides, [9]*flames* stretching out in columns.

105. Al-Fil
The Elephant

This is an early Makkan chapter, which reminds the people of Makkah how they were saved from the army of Abraha. He was a Yemenite Christian king, whose capital Sana housed a magnificent cathedral. The only rival to this cathedral in the Arabian Peninsula was the Kaaba in Makkah. Abraha was enthusiastic about spreading Christianity throughout the Arabian Peninsula, so Makkah was his natural target. He decided to attack it in 570 CE, but his plan went badly wrong, as described by this chapter. This was also the year the Messenger ﷺ was born. The defeat of Abraha was a wonderful sign that marked the beginning of a new era of spiritual change, and the coming of the Messenger ﷺ.

———————

In the name of God, the Kind, the Caring

THE DEFEAT OF ABRAHA

[1] Have you not seen how your Lord dealt with the army of the elephant? [2] Didn't He smash their plan? [3] When He sent a flock of birds against them, [4] they pelted them with flint-stones. [5] So, He turned them into *what looked like* chewed hay.

106. Al-Quraysh
The Tribe of Quraysh

This Makkan chapter highlights another favour given to the Quraysh: a good livelihood through trading. The Quraysh are reminded they can travel safely to Yemen with their caravans laden with expensive cargo during the winter months, and to Syria in the summer, and this is indeed a Divine favour on them.

In the name of God, the Kind, the Caring.

THE QURAYSH WERE SAFE

[1] For the Quraysh's feeling of security – [2] their security in the winter and summer journeys. [3] So, they should worship the Lord of this house, *the Kaaba,* [4] Who feeds them, protects from famine and gives them safety from fear.

107. Al-Maʿun
Small Kindness

This early Makkan chapter opens with a description of the character of a Qurayshi leader Abu Lahab: unwilling to accept Judgement Day and its justice, unkind to the weak, indifferent to the welfare of the needy, and so mean-spirited that he doesn't lend even small tools or utensils to his neighbours. He was the keeper of the Kaaba, taking care of its maintenance and income. Worship, which is supposed to be from the depths of one's heart, became a show rather than a symbol of true faith and genuine longings for the Divine. The lesson is that a person with such wretched character can never give even a "little kindness".

In the name of God, the Kind, the Caring.

SMALL KINDNESSES

[1] Have you seen him who denies the *Divine* Judgement? [2] He treats the orphan roughly, [3] nor encourages the feeding of the needy. [4] So, ruined are the worshippers [5] who are daydreaming whilst praying, [6] they just show off, [7] and stops others from doing small kindness.[a]

---

[a]   *Al-Maʿun* are small tools and utensils, implying that such people are so miserly that they cannot even lend these items to their close neighbours.

108. Al-Kawthar
The Abundance

This is a Makkan chapter. When the Prophet ﷺ lost both of his baby sons, Qasim and Abdullah, the Qurayshi leaders, including Abu Lahab, were jubilant and called the Prophet *Abtar*: a pejorative term meaning cut off, i.e. sonless. In other words, the taunt was that the Prophet ﷺ had no surviving male heirs, therefore his mission and campaign would come to end with his demise. The Messenger ﷺ was naturally hurt by these callous comments, so God consoled His beloved Messenger ﷺ and promised him abundant success, bliss and never-ending Divine favours. The Kawthar, abundance could be his beautiful qualities, masses and masses of followers and the lake of sweet water on Judgement Day.

In the name of God, the Kind, the Caring.

THE PROPHET WILL NOT BE CUT OFF; HIS ENEMIES WILL

¹ We gave *everything in* abundance to you, ² so, pray to your Lord and make a sacrifice. ³ Your enemy will be finished, cut off.[b]

---

[b]   Literally childless, "finished" in the sense that he will have no surviving male heirs.

109. Al-Kafirun
The Disbelievers

This chapter was revealed in the middle Makkan period, when a group of Qurayshi leaders came to the Messenger 鸞 with a proposal: "If you worship our idols for one year, we shall worship your God for one year. This way we will keep our people united." The chapter was revealed to reject this nonsensical proposal. It clearly condemns compromising with idolatry. True believers have never done so in the past; they will not do it now, nor in the future. The final verse: "For you is your religion, and for me is my religion," (6) points to the fundamental human right of religion. Despite this uncompromising tone, the chapter lays down the principle of a pluralistic, diverse society. It stresses freedom of religion, and teaches about the coexistence of different religions and ideologies. Islam does not believe in destroying other religions; instead, it preaches living alongside others in a peaceful way.

In the name of God, the Kind, the Caring.

CO-EXISTENCE OF RELIGIONS
¹Say: "Disbelievers, ²I don't worship what you worship, ³neither are you worshippers of what I worship. ⁴Nor will I be a worshipper of what you worship, ⁵neither will you be worshippers of what I worship. ⁶For you is your religion, and for me is mine."

110. An-Nasr
The Help

This is a Madinan chapter that forecasts the victory of Makkah and the ultimate success of the Messenger ﷺ, hinting his mission is nearly complete. According to some scholars, this was revealed on the occasion of the 'farewell pilgrimage', in the final year of the life of the Prophet ﷺ (622 CE). It beautifully encapsulates the humble attitude of the Prophet ﷺ to worldly victories and successes: in times of affluence and power, we must be modest.

––––––––––––

In the name of God, the Kind, the Caring.

BE GRATEFUL IN TIMES OF SUCCESS
[1] When God's help and the victory comes [2] and you see masses of people entering God's religion, [3] then glorify and praise Your Lord, and seek His forgiveness. He is ever ready to accept repentance.

111. Al-Lahab
The Flames

This is a Makkan chapter. Abu Lahab was the uncle of the Prophet ☀ but a bitter ene-my. He had considerable influence in the city. One day, the Prophet ☀ was preaching on Mount Safa near the Kaaba to an attentive crowd. He was inviting them to believe in one God, and to accept him as the Messenger ☀. Abu Lahab could not contain himself and shouted, "Damn you! Is this what you wanted to tell us?" This chapter, in contrast to other Quranic chapters, was revealed to condemn his outrageous behaviour. In other places, the Prophet ☀ and the Muslims are instructed to be patient, but here God directly confronts this abuser of His beloved Messenger ☀, and by naming him, shames him. Unfortunately, Abu Lahab and his wife continued their animosity until the end. Here God is showing His support for the Messenger ☀ and severely condemning his enemies. "Abu Lahab's hands are broken" is an idiom for "his hands are paralysed so he will not be able to confront."

In the name of God, the Kind, the Caring.

ABU LAHAB WILL BE PUNISHED

¹ Abu Lahab's hands are broken, he's ruined. ² Neither his wealth nor his achieve-ments will help him. ³ Soon he will enter the Flaming Fire; ⁴ so will his wife, the firewood-carrier – ⁵ *she* will have a rope of palm-fibre around her neck.

112. Al-Ikhlas
Sincere Faith

This Makkan chapter succinctly summarises Quranic teachings about *Tawhid*, the Oneness of God and the core of Islamic faith: all power, glory and control is in the hands of the Almighty Lord. I have translated *Al-Samad* as "The Eternal". He is the aim and goal of everything, since He is the Master of all and the final refuge. Everything depends upon Him, but He is independent of all, and He is the final cause of all causes. The chapter concisely conveys this message in four points: unique, Eternal, He is not a father nor a son. A brief but an effective refutation of idolatry.

———————

In the name of God, the Kind, the Caring.

GOD, THE ONE

[1] Say: "He is God, the One, [2] God the Eternal. [3] He is not a father nor a son. [4] None is equal to Him."

113. Al-Falaq
The Daybreak

These last two chapters of the glorious Quran (*Chapter Al-Falaq* and *Chapter An-Nas*) were revealed together in Madinah. *Chapter Al-Falaq* describes four sources of possible physical and psychological harm: from creation, including visible creatures and the invisible; darkness and what is hidden in it; the witches and their witchcraft; and jealousy. God is the only true Protector Who can shield and prevent harm from them. Aisha, the wife of the Messenger 繠 reported: "When the Messenger lay down to sleep, he would recite *Chapter al-Ikhlas* and these two chapters, and blow on his palms, then wipe over his entire body" (Bukhari).

In the name of God, the Kind, the Caring.

SEEK REFUGE WITH GOD

[1] Say: "I seek refuge in the Lord of the daybreak, [2] from the harm of all His creation, [3] from the harm of the ever-darkening night, [4] from the harm of witches who blow on knots, [5] and from the harm of a jealous person when jealous."

114. An-Nas
The People

Whilst the previous chapter described sources of physical and psychological harm, this chapter focuses on harm from our archenemy, Satan. This chapter tells us how he tries to influence our hearts and minds. Protection lies in turning to God for refuge, shield and shelter.

In the name of God, the Kind, the Caring.

SEEK GOD'S REFUGE FROM EVIL

[1] Say: "I seek refuge in the Lord of the people, [2] the King of the people, [3] the God of the people, [4] from the evil of the sneaking whisperer, [5] who whispers into people's hearts *and minds*, [6] from among the *jinn* or the people."

Index

taking souls of believers at death, 16:32
visit to Abraham, 11:69-76, 51:24-37
wings of, 35:1
anger, forgiving while in, 42:37
animals
God provides for, 29:60
as a sign of God, 36:71-73
as prostrating to God, 16:49-50
created from water, 24:45
living in communities, 6:38
proliferation of as a sign of God, 2:164
shades of colour in, 35:28
skins of, 16:80
slaughter of, 5:3
See also livestock
ants, valley of, 27:18-19
anxiousness of man, 70:19
apes, transmogrification into, 7:166
apostasy, 3:86-91
apostates, works of as fruitless, 2:216
argumentation
avoiding, 22:67-70
in the best way, 29:46-49
ark. See ship of Noah.
Ark of the Covenant, 2:248. See also
covenant
armour, 21:80, 34:11
arrogance
as disliked, 4:37
as preventing entrance to Paradise,
7:40-41
avoiding, 31:18
of disbelief, 23:75-80
of Satan, 2:31
rejecting revelation as, 16:23-29
ascension, 53:1-18
ashes, parable of, 14:18-20
associating others with God. See idolatry
atonement for breaking oaths, 5:89

awliya. See friends of God,
Azar, 6:74

B
Baal, 37:125
backbiting, wretchedness of, 104:1-8
banditry, punishment for, 5:33-34
Banu al-Nadir, expulsion from Medina,
59:1-5
barren land, metaphor of, 41:39
bath, ritual, 5:6
battle. See warfare; jihad
beast, emergence of, 27:82
Bedouins
as submitting, but not believing,
49:14-18
seeking exemption from Tabuk, 9:90
sincerity and hypocrisy amongst, 9:97-
99, 9:101
bees, 16:68-69
belief, as accepting the Messenger as
arbiter, 4:65
believers
God is friend of, 2:257
angels taking souls of at death, 16:32
as belonging to God, 9:111-12
as best community from humanity,
3:110
attitude in battle, 3:146-51, 8:45-48,
8:64-66
attributes of, 2:2-5
Christians as closest to, 5:82-86
compared with disbelievers, 11:15-24
described, 7:157, 8:2-4, 9:71-72,
23:1-11, 25:63-73, 27:2-3, 70:22-35,
76:7-11
fearing God, 3:102
half-heartedness in, 22:11-16
keeping the company of the devout,

of disbelievers, 4:54-55
  seeking refuge from, 113:5
Eve
  deception of Satan, 7:19-22
  temptation of, 2:35
evil
  protection from through worship of
  God, 2:21
  forbidding, 3:104, 3:110
  attractiveness of, 6:122-24
  seeking refuge from, 113:1-5, 114:1-6
evil eye, avoiding, 12:67-68
excuses, made by hypocrites, 9:43-49
eye for an eye, 5:45
eyes, testimony of, 41:20-22

F
factionalism, 30:32
fairness, standing up for, 4:135-36. See
also justice
faith
  arguments against rejection of, 2:28-29
  articles of, 2:177, 2:284-85
  as accepting the Messenger as arbiter,
  4:65
  as innate trait , 10:21-23
  described, 2:3-4
  migration for the sake of, 4:97-100
  of sleepers of cave, 18:13-16
  requires conviction, 5:61-63
  success through, 2:62
  true nature of, 49:14-18
false oaths, 58:14-20
falsehood, vanquished by truth, 34:48-49
family
  adopted children, 33:4-5
  caring for parents, 29:8-9, 46:15-16
  categories of relatives forbidden from
  marriage, 4:22-23

disobedient son, 46:17-20
dissolution of kinship on day of judgement, 23:101
giving charity to parents, 2:215
grieving for an absent child, 12:84-87
love between spouses, 30:21
love for relatives, 42:23
marrying disbelievers, 2:221
protecting from the fire, 66:6
rights of relatives, 33:6
sowing discord between man and wife,
  2:102
supplication for, 25:74
teaching to perform the prayer, 20:132
See also marriage; divorce; children.
famine
  in Makkah, 44:8-16
  relaxation of dietary laws during, 5:3
fasting
  as compensation for zihar divorce, 58:4
  in atonement for leaving ihram due to
  illness, 2:196
  laws of, 2:183-87
  Ramadan, 2:185
fathers, providing for children, 2:233. See
also family; children; marriage
fault-finders, 68:11
female infanticide, 16:56-60, 81:8-9
fickle nature of man, 41:49-51
fighting, in sacred months, 2:216
Final Hour. See Day of Judgement.
financial matters
  compound interest, prohibition of,
  3:130-32
  loans, 2:282-83
  mingling of orphan's and guardian's
  wealth, 2:220
  prohibition of usury, 2:275-81
  witnessing commercial transactions,

worship of golden calf, 20:83-91

Iekah, destruction of, 50:14

ihram, leaving if unable to complete Hajj or umrah, 2:196

Illiyeen (book of righteous deeds), 83:18-28

illness

    leaving ihram while suffering from, 2:196

    purification for prayer in, 4:43

iman. See faith

indecency

    prohibition of , 7:33

    repenting from, 3:133-38

    spreading, 24:19-21

infanticide, 6:137, 6:140, 6:151, 81:8-9

ingratitude, 16:53-55, 16:112-13, 80:17-32, 100:6-10

inheritance

    being content with one's share, 4:32-33

    dying childless, 4:176

    witness to the will, 5:106-108

injustice, standing up against, 4:75

innovations in Christianity, 57:27

In-sha-Allah, importance of, 18:23-24

intercession, of the truthful, 43:86

interest. See usury

iron, 57:25

iron collars, 40:71

Islam

    apostatizing from, 2:216

    avoiding those who mock, 6:66-70

isra, 17:1

Israelites

    being brought back to life after dying, 2:243-45

    breaking of Sabbath, 7:163-66

    covenant of, 2:40-46, 2:63, 2:83-84, 2:93

cow, sacrifice of, 2:67-73

crossing of the sea, 10:90-93

curse of David and Jesus on disbelievers amongst, 5:78

deliverance of, 44:30-31

dietary laws of, 3:92-93

disagreement amongst, 45:16-17

favours upon, 2:40-46, 2:47

flight from Egypt, 26:52-59

hardening of hearts of, 2:74

heedlessness of God's favours, 7:137-41

killing of prophets, 5:70

king of, 2:247-49

led out of Egypt, 20:77-82

refusal to take part in jihad, 2:246

scattering of around the world, 7:167-71

those who kept the covenant, 5:12

threats of Pharaoh, 7:127-29

traits of, 2:94-96

twelve tribes of, 7:159-62

twelve wells of, 2:60

two warnings for, 17:4-8

worship of the calf, 2:51, 2:54, 2:92-93

See also Jews

I'tikaf, abstaining from sexual relations, 2:187

J

Jannah. See Paradise,

jealousy. See envy

Jews

    acceptance of the Quran, 28:51-56

    God's favours on, 5:20

    God's willingness to pardon, 4:153-154

    as hostile to believers, 5:82

    as wanting the Prophet to follow them, 2:120

    believers amongst, 5:69

betrayal at battle of the Trench, 33:26-27

chosen people claim, 62:5-8

claim to be children of God, 5:18

claims to Paradise, 2:111

command to overlook faults of, 5:13

curse of tight-fistedness, 5:64-66

disbelievers and believers amongst, 4:160-62

in Medina, rudeness of, 4:44-46

judging in disputes amongst, 5:42-44

not taking as protectors, 5:51-53

of Medina, 2:76-82

on Christians, 2:113

paying of jizya tax, 9:29-30

rejection of the Quran, 2:89-92

righteous amongst, 3:113-15

twisting the words of God, 3:75-78

See also Israelites; Judaism

jihad

against injustice, 4:75

believers in battle, 3:146-51, 8:45-48, 8:64-66

encouragement to take part in, 2:243-45

excuses of hypocrites, 48:11-17

fleeing from, enormity of, 8:15-16

for worldly gains, 4:71-74

lacking means to contribute to, 9:91-92

prayer while engaged in, 4:102-104

staying behind from to study religion, 9:122

striving, compared with staying behind, 4:95-96

See also warfare

jinn

acceptance of the Quran, 72:1-5

control of, 34:12-14

creation of, 55:15

eavesdropping of, 72:6-12

group that accepted Islam, 46:29-32

misleading people, 6:128-31

Quran protected from, 26:210-13

setting up as partners to God, 6:100

subservient to Solomon, 21:81-82, 38:37

jizya tax, 9:29-30

journey. See travel,

Judaism

arguments over Abraham, 3:65-68

dietary laws of, 6:146-47

taking rabbis as lords besides God, 9:31-33

See also Jews; Israelites

Judgement Day. See Day of Judgement,

judges; judging

according to revelation, 5:49-50

by what God has revealed, 5:44-45, 5:47

prohibition of bribing, 2:188

justice

command to, 5:8

in commerce, 17:35

in disputes between believers, 49:9-10

of God, 41:46

standing up for, 4:135-36

K

kindness, of God, 43:32

knowledge

absolute, of God, 6:59-62, 11:6-7

and argumentation, 2:213

of Adam, 2:31

supplication for increasing, 20:114

L

landlords in orchard, 68:17-33

language, as sign of God, 30:22

mankind
        God does not speak to directly, 42:51
        as at a loss, 103:2
        as fickle, 41:49-51
        as hasty and impatient, 21:37
        as vice-regents on earth, 35:39
        blessings of God on, 14:31-34
        created anxious, 70:19
        created from a pair, 42:11
        created from water, 25:54
        creation of Adam, 15:26-40
        creation of, 40:67, 55:14
        development in womb, 23:12-16
        differences among peoples, 10:19-20
        divided, on Day of Judgement, 30:11-18
        division into two groups, 11:104-109
        enmity with Satan, 17:53, 17:61-65, 18:50-53
        first assembly of, 7:172-74
        honouring of, 17:70-72
        ingratitude of, 80:17-32, 100:6-10
        messengers sent to every community, 10:47
        natural world subjected to, 45:12-15
        old age, 16:70
        purpose of creation of, 51:56, 76:1-2
        races and tribes, 49:13
        reduced to lowest of low, 95:5
        Satan's oath to mislead, 4:116-21
        soul, 17:85
        stages of life, 22:5-7, 30:54
        things on earth as serving, 22:63-66
        will experience hardship, 90:4
        See also humanity
Manna, 2:57
Al-Mannat (idol), 53:20
manners, with the Prophet, 49:1-5
manslaughter, compensation for, 4:92-93

marital disputes, settling, 2:222
marriage
        after divorce, 2:230, 2:232
        being patient if one has not the means, 4:25
        dealing with disputes, 4:128-30
        disputes. (See marital disputes; divorce)
        forbidden relatives, 4:22-23
        helping people to, 24:32-34
        love between spouses, 30:21
        mediating marital disputes, 4:35
        of Moses, 28:25-28
        preferring believers for, 4:25
        to disbelievers, 2:221
        to fornicators, 24:3
        to People of the Book, 5:5
        to widows, 2:235
        treating wife with kindness, 4:19-21
marriage gift. See dowry
marshal, on Judgement Day, 20:108
martyrdom, martyrs as alive, 2:154
Marut, 2:102
masajid
        maintaining, 9:17-21
        established by hypocrites, 9:107-110
        performing I'tikaf in, 2:187
meat. See dietary laws
medical conditions. See illness
men
        difference in inheritance from women, 4:34
        providing for children, 2:233
menopause, divorcing after, 65:4
menstruation, avoiding sexual relations during, 2:222
mercy of God
        those who have hope of, 2:218
        decree of, 6:54

taking care of wealth of, 17:34

S

Sabbath, punishment for breaking, 2:65, 7:163-66

Sabians, 2:62, 5:69, 22:17

sacred months, 2:194

    fighting in, 2:216

    desecrating, as unlawful, 5:2

    fighting after, 9:5-11

    prohibition of fighting in, 9:36-37

Sacred Mosque

    preventing access to, 2:216

    violating sanctity of, 22:25

    See also Kaba; Qibla; Makka

sacrificial offerings

    camels, 22:39-37

    on Hajj, 22:34

    piety of reaches God, 22:37

    to atone for leaving ihram due to illness, 2:196

Safa, as sign of God, 2:158

sakinah, descent of in battle of Hunain, 9:26

salam, greeting of, responding to, 4:85-86, 4:94

Salsabil, spring of, 76:18

scales, weighing of, 7:8-9. See also deeds

Scripture

    as judging between people, 2:213

    Torah and Gospel, 3:3-4

    twisting the words of God, 3:75-78

    scrolls of Moses, 6:91

sea

    barrier between fresh water and, 55:19

    blessing of, 16:14, 35:12

    parting of, 2:50, 26:60-68

    rescue from, 6:63-64

    salty and fresh, 25:53

    sincerity when overcome by, 31:32

    subjected to mankind, 45:12

Seal of the Prophets, 33:40

secrecy, 4:114, 58:7-10

secrets, keeping, 4:34

sectarianism

    God will judge between, 2:113

    prohibition of, 3:105

    censure of, 6:159-60, 30:32

seeds, splitting of, 6:95

self defence, 42:39-42

semen, 56:58-59

senility, 16:70

seven deadly sins, 17:26-40

seven oft-recited verses, 15:87

sexual relations

    adultery (See adultery)

    as lawful only in marriage, 4:24

    during menstruation, avoiding, 2:222

    fornication (See fornication)

    having a bath following, 5:6

    homosexuality, 7:81, 27:55, 29:29

    on the nights of the fast, 2:187

    permissibility of various positions, 2:223

    purification after, 4:43

shadows

    extending of, 25:45

    in submission to God, 16:48

Shari'a

    following, 45:18

    loopholes, hypocrite tendency to look for, 4:81-82

she-camel of God, 7:73, 11:63-68, 26:155-59

ship of Noah, 11:36-39, 11:36-39

    command to build, 23:27-30

ships

    as mountains of the sea, 55:24

    as sign of God, 2:164, 42:32-35

shirk. See idolatry

Bibliography

Abdel Haleem, M.A.S., *The Quran: A New Translation* (Oxford: Oxford University Press, 2004).

Ahsan Islahi, A., *Taddabur-e-Quran*, 9 volumes (Lahore: Faran Foundation, 1983).

Al-Ghazali, M., *A Thematic Commentary on the Quran* (Kuala Lumpur: Islamic Book Trust, 2000).

Al-Mu'jam al-Wasit, fifth edition, (Cairo, Egypt: Dar al-Shruq al-Dawliyya, 2011).

Al-Razi, M., ibn Umar al-Hussain Fakhraudin, *Mafateehal Ghayb*, 16 volumes (Beirut: Dar al-Kutub al-Ilmiyyah, n.d.).

Arberry, A.J., *The Koran Interpreted* (London: George Allen and Unwin, 1980).

Asad, M., *The Message of The Qur'an* (Gibraltar: Dar al-Andalus, 1980).

Hussain, M., *The Five Pillars of Islam: Laying the Foundations of Divine Love and Service to Humanity* (Markfield: Kube Publications, 2012).

Irving, T.B., *The Qur'an* (New Delhi: Goodword Books, 2009).

Ismail ibn Kathir, *Tafsir ibn Kathir*, 3 volumes (Beirut: Dar al-Quran, n.d.).

Lane, E.W., *Arabic-English lexicon* (Beirut: Librairie du Liban, 1968).

Lings, M., Muhammad: His Life Based on the Earliest Sources (Rochester, VT: Inner Traditions – Bear & Company, 2006).

Al-Nasafi, Abdullah ibn Ahmed (d.710 AH), *Tafseer al-Madarik*, 3 volumes (Karachi: Qadimi Kutub Khana, n.d.).

Panipati, M.S., *Tafsir Mazhari*, 11 volumes (Lahore: Zia ul-Quran Publications, 2002).

Penrice, J., *Dictionary and Glossary of the Kor-an* (Beirut: Librairie du Liban, 1873).

Al-Sabuni, M.A., *Safwat al-Tafasir*, 3 volumes (Halb: Dar al-Qalam al-Arabi, 1994).

Saeh, B., The Miraculous Language of the Qur'an: Evidence of Divine Origin (London: IIIT, 2015).

Shah, P.M.K., *Tafsir Zia ul-Quran* (Lahore: Zia ul-Quran Publications, 1978).

Al-Suyuti, J.A.R., Al-Itqan fi ulum al-Quran, 2 volumes (Beirut: Dar Ihya al-Ulum, 1996).

Al-Suyuti, *Tafsir al-Jalalayn* (Mansoura: Dar al Ghadd, 2002).

Von Denffer, H., *Ulum al-Qur'an: An Introduction to the Sciences of the Qur'an* (Leicester: The Islamic Foundation, 1999).

Wehr, H., *A Dictionary of Modern Written Arabic* (Beirut: Librairie du Liban, 1980).

Yusuf Ali, A., *The Holy Qur'an* (Madinah: King Fahd Holy Qur'an Printing Complex, 1990).

Made in the USA
Las Vegas, NV
28 March 2024

87880089R00315